2
1095

Patterns of Politics

and Political Systems

in Latin America

PATTERNS OF POLITICS

AND POLITICAL SYSTEMS

IN LATIN AMERICA

Harry Kantor

Professor of Political Science, Marquette University

RAND McNALLY & COMPANY, *Chicago*

RAND McNALLY POLITICAL SCIENCE SERIES

DEDICATED TO

the many Latin Americans who made this book possible
by accepting me with gracious hospitality as a fellow American
as I wandered through the hemisphere for so many years
studying their political behavior,

and especially to
VÍCTOR RAÚL HAYA DE LA TORRE,
whose ideas helped me better to understand
Latin America's political systems,

and to my students,
whose eager curiosity and searching questions were so helpful,

and to
VIVIAN, DANIEL, and SUSAN,
who contributed so much.

Preface

The importance of Latin America to the United States increases with each passing year, and with this increasing importance there has developed a corresponding interest in the political institutions of the area. In the past, the generally chaotic conditions and dictatorial control prevalent in Latin America were not conducive to the study of governmental operations and the actual functioning of the political process, but as constitutional government has become more firmly established throughout the area, an increasing number of authoritative studies have been published. Public administration and political science are assuming more prominent positions in the curricula of Latin-American universities, and the functioning of the various Latin-American governments is more readily understood now than it was at any time in the past.

This book is an attempt to synthesize the information available about the governmental institutions of Latin America in simple and clear language. The material is organized to present a picture of the governmental process as it operates in each of the twenty Latin-American republics plus British Honduras and the Canal Zone, which, while not themselves "Latin American," are part of the general geographical picture and thus are of political consequence to the rest of the area. This method of organization has been chosen in preference to treating all of Latin America in a functional or comparative manner because experience in the classroom through the years seems to demonstrate that students can assimilate the material more easily when it is presented in this way. Although there is a certain unity in Latin America based upon history, the character of the population, and geography, the differences in governmental institutions between Uruguay and its neighbor Paraguay, for example, or between Nicaragua and its neighbor Costa Rica, are so great as to make almost valueless any general statement about governmental machinery and politics of the Latin-American countries. Each of the twenty republics is developing institutions peculiar to itself within the general framework of a Latin-American cultural pattern. This book has been prepared to help students study each country systematically.

In a book intended for the use of students bound by the rigidity of the academic year, it is impossible to devote equal time to each country. Emphasis has been placed, therefore, upon the larger, more complex countries, although none of the republics has been omitted.

All budget figures have been taken from documents of the governments to which they apply, except where I have specifically indicated otherwise.

It is difficult to discuss governments without sometimes voicing an opinion. I have tried to be as objective as possible in my judgments, but I hold a preference for democratic government and the open society, and this preference sometimes finds expression in the opinions expressed and implied.

I owe sincere gratitude to the many Latin Americans who have demonstrated their friendship and helpfulness in so many ways as I sought an understanding of their political systems. No one person can by himself study all of the Latin-American states in depth. All one can do is visit Latin America as often as possible, read everything available on the subject, and approach the area with an open mind. Having done these things, I have discovered how *simpáticos* the Latin Americans are. Without their help this book could never have been written. Needless to say, all errors are mine and are not to be attributed to anyone else. If this book helps students to understand better the way the Latin-American republics are governed, then my debt to all who have helped me will have been paid in part.

HARRY KANTOR

A Note on the Study
of Comparative Government

Man in the second half of the twentieth century is living through a period of cultural lag so serious that all organized society, if not all men, may be destroyed in a nuclear holocaust. Man can now fly faster than any bird, swim faster than any fish, communicate instantaneously with any spot on the earth. With one bomb he can kill tens of thousands of people or obliterate cities. Soon he will be visiting other planets as space travel is developed. Yet, despite these tremendous achievements in the physical sciences, man has not been able to develop governmental institutions capable of permitting the people of the world to live without suffering from war, poverty, dictatorship, political instability, and the many other ills contemporary society endures.

As the physical sciences have jumped ahead in recent decades, the art and science of government has been left behind as one of the underdeveloped areas. There are many reasons for the neglect of the study of government, but probably the most important is that control of government gives certain individuals, groups, and classes the power to exploit other individuals, groups, and classes. Those who have benefited from this exploitation have always been reluctant to permit scholars freedom to study their operations and to describe them to the public. At the same time, every government that ever existed has tried to convince those governed by it that the organizational arrangement in use was good, inevitable, desirable, and worthy of perpetuation. Through the centuries, these arguments have been repeated so many times that myths have developed to mask the actual functioning of governments. The divine right of kings, democracy, patriotism, national unity, constitutionalism, white supremacy, and many other justifications of the status quo have taken the place of a scientific study of the way governments really operate, and some people would as soon doubt that the sun rises regularly as to doubt that a certain governmental pattern was the best, and therefore must be preserved.

Governments have always been surrounded with an aura of mystery. They are like the weather: everyone talks about them, but very few investigate their functioning really scientifically; it has even been common for dictatorships and oligarchies to be considered democracies.

Another way of stating the problem is to say that everything a government does is controversial. Every time a government passes a law, it affects people favorably or adversely. Sometimes a law takes money out of their pockets (taxes), sometimes it puts money into their pockets (subsidies). One law may restrict certain individuals (segregation), another may give certain individuals special privileges (monopolies). A law may force young men into military service against their wishes, another may debase the currency. Every law passed by a government affects individuals, and no law ever passed anywhere met universal approval. Since someone always benefits from a governmental arrangement, there always is a force opposed to the objective study of government and its activities, a group so devoted to the status quo that it wants no questioning of governmental policies or forms of organization. For many persons in the United States of America, communism has become an epithet, not a subject for study; in the Soviet Union, democracy as we define it is labeled "fascism" or "imperialism" or both, and is similarly taboo as a subject of serious investigation.

All of this complicates the study of government. To understand Latin-American governments and political institutions, a student must investigate such subjects as communism, systems of land tenure, church-state relations, class systems, militarism, democracy, dictatorship, and a host of others about which controversy rages. The student must begin his study of government, therefore, conscious that he is dealing with a controversial subject, one with which the greatest minds of all times have wrestled without being able to win general acceptance for any one form of government or point of view about how governments ought to function.

There is even controversy as to how government ought to be studied. The traditional way of studying government in the past has been to study history (what governments have done or the individuals who occupied the leading positions in governments), constitutions and laws (what the written records say about governments), political theory (what a government ought to be or do), and institutions (how political parties, legislatures, cabinets, etc. function). A new view holds that what ought to be studied is political behavior, how people act in their political relationships. Yet even the behaviorists are in dispute as to how to study government. Some would have the main study be of power— who exercises it, how it is obtained, and how it can be controlled. Others maintain that what must be analyzed is the functioning of groups and how each group influences government. A third view is that what should be studied is the process of decision-making; that is, who makes the decisions announced by governments and how they come to decide as they do.

Enough has been said to emphasize how complicated and difficult the study of government is. I have started with the idea that every government is a direct outgrowth of the complicated social system in which it operates. Therefore, to understand a government, one must understand the social scene of which it is a part. This is no easy task, for the student comes to the study of comparative government with preconceptions based upon the cultural pattern to which he is accustomed. The first prerequisite for the student, then, is an open mind, an eagerness to understand what people in another culture are trying to do. The best way to go about this seems to be to learn something about how people live, what the geographical features of the country are, and what its historical development has been. This is a difficult task, for the people of every country have developed folkways and mores that sometimes are almost incomprehensible to others. The student must keep this in mind and, remembering that he is studying another culture, continuously try to overcome his inclination to judge other parts of the world by the cultural pattern dominant in his own.

Another difficulty facing the student of comparative government is the confusion about the meaning of the words used in discussing governments. Although the same word may be used in many countries, it may represent something different in each place. This is true of many kinds of words but it is especially true of political terminology. Are elections the same thing, for example, when conducted in the Dominican Republic and in Costa Rica, or in the Soviet Union and in Sweden? What is a proper example of a legislature—the United States Congress or the Supreme Soviet of the Soviet Union or both?

This problem of political terms is especially complicated in Latin America. The basic constitutional structure of the various republics was originally copied from the constitution of the United States; in fact, certain Latin-American constitutions were almost literal translations of the document written in Philadelphia in 1787. The system of local government used in most of the Latin-American republics has been copied from France, and one finds in various Latin-American countries departments, communes, and provinces not always corresponding to their originals in France. The legal system of Latin America developed out of the Spanish version of the Roman law. Thus much of the terminology of Latin-American governmental institutions has come from outside the area, but through the years the words have come to mean something different from what they mean in Europe and in the United States.

Political instability has been chronic in the area since the Spanish and Portuguese colonies were transformed into independent republics. Imposing dictatorships are overthrown by mass uprisings almost overnight and apparently stable democracies are overthrown by small groups of militarists just as rapidly. There is a constant production of new constitutions as political leaders seek the formula that will stabilize political life or perpetuate their domination.

It is impossible, therefore, for anyone to write a book describing Latin-American government and politics and expect the description to be accurate for very long. The student must continuously bear in mind that he is studying a part of the world living through a period of extremely rapid change. Much that is written about Latin America is out of date almost as soon as it is published, and it is safe to state that by the time these words are printed, at least one of the twenty republics will have completely transformed its political machinery or adopted a new formal constitution. The book can serve, therefore, not as an encyclopedia of facts to be learned, but rather as a guide to aid the student in discovering the formal constitutional framework in the Latin-American republics during the late sixties, the main groups and classes active in political life, and how the political process seems to operate.

Contents

Patterns of Politics

and Political Systems

in Latin America

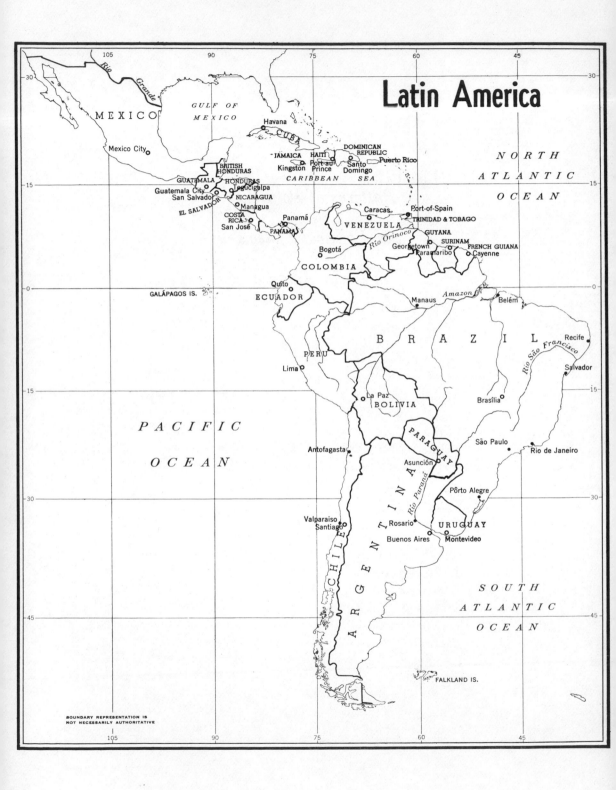

Latin America

MEXICO

GULF OF MEXICO

Mexico City

Havana

CUBA

JAMAICA HAITI
Kingston Port-au-Prince

DOMINICAN REPUBLIC
Santo Domingo Puerto Rico

NORTH

ATLANTIC

OCEAN

CARIBBEAN SEA

BRITISH HONDURAS

GUATEMALA HONDURAS
Guatemala City Tegucigalpa
San Salvador NICARAGUA
EL SALVADOR Managua
COSTA RICA Panamá
San José PANAMA

Caracas Port-of-Spain
TRINIDAD & TOBAGO
VENEZUELA
GUYANA
Bogotá Georgetown SURINAM FRENCH GUIANA
Paramaribo Cayenne

COLOMBIA

GALÁPAGOS IS.

Quito
ECUADOR

Amazon
Manaus Belém

B R A Z I L

Rio São Francisco

Recife

PERU

Lima

Salvador

La Paz
BOLIVIA

Brasília

PACIFIC

OCEAN

Antofagasta

PARAGUAY

São Paulo
Rio de Janeiro

Asunción

Rio Paraná

Pôrto Alegre

Valparaiso
Santiago

A R G E N T I N A

C H I L E

Rosario
Buenos Aires

URUGUAY
Montevideo

SOUTH

ATLANTIC

OCEAN

FALKLAND IS.

Rio Grande

Rio Orinoco

BOUNDARY REPRESENTATION IS
NOT NECESSARILY AUTHORITATIVE

LATIN AMERICA:

An Introduction

Latin America has been misunderstood ever since Christopher Columbus arrived and thought he was in Asia. As a result, much of the literature published about it is inaccurate and some of it is harmful. Students in the United States face an additional handicap because the press, radio, and television report very little of what is happening in the area. The government and the people of the United States have generally had a sort of east-west orientation which fixed their attention primarily upon Europe, secondarily upon Asia, and only incidentally upon the rest of the world.

There even is debate as to just what the term Latin America means, for the words seem to denote a unity where no real unity exists. Writers seeking a more descriptive name for the area south of the United States have suggested Hispano-America, Ibero-America, Indo-America, Eurindia, Amerindia, and other names, but none of these has gained wide acceptance. As used in this book, the term Latin America will refer to the twenty independent republics of the area, excluding the former English, Dutch, and French colonies. Although there is much that is not Latin in these republics, they have enough in common to permit one to discuss them as a group. Yet it must always be remembered that Latin America includes a vast conglomerate of peoples divided by language, culture, economic development, and physical barriers.

Latin America is almost three times larger than the United States (omitting Alaska and Hawaii). Its area is close to 8 million square miles, about three-fourths of which lies within the tropics. Variety is the best

1

word to describe the area's geography: variety in elevation, temperature, natural resources, rivers, rainfall, and soil fertility. The most distinctive feature of Latin America's topography is the series of mountain ranges that run from Mexico to Cape Horn. Temperatures range from the steaming heat of tropical lowlands to the bitter cold of mountain peaks where snow never melts. Natural resources are unevenly distributed. Latin America contains the world's largest river basin, that of the Amazon, and some of the world's driest deserts. Some of its rivers are navigable; many are not. Rainfall varies from the Atacama Desert of Chile, where practically no rain falls, to San Juan del Norte, Nicaragua, where 259.4 inches fall in the average year. Soils vary from extremely fertile plains to barren mountain plateaus.

Hurricanes and earthquakes are frequent in various parts of the area. The destruction they cause has handicapped economic development, and hence has had an indirect effect on political life.

Latin America's geographical variety has had a direct effect upon its political organization. The mountains helped to set the boundaries between the various republics and determined the location of the population. In some of the republics they served to isolate people; in Mexico, Guatemala, Colombia, Ecuador, Peru, and Bolivia, many Indians continue to live in their remote mountain valleys little influenced by the rest of the population. Since the construction of mountain roads is hazardous and expensive, much of Latin America has never been knit together. Many think the failure to build an integrated society is the direct result of the geographical features of Latin America: its tropical rain forests, its extremes of climate, its deserts, its pattern of rainfall, its very location in the Southern Hemisphere. In each of the twenty republics the combination of factors is different, but in each one geography affected the country's development.

Today Latin America has a population of more than 250 million people, or about 8 percent of the world's total, living on about 16 percent of the total land area of the world. In general, it can be said that the area is underpopulated. In the Amazon valley, the mountainous regions, the deserts, and the barren wastes of Patagonia the reasons for underpopulation are readily apparent, but there also are areas suitable for human occupation which have never been utilized. This is in great part a heritage of the Spanish and Portuguese pattern of settlement. In colonial days the metropolitan governments strictly controlled entrance into Latin America to keep non-Catholics out of the colonies, and after independence the pattern continued. While there are exceptions—Argentina and Brazil are the most noteworthy—mass immigration has never been encouraged. Since World War II some attempt has been made to promote selective immigration, but the picture has not changed much.

The population of Latin America is descended almost entirely from three ethnic strains: the American Indian, the European white, and the African Negro. It is practically impossible to estimate the number of persons in each of these groups. The majority are *mestizos*. Most of the Spaniards and Portuguese who came to America were single men —soldiers, adventurers, priests, and government officials—who came to convert the Indians to Catholicism or get rich or both. With few European women available, the *conquistadores* took the Indian women as their mates, and the children they fathered became the new group, the *mestizos*.

The third group entered America because the Indians in many areas failed to make good slaves. Many of them escaped into the mountains, where it was impossible to find them, and those that remained sickened and died in such numbers that the Spanish and Portuguese began to import Negro slaves from Africa.

A small stream of Oriental immigration also entered Latin America in the nineteenth and twentieth centuries. Many Chinese were brought in as coolie labor after the British fleet forced the discontinuance of the slave trade. Others came from India, Japan, and China as agricultural colonists or indentured servants. Peru, Brazil, Panama, Cuba, and Trinidad probably have the largest groups of Oriental inhabitants, but they are found scattered everywhere.

The social and cultural patterns of Spain and Portugal helped to mitigate racial pride in the New World. Many Spaniards and Portuguese were dark-skinned, for they were the products of centuries of mixture of all the many people who had passed through the Iberian Peninsula since the Stone Age. Celts, Phoenicians, Greeks, Carthaginians, Romans, Vandals, Visigoths, Berbers, Nubians, and many others had mingled in the Spanish and Portuguese populations even before the Moorish occupation contributed its North African strain. Racial intermingling was an old story to the Iberians, and as a result Latin America has never had the kind of institutionalized racial discrimination and segregation one finds in the United States and South Africa. The population mixed and through the years became so varied that it is not possible to estimate the proportion of each kind of people in Latin America with any degree of accuracy. This is not to say that there is no racial prejudice in Latin America. Some people regard the Indians as subhuman. Racial prejudice does exist in Latin America, and the rich are usually lighter and the poorer are usually darker. But the distinctions tend to be more cultural than racial, and in no Latin-American country is the social climate poisoned by racist political parties or Ku Klux Klans.

The best estimate of the number of Indians in Latin America is about 30 to 40 million. The largest concentrations of pure Indians are found in Bolivia, Ecuador, Guatemala, Mexico, and Peru. Estimates of the number of Negroes are very uncertain. The largest concentrations are found in Brazil, Haiti, Cuba, the Dominican Republic, Colombia, Venezuela, Mexico, and Panama.

The key to an understanding of Latin America lies in an appreciation of the great cultural conflict that has been taking place there ever since the European conquest. For thousands of years the American hemisphere was not in regular contact with the rest of the world. This isolation led to the development of people, now known as Indians, who had created cultures quite different from that of their conquerors from western Europe.[1] With the arrival of the Spaniards in the Western Hemisphere in 1492, one of the world's great dramas began: the clash between the European and American cultural patterns. In this "Americanization" of European culture, two distinctive patterns emerged, that of the United States and Canada (which can be called Anglo-American) and that of Latin America. By the twentieth century an integrated cultural pattern had emerged in Anglo-America, despite pockets of conflict with a French-speaking minority in Canada and a Negro minority in the United States. Canada and the United States have Americanized their immigrants; they are integrated nation-states structured about commonly accepted symbols of authority. In Latin America the two clashing cultures never were able to blend into a new Americanized society, and as a result political instability and underdevelopment persist in varying degrees throughout the area today.

There are basically two reasons why different cultural patterns emerged in the northern and the southern parts of America. First, the human and natural landscapes were sufficiently dissimilar to cause some sort of bifurcation. Second, the Europeans who settled in North America had different cultural patterns from those who conquered in Latin America.

Most of the immigrants who settled what is now the United States of America came from England, France, Germany, and other parts of northern Europe which had passed through the Renaissance and the Reformation. The religious, economic, and political ideas that animated

---

[1] For an interesting account of the way civilization developed in one Mexican valley over a period of about twelve thousand years, see Robert Claiborne, "Digging up Prehistoric America," Harper's, 232 (April 1966): 69–74.

these people were the products of a long development and seemed to fit well into the new geographical scene. The climate was not too different from what the immigrants had known in Europe, and relatively easy contact could be maintained with their European homelands. The soil was fairly fertile, there were many harbors along the coasts of the colonies, many natural resources were available, and great rivers, particularly the St. Lawrence, the Hudson, and the Ohio, provided transportation routes into the interior.

But even more important, there were relatively few Indians in what are now the United States and Canada, and these few were quickly pushed aside or killed. The only important non-European strain in this new society during its formative years was that of the African slaves, but these people, forcibly torn away from their homelands, soon lost almost all of their African culture and became more or less assimilated into the new American culture. No deposits of gold and silver were discovered during the colonial period to make people rich overnight, so a sort of rural democracy was able to emerge in a land of small farmers. The United States and Canada have been a great melting pot of people, but it is often forgotten that what was melting in the pot was, for the most part, a conglomeration of Europeans, and so a blend was comparatively easy to achieve.

In what is now Latin America, conditions were completely different. There the *conquistadores* found towering mountains, tropical jungles, hundreds of islands, a climate they were not accustomed to, few harbors, and no easily reached natural transportation routes. In addition, all of the pre-Columbian centers of population in America were situated south of the Rio Grande. The Mayas, the Aztecs, the Toltecs, the Chibchas, the Incas, and all the other cultural groups must have looked upon the Spanish and Portuguese conquerors about as the Romans looked upon the barbarians who stormed in to destroy the Roman Empire. The Spanish and Portuguese conquered all these peoples, but they never succeeded in turning them into Europeans on the Spanish or Portuguese model. It is not that the Spanish and the Portuguese did not kill Indians, as did their French and English neighbors to the north. During the Conquest unknown numbers of Indians died during the fighting, from the new diseases introduced by the Europeans, and from the starvation caused by the destruction of irrigation systems and farmlands; but millions of them survived to live as subjects under the Spanish and Portuguese master caste. And one further word must be said about the Conquest. The Spaniards and the Portuguese happened to be in that part of America which contained extensive resources of gold, silver, and other minerals; the mines at Potosí in Bolivia alone supplied enough wealth to cause inflation in Spain, and there were others as rich. These two factors—easily exploited mineral wealth and masses of Indians who could be forced to work—combined with a feudal land-tenure system to create a society that to this day has not developed an integrated cultural pattern around a commonly accepted symbol of authority.

There are those who claim that Rio de Janeiro, Buenos Aires, São Paulo, Mexico City, and Montevideo are modern cities, true examples of western European culture, the homes of great churches and branches of New York banks; and so they are. But these cities are only small dots on Latin America's vast area. What about Chichicastenango, Loja, Pisac, Valle Grande, and the thousands of other known and unknown towns and cities of Latin America? Are these also good examples of Western culture? The fact of the matter is that in some parts of Latin America, after some 450 years, the indigenous and European cultures continue to be almost as alien to each other as they were when the first Europeans arrived.

Outside influences have prevented the normal development of an integrated, progressive society in Latin America, if by normal development we mean one in harmony with the desires and character of the area's population. The *conquistadores* instituted their version of Iberian semifeudalism in the interests of Spain and Portugal, with no thought for the needs of the colonies or their people. The inhabitants of the Spanish and Portuguese colonies were set to work producing what was wanted in Spain and Portugal, not what they needed or wanted themselves.

Yet despite the vast cultural differences between the rulers and the ruled, after 300 years Latin America began to settle down, and it is possible that a stable, integrated society might have emerged if only it had been left alone. But it was not, for events in Europe stimulated and produced an independence movement that changed colonies into republics in a series of bloody upheavals. The only real result of independence was to replace government officials born in Spain with government officials born in America. The land-tenure system, the class system, the close relation between church and state all continued as before. The new ruling caste had practically no training for self-government, and the result was fifty to a hundred years of chaos, *caudillismo*, and retrogression.

In addition, the removal of the crown as the unifying symbol left the former Spanish colonies without a commonly accepted symbol of authority. This helps to explain the almost continuous anarchy that troubled Latin America for about a century after independence and still persists in some countries. No matter who controlled the government, there were groups that did not recognize their right to govern. Thus any adventurer or class or group felt justified in overthrowing the government in power.

Toward the end of the nineteenth century European and United States economic interests began to develop Latin America's productive capacity to supply the needs of the rapidly industrializing countries of the North Atlantic area. This increase in production did not help to stabilize Latin America's political systems because it was geared to the needs of western Europe and the United States. Meat and wheat, copper and coffee, bananas and oil, henequen and tin, cotton and many other products were produced for export as the "independent" states of Latin America became economic colonies.

In addition, the development of production for export, financed and controlled by outside interests, consumed so much of Latin America's energy and resources that not enough food was produced to feed the local population. Since the prices of the new products were set on the world market, not by the producers, most of the population became impoverished. As demand fluctuated sharply, the Latin-American countries became completely dependent on outside forces they could not control.

Expanded economic development produced a new group that was to become very important, a middle class of lawyers, exporters, importers, and others who worked for the foreign corporations. This group was just beginning to emerge when Latin America was struck by the triple blow of World War I, the depression of the 1930's, and World War II. At the same time, the international revolution in communication, transportation, and public health began to make itself felt. The airplane, the automobile, the telegraph, the telephone, the radio, television, and the movies all served to awaken the silent masses just as the other effects of the modern industrial revolution hit Latin America. Thus began what has been called "the revolution of rising expectations," the idea that one does not have to live in dirt, disease, hunger, and ignorance.

Since World War I the twenty republics of Latin America have lived through a period of rapid change. The pattern has been a trifle different in each country, but the general outlines are the same. An entrenched oligarchy exploited the people and resources of the country in cooperation with foreign economic interests. Eventually mass movements developed to challenge the traditional way of doing things. In some countries the revolution won, in others it lost; in some it came early in the twentieth century, in others it is just now gaining power.

In the chapters that follow, the student will see the pattern emerge. Economic development fostered by outside capital stimulates the creation of new groups, and as a multigroup society develops, political stability increases. In each country the contending forces have had varied strength, the process and the pace have been a little different. Most interestingly, as modern means of transportation have brought republics closer together, their populations and cultures have grown more sharply differentiated. Thus as the decades have passed, Costa Rica has become more different from Nicaragua, Uruguay more different from Paraguay, and so on.

It is of course possible that in the future the twenty republics will grow to resemble each other more than they do now. The Latin-American Common Market, the Central American Common Market, the Latin-American Parliament, and other cooperative ventures are tending to reunite the separate republics. Until this process has gone much further than it has, however, Latin America will continue to be a land of twenty different political systems, each distinct from that of its neighbors.

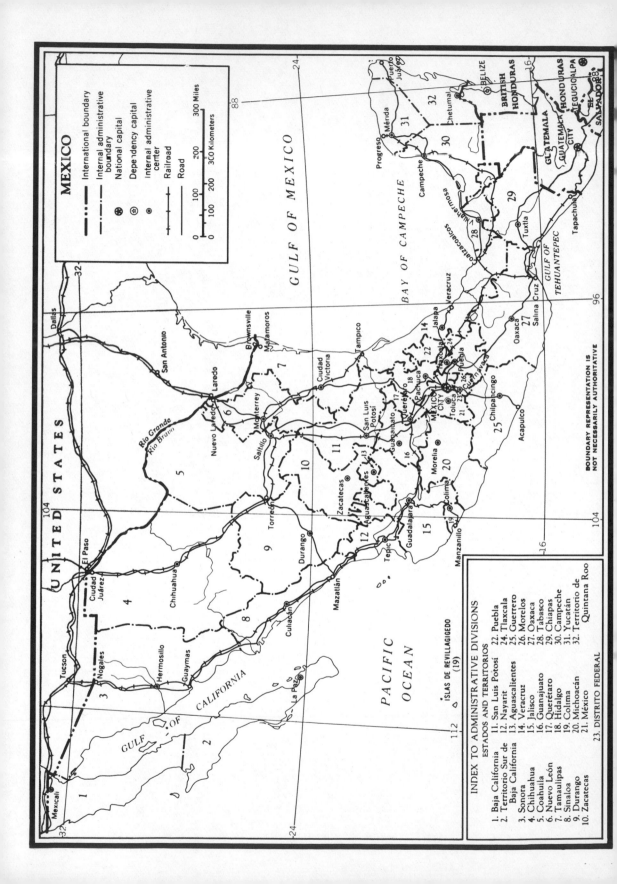

MEXICO

Legend:
- International boundary
- Internal administrative boundary
- National capital
- Dependency capital
- Internal administrative center
- Railroad
- Road

0 100 200 300 Kilometers
0 100 200 300 Miles

UNITED STATES

GULF OF MEXICO

BAY OF CAMPECHE

GULF OF TEHUANTEPEC

PACIFIC OCEAN

GULF OF CALIFORNIA

ISLAS DE REVILLAGIGEDO
(19)

BOUNDARY REPRESENTATION IS
NOT NECESSARILY AUTHORITATIVE

INDEX TO ADMINISTRATIVE DIVISIONS
ESTADOS AND TERRITORIOS

1. Baja California
2. Territorio Sur de Baja California
3. Sonora
4. Chihuahua
5. Coahuila
6. Nuevo León
7. Tamaulipas
8. Sinaloa
9. Durango
10. Zacatecas
11. San Luis Potosí
12. Nayarit
13. Aguascalientes
14. Veracruz
15. Jalisco
16. Guanajuato
17. Querétaro
18. Hidalgo
19. Colima
20. Michoacán
21. México
22. Puebla
23. DISTRITO FEDERAL
24. Tlaxcala
25. Guerrero
26. Morelos
27. Oaxaca
28. Tabasco
29. Chiapas
30. Campeche
31. Yucatán
32. Territorio de Quintana Roo

Place names:
Dallas, San Antonio, Laredo, Nuevo Laredo, Brownsville, Matamoros, El Paso, Ciudad Juárez, Tucson, Nogales, Mexicali, Hermosillo, Guaymas, La Paz, Culiacán, Mazatlán, Durango, Chihuahua, Torreón, Saltillo, Monterrey, Ciudad Victoria, Tampico, San Luis Potosí, Zacatecas, Aguascalientes, Guadalajara, Tepic, Manzanillo, Colima, Morelia, Guanajuato, Querétaro, Pachuca, Toluca, MEXICO CITY, Cuernavaca, Chilpancingo, Acapulco, Puebla, Tlaxcala, Jalapa, Veracruz, Oaxaca, Salina Cruz, Coatzacoalcos, Villahermosa, Tuxtla, Campeche, Progreso, Mérida, Chetumal, BELIZE, BRITISH HONDURAS, GUATEMALA, GUATEMALA CITY, HONDURAS, TEGUCIGALPA, EL SALVADOR

Rio Grande / Rio Bravo

—— 2 ——

MEXICO:

One-Party Politics

Mexico is a land of extraordinary geographical and human diversity which has never been completely integrated into a coordinated unit. The people of Mexico have lived cut off from the rest of the world by deserts, rain forests, mountains, and oceans, in large part occupying a series of valleys whose isolation has promoted both localism and regionalism. Since pre-Columbian times, various dominant groups have tried to knit the people into an integrated society, but it is only in recent years, as modern means of communication and transportation and a rapid growth in population have combined to break down some of the age-old cultural and geographical isolation, that a true Mexican nationalism has emerged.

Mexico is changing so fast that it is impossible to describe the situation exactly at any given moment. New roads, new irrigation projects based on gigantic dams, new factories, new schools, and important shifts in the population pattern are transforming the country. Mexico City has become one of the great and most beautiful cities of the world. Despite all the changes, however, there is still no really typical Mexican. Jet planes carrying businessmen from Mexico City to consult with colleagues in New York and Hamburg fly over tiny cornfields laboriously cultivated by Indians who have not yet graduated from the hoe to the plow. Because of this extreme cultural diversity, it has always been extremely difficult to organize a government that could even try to solve all of the country's problems, and the result was a series of dictatorships of various types.

The 1910 revolution, the first great social upheaval of the twentieth

11

century, did more to unify the country than anything that had previously occurred in Mexico. The revolution has so transformed the country that Mexico now seems well on its way to becoming a modern nation-state. After half a century the revolution has lost some of its initial impetus, but it continues to be the great dynamic force of Mexican life and a stimulus to thinkers in all parts of Latin America.

A National Profile

Mexico is located between the United States on the north and Guatemala and British Honduras on the southeast. A 1,621-mile coastline on the east faces the Gulf of Mexico and the Caribbean, and a 4,104-mile coastline on the south and west faces the Pacific Ocean. With an area of 761,600 square miles, Mexico is Latin America's third largest country, ninth largest in the world. Mexico's *mesa central,* a vast plateau from 5,000 to 8,000 feet above sea level covering approximately 14 percent of the nation's land area, contains about half of the population. On this central plateau are located Mexico's capital city, much of its industry, and about 45 percent of the country's farmers. Stretching north from the *mesa central* is a sloping, lightly populated, mostly arid area reaching to the United States. Only in recent years, with the development of modern roads and railroads, has the heart of Mexico been brought into direct contact with the United States.

To the west, cut off by towering mountains and deep ravines, is the Pacific coast, isolated, difficult of access, and very lightly populated. The Gulf of Mexico slope is a rich area easier to reach from the central plateau, but with an unhealthy tropical climate which until recent years prevented its full exploitation. South of the central plateau is a mountainous area including the states of Michoacán, Morelos, Puebla, Guerrero, Oaxaca, and Chiapas, where compact settlements are found in the various pockets and valleys. The southeastern peninsula, consisting of Campeche, Yucatán, and Quintana Roo, was finally connected to the rest of the country by road in 1960. Last, Mexico includes the arid and practically unpopulated penisula of Baja California, all but severed from the rest of the country by the Gulf of California. Except for a strip just south of the United States (around Tijuana and Mexicali), most of Baja California is relatively empty and without passable roads.

Most of Mexico lies within the Tropic Zone, but the mountains moderate the temperature, giving most of the country a pleasant climate. Three zones are recognized. The hot country extends from sea level to an altitude of about 2,000 feet. The temperate lands, where most of the population is found, extend roughly from 2,000 to 8,000 feet above sea level. Above 8,000 feet the temperatures are decidedly cool.

Mexico's population is very unevenly distributed, with the average density, in 1959, varying from 3,361.1 per square kilometer in the Federal District to 0.74 per square kilometer in Quintana Roo. In 1960, 51 percent of the population lived in urban centers, although Mexico has only two really large metropolitan centers, Mexico City, with a population of over 3 million (over 6 million in the Federal District), and Guadalajara, with over a million. In the north, Monterrey, with quick and easy access to the Texas border city of Laredo, has become Mexico's most heavily industrialized city and is fast approaching the million mark. Of the 99,028 localities enumerated during the 1960 census, only 323 were cities. The rest consisted of *villas, pueblos, haciendas, ejidos, ranchos, rancherias,* and other small centers of population.

Mexico has one of the world's fastest-growing populations, with the rate of increase estimated at 33.3 per 1,000 population in 1954. Its total population jumped from 19.7 million in 1940 to 25.8 million in 1950 to 34.9 million at the census of June 1960 to about 44 million in 1967. It was estimated that by 1969 the population would be 46.5 million. The increase has tended to alter Mexico's population pattern, for the greatest growth has come in the north, where a belt of dense population has developed close to the U.S.-Mexican border, helping to increase contact between the two peoples. The growth in Mexico's population is a result of the continuation of a traditionally high birth rate at a time when modern health techniques and improved nutrition have sharply lowered the death rate.

Although Spanish is Mexico's official language, it is estimated that about a million Mexicans speak no Spanish and about two million very little. Eric Wolf points out that in certain areas three different languages are needed to communicate with one's neighbors. "In the Huastec-speaking zone of northern Veracruz, for instance, many Indians speak Huastec at home, Nahuatl in the marketplace, and Spanish when they want to communicate with officials or outsiders."[1] In all, there are about thirty-three different language groups and twenty-one minor linguistic divisions among Mexico's Indians.

Most of the Mexicans are nominal Catholics (about 97 percent, according to the census), but for many the Catholicism has a large admixture of Indian elements. Church and state are constitutionally separated. For about a century after 1850 an intense conflict raged between the two,

---

[1] Eric Wolf, *Sons of the Shaking Earth* (Chicago: University of Chicago Press, 1959), pp. 34–35.

reaching its peak in the 1920's. By 1960 this struggle had died down, and the Catholic church and its position in the country are no longer subjects of dispute. All religious groups, including the Catholic, function freely in Mexico. In 1950, 330,111 Protestants, 17,574 Jews, and 113,834 members of other religious groups were counted.

In 1910, almost 80 percent of the population was illiterate. By 1960 this figure had been cut approximately in half, but of course that still left at least 40 percent of the population illiterate. The illiteracy rate varies greatly from region to region, with the highest rates in the rural areas and the lowest in the large cities. Mexico's geography has prevented the development of an adequate educational system despite determined efforts made during recent decades. In 1956, of 6,833,771 children between the ages of six and fourteen, only 4,106,208 were attending school. It is safe to assume that the proportion has risen since then, though there is certainly still room for improvement.

Mexico is a comparatively poor area whose economy has traditionally been based on agricultural products and mineral raw materials. Thirty-four percent of its exports in recent years consisted of minerals and petroleum, and 34 percent of textile fibers, coffee, chicle, and linseed. Its imports are mainly manufactured goods and some food products. On December 31, 1960, it was estimated that of a total population of 35,232,000 about 34.1 percent (12,014,000) were economically active, divided as shown in Table 1.

TABLE 1

MEXICO'S LABOR FORCE, 1960

Field	Number	Percent
Agriculture (including livestock raising, forestry, and fishing)	6,342,000	52.8%
Industry	2,008,000	16.7
Commerce and finance	1,092,000	9.1
Transportation and communication	423,000	3.5
Services (including government)	1,550,000	12.9
Other activities	458,000	3.8
Unemployed	141,000	1.2
Total	12,014,000	100.0%

The proportion of Mexico's population engaged in agriculture has gone down from 70.5 percent in 1930 to the 1960 figure of 52.8.

A concentrated effort has been made to increase agricultural output by developing new land and increasing production on land already under cultivation. Since only about 10 percent of Mexico's total area is arable, and of this about half is so dry that it is not utilized, Mexico remains a poor country despite the uncounted millions in minerals and petroleum the country has produced.

Mining has been important in Mexico since the Spanish arrived, and in the 1950's the country was first in the world's production of silver, third in lead, antimony, and cadmium, fifth in zinc, and seventh in copper. Petroleum, iron, and coal are also important, especially for domestic consumption.

Of all the Latin-American countries, Mexico has been most influenced by the United States. About $800 million U.S. were invested in various manufacturing, agricultural, and mining enterprises. A tremendous influx of United States tourists left about $700 million in Mexico in 1962. About 400,000 Mexican agricultural workers entered the United States legally each year from 1955 to 1958 and carried both money and new ideas back to their villages.[2] The number of Mexicans who have entered the United States as legal immigrants has risen rapidly in recent decades.

All of these United States influences have combined to affect Mexican society greatly. Associated Press and United Press dispatches and U.S. "comics" and columnists are seen in most Mexican newspapers. Large numbers of middle- and upper-class Mexicans are now learning English, and even in the smallest villages one encounters former *braceros* who know some English. There is much dispute in Mexico as to whether this influence is good or bad for the country, but the majority of articulate Mexicans seem to favor it.

Mexico's infant mortality rate went from 266.4 per 1,000 births in 1901 to 79.1 per 1,000 in 1957. Its overall mortality rate fell during the same period from 32.3 per thousand to 12.9. Millions of acres of irrigated land have been brought into production through the construction of dams and waterways. The highway system has improved and is now beginning to knit together the formerly isolated parts of the country. Just what roads can do in opening up the country is well illustrated by the small Tarascan town of Tarecuato in Michoacán. Marion Wilhelm reports that until 1953 this town had practically no contact with the rest of

---

[2] In addition to the workers who enter legally, uncounted hundreds of thousands cross the border illegally each year. Oscar Lewis, in "Mexico since Cárdenas," *Social Research*, 26 (Spring 1959): 18–30, cites a study by Gertrude D. Krichefsky, "Importation of Alien Laborers," U.S. Department of Justice, *I and N Reporter*, July 1956, pp. 4–9, which states that 1.7 million Mexican aliens were arrested in the United States and returned to Mexico in the three years 1953–55.

Mexico, although a highway passed within sixteen miles of it. In 1953, when a road was built connecting Tarecuato with the main highway, there were no cars or trucks in the town. There was no water system, no electricity, no drainage, no outside trade beyond what a man could carry on his back with the aid of a tumpline. The only contact with the rest of Mexico was by means of a radio owned by the village priest, operated by a wind-driven generator. The people wove their own cloth, made their own clothes, and ate nothing but what they grew themselves. They spoke no Spanish. With the coming of the road, a dirt lane, isolation ended. And the same thing is happening in all parts of Mexico. In La Barca in west central Mexico, the building of a road increased the tomato crop from 3,000 cases a year to 1,000,000 cases. Bank deposits doubled. The production of potatoes increased tremendously.[3]

Although Mexico is changing rapidly, the benefits of its industrial expansion have been very uneven, and about 60 percent of the population remain poorly fed, housed, and clothed. But Mexico's advances in both industry and agriculture give good reason for optimism about its future.

The Development of Modern Mexico

Man has lived in Mexico for a very long time. The oldest human bones so far discovered date from about 6,000 B.C. By 1519, when the Spaniards arrived, about 13 million people organized into a large number of tribes and other social groups inhabited the area. Some nomadic Indians lived in the north, which was otherwise largely uninhabited. On the great central plateau, the Aztecs of Tenochtitlán, a great city of 200,000 to 300,000, dominated the México-Texcoco-Tlacopan confederation of many tribes. Stretching south from Tenochtitlán (the site of today's Mexico City) to Tehuantepec was the land of the Zapotec people. Farther south, especially in Chiapas and Yucatán, lived the northern Mayas. The Indians of central and southern Mexico had developed a civilization advanced in agriculture, astronomy, mathematics, architecture, sculpture, painting, and the working of precious metals. In certain features of their culture, particularly mathematics and astronomy, the Mexican people were probably more advanced than the Spanish invaders. Unfortunately for them, they were not advanced in power politics and war, and Hernán Cortés was able to conquer the area with a force of 500 men and 16 horses. The destruction by the Spaniards of the Indians' written records has made it

---

[3] Marion Wilhelm, "Roads Bring Mexican Towns Sense of Progress," *Christian Science Monitor*, May 22, 1953, p. 3.

impossible for us ever to know the complete history of the area before 1519, although three Maya codices survive to tantalize would-be translators.

The troops led by Cortés conquered the area by utilizing the enmity between the various Indian tribes and confederations. The Spanish then set up a government that controlled all of what is now Mexico and the southwestern part of the United States. Mexico's government was typical of Spanish colonies, with Spaniards monopolizing government positions, ecclesiastical power, and foreign trade. During the colonial epoch a class of rich Creoles developed (persons born in Mexico of Spanish parents), but the basis of society was a poverty-stricken, feudally controlled Indian peasantry. John A. Crow has well described the conditions of colonial life:

> From the beginning Mexico presented extremes of poverty and wealth. The Spaniards, by and large, were well off; the Indians poor. . . . Not all Spaniards were rich, but they were relatively rich. They occupied a place in the community much like that of the white minority in some of the heavily Negro-populated communities of the United States today.[4]

The failure of Spanish culture to assimilate Mexico's Indians can be explained in part by the conflicts between the Spanish crown, the Catholic church, and the Spaniards who lived in Mexico, for each had a different object in view. Moreover, the topography of the area enabled some Indians to isolate themselves and avoid domination by the Spaniards. Whatever the cause, even after 300 years of Spanish rule many persons living in what is now Mexico had failed to adopt the most important features of Spanish culture: the Spanish language, the Catholic religion, and the Spanish system of economics.

At the time the colony became independent it is estimated that Mexico had a population of between 6 and 7 million. Professor Crow estimates that about 15,000 were Spaniards, about 500,000 were Creoles, about 2.6 million were *mestizos*, and from 3 to 4 million were Indians.[5]

When the Spanish empire collapsed after Napoleon's conquest of the Iberian Peninsula, Mexico passed through more than a decade of struggle before it became an independent state. From the abortive revolt of 1808 and Father Miguel Hidalgo y Costilla's call to independence on September 16, 1810, until the Treaty of Córdoba confirmed Mexican independence on August 24, 1821, the country lived through a series of bitter struggles that at some moments were not only wars for indepen-

---

[4] John A. Crow, *Mexico Today* (New York: Harper & Bros., 1957), pp. 87–88.
[5] *Ibid.*, p. 116.

dence, but class wars which spread racial antagonisms and stimulated a cult of violence that Mexico has not yet completely overcome.

The kind of government the leaders of independence wanted for Mexico is described in the constitution of October 22, 1814, which provided for a president, a congress of two houses, and a judiciary system headed by a supreme court. Although all males over eighteen were to vote, they were to vote only for members of an electoral college, who would select the officials of the government. Catholicism was to be the sole religion of the state. This constitution never went into effect; instead, Mexico's first government was the short-lived empire of Iturbide. Although this was soon destroyed and liberal leaders controlled the government from 1823 to 1835, Mexico's first leaders were unable to establish a stable government of any kind. It has been computed that during the twenty-five years after 1822 Mexico had seven constitutional assemblies, which produced one constitutional act, three constitutions, and one act of reform. During the same period, there were two coups d'état and a number of armed uprisings. In short, from independence until about 1876, a struggle took place between those who wanted to preserve the type of society the colony had created and those who favored a more democratic organization of the country. During this half century liberal forces were in power many times, but none of them succeeded in changing the basic organization of the country.

Mexico had had no preparation for self-government. The only real change after independence was that Spaniards born in Mexico took the place of Spaniards born in Spain. A small commercial middle class, inspired by the liberal economic ideas popular in the late eighteenth and early nineteenth centuries, formed the base of the liberal group in Mexican politics, but it was always weaker than the semifeudal landowning aristocracy left behind by the colony. The liberals, who came to be known as Federalists, favored laissez-faire economics, extension of the suffrage, separation of church and state, mass education, and a federal form of government. The conservatives, known as the Centralists, favored rule by the upper classes (particularly the landowners), the union of church and state, education only for the upper classes, a strong army, and a continuation of the landholding system then in use.

The inability of either the Federalists or the Centralists to establish a stable government led to the United States take-over of the northern half of Mexico's territory after the war of 1846–47. Some observers call the first fifty years of Mexican independence a period of anarchy, for in addition to losing half of its territory, the country lived through a period of almost constant civil wars and an attempt by Spain to reconquer the territory in 1829.

Mexico's defeat in the war with the United States led to the development of a movement known as the *Reforma*, in which the liberals tried to destroy the traditional organization of Mexico's society, set up a constitutional government modeled on that of the United States, dominate the church and the army, and extend democracy to the masses. Led by Benito Juárez, a remarkable Zapotec Indian lawyer from Oaxaca, the liberals struggled to institute their program, but the conservatives refused to cooperate, and almost continuous civil war was the result. When the conservatives called on the Spanish, English, and French governments to intervene in Mexico, Napoleon III utilized the opportunity to set up an empire headed by a romantic dreamer, Maximilian of Austria, who was kept in power by 30,000 French troops from 1864 to 1867. From 1867 to 1876 the liberal governments headed by Juárez and Lerdo de Tejada made a determined effort to reorganize the country's political and economic machinery, but although much progress was made, the country evidently was not yet ready for either constitutional or democratic government. Juárez, the most talented of the liberal leaders, died in 1872 after a series of threatened revolutions. His party had divided into two factions, one pressing for more reforms that would help the underprivileged Indians and another more interested in the economic development of the country. The second faction, headed by General Porfirio Díaz, revolted again in 1876, took power, and held control of the country until 1911.

The Díaz period was one of stability following a half century of almost continuous chaos, but it was the stability of a dictatorship. Díaz balanced the budget; national income increased as foreigners developed new economic enterprises; Mexico City grew into a large metropolitan center. This was the period when the United States and western European economic systems were expanding very rapidly, and United States and European investors obtained concessions from Díaz to exploit Mexico's mineral and agricultural wealth and to build railroads. The economic development was accompanied, however, by the concentration of all power in the hands of Díaz and his friends. The army and a hated police force (the *Rurales*) prevented all opposition. Díaz cooperated with the Catholic church by not enforcing the anticlerical provisions of the 1857 constitution, and the church became one of Mexico's largest landowners. The traditional, essentially feudal society in the agricultural areas remained undisturbed. The farm workers, particularly the Indians, were further impoverished as the government's concessions to foreign agricultural and petroleum corporations deprived them of their traditional lands. By 1913, foreign holdings were valued at more than $1.25 billion.

Díaz' dictatorship was mild as dictatorships go, but it was still a dictatorship. Mass illiteracy made a farce of a free press, and trade unions were tolerated only as long as they made no demands.

By 1910 the Díaz regime consisted of old men completely out of touch with reality. Only a spark was needed to set off the twentieth century's first great social revolution, and the spark was lit when a well-to-do landowner's son, Francisco I. Madero, published a book, *The Presidential Succession in 1910*, which criticized Díaz, proposed democratic presidential elections, and advocated other reforms that would enable the newly risen middle class to participate in the control of Mexico. The book attracted much attention and Madero became a candidate for president, but before the election could take place, Díaz arrested Madero and declared himself reelected. When Madero escaped to the United States and issued a call for revolution and a new election, the Mexican revolution began, and Díaz and his regime soon collapsed.

The 1910 revolution was a spontaneous, uncoordinated explosion. Madero, who became president in 1911, was no firebrand; he represented the landowners, industrialists, professional men, and other businessmen who had risen through the social ranks during the past decades. The revolution had no real intellectual leadership and no great names to lead it. But the people were hungry for land and for a change in the organization of the country, and once the force of the masses was unleashed, it continued to agitate Mexico until all of the old holders of power had been swept away and the traditional organization of society was completely destroyed.

The Mexican revolution was against everything that reminded the people of the past: against the continued imitation of Europe, against the semifeudal landholding system, against the preferred positions of the Catholic church, the army, the foreigners who held concessions, and the government officials who were permanently in power. The revolution was a drive to create a Mexico that belonged to its people. The Mexican revolution came as the great industrial revolution of the nineteenth century was culminating in a worldwide movement for expanded democracy, a period when social Darwinism and Marxism were capturing the imagination of millions everywhere and converting them into optimistic seekers of a utopian future. The Mexican people were swept up in this quickening current, and many looked upon their revolution as only one part of the world movement to redeem man from injustice.

Instead of ending the revolution, the installation of Madero as president, in the fall of 1911, only gave it new impetus, for Madero was unable to create a stable government to replace that of Díaz. Madero was not a good administrator, nor was he completely in favor of many of the demands raised during the fighting against Díaz. He was surrounded by men from the upper classes who had never wanted more changes than an end to Díaz' permanent domination of the country. Madero soon disappeared from the scene, murdered by the military forces of General Victoriano Huerta, who tried to reintroduced a dictatorship with himself at its head. But during Madero's short time in office, unknown people who had never before participated in politics had begun to play a role. The peasants became the driving force in the revolution as they clamored for land. Huerta's attempt to set the clock back only strengthened the efforts of the masses to achieve fundamental changes.

When Huerta took control of Mexico City in 1913, his government was recognized by the leading European powers, but the leaders of the revolution refused to accept him. War broke out and continued until about 1918. It was a chaotic, uncoordinated struggle that devastated Mexico and completely destroyed all the old mechanisms of social control. The revolutionary armies all agreed that they were against Huerta, but they could agree on nothing else. When Huerta was expelled from the country in 1914, the revolutionary armies fought each other. For five years the armies moved up and down Mexico like mass migrations, usually along the railroads. A train would contain three layers of riders: one in the boxcars, one on top of the cars, and a group in hammocks slung between the wheels. Soldiers ranged in age from seven to seventy, and women accompanied the men to cook, take care of the wounded, and help in the fighting. The rebels all called themselves Constitutionalists; Huerta's forces were known as the Federals. When Huerta was gone, General Venustiano Carranza organized a convention of generals to endorse him as the new president, but neither Villa nor Zapata, the two most powerful of the revolutionary leaders aside from Carranza himself, accepted his decision; civil war broke out again, this time with the forces lining up for and against Carranza.

Carranza was an odd figure to become the head of the Mexican revolution. He had been governor of Coahuila during the Díaz regime and was a member of Mexico's middle class. He favored curbs on United States investments, taxes on all foreign enterprise, checks on monopoly and the church, and an end to the remnants of feudalism.

Pancho Villa led what was for some years the best army in Mexico. He controlled Chihuahua and Durango and had much support from certain United States interests, although Villa himself, an uneducated peasant, did not really know what he wanted. In the south, Emiliano Zapata had mobilized the landless Indians under his slogan of "Land and liberty." His followers wanted land as quickly as possible, and operated independently of the northern rebels. Álvaro Obregón, the most brilliant of the rebel leaders, controlled Sonora. Obregón considered himself a socialist and had many labor leaders in his army.

Carranza and Obregón combined their forces in 1915 and succeeded in establishing a regime that laid the basis for an end to the revolutionary wars. While the fighting was still going on, Carranza's headquarters issued decrees to the effect that all land illegally seized by *hacendados* would be returned; that all *municipios* would have self-government; that workers would get the right to organize; and that labor legislation would be enacted to regulate wages and hours of work. These decrees progressively won Carranza more support, including that of Mexico's largest trade union, the *Casa del Obrero Mundial*, which sent its organizers out to mobilize support for Carranza.

After Carranza's forces defeated Villa's armies, a convention was organized in 1917 to write a new constitution for Mexico. Although the delegates represented the successful military factions headed by Carranza, the convention was dominated by an alliance of the Obregón radicals from the north and the agrarian radicals from the south.

The writing of a new constitution could not by itself change the character of Mexican society. When Carranza became the first constitutional president, he neither sympathized with the new constitution nor tried to put it into practice. He was opposed to the labor leaders and the unions; he was opposed to Zapata's continued efforts to get land for the landless; and he wanted personal power. Graft corrupted many of Carranza's closest associates, and when Carranza's term in office expired, he tried to install a friend as his successor. This led to an immediate revolt, and Carranza died pathetically, shot in a little Indian village as he fled toward Vera Cruz. This was the last successful revolt in Mexico. No revolt after 1920 was to succeed.

After a short interval Álvaro Obregón was elected president, and with his inauguration the active military turmoil ended. Only a decade separated the regimes of Díaz and Obregón, but during those ten years, from 1910 to 1920, the social structure of Mexico was so shaken up that it would never again return to the conditions of the past. Although many problems remained and still remain, Mexico emerged at last as a viable state.

Obregón was a brilliant political leader who set up the system which, with refinements, has continued until today. Obregón was characterized by the true spirit of Latin-American *caudillismo,* and his system made the presidency the most important element in the government. He dominated the legislature, appointed all officials, controlled the army, and with its backing installed his friends in all state governments; in short, he made all governmental decisions. This system worked so well that there has been no serious threat to the stability of the Mexican government since then. The various presidents after 1920 followed different policies, but all decided what policy to follow. Stimulated by the energy released by the revolution, the country has improved its economy, educational system, transportation, and public health. One must conclude, therefore, that despite all the power Obregón concentrated in the presidential office, his system of government was a step forward for Mexico.

But if the president is all-powerful, what happens when his term expires? As Obregón arranged the system, the incumbent president selects his successor and sees that he gets installed. Until the 1940's, each change in the presidency was accompanied by a revolt by those who thought they should have been selected, but the government always was able to put down the revolts.

Obregón's successor, Plutarco Elías Calles, was to dominate the government for ten years. These were very trying years for Mexico, as all of the forces defeated in the revolution made repeated attempts to regain power. At the same time, many of the new leaders who had emerged from the revolutionary armies, uneducated and with no traditions of public service, became corrupted by their new power and wealth. Yet the impetus of the revolution kept pushing Mexico ahead, and despite everything conditions slowly improved.

Calles held the presidency from 1924 to 1928. He greatly strengthened the labor movement, pushed land redistribution, and built roads and schools. His term in office was highlighted by a great struggle with the Catholic church and with certain forces in the United States. Yet he completed his term and supervised the election of Obregón for another term in 1928.

The year 1928 was one of the great turning points in Mexico's development. After Obregón was elected president, a religious fanatic assassinated him before he could take office. There was no other strong political leader to take his place except Calles, and the constitution forbade his continuing in office. Though Calles was the logical substitute for the dead president-elect, for the first time in the history of Mexico a man refused to take the presidency when he could have done so. Calles undoubtedly dominated the presidents who served until 1934, but he never again took the office himself, thus greatly strengthening the idea of alternation in office. Calles held the country together despite the effects of the world depression, almost continuous fighting with the pro-church elements, and graft and corruption that became notorious.

Another of Calles' enduring contributions to Mexican govern mental institutions was the creation of the National Revolutionary Party (PNR) as a mechanism to stabilize the country's political life. The PNR turned Mexico into a one-party country, but it had far more in common with the one-party system in the southeastern United States than with the totalitarian one-party regimes of Stalin and Hitler, or of Franco and Salazar in Spain and Portugal. The PNR automatically enrolled all government employees within its ranks and deducted seven days' pay from each employee's salary during the year. Thus everyone employed by the government was a party member, and the party automatically had sufficient funds to carry on its activities.

Another turning point in Mexico's development came in 1934, when General Lázaro Cárdenas was chosen as the party's presidential candidate. No one seems to know just why he was selected, but the best guesses are that the PNR did not realize what it was getting. Some scholars claim that Calles realized that someone with a revolutionary background who was personally honest was needed or the people would lose their faith in the revolutionary leadership. Cárdenas had a good military record during the revolution, he had kept his mouth shut and thus had few enemies, he had been a capable administrator as a governor and as a cabinet member, and he had a reputation for honesty.

Although Cárdenas' election was assured, he campaigned as though he would not get elected without persuading the masses to vote for him. During the campaign he visited every part of the country, promising land to the landless, help to the isolated Indian communities, and a higher standard of living for the city workers. He attacked the Catholic church and told the workers and peasants to organize to achieve their needs.

Installed in office by Calles and the PNR machinery, Cárdenas used the centralized power of the presidency to expel Calles from Mexico, take over the party machinery, and eliminate all opposition to his control. He then pushed the reforms he thought the 1917 constitution called for, particularly distribution of land to the landless. Cárdenas closed the gambling houses that had contributed to corruption in Mexico City; he strengthened the trade unions; he fostered education; and he nationalized the railroads and the petroleum industry, thereby rousing Mexico's national pride to the highest peak it had ever known. In 1938 he reorganized the official party to make it more responsive to his wishes, changed

its name to the Party of the Mexican Revolution (PRM), and strengthened the framework of the governmental machinery Obregón had begun
to organize.

Cárdenas was a great reformer and the idol of the masses, but he ran
the government in the same way Díaz, Obregón, and Calles had done
before him. Cárdenas was the government. His men held every key office,
elections were controlled, and every little detail passed through the President's office. What distinguished Cárdenas was that he won such overwhelming mass support that crude strong-arm tactics were not needed,
although two armed revolts against his rule were put down by the army.

When Cárdenas' term in office ended, he did as his predecessors had
done and selected a friend of his, General Manuel Ávila Camacho, to succeed him. Some have speculated that Cárdenas supported Ávila Camacho
because he thought Mexico needed a rest. If so, he chose well. Ávila Camacho turned out to be a dull plodder whose term in office, though it
coincided with World War II, marked the first six years of internal peace
the country had enjoyed since the revolution began. Ávila Camacho was
a Catholic who attended church services regularly, and during his term
in office the struggle with the religious faction died down. The war
brought both inflation and prosperity to Mexico, and some progress was
made in industrialization.

In 1946 a civilian, Miguel Alemán, became president. Alemán was
the first revolutionary president who had not participated in the revolution. He was conservative, but he never tried to go back to prerevolu-
tionary conditions; rather, he put the brakes on further changes and
pushed industrial expansion. With Alemán, the revolutionary generation
passed from control of Mexico, and the radicalism that reached its peak
during the presidency of Cárdenas came to an end. Alemán and the presidents who succeeded him were men who had worked their way up
through the party and governmental hierarchies as efficient administrators. Alemán represented the new Mexican middle class which had developed as a result of the revolution, men who were much more interested
in the economic, educational, and technical development of the country
than with far-reaching social reforms.

Mexico is a far different land today from what it was when its revolution began in 1910. The old semifeudal landholding society is gone;
the old holders of power have disappeared; the common people are more
closely involved in politics. The military is not as important as it was during the first 125 years of the republic's existence. A growing middle class,
including a dynamic group of entrepeneurs and bankers, plays an important role; peasant leagues and trade unions have some power; foreign

control has been weakened. There is a feeling among the Mexican people that equality and democracy are here to stay. Education is far more widespread that it ever was before. Most important, people live more normal lives, without fear of violent upheavals.

The Formal Constitutional Framework

Mexico is governed under the constitution of February 5, 1917, which describes Mexico as "a federal, democratic, representative republic composed of free and sovereign states in all that concerns their internal affairs, but united into a federation." From the promulgation of an abortive constitution on October 22, 1814, to the proclamation of the constitution of February 5, 1857, a whole series of plans, constitutions, constitutional laws, and organic bases replaced each other with great frequency. The 1857 constitution remained in effect until 1917, but many of its provisions were never observed. Thus it can be said that the constitution of 1917 is the first document that realistically describes the framework of the country's government.

A product of the Mexican revolution, the 1917 constitution incorporates within itself the philosophy of the victors in that struggle in its provisions dealing with the position of religious organizations and foreigners, the ownership of land, agrarian reform, and the rights of workers. Yet the 1917 constitution is a contradictory document, for it contains two opposing conceptions of the role of the state and the relations of the individual to government. The 1917 constitution repeats all the concepts of classic liberalism contained in the 1857 document, including guarantees of freedom of association, worship, and speech, popular sovereignty, representative government, universal suffrage, periodic elections, separation of powers, the independence of the state and local governments, the right of trial by jury, and the right to own property. *Ex post facto* laws are forbidden and due process of law is required to deprive a person of life, liberty, property, possessions, or rights. Since these clauses in the 1857 constitution did not prevent Díaz from operating a dictatorship for thirty-four years, the now famous Articles 27, 123, and 130 were added to enable the government and people of Mexico to protect themselves from the three great forces against which the revolution had been fought: the Catholic church, the large landowners, and foreign investors.

Article 27 states that "the Nation shall at all times have the right to impose on private property such limitations as the public interest may demand." Further clauses give the government direct ownership of the subsoil and all its minerals, the territorial waters, and all buildings used for religious purposes. Limitations are placed upon all property owners, and foreigners are not permitted to own land "within a zone 100 kilometers wide along the frontiers, or fifty kilometers along the coast." Aliens can own land or exploit mineral resources only if they agree to consider themselves as nationals in regard to their property, and then only if they agree in advance not to invoke the protection of their governments in disputes about their property. No religious organization can own or administer real estate. In addition, Article 27 contains various clauses protecting communal land holdings and providing techniques by which landless peasants can obtain land and set up *ejidos*, a form of agricultural cooperative. The government is also given the right to expropriate private property for public purposes after indemnification.

Article 123 outlines the rules governing relations between workers and their employers. Here workers are guaranteed the right to organize into labor unions, and Congress is charged with enacting laws regarding hours and conditions of work, compensation, and protection for workers. The constitution gives the state governments the power to enforce federal labor legislation. Article 123 is really a labor code providing for an eight-hour working day, minimum wages, compulsory paid vacations for pregnant women, and a host of other regulations governing the treatment of workers. Much of Article 123 is still little more than an aspiration, but it is important as an expression of the future the writers of the constitution wanted to bring nearer.

Article 130, after separating church and state, sets up a series of restrictions upon religious organizations and their officials, intended to prevent religious groups from interfering in the political or economic life of the nation. No religious organization can have a legal personality, or own property, or have an alien conduct its affairs, or participate in politics; nor can the clergy vote or comment on political affairs, or inherit property.

These articles of the Mexican constitution, placing group interests above individual liberties, are in direct conflict with older articles guaranteeing personal rights. What happens in Mexico when a conflict arises between the two kinds of rights? The government of the day decides this question, and it is this that has created the gyrations in Mexican policy since 1920.

The government set up by the 1917 constitution is similar in form to that of the United States. A division of powers between the central and state governments creates a federal system in which the states must "adopt for their internal government the popular, representative, republican form of government." The states are given all powers not expressly granted to federal officials, but are denied so many specific powers and are so restricted that the central government is clearly dominant.

The central government is divided into executive, legislative, and judicial branches, each with its rights and duties defined, yet with such extensive powers given to the president that the executive is the strongest branch of the government. Article 29 grants the president the power, "in agreement with the Council of Ministers and with the approval of the Congress of the Union," to suspend constitutional guarantees. In addition, the president controls the armed forces, foreign affairs, and the power of pardon, and has extensive powers in appointing and removing officials from office.

Mexico's constitution has never been fully enforced, and there has been much discussion about the intentions of the Constituent Assembly. The writers of the constitution were probably setting forth an outline of what they would like Mexico to become, rather than declaring what they thought it could be in 1917. The constitution of 1917 provided the revolution with a program after seven years of chaotic fighting during which no clear goals had emerged. As the years pass, the constitution more and more clearly reflects the reality of the Mexican political process.

This constitution was intended to be a permanent document, and its final article declares that even revolution shall not cancel its provisions. In case a revolt prevents its observance, "as soon as the people recover their liberty" the constitution goes into force again.

How the Constitution Is Amended

Mexico's constitution may be amended by a two-thirds vote of the members of the Congress present, followed by a ratification by the legislatures of a majority of the states. The Mexican constitution has been amended frequently. Changes include the abolition of the popular election of members of the Supreme Court in 1928 and replacing that system with appointment by the president; extension of the presidential term from four to six years in 1933; giving the franchise in municipal elections to women in 1946; and giving women complete suffrage in 1952. The control of all state legislatures by the PRI, as the government party is now called (for *Partido Revolucionario Institucional*) and the concentration of power in the hands of the president make any reform wanted by him easy to achieve, even though he has no formal role in the amending process. Amendments to the Mexican constitution are inserted within the body of the original document rather than being listed at the end, as is the practice in the United States.

Who Participates in Politics

Under Mexico's one-party system it is difficult to determine what proportion of the population really participates in the country's political life. Certainly the 40 to 50 percent of the population that is illiterate plays only a very minor role. In 1958 almost one out of every four persons in the country cast a ballot, but this figure is not too significant because of the kind of electoral system in use.

All persons over twenty-one, or over eighteen if married, are eligible to vote and are required to register. All registered voters must vote under penalty of a fine, but this penalty is not enforced. Women voted for a president for the first time in 1958, but their participation did not change the system in any way except to increase the number of votes.

Can one make any estimate of what proportion of the population participates in politics by looking at the membership figures of the government party? Probably not. The millions listed as members of labor unions, farm organizations, and other groups in the popular sector of the party organization may not even support the PRI, even though their leadership may do so. A larger proportion of the population is active in politics now than was the case in the past, but the majority probably still plays no role at all. Until a competitive party system develops, popular participation will develop only slowly.

The Electoral Machinery

Under the Mexican federal system, the nation and the states regulate their own elections. At the national level, the voters select only the president and the members of the two houses of Congress. Because of the preponderant position of the PRI, elections are really not decisive in selecting public officials, but as the years have gone by, rather peaceful voting became the rule. Until 1945 elections were controlled by municipal and state officials, and a great deal of violence accompanied each election; but since 1945, national elections have been under the control of a Federal Electoral Commission consisting of six persons, the Minister of Government, a senator, a deputy, and three representatives from the political parties. In actual practice the majority of the six are always members of the PRI. Each state has an electoral committee of three persons selected by the Federal Commission to which each party may send a representative with a voice but no vote. Each state electoral committee nominates the members of district electoral committees who are then appointed by the Federal Electoral Commission. The district electoral committees select the sites for the polling places and appoint the persons in charge of the actual voting.

The actual election occurs every three years on the first Sunday in July, with the polls open from 8 A.M. to 5 P.M. Each party and candidate is entitled to have a poll watcher present. The citizen is given an Australian-type ballot for each office, which he marks in private. Although votes are counted by the local and district election officials, the real decision as to who has been elected to Congress is made by the Congress itself.

The one-party system seems to make the electoral process a farce, but other political parties do exist, as we shall see, and as the habit of voting regularly develops, the electoral process will become more significant.

Campaigning for Office

Although elections are not decisive in selecting the president of Mexico, every presidential candidate since Lázaro Cárdenas in 1934 has campaigned vigorously, visiting every important center of population, participating in parades, shaking hands, and doing all the things candidates ordinarily do to win votes. Is there any purpose to all this campaigning, since everyone knows in advance who the victor will be? The Mexican presidential candidates seem to think so, and in fact the campaign is valuable for several reasons. Because the PRI nominee for president is almost inevitably an efficient functionary who has worked his way up the party and governmental ladder rather than a charismatic leader popular with the masses, he is likely to be relatively unknown to the majority of voters. An extensive campaign, therefore, makes the candidate known to many people. The painting of the candidate's name on walls, streets, mountainsides, and every other available space keeps it before the public, and when the man becomes president, his name, now known all over the country, acts as a focal point for all Mexican political life. In the second place, since there is no doubt in anyone's mind as to who will win the election, it is necessary to stimulate enough interest to get the voters to the polls. The continuous publicity over radio and television, in the newspapers, and through meetings and parades helps to arouse this interest. In addition, the PRI candidate's tour of Mexico is an educational experience for him, for he learns much about his country that few middle-class city-dwellers have had an opportunity to know. In every place the candidate stops, he is presented with lists of what the people of the locality need. Thus the candidate serves as another channel through which the people of Mexico inform the central government of their problems.

The minority-party candidates try to imitate the PRI candidate, but they have neither the following nor the resources to conduct as elaborate or widespread campaigns. At times the minority candidates meet difficulties in certain localities, and their meetings are sometimes broken up by enthusiastic opponents, but, generally speaking, they campaign freely. The PRI simply has the support of so large a percentage of the voters that little interest is shown in what the minority-party candidates have to say.

Political Parties

The PRI is a direct descendant of the PNR, organized in 1928 by Plutarco Calles. At that time local clubs were set up in all of Mexico's cities and larger towns, and all important government officials, interest-group leaders favoring the government, army officers, and intellectuals who supported the revolution became members of the PNR. The new party had within its ranks all shades of opinion. *It was not really a political party;* rather it was a mechanism to help Calles control the country.

In 1938 the party changed its name to Party of the Mexican Revolution and new sections of the population were brought into the organization. Until 1938, one was a member of the party only indirectly, by being a member of a military, labor, or agrarian organization affiliated with the PNR, but after 1938 a popular sector was added which individuals could join. In 1940 the military sector was abolished and the political officers entered the popular sector. In 1946 the party was again reorganized and its name was changed to the *Partido Revolucionario Institucional,* as it remains today.

In the past two decades the PRI has become a little more democratic and a little more representative of the total population as more groups have been integrated into its network of subsidiary organizations and as more differences of opinion have been permitted. But it remains primarily an apparatus that helps the president to control the country. A Mexican does not have to belong to the PRI and one can even be a member of an opposing party, but the PRI contains within its ranks so large a part of the politically active population that it is almost impossible to hope for a successful political career unless one belongs to it.

The organization of the PRI goes from the top down, the most important party official being the president of the National Executive Committee, who is chosen by the president of the republic. The president of the National Executive Committee is very powerful, for he serves as one of the important channels through whom an individual or a pressure group can reach the president of the republic.

Second in importance is the secretary general, who has a staff of several hundred employees. The president and secretary general more or less control the party slates at all levels of government, and they mediate disputes arising between the various sections of the party.

Next in importance to the president and the secretary general are the secretaries of the interest groups within the party: the secretaries of agrarian, labor, popular, political, women's, and youth groups, who are the channels of communication between their constituencies and the party hierarchy.

A national assembly meets every three years or at the call of the National Executive Committee. The delegates to the assembly are elected from the three sectors into which party members are organized: agrarian, labor, and popular. The National Assembly has no real power; rather it is a sort of mass meeting at which the party leaders make speeches and the delegates formalize decisions previously agreed upon by the leaders. A national council of forty-five members, fifteen from each sector, is elected by the National Assembly. It too has little power; membership is a reward to faithful party members. The National Executive Committee of six to eight persons runs the party, with its president having most of the power in his hands. The president and secretary general are elected by the National Assembly, but the president of the republic has previously designated whom he wants in these positions.[6] The other members of the National Executive Committee are the secretaries of the agrarian, labor, and popular sectors, and a senator and a representative. Theoretically these members are all elected by the groups they represent, but in actual practice they must have the approval of the president of the party.

The secretaries of the interest groups act as organizers of and advocates for their groups. They help to push legislation of interest to their groups and try to see that good party men are elected to office in the local groups. There is a close link here between the interest group and the party. In recent years the head of the largest labor union, the Mexican Confederation of Workers (CTM), has been the Secretary of Labor

---

[6] Just as the incumbent president in the United States or the leader of the government party in the United Kingdom does.

Action of the PRI. In the same way, the other secretaries are connected with their interest groups. The Political Action secretaries, for example, always are a senator and a deputy, who serve to link the party and the legislature.

Each state and territory and the Federal District has a regional executive committee similar to the National Executive Committee. This committee is elected at a meeting of the presidents of the party's municipal committees in the state. Just as the president selects the president of the National Executive Committee, the state governor selects the president of the regional executive committee. The municipal committee consists of five members appointed by the National Committee on proposal of the regional executive committee. Usually one is a woman and each of the sectors represented in the area has a member.

Having listed all this machinery, we can turn to the really important base of the PRI's strength, the sector organizations: the *Confederación Nacional de Campesinos*, the *Confederación de Trabajadores de México*, and the *Confederación Nacional de Organizaciones Populares*. The latter includes such organizations as civil service unions (the government employees), the National Cooperative Confederation, the National Confederation of Small Agricultural Proprietors, and the National Confederation of Intellectual Workers. Most of these organizations have functions other than politics which take up most of their effort. They lobby within the PRI for their constituencies, seeing that their interests are protected on all levels.

Although one party wins practically all elections in Mexico, a large number of organizations calling themselves political parties are active. Legally any group of citizens can organize a political party and enter into political activity. The law defines a political party as an association of political orientation established for electoral ends composed of Mexican citizens in full enjoyment of their political rights. All parties that seek to participate in national elections are regulated by national law, and state laws patterned on the national law regulate state and local party organizational activity.

To qualify as a national party, a political group must register with the Ministry of Government, presenting a list of 75,000 members of whom at least 2,500 must reside in each of two-thirds of the thirty-two subdivisions of the country (states, territories, the Federal District). The party must also present a program for the solution of national problems that does not allude to religious or racial matters, nor can the party be affiliated with any international or foreign political organization. It is doubtful that the rule requiring 75,000 members is strictly observed;

political considerations seem to be of first importance, and the decision as to whether a party should be registered is probably made at the highest level of government.

The National Action Party (*Partido Acción Nacional,* or PAN) is moderately conservative and sympathetic to the Catholic church. Led by business and professional men, it is the second largest party in Mexico. One of its leading efforts is to repeal Article 3 of the constitution, which bans religious teaching from the public schools. Its strength varies from election to election. In 1964 it won more than 10 percent of the vote and received twenty seats in the Chamber of Deputies, its greatest victory up to that time.

Communism functions in Mexico through four political parties and a host of front organizations, although it is not clear why four Communist parties are needed, since all are comparatively small and have basically the same program of support for the Soviet Union and opposition to United States influence in Mexico. The Mexican Communist Party (PCM), founded in 1919, has not been a registered party for many years, but it is very active, particularly in the National University, in the publication, radio, and television fields, and in the trade unions. Its failure to grow led one of its leading supporters, Vicente Lombardo Toledano, at one time an important labor leader, to found a new Communist party in 1948, called the People's Party, which later changed its name to Popular Socialist Party. The PPS is a registered party that won 0.6 percent of the votes cast in the 1961 elections and was allotted one seat in the Chamber of Deputies. In 1964 it was awarded ten seats in the Chamber and that year the PPS endorsed the presidential nominee of the PRI.

The Mexican Worker and Peasant Party (POCM) was founded in 1950 by former members of the PCM and has managed to maintain itself as an aggressive group, though it has always been small. Toward the end of 1961, the sympathizers of Fidel Castro, using the name of Lázaro Cárdenas as their ostensible leader, organized the National Liberation Movement (MLN), which has been very vocal in urging extreme programs. It probably has an overlapping membership with the other Communist-controlled organizations. No accurate estimates are available as to the membership of these organizations, but they are extremely active, well supplied with funds, and able to mobilize sizable numbers of people on specific issues. Basically, however, Russian, Chinese, or any other kind of communism is handicapped because it came on the scene later than the Mexican revolution.

Other minority parties are the Mexican Nationalist Party (PNM), which in 1952 and 1958 supported the PRI candidate for president, and the Authentic Party of the Mexican Revolution (PARM), which also supported the PRI candidate in 1958. In 1964 the PARM was allotted five seats in the Chamber of Deputies. Important at one time was the National *Sinarquista* Union (UNS), a semifascist, very pro-Catholic organization which is illegal because of its encouragement of violence. It advocates an organization of Mexico "without anarchy" based upon the Catholic faith, the Spanish tradition, the stable home, and a Christian political order. It opposes labor unions and favors Catholic censorship of the press to strengthen "law and order." Strongest in the early 1940's when the German Nazis supplied funds to the organization, it has been relatively quiet in recent years, although it apparently still functions in secret. In November 1960 the *jefe nacional* of the UNS offered volunteers to the OAS to help defend any country invaded by Communists. In December 1963 the UNS entered the Nationalist Party and was given nine seats on the executive committee of the PNM. Other minor parties continue to issue manifestos occasionally, but none has any importance.

Neither state nor federal law regulates party finances. The PAN and the *Sinarquistas* receive most of their funds from wealthy businessmen, landowners, and religious enthusiasts. The PCM and the PPS claim that they are financed by donations from workers, students, and intellectuals, but almost certainly receive the bulk of their funds from outside Mexico. The PRI collects "participation" dues from government officials, industrial and agricultural labor unions, businessmen, and civil servants in the state and local governments. Most of its money, however, comes from the treasuries of its member organizations, with some subsidy from government.

Public Opinion and Pressure Groups

Public opinion in Mexico, like everything else in the country, it centralized in Mexico City. The larger cities all have their own newspapers, but the newspapers and the radio and television stations in the capital city are the most influential in the country. At the same time, the large number of illiterates prevents any newspaper from having a really large circulation. *La Prensa* of Mexico City, with a daily circulation of 110,000 in 1961, was the most widely read daily. This is not very impressive in a city whose metropolitan area then contained around 5 million people. In the same year the more than 150 daily newspapers in the country had a total circulation of around 1.5 million daily. Just as in the rest of Latin America, the United States press is widely circulated, with *Selecciones de Reader's Digest* and *Life en Español* probably being the most widely read.

Most articulate Mexicans express themselves through functional organizations that are tied into the labor sector, peasant sector, and popular sector of the PRI. During recent decades the popular sector seems to have dominated the PRI, and the highest positions in the government have most frequently been filled by persons associated with this section of the party.

Despite the near monopoly of the PRI, two important interests are not included in the organizations affiliated with it. The Catholic church and the most important businessmen's organizations manage to function independently. Ironically, some observers point out that the country's business interests have benefited more from the Mexican revolution than any other single group in the country, and there is much evidence that this is so. The businessmen manage to influence policy-making because they have associated with them silent partners who are important officials of both the government and the functional organizations affiliated with the PRI. Most of the country's leading politicians become comparatively wealthy, and some—former President Miguel Alemán is the best example—become multimillionaires.

By law, all firms capitalized at 500 pesos ($40 U.S.) must join the national organizations representing business and industry. The Confederation of Industrial Chambers (CONCAMIN) and the Confederation of National Chambers of Commerce (CONCANCO) now represent practically all Mexican employers and have close relationships with the government, although they are not affiliated with the PRI. In addition, about 10,000 businessmen and firms are members of a private organization, the Employers' Confederation. There has been little open conflict between business and government in Mexico, and most businessmen recognize the need for the government to own and operate various economic enterprises.[7] The petroleum industry, most railroads, and the electric power industry are owned and operated by the government. Furthermore, the government plays an important part in economic development and the organization of new industries through its banks. All of the country's cooperatives, about 2,000 in number, by law must belong to the National Cooperative Confederation, which is one of the branches of the popular sector of the PRI. Through these organizations, all economic groups make their wishes known to the government.

---

[7] Of the thirty largest industrial and commercial companies in Mexico, only one is government-owned, three have mixed ownership, and the rest are privately owned. See "Mexico's Top 30 Companies," *Latin America '67*, p. 116.

Nearly 2.5 million workers, or nearly 20 percent of the economically active population, are members of trade unions. This represents about 40 percent of the nonagricultural labor force. Collective bargaining is an accepted practice in Mexico. About three-fifths of all union members belong to the Mexican Confederation of Workers (CTM), which is affiliated with the ORIT (Regional Inter-American Organization of Workers) and, along with the other labor unions, makes up the labor sector of the PRI.

The trade unions are greatly influenced by the official policy of the government, which recognizes unions through the Ministry of Labor. The leadership of the trade unions is highly bureaucratized, and many leaders serve for decades. During the 1960's there has been a stronger emphasis placed upon democracy and renovation than was the case earlier. The organized labor movement has raised the workers' standard of living, and leading labor leaders have received important positions in state, local, and national governments. The labor movement can therefore definitely be said to play an important role in the formation of public policy.

The Mexican armed forces are no longer the dominant group they used to be in Mexican life, and since 1940 no general has been the presidential candidate of the PRI. Since World War II the Mexican armed forces have become a professionally trained instrument controlled by the civilian president. During the 1960's the Mexican armed forces consisted of about 50,000 men, including about 3,500 in the officer corps. The officers are not completely out of politics, as officers often serve as government ministers, as governors of states, and in other positions, including the important post of president of the National Executive Committee of the PRI. But when President Cárdenas removed the local power base of the political generals during his reorganization of the government party in 1938, he pushed the military into the background, and there it has stayed. The army remains a powerful interest group, but today the military is, as one scholar points out, "one of several interest groups in the complicated political equations rather than, as formerly, the almost single dominant one."[8]

The Catholic church remains an important force in Mexican life, but it is not one of the most important pressure groups. The bitter church-state struggle during most of the nineteenth century and the first part of the twentieth century has ceased, and relations between the church and the government are now fairly routine. The separation of

---

[8] Howard F. Cline, *Mexico: Revolution to Evolution: 1940–1960* (New York: Oxford University Press, 1963), p. 175.

church and state has forced the church to confine itself to religious matters. Protestants and members of other religious groups function as freely as the Catholics, and all religious groups now are much more remote from political struggles than was the custom in the past.

Organized student groups play a special role in Mexican life, particularly in the capital city, where the National University students join with various political groups in demonstrations, parades, and other activities. Students often close their schools with strikes, and at times violence results.

Civil Liberties

The Mexican constitution contains an elaborate list of individual guarantees that are generally observed in all parts of the country. The people of Mexico (including noncitizens) enjoy all the rights that democratic countries usually protect: the right to speak, write, publish, worship, and petition freely, to assemble peaceably, to enjoy due process of law in any process against them, and many more. No *ex post facto* laws are valid, slavery is forbidden, and no one may be imprisoned for civil debt. As a special mechanism to protect civil rights, Mexico has created the writ of *amparo*, a judicial proceeding that combines the common-law writs of *habeas corpus, mandamus*, and *certiorari*, and is intended to prevent any government official from damaging the interests of citizens or infringing their constitutional rights.

In general, the average Mexican does as he pleases, goes where he wants, leaves the country or returns to it as he sees fit. The electoral system, as has been mentioned, is not a perfect reflection of the wishes of the population, but Communists, Fascists, Trotskyites, religious missionaries, and various other minority groups publish newspapers and speak over radio and television, hold meetings, demonstrate, and carry on various other activities freely.

Yet, under Article 29 of the constitution, the president of the republic may suspend the constitutional guarantees "in the event of invasion, serious disturbances of the public peace, or any other event which may place society in great danger or conflict." This is a most powerful weapon, and in other Latin-American countries it has been used to impose dictatorships. Fortunately, the governments of revolutionary Mexico have not utilized this article with great frequency; its last use was during World War II.

The Executive

Mexico's president is elected for a six-year term by direct popular vote and is thereafter forever ineligible for reelection. There is no vice-president. If the office of president becomes vacant during the first two years of a term, a new election is held. If the vacancy occurs after two years have passed, the Congress selects someone to complete the term. No president has died in office since the stabilization of the revolutionary regime in the 1930's, so it is not known how this method of filling the vacancy would actually work in practice.

To be eligible for the presidency one must be a native-born citizen and the son of native-born parents, at least thirty-five years old, who has lived in Mexico during the entire year preceding the election. One cannot be a member of the clergy of any religious denomination, or have "ecclesiastical status," or have been on active duty with the army or have held certain high offices within six months of the election. (This clause does not keep generals or cabinet members from becoming president, since they resign in time to become eligible if they are going to get the support of the PRI.) Although all of these formal rules are observed, in practice the incumbent president selects his successor. But to say that the incumbent president selects his successor is not to say that he can select anyone he wishes, for he must act within the limits set by practical politics. Some scholars think that all of the living ex-presidents have a veto over the selection of the new president, with Lázaro Cárdenas and Miguel Alemán being the most important of those consulted. Others believe that the pressures of the various forces in Mexican life point to a person of certain characteristics, and the incumbent president decides which political leader best meets the specifications, subject to the approval of the most important interest-group leaders.

Whatever the method of selection, it seems to have removed the charismatic leader from the Mexican presidency, as again and again the person selected has been a quiet, efficient, devoted member of the upper echelons of the party. In recent years, the person selected has been a cabinet minister when he was chosen. President Adolfo López Mateos, for example, had been a schoolteacher, secretary to a state governor, secretary to the head of the National Revolutionary Party (PNR), secretary general of the Federal District regional committee of the PNR, a functionary of the *Banco Nacional Obrero de Fomento*, the National Printing Office, and the National Treasury, rector of the National Institute of Toluca, a senator, Mexican delegate to the United Nations Economic and Social Council, secretary general of the PRI, campaign manager for Ruiz Cortines, and secretary of the Department of Labor and Welfare. Gustavo Díaz Ordaz was Minister of Government at the time he was nominated by the PRI. He had begun his career as a government employee at the age of twenty-one and slowly worked his way up the hierarchy of the judicial system. By 1937 he was president of the Superior Court of Justice in the state of Puebla and vice-rector of the University of Puebla. In later years he was a deputy and a senator of the National Congress, director of judicial affairs in the Ministry of Government, and a member of the minister's staff of that ministry. In 1958 President López Mateos appointed him Minister of Government.

The Mexican system of selecting a presidential candidate is really not very different from that used in other democratic countries. Every incumbent United States president selects his successor and obtains his party's nomination for his choice, although in the United States the incumbent president may not be able to win the election for his choice (e.g., Eisenhower and Nixon in 1960). What distinguishes the Mexican system is that once having selected his successor, the Mexican president, through his control of the government and the PRI, can install him in office.

In formal structure, Mexico has a federal system with a division of powers between the states and a central government which is divided into the three traditional branches. But in actual practice, the country is governed by the president and the executive apparatus he controls. His policy is followed by the legislature, by the courts, and by state and local governments, and if they do not follow his lead, he has the offending individuals removed and replaced by men who will follow his policy.

The power granted to the president by the constitution of 1917 is broad. In addition to his duty to promulgate and execute the laws, he has a veto over congressional bills (which is never used, since no bill he opposes is ever passed), very broad appointive powers, control of foreign relations, the power to pardon, and the power to suspend constitutional guarantees with the approval of the Congress or its Permanent Committee. Among those he freely appoints and removes from office are the members of the Cabinet, the attorney general, the governor of the Federal District, the governors of the federal territories, and all other employees whose appointment and dismissal does not require congressional action, including all officers of the armed forces below the rank of colonel. With the approval of the Senate he appoints the justices of the Supreme Court, diplomatic personnel, and the higher officers of the armed forces and the Treasury.

The president apparently does everything in Mexico. It is common to see appeals published in the newspapers asking him to settle labor disputes, help an area in distress, or solve an economic problem. According to *Time* magazine, in 1953 President Ruiz Cortines found time to issue a decree making ninety-eight changes in the rules governing bull-fights.[9]

The Civil Service

There is no formal merit system in the Mexican civil service, but the overwhelming influence of the PRI has stabilized the public service because practically all public servants are members of trade unions, which are incorporated into the popular sector of the PRI. Each agency has control over the recruitment of its employees. Since 1938 a general law has regulated government employees, but this applies only to the one-third known as "base workers" and omits the two-thirds known as "confidence workers" (political appointees). The general law refers to such things as the general conditions of work, salaries, hours, and probationary periods.

There have been many complaints concerning the quality of the government employees and their well-known tradition of *la mordida* (the bite). President Ruiz Cortines made a determined effort at enforcing high standards of honesty for government employees, dismissing hundreds of persons from their positions, but no substantial change has been noticed.

During recent years, interest in better public administration has risen markedly in Mexico. A *Revista de Administración Pública* is now published, a Society of Public Administration functions, and courses in public administration are now being offered at the university. The increasing complexity of the Mexican economy and the involvement of the federal government in many economic activities has tended to increase this interest further. Many of the government agencies operate in-service training programs for their employees.

Public Finance

Mexico's president dominates the government's budget process, as he does all other aspects of government, and the legislature never makes

---

[9] *Time*, December 7, 1953, p. 42.

any substantial changes in the figures submitted by the president before it approves the budget. The president submits the budget to the Chamber of Deputies by December 15. This leaves the Chamber fifteen days (including Christmas) in which to consider this important document, so only the most cursory revision is possible if the budget is to be approved before January 1, when it goes into effect. If the Chamber does not approve the budget by January 1, the previous year's figures automatically are appropriated.

The income and expenditures of the Mexican government have multiplied rapidly during the years since World War II, although it is almost impossible to give exact figures describing the government's financial position, since the regular budget does not include the transactions of the government's decentralized agencies and the private businesses owned in part by the government. The Mexican peso has remained steady (at $0.08 U.S.) since April 1954, yet in nine years the annual receipts and expenditures nearly tripled, from 5.681 billion pesos in 1955 to almost 16 billion pesos in 1964.

The 1964 budget of the national government, as shown in Tables 2 and 3, is typical of Mexico's revenues and expenditures during the

TABLE 2

ESTIMATED REVENUE OF MEXICO, FISCAL YEAR 1964

(000,000 Omitted)

Source	Amount in Pesos	Percent of Total
Income tax	$6,004	37.63%
Taxes on lotteries, gambling, etc.	108	0.68
Export taxes	759	4.75
Taxes on exploitation of natural resources	248	1.56
Taxes on commerce and production	2,170	13.60
Taxes on mercantile incomes	1,612	10.10
Import taxes	1,736	10.88
Stamp taxes	279	1.75
Other taxes	328	2.06
Fees for government services	620	3.89
Earnings from exploitation or use of national property	682	4.28
Profits	758	4.75
Total ordinary revenue	$15,304	95.93%
Earnings from sales and capital earnings	50	0.31
Loans and financing	600	3.76
Total revenue	$15,954	100.00%

TABLE 3

ESTIMATED EXPENDITURES OF MEXICO, FISCAL YEAR 1964

(000 Omitted)

	Amount in Pesos	Percent of Total
Legislature	$69,480	0.43%
President's office	45,323	0.28
Judiciary	62,631	0.40
Attorney General's office	32,346	0.20
Ministry of Government	104,692	0.66
Ministry of Foreign Relations	165,680	1.04
Ministry of Finance and Public Credit	571,889	3.59
Ministry of National Defense	1,062,197	6.66
Ministry of Agriculture and Livestock	324,914	2.03
Ministry of Communications and Transport	999,212	6.26
Ministry of Industry and Commerce	129,179	0.81
Ministry of Education	4,062,066	25.46
Ministry of Public Health and Welfare	778,424	4.88
Ministry of Navy and Marine	422,078	2.65
Ministry of Labor and Social Security	51,762	0.33
Ministry of Agrarian Affairs and Colonization	99,643	0.63
Ministry of Hydraulic Resources	1,405,212	8.81
Ministry of National Patrimony	161,609	1.02
Ministry of Military Industry	77,248	0.48
Ministry of Public Works	1,243,811	7.74
Tourism	65,710	0.41
Investments	768,305	4.81
Additional expenses	2,287,004	14.33
Public debt	972,126	6.09
Total	$15,953,541	100.00%

1960's. As the figures demonstrate, Mexico devotes a large part of its regular budget to economic development, public education, and social welfare, with education receiving the largest single share, 25.46 percent of the total funds expended in 1964. Mexico's tax structure is much sounder than that of most of the other Latin-American republics, with 37.63 percent of its revenue coming from income taxes. Nevertheless, there is much criticism of the country's tax structure, mainly because it continues to be regressive, and Mexico apparently is one of the least heavily taxed countries in Latin America. Mexico's income-tax law differentiates between different kinds of income, with rates on salaries and wages being lower than those on interest and profits. Only the tax on salaries and wages is withheld at the source.

The Legislative Power

Mexico's legislature is a bicameral Congress consisting of a Senate and a Chamber of Deputies. One deputy is elected for each 200,000 inhabitants or fraction over 100,000, with each state receiving a minimum of two deputies and each territory at least one. In 1963 the total membership of the Chamber of Deputies was 178: 172 from the PRI, 5 from the PAN, and 1 from the PPS. Each house is the judge of its own members. After the election is held, the preparatory committee of the new session decides who has been elected. In the Senate, all the seats in recent decades have gone to members of the PRI, and in the Chamber of Deputies only a few seats have gone to parties other than the PRI.

The Senate is composed of sixty members, two from each state and two from the Federal District. Deputies serve for three years and senators serve for six years. Both are elected by direct vote, with alternates elected at the same time. Members of the Congress cannot be reelected, although their alternates can be elected for the following term. Senators and deputies cannot be alternates for the following term, but become eligible again after a term has intervened. In order to be a deputy, one must be a Mexican by birth, at least twenty-five years old, a native of or a resident of the state or territory from which he seeks election, and in possession of his political rights. Not eligible are those on active service in the army, various national officials (unless they have resigned their positions ninety days before the election), the governor of a state, or clergymen. In order to be a senator, one must meet all of the deputy's requirements and be at least thirty-five years old. The Mexican Congress meets regularly on September 1 of each year and must adjourn not later than December 31. Special sessions can be called by the Permanent Committee of the Congress, but such sessions can consider only the matters presented by the Permanent Committee. When in session the Congress usually meets twice a week, usually for an hour or two each time. The shortness of the Congress' meetings and the overwhelming power of the president of the republic, as well as the near monopoly of the PRI on membership, relegates Congress to a minor position in Mexican life.

Between sessions, a Permanent Committee of fifteen deputies and fourteen senators handles the business of the Congress, but the Permanent Committee cannot legislate. The Congress has the power to admit new states to the Union, change the boundaries of the states, legislate on all matters dealing with the Federal District and national territories, levy taxes, and legislate on the subjects of hydrocarbons, mining, the motion-picture industry, commerce, gambling, credit institutions, electric power, and education. In addition, the Senate ratifies treaties made by the president and approves certain appointments made by him.

The weakness of the Congress and the pressure for a greater popular voice in government led the PRI to amend the constitution in 1962 so that any political party that receives at least 2.5 percent of the total votes cast but does not get proportional representation in the Chamber will be given five seats in the Chamber of Deputies plus an additional seat for each additional 0.5 percent of the votes cast over 2.5 percent up to a maximum of twenty deputies. It is impossible to say whether this will improve the functioning of the Congress, but the sponsors of the amendment thought that it would encourage the development of a responsible opposition in the Chamber of Deputies. In recent decades, most of the bills passing through the Congress have been introduced by the president or the state legislatures. Adding the few opposition members will not really change the character of the legislature, which will remain weak as long as it is dominated by a single party and meets only for a short time each year. Unable to be reelected, no legislator in Mexico can build a basis of power within the Congress, and the positions of deputy and senator are usually held by young politicians just starting their careers or by old politicians losing their effectiveness, who receive a congressional seat as a reward for past services.

The Judicial Power

Mexico's judicial power rests in a Supreme Court of Justice of twenty-one members and subsidiary tribunals. The Supreme Court justices are appointed by the president with the consent of the Senate. The Supreme Court appoints the judges of the lower courts and has administrative jurisdiction over them. Supreme Court justices serve for life. Judges of the lower courts are appointed for four years, but receive life tenure if they are reappointed or promoted. Judges with life tenure can be removed only for improper conduct after a recommendation by the president and a majority vote of the Congress. The Supreme Court serves either as a plenary court or in four divisions of five justices each, each division dealing with a different subject.

Below the Supreme Court there are six circuit courts, each headed by a single judge, which deal with appeals from the lower district courts, of which there are forty-eight. There also are five circuits with more than one judge in each court which deal with writs of *amparo*.

The Mexican judicial system is based on the civil law system brought from Europe. Under this system the judges look for the law in codes, which are elaborate collections of laws passed by the legislature. Mexico's great contribution to law has been the development of the writ of *amparo*, under which any person can appeal to the courts for justice to prevent a government official from harming him or taking away his constitutional rights. Generally speaking, in civil cases the Mexican courts function well, but the court system is distinctly subordinate to the executive power. There is no such thing as judicial review of legislative or executive acts. In cases of conflict, most judges seem to take into consideration the wishes of the executive.

Mexican Federalism

Mexico's constitution sets up a federal republic which consists of twenty-nine states, two territories, and the Federal District. Despite its constitution, federalism is an exotic growth in Mexico. Opposition to the centralized character of the colonial government and admiration of United States federalism led most liberal Mexicans to associate unified centralized government with tyranny. In a reaction to tyrannical centralization, federalism was proposed as the proper form of Mexico's republican government. It is important to note that the members of the 1917 constitutional assembly did not even debate the issue. But despite such long-standing agreement, it is doubtful whether true federal government has ever functioned in Mexico.

Three forces have tended to negate federalism in Mexico. The geographic and human diversity of the country have always promoted localism and regionalism. One would think that this would be a good basis for the federal form of organization, but in actual practice the social organization of the country required a strong central government. As has been pointed out, since the days of the Aztecs each dominant group in Mexico has had difficulty in organizing the country. The loss of half the country (Texas, New Mexico, Arizona, and California) to the United States well illustrates this difficulty. Federalism could not operate as long as the country was not joined together into a functioning whole.

Several scholars have pointed out that Mexico was made into a federal state from the top down, whereas the successful federal countries of the world, such as the United States and Australia, were created by the fusion of previously existing organized political units. The component parts of Mexico never grew together, but rather were forcibly united by the Aztec, Spanish, or republican armies, and throughout history have been kept united by force. The Constituent Congress of 1824 simply divided the Mexican territory into states and expected them to behave like states.

The character of the one-party system in Mexico also prevents the functioning of federalism by enforcing a centralized policy. And finally, the Mexican constitution contains articles giving the central government the power to intervene legally in the functioning of the states. Utilizing these clauses and his power over the PRI, the president of the republic, acting through the Minister of Government, sees that no one who is unacceptable to the president is elected in any state. The question of the governorship of a state comes before the federal government usually because two or sometimes three governors, each with a legislature, claims to have been elected. All election results must be accepted by the federal government, so each candidate sends telegrams to the president, the Minister of Government, and the Senate to announce his victory. The office of the Minister of Government, acting through the Senate or the Senate's Permanent Committee, decides which candidate is to be recognized and tells the local military commander to see that the winning candidate and his legislature are installed in office. Nor is this all. The constitution also authorizes the central government to see that democratic governments prevail in the states, that the constitution and the federal laws are published and executed by the state officers, that constitutional guarantees are not denied, and that peace is maintained between the different sections of the state government. The central government can intervene in the states for any of the above reasons, and it has frequently done so.

In recent decades the federal government has only on rare occasions intervened in the states, but this does not mean the states are any more independent that they ever were. The PRI is so overwhelmingly in control of the country that it can obtain the resignation of any governor who has lost the confidence of the national government.

The standard definition of federalism is that it is a government system in which the power to govern is divided between the national government and the governments of the component parts, with each of these receiving its powers from the written constitution, which cannot be changed without the consent of both the national government and two-thirds or three-fourths of the state governments. In describing federalism Professor K. C. Wheare, a leading authority on the subject, uses the phrase "the general and the regional governments being co-ordinate and independent in their respective spheres."[10] Using this definition, it can be said that Mexico does not truly have a federal system of government. The money at the disposal of the state and local governments also seems to testify to this, for in 1954, when the national government spent

---

[10] K. C. Wheare, *Federal Government* (London: Oxford University Press, 1953), p. 5.

7,916,807,418 pesos, all of the states combined spent only 1,359,239,000 pesos.

The Formal Structure of the States

Mexican states vary greatly in size, population, and resources. The larger states are in the less populated dry north, the smaller states in the mountains of the central area. State population in 1967 varied from a low of 221,000 in Colima to a high of 3,409,000 in Vera Cruz. Only seven of the twenty-nine states had more than 2 million population.

The national constitution requires the states to have governments that are "popular, representative, and republican," and which create the free *municipio* as the form of local government. The states are given the powers reserved to them by the constitution, but their role is restricted by the concurrent powers exercised by the national government and by definite prohibitions upon what they can do. States cannot, without the consent of the national Congress, levy import or export duties, maintain permanent troops, or make war except when invaded or when invasion is imminent. They are prohibited from making treaties, issuing money or stamps, taxing the transit of persons and goods, or negotiating loans that are not for revenue-producing purposes. States are also obligated to render criminals wanted in other areas, to publish and enforce federal law, and to give full faith and credit to the public acts, registers, and judicial proceedings of the other states. Since the national government exercises power in the fields of education, public health, mineral industries, commerce in general, social security, religion, and labor relations, not much is left for the states to do.

Mexican state constitutions are long, involved, and easy to amend; that of the state of Mexico was amended 139 times between 1921 and 1951. The formal structure of the various states is similar. Each has a governor who serves a four- or six-year term. There is no lieutenant governor. All states have unicameral legislatures serving three- or four-year terms; the incumbents cannot be reelected. All have courts whose judges are appointed by the governors or elected by the legislatures or the people.

The states exercise limited powers over and spend money for public works, education, public services, courts, welfare, and public health, receiving their money from taxes and federal grants.

The real key to state power is the regional executive committee of the PRI, which, through its president, is the link to the national PRI and the president of the republic.

In its turn, the state government exercises close control over the *municipios* into which each state is divided for purposes of local government. The *municipio* is more like a county than like a municipality as the term is generally used in the United States. Each *municipio* is governed by an elected council, but the state governor, through the local PRI unit, keeps a close check on the *municipio* governments. As one close observer of Mexican *municipio* government has written: "In practice, the *municipio* is a decentralized agency of the state for administrative purposes, with as many powers as the state legislature may be willing to confer on it."[11]

Some of the Indian communities have kept their old form of government, but these exercise only local power in cooperation with the *municipio*. Among the Tarahumaras, for example, the authority is an assembly of adults which elects a governor to exercise its powers.

The Federal District, with a population of over 6 million (which is far more than that of any of the twenty-nine states), has no local self-government. It is run by the national government with the national Congress legislating for it and the executive power in the hands of a *jefe* (chief) appointed by the president. The *jefe*, with the president's approval, appoints all other officials, and has a Consultative Council which he appoints to advise him.

The two territories, Baja California Sur and Quintana Roo, are ruled by governors appointed by the president. The national Congress legislates for the territories, and each territorial governor has an appointed Consultative Council to advise him. The governor also appoints the other needed officials in his territory.

The weakness of state and local government led President Ruiz Cortines to stimulate the creation of local Committees of Moral, Civic, and Material Improvement in 1953. He started such groups in Vera Cruz in 1944, when he was governor of the state, and their success there led him to sponsor the organization of similar committees on a national scale. By 1955, more than 5,000 of these committees were functioning. Not really government bodies, the committees functioned as stimulators of public works and propagandists for community development. Where they were most effective, the people became more interested in politics, and certain local improvements were pushed to completion.[12]

---

[11] Leonard Cárdenas, *The Municipality in Northern Mexico*, Texas Western College Southwestern Studies, 1, no. 1 (Spring 1963): 33.

[12] See Frank R. Brandenburg, "Mexico's Blueprint for Democracy," *Latin American Report*, 1 (July 1956): 16–19. For an account of the activity of these committees in Sonora, see Marvin Alisky, "Surging Sonora," *Arizona Highways*, 40 (November 1964): 35.

So little empirical research has been done on Mexico that it is difficult to say exactly how important the organs of local government are. One study made of the power structure and decision-making process in Tijuana, a border city near San Diego, California, came to the conclusion that the real center of power was outside the city; that is, the important decisions for Tijuana were made in Mexicali, the state capital, and in Mexico City, with substantial influence from southern California.[13]

This pattern seems to prevail throughout Mexico. The Mexican government is so centralized that state and local governments are relatively unimportant; most decisions affecting states and localities are made in Mexico City.

Mexico: A Last Word

Although Mexico has passed through the most important and significant revolution yet experienced by Latin America, it has not yet developed a democratic political system. The most that can be said is that it is developing toward democracy. The revolution succeeded in eliminating those groups that had dominated Mexican life as heirs of the colonial system. However, in the establishment of the new revolutionary government, so much emphasis was placed on perpetuating the revolutionary leaders in power that little opportunity for democratic functioning was permitted to develop.

The greatest achievement of the Mexican revolution was the winning of personal liberty for a much larger proportion of the population than had enjoyed such liberty at any earlier time. A freedom that is still lacking is the freedom to seek election to public office with any realistic hope of winning without government backing, since the electoral system together with the near monopoly held by the PRI prevents any accurate reflection of the wishes of the voters in an election. At the same time, a Mexican's freedom includes the ability to rise through the hierarchy of the power structure to the highest position in Mexico, the presidency of the republic. Any Mexican can strive to become rich through business activity, he can acquire an education and achieve a position as a professional man or educator, or he can enter political life as a young man and eventually achieve high office.[14]

Although Mexico is a one-party state, democratic trends are at work

---

[13] Orrin E. Klapp and L. Vincent Padgett, "Power Structure and Decision-Making in a Mexican Border City," *American Journal of Sociology*, 65 (January 1960): 400–406.

[14] See Frank Brandenburg's interesting description of the twelve levels on the "ladder of political prestige" in his *The Making of Modern Mexico* (Englewood Cliffs, N.J.: Prentice-Hall, Inc., 1964), pp. 158–59.

within the PRI. While a broadening of the democratic process through the growth of an opposition party remains a possibility, it seems more likely to come about through an eventual split within the PRI and a resultant balance between the factions. Some scholars go so far as to identify a right wing in the PRI, led by former President Alemán, and a left wing, led by former President Cárdenas. Neither of these wings, however, is in any real sense an organized group, and the center of power continues to rest in the president of the republic and his associates.

In the first year of President Díaz Ordaz' term, a determined effort was made to democratize the PRI, but the attempt disrupted the functioning of the party to such an extent that it was abandoned. Yet the government and the PRI are more responsive to public pressure than ever before. The great weakness has been the failure to devise a system of rotation of leadership in many of the interest groups, particularly the trade unions and the armed forces. Fidel Velásquez, for example, has been the dominant figure in the Confederation of Mexican Labor since 1941, and most generals in the army saw service in the revolution and the civil wars that accompanied it. At the same time it must be pointed out that in these men and others like them, the members of the various functional interest groups incorporated into the sectors of the PRI have effective spokesmen through whom they can make their wishes known to the decision-makers.

The second great achievement of the Mexican revolution has been the development of a modern transportation system, which is enabling Mexico to become an integrated nation-state. It is still true that some millions of Mexican peasants live in isolated areas, largely cut off from the mainstream of developments within the country, but the number of such people living at a very low level of subsistence has been going down through the years. The development of tremendous irrigation projects in various parts of the country has brought new lands into cultivation and enabled swamps and deserts to be transformed into flourishing areas of settlement.

Mexico's revolution brought with it into political activity new sections of the population that had not previously participated in Mexican political life. At the same time, the desires of the Mexican masses for education and a better standard of living have so stimulated the country's political leaders that the share of Mexico's national budget devoted to education, some 25 percent in recent years, is one of the highest in the world, and the illiteracy rate has plummeted from about 78 to about 40 percent. At the same time, the enthusiasm engendered by the revolution has stimulated a flowering of artistic life, most notably in the fields of painting and architecture. The campus of the National University of Mexico contains some of the most strikingly beautiful university buildings ever built in the world. All these things enable the Mexicans to say that their revolution has been worthwhile. Mexico has amply demonstrated its ability to cope with its problems and move forward in ways acceptable to the great majority of its people, and there is little room for doubt that it will continue to do so in the years ahead.

SELECTED READINGS

ALISKY, MARVIN. *The Governors of Mexico.* Southwestern Studies, monograph no. 12. El Paso: Texas Western College Press, 1965.

———. "Government of Arizona's 'Other' Neighbor: Baja California," *Arizona State University Public Affairs Bulletin* 2 (1963): 1–3.

———. *State and Local Government in Sonora, Mexico.* Tempe: Arizona State University, Bureau of Government Research, 1962.

ALLOWAY, C. S. *Mexico: A Symposium on Law and Government.* Miami, Fla.: University of Miami Press, 1959.

BARNES, WILLIAM SPRAGUE. *Taxation in Mexico.* Boston: Little, Brown & Co., 1957.

BENÍTEZ, FERNANDO. *In the Footsteps of Cortez.* New York: Pantheon Books, 1952.

BETETA, RAMÓN. *El Pensamiento y la dinámica de la revolución mexicana.* 2nd ed. Mexico City: Editorial México Nuevo, 1951.

BRANDENBURG, FRANK. *The Making of Modern Mexico.* Englewood Cliffs, N.J.: Prentice-Hall, Inc., 1964.

———. "Mexico's Blueprint for Democracy." *Latin American Report* 1 (July 1956): 16–19.

———. "Organized Business in Mexico." *Inter-American Economic Affairs* 12 (Winter 1958): 26–50.

BRENNER, ANITA, and LEIGHTON, GEORGE R. *The Wind That Swept Mexico: The History of the Mexican Revolution.* New York: Harper & Bros., 1943.

BUSEY, JAMES L. "Mexico," *Latin America: Political Institutions and Processes,* pp. 10–49. New York: Random House, 1964.

CÁRDENAS, LEONARD. *The Municipality in Northern Mexico.* Texas Western College Southwestern Studies 1, no. 1 (Spring 1963).

CLINE, HOWARD F. "Mexico: A Matured Latin American Revolution." *Annals of the American Academy of Political and Social Science* 334 (March 1961): 84–85.

———. *Mexico: Revolution to Evolution, 1940–1960.* New York: Oxford University Press, 1963.

———. *The United States and Mexico.* Rev. ed. New York: Atheneum Publishers, 1963.

"Cómo funcionan nuestras secretarias y departamentos de estado." *Revista Internacional y Diplomática,* no. 100 (February 28, 1959), pp. 42–53.

CROW, JOHN A. *Mexico Today.* New York: Harper & Bros., 1957.

CUEVA, MARIO DE LA, et al. *México, cincuenta años de revolución.* Vol. 3, *La Política.* Mexico City: Fondo de Cultura Económica, 1961.

DELMAS, GLADYS. "Mexico: The Middle-Aged Revolution." *Reporter,* September 28, 1961, pp. 32–38.

EBENSTEIN, WILLIAM. "Public Administration in Mexico." *Public Administration Review* 5 (Spring 1945): 102–12.

FERNÁNDEZ BRAVO, VICENTE. "La Revolución y la política: Los Cambios operados en México a partir de la revolución." *Revista de las Ciencias Sociales* (Puerto Rico) 7 (September 1963): 231–45.

FLORES OLEA, VÍCTOR, *et al.* "Tres interrogaciones sobre el presente y futuro de México." *Cuadernos Americanos* 18 (January–February 1959): 44–75.

FUENTES DÍAZ, VICENTE. *Los partidos políticos en México.* 2 vols. Mexico City: Fuentes Díaz, 1954–56.

GONZÁLEZ NAVARRO, MOISÉS. "Mexico: The Lop-sided Revolution." In *Obstacles to Change in Latin America*, edited by Claudio Veliz. New York: Oxford University Press, 1965.

GOODSPEED, STEPHEN S. "The Development and Use of *Facultades Extraordinarias* in Mexico." *Southwestern Social Science Quarterly* 34 (December 1953): 17–33.

———. "El papel del jefe del ejecutivo en México." *Problemas industriales y agrícolas de México* 7 (January–March 1955): 13–208.

GRAHAM, D. L. "The Rise of the Mexican Right." *Yale Review* 52 (Autumn 1962): 102–11.

HANKE, LEWIS. "Mexico," *Mexico and the Caribbean*, pp. 68–95. New York: D. Van Nostrand Co., Inc., 1959.

JAMES, DANIEL. *Mexico and the Americans.* New York: Frederich A. Praeger, Inc., 1963.

JOHNSON, JOHN J. "Mexico," *Political Change in Latin America: The Emergence of the Middle Sector*, pp. 128–52. Stanford, Calif.: Stanford University Press, 1958.

JORDAN, HENRY P. "Mexico: From Revolution toward Constitutionalism." In *Foreign Governments*, edited by Fritz Morstein Marx. New York: Prentice-Hall, Inc., 1949.

KLAPP, O. E., and PADGETT, L. V. "Power Structure and Decision-Making in a Mexican Border City." *American Journal of Sociology* 65 (January 1960): 400–406.

KLING, MERLE. *A Mexican Interest Group in Action.* Englewood Cliffs, N.J.: Prentice-Hall, Inc., 1961.

LEWIS, OSCAR. "Mexico since Cárdenas." *Social Research* 26 (Spring 1959): 18–30.

LIEUWEN, EDWIN. "Curbing Militarism in Mexico: A Case Study," *Arms and Politics in Latin America*, pp. 101–26. New York: Frederick A. Praeger, Inc., 1961.

MACDONALD, AUSTIN F. "Mexico," *Latin American Politics and Government*, pp. 200–82. 2nd ed. New York: Thomas Y. Crowell Co., 1954.

MADDOX, JAMES G. "Economic Growth and Revolution in Mexico." *Land Economics* 36 (August 1960): 266–78.

MANTILLA PINEDA, B. "La Filosofía del derecho en México." *Estudios del Derecho* (Medellín, Colombia) 18 (February–May 1959): 7–17.

MECHAM, J. LLOYD. "Mexican Federalism—Fact or Fiction?" *Annals of the American Academy of Political and Social Science* 208 (March 1940): 23–38.

———. "The Origins of Federalism in Mexico." In *The Constitution Reconsidered*, edited by Conyers Read. New York: Columbia University Press, 1938.

MENDIETA Y NÚÑEZ, LUCIO. *La Administración pública en México.* Mexico City: Imprenta Universitaria, 1948.

———. "Ensayo sociológico sobre la burocracia mexicana." *Revista Mexicana de la Sociología* 3 (September–December 1941): 63–111.

———. *Los Partidos políticos.* Mexico City: Instituto de las Investigaciones Sociales, Universidad Nacional, 1947.

MIRANDA, JOSÉ. *Las Ideas y las instituciones políticas mexicanas.* Mexico City: Imprenta Universitaria, 1952.

MORTON, WARD M. "Mexican Constitutional Congress of 1916–17." *Southwestern Social Science Quarterly* 33 (December 1953): 17–27.

NEEDLER, MARTIN C. "Mexico: Revolution as a Way of Life," *Political Systems of Latin America*. Princeton, N.J.: D. Van Nostrand Co., Inc., 1964.

———. "The Political Development of Mexico." *American Political Science Review* 55 (June 1961): 308–12.

NEEF, ARTHUR. *Labor in Mexico.* Washington: U.S. Department of State, Agency for International Development, Communications Resources Division, 1963.

PADGETT, L. VINCENT. *The Mexican Political System.* Boston: Houghton Mifflin Co., 1966.

———. "Mexico's One Party System: A Re-evaluation." *American Political Science Review* 51 (December 1957): 995–1008.

PAZ, OCTAVIO. "The Mexican Revolution Today." *Dissent* 9 (Autumn 1962): 319–31.

PINNEY, EDWARD L., and CONLEY, JAMES E. "On Political Modernity in Mexico: Consensus and Recruitment." *Southwestern Social Science Quarterly* 44 (December 1963): 225–36.

"El Programa económico del Partido Revolucionario Institucional." *Revista de la Economia* 26 (March 1963): 74–102.

SCHMITT, KARL M. *Communism in Mexico.* Austin: University of Texas Press, 1965.

———. "Communism in Mexico Today." *Western Political Quarterly* 15 (March 1962): 111–24.

SCOTT, R. E. "Budget Making in Mexico." *Inter-American Economic Affairs* 9 (Autumn 1955): 3–20.

———. *Mexican Government in Transition.* Urbana: University of Illinois Press, 1959.

———. "Mexico: The Established Revolution." In *Political Culture and Political Development,* edited by Lucian W. Pye and Sidney Verba. Princeton University Press, 1965.

SENIOR, CLARENCE. *Land Reform and Democracy.* Gainesville: University of Florida Press, 1958.

SOLÍS QUIROGA, HÉCTOR. *Los Partidos políticos en México.* Mexico City: Orion, 1961.

SPAIN, A. O. "Mexican Federalism Revisited." *Western Political Quarterly* 9 (September 1956): 620–32.

TANNENBAUM, FRANK. "Agrarismo, indianismo y nacionalismo." *Hispanic American Historical Review* 23 (August 1943): 394–423.

———. *Mexico: The Struggle for Peace and Bread.* New York: Alfred A. Knopf, Inc., 1950.

———. "Personal Government in Mexico." *Foreign Affairs* 27 (October 1948): 44–57.

TAYLOR, PHILIP B., JR. "Political Ambivalence: Simplicity or Complexity?" *Texas Quarterly* 2 (Spring 1959): 92–112.

———. "The Mexican Elections of 1958: Affirmation of Authoritarianism." *Western Political Quarterly* 13 (September 1960): 722–44.

TENA RAMÍREZ, FELIPE. *Derecho constitucional mexicano.* 3rd ed. Mexico City: Editorial Porrua, 1955.

TUCKER, WILLIAM P. "Mexico: A Developing Democracy." *Parliamentary Affairs* 2 (October 1958): 432–42.

———. *The Mexican Government Today.* Minneapolis: University of Minnesota Press, 1957.

U.S. DEPARTMENT OF LABOR. *Labor Law and Practice in Mexico.* Bureau of Labor Statistics report no. 240. Washington: U.S. Government Printing Office, 1963.

WOLF, ERIC R. *Sons of the Shaking Earth.* Chicago: University of Chicago Press, 1959.

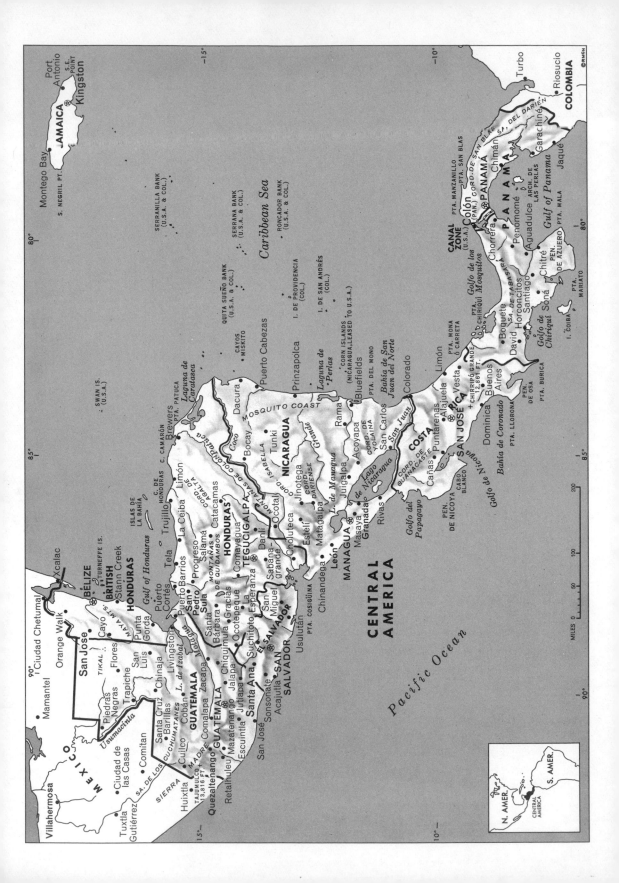

©RMcN

Port
Antonio
S.E.
POINT
Kingston
Montego Bay
JAMAICA
S. NEGRIL PT.
Turbo
Riosucio
COLOMBIA
PANAMÁ
PANAMA
Chimán
Garachiné
Jaqué
SA. DEL DARIÉN
CORD. DE SAN BLAS
PTA. MANZANILLO
PTA. SAN BLAS
Colón
CANAL
ZONE
(U.S.A.)
Chorrera
Penonomé
Aguadulce
ARCH. DE
LAS PERLAS
Santiago
Chitré
Gulf of Panama
PTA. MALA
PEN.
DE AZUERO
Gulf of
Chiriquí
Soná
PTA.
MARIATO
I. COIBA
PEN.
DE BURICA
PTA. BURICA
Horconcitos
David
Boquete
PTA. LLORONA
CHIRIQUÍ GRANDE
12,861 FT.
+CHIRRIPÓ GRANDE
PTA. MONA
Golfo de los
Mosquitos
S.A. DE TABASARÁ
PTA.
Bahía de Coronado

Caribbean Sea
SERRANILLA BANK
(U.S.A. & COL.)
SERRANA BANK
(U.S.A. & COL.)
RONCADOR BANK
(U.S.A. & COL.)
QUITA SUEÑO BANK
(U.S.A. & COL.)
I. DE PROVIDENCIA
(COL.)
I. DE SAN ANDRÉS
(COL.)
CAYOS
MISKITO
CORN ISLANDS
(NICARAGUA,LEASED TO U.S.A.)
Laguna de
Perlas
PTA. DEL MONO
Bahía de San
Juan del Norte
Colorado
Límón
Puerto Cabezas
Prinzapolca
Bluefields
Rama
Acoyapa
San Carlos
Buenos
Aires
Dominica
Alajuela
Vesta
SAN JOSÉ
RICA
COSTA
Puntarenas
Cañas
CORD. DE
GUANACASTE
CABO
BLANCO
PEN.
DE NICOYA
Golfo de Nicoya
PTA.
CARRETA
Golfo del
Papagayo
Rivas
Granada
Masaya
MANAGUA
L. de Managua
Lago
de Nicaragua
Juigalpa
CORD. DE
YOLAINA
San Juan
CORD. CHONTALEÑA
Laguna de
Caratasca
PTA. PATUCA
Brewers
C. CAMARÓN
C. DE
HONDURAS
Dacura
Mosquito Coast
Bocay
Coco
Tunki
ISABELLA
CORD.
Jinotega
Matagalpa
Grande
CORD.
DARIENSE
NICARAGUA
León
Chinandega
Estelí
Ocotal
Danlí
Choluteca
PTA. COSIGÜINA
San
Miguel
El SALVADOR
SAN
SALVADOR
Usulután
Sabana-
grande
TEGUCIGALPA
Comayagua
La
Esperanza
San
Salama
MONTAÑAS
DE GUIDAMBOS
Gracias
Catacamas
Juticalpa
Trujillo
La Ceiba
Límón
Tela
Progreso
Puerto
Cortés
Puerto Barrios
San
Pedro
Sula
Santa
Bárbara
Ocotepeque
HONDURAS
Chiquimula
Zacapa
Jalapa
Jutiapa
Santa
Ana
Sonsonate
Acajutla
San José
Retalhuleu
Mazatenango
Escuintla
GUATEMALA
Quezaltenango
Comalapa
Cobán
Chinaja
L. de Izabal
Livingston
SIERRA MADRE
SA. DE LOS
CUCHUMATANES
TAJUMULCO
3,816 FT.
Huixtla
Cuilco
Barillas
Santa
Cruz
San
Luis
Flores
TIKAL
Trapiche
Piedras
Negras
Comitán
Ciudad de
las Casas
Tuxtla
Gutiérrez
MEXICO
Villahermosa
Mamantel
Ciudad Chetumal
Orange Walk
Xcalac
San José
Cayo
Punta
Gorda
Stann Creek
BELIZE
BRITISH
HONDURAS
TURNEFFE IS.
ISLAS DE
LA BAHÍA
SWAN IS.
(U.S.A.)
MAYA MTS.
USUMACINTA
Gulf of Honduras

Pacific Ocean

CENTRAL
AMERICA

MILES 0   50   100   200

N. AMER.   S. AMER.
CENTRAL
AMERICA

−15°
80°
85°
90°
15°
10°
−10°
80°
85°
90°

——— 3 ———

CENTRAL AMERICA

Central America is the name given to the area lying between Mexico and South America. It is divided into six republics (Guatemala, El Salvador, Honduras, Nicaragua, Costa Rica, and Panama) and two colonies (British Honduras and the Canal Zone). Central America ought to be one political unit, for none of the colonies or republics contains enough people, land, or resources to enable it to develop into a prosperous modern nation-state. The preservation of the present political divisions has left most of the area's people impoverished, its natural resources in large part unexploited, and transportation and communications rudimentary. Vast areas in Central America remain forested, largely unexplored and almost completely uninhabited, waiting for man to utilize their untapped resources.

During Spanish colonial days all of Central America except Panama was one political unit, the Captaincy General and *Audiencia* of Guatemala, and it was a mistake to divide it into five republics when one would have sufficed. Yet this disintegration was probably inevitable, for the population had no experience in self-government, there were no roads knitting the area together, and the total population was too small to provide the resources with which roads could be built. At the time of independence from Spain, each small nucleus of population was anchored to its mountain plateau or fertile valley, isolated from the rest. The economy was based almost entirely on subsistence agriculture and poverty was endemic.

It is extremely difficult to get exact population figures for Central

America; the best estimate available is that in 1823 all of Central America, excluding Panama, had about one million people, divided roughly as follows: Costa Rica, 65,393; Nicaragua, 174,213; Honduras, about 100,000; Guatemala, about 400,000; and El Salvador, about 200,000. This is probably an inflated figure, for in 1855 it was estimated that the area's population was only 1,325,174. When Costa Rica took its first census, in 1864, the population totaled 120,499; of this number, 64,194 were under the age of twenty, leaving 56,305 adults. In other words, in 1864 Costa Rica did not even have enough people to create an effective city-state, much less a modern nation-state. The same was true of its sister republics in the isthmus.

The population has grown enormously during the twentieth century, especially since modern techniques of public health were introduced into the area, but even in the 1960's the area remains greatly underpopulated, with the possible exception of El Salvador. The total population in 1960 was less than 12 million, divided as follows: Costa Rica, 1,171,441; Guatemala, 3,584,684; Honduras, 1,850,000; El Salvador, 2,434,000; Nicaragua, 1,380,000; Panama, 995,000; British Honduras, 85,000; and the Canal Zone, 40,000. This total was less than the population of metropolitan New York City, which had about 14,093,000. The rate of natural increase in the area is high, but vast parts of the territory still remain completely unpopulated.

When independence came to the area in 1821, as a result of events in Mexico, the leaders of the Captaincy General tried to preserve its unity. In fact, an attempt was made to combine it with Mexico in 1822, but this union ended almost as soon as it began except for one Guatemalan province, Chiapas, which is still a part of Mexico.

On July 1, 1823, the Captaincy General of Guatemala became the United Provinces of Central America, "free and independent of old Spain, of Mexico, and of every other power," but this attempt at preserving the unity of the area continued only until 1838, when the five present republics started their lives as independent states. The United Provinces fell apart for many reasons, the most important of which was that what is now Guatemala, having been the seat of the Spanish colonial administration, became the center of the conservative elements in the new country. The other, smaller colonies became centers of liberal power. At the same time, because Guatemala had almost as large a population as the rest of the area combined, it was bound to dominate the United Provinces. This the liberal leaders of El Salvador, Honduras, Nicaragua, and Costa Rica refused to allow.

The result of this split was almost constant civil war. When the conservatives consolidated their power in Guatemala under General Rafael Carrera and expelled the then president of the confederation, the Honduran Francisco Morazán, from Guatemala in 1838, the end of the United Provinces had come. Many attempts have been made to reunite the republics since then, but all have failed. Nevertheless, the republics are now cooperating with each other through the Organization of Central American States, with headquarters in San Salvador; the people of the area have a feeling of belonging to Central America; and there is much sentiment favoring political and economic unification of the independent republics.

One factor that hindered the unification and development of Central America was the exceptional amount of pressure to which it was subjected by the United States and Great Britain as these two world powers jockeyed for canal rights across the territory during the past century. As a result of this struggle, Britain retains possession of British Honduras (though independence has been promised for the near future) and the United States has a permanent lease on the Panama Canal Zone.

Central America's only real hope lies in the unification of the six small republics and two colonies into one country. If this could be accomplished and the economic system developed, it is possible that the people of the area could reach a level of living sufficiently high to give the political system some basic stability. Most intelligent leaders of the area believe and hope that through the Organization of Central American States, a loose cooperative arrangement in which each state preserves its full sovereignty, they will eventually reach economic and political unification.

The Organization of Central American States was founded on October 14, 1951, and formally organized in August 1955 to coordinate the efforts of the five northernmost republics toward improving their educational and economic systems and to sponsor activities that would lead to the economic and political unification of the isthmus. Some progress has been made, but Panama has not yet joined, although it has participated in some of the activities of the organization.

The constitutions of four of the republics contain clauses referring to the ideal of unification. That of Honduras, for example, states in Article 9 that "Honduras is a State separated from the Federal Republic of Central America. Consequently, it recognizes the primary necessity of restoring a union with one or more States of the former Federation. To this end, the legislative branch is authorized to ratify treaties aimed at accomplishing this partially or in full, provided this is proposed in a fair and democratic manner."

In addition, the constitutions of the Central American republics contain clauses treating the nationals of the other republics in a special manner. Article 6 of the constitution of Guatemala, for example, states that "Citizens by birth of the other republics which constituted the Federation of Central America are also considered to be native Guatemalans provided they acquire domicile in Guatemala and declare their desire to be Guatemalans before the appropriate authority. In this event, they may preserve their nationality of origin."

The greatest advances in cooperation have taken place in the economic field. By the General Treaty of Central American Economic Integration, the five northern republics are trying to set up a Central American Common Market. A Central American Bank for Economic Integration is functioning to stimulate new economic enterprises. A Central American Clearing House has created a Central American peso to simplify settling commercial debts without utilizing foreign currency. Other Central American cooperative organizations are the Central American Research Institute for Industry and Technology, the Nutrition Institute, the Higher University Council, which coordinates the work of the various universities, and the Graduate School of Public Administration for Central America and Panama, which has become a valuable training center. Events are pushing the area toward increased cooperation, and the future will almost assuredly see more and more joint activities. Yet, until one integrated state takes the place of the eight units now in existence, the area will continue to be a backward collection of impoverished peoples.

SELECTED READINGS

BUSEY, JAMES L. "Central American Union: The Latest Attempt." *Western Political Quarterly* 14 (March 1961): 49–63.

FACIO, RODRIGO. *La Federación de Centroamérica, sus antecedentes, su vida y su disolución.* San José, Costa Rica: Escuela Superior de Administración Pública de la América Central, 1957.

FERNÁNDEZ-SHAW, FÉLIX. "Estado actual de la integración económica centroamericana." *Revista de la Política Internacional* (Madrid), no. 76 (November–December 1964), pp. 75–106.

FEUERLEIN, W. J. "Interregional Development and Industrialization in Central America." *Economic Leaflets*, vol. 16 (July 1957).

FITZGIBBON, RUSSELL H. "*Continuismo* in Central America and the Caribbean." *The Inter-American Quarterly* 2 (July 1940): 56–74.

———. "Executive Power in Central America." *Journal of Politics* 3 (August 1941): 297–307.

KARNES, THOMAS L. *The Failure of Union: Central America, 1824–1960.* Chapel Hill: University of North Carolina Press, 1961.

LIND, HUGO, and MARTÍNEZ M., ALFREDO. *Movimiento unionista centroamericano.* Santiago, Chile: Instituto de Ciencias Políticas y Administrativas, 1958.

MEEK, GEORGE. "Coordination in Central America." *Americas* 16 (July 1964): 20–22.

Moses, Carl C. "Contemporary Relations among the Central American States." In *The Caribbean: The Central American Area*, edited by A. Curtis Wilgus. Gainesville: University of Florida Press, 1961.

Munro, Dana G. *The Five Republics of Central America*. New York: Oxford University Press, 1918.

O'Shaughnessy, Hugh. "Central America: The Road from Poverty and Disunity." *The World Today* 20 (July 1964): 314–18.

Padelford, Norman J. "Cooperation in the Central American Region: The Organization of Central American States." *International Organization* 11 (Winter 1957): 41–54.

BOUNDARY REPRESENTATION IS
NOT NECESSARILY AUTHORITATIVE

MEXICO

Orange Walk

TURNEFFE
ISLANDS

BELIZE

CARIBBEAN
SEA

El Cayo
Middlesex
Stann Creek

BRITISH
HONDURAS

Río Hondo
Belize
Río Chocop
Río San Pedro

Tenosique

INDEX TO
DEPARTAMENTO NAMES
1. EL PETÉN
2. HUEHUETENANGO
3. SAN MARCOS
4. TOTONICAPÁN
5. QUEZALTENANGO
6. RETALHULEU
7. EL QUICHE
8. SOLOLÁ
9. SUCHITEPÉQUEZ
10. CHIMALTENANGO
11. SACATEPÉQUEZ
12. ESCUINTLA
13. ALTA VERAPAZ
14. BAJA VERAPAZ
15. GUATEMALA
16. SANTA ROSA
17. EL PROGRESO
18. JALAPA
19. JUTIAPA
20. IZABAL
21. ZACAPA
22. CHIQUIMULA

Lago
Petén Itzá

1

Flores

La Libertad

Río Usumacinta
Río de la Pasión
Río Lacantum
Río Jataté

Puerto
Cortés

2

13

Río Salinas

Modesto
Méndez

Livingston

Puerto
Barrios

Ciudad
Cuauhtémoc

7

Cobán

20
Lago
de Izabal

Matías de
Gálvez

El Estor

Río Cuilco

HONDURAS

Huehuetenango

Los Amates

Río Motagua

Salamá

Santa Cruz
del Quiché

3

14

Río Hondo

17

21

San Marcos

4

Zacapa

Totonicapán

Río Grande

10

Quezaltenango

5

15 El Progreso

Coatepeque

Sololá

Chimaltenango

Chiquimula

22

Ciudad
Técun Umán

Lago de
Atitlán

Jalapa

Mazatenango

18

Ocós

Antigua
Guatemala

GUATEMALA
CITY

Asunción
Mita

GUATEMALA

Retalhuleu

9

11

Champerico

6

Pueblo
Nuevo
Tiquisate

Escuintla

Cuilapa

Jutiapa

19

International boundary
Departamento boundary
National capital
Departamento capital
Railroad
Inter American Highway
Other road

Río Samalá

Río Madre Vieja

12

16

Río Lempa

indefinite

0   10   25   50 Miles

0 10 25   50 Kilometers

Tecojate

San José

Iztapa

EL SALVADOR

PACIFIC OCEAN

SAN SALVADOR

—— 4 ——

GUATEMALA:

The Aftermath of a Frustrated Revolution

Guatemala, a fascinating land whose charm centuries of misrule and exploitation have been unable to destroy, is a case study in the ways in which the heritage of Spanish colonial culture hinders the development of a modern state. Guatemala's political life since independence in 1821 has featured an alternation of chaos and dictatorship. A revolution in 1944 initiated a process of rapid change which led many to believe that at last Guatemala was on the road to political stability, but the capture of the revolution by Communists and their sympathizers distorted the objectives of the revolution and led, after the left-wing regime of Jacobo Arbenz was toppled in 1954, to another period of undemocratic government. After a new constitution was adopted in 1956, another attempt was made to govern Guatemala constitutionally, but this too broke down. A new constitution was adopted in 1965 and after an election constitutional government was reintroduced on July 1, 1966. The new government is under constant attack by totalitarian gangsters trying to imitate Fidel Castro and by others who want to preserve the traditional organization of Guatemala. Why it has been so difficult to establish a stable political system will become clear after we have reviewed Guatemala's geography and history.

A National Profile

Guatemala is bordered on the east by British Honduras (known in Guatemala as Belize), the Gulf of Honduras, and the republics of Honduras

63

and El Salvador, on the south by the Pacific Ocean, and on the north and west by Mexico. With an area of 42,042 square miles, Guatemala consists of four distinct parts. To the north lies an area known as the Petén, containing 33 percent of the country's area and 0.6 percent of its population. This is an almost untouched lowland lying between Mexico and British Honduras. Once the center of the Mayan civilization, it awaits development. The Pacific lowlands, 8 percent of the area, are inhabited by 13.5 percent of the population. Much of the country's sugar and cotton, two of its most important cash crops, are produced in this area, yet it has much undeveloped land. The Caribbean lowlands, 9 percent of the territory, contain 2.7 percent of the population. This area is greatly underdeveloped, although the ports of Puerto Barrios and Livingston are important. The last and most important part of Guatemala is the highlands, Guatemala's section of the great cordillera, a series of chains of volcanic mountains and fertile valleys, extending southeast from Mexico. Here, on 50 percent of the national territory, are found 83.3 percent of the country's population, most of its coffee plantations, and the political, religious, financial, and educational centers.

Guatemala is a tropical country with two seasons, a dry "summer" from November to April and a rainy "winter" from May to October. The lowlands can be very steamy indeed, but in the highlands, between 3,000 and 8,000 feet above sea level, the climate is pleasant and mild all year round, with no extremes of heat or cold.

Guatemala's population, at the time of the 1964 census, was 4,284,473, about 50 percent Indian, 45 percent *mestizo* and *ladino*,[1] and 5 percent white, primarily of Spanish origin. Most of the Indians are rural and illiterate, still speaking about twenty different ancient languages of the Maya-Quiché family. The population has grown in recent years at the rate of 3.1 percent annually. Over 66 percent of the country is rural and there is only one large city, Guatemala, the capital, with 572,937 inhabitants in 1960. The next largest cities in 1960 were Quezaltenango, 45,195; Escuintla, 24,832; Puerto Barrios, 22,242; and Mazatenango, 19,506.

Spanish is the official language, but about 40 percent of the population continues to use the ancient Indian languages. Although a minimum of common education, according to the constitution, is compulsory and free, the majority of children do not attend classes, and from 70 to 85 percent of the population is illiterate. In 1957, only 203,448 of the

---

[1] A *ladino* in Guatemala is anyone who has adopted European cultural standards, especially the Spanish language and a European style of dress, even though he may be Indian, *mestizo*, European, Chinese, or Negro.

country's 644,420 children between the ages of seven and fourteen attended school. By 1960 the number of students had risen to 238,118, attending 3,716 primary schools staffed by 8,879 teachers. Only about 12 percent of the annual budget is spent for education, and the outlook for any improvement in the educational level is dim unless much more intensive efforts are made. Over 96 percent of the population are counted as Catholics and 2.8 percent as Protestants, but many of the Indians have been only slightly affected by Catholicism.

Although Guatemala is an agricultural country, it is an importer of foodstuffs because the pattern of production puts emphasis upon the growing of export crops, primarily coffee, for the world market. Guatemala was once one of the world's largest exporters of bananas, but a few years ago a combination of political and natural disasters caused the virtual withdrawal of the United Fruit Company from its once extensive operations in the country, and bananas are no longer of prime importance to the economy. The country has an extremely low per capita income, the gross national product in 1957 amounting only to $180 U.S. per capita, the lowest in Central America. And even this low average per capita income does not tell the whole story, as the gross national income is very unevenly distributed, with 73 percent of the population averaging $83 per year. Landownership in Guatemala is concentrated in the hands of a few, a fact that tends to perpetuate the poverty of the masses. Redistribution of the land is a burning political issue, and in the years after the Castillo Armas revolution in 1954, 16,909 farmers received title to 352,000 acres, but this only began to touch the problem. The government is the country's largest landowner, controlling about a hundred large farms, most of which are coffee plantations expropriated from German owners during World War II. Some of these farms are being divided and distributed to individual farmers as part of the land-reform program.

In addition to coffee, which accounted for 75 percent of all exports in 1958, Guatemala exports cotton, chicle, bananas, abacá, and wood of various types. Produced for domestic consumption are maize (the staple food of the Indian population), sugar, wheat, beans, rice, and leaf tobacco. Cattle raising is important in the Pacific coastal area. About 943 industrial establishments employed about 36,000 workers in 1958. The principal products were textiles, leather, cement, cigars, cigarettes, beer, liquors, soft drinks, refined sugar, vegetable oils, and chemical products. A tire and tube factory began operation in 1958. The subsoil contains gold, silver, copper, iron, lead, zinc, and manganese, but production is low. Exploration for petroleum has been carried on, and there are almost certainly important deposits in the Petén, but this is jungle country, and exploiting them would be prohibitively costly under present conditions. Membership in the Central American Common Market has stimulated economic growth, but Guatemala still has a long way to go.

Guatemala's main problems are the poverty in which most of the population lives and the great cultural gap between the Indians and the rest of the population.

Here is how a newspaperman described the life of a Guatemalan Indian in 1966:

> His home has stone walls about thigh-high forming the base. Atop this are corn stalks which go up to a height of six or seven feet. The roof is thatched. Inside Gaspar and his wife sleep on a straw mat scarcely softer than a board. At the foot of the bed are two big bags and a rack full of ears of corn. The corn, beaten and fried into pancakes called tortillas, is practically all the Indians get to eat. The floor is dirt and a primitive kerosene lamp gives light. The kitchen, which is little more than a crude hearth for making tortillas, is in another hut which has no chimney. The inside of the roof is black as coal from the smoke which has gathered there through thousands of mealtimes. Like his neighbor, Gaspar is a farmer. He farms with a broad metal hoe. There are no tractors here, or even plows. One man and one hoe is a piece of machinery, and it earns very little. About eighty cents a day is the wage on the big coffee plantations, but this is far from average. Sixty cents a day is about the median for men. Women get only fifteen to thirty cents.[2]

Despite the poverty and miserly wages, custom keeps the mass of Indians chained to the uplands, where arable land is so scarce that their cornfields tilt at dizzy angles far up the mountainsides. Transportation remains poorly developed, in part because of the expense of building and maintaining roads and railroads in mountainous terrain. And to complicate matters further, the most important economic enterprises are foreign-owned, including much of the coffee, the railroad system, the telephone company, and the electric power company. And those Guatemalans who have grown rich on coffee and commerce tend to place their profits in safe bank accounts in the United States or Switzerland, rather than reinvest them in enterprises that would create jobs for Guatemalans. All this combines to make it very difficult to establish a stable political system and tends to perpetuate the traditional organization of the country.

---

[2] Lee Winfrey, "Elections Mean Little to Guatemalan Indians," *Miami Herald*, March 6, 1966, p. 2D.

The Development of Modern Guatemala

What is now known as Guatemala was once part of the great Maya empire, probably the most advanced civilization developed in the Americas before 1492. By the time the Spaniards arrived in 1524, Maya civilization had decayed, and the Spanish soon conquered the area, although they had to fight bloody battles before they succeeded in dominating the Indians, particularly the Quichés. Once the conquest was completed, the land and its Indian inhabitants were divided among the *conquistadores* as *encomiendas* (see page 507), thus beginning the construction of a semifeudal society that has endured into the twentieth century.

As we have seen, Guatemala was once the seat of government for all of Central America, and as such it acquired a conservative character that is still very much in evidence. With only occasional lapses into melodrama, colonial Guatemala lived tranquilly between earthquakes. The capital city has been destroyed by earthquakes and relocated twice, and the present capital (its third) had to be largely rebuilt after a series of quakes in 1917–18. Before its destruction in 1773 the second capital, now known as Antigua, was an impressive place of vast churches, monasteries, government palaces, and a university (founded in 1681). Wandering among their ruins today, the visitor can see that this was once a center of great wealth and culture. But the culture was that of a small upper class that exploited the labor of the Indian masses, who continued to live much as their ancestors had lived, except that now they worked for the Spanish ruling class. As Thomas Gage, an English Catholic priest who lived in Guatemala for twelve years during the seventeenth century, wrote:

> The miserable condition of the Indians of that country is such, that though the kings of Spain have never yielded to what some would have, that they should be slaves, yet their lives are as full of bitterness as is the life of a slave. . . . Thus are the poor Indians sold for threepence a peece for a whole week's slavery, not permitted to goe home at nights unto their wives, though their worke lie not above a mile from the Town where they live; nay some are carried ten or twelve miles from their home who must not returne till Saturday night late, and must that week do whatsoever their Master pleaseth to command them. The wages appointed them will scarce find them meat and drinke, for they are not allowed a Riall a day, which is but sixpence, and with that they are to find themselves, but for six daies worke and diet they are to have five Rials,

which is halfe a crowne. This same order is observed in the city of
Guatemala and Townes of Spaniards, where to every family that
wants the service of an Indian or Indians, though it be but to fetch
water and wood on their backs, or to goe of arrants, is allowed the
like service from the neerest Indian townes.[3]

Guatemala's first years of independence were complicated by an
almost continuous war between the Liberals and the Conservatives over
the question of confederation with the rest of Central America. In 1829
the Liberals, led by Francisco Morazán of Honduras, captured power and
launched a reform program that included such measures as the expulsion
of the leading Conservatives and confiscation of church property. By
1838 Rafael Carrera, a Conservative, had organized an army of Indians,
defeated Morazán, destroyed the confederation, and begun his years of
dictatorial rule.

Carrera maintained control of Guatemala until he died in 1865, although he did not always have the title of president. In 1851 he introduced a constitution that, by conferring citizenship only upon the upper
classes, legalized his dictatorship. Under this constitution, the president
was elected by an assembly consisting of the lower house of Congress, the
archbishop, the Supreme Court justices, and the Council of State. This
system remained in force until 1871, when the Liberals siezed power in
an armed revolt.

In the 1870's Guatemala began to feel the impact of the liberal ideas
that flowered in western Europe during the first half of the nineteenth
century as a result of the industrial revolution. Animated by such
ideas, a group of liberal politicians led by General Justo Rufino Barrios
seized power in 1871 and made an attempt to reorganize the country.
Barrios' government fostered education, restricted the power of the
Catholic church and confiscated some of its lands, improved communications, and built many public works. Among his many other reforms
was the introduction of a new constitution, in 1879, which provided for
the election of the president and the Congress by popular vote.

Despite his efforts, Barrios did not succeed in transforming Guatemala; in fact, he made things worse, if possible, although some writers
call him the founder of Guatemalan democracy. In an attempt to improve agricultural production, he expropriated some of the Indians' communal lands, set up large plantations, introduced the commercial production of coffee, and fostered immigration. As a result, the Indians

---

[3] Thomas Gage, *The English-American His Travail by Sea and Land: Or a New Survey
of the West Indies* (London: R. Cotes, 1648), pp. 139–40.

were further alienated from the rest of the population, and the basic split in Guatemalan society was continued into the twentieth century.

The dictatorial practices of Barrios were continued by his successors, who, although calling themselves Liberals, introduced no liberal reforms. Manuel Estrada Cabrera, who ruled from October 2, 1898, to September 1920, was of this type. Some economic development took place during Cabrera's[4] rule, and the Rockefeller Foundation helped to improve public health, but Cabrera did nothing to solve the country's basic problems or to train the population for self-government.

The post–World War I depression stimulated the creation of labor unions and the Union Party, which, by combining their efforts, succeeded in overthrowing the Cabrera dictatorship in 1920. Here again the Guatemalan people demonstrated their political immaturity, for they did not have enough experience to set up a constitutional government that would endure. Despite their efforts, the world financial crisis of 1929 brought General Jorge Ubico to power in 1930, to rule until 1944 as Guatemala's last old-fashioned dictator.

General Ubico fostered economic development, but under his regime foreigners completed their domination of Guatemala. Bananas and coffee made up about 90 percent of the country's exports, with the United Fruit Company controlling the banana industry and Germans controlling the coffee industry. Under Ubico, the conditions of the Indian farmers went from bad to worse. It is reported that the average wage for plantation workers was about fifteen cents a day, and dockworkers earned seven to twelve cents an hour. In addition, Ubico collected "taxes" from the Indians in the form of forced labor on plantations and on road building. He stayed in power by utilizing a national police force which replaced local government.

In 1944 Guatemala remained about as it had been all during its existence as an independent republic: a backward agricultural dictatorship in which about 2 percent of the landowners possessed about 70 percent of the country's arable land and more than half of the population consisted of illiterate non-Spanish-speaking Indians who lived much as their ancestors had before the Spaniards arrived. It is estimated that not

---

[4] Students of Spanish may wonder why he is called Cabrera, his mother's name, rather than Estrada, his father's name, as would be customary. The explanation is revealing of much about the man and his society. Following an old Latin custom, the father legally recognized his infant son and gave him the family name, without, however, going so far as to marry the child's mother. The son never forgave him, and insisted on being called by his mother's name throughout his life. He did it, he said, to "honor" his mother; yet surely he must have recognized that he was unnecessarily calling public attention to her unmarried status.

more than 5 percent of the adult male population had an education comparable to that of a United States high school graduate.

On the other hand, as foreign capital entered the country it stimulated the growth of a small middle class, and the automobile, airplane, and other modern means of communication revolutionized the archaic transportation and communication systems. These forces produced merchants, professionals, educators, and technicians who found they had little opportunity to develop new enterprises or to practice their professions in the poverty-stricken stagnant society Ubico dominated.

During World War II the slogans of the Four Freedoms and the general emphasis on democracy fired the ambition of these people to reform Guatemala into a modern democratic state. When they pressed for reforms, Ubico's imposing dictatorship quickly collapsed. The 1944 revolution began with apparently simple activities. Forty-five lawyers petitioned Ubico to remove an unfair judge. Two hundred teachers petitioned for an increase in salary. The university students asked to have the university's autonomy restored. Ubico refused to grant these requests, and instead further tightened controls. A mass demonstration was organized in response, and when this was broken up by the police, a general strike developed. Students, teachers, physicians, lawyers, storekeepers, and transportation workers all went on strike. Ubico tried to force the retail shops to open, but this only stiffened the opposition.

Faced with almost complete noncooperation, Ubico resigned on July 1, 1944, and left the country, turning his power over to a three-man military junta headed by General Federico Ponce Vaídes, who became provisional president on July 4. When Ponce tried to become the new strong man, he was overthrown in another revolt on October 19–20, 1944, and a three-man junta composed of two military men, Francisco Javier Arana and Jacobo Arbenz Guzmán, and a civilian, Jorge Toriello Garrido, took control of the government. The junta organized the election of a constituent assembly and another election to choose a president, and turned its power over to the victor in that election, Dr. Juan José Arévalo.

Then began a most interesting experiment, as the young teachers, army officers, and professionals who had led the revolution tried to organize a democratic government. Unfortunately, they were completely untrained in political activity and had no real grasp of what had to be done to achieve their aims. Guatemala's experience from 1944 to 1954 is an almost classic example of how difficult it is for a group that has never known democracy suddenly to begin practicing it.

The revolution of 1944 did not have the support of the majority of the population, which was completely out of politics. Rather, it represented the middle class in the professions, the army, and the urban working class. While this group was a larger fraction of the population than the small clique around Ubico, it too was far from being a majority. The revolution was an expression of the articulate section of Guatemala's population seeking political liberty and the economic development of their country. It is possible that if these enthusiastic young people had received adequate support and encouragement from the other governments of Central America and from the United States, they might eventually have developed some kind of stable government that would have improved life for the average Guatemalan. Unfortunately, they did not receive much help from other governments, and in addition two forces within Guatemala destroyed the revolutionary movement.

The country's traditional oligarchy, the landowners and other rich, refused to admit that it was necessary for Guatemala to improve the health, education, and standard of living of the masses, and they continuously plotted to restore the old order. President Arévalo had to face an almost continuous series of armed revolts, plots, and attempted coups d'état, some serious and some little more than rumors, which forced him to suspend constitutional liberties during about half of his term in office. So much of the government's energy had to go into staying in power that it never could devote itself completely to implementing the important reforms the country needed.

In addition, a strong Communist movement developed during this period because the Guatemalans, deprived of all liberty for so many generations, had no experience of democratic institutions. To many Guatemalans, "democracy" meant only the hated United Fruit Company, which contributed much to Guatemala, but not so much, they believed, as it took away in land, money, and pride. (For a glimpse of United Fruit's methods of operation, see pages 134, 137; the company followed basically the same pattern here as in Honduras.) After 1944, Communists came to dominate the trade unions, the peasant organizations, and many of the embryonic political parties that had been organized. Every attempt made by Arévalo to build a strong political party was frustrated by the Communists, who followed their traditional policy of rule or ruin.

These two forces—the refusal of the defenders of the status quo to permit reform and the refusal of the Communists to permit the Guatemalan reform movement to develop naturally—were to destroy the revolution before its aims could be achieved. Yet the period from 1944 to 1954 saw many changes in the organization of Guatemalan life, and the country will probably never go back to the kind of life it knew before 1944.

The moderate objectives of the revolution are probably best expressed in Decree 17 of the revolutionary junta, which listed the principles of the revolution as:

1. Decentralization of the executive power and separation of the state powers.
2. Abolition of the position of president designate and his replacement with an elected vice-president.
3. Alternation of power, no reelection, and recognition of the people's right to revolt when anyone attempts to continue in office beyond the expiration of his term.
4. Removal of the army from politics and creation of a superior army council to control the armed forces as a technical force to defend liberty, the constitution, and the national integrity.
5. Election of local governments, rather than appointment by the executive.
6. Effective autonomy of the judicial system.
7. Autonomy for the national university.
8. Constitutional recognition of democratic political parties and minority representation in the electoral machinery.
9. The obligatory secret vote for literate males; obligatory open vote for illiterate males in local elections only; the right to vote for literate women.
10. Honesty in public administration.

Decree 17 ends by stating: "These principles are essential to consolidate the ideology of the Revolution of October 20 and will be incorporated into the Constitution of the Republic."

The new constitution was put into effect on March 15, 1945, the date of Dr. Arévalo's inauguration as Guatemala's president. Under Arévalo, a fundamental social revolution was attempted. The most important steps taken were the strengthening of the educational system and the system of local government, the abolition of forced labor, the promulgation of an advanced labor code, the creation of the Social Security Institute, the beginning of the reorganization of the army, encouragement of Indian participation in government, and the construction of many schools, low-cost housing units, and sanitation systems. At the same time, the organization of labor unions was encouraged, studies were begun looking toward agrarian reform and the breaking up of the large landholdings, and civil liberty was protected.

The great lack in the developing revolution was a political party strong enough to continue the process begun under Arévalo. In addition, the lack of trained personnel enabled the Communists to infiltrate the existing political parties, trade unions, and other organizations, including the government. By 1949 the lines were beginning to be drawn for the 1951 election. The two most important candidates were the former members of the 1944 junta, Colonel Francisco J. Arana, chief of the armed forces, and Lieutenant Colonel Jacobo Arbenz, the Minister of Defense. Arana seemed to be the only noncommunist associated with the government popular enough to win the election of 1951, and he controlled the armed forces. Arbenz, a rather stupid militarist, was a friend of the Communist Party and unpopular.

In July 1949 Arana fired one of Arbenz' friends as chief of the air force and replaced him with one of his own friends. Shortly after that, on July 18, Arana was murdered, apparently by agents of Arbenz. Arana's friends in the army immediately revolted, but were defeated. Soon all of Arana's supporters were purged from the government and the army, and Arbenz took over undisputed control of the armed forces. There was nothing now to prevent his becoming president, and in 1951 he was elected to that office. It is possible that if President Arévalo could have run for reelection, the Communists might have been kept under better control, but the no-reelection clause in the constitution prevented that. In fact, Arévalo left the country to become an ambassador at large in Europe, and played no role in the Arbenz regime.

Under Arbenz, the Communists increased their influence until they dominated the government. How they did this makes an interesting story and is important, for the same techniques were to prove even more successful in Cuba a few years later.

The Communists in Guatemala were few in number, but they were the best organized force in the country and were able to utilize the inexperience and naïveté of the young middle-class reformers who were their associates. Although the Communist Party of Guatemala was first organized soon after World War I, it played no part in the 1944 revolution. From 1921 to 1944 its fortunes varied, but the dictatorial governments of the period were able to keep it from developing any real force. The party grew important in the period after 1944, mainly because the leaders of the revolution had little political experience. It must be remembered that the Guatemalan revolution came at a time when the "honeymoon" between the democratic leaders of the world and Stalin's Russia was at its height, and many Guatemalans simply never left that stage, but continued to look upon the Communist Party as only another reformist organization, or one they could use to further their own aims of national development.

Under Ubico, every opponent, whether a liberal, a labor leader, a democrat, a socialist, or a Communist, was labeled Communist. In addition, the conservative opposition to the 1944 revolution attached the label of communism to such reforms as labor legislation, social security, and agrarian reform, and eventually the Communist Party was able to cover itself with the prestige of the revolution to such an extent that opposition to the Communists became opposition to the revolution.

The Communists had another great advantage. After the revolution, they swarmed into Guatemala from Mexico and other parts of Latin America in the guise of labor leaders to organize industrial and agricultural organizations. At that time the Communists controlled the Latin-American Confederation of Labor (CTAL), headed by Vicente Lombardo Toledano, and using its machinery they soon gained control of the Guatemalan agricultural organizations and trade unions. The Communists who came to Guatemala had years of experience in organizational techniques in many parts of the world, and their competition for control of the trade unions consisted of eager young middle-class ideologists with little or no political or trade-union organizational experience.

This lack of training can be clearly seen in the involved history of the "revolutionary" political parties. Despite all efforts made, a strong political party was never developed, and those in existence were infiltrated and manipulated by the Communists. By 1952 the Communist Party was not only the strongest, best organized party in the country, but the only well-organized political group in Guatemala. During Arbenz' administration the Communists controlled the legislature, the national radio station, the social security system, the peasant and trade-union organizations, the student movement, the most important pro-government political parties, and the machinery of the land-reform program.

Because of the growing power of the Communists, the Arbenz regime became increasingly unpopular as time passed, both despite and because of its initiation of land reform, something much needed in Guatemala. At least 495,000 acres in 269 private farms were distributed to landless peasants, but the Communists held most of the key positions in the land distribution agency, and they utilized their positions to favor their supporters. One of Arbenz' actions that increased his unpopularity was the impeachment of four Supreme Court justices because they had handed down a decision temporarily restraining the government from carrying out the agrarian-reform law until a study of its operation could be made. This action stimulated an estimated 7,000 persons to demonstrate in front of the National Palace on February 9, 1953. In the ensuing riot, at least one person was killed and several others were wounded. This helped to widen the breach between Arbenz and his Communist allies and the rest of the population. In addition, the Arbenz government alienated the rest of Central America. The government of Honduras became alarmed after the Guatemalan government radio station encouraged a strike in the Honduran banana area by 20,000 workers. In 1953 Arbenz withdrew Guatemala from the Organization of Central American States, and he permitted the Communists to carry on an extensive campaign against "Yankee imperialism" with pro-Soviet overtones which frightened the neighboring countries.

When it became known that Arbenz had received a whole shipload of arms from Poland, this so alarmed the governments of the United States and of Guatemala's Central American neighbors that they helped an unknown Guatemalan refugee, Colonel Carlos Castillo Armas, to organize an invasion from Honduras, probably with financial help from the United States Central Intelligence Agency. On June 18, 1954, the Castillo Armas army invaded Guatemala, set up a provisional government at Chiquimula, bombed several cities, and destroyed Arbenz' army's fuel supplies by air attack. When the Guatemalan army refused to fight against the invasion, Arbenz resigned and took refuge in the Mexican embassy on June 27. A military junta took over control of Guatemala, and after some negotiations Castillo Armas entered the junta. By September 1 the junta was dissolved and Castillo Armas became president of the republic.

For three years Castillo Armas ruled as a virtual dictator and tried to stabilize the country with the help of large grants of money from the United States. He failed primarily because he was incompetent, although he was a surprise both to those who thought he would restore an Ubico-type dictatorship and to those who believed his statement that he would continue the revolution without its Communist trimmings. He turned out to be a centrist who maneuvered between the oligarchy, which refused to support any change in the traditional order of society, and the masses, who refused to see abolished the meager steps taken toward reform.

Castillo Armas "legalized" himself in power by conducting an oral plebiscite. His conservative opponents revolted in January 1955, but were easily defeated. They especially objected to the taxes Castillo Armas levied on the rich in an attempt to secure the funds necessary to operate the government. The money was needed because the Arbenz regime had transferred large sums out of the country and Castillo Armas found the treasury almost empty when he took control. In addition, the United States, which had promised to help the new government, did not supply substantial amounts until about 1956. Other steps that increased Castillo

Armas' unpopularity with the rich were his amending of the land-reform law to improve its operation instead of repealing it, his law to tax unused land to force its cultivation, and his stimulation of foreign investments in new industries and in oil exploration.

Castillo Armas dissolved all political parties and trade unions and refused to permit new ones to be created. During his regime there were only two organized groups in the country: the army and the government. On the other hand, Castillo Armas did try to stimulate the economic development of the country, and had the National Council for Economic Planning draw up a plan for the period from 1955 to 1960 which had much to commend it. The injection of about $68 million in grants and loans by the United States government for road construction and other activities helped to improve the economic situation. By the middle of 1957, Guatemala began to show signs of recuperating from the chaos caused by the overthrow of the Arbenz government.

Just as it appeared that Castillo Armas would finish his term and the country would return to constitutional government, he was assassinated on July 27, 1957, in the Presidential Palace by one of his own bodyguards. Luis Arturo Gonzáles, a lawyer and former president of the Congress, who was a close personal adviser and friend of Castillo Armas, automatically became president as first designate elected by the Congress. He pledged to uphold the constitution, not to run for reelection, and to conduct an honest election.

The calling of elections stimulated the organization of political parties. The noncommunist supporters of the 1944 revolution organized the Revolutionary Party; the friends of Castillo Armas continued with his organization, which they named the Democratic Nationalist Movement (MDN), and General Miguel Ydígoras Fuentes organized a moderate conservative party, the National Democratic Reconciliation Party. The government, however, refused to permit the Revolutionary Party to participate in the election, claiming its leaders were Communists. It so dominated the election, held on October 20, 1957, that the candidate backed by the government appeared to be an easy victor. The other candidate, General Ydígoras, cried fraud and organized mass demonstrations which were so successful that the army took over the government, canceled the election, and named a new acting president, Guillermo Flores Avendaño, who was second designate at the time.

Another election was organized for January 19, 1958. President Flores Avendaño is reported to have said, "For the first time in history Guatemalans will be absolutely free to vote for the candidate of their choice." Most observers are in agreement that this turned out to be Guatemala's first relatively free and fair election in 137 years of independent political life. The choice the voters had was between three military officers and a lawyer. General Miguel Ydígoras Fuentes, the moderate conservative candidate of the National Democratic Reconciliation Party, received 190,972 votes; Colonel José Luis Cruz Salazar of the Democratic Nationalist Movement, the conservative party founded by Castillo Armas, received 138,488 votes; Mario Méndez Montenegro, candidate of the Revolutionary Party, received 132,824 votes; and José Enrique Dardón received 5,834 votes. An additional 24,156 votes were voided, giving a total of 492,274 votes cast in the election. Since no candidate had a majority, the election of the president was thrown into the Congress, where the Democratic Nationalist Movement had a majority. General Ydígoras had received more votes than any of the other candidates, and Cruz Salazar was persuaded to throw his support to him in exchange for a lucrative cabinet position. Ydígoras was inaugurated on March 2, 1958.

The difficulty in developing constitutional government in a country such as Guatemala is illustrated by what happened during General Ydígoras' years as president. He was a moderate conservative who had begun his career serving General Ubico. He was a poor administrator, and once he had achieved his goal of becoming president he seemed to have no program beyond preserving the country's traditional land-tenure system. As a result, his years in office were marked by crisis after crisis, and much of the time he ruled by imposing a state of siege.[5]

The failure of the Ydígoras government to improve conditions stimulated the growth of opposition political parties, the most important of which was the Revolutionary Party. The Revolutionary Party won elections for local offices in the capital and some of the other cities, where its organization prevents the elections from being manipulated, but it lost the elections in the rural areas, where the traditional class system facilitated electoral frauds.

Political life in Guatemala under General Ydígoras Fuentes was complicated by the Communists, who, with financial help from the Castro regime in Cuba, were very active. In addition, the Ydígoras government was notorious for graft at the highest levels. The United States tried to help the country, giving it $3,669,000 during the first year of the

---

[5] Some of the background information for this chapter was gathered in Guatemala in July and August 1961, during a state of siege declared after a cache of arms and homemade flamethrowers was accidentally discovered by the police.

Alliance for Progress (1961–62), but the government was so corrupt and inefficient that the foreign aid helped little. Finally, armed revolts began once again to break out.

The situation came to a head with the congressional by-elections of December 3, 1961, in which thirty-three of the sixty-six congressional seats were at stake. After the votes were counted, Ydígoras claimed that twenty-five of the thirty-three seats had been won by his followers, giving the government a total of fifty of the sixty-six seats in the Congress. The Revolutionary and the other opposition parties were strong, as usual, in the city and weak in the rural areas. A cry of fraud went up, and all the opposition parties united in efforts to force Ydígoras to resign. On January 24, 1962, the chief of Ydígoras' secret police force was shot dead. In February a revolt was crushed. In March large demonstrations against the government were put down by the army, and at least 20 were reported killed and 530 wounded. Ydígoras instituted a strict state of siege and managed to hold on to his office. The Revolutionary Party, the National Liberation Movement, and the Christian Democratic Party combined their efforts and appealed to the army to oust Ydígoras and permit a neutral anticommunist junta that could then organize elections. But still Ydígoras managed to stay in power.

On November 24, 1962, the Congress passed a more stringent income-tax law. This provoked a serious effort, led by conservative military officers, to overthrow the government. On November 25 the air force bombed the National Palace, but Ydígoras crushed the revolt. Meanwhile, a group of army officers and middle- and upper-class youths had organized a band called MR 13, which tried to emulate Fidel Castro and overthrow the government by guerrilla activities. The Ydígoras government proved incapable of destroying the guerrillas. The situation deteriorated, and finally, just before the elections of 1963, Ydígoras was overthrown by a coup d'état led by his Minister of Defense, Colonel Enrique Peralta Azurdia. When the various political groups began campaigning for the presidency in 1963, Dr. Juan José Arévalo, who had been out of the country since 1952, announced from Mexico that he was a candidate for the presidency. When Dr. Arévalo secretly returned to Guatemala late in March, Colonel Peralta took control of the government, suspended the constitution, dissolved the legislature, banned all political activity, and enforced his wishes by use of the military and a state of siege. Since Ydígoras had lost practically all his support by then, Colonel Peralta had no trouble taking power and expelling Ydígoras from the country.

Colonel Peralta justified his action by stating that Guatemala was "on the brink of internal conflict as a result of subversion promoted by pro-Communist sectors, and because of the infiltration of communism, which has become more alarming each day." The Colonel declared himself Chief of State and took over all executive and legislative functions. There was so much opposition to Peralta's cancellation of the 1963 election that he was unable to institute a personal dictatorship. By August 1964 he had created a constituent assembly, which he dominated. This group created a new fundamental document, which was proclaimed on September 15, 1965. An election was held on March 6, 1966, and constitutional government was reinstituted on July 1, 1966. All during Peralta's period in office, the country was kept in an unsettled state by the activities of guerrilla forces, which fought the army, kidnapped rich men and held them for ransom, threw bombs, and caused much unrest.

When the election took place, the forces behind Colonel Peralta organized the Institutional Democratic Party (PID) and nominated Colonel Juan de Diós Aguilar de León for president. The followers of Castillo Armas, reorganized as the National Liberation Movement, nominated Colonel Miguel Ángel Ponciano, and the Revolutionary Party nominated its leader, Mario Méndez Montenegro. Méndez Montenegro was murdered during the campaign, whereupon the party nominated his brother, Julio César Méndez Montenegro. To the surprise of the colonels and the Peralta government, Méndez won the largest number of votes, 201,070. Aguilar received 146,085 and Ponciano 110,145. The PR also won a majority of the seats in the legislature. Méndez Montenegro was then elected president by the legislature by a vote of 35 to 19, the first opposition candidate ever to win the presidency in Guatemala without violence. This was probably only the second fair election ever held in the country.

Upon taking office on July 1, 1966, Méndez Montenegro offered an amnesty to the guerrillas if they would stop fighting. The guerrillas rejected the offer and launched a campaign of terror upon what they termed "right-wing" elements. This provoked the development of counteractivity by terror gangs known as the National Resistance Front and the White Hand, led and financed by wealthy conservatives who were frightened because of the kidnappings some of them had suffered. The President broadcast an appeal to the various gangs to quit fighting and allow his government to begin the reforms it was pledged to achieve. One of the armed groups, the Armed Forces of the Revolution (FAR), offered a truce if the army would leave it alone, but reiterated its goal of overthrowing the government and installing a "people's government." When the violence continued, the government had the army begin a sustained drive against the various armed bands, which was fairly successful. The FAR and other terrorist groups reacted by redoubling their efforts. A police station in Guatemala City was attacked; a wholesale firm was looted; fuel storage tanks were set afire. The armed bands of the businessmen then intensified their activities, claiming that the government had sold out to the Communists and that therefore they had to take the law into their own hands to prevent the spread of violence.

On November 2, 1966, President Méndez Montenegro finally declared a state of siege in a desperate attempt to stop the carnage. His government, which was elected in a fair election, is pledged to reform Guatemala. It is pushing agrarian and tax reform, and has signed for several developmental loans with international agencies. These meager steps infuriated both the Communist true believers and the defenders of the status quo, both of whom redoubled their efforts to destroy the government. The experience of the years since 1944 has tempered the Guatemalan people, however, and the government seems to have the support of a majority.

The history of Guatemala clearly demonstrates how impossible it is to construct a stable political system when there is no concensus among the population. Although President Ydígoras was elected in what was probably the fairest election ever conducted in the country until then, his government could not finish its term. With the new attempt at constitutional government under Méndez Montenegro, again the lack of concensus prevents any orderly development. The Communist-inspired terrorist gangs keep insisting that only they can lead Guatemala, and the terrorist gangs inspired by the defenders of the antiquated social system call every reformist step taken by the government "communism."

Thus Guatemala struggles with its perennial problem: how does one stabilize a country containing a mass of illiterate, non-Spanish-speaking Indian farmers and a tiny aristocratic traditional-minded caste that tries to prevent the changes needed to solve the country's problems?

The Formal Constitutional Framework

Guatemala is governed under the constitution that was adopted September 15, 1965, and became effective May 15, 1966. This replaces the "Fundamental Charter of Government" introduced by the *de facto* military government of Colonel Peralta.

Guatemala has had more constitutions than it needed and practically none was ever completely observed. The first constitution for independent Guatemala was that of October 11, 1825, when it was a province of the Central American Confederation. After the confederation was destroyed, new constitutions were adopted in 1851, 1876, and 1879. With extensive amendments in 1887, 1897, 1927, and 1935, and lesser changes in other years, the 1879 document remained in force until the overthrow of Ubico in 1944.

The 1944 revolution produced the constitution of March 15, 1945, which reflected the newer trends in Latin-American constitutionalism. This established a unitary government with much power in the legislature, included extensive guarantees of political, social, economic, and cultural rights, and provided specific restrictions on presidential succession and on the various branches of the government. It was intended to prevent dictatorship and foster democratic government. In actual practice, the 1945 constitution was often ignored. Because Article 32, forbidding the "formation and functioning of political organizations of an international or foreign character," was not applied against the Communist Party, the 1945 charter came to be identified with Communist infiltration, and in 1954 the new holders of power abolished the 1945 document and governed until March 1, 1956, under a forty-five-article "political statute." A new constitution was proclaimed in 1956, but President Ydígoras often ignored it and for long periods governed under a state of siege. In actual practice, during most of Guatemala's history there has not been much difference in the style of government whether a constitution was in force or not.

The 1965 constitution sets up a representative democratic republican form of government organized "to guarantee Guatemala's inhabitants the enjoyment of liberty, security, and justice," with power divided between a president, a unicameral legislature, and a court system. A Council of State serves as an advisory group. This constitution is typical of recently written Latin-American constitutions: it is too long, containing much material that could have been better left to congressional action; it recognizes the special relationship of Guatemala to the rest of Central America; and after listing pages of constitutional rights, it then gives the president, "in case of invasion of the territory, of grave perturbations of the peace, of public calamity, or of activities against the security of the state," the power to suspend the most important constitutional guarantees.

How this constitution will work out cannot be determined, because of the short time it has been in effect. If one can judge by Guatemala's past history, it will not last long.

How the Constitution Is Amended

For ordinary changes in the constitution, a two-thirds vote of the Congress is needed to propose an amendment and a majority of a specially convened constituent assembly is needed to ratify the proposal. No changes can be made in the clauses banning the reelection of the president, nor can the clauses dealing with the presidency be deleted from the constitution.

A special arrangement is provided for constitutional amendments dealing with the partial or complete union of the Central American states or to incorporate Belize into Guatemala. In these cases, a joint meeting of the Congress and the Council of State can amend the constitution by a two-thirds vote of the combined membership.

Who Participates in Politics

The great majority of Guatemala's population has never effectively participated in the political life of the country, although the percentage of those that do has been rising since 1944. The election of 1966 was the first time all citizens over eighteen were permitted to vote.

The vote in Guatemala is theoretically obligatory for all literate citizens over eighteen and voluntary for illiterates. Until 1966 illiterate females could not vote. The percentage of the voting population rose from 12.9 percent of the total in 1940 to 20.5 percent in 1958. In 1964, 839,800 were registered to vote, and 333,643, 39.7 percent of those registered, cast their ballots in the uncontested election for the constituent assembly. For the 1966 election about a million were registered and more than 456,000 actually voted.

The only citizens not permitted to vote are the mentally disabled and men on active duty with the armed forces and the police.

The Electoral Machinery

Under the 1965 constitution, elections will be controlled and organized by the Electoral Council, made up of the director of the Electoral Registry, one representative of each legally registered party that obtained 15 percent of the votes in the last previous election, a representative elected by the Congress, and one elected by the Council of State. The election of 1966 was organized by a special electoral council set up by decree, but similar to the council set up by the constitution. The Electoral Registry is to be the permanent body concerned with elections; the Electoral

Council is to be set up just before each election and to disband after the election is over.

Under an electoral law originally adopted during the Castillo Armas regime and amended several times since then, the Electoral Registry and the Electoral Council control all aspects of the electoral process, their most important duties being to set up and verify the register of voters, to set up and keep a register of political parties, to prepare and distribute instructions about the elections, to organize elections, to prepare the election returns except in the case of presidential elections, to appoint and dismiss departmental delegates and employees of the Electoral Council, and in case of a tie vote in any election to pick a winner by lot.

The electoral law was carefully drawn up to create as fair a system as was possible. Government employees cannot serve as members of the local committees that control the elections, and only one voter at a time can enter the polling place. No electoral propaganda can be distributed the day of the election, nor can political meetings be held on that day. In addition, the political parties and independents running for office are given free use of the telephone, telegraph, and radio system, so that they can be in contact with the officials of the Electoral Council on election day. The sale or drinking of liquor is forbidden on election day.

During the Arévalo and Arbenz regimes, each party prepared its own ballot and the government supplied an official envelope to put it in. Thus the voter could not divide his vote among the several parties. And he still can't. Under the system now in use, the electoral tribunal prepares a party column ballot and each voter casts his ballot for all the candidates of one party. Elections are held on a Sunday with the polls opening at eight A.M. and closing at six P.M., unless additional voters are present and waiting to cast their ballots at six, in which case the polls remain open until all have voted but no later than midnight.

Although the mass illiteracy still permits some controlled voting in the rural areas, the votes are fairly counted wherever the political parties are well organized, and whatever cheating takes place is the exception rather than the rule. It was for this reason that the December 1963 election never took place: the incumbent power holders were sure to lose. That the opposition candidate won in 1966 and was permitted to take office demonstrates how much Guatemala has changed since 1944.

Political Parties

During most of its history, Guatemala's political leaders operated through the traditional Liberal and Conservative Parties. These two groups had many features in common. Both came out of the upper classes. Both had definite ideologies but little program. Both were combative and had a tendency toward *caudillismo*. They were active only in the cities and primarily in the capital. Both were intransigent, neither of them ever accepting anything the other proposed. Each was organized as an oligarchy around a small group of leaders who eventually became a parliamentary bloc. Both were financed by the rich when out of power and by the government treasury when in power.

Until the end of the nineteenth century, the Liberals were the more progressive group. They supported the republic, federalism, agrarian and fiscal reform, economic development, and separation of church and state. The Conservatives, as their name implies, were for the preservation of the status quo. During the dictatorships of Carrera and Ubico, the Conservative and Liberal Parties so discredited themselves that with the 1944 revolution they completely disappeared.

From 1944 to 1954 many attempts were made to build modern political parties. But, as we have seen, the Communist Party, the only well-organized political group in the country, was able to infiltrate every party organized and prevent its normal development. Thus a healthy party system never developed. Professor K. H. Silvert reports that twenty-four different parties appeared between 1944 and 1952, yet on December 2, 1952, only nine were legally registered with the Civic Registry.[6] All except the Communist Party were weak, and all the parties that supported the government were financed by the government. The opposition functioned through a number of different organizations, the most important being the Party of Anticommunist Unification (PUA). After Castillo Armas came to power, he dissolved all political parties and banned all party activity. In the "election" of October 10, 1954, Castillo Armas presented his candidates under the name of the National Anticommunist Front. After his death political parties began to develop again, and a large number were organized, most of them small personalistic groups. From 1944 to 1967 about fifty different organizations calling themselves parties appeared on the scene, most of them to disappear as suddenly as they had appeared.

Under the 1965 constitution, political parties can participate in electoral activities when they are registered with the Electoral Registry in accordance with rules governing parties. Before 1965, only 10,000 signatures of registered voters were needed with the petition filed for registration, but this number was increased to 50,000 in an attempt to cut

---

[6] K. H. Silvert, *A Study in Government: Guatemala* (New Orleans: Middle American Research Institute, 1954).

down on the number of small parties. Under the 1965 rule, only three parties were able to qualify for the election held in 1966. No party propagating Communist ideology can be registered, nor any having international ties or opposing the democratic organization or the sovereignty of Guatemala.

In 1967 Guatemala's largest party was the Revolutionary Party (PR), which looks upon itself as the heir of the 1944 revolution. The PR was organized on August 20, 1957, but did not gain legal recognition until just before the January 1958 election. During the 1950's the PR won several elections in Guatemala City, Quezaltenango, and other cities, but did not become strong enough to prevent the 1963 coup d'état. When its president and the party's candidate for the presidency of the republic, Mario Méndez Montenegro, was mysteriously killed in 1965, it won great public sympathy and went on to win the election of 1966.

The PR is an attempt to continue the 1944 revolution without the mistakes made from 1944 to 1954, which the PR leadership attributes to inexperience. It is a multiclass, nationalistic party that favors the capitalist system based on social justice and representative democracy. It is against illegal and subversive activity and favors strengthening democratic instruments, including political parties, trade unions, and cooperatives. It is for agrarian reform, municipal and university autonomy, complete observance of human rights, advanced social legislation, and economic development based upon a plan. The PR is associated with the other noncommunist reformist and popular parties in Latin America in the League of Popular Parties. Democracy, the PR states, "is the only political system compatible with human dignity capable of winning complete social justice and the exaltation of the highest spiritual values."

The PR is attempting to develop a modern structure and is continuously active in all parts of the country. It had about 85,000 members in 1961, of whom about 73 percent were Indians. Most of the important national leaders are intellectuals, workers, or professionals, but many of the local leaders are Indians. It has had some trouble with Communist infiltration, but expels any members who cooperate with the Communist Party. Its members hold a majority in the 1966–70 legislature, thirty-one of the fifty-five seats.

The Institutional Democratic Party (PID) is the second strongest party in Guatemala. Founded in 1965 by the leaders of the Peralta *de facto* government, it includes within its ranks most of the followers of former President Ydígoras who functioned as the National Democratic Reconciliation Party until 1965, and most of the conservative landowners and military leaders. In the 1966 election it was considered to be the "official" party, and advocated the continuation of the policies of the Peralta regime, particularly in the field of economic development. The PID tends to minimize the importance of guerrilla activities and generally looks to a Guatemala in the future not much different than it has been in the past. Its members hold nineteen of the fifty-five seats in the 1966–70 legislature.

A third important registered political party, the Movement of National Liberation (MLN), is an outgrowth of the Democratic Nationalist Movement (MDN), the party founded by Castillo Armas. The MDN steadily decreased in strength after Castillo Armas was killed, and in 1960 the party split, with the core of the original group founding the MLN. The MLN is led by Mario Sandoval and consists of moderate conservatives who have strong ties to the Catholic church and are strongly anticommunist. Its members hold five of the fifty-five seats in the 1966–70 legislature.

Of the unregistered parties in Guatemala, the most important is the Guatemalan Labor Party (PGT), which is the name adopted by the Soviet-oriented Communists in 1952. From 1944 to 1954 this group consisted of young *ladino* intellectuals of the lower middle class. The best evidence is that it never had more than three or four thousand members. The leadership never included any workers or Indians, and today the PGT continues to be of the same character, working through numerous front organizations and infiltrating other organizations, with its members posing as liberals, socialists, and other types of reformers. There is some evidence that President Ydígoras encouraged them in an attempt to weaken the Revolutionary Party and to stampede conservative elements to his banner. Guatemalan Communists have proven their skill at political operations and campaigning, and noncommunist political groups and parties have frequently yielded to the temptation to include them in their operations, only to find themselves the eventual victims of astute manipulation.

Other parties continue to function. The Christian Democratic Party (PDCG) held four seats in the national Congress abolished by Colonel Peralta. The PDCG is a highly doctrinaire group, closely associated with the Catholic church, and in recent years has called for reforms. In the summer of 1966 it was able to become a registered party. A number of organizations that seek the reelection of former President Arévalo have also been functioning in recent years. The most important of these has been a group calling itself Democratic Revolutionary Unity (URD), led by Francisco Villagrán Kramer. This began as a registered party during the Ydígoras regime and at one time had six seats in the national Congress. Unregistered in 1966 and 1967, this party maintains a clandestine organization in Guatemala and issues propaganda from Mexico, where Villagrán Kramer lives in exile. The URD considers itself the spokesman for the "new revolutionary generation"; most of its followers are students and intellectuals. Its program is nationalistic and oriented toward rapid social reform.

Not strictly political parties are the two Communist-led terrorist groups functioning in Guatemala, although they are political organizations. One is known as the Armed Forces of the Revolution (FAR). The other, which the Communists attack as "Trotskyist," is known as the Revolutionary Movement of November 13, or MR 13. The two groups were united at one time, but they split in April 1965. The FAR was led originally by Luis Turcios, who received much publicity in the United States as a new Fidel Castro, until his death in October 1966, when the leadership was taken over by someone known as César Montes.[7] The MR 13 is led by a former army officer, Marco Antonio Yon Sosa. Both organizations have their headquarters in the undeveloped jungle and spend their energies in fighting the army, kidnapping the rich and holding them for ransom, perpetrating hit-and-run atrocities in the capital, and making propaganda. Both seem to get some of their money and guns and much of their training in Cuba and other Communist countries.[8]

Guatemala has had too many political parties since 1944, and it still has too many. With the new rules requiring 50,000 signatures before a party can be registered, perhaps it will be possible at last to keep the number of parties functioning down to a few. Most parties during recent years, except for the Revolutionary, Communist, and Christian Democratic, were simply vehicles for politicians looking for power. Nine different organizations participated in the 1959 congressional elections, and at least sixteen were apparently preparing to enter the 1963 election before it was canceled. If a stable party system is to be built, the population must become more integrated and the political leaders will have to learn how to cooperate with each other.

Public Opinion and Pressure Groups

Public opinion in Guatemala is an expression of the urban middle class and is centered in Guatemala City. The majority of the illiterate Indians

---

[7] See, for example, "Red Riding Hood," *Newsweek*, October 17, 1966, p. 61.

[8] In the summer of 1965 the Guatemalan police arrested a man riding a second-class bus who was carrying $125,000 and a passport showing he had just come from Cuba. It was assumed this was a courier carrying funds to the guerrillas from Communist sources.

remain inarticulate and make no impression upon events. Most Guatemalans have no channel through which to express themselves. The political parties, trade unions, interest groups, and professional associations are all weak. Their opinions are expressed through speeches, letters to the press, memorials signed by groups, public meetings, and parades that invariably end in the public square facing the National Palace.

The best organized group in Guatemala consists of the officers in the armed forces. Other groups that make their influence felt are the Guatemalan Association of Agriculturists (the large landowners), the Chamber of Commerce, the Association of Industries, the Association of Journalists, the Catholic church, the Bar Association, the trade unions, and the organized student groups, particularly the university students' association. Because of the mass illiteracy, no really good newspapers are published in Guatemala, but the quality has been improving in recent years. The few well-organized groups tend to monopolize attention, and any determination of public opinion is therefore almost impossible.

In the 1960's the army consisted of about 10,000 officers and men. Its organization puts it into contact with all sections of the country, and the tradition of officer involvement in politics has led to an almost constant stream of military presidents. From 1930 to 1967, the only civilian presidents were Dr. Arévalo and Méndez Montenegro. There is some evidence that the officer corps has been changing in composition. Traditionally, the Guatemalan officers came from the upper classes, but the broadening of the economy has cut down the number of sons of the aristocracy who adopt a military career. On the other hand, the growing lower middle class has found few outlets for its ambition, and the army has absorbed many young men of this strata. As a result during the last decade the officers in Guatemala have tended to be among the more progressive groups.

During the 1960's the armed forces began to carry out civic-action programs financed in large part by the United States government. The military forces have been drilling wells and building roads, sending military physicians to treat the sick in isolated areas, feeding schoolchildren, and sponsoring literacy campaigns. In 1965 the armed forces were providing meals to 301,000 schoolchildren, using food provided by the United States government. Since about 70 percent of the recruits into the armed forces are illiterate, the military is now teaching its recruits to read and write. But despite its civic-action programs, the Guatemalan military continues to be inefficient and unpopular, and it has been unable to stop the terrorist activities.

The Catholic church has experienced ups and downs in Guatemalan political life. During the Conservative regime of Rafael Carrera and his successor, the church was the dominant institution in public life. A visitor to the national Congress during this time reported that more than half the congressmen were priests. The aftermath of the revolution of 1871 permanently changed this situation. Justo Rufino Barrios instituted a number of reforms, including nationalization of church lands and properties, confiscation of religious endowments, abolition of nunneries, and legalization of civil marriage and contract, which permanently broke the power of the church in civil matters. The church has subsequently been very discreet with respect to direct intervention in political affairs. Only one protest was publicized by the church during the period of Communist infiltration into the Arbenz regime, but the archbishop of Guatemala did praise the triumph of the forces of Castillo Armas as a "true national liberation" in 1954, and the church has subsequently been a focal point of attack by Dr. Arévalo and his supporters.

Religious freedom and tolerance are practiced in Guatemala today, and there are missionaries of Protestant faiths, notably Presbyterians, active in the country. At least nominal Catholicism is the professed religion of the vast majority of the population.

Labor was weak and practically unorganized before the 1944 revolution. A fairly strong labor movement developed during the 1945–54 period, but because the trade unions were controlled by the Communists, Castillo Armas dissolved them all. Since that time the organized labor movement has slowly revived, but by 1966 only 18,000 of the total labor force of about one million were in labor unions. Even these workers did not have much influence as a pressure group, since they were split into four different kinds of unions. As is common in Latin America, the government exercises much control over labor unions through the laws governing their recognition.

Students, especially university students, play a significant role in Guatemala, probably because they also are one of the few well-organized groups in the country. They are very prone to strike, sometimes for political reasons, sometimes for trivial ones. Since the university students are practically all from the middle and upper classes, governments have been loath to treat them harshly. Students graduate directly from student politics into national politics, and there is always a close connection between the political parties and the students.

Civil Liberties

The majority of Guatemalans have almost never enjoyed true civil liberty, except during parts of the constitutional regimes headed by Arévalo and his successors. Despite the fact that the country's early constitutions guaranteed individual liberties, the Guatemalan dictators paid scant attention to human rights, and under General Ubico people lived in constant fear. Consequently the 1945 constitution listed at length all the civil liberties to be guaranteed, and also included a long list of social, economic, cultural, and family rights. The continuous revolts against the Arévalo government forced it to suspend these rights from time to time, but, generally speaking, the period from 1945 to 1951 was the freest the Guatemalan people ever enjoyed. Under Arbenz, civil liberties slowly disappeared, and as the resulting protests increased, censorship and restriction became tighter. During the last six months of the Arbenz regime (January to June of 1954), the anticommunists were ruthlessly crushed in a reign of terror that featured many of the techniques of eastern European totalitarianism, including torture, looting, exile of opponents, homes broken into, meetings broken up, etc. At the same time, it must be admitted that such techniques were hardly recent imports. Similar methods have been used on far too many occasions in Guatemala, by both left- and right-wing factions.

The Castillo Armas government ruled most of its life under a state of siege. It jailed thousands of persons and did little to safeguard individual rights, although it never tried to set up an all-out dictatorship. The same was true of Ydígoras Fuentes, who ruled most of the time under a state of siege. The military government that took his place simply suspended the constitution and continued the state of siege Ydígoras had instituted. Even under the constitutional government of Méndez Montenegro, a state of siege has been necessary to control the terrorists.

The many articles listing individual guarantees in the various Guatemalan constitutions have been only idealistic hopes for the future. The 1956 constitution was typical of constitutionalism in Latin America: Article 77 clearly stated that "It is the obligation of the authorities to see to it that the inhabitants of the Republic enjoy the rights which this Constitution guarantees," and then went on: "Nevertheless, in the event of an invasion of Guatemalan territory, a serious disturbance of its peace, activities against the security of the State, or a public calamity, full enjoyment of the guarantees referred to . . . will cease." Provisions such as these make a farce of civil liberties, and individual rights will probably always be insecure until such clauses disappear from Guatemala's constitution.

The Executive

The Guatemalan executive under the 1965 constitution is a president elected by direct vote for a four-year term and never eligible for reelection. The constitution contains several clauses making it illegal to advo-cate changing this rule. A president must be a Guatemalan by birth, more than forty years old, in full possession of citizenship rights, and not a member of the clergy. Not eligible to be president, in addition to clergy-men, are the leaders of a coup d'état that alters the constitutional order, the person occupying the office of president within six months of an election, relatives of the president or of the leaders of a coup d'état within the fourth degree by blood and the second degree by affinity, and min-isters of state and high military officers, unless they have resigned their positions at least six months before the election.

A vice-president is elected at the same time as the president, and he takes over the presidency if the incumbent dies. If both the president and vice-president should die, someone is elected to fill the unexpired term by a two-thirds vote in a joint session of the Congress and the Council of State.

The president of Guatemala is a strong executive, with thirty-four specified constitutional duties (preserving public order, enforcing the constitution and the laws, being commander in chief of the armed forces, administering the public treasury, and so on). The president can veto bills passed by Congress and can issue decrees, resolutions, regulations, and orders looking toward strict compliance with the laws of the land. Although the president exercises "the executive functions of the state with his ministers either individually or assembled in council," and a minister or ministers must countersign all decrees, agreements, and regu-lations issued by the president, this is no limitation, as the president appoints and removes ministers as he sees fit.

An attempt was made in the 1945 constitution, and continued in the 1956 and 1965 charters that took its place, to make the executive more re-sponsible to the Congress by giving that body the power to vote a lack of confidence in a minister, who must then resign. But the president may call for a revote on the lack of confidence, which requires a two-thirds vote of the total membership of the Congress. And if the president's man is still voted out, there it nothing to prevent him from appointing another minister who will follow the policy to which the Congress objected.

The president has ten ministers assisting him, each in charge of a branch of the public service. Government employees in Guatemala are recruited without the use of a formal civil service system, although as long ago as January 1958 a Department of Civil Service was set up under the Ministry of Labor to proceed with job evaluation and classification of positions until such time as the Congress approved a statute for state workers.

Professor Silvert computed the total number of government employees on all levels in 1952 as about 50,000, all appointed by the executive. The only government employees the executive cannot appoint are the president, the vice-president, the deputies of the Congress, judges, and members of the councils of the *municipios*.

Some attempts are being made to improve the functioning of the administration, the most important being the creation of a training center in public administration operated cooperatively by the Guatemalan government and the International Cooperation Administration of the United States. By January 1, 1960, this center had trained 1,933 employees in various branches of administration.

The Legislative Power

Under the 1965 constitution, Guatemala's legislative power rests in a unicameral Congress consisting of fifty-five members serving four-year terms. Members cannot be reelected, but they can be elected for a second term after one term has intervened. Guatemala does not have a fixed membership in its Congress; each district (there are twenty-two) elects two deputies and all districts with more than 200,000 population elect an additional deputy for each additional 100,000 inhabitants. To be a deputy, one must be a native Guatemalan more than thirty years of age and of secular status. Those not eligible to be deputies, in addition to churchmen, are all officials of the executive and judicial branches and all employees of the executive, the judiciary, and the Congress. The only exceptions to this rule are those who occupy teaching positions and professionals in the service of the government's social welfare establishments. Also ineligible to be deputies are contractors on public works, their guarantors, and those who have financial claims pending for public works; relatives of the president of the republic within the fourth degree of consanguinity or the second degree of affinity; military men on active service; those who represent the interests of companies or persons who operate public services or their attorneys; and those who have administered or collected public funds and have not obtained a settlement of their accounts at the time of their election. When the deputies are elected, one alternate is also elected for each district, to serve if a regular deputy dies or is otherwise unable to carry out his duties. Thus there are no by-elections in Guatemala.

Deputies receive a salary of 650 quetzales each month. (The quetzal is on a par with the dollar.) There is much grumbling in Guatemala about the cost of the Congress, although its total cost is only a tiny fraction of the annual budget, Q751,218 during the 1961–62 fiscal year. The Congress meets in regular session on June 15 for four months and can extend its session if necessary. Special sessions can be called by the president or by the Permanent Committee of the Congress, at which time the Congress can consider only the matters that gave rise to the convocation, unless two-thirds of the total number of deputies vote to deal also with other matters.

The principal powers of the Congress are to enact, amend, and repeal legislation; to approve the budget; to vote taxes; to declare war and approve or disapprove treaties of peace; to initiate legal proceedings against the president, chief justice of the Supreme Court, magistrates, ministers of state, the attorney general, and congressional deputies; to issue the call for presidential elections; and to approve or disapprove treaties by a two-thirds vote. When no presidential candidate has received an absolute majority in an election, as happened in the case of Méndez Montenegro, the Congress has the duty of electing the president from between the two highest vote-getters.

When Congress is not in session, its place is taken by a Permanent Committee made up of the presiding officer of the Congress and eight elected members. (Three alternates are also elected.) The Permanent Committee has the duty of dealing with all matters left pending in the Congress or assigned to it by the Congress. It can call the Congress into special session when necessary.

Members of the Congress, the executive, the Council of State, the Supreme Court, and the College of Professionals all have the right to introduce bills, but most bills continue to come from the president. The Congress has traditionally followed the lead of the president, and only during the few years since Castillo Armas' death has it displayed any initiative. President Ydígoras Fuentes did not control the activities of the Congress, although the majority of members were from his party. The president has the power to veto bills, but Congress can override his veto by a two-thirds vote. During 1961 it appeared as if the Congress were developing more strength than it had ever enjoyed in the past. The members of the various parties were working through organized caucuses, and the reelection of congressmen was strengthening the legislature by giving permanence to a portion of the membership. (Immediate reelection was then permitted.) The president remained the dominent force in Guatemala, but he was far weaker than any of his predecessors. In the annual election for the officials of Congress in March 1961, Ydígoras' opposition succeeded in electing their men to four of the seven posts. This perhaps accounts for the fact that Colonel Peralta's first act after taking power was to disband the legislature. It seems doubtful that this development of congressional strength will continue into the future, for the 1965 constitution prohibited the immediate reelection of a congressman.

Public Finance

Guatemala's budget is prepared by the Ministry of Finance under the supervision of the president and submitted to the Congress not later than October 15 annually. If the Congress does not approve the proposed budget by December 15, that of the previous year remains in effect. Generally, the Congress follows the budget as submitted by the president with relatively few changes.

The income and expenditures of the Guatemalan government have risen rapidly during recent decades. Income in 1939 was Q12,356,700. By 1951, this had risen to Q49,296,900. Arbenz' last budget, that for 1953–54, was close to Q70 million, and by 1961–62 the Congress was adopting a budget calling for receipts and expenditures of Q121,028,834. In 1965 the total had risen to Q166,899,726, but in 1966 it fell to Q155,245,691.

As is typical of many Latin-American countries, Guatemala gets most of its money from those least able to pay taxes. The total collected

TABLE 1
REVENUE OF GUATEMALA, 1966

Source	Amount in Quetzales	Percent of Total
Taxes		
On imports	Q30,644,500	19.7%
On exports	9,169,100	5.9
On alcoholic drinks	12,552,893	8.1
On tobacco	4,825,500	3.1
Tax stamps and official paper	17,502,197	11.3
On income	13,305,700	8.6
On petroleum products	10,963,228	7.1
On land and real property	2,649,000	1.7
Others	4,707,200	3.1
Nontax income		
Public services, sales, profits by government corporations, etc.	4,476,240	2.8
Miscellaneous	18,092,966	11.6
Loans	5,379,952	3.5
Public bonds	20,977,215	13.5
Total	Q155,245,691	100.0%

TABLE 2
EXPENDITURES OF GUATEMALA, 1966

	Amount in Quetzales	Percent of Total
Legislative branch	Q757,537	0.5%
Judicial branch	2,334,834	1.5
Executive branch		
Presidency	4,628,737	3.0
Ministry of Foreign Relations	2,924,567	1.9
Ministry of Interior	6,483,776	4.2
Ministry of National Defense	14,448,365	9.3
Ministry of Public Finance	44,990,908	29.0
Ministry of Education	21,481,980	13.8
Ministry of Public Health	12,521,459	8.1
Ministry of Labor	633,528	0.4
Ministry of Economics	3,293,391	2.1
Ministry of Agriculture	5,150,960	3.3
Ministry of Communications	34,595,365	22.2
Miscellaneous	1,000,284	0.7
Total	Q155,245,691	100.0%

in income and real estate taxes in 1966 was only 10.3 percent of the government's income. The largest sums came from taxes on exports, imports, and consumer products; 19 percent was borrowed. The failure to tax the rich is reflected in the continuing mass illiteracy, and only 13.8 percent of the total budget in 1966 went for education. The 1966 budget, shown in Tables 1 and 2, is typical of Guatemala's pattern of revenue and expenditure during the 1960's.

Local Government

For administrative purposes Guatemala is divided into departments, *municipios*, cities, *villas*, *pueblos*, *aldeas*, and *caserios*, but local government is carried on at only two levels, that of the department and that of the *municipio*; the other subdivisions are governed as part of either the department or the *municipio*. Guatemala is divided into twenty-two departments, each headed by a governor appointed by the president of the republic. The office of the governor is weak, and is made weaker still by the fact that the national government maintains branch offices of various national organizations, functioning independently of the governor, in each department. Professor Silvert found in 1952 that the governor of the department of Alta Verapaz had a staff of only four persons, and his office served mainly as a communications center, forwarding problems to the capital and applying decisions made there. The governor also has some ceremonial and judicial functions, but the majority of departmental government work is done by the branches of national entities (the social security system, etc.).

Local governmental divisions in Guatemala are in great part continued from colonial days, and the departmental boundaries especially are completely unrealistic. There are departments that extend from the tops of mountains to sea level, and many have no relationship to the topography at all. Departmental government has traditionally been weak, and the department is considered as a unit only for the purpose of electing the members of the national Congress. There never have been any departmental assemblies of any kind.

Each department is divided into *municipios*, of which there are 324. The Guatemalan *municipio* resembles a United States county, and consists of both rural and urban areas. The cities, *villas, pueblos, aldeas,* and *caseríos* are all parts of *municipios* and have no independent governmental apparatus. The government of the *municipio* may designate police officers or other unpaid officials for these subdivisions, but the governing authority is located in one city or town within each *municipio*, which corresponds to a United States county seat. Each *municipio* is governed by an autonomous elected council presided over by one or more *alcaldes* (mayors). The *municipio* in theory is independent, but in practice all are dependent for funds on the national government, since they can levy taxes only with the approval of the president of the republic.

Until 1936 the principal officer in each department was a *jefe político*, appointed by the president, who was responsible for all the *municipios* in his department. Each *municipio* was under a council consisting of an *alcalde*, a number of *regidores* (aldermen), and a *síndico* (a legal representative, though not necessarily a lawyer). The council was elected annually, but the general rule seems to have been that the retiring *alcalde* would present a single slate of names approved by the *jefe político*, and the voters would automatically vote for the list of names. In the Indian *municipios*, a council of elders apparently prepared the slate of names, but again only one list was presented to the voters. In many *municipios*, the *alcalde*, the theoretical head, was actually subordinate to a military commandant or the secretary of the *municipio*, who was a paid official and usually a *ladino*.

In 1935 President Ubico introduced a new variation by abolishing the elected *alcalde* and replacing him with an appointed *intendente*, who generally was a literate *ladino* from outside the area he served. After the

1944 revolution, the new constitution provided for a return to the elected *alcalde* and town councils. Since then, local government has had more vitality than it ever had before, as the national political parties spread to the *municipios* and true elections began to be held.

Castillo Armas removed all elected and appointed local officials and replaced them with his own appointees in 1954. After the 1956 constitution was adopted, the system of electing the officials of the *municipio* was restored, and by the 1960's true elections were the rule. The scope of the *municipio's* activity is still limited, and the local political leaders are further weakened by the constitutional ban on reelection, which prevents the consolidation of local bases of power. However, there is some vitality at this level, and the growth of political parties is transforming the system of local elections into a school of political activity. An innovation that may strengthen local government was the creation in 1956 of an Institute for Municipal Development, which loans money to *municipios* for improvements. Although the money still comes from the national government, the institute is a new channel, and the *municipios* are benefited by it.

Many of the officials of the *municipios* serve without pay. *Alcaldes* receive salaries if they are elected for three years, which is the term in the larger *municipios*, except for the capital, where the term is four years. Professor Silvert reported that Quezaltenango, a *municipio* with about 27,700 urban and 8,300 rural inhabitants in 1952, had at that time a governing council consisting of a paid *alcalde*, two *síndicos* and nine councilmen who served without pay, and about ninety paid employees. He computed that the total number of paid and unpaid employees at all levels of government in the *municipio* of Quezaltenango was about 660. In addition to this number, the armed forces had an unknown number of soldiers in the *municipio*.

Most of the *municipio* activity consists of local policing and regulation and distribution of water, electricity, and community-owned land. At the time of Professor Silvert's study, Quezaltenango received most of its income from the sale of electric current, head taxes, slaughter fees, the sale of water, municipal market charges, and miscellaneous property and business taxes. Most of the *municipio's* income goes for salaries; the balance goes for local improvements.

The Judicial Power

Guatemala's judicial power under the 1965 constitution rests in a Supreme Court of Justice, subsidiary tribunals, and a series of special courts.

The members of the Supreme Court, the Appeals Court, and special courts are elected by the Congress, and the judges of the lower courts are appointed by the Supreme Court. In minor local cases, municipal officials serve as judicial officials. The judges elected by the Congress serve four-year terms, but if they have served two complete terms they may then continue to serve until retirement at the age of seventy.

In addition to the regular court system, the armed forces operate a series of military tribunals with jurisdiction over crimes and misde-meanors committed by members of the armed forces and by leaders of armed insurrections. The Court of *Amparo* is made up of regular judges to hear cases dealing with threats to a person's political rights or constitu-tional guarantees. The Court of Jurisdictional Conflict and the Court of Administrative Conflict deal with administrative disputes. The Court of Accounts examines and reviews all receipts and expenditures of all gov-ernmental agencies and all semi-independent and other organizations operating with government funds. The Constitutional Court is also made up of regular judges (the chief justice, four other Supreme Court justices, and eight members of the Appeals and Administrative Conflict Courts chosen by lot), who vote on the constitutionality of legislation and by a two-thirds majority can declare an act unconstitutional. This power has not yet been exercised enough to allow a judgment on the operation of judicial review in Guatemala.

The Scope of Governmental Activity

Despite its comparatively small budget, the Guatemalan government is the most important social group in the country, for it is the largest em-ployer, the largest landowner, and the largest purchaser, seller, and banker. The economic welfare of the country depends upon it. It controls the educational system, the health services, public assistance, and even sports, through the subsidies it gives the National Sports Commission. Its coffee *fincas* produce more than any individually owned farms. It owns the subsoil, including anything found therein. Its activities determine whether the country prospers or stagnates.

Guatemala: A Last Word

Guatemala has not achieved democracy, nor has it ever been governed democratically. Events since the end of World War II have so shaken up the population that the country will probably never turn back from its road away from the semifeudal social system that produced misery for the overwhelming majority of the population and luxury for a tiny aristocratic minority, though it has not yet left that system completely behind. The rise in population, the improvement in the transportation system, and the increase in educational facilities are all contributing to the development of a more widely based public opinion than ever existed before.

Yet Guatemala faces tremendous problems before it can become a modern state. Too much money goes to the support of a useless army and not enough to education. The broadening of the economy is creating a larger middle class, but almost half of the population continues to consist of illiterate agricultural Indians. Landless male Indians continue to work a whole day in the fields for fifty or sixty cents, while their wives walk barefoot for miles to the nearest market to sell their handicrafts. In such a society, the children receive little education, the diet is poor, the cultural level is low. The gap between the Indians and the *ladinos* in Guatemala is probably just as wide today as it has ever been.

The Indian culture, while poor in its material aspects, has an extremely strong hold on its people. To an overwhelming extent most Indians will accept only minor elements of modern culture, and these only so long as they in no way interfere with their traditional life. Any real change is rejected. It is not enough that an Indian continue to cultivate maize on the ancestral land; he must cultivate it in precisely the same way as his ancestors did. He must not irrigate it or fertilize it, or replace the traditional hoe with a more modern implement, even if he could afford these things—and there are those who could—for that is not "the custom." If an exceptional Indian does try to change his life in any way not sanctioned by ancient custom, he and his family are ostracized by his village. This is a price few have cared to pay. Most Indians seem to understand intuitively that any real acceptance of modern ways would mean the quick death of their whole culture, and they cling to it with a tenacity that has been the despair of many sincere reformers who have tried to help them. Thus the problem of Indian poverty will be a particularly hard one to solve, even if exploitation should miraculously cease.

Meanwhile the president continues to dominate the larger society, and is himself bedeviled by the organized violence of the Communists and the old-fashioned conservatives who dream of a return to the past.

The long hoped-for integration of Central America would almost certainly be of great help to Guatemala in dealing with its problems, and recent presidents, recognizing this, have been among the most vigorous supporters of cooperation among the Central American republics. The coming to power of the Revolutionary Party in 1966 has led some to prophesy faster progress for Guatemala, but the problems facing the country are so gigantic that it is difficult to be optimistic about its future. Perhaps the completion of the Central American Common Market in the near future will turn the eyes of the Central Americans toward greater political and economic unification, and Guatemala's neighbors will be able to help it to solve its age-old problems.

SELECTED READINGS

ADAMS, RICHARD N., comp. *Political Change in Guatemalan Indian Communities.* New Orleans: Middle American Research Institute, 1957.
ADLER, J. H., *et al. Public Finance and Economic Development in Guatemala.* Stanford: Stanford University Press, 1952.
ALEXANDER, ROBERT. "Communism's Bid for Power in Guatemala," *Communism in Latin America.* New Brunswick, N.J.: Rutgers University Press, 1957.
CEHELSKY, MARTA. *Guatemala: Election Factbook, March 6, 1966.* Washington: Institute for the Comparative Study of Political Systems, 1966.
FERGUSSEN, ERNA. *Guatemala.* New York: Alfred A. Knopf, Inc., 1937.
GEIGER, THEODORE. *Communism versus Progress in Guatemala.* Washington: National Planning Association, 1953.
GRANT, J. A. C. "Due Process for Ex-Dictators: A Study of Judicial Control of Legislation in Guatemala." *American Political Science Review* 41 (June 1947): 463–69.
INMAN, SAMUEL GUY. *A New Day in Guatemala.* Wilton, Conn.: Worldover Press, 1951.
INTERNATIONAL BANK FOR RECONSTRUCTION AND DEVELOPMENT. *The Economic Development of Guatemala.* Washington, 1951.
JAMES, DANIEL. *Red Design for the Americas: Guatemalan Prelude.* New York: John Day Co., 1954.
JOHNSON, KENNETH F. *The Guatemalan Presidential Election of March 6, 1966: An Analysis.* Washington: Institute for the Comparative Study of Political Systems, 1967.
MACDONALD, AUSTIN F. "Guatemala," *Latin American Politics and Government,* pp. 613–21. 2nd ed. New York: Thomas Y. Crowell Co., 1954.
MÉNDEZ MONTENEGRO, MARIO. "La Revolución Guatemalteca." *Combate* 1 (March–April 1959): 63–67.
MONTEFORTE TOLEDO, MARIO. *Guatemala, monografía sociológica.* Mexico City: Instituto de Investigaciones Sociales, Universidad Nacional Autónoma de México, 1959.
NÁJERA FARFÁN, MARIO EFRAÍN. *Los Estafadores de la democracia.* Buenos Aires: Editorial Glem, 1956.
NASH, MANNING. "Political Relations in Guatemala," *Social and Economic Studies* 7 (March 1958): 65–75.
RAY, JULIO ADOLFO. "Revolution and Liberation: A Review of Recent Literature on the Guatemalan Situation." *Hispanic American Historical Review* 38 (1958): 239–55.
RODRÍGUEZ, MARIO. "Guatemala in Perspective." *Current History* 51 (December 1966): 338–43, 367.
SALAZAR, GUILLERMO, ed. *Democracia en Guatemala.* Guatemala, 1951.
SCHNEIDER, RONALD M. *Communism in Guatemala, 1944–1954.* New York: Frederick A. Praeger, Inc., 1958.

SILVERT, K. H. *A Study in Government: Guatemala.* New Orleans: Middle American Research Institute, 1954.

TAX, SOL. *Heritage of Conquest: The Ethnology of Middle America.* Glencoe, Ill.: Free Press, 1952.

————. *Penny Capitalism: A Guatemalan Indian Economy.* Washington: U.S. Government Printing Office, 1953.

U.S. DEPARTMENT OF STATE. *Penetration of the Political Institutions of Guatemala by the International Communist Movement: Threat to the Peace and Security of America and to the Sovereignty and Political Independence of Guatemala.* (Information submitted by the delegation of the United States of America to the fifth meeting of consultation of Ministers of Foreign Affairs of the American republics, serving as organ of consultation.) Washington, 1954. (See especially "The Partido Guatemalteco del Trabajo, A Basic Study," Annex B.)

WHETTEN, NATHAN L. *Guatemala—The Land and the People.* New Haven: Yale University Press, 1961.

YDÍGORAS FUENTES, MIGUEL. *My War with Communism,* as told to Mario Rosenthal. Englewood Cliffs, N.J.: Prentice-Hall, Inc., 1963.

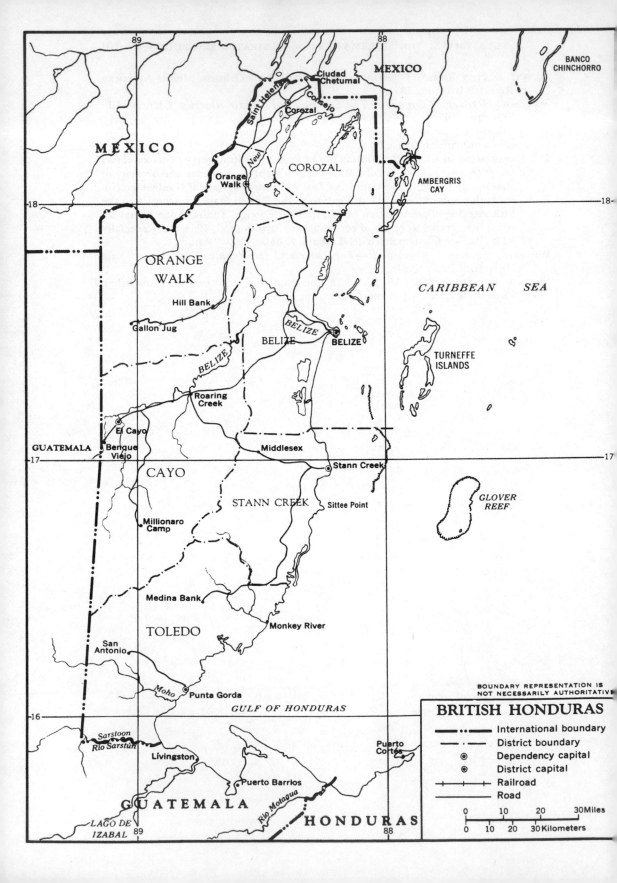

MEXICO

89

88

MEXICO

BANCO
CHINCHORRO

Saint Helena

Ciudad
Chetumal

Consejo

Corozal

18

COROZAL

Neul

Orange
Walk

18

AMBERGRIS
CAY

ORANGE

WALK

Hill Bank

CARIBBEAN SEA

Gallon Jug

BELIZE

BELIZE

BELIZE

BELIZE

TURNEFFE
ISLANDS

Roaring
Creek

GUATEMALA

17

El Cayo

Benque
Viejo

CAYO

Middlesex

Stann Creek

17

STANN CREEK

Sittee Point

GLOVER
REEF

Millionaro
Camp

Medina Bank

Monkey River

TOLEDO

San
Antonio

Moho

Punta Gorda

GULF OF HONDURAS

16

Sarstoon
Río Sarstún

Lívingston

Puerto
Cortés

BOUNDARY REPRESENTATION IS
NOT NECESSARILY AUTHORITATIVE

BRITISH HONDURAS

Puerto Barrios

GUATEMALA

LAGO DE
IZABAL

89

Río Motagua

HONDURAS

88

International boundary

District boundary

⊛ Dependency capital

◉ District capital

Railroad

Road

0   10   20   30 Miles

0   10   20   30 Kilometers

——— 5 ———

BRITISH HONDURAS or BELIZE

Physically connected to Guatemala and Mexico but almost completely isolated from them until recent years, the territory of British Honduras or Belize is never considered a part of Central America, although it is an integral part of the isthmus. Located on the Atlantic coast to the south of the Mexican territory of Quintana Roo and east of Guatemala, British Honduras consists of 8,866 square miles of mostly unoccupied forest land. During colonial days this sparsely settled area was used as a refuge by English pirates, and later the English received permission from the King of Spain to exploit the lumber found there. In 1859 Guatemala signed a treaty granting British sovereignty over the area in return for certain concessions, the most important of which was Britain's promise to build a road from the Atlantic coast to Guatemala City. Because this road was never built (Guatemala finally did the job itself in the 1950's), in 1938 Guatemala declared the 1859 treaty void, but the British have refused to recognize Guatemala's claim to sovereignty over the area. Mexico has also claimed the territory, but the British have preserved their control over the almost unpopulated area, governing it as a crown colony until the 1950's.

British Honduras is a poor, practically empty, and neglected stretch of jungle with a population estimated in 1966 at 109,000. The inhabitants, a mixture of Negroes and *mestizos* with some East Indians, gain their livelihood by exploiting the colony's lumber resources and farming.

After World War II the people began to agitate for self-government, and by 1951 George Price had organized the People's United Party, which gained the support of the majority of the population. When some local self government was granted in 1954, the PUP won eight of the nine seats in an election to the Legislative Council, which had little power. In 1957 the PUP won all nine seats. In 1960 the British government instituted a new constitution that raised the Legislative Council to eighteen elected and five nominated members and decreased the governor's powers. The PUP won all eighteen seats in the 1961 election, and George Price became the First Minister of the colony. After further agitation and negotiation, on January 1, 1964, the United Kingdom granted complete internal self-government to British Honduras.

British Honduras has a parliamentary system of government. The executive consists of a premier and the members of his cabinet, who are elected by the House of Representatives. The House's eighteen members are elected by universal suffrage. A senate of eight members is appointed by the governor. Five senators are appointed on the advice of the premier, two are appointed upon the advice of the leader of the opposition, and one is appointed by the governor as he sees fit. At this writing George Price is the premier and his party holds a majority of the seats in both houses. Price and his party look forward to complete sovereignty for British Honduras someday and membership in the British Commonwealth of Nations.

On December 31, 1960, President Ydígoras of Guatemala offered to make British Honduras a self-governing, free associated state if it would join Guatemala. This offer was refused. The dispute with Guatemala was subsequently submitted to the U.S. State Department for mediation. At this writing no decision had yet been reached. Economically speaking, unification of the area with Guatemala makes sense. Belize or British Honduras, no matter what name it is called, has no future as an independent state. Its only possible future lies in becoming part of something else; if not of Guatemala, then perhaps of a United Central American Republic. The local political leaders, however, opposed the entrance of the colony into the British West Indies Federation, and they continue to oppose any ties with Guatemala. Yet one of its problems is that its governmental machinery is too elaborate for its small population to support. The Mexican government has recently built a bridge across the river separating Quintana Roo and British Honduras. Perhaps as communications improve, the tiny country will be drawn closer to its neighbors. Meanwhile, it continues to be supported by the United Kingdom and gives Guatemalan politicians an issue to discuss.

SELECTED READINGS

ANDERSON, A. H. *Brief Sketch of British Honduras*. Rev. ed. Belize: Government Printing Department, 1958.

BIANCHI, WILLIAM J. *Belize: The Controversy between Guatemala and Great Britain over the Territory of British Honduras in Central America*. New York: Las Americas Publishing Co., 1959.

BOULDING, KENNETH E. "Notes on British Honduras." Mimeographed. Rio Piedras: University of Puerto Rico, 1960.

BRITISH HONDURAS. *Report for the Years 1962 and 1963*. London: Her Majesty's Stationery Office, 1965.

BRITISH HONDURAS PUBLIC RELATIONS OFFICE. *British Honduras, Portrait of a Colony*. Belize, 1953.

CAIGER, STEPHEN L. *British Honduras, Past and Present*. London: George Allen & Unwin, 1951.

CAREY JONES, N. S. *The Pattern of a Dependent Economy*. Cambridge: Cambridge University Press, 1953.

WADDELL, D. A. G. *British Honduras: A Historical and Contemporary Survey*. New York: Oxford University Press, 1961.

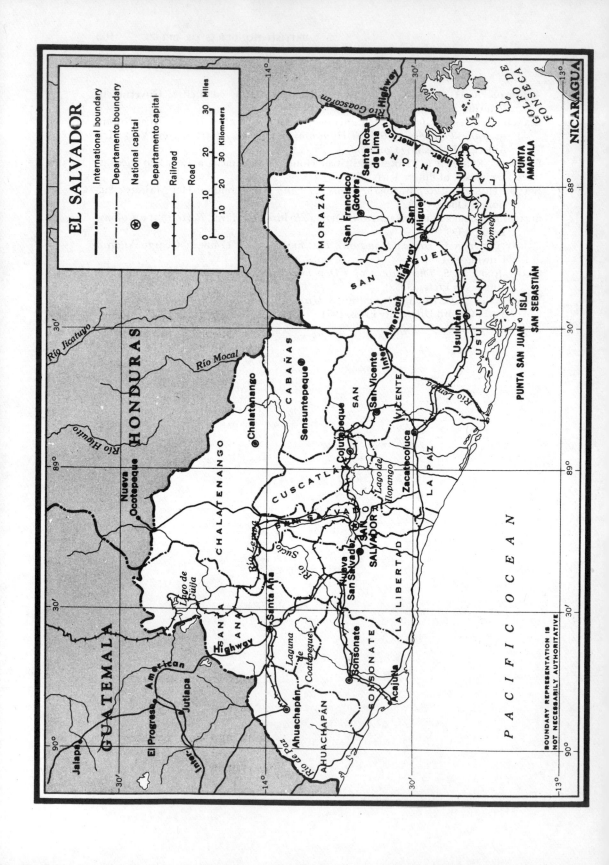

EL SALVADOR

International boundary
Departamento boundary
⊛ National capital
● Departamento capital
Railroad
Road

Miles
0   10   20   30
0   10   20   30   Kilometers

GUATEMALA

HONDURAS

NICARAGUA

Río Jicatuyo

Río Mocal

Río Higuito

Nueva Ocotepeque

Jalapa

El Progreso

Jutiapa

Inter-American Highway

Santa Rosa de Lima

Río Goascorán

San Francisco Gotera

MORAZÁN

SAN MIGUEL

San Miguel

UNIÓN

La Unión

LA

PUNTA AMAPALA

GOLFO DE FONSECA

Usulután

USULUTÁN

Laguna de Olomega

American Highway

Inter-

Chalatenango

CABAÑAS

Sensuntepeque

CHALATENANGO

CUSCATLÁN

SAN VICENTE

San Vicente

Cojutepeque

SAN

Lago de Ilopango

Zacatecoluca

LA PAZ

Río Lempa

PUNTA SAN JUAN

ISLA SAN SEBASTIÁN

SANTA ANA

Santa Ana

Highway

American

Inter-

Lago de Güija

Río Lempa

Río Sucio

SAN SALVADOR

Nueva San Salvador

SAN SALVADOR

LA LIBERTAD

Laguna de Coatepeque

AHUACHAPÁN

Ahuachapán

SONSONATE

Sonsonate

Acajutla

Río de Paz

P A C I F I C   O C E A N

BOUNDARY REPRESENTATION IS NOT NECESSARILY AUTHORITATIVE

90°

30'

89°

30'

88°

30'

14°

30'

14°

13°

30'

13°

—— 6 ——

EL SALVADOR:

The Military as Reformists

El Salvador is a small country in which an entrenched agricultural aristocracy for centuries dominated a mass of poverty-stricken, largely illiterate peasants. Its location on the Pacific isolated it from direct contact with Europe and with the East and Gulf Coasts of the United States until the Panama Canal was built and modern means of transportation were developed. In this isolated area, there was nothing to hinder the development of a traditional oligarchically controlled society. So small is the oligarchy that one frequently encounters the phrase "the fourteen families that run the country" in works about El Salvador. Yet fertile soil permitted El Salvador's hard-working population to develop one of the two countries in Latin America where practically all the land is occupied. Democratic government never flourished, however, and the presidents have usually been military men. In 1962 El Salvador began a new attempt to establish constitutional government which has attracted much attention; this little country finally seems to be developing a functioning constitutional political system.

A National Profile

El Salvador, the most densely populated of the Central American states, is a comparatively small, oblong-shaped country located between Guatemala and Honduras on the southern coast of Central America. Its area of 8,260 square miles includes nine islands in the Gulf of Fonseca. Its maximum length is only 160 miles and the average width is 60 miles. Guatemala lies to the west, the Pacific Ocean to the south, and Honduras and the Gulf of Fonseca are to the north and east.

Two mountain ranges cross the country from west to east, one along the coast, the other along the interior border. Between the two ranges lies a region of plateaus about 2,000 feet above sea level. Here, around the city of San Salvador, live the majority of the Salvadorans. A coastal plain from ten to fifteen miles wide gives access to the Pacific Ocean. The land is less broken up by mountains here than in the rest of Central America, a fact that in large part explains El Salvador's comparatively heavy population and almost complete racial mixture, for there were few isolated valleys in which the Indians could protect their ancient way of life from adulteration by Spanish culture. The climate in the coastal lowlands is hot and humid. On the plateaus it is semitropical, mild and almost uniform all year long. Two seasons are recognized, a wet "winter" from May to October and a dry "summer" from November to April.

El Salvador's population in 1966 was 3,037,000. The overwhelming majority of the people are *mestizos*, with a small minority of Indians and whites. There are no longer any tribal Indians, and El Salvador has one of the most homogeneous populations in Central America. With 376 persons per square mile, El Salvador has the highest density of people in Latin America next to Haiti. About 61 percent of the people live in the rural areas, and there are only two large cities, San Salvador, the capital, with 248,100 at the census of 1961 (350,730 in the metropolitan area), and Santa Ana, with 72,866 (106,550 in the metropolitan area). The population has been increasing at a rate of about 2.82 percent per year. The actual rate of increase is higher, but a large number of people leave each year to search for work in Guatemala, Honduras, and Nicaragua, where jobs are hardly more plentiful but the competition seems less severe, at least from a distance.

Spanish is the official language and the bulk of the population is Roman Catholic. Education is free and obligatory, but a shortage of schools and teachers has left the majority of the population illiterate. In 1964, 56 percent of all over the age of fifteen were unable to read and write. The cities provide six years of schooling and the rural areas three, but in 1966 only about 60 percent of the children in the primary-school age group were attending classes. The country's only university had an enrollment of only 2,705 in 1964. From 1954 to 1964, the university graduated an average of only sixty-two students each year. The lack of education hampers economic development and there is a great shortage of skilled labor. The census of 1961 showed only 2,850 university graduates for the whole country.

El Salvador is primarily an agricultural country; 59 percent of the labor force was engaged in agriculture in 1961, and 80 percent of the country's total area is used for cultivation or grazing, a high percentage for Central America. Coffee is the most important crop, supplying about 75 percent of the value of all exports in most years. Other important crops are cotton, rice, maize, cocoa, tobacco, indigo, henequen, sugar, and rubber. Livestock is an important product, and El Salvador is the world's principal source for a medicinal gum, balsam.

In spite of the dominance of agriculture, great emphasis upon economic development since 1948 has made El Salvador the most industrialized country in Central America. Shrimp fishing in the Pacific has become a major industry since 1960. An oil refinery is located at Acajutla. There is some mining and a small tourist industry. The small size of the country helped to make road construction less costly than in the neighboring countries, and El Salvador has a good road system.

Despite industrialization and an economic growth rate of about 6.3 percent from 1961 to 1965, an antiquated social structure keeps El Salvador's people desperately poor. In 1965 about 8 percent of the population received about 50 percent of the country's total income. Of the 224,289 farms counted in the 1961 census, 2,058, or 0.0092 percent, included within their boundaries 44.86 percent of all the farmland in the country. Housing conditions are very bad for the bulk of the population, and there has been a high rate of unemployment during recent years. The gulf between rich and poor in El Salvador is about as great as anywhere in Latin America, and this helped to produce the militarized semidictatorship that served to preserve an unhealthy status quo into the 1960's. El Salvador's politics has been a dreary alternation of dictatorships, revolutions, attempts at reforms, and new dictatorships that in their turn brought new revolutions. The rapid economic development during the years since 1948 produced new forces in El Salvador which stimulated great political conflict. As a result, new measures to improve education, the economy, and health were introduced, and El Salvador is now changing so rapidly that any description fails to picture the actual situation. Why El Salvador had so much difficulty establishing a stable, effective political system and why in recent years the situation has begun to change will become clear after a survey of the country's historical development.

The Development of Modern El Salvador

El Salvador's location and small size have made it one of the least known Latin-American countries. It began life with a population of about

200,000, with the vast majority illiterate peons working on the farms of a small group of landowners. These landowners, probably as a reaction to Guatemala's attempt to dominate the Central American Confederation, became the leadership of the Liberal Party in Central America, and a Salvadoran, Manuel José Arce, became the first president of the United Provinces of Central America. When Arce aligned himself with the Guatemalan Conservatives, El Salvador's leaders cooperated with Francisco Morazán, the Honduran Liberal. When Morazán was defeated in 1838, Francisco Malespin was installed as president of El Salvador by the victorious army. Thus began a half century of political chaos during which almost continuous war tormented the little country, and Guatemala, Honduras, and Nicaragua repeatedly intervened on one side or the other. Any Salvadoran political leader out of power could always obtain support in a neighboring country, for the liberal-conservative struggle was going on in all parts of Central America. This period left a deep impression upon the political system of El Salvador. In the first place, democratic institutions never developed, for with the incessant fighting, coups, and intrigues there was no time for elections, reforms, debates, and the other aspects of orderly government to become the habitual means of settling political problems. The army became the most important social group after the landowning aristocracy, for only the army could ensure peace of any kind.[1] At the same time a deep desire for the unification of Central America developed, for this seemed to be the only way to prevent the constant meddling in Salvador's affairs by its neighbors. El Salvador remains the most vigorous proponent of the unification of Central America, and the office of the Organization of Central American States is located in San Salvador.

With the beginning of the twentieth century and the rise of the United States as the dominant power in Central America, outside intervention in El Salvador ended. The United States intervened when Guatemala threatened invasion in 1906, and again when Nicaragua threatened attack in 1907. After the latter incident, the United States pressured the Central American states into signing the Washington Treaty of 1907, which pledged the Central American republics to settle their differences peacefully. After that El Salvador became more stable as intervention and war became less frequent.

An aristocracy of landowners still ran the country in their own in-

---

[1] In 1911, for example, there were 82,881 officers and men in the Salvadoran army, and of 10,371,869 pesos (at $0.403 U.S. gold per peso) total expenditures for 1910–11, 2,573,510 pesos went to the Department of War and Marine (Percy F. Martin, *Salvador of the Twentieth Century* [London: Edward Arnold, 1911], pp. 59, 87).

terests, however, and whenever any step toward a more liberal regime was attempted, the aristocracy called a halt to it. Romero Bosque, president from 1927 to 1931, ended martial law and press censorship and ran a fair election in 1931. When Arturo Araujo, who favored liberalization and reform, won the presidential election in that year, the oligarchy refused to accept the results, overthrew the Araujo government, and made Maximiliano Hernández Martínez president.

Hernández Martínez was probably insane. He was a peculiar combination of ruthless dictator and mystic theosophist who thought God was communicating with him daily. To protect the country from what he called communism, he crushed all opposition brutally. Perhaps 17,000 were killed in 1932 when Hernández Martínez claimed the Communists were revolting. Thousands of others were killed, jailed, and exiled during his stay in power. Hernández kept extending his term in office until thirteen years had passed. Although he had gone through the constitutional procedures to extend his term in office until 1949, he was forced out of office in 1944 when the population refused to cooperate with him any longer. In one of the most complete passive-resistance movements ever seen in Latin America, all activities in the country came to a halt. Government employees did not report for work. Trains and streetcars did not run. The schools and all businesses remained closed. Facing such opposition, Hernández Martínez resigned and went into exile.

Hernández Martínez left behind him a country ill prepared for self-government, and no leadership had emerged from the mass strike that overthrew him. And so another military man, General Andrés Menéndez, became acting president, to be followed soon by Colonel Osmín Aguirre Salinas. The old system of government continued until a one-candidate "election" was arranged the following year and yet another military man, General Salvador Castañeda Castro, became the new president. He was a milder conservative than most of his predecessors, and meager reforms were instituted during his term in office. But he governed as he pleased, and civil liberties were ignored. When he tried to extend his term in office in 1948, a younger group of army officers evicted him from the Presidential Palace after three hours of battle.

By 1948 the Guatemalan revolution had evidently awakened a desire for reform in El Salvador, for with the majors and colonels in power instead of the generals, El Salvador for the first time in its history began to hear talk about the reorganization of its archaic social structure. The young officers talked about a new era for their country, about the dawn of democracy and reform, and they seem to have made a real attempt to change the course of Salvadoran history. But, just as in Guatemala, this was a revolution that failed. The lack of practice in operating governmental institutions found the people untrained for active democratic participation, and power soon corrupted the young idealistic army officers. Interestingly enough, they received the cooperation of some of the younger coffee millionaires, who, not unmindful of the lessons taught by the Guatemalan revolution, were ready to aid the underprivileged masses to prevent the complete destruction of their position as a privileged oligarchy.

Major Oscar Osorio was the leader of the young army officers, and he tried to institutionalize the revolution by creating a political party to carry on its program. The Revolutionary Party of Democratic Unification (PRUD) was apparently modeled on the Mexican PRI, but it never developed the strength of that organization. On March 26, 1950, in the first free election El Salvador had known since 1931, Major Osorio won the presidency as the PRUD candidate with 345,239 votes against 266,271 votes for the opposition, organized as Renovating Action *(Acción Renovadora)*. The PRUD also won the majority of the National Assembly seats. This was a peaceful election in which women voted for the first time.

The country made substantial progress under Major Osorio's leadership. The Korean War was then in progress and the price of coffee was high. In addition, the country had exceptionally good coffee crops at that time. Much of the extra income the government received was well invested. A new constitution was adopted in 1950. The Public Administration Service of Chicago was contracted to help introduce modern techniques of public administration, and after some reorganization and the installation of modern systems, one of the better administrations of Latin America was developed. The *municipios* were given greater autonomy. Efforts were made to improve and diversify agriculture. Industry developed. Campaigns were begun against poverty, alcoholism, illiteracy, and poor public health. Education was stimulated. (The United States technical assistance program was helpful in many of these fields.) Some workers were given the right to organize unions. The unification of Central America was pushed.

Loans from the International Bank financed new highway developments. An excellent agricultural extension service was built up. The Armour Research Foundation of the Illinois Institute of Technology set up a scientific laboratory that stimulated and fostered new industry. Many international organizations were invited to help the country's development. One newspaper reported:

... the people are eager to learn new methods, according to technicians. This explains the presence of more foreign specialists per square mile than perhaps in any other country of the world. In addition to the United States Point Four Mission, experts from the World Health Organization, the U.N.E.S.C.O., the International Labor Organization, and the United Nations Children's Emergency Fund and private groups such as I.B.E.C., a Nelson Rockefeller group, are busy applying modern techniques to Salvador's age-old problem of poverty, lack of adequate housing, illiteracy, poor water supply, etc.[2]

Probably the most important of the new industries were a cement factory and a textile factory financed by Japanese capital. The construction of the Lempa River Dam doubled the country's electricity production and provided water to irrigate 85,000 acres of previously unused land. The port of Acajutla was expanded with help from the United Nations.

Yet despite the economic and social developments, the country's basic social structure was not drastically changed. City workers, for example, were given the right to organize in the 1950 constitution, but they could not set up a national labor center, and agricultural unions were banned. Nor was much encouragement given to the creation of a legal opposition, and what opposition existed was so poorly led that in 1952 the opposition parties withdrew from the election, claiming Osorio was going to steal it.

There was much resistance to the Osorio government from the traditional holders of power and from those influenced by the Communists. Revolts had to be put down regularly, and a state of siege was imposed from time to time. Nevertheless, El Salvador seemed to have made a turn toward a more stable political system, and its future looked bright. Unfortunately for El Salvador, the tradition of no reelection prevented President Osorio from continuing in office after 1956, and his successor was incapable of continuing the progress initiated by Osorio. In addition, a drastic drop in coffee prices in the late 1950's upset the country's economic balance, and by 1960 near anarchy returned to El Salvador.

Osorio's successor as president was Colonel José María Lemus, the candidate of the PRUD. Other parties tried to contest the election, but by February 28, 1956, the day of the election, most of them either had

[2] Robert M. Hallett, "Food for El Salvador," *Christian Science Monitor*, April 30, 1953, p. 9. (Copyright © 1953 The Christian Science Publishing Society. All rights reserved.)

withdrawn their candidates, claiming that the government was not going to permit a fair election, or had been banned from the ballot by the Central Election Council. Thus, in a most confusing election campaign that at best could be called "controlled" and at worst "managed," Colonel Lemus was reported to have won 677,748 votes to about 40,000 votes for the opposition candidates whose names were on the ballot.

Lemus began his term in office as though he intended to govern constitutionally. He set up a coalition cabinet and issued a general amnesty for political refugees who had fled or been exiled during the Osorio administration. Some factories were built during his years in office, the largest probably being a Sherwin Williams paint factory, financed by nationals of the five Central American republics, and a sugar refinery. But when coffee prices dropped drastically in 1957 and 1958, unrest rapidly developed, and Lemus never finished his term in office.

The rise of Fidel Castro in 1959 encouraged his admirers in El Salvador to become very active in advocating instantaneous revolution. At the same time, the extreme conservatives whose profits had declined because of the drop in coffee prices redoubled their opposition to the government's halting steps toward reform. The opposition came to a head at the time of the congressional and local elections of April 24, 1960. For the first time since 1950, the opposition participated in the election, united as the National Front of Civic Orientation. Claiming this organization was infiltrated by Communists, Lemus had the rules regulating political parties changed so that 5,000 signatures were needed to register, instead of 2,000, as had been the rule (and is now the rule again). The opposition claimed this requirement would make it too difficult for it to get on the ballot. The new law also banned parties with Communists or anarchists as members. A widespread campaign was launched against the law and temperatures began to rise.

During the August 1960 meeting of the Foreign Ministers of the American states in San José, Costa Rica, to consider the Cuban situation, mass demonstrations and riots took place in San Salvador. President Lemus used the army to crush the riots, thus intensifying opposition to his rule. Groups of students went on strike on August 25. The legislature voted a state of siege on September 5. Lemus announced he had discovered a Communist plot. In the confused rioting and demonstrations, students and others were wounded and killed. Finally, on October 26, the army deposed Lemus in a bloodless coup and installed a junta to govern the country.

The junta consisted of three army officers and three civilians, a peculiar combination of military men and Castro sympathizers. It released all political prisoners, purged the public administration, and announced it would reform El Salvador. But the Communists and *Fidelistas* seemed to be in control of the streets of San Salvador, and mass demonstrations were the order of the day. Some think former President Osorio had something to do with the new junta, for by December he had announced the creation of a new organization, the Social Democratic Party. A party with a *Fidelista* orientation, the Revolutionary Party of April and May, also was recognized by the Supreme Court in December 1960.

The junta was unable to stabilize the government. On January 25, 1961, there was another coup d'état, and this time a civic-military directorate took over the country, pledging to fight communism and reform the country's social system. Opposed by the diehard reactionaries and the Communists and their supporters, the new directorate issued 335 decrees in a short time, all intended to transform the country. The leaders of the old junta and Osorio were exiled and the new government organized the National Conciliation Party as a mechanism through which it could control the country.

The reforms instituted by the new government were revolutionary for El Salvador. A higher minimum wage was decreed. Rents were reduced 30 percent and rent ceilings were instituted. A system of social security was established. Income taxes were raised. Exchange controls were set up to keep the rich from transferring their money out of the country and the national bank was taken over by the government. All farm workers were to be given a compulsory day off with pay on Sunday. The civil service system was improved. The military directorate even resigned from office after a newly elected National Assembly elected a provisional president, Dr. Eusebio Rodolfo Cordón Cea. The National Conciliation Party had won all fifty-four seats in the Assembly that was to hold office until 1964.

The junta had abrogated the constitution of 1950. On January 3, 1962, the National Assembly readopted the 1950 constitution with amendments and set an election for April 29, 1962, when a president would be elected. Upon his inauguration for a five-year term, the country would return to constitutional government. Only one candidate, Julio Adalberto Rivera, sponsored by the National Conciliation Party, was on the ballot. Declared elected, he was inaugurated on July 1, 1962. The withdrawal of all the other political parties from the election in April makes it impossible to state how much support the new president had in the country at the time. He received only 368,801 votes when about 800,000 could have voted. He was vigorously opposed by the Communists and *Fidelistas*, and from April to July 1962 a series of minor bombings in public and private buildings caused unrest. Antigovernment and anti-U.S. signs were painted all over the capital city. On September 15, 1962, the national Independence Day, the *Fidelistas* staged a demonstration at the Independence Monument and covered the monument and surrounding buildings with slogans in red paint. The government immediately called a special session of the Assembly, which passed a stiff anticommunist law that went into effect on September 19, 1962. The law provided three to five years' imprisonment for anyone who "praises, diffuses, indoctrinates, or propagates" Communist or any other doctrine contrary to democracy. It also provided severe penalties for marking provocative statements on walls and banned the organization or encouragement of work stoppages "inimical to public order." The new law also provided a heavy penalty for inciting disorder by causing an explosion.

About this time, the government began to concern itself with the lack of a responsible opposition, and in August 1963 a law was passed creating a system of proportional representation for filling the seats in the National Assembly. There had been no legislative opposition for years, but in 1964 two of the opposition parties won twenty of the fifty-two seats in the Assembly and a Christian Democratic Party member was elected mayor of San Salvador. In the March 13, 1966, election the opposition parties again won twenty seats: the Christian Democratic Party was represented with fifteen seats, the Renovating Action Party with three, and two minor parties with one each. And again José Napoleón Duarte, of the Christian Democratic Party, was elected mayor of San Salvador.

Thus as the country prepared for presidential elections in 1967, it appeared as if at last constitutional government were becoming established. Even though the "revolution" of 1948 had been a failure, it apparently had set in motion forces that had changed the country so much that the old system no longer could be preserved. The economic development, the campaigns to improve health and education, and the maturing of the political parties had all contributed to the creation of a new atmosphere in El Salvador. How different the situation was from the past was demonstrated during the election campaign. The Renovating Action Party's candidate for president was Fabio Castillo, who had been a member of the short-lived junta that had tried to control the country from October 1960 to January 1961. Upon the announcement of his nomination, a great furore arose over Castillo's alleged communism. The Central Electoral Council, however, rejected a petition filed by the government asking that the PAR be banned from the ballot as a subversive organization. When election day came on March 5, the voters peacefully went to the polls and made their choice. This was the first election in the country's history in which several candidates campaigned for office, the election was fairly conducted, and the overwhelming majority of the population accepted the result. Colonel Fidel Sánchez Hernández, the candidate of the National Conciliation Party, won with 223,746 votes. Abrahán González, candidate of the Christian Democratic Party, received 90,089 votes; Fabio Castillo received 49,537 votes; and Álvaro Martínez, of the Popular Salvadoran Party, received 38,647 votes.

Under the National Conciliation Party slogan of "Evolution in liberty," Rivera and Sánchez seemed to represent the forces that recognized that drastic reform was needed and were pushing it with emphasis on economic development and strengthening the machinery of government in order to deal effectively with the country's problems. The two leading opposition parties, the Christian Democrats and Renovating Action, insisted that socal reform, especially agrarian reform, had to come much faster, but the majority of the voters seemed to agree with the National Conciliation Party.

Today El Salvador is closer to having a stable, functioning constitutional system than ever before in its history. The high economic growth rate in the country during the 1960's, the improvements in housing, education, public health, and transportation are all signs that the traditional ruling aristocracy no longer controls the country and that a viable political system is emerging.

The Formal Constitutional Framework

El Salvador is governed under the constitution of January 8, 1962, which sets up a government described as "republican, democratic, and representative." The state has the obligation, according to the constitution, of "assuring to the inhabitants of the Republic the enjoyment of liberty, health, culture, economic welfare, and social justice." This is El Salvador's twelfth constitution.

Power is divided between the president, a unicameral legislature, and the courts; all three governmental branches are independent, although each is supposed to collaborate with the others. The constitution authorizes the executive, with the consent of the legislature, to affiliate El Salvador with a new Central American federation.

The Salvadoran constitution is typical of Latin-American constitutions: unnecessarily long and detailed, listing elaborate individual and social rights, including family rights, labor and social security rights, cultural rights, and even public-health and social-assistance rights, most of which are declared suspended in case of "war, invasion, rebellion, sedition, catastrophe, epidemic, or other general calamities or disturbances of the public order."

How the Constitution Is Amended

To amend the constitution a two-thirds vote of the elected members of the National Assembly is needed, in two consecutive Assemblies, followed by the convocation of a Constituent Assembly which must approve the proposed amendment.

Who Participates in Politics

Until after World War II, the majority of El Salvador's population never really participated in the country's political life at all. Mass illiteracy, the rural character of most of the population, and the refusal of the various governments to draw the masses into active participation all combined to restrict political participation to a minority. The political parties are partly to blame for this, for they have on many occasions urged the boycotting of elections because they claimed the votes would not be counted accurately. In 1950, in what was probably the freest presidential election held until then, only 611,379 votes were cast when the population was close to 2 million. In 1962, when the population had passed 2.5 million, only 400,118 votes were cast in the presidential election. With the introduction of competitive elections in 1964, the registration of voters went up, but the votes cast remained about the same as previously.

Until 1950 suffrage was restricted to males, but since then all over eighteen have had the right to vote except those who have lost the vote by judicial process after conviction for certain crimes, the insane, those who buy or sell votes, those who have been elected to public office and refused to serve, and anyone who interferes with the freedom of the suffrage.

The Electoral Machinery

The political struggles after the Second World War led to the introduction of a modern electoral system headed by a Central Electoral Council (CEC). The practice of political parties' boycotting elections and the attempt by some of the governments in the 1950's to control elections make it impossible to state whether El Salvador has satisfactory electoral machinery, but the electoral law, if observed in all its features, would produce fair elections. The National Assembly elects the three members of the CEC for three-year terms. The Assembly must choose one member from those nominated by the executive and one member from those nominated by the Supreme Court. At the same time the members are elected, three alternates are elected in the same manner.

The low vote cast in the presidential election of 1962 led the government to introduce proportional representation in the congressional election of 1964. After that election, for the first time in some years the opposition was officially represented in the legislature. The constitution provides for congressional and presidential elections held at different times. Another unusual provision forbids electoral campaigning more than four months before a presidential election, more than two months before congressional elections, and more than one month before local elections.

Political Parties

Political parties must be registered with the Central Electoral Council and must observe all rules governing parties set down in the electoral law. To be registered, a party must have at least 2,000 members, and to keep its registration it must receive at least 1 percent of the votes cast in a national election. No party can be registered or function in El Salvador if it upholds "anarchist, communist, or any other doctrine which tends to destroy or alter the democratic structure of the government," or if it is based upon sexual, racial, or religious prejudice, or if it has connections with or receives financial or other aid from outside the country. The only exception to the last rule permits democratic fraternal cooperation to promote Central American union or continental or universal cooperation. These rules have been interpreted to outlaw the Communist Party of El Salvador.

The dominant political party today is the National Conciliation Party (PCN), which includes within its ranks many of the same groups and individuals that had been in the PRUD. Military officers are the most important leaders, but many of the educated rich support the party. Like the PRUD, the PCN hopes to become an institutionalized party which, like the Mexican PRI, will be able to lead El Salvador through the changes the country needs. There seem to be two factions within the PCN, one that welcomes opposition parties and another that wants to limit the activity of the opposition. Under former President Rivera the first group was dominant. The PCN held thirty-two of the Assembly's fifty-two seats during the 1966–68 term. It seems to be less personalistic than its predecessor, the PRUD, but it has not functioned long enough to permit a forecast of its future.

The second largest party in recent years has been the Christian Democratic Party (PDC), founded in 1960 in emulation of the other Christian
Democratic parties functioning in Latin America. Under the constitutional rule banning international party connections, the PDC has no
formal ties with the other Christian Democratic parties, but it founded
the Christian Democratic Organization of Central America and is trying
to promote the growth of this type of party in the other Central American
republics. The PDC favors reform, democracy, and limiting the power
of the military; it bases its ideology on Catholic social-action doctrines.

The third largest party in El Salvador, the Renovating Action Party
(PAR), is, next to the Communist Party, the oldest party functioning at
this writing. Founded in the 1940's by participants in the movement that
overthrew the dictator in 1944, it was the chief opposition party to the
governments in power until 1964. In 1950 it lost the presidential election
by only 80,000 votes. During the years from 1944 to 1964, the party
changed its program and its leaders. Its decision to boycott most of the
elections held during the 1950's weakened it greatly. In 1964 a younger,
more aggressive group won control of the party, made contact with some
of the popular parties of Latin America, and tried to transform the PAR
into a popular party. It never developed a clear program and lost some
of its support when the more conservative members left to found the
Salvadoran Popular Party. The PAR has been called Communist by unin-
formed observers, but its leaders are all devoted democrats whose ideal is
Peruvian *Aprismo*. It has some strength among the organized workers
and the rising middle class, especially the young professionals.

Two minor parties were represented in the 1966–68 legislature, with
one deputy each. The Salvadoran Popular Party (PPS) was created by a
group of the old leaders of the PAR who lost their positions in 1964 and
disagreed with the new line of the party. Its candidate for president in
1967 received the lowest vote of the four candidates. The Republican
Party of National Evolution (PREN) is a personalistic organization consisting of the following of Colonel Luis Roberto Flores.

Although it is not legally recognized, a Communist party has been
functioning in El Salvador since 1925 and is probably the best organized
of all the parties, although it remains small. In 1932 the Communist Party
was involved in the military revolt that gave Hernández Martínez the
excuse to butcher thousands of peasants and institute his dictatorship.
From 1944 to 1954 the Salvadoran Communists received much help from
the Guatemalan Communists, but they never grew strong until *Fidelismo*
swept Latin America in 1959. Combining their efforts with those attracted by Fidel Castro, the Communists helped to organize the Revolu-

tionary Party of April and May (PRAM). By 1960 the PRAM was able to control the streets of San Salvador with crowds of almost permanent demonstrators, and the party had a great deal of influence in the governmental junta that ruled from October 26, 1960, to January 25, 1961. Since then the Communists have lost much of their influence, but they continue to be an important force operating through the PRAM and other organizations, particularly the student group, University Student Action (AEU).

El Salvador has a long way to go before its political parties play the role they should in articulating the needs of the population, but the new system of proportional representation may well strengthen them. In recent years several of the parties have maintained headquarters in the capital city to enable them to engage in continuous activity between elections. The habit of boycotting elections tended to weaken the opposition parties in the past, but the PDC and the PAR seem to have abandoned that tactic.

Public Opinion and Pressure Groups

Public opinion is centralized in the capital city, as is all political power in El Salvador. Until the Second World War, no attention was paid to the opinion of anyone except the landed aristocracy and the military officers, but slowly since then other groups have begun to affect public policy, though the high illiteracy rate keeps much of the population from making its sentiments known.

In 1961 only seven daily newspapers with a total circulation of around 100,000 were published in the country, with the four in San Salvador circulating about 96,000 copies. The most important dailies for many years have been *La Prensa Gráfica*, with a circulation of about 45,000, and *El Diario de Hoy*, which circulates about 30,000 copies.

The strongest and best organized groups in El Salvador are still the army officers and the landed oligarchy. Army officers have dominated the governmental machinery during most of the twentieth century. As the decades passed, the composition of the officer corps apparently changed somewhat as more education became necessary to handle modern armaments. Thus the colonels and majors who were so prominent from 1948 to 1965 were young men with lower- or middle-class backgrounds who had been educated in the U.S. or other foreign military schools, while the generals and older officers were more likely to have upper-class connections and not to have been educated outside of El Salvador. The actual fighting and the years of dictatorship seem to have given the younger army officers a high degree of political sophistication and an interest in improving the country. By 1965, civic action was an important part of the military's activity. Despite its importance, the military is relatively small, the total number of men in the armed forces being 6,900, despite compulsory service for all males.

The traditional aristocracy in El Salvador is based on family, landed wealth, and close association. The upper-class family is a closely knit extended unit, with all important positions in its enterprises tightly held by members of the family. In El Salvador the custom has developed that when a family does not have a male head, a mother or a grandmother may become the leading member of the family. The aristocracy functions through social clubs and a series of organizations founded to protect and foster certain economic interests, including the Chamber of Commerce and Industry, the Association of Industrialists, the Union of Textile Industries, the Commercial and Industrial Society, the Cattle Raisers', Sugar Producers', Coffee Processors' and Exporters', and Coffee Growers' Associations, and the Cotton Growers' Cooperative.

Organized labor is very weak in comparison with the organized employers. In 1966 there were only about 30,000 trade-union members in the whole country out of an estimated labor force of 800,000, split into three confederations and a group of independent unions. The largest organization is the General Confederation of Labor (CGS), which is affiliated with the International Confederation of Free Trade Unions and its Inter-American Regional Organization (ORIT). In 1966 it had about 19,000 members organized into sixty-three trade unions. This was about 79 percent of all trade-union members. The Trade Union Unity Committee of Salvadoran Workers (CUS) had about 2,500 members in eight trade unions. The Communists have been prominent in the leadership of the CUS, and from 1957 to 1960 they played an important role in supporting the PRAM. When the PRAM declined in importance as Fidel Castro lost his appeal, the CUS also declined in size. Twenty-three independent labor unions had 6,827 members in 1963. Salvadoran law confines trade unions to nonagricultural labor, which prevents much growth in the labor movement, and only about 6 percent of all wage and salary earners are organized.

Although there are less than 3,000 students enrolled in the country's only university, they are among the most vociferous critics of the government. Most university students have been radical, and the Communists have generally been strong among them. The autonomy of the university enables the students to speak out when other groups may be silent, but there are so few students that they do not play a really important role.

The peasants, because they are not organized, play practically no role at all in the country's political life. And in El Salvador, unlike most other Latin-American countries, the Catholic church has been a silent factor until comparatively recently. With the growth of the Christian Democratic political party and the attempt to create Christian trade unions, the church is assuming more importance, but it has little weight in politics, and priests cannot belong to political parties or be elected to public office.

Civil Liberties

The 1962 Salvadoran constitution guarantees all of the individual rights usually found in democratic constitutions. Discrimination based on differences of nationality, race, sex, or religion is forbidden. Religion, speech, correspondence, and association are all guaranteed, and all persons are entitled to due process of law before they can be deprived of life, liberty, or property. Similar provisions were part of all previous constitutions, but they were never observed; and, as we have seen, they can still be suspended in case of any grave disturbance of public order, although the only constitutional limitation on liberty is the clause prohibiting the propagation of doctrines contrary to the exercise of democracy.

The 1962 constitution has not been in force long enough, as this is written, to warrant any judgment as to how civil rights will be treated under its provisions, but since the turmoil of 1960–61 there has been an effort by the government to permit free expression and organization for all except the followers of Russian, Chinese, and Cuban communism. At this writing the atmosphere in El Salvador is much freer than it has ever been before, and most competent observers were fairly optimistic about the future of constitutional government in El Salvador.

The Executive Power

El Salvador's executive is a president elected by direct popular vote for a five-year term who cannot be reelected for the following term. A vice-president is elected when the president is chosen, but in addition the legislature elects three *designados* for two-year terms who take the place of the president when necessary.

To be a president one must be a Salvadoran by birth at least one of whose parents was a native Salvadoran, not a clergyman of any denomination, over thirty years of age, and in possession of all rights as a citizen. Not eligible to be president, in addition to the incumbent, are the relatives of the incumbent president to the fourth degree of consanguinity or to the second degree of affinity; all who during the previous year have been ministers or subsecretaries of state; all who during the previous six months have been high officers of the armed forces; and certain types of persons, listed in the constitution, who have handled government funds or contracted with the government to do certain public works.

The president of El Salvador is a strong executive who freely appoints and removes his ministers and subsecretaries of state and certain other officials, serves as commander in chief of the armed forces, draws up the budget for submission to the legislature, directs foreign relations, supervises the administration, and executes the laws. He is aided by a cabinet of ten who head the various ministries. In addition, the president is assisted by the National Council of Planning and Economic Coordination, an attorney general, and an official in charge of helping the poor. As is common in Latin America, a series of automonous agencies is entrusted with certain functions that for various reasons have been removed from the regular ministries.

The Legislative Power

El Salvador's legislature is a unicameral National Assembly consisting of fifty-two members. Each department elects one deputy and one alternate deputy for each 50,000 persons, and one more for any remaining fraction over 15,000. The term is two years and deputies can be reelected. To be a member of the Assembly one must be twenty-five years old and a Salvadoran by birth, must not have lost his citizenship rights during the past five years, and must have been born or live in the department from which he runs for election. A great many persons are ineligible to be deputies, including the president, his ministers and subsecretaries, the justices of the Supreme Court, the functionaries of the electoral organizations, high military officers, and persons who owe debts to the government because of their positions or because they are carrying out public works financed by the government. In addition, no relative of the president to the fourth degree of consanguinity or the second degree of affinity can be a deputy. Most of the public officials listed can become candidates by resigning their positions at least three months before the election. Deputies cannot hold any other position in the government except for teaching and certain professional posts in social-assistance organizations; nor can a deputy resign his position to accept an appointment from the president without permission of the Assembly.

Deputies receive a salary of 600 colones a month ($240 U.S.) and have the immunity customary in legislatures in democratic countries. The National Assembly is endowed with a long list of powers by the constitution; in addition to passing laws, it elects many officials, including the justices of the Supreme Court and judges of the lower courts, members of the Central Electoral Council, three substitutes for the president, and the president and vice-president when no one has received a majority in an election. Bills may be introduced into the Assembly by the deputies, the president of the republic, and the Supreme Court. A formal procedure is used in considering legislation and the president has the right to veto bills, but the Assembly can override the veto by a two-thirds vote. When the president vetoes a bill on the grounds that it is unconstitutional, if the Assembly votes by a two-thirds majority that it is not, the bill is sent to the Supreme Court within three days. The court must hand down a decision within fifteen days, and if the decision is that the law is constitutional, it must be proclaimed by the president.

Traditionally the legislature in El Salvador has been subservient to the executive, and this was especially so during much of the time from 1952 to 1964 because one party had all the seats in the Assembly. The election of opposition candidates in 1964 and 1966 has put more life into the legislature, but the opposition has never controlled the Assembly, and it continues to follow the lead of the president.

When the Assembly is not in session, it is represented by a Permanent Commission consisting of nine members and nine substitute members. The Permanent Commission prepares bills for consideration, considers charges of impeachment, and has the power to call the Assembly into special session. The Assembly meets twice a year, on June 1 and December 1, and can stay in session as long as necessary to transact its business.

Public Finance

El Salvador's budget is prepared by a budget office within the Ministry of Finance and submitted to the National Assembly by the president. The Assembly can lower amounts or delete items, but it cannot increase any item. Once the budget is approved, it is supervised and audited by an agency independent of the executive, the Court of Accounts. The members of the Court of Accounts are elected by the Assembly for a three-year term and can be reelected.

Income and expenditures have risen rapidly during the 1960's. In 1950 the total budget amounted to only C77,777,777, which equaled about $31 million U.S. (There are 2.5 colones to the dollar.) By 1960, the total was around C188 million; by 1964, C222,288,407. Tables 1 and 2, summarizing the 1964 budget, show where the money came from and how it was being spent under the constitutional government headed by President Rivera.

Although El Salvador taxes personal income and business profits, most of its income comes from import and export duties and indirect taxes. In 1960 taxes on income and wealth provided 16.40 percent of receipts; import duties, 36.59 percent; export duties, 15 percent; other indirect taxes, 22.38 percent. The 1964 budget demonstrates the efforts the government is making to modernize. The largest expenditure, 22.9 percent of the total, goes to education. Together education, public health and social assistance, and public works account for 49.7 percent of the total, while the armed forces received only 10.8 percent of expenditures.

TABLE 1
REVENUE OF EL SALVADOR, 1964

Source	Amount in Colones	Percent of Total
Taxes	C193,501,700.00	86.00%
Nontax income	9,667,700.00	4.06
Miscellaneous	924,807.93	0.04
Deficit	2,000,000.00	0.90
Loans	16,328,000.00	7.30
Transfers of capital	3,866,200.00	1.70
Total	C222,228,407.93	100.00%

Local Government

For the purposes of local government, El Salvador is divided into fourteen departments which are subdivided into thirty-nine districts. At the same time, the fourteen departments are divided into 260 *municipios*. The system is extremely centralized, yet not really a system of local government, as the various branches of the national government function in all parts of the country with little coordination between the various groups at the local level.

The departments vary greatly in area and in population, ranging in 1961 from 732 to 2,167 square kilometers and from 97,450 to 459,390 inhabitants. In each department there is a governor who is appointed by the president of the republic and is responsible to the Minister of the Interior. The governor has only a small staff and serves as a sort of report-

TABLE 2

EXPENDITURES OF EL SALVADOR, 1964

	Amount in Colones	*Percent of Total*
National Assembly	C1,201,527.00	0.60%
Judicial system	4,563,073.00	2.10
Court of Accounts	2,174,083.00	1.00
Central Electoral Council	581,611.00	0.03
Civil Service Tribunal	159,139.00	0.01
Attorney General's office	702,805.25	0.08
President of the republic	3,386,094.00	1.50
Ministry of Finance		
Administration	13,108,808.80	6.00
Public debt	9,627,403.00	4.40
Administration of pensions, social security, and retirement system	12,718,000.00	5.70
Ministry of Foreign Relations	4,189,189.00	1.90
Ministry of the Interior, including administration of post office, publication of *Diario Oficial*, immigration, and radio	5,141,733.00	2.30
Ministry of Defense	23,928,532.50	10.80
Ministry of Justice, including administration of jails	3,392,448.30	1.50
Ministry of Education	50,864,468.00	22.90
Ministry of Public Health and Social Assistance	22,423,998.00	10.20
Ministry of Labor	2,474,555.00	1.10
Ministry of Economy	14,555,340.00	6.50
Ministry of Agriculture and Livestock	17,111,674.00	7.60
Ministry of Public Works	27,886,745.08	12.60
Office of Social Welfare	2,097,181.00	1.00
Total	C222,288,407.93	99.82% *

* Figures do not add to 100 because of rounding.

ing agency to keep the ministry informed about conditions in the department. The governor also supervises the governments of the *municipios*, but he does not actually supervise the employees of the national government within his department.

In each *municipio* there is a council composed of an *alcalde* (mayor), a *síndico* (legal official), and from two to twelve *regidores* (councilmen), all of whom serve four-year terms and are elected by popular vote. The central government supplies the communities' basic services; the *municipio* governments provide such supplementary services as their resources permit, including extra educational programs, recreation and cultural-affairs programs, some policing, public health and sanitation, and such public works and services as markets, cemeteries, ambulance service, etc. A municipal secretary handles most of the office work for the *municipio*. The position of the municipal secretary has by law become part of a career in public service, and competent secretaries are promoted to larger *municipios* after serving in smaller ones.

The *municipio* has little independence. In addition to the supervision it receives from the departmental governor, the Court of Accounts exercises broad preaudit and postaudit powers. Inspectors from the Division of Municipal Inspection and Administrative Control of the Ministry of the Interior are a further control over local autonomy.

The Judicial Power

El Salvador's court system is headed by a Supreme Court of Justice consisting of ten members elected for three-year terms by the National Assembly. If a justice is elected three times, he then holds the position for life. Under the Supreme Court are appeals courts, whose members are also elected by the Assembly, and local courts, whose judges are selected by the Supreme Court. The Supreme Court has general jurisdiction over the entire judicial system, including authorizing lawyers to practice their profession. The Supreme Court is the only court capable of declaring laws, decrees, and executive orders unconstitutional, and it can do this upon the request of any citizen.

El Salvador: A Last Word

El Salvador is closer to having institutionalized constitutional government than at any previous time since the republic was established, yet it is far from having a democratic government. Most competent observers rank El Salvador second, after Costa Rica, among the five Central American states in progress made in establishing a stable political system since World War II. It is surprising how well this country has done in view of the tremendous handicaps it had when the period of change began in the late 1940's. The mass illiteracy, the rigid oligarchic land-tenure system, and the tradition of military interference to prevent meaningful change handicapped the development of the kind of organizations a pluralistic society needs. But the fluctuations in the world price of coffee helped to stimulate industrialization, and as industry developed, inevitably new groups emerged which clamored for a share in the country's decision-making process. Thus public opinion in favor of a more equitably organized society could develop.

The series of "revolutions" which began with the overthrow of Hernández Martínez in 1944 had the effect of forcing change upon the country. Many critics point to the slowness of the changes, but in total they amount to more than the sum of the individual reforms. The process of development seems to be cumulative; each year it moves faster. Most important, the growth of a middle class of white-collar technicians, professionals, and small businessmen came at the same time that a group of rich upper-class leaders, recognizing the need for change, provided leadership to the new political parties, trade unions, and pressure groups now accepted as normal features of life in El Salvador.

All things considered, El Salvador seems to be on the brink of establishing democratic government. The introduction of proportional representation in the National Assembly has tended to strengthen the political parties and to make opposition to the government respectable, so there seems reason to hope that El Salvador will abandon the coup d'état, revolution, and violence as political techniques in favor of democratic processes that will transform it into a progressive state of literate, prosperous people.

SELECTED READINGS

ALEXANDER, ROBERT. "El Salvador," *Communism in Latin America,* pp. 366–71. New Brunswick, N.J.: Rutgers University Press, 1957.

ANDERSON, CHARLES W. "El Salvador: The Army as Reformer." In *Political Systems of Latin America,* edited by Martin C. Needler. Princeton, N.J.: D. Van Nostrand Co., Inc., 1964.

EL SALVADOR, MINISTERIO DEL INTERIOR. *Ley electoral y sus reformas, 1961.* San Salvador: Imprenta Nacional, 1962.

———, SECRETARÍA DE INFORMACIÓN DE LA PRESIDENCIA DE LA REPÚBLICA. *Memoria de las elecciones de 1950.* San Salvador: Imprenta Nacional, 1951.

ENGLISH, BURT H., ed. *El Salvador Election Factbook, March 5, 1967.* Washington: Institute for the Comparative Study of Political Systems, 1967.

GALLARDO, RICARDO. *Las Constituciones de El Salvador.* Madrid: Ediciones Cultura Hispánica, 1961.

HUMES, SAMUEL, and MARTIN, EILEEN M. "El Salvador," *The Structure of Local Governments throughout the World.* The Hague: Martinus Nijhoff, 1961.

MACDONALD, AUSTIN F. "El Salvador," *Latin American Politics and Government,* pp. 621–27. 2nd ed. New York: Thomas Y. Crowell Co., 1954.

PUBLIC ADMINISTRATION SERVICE. *Informe sobre la conveniencia de introducir mejoras en la organización del gobierno de El Salvador.* San Salvador: Editorial Ahora, 1950.

"Report on El Salvador." *Latin American Report* 4 (October 31, 1960): 5–24.

U.S. DEPARTMENT OF LABOR. *Labor Law and Practice in El Salvador.* Bureau of Labor Statistics report no. 280. Washington: U.S. Government Printing Office, 1964.

WALLICH, HENRY C., and ADLER, JOHN H. *Public Finance in a Developing Country: El Salvador—A Case Study.* Cambridge: Harvard University Press, 1951.

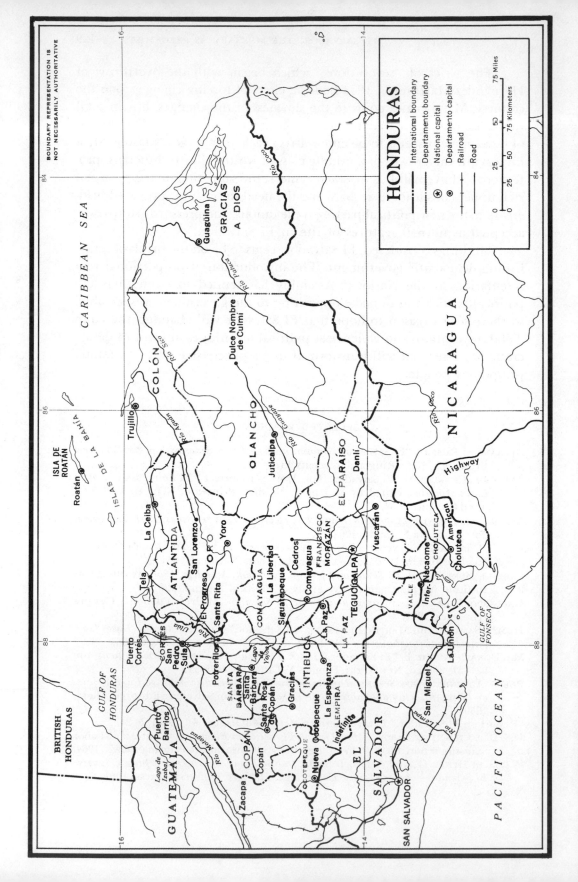

HONDURAS

International boundary
Departamento boundary
National capital
Departamento capital
Railroad
Road

75 Miles
75 Kilometers
50
50
25
25
0

CARIBBEAN SEA

GULF OF HONDURAS

BRITISH HONDURAS

ISLA DE ROATÁN
Roatán
ISLAS DE LA BAHÍA

GUATEMALA

Zacapa
Puerto Barrios
Lago de Izabal
Río Motagua

Copán
COPÁN
Santa Rosa de Copán
Nueva Ocotepeque
OCOTEPEQUE
indefinite

EL SALVADOR
SAN SALVADOR
San Miguel
Río Lempa

PACIFIC OCEAN

GULF OF FONSECA

La Unión

VALLE
Nacaome
Inter-American
CHOLUTECA
Choluteca
Highway

Río Coco

NICARAGUA

EL PARAÍSO
Danlí
Yuscarán

Juticalpa
OLANCHO
Río Guayape
Río Guayambre

Dulce Nombre de Culmí

GRACIAS A DIOS
Guagüina
Río Patuca

COLÓN

Río Sico
Río Aguán

Trujillo

La Ceiba
ATLÁNTIDA
San Lorenzo
YORO
Yoro

Tela
El Progreso
Santa Rita
Puerto Cortés
CORTÉS
San Pedro Sula
Río Ulúa
Potrerillos
Lago de Yojoa
SANTA BÁRBARA
Santa Bárbara
Gracias
LEMPIRA
La Esperanza
INTIBUCÁ

COMAYAGUA
La Libertad
Siguatepeque
Cedros
Comayagua
FRANCISCO MORAZÁN
La Paz
LA PAZ
TEGUCIGALPA

——— 7 ———

HONDURAS:

The Politics of Underdevelopment

Honduras, because of its location in the center of Central America, has been greatly affected by outside interference in its affairs. It is a poor country, and the constant invasions from El Salvador, Guatemala, and Nicaragua during the nineteenth century, combined with almost continuous civil wars, did nothing to create the kind of climate needed for economic development. When some development did begin at the end of the century, it was brought in by foreign interests that were more interested in maximizing their income than in aiding Honduras. It was not until after World War II that the people of Honduras could begin an effort to create a modern state. From about 1950 to 1963, under the leadership of a series of governments, the country tried desperately to overcome the heritage of its past, but this attempt came to an end when the army forcibly expelled the president and reintroduced dictatorship in 1963.

A National Profile

Spanning the Central American isthmus, with an area of 43,227 square miles, including some islands off each coast, Honduras is roughly triangular in shape. In the north it stretches for 495 miles along the Caribbean Sea. In the south, an eighty-nine-mile coast on the Gulf of Fonseca faces the Pacific Ocean. Guatemala lies to the west and northwest, El Salvador to the south, Nicaragua to the south and southeast.

The most mountainous of the Central American republics, Honduras has peaks rising to nearly 10,000 feet. These mountains have created a series of small valleys in which the bulk of the country's population is found. To the north and south, flat coastal plains lie drenched in tropical heat and rain. The mountains help to moderate the temperature, but they make road building exceedingly costly and difficult. At the end of 1955 the country had only 24 miles of paved road and only 1,400 miles of roads of any kind, of which only about half were usable during the rainy season. By 1967, after great efforts, the total miles of road had reached about 2,120, 239 of them paved. Tegucigalpa is the only capital city of an American republic that is not located on a railroad; all of the country's railroads are located in the banana-producing area on the north coast. Off the north coast are the Bay Islands, which were controlled by the British from 1642 to 1861.

In the highlands, a rainy season lasts from May to the middle of November. The population has traditionally been concentrated in the central and western part of the country, leaving the northeast largely uninhabited. During the twentieth century, the development of the banana industry on the north coast has increased the population in that section.

At the time of the April 1961 census, Honduras had a population of about 1,860,000, which by 1966 had grown to 2,363,000, mostly rural; only about 25 percent of the population is urban. There are no large cities in the country; the capital, Tegucigalpa, is the largest, with a population in 1967 of only 170,535. The population is increasing at a rate of 3.1 percent per year and the average age is very young because the fertility rate remains high while improvements in health and medicine have lowered the number of deaths, particularly among the young. Most of the people of Honduras are *mestizos*, with about 10 percent white and about 5 percent Negro. About 35,000 aboriginal Indians continue to live in isolated areas.

Spanish is the official language of practically the entire population, except for some of the descendants of the English settlers of the Bay Islands and a few of the aboriginal Indians. Primary education is supposed to be free, compulsory, and secular for all children from seven to fifteen years of age, but in 1960 only 209,483, 49.5 percent of the 423,245 school-age children, were enrolled in the country's primary schools. By 1963 this had increased to 249,277. This is a great improvement over past years, for in 1950 only 33.6 percent of the children were enrolled. Since 1945, strenuous efforts have been made to improve the educational system, but results have not been spectacular, even though the budget for education went up from 463,000 lempiras in 1934–35 to L1,397,500 in 1944–45 to L9,992,200 in 1954–55, when this amount constituted 13.7 percent of the national budget. By 1963 this sum had risen to L19,628,180, or 17.81 percent of the budget, and by 1965 had leaped to L27,054,127. This expenditure is essential if the country is to develop. In 1961 only 6.1 percent of the total population had completed six years of primary education, and the illiteracy rate was 53 percent. This figure is actually misleadingly low, since many of those considered literate never went to school more than two years and have lost their once sketchy ability to read and write through lack of practice. Catholicism is the religion of most of the population, but the government does not contribute to its support. About 22,000 Protestants and a few members of other religions worship freely.

Honduras' economy is based on agriculture. The leading products are bananas, coffee, timber, cotton, tobacco, dairy and beef cattle for export, and rice and maize for local consumption. Mining had some importance in the past; the leading products in 1958 were silver, lead, and a little zinc. The most important mines are owned by United States firms. There has traditionally been little industrial production, but efforts to industrialize began after World War II. The creation of the Central American Common Market and the location of the Central American Development Bank in Tegucigalpa stimulated industrial ventures in the 1960's. Much of the new industry is being financed by merchants who see the opportunities offered by the larger markets the economic integration of Central America will provide. Agriculture occupies 70 percent of the economically active population, who themselves represent only 27 percent of the population, and productivity is very low. The landownership pattern helps to explain why Honduras is so unproductive. Almost 75 percent of the farms total only 16 percent of the country's farmland. Less than 2 percent of the farms include within their area about 46 percent of the land in use.

As can readily be understood from this brief survey, Honduras is desperately poor.[1] The gross national product in 1964 came to only $439 million U.S. In 1965, the last year for which figures are available, the per

---

[1] Even the water supply is bad. In Tegucigalpa, the capital, for example, during the dry season water mains have been closed for long periods each day in recent years because not enough water was available. By 1965 work was at last under way to improve Tegucigalpa's water supply. See Harris Seidel, "Empty Water Mains," *The American City*, 78 (April 1963): 33.

capita gross domestic product was only $215 U.S. Not only is there a great gap between the rich and the poor, but foreign ownership of the most important economic assets drains much of the national income out of the country. On the north coast, where the bananas are grown, the United and Standard Fruit Companies form a sort of state within a state. Not only do they own practically all the land where they operate, but they have their own public services, including education and housing, and until about 1950 they completely controlled and politically dominated the area. The major Atlantic ports, Tela, La Ceiba, and Puerto Cortés, as well as almost all the railroads, are operated by the fruit companies. In 1956 bananas made up 46 percent of the country's total exports and made the banana companies the country's most important economic factor. By 1964 bananas had gone down to 36 percent of the total exports, but from 1961 to 1964 the average was 42.6 percent, and in 1967 bananas constituted a whopping 65 percent of exports.

It is difficult for any Honduran government to do very much to improve conditions, as sufficient funds are never available. In addition, the mass illiteracy, the poor health of much of the population, and the poor transportation system make Honduras a difficult country to govern. During the period from 1948 to 1957, the gross domestic product, at constant prices, rose at the average annual rate of 3.8 percent, but at the same time the population increase averaged 3.4 percent each year. Thus, for all practical purposes, Honduras was standing still.

The effects of the policies of the Liberal government of the late 1950's and of the Central American Common Market seem to have helped, for from 1962 to 1965 the gross domestic product rose by 7.1 percent annually and in 1965 rose at the rate of 11.2 percent while the population rose only 3.5 percent, permitting a rise in per capita income. Yet the country still has a very long way to go.

The Development of Modern Honduras

Honduras was the first place on the American mainland visited by Columbus (1502), and its political history ever since has been a constant chaotic struggle for power that has prevented the development of its human and natural resources. Perhaps because Honduras was known so early, it became a prize fought over by many Spaniards from Mexico, Panama, and Santo Domingo. Spaniards fought Spaniards, the indigenous population fought them all, and when the Spaniards brought in their Indian allies from Mexico and Guatemala, the Honduran Indians had to fight them too. When the native population began to decline, Negro slaves were brought in to take their place.

One of the early *conquistadores* has left a graphic picture of Honduras in the early sixteenth century in a letter to Charles V:

> I do not know, Your Holy Catholic Majesty, what evil fortune it can be which pursues this land, nor what saturnine planet reigns over it, for since the Christians first came to conquer, pacify and settle it, dissension and mutinies have never ceased among the governors who until this time have held authority, as is clear from that which befell under Cristóbal de Olid, who was the captain who went to the conquest, and then what befell under Diego López de Salcedo and a nobleman who was called Saavedra, whom the Marqués del Valle [Hernán Cortés] had left in the land as his lieutenant. Likewise that which happened to Vasco de Herrera and Diego Méndez [de Himostrosa]. Because Diego Méndez wished to hold power, he had Vasco de Herrera, who then governed, killed, and then forced everyone to obey himself as governor. [Diego Méndez] governed until the blood of Vasco de Herrera called out for vengeance to God, who was pleased to have the Christians who were in Trujillo at that time elect the Contador Cerezeda as governor and chief officer of justice in the name of Your Majesty. And the majority of the Christians joined together and took Méndez and quartered him, and hanged, flogged and cut off the hands and feet of many of his partisans. A little while later the Treasurer Diego García de Celís arrived in the province . . . and as soon as he came he began to quarrel with Andrés de Cerezeda, who then governed, so that rival parties formed just as though they were citizens of Cáceres and Trujillo [in Castile]. The Treasurer [García de Celís] and others who joined him ridiculed Cerezeda, and scarcely wished to obey him in that which he ordered. Those who followed the Treasurer wished that he [alone] should govern and that the other [Cerezeda] should be destroyed. Then they tried to destroy [the Contador], for [the Treasurer] came back to Castile and placed many charges against him before the Royal Council. . . . At the time I went out to the province I went there with the Treasurer, and upon my arrival there the first thing which I did was to set myself the task of making [García de Celís and Cerezeda] friends. Afterwards [I composed a quarrel between] the Adelantados Montejo and Alvarado. [Quarrels] such as these have caused much destruction in the land and

have led to the dispersal of the Indians, for upon observing the killings, disorders and harm which came down upon [all Indians] many of those who still remained in their pueblos fled to the mountains, where they have stayed to this very time . . .[2]

With such a beginning, it is not difficult to imagine what Honduras became during the remaining centuries of the colonial period. Some Spaniards settled down as *encomenderos,* some government officials came to rule the colony, some silver and gold were exploited, but the basic population continued to live by hunting, fishing, and farming. The English began to settle on the north coast and there was constant conflict between English "pirates" and the Spanish authorities and population. Although efforts were made to set up independent colonial government, eventually Honduras became a subdivision of Guatemala. Few schools were organized, and the only institution of higher learning in all Central America was in Guatemala. Thus, when independence came, what is now Honduras was a rural backwater of the Spanish empire with a population of about 100,000, completely innocent of any practice in self-government.

When the United Provinces of Central America was set up, the leaders of Honduras resented the dominant position of Guatemala in the federation. Under Francisco Morazán, Honduras became one of the leaders of the so-called Liberal forces, and when the Conservatives under Rafael Carrera consolidated their power in Guatemala, Honduras declared its independence in 1838. Since Honduras had neither the population, the wealth, nor the cultural background for existence as an independent state, chaos resulted. Internal strife and outside intervention were standard features of life in the newly independent country, and the turmoil continued for a hundred years. The only distinction between the Liberal and Conservative leaders during that century was in their attitudes toward the Catholic church: the Liberals tended to dislike the church's special privileges while the Conservatives upheld ecclesiastical power. But they were all, of course, "good" Catholics, and political leaders often transferred their allegiance from one faction to the other. The only real principle any political leader seemed to have was that power ought to be his.

Honduras was so centrally located that Nicaragua, El Salvador, and Guatemala had little difficulty in finding reasons to interfere in its affairs, and any defeated Honduran politician could get aid from one of the

---

[2] Bishop Cristóbal de Pedraza to Emperor Charles V, December 16, 1544, quoted in Robert S. Chamberlain, *The Conquest and Colonization of Honduras, 1502–1550* (Washington: Carnegie Institution, 1953), pp. 247–48.

neighboring republics to support a new revolution. British control of the Bay Islands and the Mosquito Coast added another international complication to the country's problems. After the British relinquished claims to everything except what is now British Honduras, United States adventurers[3] and businessmen brought a new foreign influence to Honduras.

During the first hundred years of Honduras' existence as an independent republic, various constitutions were adopted, attempts were made to reconstitute the Central American Federation, dictators tried to pacify the country. Nothing helped. The wealthy families fought for control of the presidency, which dominated all other parts of the government. Because economic opportunities were limited, government jobs became one of the few roads to personal advancement, and the competition for these jobs made politics a bitter struggle. Graft and corruption were standard features of administration.

Change finally began with U.S. development of large-scale banana production at the beginning of the twentieth century. This became the largest economic enterprise in the country and eventually made Honduras the world's leading banana producer for some years. Yet the first result of the banana industry was an increase in outside meddling in Honduras' internal affairs, for the banana companies wanted large land concessions and favorable treatment from the government, and the easiest way to get them was to install a president. The classic example probably was the revolution led by General Manuel Bonilla in 1910–11. Bonilla, a former president of Honduras living in exile in New Orleans, was financed by Samuel Zemurray, then president of Cuyamel Fruit Company. Because the United States government was trying to prevent the organization of invasions into Honduras, Bonilla and his aides and their armaments were taken in Zemurray's private launch and put aboard the invading vessel, the *Hornet*, on the high seas. The invasion triumphed, the incumbent president was ousted, Bonilla became the new president, and Zemurray became a multimillionaire and president of the United Fruit Company.[4]

In 1907 the chaos in Honduras led the governments of the United States and Mexico to bring the five Central American republics together

---

[3] There was, for example, a rogue with the unlikely name of Lee Christmas, an illiterate railroad worker, who became at various times, without ever giving up his United States citizenship, director of police in Tegucigalpa, a general in the Honduras army, commander in chief of the Honduras army, *comandante* of Puerto Cortés, and inspector general of the north coast. See Herman B. Deutsch, *The Incredible Yanqui, The Career of Lee Christmas* (New York: Longmans, Green & Co., 1931).

[4] The story of the 1910–11 revolution has been retold many times. See, for example, "United Fruit II: The Conquest of Honduras," *Fortune*, 7 (March 1933): 31–33, or Deutsch, *Incredible Yanqui*, pp. 102–69.

in a conference in Washington, D.C., where an attempt was made to re-create the Central American Confederation. This could not be achieved, but the representatives of the five governments did agree to refer future disputes to a Central American Court of Justice which was set up at San José, Costa Rica. The delegates also agreed to neutralize Honduras and stop interfering in one another's affairs. Unfortunately, the United States, which had helped to create the Central American Court, helped to destroy it a few years later by refusing to accept its decisions.

As the production of bananas increased through the years, comparative stability with some liberty finally came to Honduras in the late 1920's and early 1930's. But the world depression cut the government's income, and in 1933 General Tiburcio Carías Andino set up a dictatorship that lasted until the end of 1948. Like so many of his type, Carías changed the constitution whenever his term expired and managed to squelch every attempt to get him out of office. Meanwhile, the continued development of foreign economic enterprises increased the size of the middle class as the foreign corporations gave opportunities to lawyers, accountants, insurance men, retail and wholesale dealers, and others of this sort. A working class began to develop. Attempts were made to organize trade unions, but they remained illegal. At the same time, the efforts of the Pan American Sanitary Bureau and other international organizations to improve sanitary conditions were so successful that the population began to grow at a much faster rate than had been customary. By 1948, it was over a million, more than double what it had been in 1930. By 1966 it was over two million. This enlargement of the population helped to create a more vigorous public opinion.

These developments seem to have had some effect on General Carías, for in 1948 he amazed everyone by announcing that he was finally leaving the presidency. However, through his political organization, the National Party, he dictated the nomination of his successor, Juan Manuel Gálvez, one of his trusted henchmen who had been a judge, a deputy, an ambassador, a cabinet minister, and the secretary to the president. He had also been a lawyer for one of the United States fruit companies. The demoralization of political life in Honduras after fifteen years of Carías can be seen by the opposition Liberal Party's choice of a candidate to oppose Gálvez: none other than Ángel Zúñiga Huete, an exile who had opposed Carías in the elections of 1932. The government interfered so much in the electoral process that the Liberals finally refused to participate, and as the sole candidate Juan Manuel Gálvez was declared elected and took office on January 1, 1949.

To the surprise of all observers of the Honduran political scene, President Gálvez ruled in a constitutional manner. All political refugees were invited to return to Honduras, a free press and the free organization of political parties were permitted, and, most remarkable, Carías refrained from interfering. With the aid of the United States, the United Nations, and various international agencies, progress was made in road construction, industrial development, forestry, tax reform, education, and social services.

When municipal elections were held in December 1950, the Liberal Party actually won in one *municipio*, Nacaome, and was allowed to take office. The vote in the 1950 election, one of the fairest ever held until then, demonstrates how few voters Honduras has traditionally had, for the official result gave the National Party 77,593 and the Liberal Party 8,104, a total of 85,697 at a time when the country's population was 1,428,089.

Despite all the good he did, Gálvez could not hand over his office to his elected successor. When his term expired in 1954, three candidates competed for the votes. The National Party nominated its *caudillo*, the former dictator Carías Andino. A split-off faction of the National Party, using the name National Reform Movement (MNR), nominated the former vice-president, General Abrahán Williams. The Liberal Party nominated a young physician, Dr. Ramón Villeda Morales. After a free election marked by spirited campaigning and some violence, the traditional holders of power were surprised to discover that Villeda Morales had received 121,213 votes, 48 percent of the total cast. Carías received 77,726 and Williams 53,041. Under the constitution then in force, if no candidate received a majority the Congress of Deputies was to pick the president from the two candidates with the greatest number of votes. The logical new president was Villeda Morales, who had so many more votes than either of his rivals, but the old political leaders refused to allow him to be elected.

Just before the Congress was to meet, Gálvez suddenly left the country "for reasons of health." He turned his office over to the vice-president, Julio Lozano, who on December 5, 1954, abolished the constitution and proclaimed himself constitutional dictator. Lozano claimed he was forced to do what he did because there was no Congress. The Congress required the attendance of two-thirds of its membership for a quorum. Generals Carías and Williams had their parties' deputies boycott the session. Thus no quorum, no Congress, no new president, and the declaration of a constitutional dictator. This maneuver completed, Gálvez recovered from his "illness" and returned to Tegucigalpa on December 7, two days after the assumption of dictatorial power by Lozano. Lozano appointed the deputies whose failure to meet had given him his post as members of an advisory council charged with drafting a new constitution.

Not surprisingly, there was great unrest during Lozano's term in office. Strikes and other labor disputes became common. But by 1956 President Lozano thought he had everything organized, and he set an election for October 7. This only made the conflict more bitter, and in July Lozano expelled from the country Dr. Villeda Morales, the leader of the Liberal Party; Oscar Flores, the editor of the Liberal paper *El Pueblo*; and Francisco Milla Bermúdez, a former member of the Honduras Council of State. This arbitrary action provoked a strike of university and high-school students. On August 3, 1956, an unsuccessful revolt took place. Lozano instituted complete censorship and a state of emergency in the department of Morazán, in which Tegucigalpa is located. Many arrests took place and the Liberal newspapers *El Pueblo* and *El Cronista* were shut down. In September there was some shooting.

Juan Gálvez was then president of the Supreme Court. As election day drew near, President Lozano suddenly discovered that he needed "medical treatment" and left the country for Miami after turning his office over to Gálvez. But he returned just before the election, and on October 7 the election took place. The government announced that its organization, the National Union Party, had won 370,318 votes and all fifty-six seats in the Constituent Assembly that was to elect the new president. The Liberal Party was awarded 41,724 votes, the National Party 2,003. Two weeks later, on October 21, without a shot being fired, a coup d'état expelled the Lozano-Gálvez government from office and set up a three-man military junta to run the country while a fair election was organized.

The fake election conducted by Lozano had evidently so stirred up the population that a revolt was inevitable. Interestingly enough, one of the young army officers in the new junta was Major Roberto Gálvez Barnes, the son of former President Gálvez. The first action by the new junta was to cancel the election of October 7. Within a week, the neighboring countries and the United States had recognized the new government. The junta tried to organize a fair election so that the country could return to constitutional government. All of the military commanders in the seventeen departments were replaced with younger officers. The entire Supreme Court was persuaded to resign. The rector of the university was appointed the new Minister of Education and Dr. Villeda Morales was appointed ambassador to the United States. All political prisoners were freed.

A wave of enthusiasm swept over Honduras. All the political parties became active and an election was organized for September 22, 1957. This was the first election in the country's history not dominated by the armed forces, the first to include women voters, and the first to use the system of proportional representation. The political leaders had finally begun to understand that a country must have a loyal opposition, and therefore all parties must be represented in the Congress. That year 522,359 persons registered to vote, including 213,065 women and 313,373 illiterates. About 62 percent actually voted, and the Liberal Party won a smashing victory, gaining 209,109 votes, 62 percent of the total. The National Party received 101,274, or 31 percent of the votes, and the National Reform Movement won 29,489, or 7 percent. The Liberals received thirty-six seats in the Congress, the National Party eighteen, and the MNR four seats. On November 16 the Congress elected Dr. Villeda Morales president of the republic and he was inaugurated on December 21, 1957, for a six-year term. On December 19, 1957, the Congress adopted a new constitution.

Under President Villeda, an intensive drive was made to transform Honduras into a modern state. President Villeda had spent his exile in Costa Rica, where he had become friends with José Figueres, the leader of that country's National Liberation Party, and through Figueres, Villeda had been put in touch with the other "popular" parties of Latin America. During his stay in office he tried to transform the Liberal Party into a modern reformist party that could serve as the instrument to institutionalize constitutional government. While many of his efforts were realized only on paper and others were only partially completed, the government and the Liberal Party gave a great impetus to the development of Honduras. Efforts at land reform were initiated. During his term in office Dr. Villeda Morales saw more schools, health centers, roads, and bridges built than the total number the country had had when he took office. Labor's right to organize unions had at last been recognized under President Gálvez, and now under Villeda a modern labor code was adopted which assured workers collective bargaining, a guaranteed minimum wage, hospital benefits, vacations with pay, and terminal leave. The labor movement was growing stronger.

The United States and various international organizations helped with loans and technical assistance to build roads and a hydroelectric plant. Efforts were made to create new industries and to improve those already in existence. President Villeda Morales supported the efforts of the Organization of Central American States to set up a common market for Central America.

Yet Villeda Morales too did not succeed in institutionalizing constitutional government, and he failed to finish his term in office. He had a
great deal of difficulty in staffing his government because there were too
few trained people to do all that had to be done. The few educated and
capable Liberals had had little opportunity to get administrative experience under the previous governments, and Villeda's efforts to obtain
bipartisan participation in the government failed, as did his attempt to
stabilize the bureaucracy by getting a civil service law passed. Because of
these failures, many of the traditional followers of the National Party
who had supported him because they thought he could accomplish these
things turned away from him and joined the army officers in efforts to
expell him from the presidency.

Another problem facing Villeda, and a big one, was the disruptive
influence of *Fidelismo*. The rise of Fidel Castro coincided with Villeda's
term in office, and the Maximum Leader's Honduran admirers kept the
country in turmoil and disrupted Villeda's attempts at orderly government and reform. The *Fidelistas* attempted to infiltrate the Liberal
Party and the government and met with some success. At last, convinced
that the Castro government was financing the armed revolutionaries in
Honduras, Villeda broke relations with Cuba. Meanwhile, the army officers and their ultraconservative backers posed constant threats. To protect his government, Villeda set up a Civil Guard made up primarily of
young members of the party. The army did not like the idea of a second
military force, and all through Villeda Morales' term in office there were
armed clashes between the regular army and the Civil Guard. In the end
it was the army and the conservative elements rather than the *Fidelistas*
that were to overthrow the Liberal government of Villeda Morales.

In 1962 the legislature adopted an agrarian-reform law that aroused
much opposition from the country's landowners.[5] The United Fruit
Company was particularly disturbed and protested to the U.S. State Department.[6] There is no evidence that there was any connection between
the United Fruit Company's activities in Washington and the successful
overthrow of the government in 1963, but the fruit company's activities
strengthened the will of the landowners who did actively participate in
the overthrow of the government.

Soon after that, the political parties met to nominate candidates for
the presidential election due in the fall of 1963. The Liberal Party nomi-

---

[5] See "Agrarian Reform Law in Honduras," *International Labour Review*, 87 (June
1963): 573–80.

[6] See the letters from officials of the United Fruit Company to the Assistant Secretary
of State and to U.S. Senator Hickenlooper, *Congressional Record*, 87th Cong., 2nd sess.,
vol. 108, pt. 16 (1962), pp. 21618–19.

nated Modesto Rodas Alvarado, the president of the Congress. The National Party, by a vote of 30 to 27, nominated Judge Ramón E. Cruz. The defeated candidate for the nomination, Gonzalo Carías Castillo, a son of the former dictator, then split the party and started a new organization, the Popular Progressive Party, to sponsor his candidacy. This split in the opposition to the Liberal Party practically guaranteed victory to Rodas Alvarado, but the traditional power holders of Honduras refused to reconcile themselves to his expected electoral victory.

Another complicating factor was the peculiar constitutional provision that removed the country's armed forces from the president's control. The 1957 constitution provided for an officer with the title of Commander of the Armed Forces to be elected by the Congress from a list of names sent to it by the Superior Council of National Defense, consisting of officers of the armed forces. In practice, this meant that the officers of the armed forces nominated the head of the armed forces. This created a bifurcation in government that inevitably led to conflict. Rodas Alvarado was known to be opposed to this system and in favor of a constitutional amendment that would give the president effective control over the armed forces.

On October 3, 1963, ten days before the scheduled election, when it was apparent that Rodas was headed for electoral victory, the army revolted. Estimates of those killed vary between 200 and 1,000. Some civilians joined the Civil Guard in fighting the army, but the army won, expelled the president from the country, and set up a dictatorship headed by the commander of the armed forces. The officers' justification for their revolt was that they were trying to halt "restlessness and anarchy" and end "flagrant violations of the constitution and obvious Communist infiltration." This was nothing but demagogic verbiage, as Villeda Morales was one of the few presidents in Latin America with the courage publicly to fight communism and Castro. It is true that some Communists managed to infiltrate the schools and labor unions; but they could do this only because Villeda Morales was trying to run a democratic government.

Some critics blame Villeda Morales for his own downfall, claiming that in 1957 he was strong enough to have refused to grant autonomy to the armed forces and to have been able to end the vicious vendetta-like rivalry between the Liberals and Nationalists which is the basic reason for Honduras' political instability, since neither group is willing to recognize the other's right to exist. In Villeda's defense it can be said that the writers of the 1957 constitution thought they were removing the armed forces from politics. It turned out they were wrong, but the evidence is that this was their intention. As for the cutthroat politics, this can end only when the people of Honduras are willing to accept a common symbol of authority: a constitution, the myth of democracy, or whatever it may be. As long as the society continues to be as unintegrated, as illiterate, and as poverty-stricken as it is, all governments will have difficulty finding acceptance by the entire population.

As this is being written, the military remains in power. On February 16, 1965, an election for the Congress of Deputies resulted in a victory for the National Party, which received, according to the official results, 328,412 votes to 267,808 votes for the Liberal Party. Reports of voting irregularities came from many observers and there was much suspicion that the election was not altogether honest, for the National Party had announced in advance its intention to elect Colonel Oswaldo López Arellano, head of the *de facto* government, as constitutional president. But the Liberal Party, after a struggle between its various factions, decided to accept the results of the election, and on March 24, 1965, the Congress duly elected Colonel López Arellano constitutional president for the 1965–71 term.

Honduras therefore returned to "constitutional government" during 1965 under the auspices of the same groups and individuals that had destroyed its last constitutional system. Whether the new government will prove stable cannot be said. Meanwhile, Honduras remains the poorest and most underdeveloped of the Central American republics. To add to the country's problems, in 1964 and 1965 its most valuable natural asset, the unused forests, were attacked by an insect that threatened to destroy the country's timber resources. No one can forecast what the future holds for Honduras. At the moment the only hopeful sign is a modest improvement of the economy, due in large part to the effects of the Central American Common Market and the inflow of money from international financial institutions.

The Formal Constitutional Framework

Honduras is governed under the constitution of June 6, 1965, which describes Honduras as "a sovereign and independent state, erected as a democratic republic, to ensure the enjoyment of freedom, justice, social and economic well-being, and the individual and collective betterment of its inhabitants." This is Honduras' twelfth constitution since it began life as an independent state, but none of the twelve was ever completely observed and the only president in the country's history who made an effort to govern constitutionally was Villeda Morales.

The 1965 constitution sets up a presidential form of government

with three separated powers, the legislative, the executive, and the judicial. At the same time, however, the constitution continues the independent control of the armed forces introduced in the 1957 constitution.
Thus Honduras has a bifurcated government with a self-perpetuating
officer corps heading the military. The chief of the armed forces has a
term of six years, just like the president of the republic, and can be removed only by a two-thirds vote of the Congress of Deputies. The armed
forces are asked by the constitution to "cooperate with the executive
branch in tasks of literacy, education, agriculture, conservation of natural resources, highways, communications, health, land settlement, and
emergency activities." The constitution adds that "orders given by the
President of the Republic to the armed forces, through their chief, must
be obeyed," but it is easy to forecast who will dominate the military in
Honduras.

Except for this section on the armed forces, Honduras' constitution
is typical of Latin-American constitutions. Many pages (Articles 51 to
164) are taken up with listing "declarations, rights, and guarantees," including elaborate individual, property, family, labor, and cultural rights.
At the same time, the most important individual rights can be suspended
by executive decree "in the event of invasion of the national territory,
serious disturbance of the peace, an epidemic, or other general disaster."

Much of the Honduras constitution is a picture of what the delegates to the convention hoped to see someday in their country. Until the
political, economic, and social situations of the country have improved,
they will remain in effect only in the articles of the constitution.

How the Constitution Is Amended

The constitution can be amended by a two-thirds vote of the total membership of the Constituent Assembly voting in two consecutive yearly
regular sessions. Certain articles cannot be changed: those dealing with
the president's term in office, the ban on reelection of the president, and
the state's rights over natural resources in the continental and insular
seas. How this will work out cannot be forecast as this is written.

Who Participates in Politics

The majority of Honduras' population has never really participated in
the country's political life. The mass illiteracy, poor road system, and traditional mores combine to restrict political participation to a minority.
In what William Stokes writes of as "without doubt the freest election in

the history of Honduras,"[7] that of 1923, 106,266 votes were cast. In 1929, the number was 100,064; in 1932, 142,854; in 1953, 251,295; in 1957, 339,872. These low totals occurred regularly, even though all males over twenty-one (over eighteen if married or literate) had the vote after 1936 and voting was legally obligatory. After 1956, women could vote under the same conditions as the men. The election of 1965 saw the largest number of voters in the history of the country participating, 596,230, which was about 71 percent of the estimated 840,000 of voting age. This was because the 1965 constitution granted the vote to all over eighteen. The compulsory voting law is not generally enforced, although one does hear now and then of someone being fined for not having voted.

Despite the theoretically compulsory vote and the striving for a more democratic political system evidenced by the events of the 1950's and 1960's, there remains a lack of meaningful participation in both the economic and the political life of the country. In many cases, the illiterate *campesino* is duped, intimidated, or simply ignored. In other cases, he lives in so isolated an area that he might as well be on Mars for all the effect he has on the country's economic or political institutions.

The Electoral Machinery

During the 1950's an elaborate system for conducting elections developed, and in 1961 President Villeda Morales asked the Organization of American States to send a commission to Honduras to recommend improvements in the country's electoral laws. The committee, consisting of U.S. political scientist Henry Wells, Víctor F. Goytía of Panama, and José Antonio Bonilla Atiles of the Dominican Republic, drew up recommendations for the government.[8] The election of February 16, 1965, was conducted by a bipartisan electoral council similar to that set up before the 1963 election, with party representatives sharing equally on the electoral boards and at the local polling places. The electoral machinery is probably adequate; what prevents the system from functioning better than it does is the vendetta-like campaigning conducted by the political parties. Especially in the remote rural areas, where the local strong man still is important, it is unusual for an election to be conducted calmly. The incumbent, whoever he may be, usually has a great advantage. As long as the majority of the population remains illiterate, the quality of

---

[7] William Stokes, *Honduras* (Madison: University of Wisconsin Press, 1950), p. 247.
[8] Unión Panamericana, *Informe de la misión de asistencia técnica de la Organización de los Estados Americanos a la República de Honduras en materia electoral* (Washington, 1963).

the election will be a reflection of the wishes of the man in charge of the voting machinery.

Political Parties

Honduras, like its neighbors in earlier days, developed a two-party system, here consisting of the Liberal and National Parties, but while almost all the other Latin-American republics went on to develop a variety of political factions, these two continue to be the only important parties in Honduras. (The Communist Party, small but typically active, gives Honduras a third organized political group, but it has never been permitted to operate legally or to present its own candidates.) In many ways the two-party system in Honduras resembles that of Colombia, although in Honduras the violence and bloodletting never reached such peaks as in Colombia. In both Honduras and Colombia the two parties incorporate into their ranks almost all the politically active population, in both countries the parties' programs are similar, and in both countries the partisan rivalry is so fierce that stable government has difficulty in operating.

The largest party in Honduras is the Liberal Party. It originally developed out of the nineteenth-century anticlerical movement, but about the time of the Second World War it began to adopt the programmatic ideas being advocated by "popular" parties in the other Latin-American republics. By the 1950's the Liberal Party was closely cooperating with such groups as the Costa Rican National Liberation Party. Its program called for agrarian reform, industrialization, and most of the other reforms sponsored by popular parties in Latin America. It "repudiated dictatorship" and advocated state intervention in the social and economic life of the nation to "prevent abuse by private interest" and "to further the general welfare." During President Villeda Morales' term in office, the party was anticommunist and opposed the Cuban dictatorship of Fidel Castro. It had a formal structure and rules to conduct its business. Headquarters were opened in the most important towns, and it developed into a mass party. The Liberal Party won the largest vote in the national elections of 1954 and 1957 and in the municipal elections of 1962. It seemed headed for certain victory in 1963 before the army takeover. In the 1965–71 legislature it held thirty of the sixty-four seats in the Congress of Deputies. The Liberal Party has traditionally suffered from internal dissension. It was a split in the party in 1932 that permitted Carías Andino to win and thus gain the opportunity to establish his dictatorship. In 1963 there were two factions in the party: the Rodas group, whose leader won the nomination, and the *Acción Liberal* faction, led by Andrés Alvarado Puerto. However, once Rodas won the nomination, most Liberals united behind him; a small conservative splinter led by Roque Rivera operated under the name of the Republican Orthodox Party, but it was refused recognition by the Electoral Council.

The National Party is descended from the nineteenth-century Conservative Party. Until the years of the world depression, there was little difference between the Liberals and Nationalists in either ideology or the social and economic classes from which they drew their followings. Under Carías Andino, however, the National Party came to be the spokesman for the aristocracy. Labor could not organize, and there were no labor reforms until Gálvez was president and the Liberals won the support of the majority of the organized workers and their leaders. Yet while the Liberal Party has been moving in the direction of a "popular" party, as we have seen, and the National Party has tended to remain a power-seeking machine with a bias toward the richer sections of the population, there is still not a great deal of difference between them.

Some kind of Communist party has functioned in Honduras since the late 1920's, usually working through other organizations. In the period after 1948, the Communists controlled the Democratic Revolutionary Party (PDRH), which assumed some importance during the Gálvez administration. With the growth of the Liberal Party as a reformist organization, the Communist Party and the PDRH lost most of their following until the victory of Fidel Castro in Cuba revived procommunist activity. The Honduran Democratic Youth Front is a pro-*Fidelista* student group that probably includes Communists within its ranks.

Public Opinion and Pressure Groups

The mass illiteracy and the overwhelmingly rural character of the population impede the development of an informed public opinion. There are no good daily newspapers. The four in existence in 1961 had a total circulation of about 32,000, with *El Día* and *El Cronista* of Tegucigalpa, the largest, both circulating about 10,000 daily. The newspapers reach only the articulate urban groups. Radio is more important as a means of communication. Both the Liberal and National Parties own their own newspapers.

The army is the best organized group in the country, and the attempt to keep it out of politics by giving it constitutional independence only strengthened its importance. Obligatory military service supplies the rank and file. President Villeda Morales tried to create a balancing force in the Civil Guard, made up primarily of young Liberals, but this force was dissolved after it was crushed by the army in 1963. With a military man currently president, the army clearly is the dominant group in the country.

The landed aristocracy and the business and professional men of the cities make up the second most important group in Honduras. This is a face-to-face group, as their activities throw the well-to-do urban and rural families into continuous contact with each other. They can be found in support of both the Liberal and National Parties. It must be remembered that there are very few extremely wealthy people in the country, and that once one has managed to get out of the *campesino* class, social mobility is possible. Education, energy, intelligence, and a little bit of luck can transform one into a landowner, a professional, or a businessman. There is a group of businessmen of foreign birth (many are Christian Arabs and Chinese) who have played little role in politics, but with the development of industrialization this group has begun to assume more importance.

The Catholic church,[9] the organized university students, and the United Fruit Company all play roles as pressure groups, but none is of great importance compared to the army, the landowners, the businessmen, and the political parties. The organized workers, especially those employed on the north coast in the banana and related industries, exert some pressure, but since the total amount of industry is small, the organized workers are weak. On December 31, 1962, there were only seventy-five trade unions in the country with a total membership of 18,848. Of this total, eight unions in the north-coast banana and associated industries, with 9,510 members, made up 50.46 percent of the organized workers. Most of the organized workers are affiliated with the Honduras Confederation of Labor (CTH). The unorganized *campesinos*, who make up about 70 percent of the population, play practically no role in the country's political life except when they get a chance to vote.

Civil Liberties

While Honduras has never had to suffer the kind of dictatorships that Rosas and Trujillo provided their countries, civil liberty has not been

---

[9] The weakness of the Catholic church can be seen in the fact that there are 632 Catholic churches and only 156 priests, or one priest for each 9,950 Catholics. Most of the priests are from the United States, Canada, and Spain (Franklin D. Parker, *The Central American Republics* [London: Oxford University Press, 1964], p. 216).

well protected. As long as politics was reserved to the landowners, the well-to-do, and the educated, there was a sort of tacit understanding that the "ins" would never be too harsh to the "outs," especially to the "outs" who were "*gente decente*," the wellborn or those well endowed with money. Usually these people went into exile to wait for a change in government. The *campesinos* were the ones who went to jail or were killed when trouble started.

The real birth of freedom in modern Honduras came when Gálvez became president and lifted the restrictions imposed by Carías Andino. With the growth of the Liberal Party into the dominant party in the 1950's, personal liberty became the rule, and all could express themselves. In fact, many have accused Villeda Morales of being "soft" on communism because he did not persecute Communists, and during his term in office he had considerable difficulty with an extremist militarist, Colonel Armando Velásquez Cerrato, who attempted a coup d'état in 1959. The military government of 1963–65 never was very oppressive, and even permitted Villeda Morales to return from exile to campaign for the election of February 1965.

The Executive

The executive power in Honduras is headed by a president who is elected for a six-year term and can never be reelected. At the same time that the president is elected, three president designates are elected to take the president's place when necessary in the order set by the Congress. To be president or designate, one must be a Honduran by birth, over thirty years of age, a citizen, and a layman. As is common in Latin America, many persons are barred from becoming candidates for the presidency. The list includes all former presidents, the president of the Congress, members of the cabinet, assistant secretaries of state, the chief of the armed forces, the members of the National Electoral Council, officials elected by the Congress, and the relatives of the president, of the chief of the armed forces, and of members of the Electoral Council. Many of these can become eligible by resigning their positions twelve months before the election.

Because of the practically independent armed forces, the Honduran president is not as powerful an executive as is the rule in most of Latin America. Not only must the president give his orders to the armed forces through its chief, but the constitution also gives "the administration of funds appropriated for the Department of Defense" to the disbursement office of the armed forces, which the president does not control. The president is in charge of the general administration of the country and has forty-five specific duties assigned to him, but he must have the signature of a minister on all his actions. He freely appoints all the ministers and many other officials. When the president is a military man who has influence with the army officers, he can be a strong president; otherwise he is in a relatively weak position.

Because of the underdeveloped economy in Honduras, the importance of a government position as a way of personal advancement always has been great, and no formal civil service system has ever replaced the traditional spoils system. In 1959 a School of Public Administration began to function, but it has not been in operation long enough to have produced observable results.

The Legislative Power

The legislature of Honduras is a unicameral Congress of Deputies consisting of sixty-four deputies in 1967, each elected for a term of six years. One deputy and one alternate deputy are elected for each 30,000 inhabitants or fraction over 15,000. Deputies are elected by departments, with one deputy and one alternate being elected for each department with a population of less than 30,000. There are no by-elections; if a seat is vacant, an alternate takes the missing deputy's place. Unlike most constitutions, that of Honduras names no requirements for the office of deputy, but it lists so many disqualifications that a large portion of the country's leadership is banned from the Congress. Among those who cannot be elected deputies are the president of the republic and persons attached to his office; members of the cabinet and assistant secretaries; all public employees and all members of the military on active duty; all members of election agencies; the members of the National Economic Council; all diplomatic and consular representatives; the presidents, directors, and managers of national banks and autonomous government institutions; the relatives of the president of the republic, of his spouse, of the members of the cabinet, of the chief of the armed forces, and of the justices of the Supreme Court, all this within the fourth degree of consanguinity and the second degree of affinity. This would seem to carry the safeguards against nepotism to quite sufficient lengths, but apparently not for Honduras: the relatives of the chiefs of military zones, of the commanders of military units, and of other military officers who are serving in the department one wants to represent are also barred from becoming candidates, as are those who have concessions to exploit natural resources, contractors on public works, and delinquent debtors of the national treasury. Since more than 50 percent of the people are illiterate, one can only wonder who is left to become a deputy. Surprisingly, however, the deputies can be reelected.

The Congress has always been a minor power in Honduras. In 1963, for example, the budget provided L13,000 (about $6,500 U.S.) for professional and technical services for the Congress for the entire year. Under previous constitutions, deputies could not be reelected; now that reelection is possible, the deputies may be able to build up bases of power to strengthen this branch of the government. The constitution gives the Congress a long list of forty-one powers, but certain of them are only formal in nature. Among the normal powers of the Honduras legislature are the power to enact laws, to regulate its internal functioning, to impeach the president and various other officials, to grant amnesty, to declare war and make peace, to fix the strength of the permanent army, and to exercise ultimate control over public finances.

When the Congress is not in session, it is represented by a Permanent Committee of nine deputies who are appointed by the congressional leaders (the directorate). The Permanent Committee has the power to call the Congress into special session, temporarily to elect certain officials, to prepare bills for the consideration of the Congress, and to handle various other tasks. Deputies can be appointed as members of the cabinet or as assistant secretaries or to diplomatic positions. While they serve in these posts, their seats are held by alternate deputies.

Public Finance

The Honduras budget is prepared by the executive and presented by the president to the Congress. If the Congress does not approve it by the end of the fiscal period, the previous budget continues in force until a new budget is voted. The underdeveloped nature of the economy means that the government never has enough money for everything that ought to be done, even though in recent years the budget has risen rapidly. In 1963, for example, the total budget amounted to only a trifle more than $55 million U.S.[10] In addition, the Honduras government depends too much on the taxes on its banana companies. In 1957, when a storm destroyed seven million banana plants, the United Fruit Company, which had paid $2,665,157 in income tax for 1956, paid only $30,500 in taxes.

The tax structure of Honduras depends heavily on indirect taxes,

---

[10] In 1939 the government's income was only $4.5 million U.S.; in 1944, $6.5 million; in 1949, $14 million; in 1953, $22 million; in 1956, $29.5 million; and in 1958, $45 million. See Parker, *Central American Republics*, p. 199.

which in 1963 raised 55.68 percent of the government's income. In that year 18 percent of the total came from foreign loans. The 1963 budget, shown in Tables 1 and 2, is typical.

TABLE 1
REVENUE OF HONDURAS, 1963

Source	Amount in Lempiras	Percent of Total
Direct taxes		
On income	L3,070,000	2.83%
On profits of businesses	7,930,000	7.04
Social security tax	90,000	0.07
On property	700,000	0.62
Total direct taxes	L11,790,000	10.56%
Indirect taxes		
On autos	1,133,000	1.00
On public entertainment	330,000	0.29
On beer	8,000,000	7.17
On liquor	5,200,000	4.61
On soft drinks	550,000	0.48
On cigarettes	3,100,000	2.75
On matches	400,000	0.35
On sugar	840,000	0.74
On production, commerce, and consumption	2,497,000	2.21
On imports	35,700,000	32.40
On exports	4,032,891	3.58
Miscellaneous	120,000	0.10
Total indirect taxes	L61,902,891	55.68%
Nontax income		
Services by the government including ports, airports, post offices, telegraph, sales of goods and services	5,227,600	5.00
Commercial and industrial activities conducted by the government	241,500	0.21
Miscellaneous, including income from autonomous organizations and national lottery	2,630,500	2.50
Adjustment to balance budget	60,000	0.05
Total nontax income	L8,159,600	7.76%
Total regular income	L81,852,491	74.00%
Internal loans	8,350,000	8.00
External loans	20,060,000	18.00
Total budgeted income	L110,262,491	100.00%

TABLE 2
EXPENDITURES OF HONDURAS, 1963

	Amount in Lempiras	*Percent of Total*
Legislature	L1,599,960	1.42%
Court system	1,796,160	1.59
General administration, including office of the president, foreign relations, electoral system, etc.	7,909,727	7.17
Education	19,628,180	17.81
Public health	6,668,440	6.06
Social welfare	1,963,000	1.81
Labor and social security	1,425,770	1.30
Transport and communications	31,655,242	28.72
Urban services and housing	1,218,200	1.10
Economic development	4,368,320	3.97
Agriculture and natural resources	2,010,760	1.82
National defense	8,565,872	7.79
Internal security (police, firemen, jails)	5,000,312	4.53
Fiscal administration	4,584,338	4.16
Service of public debt	11,855,730	10.75
Miscellaneous	12,480	. . .
Total	L110,262,491	100.00%

Local Government

For purposes of local government, Honduras is divided into eighteen departments, which are divided into 275 *municipios*, which include within their boundaries 1,606 *aldeas* and 6,970 *caseríos*. Each department is headed by a governor who is appointed and may be removed by the national executive. The governor plays a double role: he is the agent of the national government and at the same time the president of the department council, made up of the governor and two councilors. Each *municipio* elects a council to manage its local affairs. Generally speaking, the ministry in charge of local government through the governors dominates the system. The system has worked fairly well because there are no large cities in Honduras, and hence no problems of urbanization have developed, except to some extent in Tegucigalpa, the national capital, and San Pedro Sula, the north-coast center.

The Judicial Power

Under the 1965 constitution, Honduras has a centralized court system headed by a Supreme Court whose seven justices are elected by the Congress for six-year terms. Judges of the lower courts are appointed by the Supreme Court, with those on the lowest level appointing justices of the peace for the rural areas. The court system is completely controlled by the executive, and the six-year term for Supreme Court justices tied to the presidential term prevents any judicial independence. Under the military government of Colonel López, the court system continued in a subordinate position as before. The 1965 constitution provided for judicial review by giving the Supreme Court the power, under certain conditions, of declaring laws unconstitutional because of their form or content, but not enough time has gone by to warrant any conclusion as to how this will work in Honduras.

Honduras: A Last Word

At this writing Honduras is being governed "constitutionally" with Colonel Oswaldo López Arellano, the leader of the coup d'état in 1963, serving as president of the republic for the 1965–71 period. It is impossible to describe the Honduran government as a democracy, nor has the country ever really known democratic government. Except for the few years in the 1950's and 1960's under Presidents Gálvez and Villeda Morales, no government has really tried to develop democratic institutions in Honduras. When William Stokes made his study of Honduras in 1942, he came to the conclusion that

> unrestrained executive authority sanctioned by force has been more the rule than the exception. However the subject of government is examined, by the microscope or the telescope, the result is the same. Government in action is government by *caudillo, él que manda* (the one who commands), the military man on horseback, the *doctor en filosofía* from the lecture hall. The average Honduran knows that wherever government is able to operate, the final authority is the executive.[11]

This was a fair description of government under the dictatorship of Carías Andino, and there has been little real change.

Since 1942 the population of Honduras has increased rapidly, the completion of the Inter-American Highway has brought the people more in contact with the world, plant diseases tend to temper the importance of the banana crop, and some economic development has taken place. Yet the government, as this is written, is controlled by a colonel whose chief reason for being in the Presidential Palace is that he commands the

---

[11] Stokes, *Honduras*, p. 294.

country's armed forces. Why has political development not proceeded faster than this in Honduras? The only answer is that the social and physical settings within which Honduras operates have not been such as to foster the growth of the social structures and secondary organizations needed to produce a stable political system.

Despite the history of the country, one Honduran politician, speaking at the University of Florida in 1954, said that in his opinion, "properly ruled, Honduras could be easily transformed into a model country."[12] This is nonsense. Honduras simply does not have the resources to finance the country's needs. There is no extensive wealth, mineral or otherwise, in its mountains and tropical jungles. In 1963, 18 percent of the government's budget came from international loans, and 10.75 percent of the expenditures went to service the public debt. In other words, over L20 million were borrowed so over half the sum could be paid out in interest on the debt previously contracted. Honduras needs massive amounts of money to make up for the misgovernment and neglect of more than 400 years, and there does not seem to be any place these funds can be found. The human and natural resources of Honduras must be developed if the country is ever to progress, but even if the parasitic army were abolished there would not be enough money available.

Honduras is so little developed that in many cases it cannot even take advantage of its opportunities. The Inter-American Development Bank, in discussing planning for development in Honduras, pointed out:

> Honduras' earlier planning efforts were hampered by the limited availability of financial resources, trained local manpower and adequately studied projects. The two previous plans, for 1956–1961 and 1962–1965, obtained substantial foreign commitments, but had to be drastically reduced, due to delays in project preparation and implementation and a shortage of local resources for counterpart funds.[13]

In addition, Honduras finds itself caught up in the cold war. Its nearness to the Communist base in Cuba makes it easy for the Communists to smuggle arms and personnel into the country. As the little Communist Party organizes guerrilla groups and provokes violence from time to time, the intransigent upper class clings more firmly to the status quo. Its failure to cooperate closely with the Liberal Party government from

---

[12] Jorge Fidel Durán, "Culture and the Economy in Honduras," in A. Curtis Wilgus, *The Caribbean: Its Culture* (Gainesville: University of Florida Press, 1955), p. 187.

[13] *Socio-Economic Progress in Latin America*, Social Progress Trust Fund sixth annual report, 1966 (Washington: Inter-American Development Bank, 1967), p. 267.

1957 to 1963 helped bring a reintroduction of dictatorship. Meanwhile, illiteracy, poverty, and underdevelopment continue. Yet modern means of communication bring the illiterate peasants news of attempts in all parts of the world to improve conditions in underdeveloped countries such as theirs. The only result of a continuation of the type of government Honduras has had through most of its history must be chaos, with the possibility that eventually communism may capture the country.

Probably the only real hope for Honduras is incorporation into some kind of larger political unit, perhaps a United States of Central America. The money now wasted on the trappings of sovereignty, the army, a diplomatic corps, etc. would at least help to start the process of development, and as part of a larger unit perhaps the area could find more financial resources internationally, and the latent energies of the Hondurans could be released to begin the construction of a more rational social system. Until that happens, the majority of the people of Honduras will be doomed to continue living as they have for over 400 years.

SELECTED READINGS

ALEXANDER, ROBERT. "Honduras," *Communism in Latin America*, pp. 371–77. New Brunswick, N.J.: Rutgers University Press, 1957.

ANDERSON, CHARLES W. "Honduras: Problems of an Apprentice Democracy." In *Political Systems of Latin America*, edited by Martin C. Needler. Princeton, N.J.: D. Van Nostrand Co., 1964.

"Blue and White or Red." *Time*, May 19, 1961, pp. 36–39.

CHECHI, VINCENT, et al. *Honduras: A Problem in Economic Development*. New York: Twentieth Century Fund, 1959.

Estatutos y programa del Partido Liberal de Honduras, 1953. Tegucigalpa: Diario El Pueblo, 1953.

GARDNER, MARY A. "The Press of Honduras: A Portrait of Five Dailies." *Journalism Quarterly* 40 (Winter 1963): 75–82.

HIDALGO H., CARLOS. "Honduras." *Cuadernos Hispanoamericanos*, no. 151 (July 1962), pp. 79–94.

JAUREGUI, ARTURO. "The Young Free Trade Union Movement in Honduras." *Free Labour World*, no. 59 (May 1955), pp. 26–31.

MACDONALD, AUSTIN F. "Honduras," *Latin American Politics and Government*, pp. 632–37. 2nd ed. New York: Thomas Y. Crowell Co., 1954.

PAREDES, LUCAS. *Drama político en Honduras*. Mexico City: Editora Latinoamericana, n.d.

STOKES, WILLIAM S. *Honduras: An Area Study in Government*. Madison: University of Wisconsin Press, 1950.

————. "Honduras: Dilemma of Development." *Current History* 42 (February 1962): 83–88.

UNIÓN PANAMERICANA. *Informe de la misión de asistencia técnica de la Organización de los Estados Americanos a la República de Honduras en materia electoral*. Washington, 1963.

U.S. DEPARTMENT OF LABOR. *Labor Law and Practice in Honduras*. Bureau of Labor Statistics report no. 189. Washington: U.S. Government Printing Office, 1961.

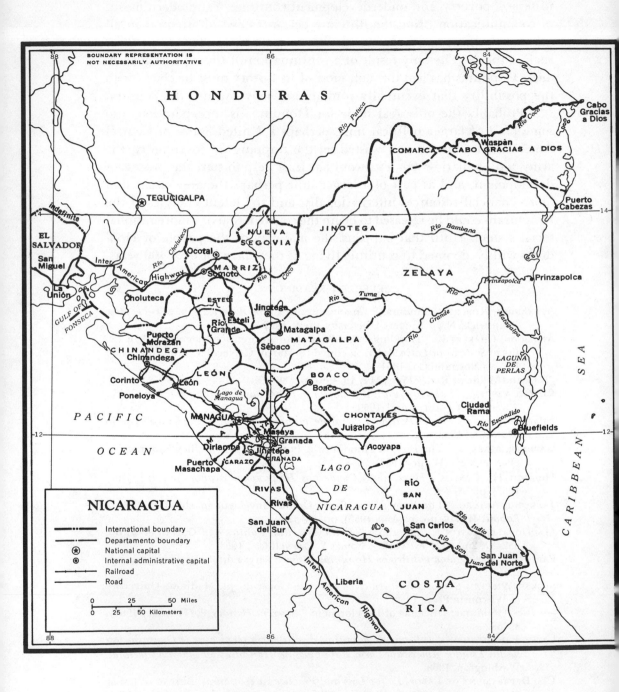

NICARAGUA

International boundary
Departamento boundary
★ National capital
◉ Internal administrative capital
Railroad
Road

0   25   50 Miles
0   25   50 Kilometers

BOUNDARY REPRESENTATION IS
NOT NECESSARILY AUTHORITATIVE

H O N D U R A S

TEGUCIGALPA

Rio Patuca

Rio Coco

Cabo Gracias a Dios

COMARCA — CABO GRACIAS A DIOS

Waspán

Puerto Cabezas

EL SALVADOR

San Miguel

Indefinite

Inter American Highway

Rio Choluteca

NUEVA SEGOVIA

Ocotal

MADRIZ

Somoto

JINOTEGA

Rio Bambana

ZELAYA

Prinzapolca

Prinzapolca

La Unión

Choluteca

ESTELÍ

Rio Coco

Rio Esteli

Jinotega

Rio Tuma

Rio Grande

Rio de

Matagalpa

GULF OF FONSECA

Puerto Morazán

Rio Grande

Esteli

Sébaco

Matagalpa

MATAGALPA

LAGUNA DE PERLAS

CHINANDEGA

Chinandega

LEÓN

BOACO

SEA

Corinto

León

Boaco

Poneloya

Lago de Managua

CHONTALES

Ciudad Rama

PACIFIC

MANAGUA

Masaya

Juigalpa

Rio Escondido

Bluefields

OCEAN

Dirlamba

Jinotepe

Granada

Acoyapa

CARAZO

GRANADA

LAGO

Puerto Masachapa

RIVAS

DE

RÍO SAN JUAN

Rivas

NICARAGUA

San Carlos

Rio Indio

C A R I B B E A N

San Juan del Sur

San Juan del Norte

Inter American Highway

Liberia

COSTA RICA

Rio San Juan

———8———

NICARAGUA:

America's Only Hereditary Dictatorship

During the nineteenth century Nicaragua had far greater importance than its size, population, or natural resources warranted, for it contains within its territory what is probably the best site for an interoceanic canal in America. As a result, Nicaragua was long used as a road from the Atlantic to the Pacific, especially from the time of the California gold rush to the opening of the Panama Canal. Nicaragua's canal site brought her an unusual amount of outside intervention, as soldiers of fortune and the governments of the United States and Great Britain competed to control the area.

The outside interference combined with the political system inherited from the Spanish colony to produce a situation so chaotic that in the early years of the twentieth century, Nicaragua, for all practical purposes, became a protectorate of the United States. The protectorate produced an efficient armed force, which, led by Anastasio Somoza, took over control of the country in the 1930's and created the longest-lasting hereditary political machine developed in Latin America. As this is written Nicaragua continues to be the private domain of one family. Nicaragua has interesting lessons to teach the student of government, for it has the closest thing to a legal dictatorship ever developed in America.

A National Profile

Nicaragua, with an area of 57,143 square miles, is the largest of the Central American states, but at least half this territory lies completely unused.

Bounded on the north by Honduras, on the east by the Caribbean Sea, on the south by Costa Rica, and on the west by the Pacific Ocean, Nicaragua is a roughly triangular-shaped area whose most distinctive feature is a belt of lowland about fifty miles wide running from the Gulf of Fonseca southeast to the Caribbean. In this small section of the country's territory, especially around Lakes Managua and Nicaragua, most of the country's population is found. Coming down from Honduras, two ranges of the Central American mountain chain provide an area of high plateau that makes up Nicaragua's second region. To the east, along the Caribbean coast, is the country's third area, a belt of heavily forested, very rainy, humid, and hot plain, which is lightly populated by people who follow a culture pattern different from that of the rest of the country. Nicaragua is a tropical country, but in the mountains, which rise 5,000 to 7,000 feet above sea level, the climate is moderated.

With 1,715,000 people in 1966, Nicaragua had the lowest population density in Central America, but this is deceiving, as about 70 percent of the population is concentrated in the area around the two lakes. The population has been increasing rapidly, at a rate of 3.5 percent from 1958 to 1962. The great majority of the people are *mestizos* (69 percent) with a heavy dominance of Indian and Negro in their ancestry. Seventeen percent are white, 9 percent Negro, 5 percent Indian. Some pure Indians and some English-speaking descendants of immigrants from the British Caribbean islands and British Honduras are found in the eastern part of the country. There are few foreigners in Nicaragua; the census of 1950 showed only 10,193, of whom 7,129 had come from other Central American states. There is no real discrimination for racial reasons, but the richer upper class is much lighter in complexion that the rest of the population. Over 59 percent of the population is rural. There is only one large city, Managua, the capital, with about 275,000 inhabitants. The next largest cities are León, with about 50,000, and Granada, with a little more than 30,000.

Spanish is the official language. Education is very poorly developed; the total number of students enrolled in all schools during the 1960–61 school year was 177,645, less than half of the school-age population when the total population was 1,480,251. At least 50 percent of the total population remained illiterate in 1964. In 1950 only 0.3 percent of the population had received any university training, and in the 1965–66 school year the total enrollment in all of Nicaragua's universities was about 3,000. The majority of Nicaragua's children probably still do not attend school. Not very much emphasis has been given to education until recent years, but since 1965 there has been a sharp increase in government expenditures for schools. The low educational level of the population helps keep the country unproductive and backward. The majority of the population is supposed to be Roman Catholic (the 1950 census gave the figure at 95.9 percent), but many Nicaraguans are not firmly attached to the church. Protestant organizations are strong, especially on the east coast, and there are about 400 Protestant places of worship in the country. Religion has never been as important an issue in Nicaragua as it has been in most of the other Latin-American countries.

Nicaragua is basically an agricultural country, although its productivity is so low that only 35 percent of the gross national product came from agriculture in 1965. Fifty-eight percent of the economically active in 1965 were in agriculture, only 12 percent in industry. The main products are coffee, sugar cane, cotton, cacao, rice, maize, and cattle and other livestock. Only about one-sixth of the country's area is laid out in farms, and most of these are subsistence plots. Of the country's 51,581 farms in 1959, 362, or 0.7 percent, contained 32.8 percent of the total area in farmland. The few large farms produce most of the export crops. Some industry has been developed, especially since the 1950's. The main products are processed foods, footwear (although most of the population goes barefoot), wearing apparel, cement, and lumber. An oil refinery has been established and some minerals are mined, gold and silver being the most important.

From 1954 to 1960, Nicaragua's gross domestic product grew at a rate of 8.2 percent, which is very high for Latin America, but most of this was attributable to an increase in the production of cotton, which is grown on the very large farms owned by a small number of families. It is thought by some that the rapid economic growth in the 1960's will generate forces that will lead to change in the organization of Nicaragua. The development, however, has taken place in only a small part of the country, the area in and around Managua, leaving most of the rest of the country untouched.

In summary, it can be said that Nicaragua is an underdeveloped country most of whose people are rural, illiterate, and in poor health. Yet a mission from the International Bank in 1952 "concluded that few underdeveloped countries have so great a physical potential for growth and economic development as does Nicaragua."[1] What has held Nicaragua back is a political system that operates to make one family the owner of perhaps hundreds of millions of dollars' worth of property while the overwhelming majority of the population owns practically nothing.

---

[1] International Bank for Reconstruction and Development, *The Economic Development of Nicaragua* (Baltimore: Johns Hopkins Press, 1953), p. 3.

The International Bank mission, writing in 1952, reported that "more than twenty-five percent of the national income accrues to about one percent of the population. Within the top one percent there is a further concentration of income at the upper level."[2] There is no evidence that this has changed in the years that have passed since then. Marvin Alisky analyzed the population characteristics of Managua, the most prosperous city in the country, in 1960, and computed that only 1.1 percent of the 200,000 residents were well-to-do; 7.9 percent were in the middle class, 39 percent were in the working class, and 53 percent lived in utter poverty.[3]

Only 49.5 percent of the urban and 1.4 percent of the rural population had potable water in 1966. Only about 28 percent of the people in Managua and 8.4 percent of the rest of the population had sewer facilities in 1966. To complicate matters, the great wealth amassed by one family forces that family to monopolize all political power and fight strenuously to prevent any change. Any substantial improvement in the population's literacy or health or any real growth of the economy would develop forces whose first effort would be to rid the country of the dictatorship that has ruled it for thirty years. Since the dictatorship shows no signs of giving up any of its privileges, Nicaragua is living through a period of crisis.

The Development of Modern Nicaragua

Although Columbus touched the Atlantic coast of Nicaragua on his fourth trip, in 1502, the Spaniards never flocked in to settle the area, for eastern Nicaragua was as hot, as wet, and as forested as it is today, and quite unappetizing to any Spaniard looking for easy ways to get rich. With the passage of time, however, the San Juan River became part of a route to the west coast of Mexico, for it is only twelve miles from Lake Nicaragua to what became the town of San Juan del Sur on the Pacific coast. Slowly some Spaniards did settle on the plains around Nicaragua's two lakes, for they found sedentary Indians there who could be forced to work the land. Thus a typical Spanish colony grew up, and it never was really isolated as long as the San Juan River–Lake Nicaragua route was used to reach the west coast.

As the centuries passed, two nuclei of population developed: one near the north end of Lake Nicaragua, which became the town of Granada, and the other to the north of Lake Managua, in the center of a rich

---

[2] *Ibid.*, p. 75.
[3] Marvin Alisky, "Public Opinion under Dictatorship in Nicaragua," *Nieman Reports*, 16 (April 1962): 12.

agricultural area centered around the city of León. Apparently because it was the point at which land travelers took to boats, Granada became a richer center than León, and when independence came to Central America, the leading families of León and Granada began to dispute for hegemony of the new Republic of Nicaragua. The people of León called themselves Liberals, the people of Granada called themselves Conservatives, and whatever the one group favored, the other opposed. Thus for the first thirty years of independence, until the 1850's, the country lived a hectic and turbulent political life.

It should not be supposed that the two groups were separated ideologically, for the differences were primarily products of a spirit of localism. Each group sought and found allies in the other Central American states. When the Liberals were in control of the federation, the leading families of León dominated Nicaragua; when the Conservatives controlled the federation, power passed to the leading families of Granada. This type of political struggle was inevitable, for, just as in the other Spanish colonies, no group or class in Nicaragua was prepared for self-government. The poorer peasants followed their richer neighbors because of semifeudal loyalties, and the habit of supporting one party or the other became so ingrained that people still call themselves Liberals and Conservatives in Nicaragua today.

Because of its location, Nicaragua was always subject to more than its share of outside influence, and for many decades in the nineteenth century the British tried to control the country's east coast through the Mosquito Kingdom, "ruled" by various Indians kept in power by the British. When the gold rush to California started, Commodore Cornelius Vanderbilt, the United States capitalist, established a route by steamer and land across the isthmus. This transportation route also became involved in politics, and in 1855 the León Liberals were helped by a United States soldier of fortune, William Walker, who succeeded so well that he was soon president of Nicaragua and Vanderbilt lost his transportation concession. Naturally Vanderbilt was soon financing the armies of Nicaragua's neighbors, who were fearful Walker might conquer them also. A coalition of Central American powers defeated Walker and he fled the country in 1857. By this time, however, the Commodore had apparently become disillusioned, for the next year he sold out to competitors operating a route across Panama.

Now it was the turn of the Conservatives, who dominated Nicaragua from 1863 to 1893. Tired by all the chaos of civil war, the country settled down. Agricultural production increased, gold was mined, bananas began to be grown in quantity, but the majority of Nicaragua's population remained illiterate subsistence farmers living in isolated poverty. Education was neglected, tropical diseases were endemic, the government was the traditional do-nothing force so typical of the area. In 1893, after a split among the Conservatives, a Liberal *caudillo,* José Santos Zelaya, captured the government and set up a harsh dictatorship that lasted for sixteen years. Zelaya promoted some economic development, including a little railroad construction. At the same time, graft and corruption became the rule, liberty completely vanished, and concessions of all kinds were sold to foreigners. Zelaya aspired to be the president of a reunited Central America, and kept the area in turmoil with his constant plotting and interference in the affairs of the neighboring republics.

By the 1900's the United States had become deeply involved in interoceanic canal planning. Nicaragua was at one time seriously considered for the route of the new canal,[4] but eventually the Panama route was chosen. The United States government, however, maintained its interest in Nicaragua, and when two United States citizens were executed there in 1909, in one of Zelaya's attempts to crush opposition, the United States expelled the Nicaraguan ambassador from Washington and Zelaya was soon out of office.

Here began a period of United States intervention in Nicaraguan affairs.[5] When Zelaya had left the country, the Conservative leaders, who took control, found the government bankrupt and asked the United States for help. The U.S. State Department sent a Mr. Thomas D. Dawson, who devised a plan under which a United States collector of customs would collect the receipts of the customhouse and divide them between the country's foreign creditors and the Nicaraguan government. At the same time, a loan from New York bankers retired certain British loans and gave the government some working capital. Under this arrangement, a Conservative, Adolfo Díaz, became president, whereupon the Liberals revolted under the slogan "Down with Yankee Imperialism." When they appeared to be winning, the United States Navy landed the Marines and put down the rebellion. Díaz thus remained in office, but during nineteen of the twenty-one years after 1912, United States Marines were stationed in Nicaragua. Sometimes the total number of Marines went down to about a hundred men, but they were there, and additional forces were

---

[4] For an account showing how close Nicaragua came to being the site of the new canal, see Philippe Bunau-Varilla, "The Fight to the Death for the Triumph of Panama and the Defeat of Nicaragua," *From Panama to Verdun* (Philadelphia: Dorrance & Co., 1940), pp. 85–124.

[5] For the official United States explanation of the U.S. occupation, see U.S. Department of State, *The United States and Nicaragua: A Survey of the Relations from 1909 to 1932* (Washington: U.S. Government Printing Office, 1932).

available whenever they might be needed. At the same time, citizens of the United States, in addition to controlling the collection and distribution of customs receipts, ran the country's national bank and the government-owned railroad.

In 1925, after the New York bankers had received full payment for their loans, the Marines were withdrawn. Immediately civil war broke out. Soon a Conservative government, headed by Adolfo Díaz and backed by the United States, was in power in Managua, and a Liberal government, headed by Juan B. Sacasa and backed by Mexico, was functioning on the east coast. When it appeared that Díaz was about to lose the civil war in 1927, the United States landed 2,000 Marines and sent a prominent United States politician, Henry L. Stimson, to arrange a truce in the fighting. Stimson succeeded in getting most of the struggling politicians to cease military action, arranged for an election in 1928 to be supervised by the Marines, and presided over the inauguration of a Liberal president, José María Moncada. One Liberal leader, however, César Augusto Sandino, refused to accept the arrangement and continued to fight against both the Nicaraguan government and the United States Marines. Until 1934 he continued to harass the government, and although he never could overthrow it, the Marines were equally unsuccessful in their efforts to defeat or capture him. He became a great hero to all in Latin America who objected to United States intervention, and probably was the best known of all Latin Americans during the late 1920's. His struggle assumed the proportions of myth, and even today his name is still invoked by political leaders in nationalistic speeches.

It has been suggested that the reason the Marines intervened in Nicaragua was that the United States government was still interested in the possibility of building a canal there someday, even though it was already building one in Panama. Whether this was the case or not, soon after the Marines landed, a treaty known as the Chamorro-Bryan Treaty was drawn up and ratified on June 24, 1916, granting the government of the United States in perpetuity, free of taxation, exclusive rights to a canal across Nicaragua. At the same time Nicaragua leased the Great Corn and Little Corn Islands to the United States for ninety-nine years and gave the United States the right to set up a naval base on Nicaraguan territory bordering the Gulf of Fonseca. In return for all this, the United States gave the Nicaraguan government $3 million.

During their years in Nicaragua the United States Marines ran several elections, built some roads, and improved public health. They also did something that was greatly to influence future political developments in the country: they disarmed almost all the population and organized a national constabulary. Thus, when the United States launched its "Good Neighbor" policy in 1933 and withdrew the Marines, Nicaragua discovered that the newly created constabulary under its new leader, General Anastasio Somoza, was the only armed force in the country. In 1934 Somoza had Sandino assassinated. In 1937 he illegally took over the presidency, and from then on he ruled as a dictator until he was assassinated on September 21, 1956, leaving power in the hands of the armed forces, headed by his sons, Luis and Anastasio, Jr., thus creating Latin America's first hereditary dictatorship in the twentieth century.

Anastasio Somoza was a very clever politician who was able to control the Nicaraguan government with a minimum of brute force. Somoza had married the daughter of one of Nicaragua's leading families. The English he had learned at Pierce Commercial College in Philadelphia enabled him to become one of the interpreters between the Nicaraguan officials and the military and civilian officials of the United States occupying forces. Soon he became the personal friend of many of the officials from the United States who knew no Spanish, for he was a robust, fun-loving, energetic young man, fond of drinking and dancing, a baseball fan who talked the language the United States Marine officers and embassy officials understood. When his wife's uncle became president of Nicaragua in 1932, he appointed Somoza head of the National Guard. Using this position to build up his power, Somoza was running the country soon after the Marines left.

Unlike most other dictators, Somoza was clever enough to see that more than force was needed to stay in power. He juggled the constitution until he had a document that enabled him to be a dictator legally. After becoming president in 1936, Somoza had a new constitution proclaimed in 1939, another in 1948, and another in 1950, and he changed that in 1955. The purpose of all the changes was to create a legal framework under which he could do whatever he wanted to do. Under his personally dictated constitution he was the commander in chief of the armed forces, and he could issue decree-laws when Congress was not in session (and Congress met for only sixty days each year), oversee the official conduct of the courts, supervise the spending of the government's money, confer military ranks up to brigadier general, appoint and remove all government employees including all *local* government officials, suspend or restrict constitutional guarantees, and do just about anything else that occurred to him without any check from anyone. He controlled the press and radio, ran managed "elections," and exiled or jailed anyone who opposed him too vigorously.

In addition to his military power as head of the armed forces and his political power as head of the government, Somoza amassed great economic power by becoming the richest man in Central America. It is impossible to document the ways in which he accomplished this, but there is general agreement that he made full use of his political and military power plus a generous measure of unscrupulousness. One example became public knowledge through a United States congressional hearing whose report included the following:

> On June 27, 1934, Mr. Frank Jonas, an agent for Remington, which is controlled by the Du Pont Company, wrote Mr. Monaghan, export manager of the Remington Arms Company, that General Somoza in Nicaragua intended to equip the army with .45-caliber Colt automatic pistols as standard equipment. Jonas suggested that Monaghan communicate with Mr. Nichols of Colt's and tell him to write General Somoza offering to sell direct to him. "I would suggest that in this quotation he should include a 10 percent commission for General Somoza." Remington was naturally anxious to have Colt's supply the guns, for which they could then supply the ammunition. The guns had to come first.[6]

It takes only a few deals like this before one has enough money to start buying up plantations, airlines, etc., which, in their turn, pour more money into the bank. Somoza's income was estimated at $1 million a year and his assets at about $100 million. One estimate is that he personally owned 360 pieces of agricultural land, plus 72 apartments and homes in Managua, plus most of Nicaragua's industry, including the merchant marine and national airline, plus various properties in other countries. Somoza put every relative he had on the public payroll; soon after his grandson was born, the baby was made a captain in the army with full pay and privileges.

From 1937 to 1956 there was a little economic development in Nicaragua. Roads, schools, hospitals, and hydroelectric plants were built, and agriculture was diversified by stimulating the production of sugar and cotton, but basically the population continued to live as before, since the Somoza family seemed to own all or part of practically every enterprise that was developed.

Somoza had many kind words to say about democracy, though he felt no need to practice it, and he enjoyed advertising his friendship with the United States. He succeeded in winning many admirers in important posi-

---

[6] *Munitions Industry* (report of the Special Committee on the Investigation of the Munitions Industry, Senate report no. 544, pt. 3. 74th Cong., 2nd sess. [Washington: U.S. Government Printing Office, 1936]), pp. 70–71.

tions in Washington, and as a result the United States government almost always supported him, supplied his army with the equipment it needed, and loaned and gave him a great deal of money for "development." He could hardly have asked for a redder carpet than the one rolled out for him when he paid a state visit to Washington. It seems President Roosevelt wanted to rehearse the ceremonies to be held in connection with the planned visit of the British monarch to the United States. And so, to the amazement of all who understood what kind of government there was in Nicaragua, President Roosevelt and his cabinet personally went to the railroad station to greet the dictator. Guns were fired, bands played, and government employees were given three hours off so the streets would be full during the parade. This may have been a useful rehearsal, but it helped to convince many in Latin America that the United States supported the Nicaraguan dictatorship and strengthened Somoza's hold on Nicaragua.[7]

Somoza managed to maintain his warm relationship with the United States government all during his years in power. When he was assassinated, President Eisenhower sent a team of physicians from the Canal Zone as well as the commander of Walter Reed Hospital in Washington to Managua in an attempt to save the dictator's life. When their efforts produced no improvement in his condition, a United States plane carried the dying tyrant to the Canal Zone in a further attempt to save his life. After Somoza nevertheless died, President Eisenhower issued a statement that went far beyond diplomatic courtesy; he called the attack on Somoza "dastardly."[8] (Meanwhile, the Uruguayan legislature passed a resolution honoring the young Nicaraguan who had been killed after assassinating Somoza.)

With Somoza dead, his tame legislature elected his son Luis president of the republic, and his other son, Anastasio, Jr., continued as commander of the armed forces. His daughter's husband continued as Nicaraguan ambassador to the United States, a position he had held so long that he became the dean of the diplomatic corps in Washington.

Some thought that under the Somoza sons there would be a relaxation of the dictatorship. There was, but the relaxation was so slight that

---

[7] A story has been reported many times that President Roosevelt was once asked by a visitor why the United States had such good relations with Somoza—didn't he realize Somoza was an S.O.B.? Roosevelt is supposed to have replied, "Of course, but he's our S.O.B."

[8] The party hack who was the United States ambassador to Nicaragua went further, saying in his funeral address, "We feel that we have lost a great friend whose attractive personality and generosity made us feel as if he were one of us" (Thomas E. Whelan, "Discurso," in *Discursos oficiales pronunciados en las honras funebres del excelentísimo señor General don Anastasio Somoza, Presidente de Nicaragua* [Managua: Ministerio de Relaciones Exteriores, 1956]).

for all practical purposes there might have been none. From 1956 to 1967 economic development speeded up and new roads, housing, and other public works were built, but the Somozas continued to dominate the country. They still owned all the property their father had amassed, they still had the armed forces under their command, and they still had the constitution that made the president a legal dictator. During Luis Somoza's presidency the constitution was amended to bar relatives of the president from being candidates for the presidency, but all this meant was that Luis was succeeded by a friend instead of by his brother, who by 1965 was already campaigning for the 1967–71 term.

The National Guard kept busy repelling real and imaginary invasions. On September 30, 1960, the Guard officially announced it had repelled the twentieth armed invasion since Luis Somoza had become president. The invasions were a result of the opposition's firm grasp of the fact that it could win control of the government only by armed force, for all power remained concentrated in the hands of the Somoza family. Even though the opposition was allowed to carry on its activities in Nicaragua, it refused to participate in the election of January 1963 because Luis Somoza refused to permit supervision of the election by the Organization of American States. Since the opposition boycotted the election, Somoza was able to announce quite truthfully that his candidate, Dr. René Schick, had won an overwhelming victory. Under Dr. Schick, everything went on as before. When he died in 1966, the vice-president, Lorenzo Guerrero Gutiérrez, succeeded him, and in February 1967, after a scandalous "election," Anastasio Somoza, Jr., was declared president-elect for the 1967–71 term. In this campaign the opposition succeeded in uniting its forces behind Dr. Fernando Agüero, but there was much violence with many deaths during the campaign. Thus at this writing Nicaragua continues to be ruled by America's only hereditary dictatorship. Luis Somoza died in 1967; the family goes on.

The Formal Constitutional Framework

Nicaragua is governed under the constitution of 1950 as amended, which describes Nicaragua as a "unitary, free, sovereign, and independent state" with a "republican and democratic-representative" government. Not only does the constitution talk of representative democracy, which has never existed in Nicaragua, but it officially "accepts the principles of the Atlantic Charter, the American Declaration of the Rights and Duties of Man, and the principles of the Inter-American Charter of Social Guarantees." If any of this verbiage had ever been observed, Nicaragua might have become a paradise, but these clauses are only words written on paper; they have no relation to the actual way in which the undernourished, diseased, poverty-stricken, mostly illiterate peasants of Nicaragua are governed.

The constitution of 1950 is Nicaragua's eighteenth, but actually Nicaragua has never been governed constitutionally, despite the stream of constitutions, proposed constitutions, *leyes provisionales*, and constitutional amendments. Somoza, who was an exceedingly clever politician, kept changing the constitution until he had one that legally gave him so much power that for all practical purposes he was a constitutional dictator. Almost nothing was left to chance. One day he began to wonder what would happen if he were assassinated, and it occurred to him that his sons were under thirty, the minimum constitutional age for a president. So he changed the required age to twenty-five.

The 1950 constitution devotes about six pages merely to Articles 190 to 199, which list the "powers and duties of the Executive Power." So much power is vested in the president that he can do almost anything he wants to do, unless he does not control the armed forces; in that case he becomes a puppet and the commander of the armed forces dominates the executive. Thus a Somoza does not necessarily have to have the title of president in order to rule. In the 1940's the elder Somoza installed three consecutive puppet presidents but retained control of the National Guard. When one of the puppets proved disappointing in 1947, Somoza ejected the man from the presidency only twenty-six days after he had been inaugurated.

How the Constitution Is Amended

The Nicaraguan constitution can be amended in part by an involved process that requires the approval of both houses of the Congress in two different sessions. The constitution as a whole can be amended only by a constituent assembly set up by the legislature after it has gone through the involved process needed for amendments. The complicated system does not seem to prevent amendments, as they are passed whenever the Somozas want them passed; in 1962, for example, Luis Somoza pushed through a whole series of amendments as part of his "liberalization" policy.

Who Participates in Politics

The majority of Nicaraguans probably have never actively participated in the country's political life. Until the epoch of the Somozas, politics was an aristocratic pastime for the influential few of Managua, León, and Granada. With the rise of Somoza, the Chamorros, Sacasas, and other important families continued to occupy positions in the government, but all decision-making was in the hands of the Somozas.

The vote is officially obligatory in Nicaragua, but this rule is not enforced. All over twenty-one have the right to vote, plus all from eighteen to twenty-one who are literate and/or married, and all under eighteen who have academic degrees. Women have had the vote since 1955. The way elections are conducted, however, the vote is not of much importance. In 1950, when 202,698 votes were cast, all voting was done in public, and everyone who voted for Somoza received a card the possession of which was required for employment with the government. National Guardsmen observed each vote cast. Somoza received a majority of three to one.

The Electoral Machinery

The United States authorities tried to introduce a fair electoral system during the occupation and supervised some elections to that end, but there has never been a fair election since Somoza came to power. The electoral system developed by the older Somoza put the electoral machinery in the control of a three-member National Council of Elections. One member was appointed by the Supreme Court and one by each of the two traditional political parties. Since Somoza always dominated the Supreme Court, he always had a two-to-one majority.

One of Luis Somoza's reforms as part of his "liberalization" policy was to change the three-man National Council of Elections into a five-man Supreme Tribunal of Elections. One member is appointed by the Congress, one by the Supreme Court, one by the majority party, one by the party that won the second largest number of votes (the official opposition party), and one by the party that obtained the greatest number of signatures on its registration petition. As it worked out, this meant there were four supporters of Somoza on the tribunal and only one opponent.

In 1967 the three most important opposition parties united their efforts in an organization known as the National Union of the Opposition (UNO). About 836,000 were registered to vote. The election campaign suddenly ended when the National Guard broke up a meeting of the UNO supporters in Managua on January 22, 1967. Various reports gave the number of dead as from 32 (the government figure) to 300 or 400 (Fernando Agüero's estimate). On January 25 the Congress passed a censorship law to curb "political agitation by news media," and the rest of the "election" campaign was carried on under the rules of the new law.

The lack of local elections before 1962 contributed to the voters' lack of experience in the operation of electoral machinery, and Somoza's managed elections came only every six years. The occasional boycotts advocated by the Conservative Party did little to train Nicaragua's voters. Until such time as literacy is more widespread and the opposition political parties develop much more strength than they have had, it does not appear that meaningful elections will take place in Nicaragua.

Political Parties

In Nicaragua, as in a number of other Latin-American countries, the two-party system developed in the nineteenth century continued into the twentieth century. That is not to say that modern political parties developed in Nicaragua in the last century; during the power struggles between the dominant families of Granada and León, the two groups merely received names. From 1821 to 1856 the groups were known as the *Timbucos* and the *Calandracas,* from 1856 to 1893 as the *Legitimistas* and the *Democráticas,* and after 1893 as the Conservatives and the Liberals. Until the Somoza era, the Conservatives and Liberals were regional groups, their members bound together by close interpersonal ties. People were born into their party as they were born into a family. There were no real ideological differences between the two. In the struggles between them, each sometimes tried to destroy the enemy's city, and in their zeal the Liberals of León even brought the adventurer William Walker and his army of soldiers of fortune into Nicaragua, with the tragic results that we have noted. In 1852, Managua, located between the two rivals, was made the capital city in an effort to end the competition between them, but the bitter rivalry went on.

To register a legal party a group of voters must present a petition containing the signatures of citizens equal to 5 percent of the total vote cast in the previous election. The parties that received the highest and second highest number of votes in the last election are automatically registered and are eligible to offer candidates in subsequent elections. To create a legal opposition, the constitution contains clauses under which minority parties automatically are given at least one-third of the seats in the Chamber of Deputies, the Senate, the Supreme Court of Jusice, and the Supreme Tribunal of Elections. The only parties banned from functioning by the constitution are those with international connections. This has been interpreted to ban the Communist Party, which as a result works through the National Liberal Party of the Somozas.

Anastasio Somoza had married into the Sacasa family, one of the leading families in the Liberal Party, and he continued to call himself a Liberal after he became dictator, and even after the party became only a mechanism used to keep him in power. There was so much opposition to his dictatorship within the organization known as the Liberal Party that it split, and there are now two groups using the name Liberal. The dominant group is the National Liberal Party (PLN). This includes within its ranks a few of the traditional "Liberals," but basically it consists of the governmental apparatus through which the Somozas operate. Party membership is practically a prerequisite for government employment or a position in any of the many Somoza-controlled private enterprises. A loyal party member receives many privileges, the most important of which is the seal of respectability so vital in a dictatorial society. Since all candidates for office are nominated by the party leadership, which is the Somozas, they can exact obedience from the party and at the same time maintain a mechanism by which their dictatorship is made to look like representative government.

When the Liberal Party split in 1944, the anti-Somoza group took the name Independent Liberal Party (PLI). Most of the leaders of the PLI have lived outside of Nicaragua most of the time since then, plotting the overthrow of the Somozas, leading abortive invasions into the country, and conducting propaganda campaigns. Practically all of them have been imprisoned at one time or another, and some bear the scars to prove it.

The Conservative Party also split over the issue of what to do about Somoza. During the 1930's and 1940's there were two main factions, one in favor of participating in the government as a minor party and one that favored complete boycott and opposition. By the late 1950's both of these had declined to ineffectual little groups, but after the elder Somoza was killed the party revived. In 1960 a younger, more imaginative group captured the leadership of what came to be known as the Traditional Conservative Party (PCT). Led by Dr. Fernando Agüero, the PCT tried to organize itself into a modern "popular" party. It established contacts with the other popular parties of America and began to emphasize a thorough reform of Nicaragua, beginning with the expulsion of the Somozas. By 1967 it had probably become the country's largest political group. There is no way of knowing its exact strength because of the way elections are conducted, but it was the most important element in the National Union of the Opposition (UNO) in 1967. The other faction of the Conservatives is known as the Nicaraguan Conservative Party (PCN). Because it participated in the 1963 election, it was the official opposition party from 1963 to 1967, and its members made up one-third of the legislature. It is only a small group without a distinctive program and was not permitted to join the UNO in 1967.

Three small parties are active. The Social Christian Party (PSC), founded in 1957, is a small group similar to the Christian Democratic parties in other countries and is oriented by the social doctrines of the Catholic church. In 1967 it was part of the UNO. The Communist Party is illegal and it cannot present candidates, but the Somozas have helped the Communists in order to utilize them in fighting their opposition. With help from the Somozas, the Communists, who use the name Socialist Party of Nicaragua, have built themselves a base, particularly in the labor movement, the Ministries of Education and Labor, and in the National Liberal Party.[9] After the rise of Fidel Castro in 1959, the Communists tried to start armed revolts several times, but they never attracted very much support because of their record of cooperation with the Somozas. In addition to their positions in the government, in the official party, and in the labor movement, they operate through a series of front organizations, the most important of which are the Republican Mobilization, the Revolutionary Youth Front, and the National Liberation Front. The Revolutionary Action Party is a small group of no importance. In 1967 it supported the candidate of the UNO for the presidency.

There have been many attempts through the years to unite all of the opposition in a force capable of destroying the Somoza regime. The UNO, created for the 1967 election as a united front of the Traditional Conservative Party, the Independent Liberal Party, and the Social Christian Party, is the latest attempt. Since this group automatically received one-third of the seats in the Congress and the Supreme Court, it is possible that it may be able to continue to function. There really is no reason why the three components of the UNO should not unite. These parties resemble each other in their programs, their composition, and their objectives. Unfortunately, there is something in the Nicaraguan ambience that makes Conservatives and Liberals cling to their traditional names.

As long as the population remains as rural and as illiterate as it is, it is unlikely that a viable party system will be created. All parties function only sporadically, and then mainly in Managua, León, and one or two other places. Many of the Independent Liberal leaders remain in exile in Mexico.

---

[9] A newspaperman who asked Luis Somoza why the Communists were permitted to be members of the National Liberal Party quoted Somoza as saying, "When the Communists get too far out of line, we try to persuade them to be more reasonable. If they refuse, we kick them out of our party" (Gerry Robichaud, "Nicaragua's Somoza Taking Softer Line," *Miami Herald*, December 1, 1960, p. 11A).

Public Opinion and Pressure Groups

Public opinion is centralized in Managua, which completely dominates the country. At times the students and newspapers in León make themselves heard, but only faintly. The Somozas dominate communications as they dominate everything else. The high rate of illiteracy makes the radio probably the most pervasive influence, but in 1960 there were only 18 radio receivers per 1,000 inhabitants; at the same time, only 56,000 daily newspapers circulated in the whole country, but the press reached the more influential part of the population. Seven daily newspapers were being issued in Nicaragua in 1959. The most important were *Novedades*, owned by the Somozas, with 20,000 circulation; *La Prensa*, the leading opposition paper, with 20,000; and *La Noticia*, with 15,000.

The strongest and most important group in Nicaragua is the National Guard, the country's only armed force, which enabled Somoza to get control of the country in the beginning. The officers are trained in a national military academy and have had many privileges bestowed upon them. The armed forces traditionally get a sizable share of the national budget (16.14 percent in 1963–64) and are involved in many activities not normally considered military. The Nicaraguan National Guard controls all internal communications (post office, telephone, and telegraph), the border stations, immigration, and ports, and local criminal investigation, policing, and traffic regulation. There are many ways for an officer to get rich, including importation of cars and other readily salable items without paying customs. A lavish military club in Managua and others scattered over the country help make the officers a people apart. These are far and away the most important men in the country after the Somoza family itself, which they faithfully serve.

Because the Somozas never set up a crude dictatorship, but always tried to have an aura of constitutionality about them, the traditional landed aristocracy and the newer wealthy groups in the city have remained an important force. Practically all the political leaders are professionals, landowners, or merchants. The great fortune the Somozas have amassed helps them to keep the landowners and businessmen under control, for one can hardly do business in Nicaragua without utilization of the Somoza factories, airlines, steamship company, etc. The various producers' associations, chambers of commerce, and miscellaneous business groups do not play effective roles as pressure groups, but rather serve as agencies for collective bargaining and to handle noncontroversial matters. The influence of the professional men and businessmen comes through personal relations with those in power and through family connections.

The organized labor movement is very weak in Nicaragua. In 1960, 304,885 of the total labor force of 477,338 were in agriculture and only 58,882 were in manufacturing. The rest were in services, commerce, construction, transportation, mining, and electricity production. Thus there are no large groups of workers to be organized. In addition, the Somozas, by favoring the Communists to fight their democratic opposition, have enabled them to keep their influence in what trade unions there are, and they have managed to split the anti-Somoza unions into a series of weak organizations. In 1963 it was estimated that only about 16,000 workers, or 6 percent of the total salaried employees and wage earners, were organized. Of this number only 11,000, or 4 percent of the total labor force, was enrolled in the 89 most active trade unions. The largest group of unions is associated with the General Confederation of Labor (CGT), which in the 1950's was part of Perón's ATLAS international organization. In 1963 the CGT was estimated to have about 5,000 members split into two factions, one of which is not recognized by the Ministry of Labor. The National Confederation of Workers (CNT) has about 4,000 members. The Autonomous Trade Union Movement of Nicaragua is affiliated with the Latin American Confederation of Christian Unions but had only 625 members in 1963. In addition there are several other independent confederations, but all together amount to very little. None of the unions is affiliated with the ORIT, although that organization has been actively trying to develop the labor movement in Nicaragua. As a result of its weakness, the labor movement plays very little role in determining public policy.

There are so few university students that they too play little part in politics. The peasants are almost completely unorganized and play no part at all. Society is so primitive in Nicaragua that there really is no organized system of interest groups. The extended family is the channel through which a man takes care of his needs, and this system has been extended into the party organizations, which function more like very large families than like coordinators of the wishes of varied classes and groups.

Civil Liberties

The Nicaraguan constitution contains pages of "rights and guarantees" that have practically never been observed. Article 113, for example, states: "No one may be molested or persecuted for his opinions. The State guarantees the free utterance and dissemination of thought, without prejudice to any liability that might arise for crimes and abuses committed in the exercise of such freedom." Yet on August 21, 1960, the Associated Press reported:

> The government has banned political discussion on radio news programs. General Anastasio Somoza, Commander of the National Guard, called radio station owners into his office and read them the new regulations, which he said would be stringently enforced. He was quoted as saying, "We have had enough of propaganda and political news which has caused bloodshed—from now on there will be no politics at the microphone." At the same time, national guardsmen who have occupied radio stations for the last month were withdrawn.[10]

It is common to come across such news items emanating from Nicaragua. Lester Velie, writing in *The Reader's Digest*, reported that "Tortures, shootings and jailings are part of everyday life in Nicaragua."[11] Although the Somozas never tried to operate as rigid a dictatorship as many other Latin-American strong men, they have never hesitated to use enough force and terror to keep themselves in power. Whenever the opposition seemed to be getting too strong, they would have recourse to Article 197, which gave the president the power to suspend constitutional guarantees. In addition to everything else, until well into the 1950's the armed forces maintained strict control of the movement of all people, and outside every town there was a police post to keep track of travelers. Under President Schick, people were let alone more than had been the custom under the Somozas, but Nicaragua still has a very long way to go before its people can say they have civil liberty.

The Executive

Nicaragua's executive is a very powerful president who serves for five years and cannot be reelected until one term has intervened. Nor can his relatives be candidates for the presidency. Under the elder Somoza the constitution allowed a six-year term and reelection, but his son Luis had these clauses changed as part of his "liberalization" program.

The Nicaraguan president is given the power by the constitution to command the armed forces, to "enact laws during adjournment of Congress [or ten months out of every twelve] by use of his delegated legislative power," to veto the laws passed by Congress (although a two-

---

[10] *Miami Herald*, August 21, 1960, p. 29A.
[11] Lester Velie, "Bomb in the Caribbean," *Reader's Digest*, January 1962, p. 206.

thirds vote of the legislature can override his veto), to "oversee the official conduct of the members of the Judicial Power," to supervise the proper disbursement of the budget, to appoint and freely remove practically all government employees, to "direct and inspect public education," to detain persons whenever he thinks it necessary, and to declare the suspension of constitutional guarantees whenever he wants to do so.

In addition, he has a host of other duties, including such things as granting and canceling naturalization certificates and granting patents. The only check upon all this power is that for certain duties, the president's orders must be countersigned by a minister, but this is no real check, as the president can appoint or remove ministers at any time for any reason.

There are two vice-presidents elected at the same time as the president, but they have no duties except to wait for the president to die. There is no formal system of recruiting public servants; political reliability and loyalty to the Somozas are the chief qualifications.

The Legislative Power

Nicaragua's legislature is a bicameral Congress consisting of a Chamber of Deputies of fifty-four members and a Senate of sixteen members. The presidential candidate who was second in votes and all ex-presidents also are members of the Senate. Alternates are elected at the same time as the regular members. The members of both houses serve five-year terms that are coterminous with that of the president. All are elected by a system of proportional representation under which the majority party gets thirty-six deputies and eleven senators and the minority parties get at least eighteen deputies and five senators.

The method of electing the legislature tends to strengthen the Somozas, for through their control of the National Liberal Party they determine who shall be its candidates, and since no one represents a geographical district, it is difficult for anyone to build up any independent power. When the elder Somoza was killed, his son Luis was the president of the Congress and soon was elected to succeed his father. The formal rules governing eligibility are of no significance, since the Congress itself is of little significance. The constitution has elaborate rules governing the composition of the Congress, the powers of the two houses, individually and meeting together as the United Chambers, and the ways in which laws shall be enacted, but under the Somoza family the Congress has played a very minor role in government. Practically all the laws originate with the executive. The Congress' annual sixty-day sessions can be extended for thirty days, and special sessions can be called under special circumstances.

Public Finance

The president of the republic is the key figure in the drawing up of Nicaragua's budget. Although the Congress must approve the budget, by a constitutional provision it cannot "alter fixed charges," nor can it increase the amount for any specific budget item, since "the initiative for increasing [budget items], as well as for changing the estimate of revenues, is the exclusive function of the Executive." In addition, if the Congress does not approve the budget before the day it is to go into force, the president's draft budget goes into effect.

Income and expenditures have been rising during the postwar years. Income went from 249,581,000 córdobas in 1956–57 to C$465 million ($65 million U.S.; there are 7.05 córdobas to the dollar) in 1965, and the total of expenditures has risen correspondingly. In six of the years from 1956–57 to 1963–64 there was a small deficit, in two years a small surplus. Tables 1 and 2 show where the money comes from and how it has been spent in recent years.

Nicaragua has an income tax, applicable to all income earned in the country, which ranges from 16 percent on incomes of C$300,000 to C$350,000 to 30 percent on all income over C$2 million. Both the low level of the average person's income and the failure of the rich to pay up can be seen in the receipts for income taxes in the fiscal year 1963–64: slightly less than C$26 million, or only 7.74 percent of the government's income that year. If we add the tax on capital and the receipts from the inheritance tax, the total from all direct taxes comes to a little over C$45 million, or 13.65 percent of revenue. A regressive system of indirect taxes on exports, imports, and consumption raised 73.67 percent of the year's revenue. Nor was the country's income spent any more intelligently. Whereas 16.14 percent went to the armed forces, only 3.08 percent went to the Ministry of Agriculture and only 4.07 percent was spent for public health.

Local Government

Nicaragua is divided for administrative purposes into sixteen departments, each of which is in charge of a *jefe politico* appointed by the president. The *jefe politico* is assisted by the National Guard in enforcing the law. The cities, towns, and villages within the departments (122

TABLE 1

REVENUE OF NICARAGUA, FISCAL YEAR 1963–64

(000 Omitted)

Source	Amount in Córdobas	Percent of Total
Direct taxes		
On income	C$25,850	7.74%
On capital	17,800	5.33
On inheritance	1,960	0.58
Total direct taxes	C$45,610	13.65%
Indirect taxes		
On imports	115,615	34.60
Consular fees	22,706	6.80
On exports	6,570	1.97
On consumption	87,592	26.21
Miscellaneous	13,669	4.09
Total indirect taxes	C$246,152	73.67%
Nontax income		
From services	17,455	5.24
From government corporations	5,820	1.74
From donations	510	0.16
Miscellaneous	3,183	0.93
Total nontax income	C$26,968	8.07%
Total regular income	C$318,730	95.39%
Loans	15,412	4.61
Total budgeted income	C$334,142	100.00%

of them) until 1962 were headed by a group of officials known collectively as the *municipalidad,* who were appointed by the president. Since 1962 the *municipalidades* have been governed by a council of five *regidores* elected at the time of the national elections by a system of proportional representation under which three *regidores* represent the majority party and two the second party. The president of the republic, however, must still approve the local tax schedules. Until 1962 Managua was governed directly by the national president, but since 1962 the voters have elected a council of six *regidores* by proportional representation for five-year terms. Their meetings are presided over by a minister appointed by the country's president.

It is too early to judge how the new system of local government will work, especially as the armed forces and the agencies of the national government all continue to function in each locality. Centralization is the rule in Nicaragua, and the creation of a few elected positions does not

TABLE 2

EXPENDITURES OF NICARAGUA, FISCAL YEAR 1963–64
(000 Omitted)

	Amount in Córdobas	*Percent of Total*
Legislature	C$4,917	1.44%
Executive		
Office of President	4,574	1.34
Ministry of Government	24,570	7.19
Ministry of Foreign Relations	10,830	3.17
Ministry of Economy	6,874	2.01
Ministry of Finance	31,878	9.33
Ministry of Education	58,462	17.12
Ministry of Development	61,783	18.09
Ministry of War	55,141	16.14
Ministry of Agriculture	10,510	3.08
Ministry of Public Health	13,894	4.07
Ministry of Labor	2,612	0.76
Judiciary	7,200	2.11
Transfers to public corporations	26,202	7.67
Government monopolies	3,500	1.02
Public debt	18,635	5.46
Total	C$341,582	100.00%

radically change the system. At the departmental level there still is no council, either elected or appointed, to control the *jefe político* appointed by the president.

The Judicial Power

The Nicaraguan courts, like everything else in the country, are subservient to the executive. Although most of the judges are elected by the Congress and the rest by the Supreme Court, the judges are well under the control of the executive, who, as we have seen, has the power to "oversee the official conduct of the members of the Judicial Power." In addition, until 1962 the terms were fixed, six years for the seven-member Supreme Court and terms of four years, two years, and one year for lower-court judges. In 1962 the six-year term for Supreme Court justices was changed to life for those elected in 1963. The constitution recognizes the political character of the courts by requiring that three of the Supreme Court justices must be members of minority parties. During the Somoza era the courts have always been subservient to the executive power.

Nicaragua: A Last Word

Nicaragua is a dictatorship masquerading as a constitutional republic. That Anastasio Somoza was able to pass his power on to his family when he died, something neither Rafael Trujillo nor Juan Vicente Gómez could do, is indicative of how clever a politician he was and how little Nicaragua changed during thirty years of Somoza rule. In the last analysis, the chief cause of change in a society such as Nicaragua's is the emergence of new groups into positions of power. As long as Nicaragua continues to be a land of largely illiterate, barefoot peasantry, subject to all kinds of endemic diseases, poor and rural, the Somozas will continue in power.

A complicating factor in Nicaragua is the tremendous wealth amassed by the Somozas. There were rumors that perhaps Luis Somoza, before he died, and other members of the family would have liked to relax the controls they exercised, but they could not see how to do it and still preserve their wealth in land and business enterprises. Nor can the Somozas take the farms and factories with them if they should decide to leave the country. Meanwhile, their economic power serves as one of their means of control.

Nicaragua's future is very difficult to predict. At this writing it remains an unintegrated country lacking roads, schools, electric power, adequate public health, and a population trained to live in the modern world. Where can a country that had only about 3,000 university students in the 1965–66 school year expect to get the administrators, technicians, and professionals a modern society needs? Even when one adds the Nicaraguans educated outside of the country, there simply are not enough trained persons to operate a modern nation-state. With Nicaragua's high illiteracy rate, the productivity is necessarily low, so either the country pulls itself up by the bootstraps or gets the money from outside sources. If rapid change does not come, the Communists may well capture the country eventually, since they do have access to foreign resources in Moscow, Peiping, and Havana.

The only bright hope for Nicaragua seems to be the economic spurt of the 1960's and the opposition to the Somozas. The Central American Common Market and the attempts by the Somoza sons to liberalize the regime have contributed to a rapid rate of economic growth. The middle class is growing and a more sophisticated group of young entrepreneurs is developing, many of them educated in the United States. As this group grows, it may insist on having a larger role in determining the government's policy. The opposition is a force for modernization because its leaders are regularly expelled from the country or flee to save their lives, and thus have a chance to acquire new ideas in the countries where they spend their exile. It is no accident that the leader of the Traditional Conservative Party, Fernando Agüero, lived for some years in New York, and that the leadership of the Independent Liberal Party lived for many years in Costa Rica and Mexico.

As economic development advances and as the opposition grows more sophisticated, the United States programs of economic assistance and loans finance new developments. Roads get built, housing improves, the radio continues to bring new ideas to out-of-the-way places, and the new ideas begin to grip the people. The fast growth in population, largely brought about by the work of international health organizations, also must be considered a positive factor. Even the army serves as a modernizing influence, as it drafts farm boys and inevitably teaches them something about the modern world. Thus the forces of change are being stimulated. Whether the entrenched power of the Somoza military, economic, and governmental machinery can prevent drastic change is doubtful. There probably is a race in Nicaragua between the agents of instantaneous change controlled by the communist ideology and the now awakening Nicaraguans who work through the Conservative, Independent Liberal, and Social Christian Parties. When the Somoza type of legalized one-family dominance will disappear cannot be predicted, but that it will go is inevitable. The nuclear age is not propitious for hereditary governments, whether they are called monarchies or republics.

SELECTED READINGS

ALEXANDER, ROBERT J. "Nicaragua," *Communism in Latin America*, pp. 377–83. New Brunswick, N.J.: Rutgers University Press, 1957.

ÁLVAREZ LEJARZA, EMILIO. *Las Constituciones de Nicaragua*. Madrid: Ediciones Cultura Hispánica, 1958.

ANDERSON, CHARLES W. "Nicaragua: The Somoza Dynasty." In *Political Systems of Latin America*, edited by Martin C. Needler. Princeton, N.J.: D. Van Nostrand Co., Inc., 1964.

BORGE GONZÁLEZ, EMILIO. "Nicaragua por dentro." *Combate* 1 (March–April 1959): 33–42.

BRIONES TORRES, IGNACIO. "Angustia y esperanza de Nicaragua." *Combate* 3 (July–August 1961): 44–50.

BUSEY, JAMES L. "Foundations of Political Contrast: Costa Rica and Nicaragua." *Western Political Quarterly* 11 (September 1958): 627–59.

COLGROVE, ALBERT M. "Nicaragua: Another Cuba." *Nation* 193 (July 1, 1961): 6–9.

ENGLISH, BURT HAROLD. "Nicaragua: A Study in the Evolution of One-Family Rule." Master's thesis, University of Florida, 1964.

———. *Nicaragua Election Factbook, February 5, 1967*. Washington: Institute for the Comparative Study of Political Systems, 1967.

GOLDWERT, MARVIN. *The Constabulary in the Dominican Republic and Nicaragua*, pp. 22–53. Gainesville: University of Florida Press, 1962.

GONDI, OVIDIO. "All Nicaragua Is His Hacienda." *United Nations World* 2 (March 1948)· 30–33.

HAFTER, RUDOLPH P. "Nicaragua: La Dinastía de los Somoza." *Cuadernos*, no. 66 (November 1962), pp. 77–80.

HALLETT, ROBERT M. "Somoza Runs Nicaragua like a Sugar Plantation." *Christian Science Monitor*, December 20, 1952, p. 13.

INTERNATIONAL BANK FOR RECONSTRUCTION AND DEVELOPMENT. *The Economic Development of Nicaragua*. Baltimore: Johns Hopkins Press, 1953.

JAMES, PRESTON E. "Nicaragua as a Political Unit," *Latin America*, pp. 647–48. Rev. ed. New York: Odyssey Press, 1950.

LENS, SIDNEY. "Nicaragua: Portrait of a Dictatorship." *Fellowship* 28 (January 1, 1962): 13–16, 21–25.

MacDONALD, AUSTIN F. "Nicaragua," *Latin American Politics and Government*, pp. 627–32. 2nd ed. New York: Thomas Y. Crowell Co., 1954.

NICARAGUA, CONSEJO NACIONAL DE ELECCIONES. *El Juicio Electoral en 1950*. Managua: Talleres Nacionales, 1956.

PARKER, FRANKLIN D. "Nicaragua," *The Central American Republics*, pp. 219–55. London: Oxford University Press, 1964.

ROBICHAUD, GERRY. "Nicaragua: It's Still a Vast Poorhouse and Pesthole." *Miami Herald*, December 8, 1960, p. 4E.

U.S. DEPARTMENT OF LABOR. *Labor Law and Practice in Nicaragua*. Bureau of Labor Statistics report no. 265. Washington: U.S. Government Printing Office, 1964.

VELIE, LESTER. "Bomb in the Caribbean." *Readers' Digest*, January 1962, pp. 205–14.

COSTA RICA

—·—·—	International boundary
—·—·—	Provincia boundary
⊕	National capital
○	Provincia capital
+++	Railroad
——	Road

0   25   50 Miles
0   25   50 Kilometers

COCOS ISLAND
0   1   2 Miles

5°
32'N

87°04'W

NICARAGUA

ISLA DE OMETEPE

LAGO DE NICARAGUA

Rivas

La Cruz

San Carlos

San Juan del Norte

CARIBBEAN SEA

ALAJUELA

HEREDIA

Puerto Viejo

GUANACASTE

Liberia

Arenal

Las Cañas

Santa Cruz

Nicoya

Puerto Jesús

Villa Quesada

Naranjo

Alajuela

Heredia

SAN JOSE

Siquirres

Matina

Limón

Turrialba

Atalanta

LIMON

GOLFO DE NICOYA

Puntarenas

Esparta

Santiago

San Ignacio

San Marcos

Pirris

Cartago

CARTAGO

SAN JOSE

Ureña

Puerto Quepos

Dominical

PACIFIC

OCEAN

PUNTARENAS

American Highway

Palmar Sur

Golfito

GOLFO DULCE

Puerto Jiménez

Corredor

Concepción

Puerto Armuelles

PANAMA

BOUNDARY REPRESENTATION IS
NOT NECESSARILY AUTHORITATIVE

——9——

COSTA RICA:

A Progressing Democracy

Costa Rica has been a misunderstood land ever since someone named a comparatively poor area "Rich Coast." During the twentieth century this misunderstanding continued as most writers pictured the little country as a peaceful rural Eden where progress, brotherhood, and democracy were solidly entrenched, an oasis of orderly government surrounded by unstable, more typically Latin-American governments. Costa Rica *is* different from its neighbors, but the contrast has not always been so striking as some of the writings about the country have implied. Costa Rica is and always has been poor, underdeveloped, and under-populated.

The Costa Ricans must be admired for their achievements in transforming one of Spain's most impoverished colonies into a progressing democracy. The transformation cannot be understood, however, if one begins by accepting the myth that Costa Rica has been an idyllic rural democracy without a controlling aristocracy. Actually, from 1940 to the 1960's, the people lived a most intense political life. The country was torn apart by civil war, armed invasions, and fierce electoral struggles as the position of a traditional oligarchy was challenged by the aspirations of the bulk of the population to achieve a better life. As the decade of the sixties drew toward its close, Costa Rica's people were demonstrating that a stable, integrated society based on democratic political institutions could be built in an area that had been plagued by political instability and economic backwardness for over a century. This has been a great achievement.

A National Profile

Costa Rica is bordered on the east by Panama and the Caribbean, on the north by Nicaragua, and on the west and south by the Pacific Ocean. It is 288 miles long, with widths varying from 74 to 170 miles. Its area is estimated to be 19,631 square miles, including some small islands with a total area of 38.6 square miles.

Varying topography and climate divide Costa Rica into three main regions. The central highlands extend from northwest to southeast, reaching elevations above 12,000 feet south of San José. Nestled in the highlands are a number of basins, the most important of which is the *meseta central* with an elevation of 3,000 to 4,000 feet. Here, on approximately 770 square miles of fairly level, fertile terrain with a pleasant climate, are found about 72 percent of the population, the centers of culture and government, and the bulk of the important coffee industry. On the Caribbean side of the highlands is located some 30 percent of the country's area, low, swampy, hot, excessively rainy, heavily forested, and insect-infested. About 5 percent of the country's population live here. On the Pacific side of the highlands is located another 30 percent of the national territory, inhabited by about 23 percent of the total population. The rainy southwest resembles the Caribbean lowlands in climate. To the northwest is Puntarenas and the province of Guanacaste, a dry area resembling west Texas, whose main products are cattle and grain. Costa Rica is a tropical country with two seasons, a dry "summer" and a rainy "winter."

Costa Rica's population in 1966 was 1,486,000. The population has been growing at the rate of about 3.9 percent a year, one of the world's highest growth rates. There is only one large city in the country, the capital, San José, with a population on December 31, 1964, of 176,219 (335,396 including the metropolitan area). Puntarenas, Alajuela, Cartago, Heredia, Liberia, and Limón, all provincial capitals, are the other important cities, but their populations are small, ranging from about 7,000 to 25,000. At the census of 1963, 34 percent of the population was urban.

The population of Costa Rica is fairly homogeneous; the people are primarily of European descent, chiefly Spanish. There is a substantial *mestizo* minority, especially in Guanacaste province. Only about 2,600 Indians remain, most of them on isolated reservations out of contact with the bulk of the population. About 15,000 Negroes and mulattoes live in the province of Limón on the Caribbean coast.

Spanish is Costa Rica's national language, although English is used as a first language by a large proportion of the descendants of the

Jamaicans living on the Atlantic coast. The government supports the Roman Catholic church and contributes to its maintenance, but the constitution guarantees freedom for all religions that do not oppose universal morality or "good customs." Most of the population is nominally or actively Catholic, but there are small organized groups of Protestants and Jews.

Costa Rica has fostered education, and as a result it has one of the most literate populations in Latin America. In 1964, 24.8 percent of the government's annual budget was spent for public education. Only in rural areas is education a problem; by 1963 illiteracy had gone down to just over 6 percent in the urban areas, but was about 22 percent in the rural areas. The 1963 census showed that 84 percent of the population over ten years of age was literate. Costa Rica's poverty has prevented it from having an even better educational system than it now has. Although it has surpassed its neighbors, there is a very large dropout rate each school year, and only a small fraction of those entering the first grade graduate from high school. In 1963, of the economically active population only 4 percent had completed secondary school and 3 percent had university degrees.

Costa Rica is primarily an agricultural country (about half the economically active population is occupied in agriculture and related activities), yet most of the country's area is not utilized. About 36 percent of the land is in farms, but of this amount only 12.3 percent was reported arable in 1950. This percentage gave Costa Rica 931 persons per square mile of arable land, a rather high amount. There is a great need for the development of some of the thousands of square miles of uncleared public land into additional farmland. Coffee is the leading crop, followed by bananas, cocoa, sugar, cattle, and Manila hemp. Dairy farming, poultry raising, and fishing supply the local market. Some gold and salt are the most important minerals. Manufacturing is on a small scale. A number of international educational institutions bring income from outside the country, the most important being the OAS' Inter-American Institute of Agricultural Sciences, the UN's Graduate School of Public Administration for Central America and Panama, and a Protestant missionary language school. The Central American Common Market has stimulated industrialization, but this effort has been hampered by constant changes in government programs as the National Liberation Party and its opponents alternated in control of the executive.

Costa Rica's main problem is its poverty. Despite the importance of agriculture, domestic food prices are high. Transportation is inadequately developed, especially in areas outside of the *meseta central*. It is still impossible to go by automobile from the *meseta central* to the Caribbean coast. Housing is poor for many, with 41 percent of all homes having only one room and 31 percent having no water supply. Unemployment in 1963 was estimated at 8 percent of the economically active population, and there is high seasonal unemployment. Yet, in comparison to its neighbors, Costa Rica is doing well. Its 1965 per capita domestic product of $416 was the highest in Central America and exceeded the regional median by more than 25 percent. Why this is so will be clear after we have surveyed Costa Rica's development since independence.

The Development of Modern Costa Rica

A more pitiful picture than that of the people of Costa Rica at the beginning of the eighteenth century it would be hard to imagine [writes Chester Lloyd Jones]. The country population lived in unbelievable ignorance and squalor. The growth of the population and greater extension of agriculture did not make the community stronger, for local manufactures had not developed and trade with the outside world was so small in volume that it did not provide the minimum of imported goods necessary for civilized life. The poorer people of Cartago had been forced to go to the adjacent country districts to take up small farms to keep themselves from starving. Many of them had to clothe themselves with bark of trees for lack of textiles. Families for years did not go to church for lack of clothes.[1]

The condition described by Professor Jones was the pattern of life in Costa Rica all through colonial days. With neither mineral wealth nor a docile Indian population to make it interesting to Spanish eyes, Costa Rica was one of the stepchildren of the empire. What agriculture existed was subsistence farming. When Costa Rica became an independent state it had less than 70,000 inhabitants, and it remained an isolated and poverty-stricken community until the middle of the century. It was not until the development of coffee production during the nineteenth century that change came, for coffee at last gave the country something that could be sold on the world market. With the income from coffee, Costa Rica began to import the products of Europe and the United States. Coffee also stimulated the improvement of communica-

---

[1] Chester Lloyd Jones, *Costa Rica and Civilization in the Caribbean* (Madison: University of Wisconsin Press, 1935), p. 17.

tions, and eventually railroads linked San José with both the Caribbean port of Limón and the Pacific port of Puntarenas. The rise of coffee production did not, however, mean that the heritage of centuries disappeared overnight.

During the nineteenth century, government in Costa Rica was the monopoly of a small aristocracy. From the gaining of independence till 1889, popular representation in government was nonexistent or only of the most formal sort. The election of 1889 was the first in the country's history in which freedom of speech was guaranteed. The people were aroused during this presidential campaign and from then on were a factor to be considered. This is not to say that democracy came to Costa Rica in that year, for it did not. Political habits change slowly, and after so many years oligarchic rule was well entrenched. Constitutional literacy and financial requirements for election to office remained in force until 1949. Suspension of the guarantees of civil liberty, refusal by the executive to respect decisions of the courts, arbitrary imprisonments, exiling of adversaries by the government, controlled elections, dictatorships, attempted and successful coups d'état, violence—all these can be observed in Costa Rica after 1889, but not with the frequency of previous years.

It was not until 1913 that a constitutional amendment provided for the direct election of the president and the legislature. Until that date popular conventions were held in the various localities to elect a limited number of electors, who then met in a body called the Electoral Assembly and elected the president, the legislature, and the local government officials. To be a member of the Electoral Assembly, one had to be over twenty-one, literate, a resident of the province in which elected, and possessed of not less than 500 colones or an annual income of not less than C200. It is estimated that about 70 percent of all adults were included in the list of those eligible, but, generally speaking, those elected were the wealthier men in the community.

Even after the introduction of popular elections, the great majority of the people took little interest in political affairs. A small group of landowners, professional men, and politicians continued to dominate the government. This small group was divided into cliques coalescing around leaders of the typical *caudillo* type, except that in Costa Rica military men were not conspicuous, since there was only a very small army and little money to develop a larger one.[2]

Only a part of the eligible population voted in the elections. The

[2] The description given here is paraphrased from Dana G. Munro, *The Five Republics of Central America* (New York: Oxford University Press, 1918), pp. 150–56.

average number of registered voters from 1889 to 1949 has been estimated at about 20 percent of the country's population. Of this 20 percent, some 80 percent usually voted in each election, or about one in
every six persons in the country. This was the average election; sometimes the proportion decreased to one in nine or one in ten.[3]

Costa Rica had no merit system for selecting government employees;
each winning political clique could award the spoils of office to its followers, and then finance subsequent campaigns by compulsory assess-
ments upon government employees. No political programs had any
importance; each politician sought office for the power and the money
it could bring him. Politicians transferred their allegiance from one
clique to another overnight. The so-called political parties had no real
organizational structure, just as they had no permanent ideas.

Alberto Quijano Quesada, writing in 1939, has well described the
Costa Rican political party system as it operated until that time:

> Political parties with definite ideas do not exist in Costa Rica.
> Every four years, in the year before the presidential term expires,
> as many groups organize themselves for the electoral campaign
> that is about to begin as there are candidates. The political parties
> organize themselves around a man of merit and sufficient prestige
> to attract public attention. The distinction between the parties
> is reduced to adding the syllables *ista* to the name of the candidate,
> and with this and an emblem of one or more colors, the party is
> ready to enter fully into an ardent struggle, utilizing the press,
> personal propaganda, speeches, parades, and insults to the op-
> posing candidates. . . . The struggle ended, the waters regain
> their normal level, the insults are forgotten, the enthusiasm dies
> down, and life returns to its normal condition of complete tran-
> quillity, to repeat itself with the same procedure four years later
> with another name and its indispensable *ista*.[4]

The man who became president as a result of this process had almost
absolute control of the government. He appointed all administrative
officials, dominated the Legislative Assembly, and controlled the money
allocated to public works. The courts were fairly independent; the
Supreme Court was elected by the Legislative Assembly every four years
at the middle of the president's term, and its justices appointed and

---

[3] Juan Rafael Guzmán, "Datos estadísticos sobre las elecciones habidas en Costa Rica
desde Noviembre de 1889 hasta el 2 de Octubre de 1949," *Diario de Costa Rica*, July 24, 1953,
p. 17.

[4] Alberto Quijano Quesada, *Costa Rica ayer y hoy: 1800–1939* (San José: Editorial
Borrasé Hnos., 1939), p. 33; my translation.

removed the subordinate judges in all parts of the country. But local administration was highly centralized and dominated by the president.

On the bright side, law and order were fairly well maintained during this period, education flourished, and the population increased at a fairly rapid rate. All these factors contributed to the creation of a more alert public opinion, and when new conditions developed, the people of Costa Rica were ready to meet the challenge. It is difficult to state with certainty just what were the factors that led to the new developments, but I would hazard the opinion that the following were most important: In the first place, Costa Rica was always too poor to afford the luxury of an army of any size and did not participate in the wars of independence. Thus a stimulus for the development of militarism and a society dominated by a military caste was lacking. In the second place, although landownership was typically uneven, most Costa Ricans received some education. By our standards it would be considered very little, but even a little is better than none at all.

A few figures will illustrate the pattern of landownership in Costa Rica. The agricultural census of 1963 revealed that there were 64,621 farms in the country when it had a population of 1,333,432. Thus, just over 5 percent of the population owned farms. Of these 64,621 farms, 419, or 0.0064 percent, were more than 1,000 *manzanas*[5] in area and contained 31 percent of the country's farmland. In 1963 there were fifty-nine farms of more than 3,500 *manzanas* each, employing 21,771 workers. In coffee production, about 6 percent of all the farms, each of which was larger than 100 *manzanas*, included 36 percent of all the land in coffee and produced about half the country's crop. Near Cartago there is a farm called Aguiares, extending over 1,372 *manzanas*. In 1950–51 there were living on Aguiares 137 families, totaling 664 people, in which the men worked as day laborers, and 78 families, totaling 547 people, in which the men worked as sharecroppers. From 1940 to 1950, this one farm had an average annual production of 1.4 percent of all the coffee grown in Costa Rica. With this pattern of landownership, poverty for the masses under an aristocratic landowning class was inevitable.

Throughout the nineteenth century and the first half of the twentieth, the country did not produce enough food for its population, and importation of food further impoverished most of the population. Foreigners practically monopolized business, banking, and the most important agricultural enterprises. There were far too few engineers and agricultural technicians and too many lawyers and politicians. The

---

[5] A *manzana* equals 1.727 acres.

government spent its time handling foreign relations, operating schools, and preserving law and order. No planning for the future was done. In short, Costa Rica was only one more sleepy Central American republic.

But with the world depression of the 1930's, when the drop in the prices of coffee and bananas lowered the people's already low living standards, the fact that a fairly high proportion had some education stimulated intelligent thought about the problems of the country. As in many other areas of the world, a portion of the thinking population embraced communism, but—and this is one of the things that sets Costa Rica apart—the majority of the students, teachers, and other thinking persons rejected the political pattern of the Soviets and turned their efforts to a searching examination of their own country. Slowly three distinct ideological groups developed and became the protagonists in the political struggle that led to the creation of a democratic political system.

The group that controlled the government of Costa Rica from 1940 to 1948 included most of the traditional politicians and most of the wealthy landowners, who were primarily interested in power and preserving the status quo. Led by Dr. Calderón Guardia, who was president from 1940 to 1944, this group functioned through the National Republican Party. Dr. Calderón Guardia, forty-two years old when he was elected in 1940, was so skillful a politician that no other important political leader ran against him, and he received 100,000 of the 110,000 votes cast in the election.

The second most important group active in politics during and just after World War II was the Communist Party, which had been founded in 1929 by Manuel Mora, a nineteen-year-old university student. During the 1930's the Communist Party was practically the only outspoken supporter of the rights of the workers and poor peasants. In addition, Mora won the support of many of the more socially conscious university students. In 1933 Mora was elected to the national legislature and in 1934 he led a strike of about 15,000 workers against the United Fruit Company and won concessions for the workers. In 1936 the Communist Party received 4,500 of the 85,500 votes cast in a national election. It published a weekly newspaper and functioned freely. Despite these achievements, the Communist Party did not grow spectacularly until its cooperation with the government during the war gave it a golden opportunity.

The third group active in Costa Rican politics had its roots in two different social groups. Certain college professors and their students, led by Professor Carlos Monge Alfaro, had begun to meet to discuss the problems facing the country, and these informal discussions grew into a formal organization, the Center for the Study of National Problems. At the same time, a group of businessmen and farm operators also were meeting to discuss the country's problems, and out of these meetings grew an organization known as Democratic Action. Both the Center for the Study of National Problems and Democratic Action looked to a more democratic form of government as the mechanism that would permit the country's economy to be reorganized and modernized. Both organizations believed that the creation of permanent ideological political parties was a necessity if democratic government was to be strengthened in Costa Rica.

Dr. Calderón Guardia's administration was inefficient, corrupt, and riddled with nepotism. His father, for example, was the first vice-president and his brother was the third vice-president. Calderón Guardia soon lost his popularity and, seeking support, turned to the growing Communist Party. The Communists were ready to cooperate with him. When Hitler broke his 1939 pact with Stalin and sent his troops into the Soviet Union in 1941, Communist policy all over the world changed. Since Calderón Guardia had declared war on Germany even before the United States Congress, the Communists supported him vigorously as part of their world program of supporting all governments opposed to the enemies of the Soviet Union.

During the period in which Calderón Guardia cooperated with the Communists, he claimed he was a liberal and supported various laws of the type known as liberal: paid vacations for workers, unemployment insurance, an income tax, social security, workmen's compensation. Much of this legislation, sponsored by the Catholic archbishop of San José, was enacted during the 1940's, and the Communists helped to set up and to staff the organizations created to carry it out. At the same time, however, Calderón Guardia's government included old-style politicians who were accused of feathering their nests at the public's expense. This group apparently had no objection to advanced social legislation since much of it remained unenforced. Thus the Costa Rican government was a curious amalgam of the National Republican Party, consisting of the largest landowners and the traditional politicians, and the Communist Party.

The first dramatic act in the unfolding struggle came in 1942. Calderón Guardia and his policies caused much discontent. On July 2 of that year, a German submarine sank a United Fruit Company vessel in Puerto Limón, killing several Costa Rican longshoremen unloading the vessel. This action stimulated anti-German riots in San José, which caused much property destruction. On July 8 José Figueres, one of the leaders of Democratic Action, an unknown farmer who had never been active in politics, began a speech over a San José radio station attacking the government and suggesting that if it could not keep German submarines out of the harbor of Puerto Limón or destructive mobs off the streets of San José, it ought to resign for the good of the country. The speech was never finished. When he was halfway through it the police burst into the radio station; the audience heard curses, shouts, scufflings, then silence. In a few seconds it was announced that Señor Figueres' speech had been canceled by order of the chief of police.

Figueres was jailed, accused of being a Fascist, and exiled. From that time on the government became increasingly tyrannical and the Communists increased their influence, gaining important posts in the leadership of the trade-union movement and in the public service. In addition, the hierarchy of the Roman Catholic church seemed to be giving them unofficial support. The Communist Party had announced its support of the social policies of President Calderón Guardia based on the papal encyclicals. It also changed its name, in 1943, to *Partido Vanguardia Popular* in an attempt to avoid the stigma attached to the name Communist. When the Communist leaders addressed a letter to the archbishop of San José asking him if there were any obstacles to a Catholic's collaborating with the *Partido Vanguardia Popular,* the archbishop replied that he thought all parties were equal and a Catholic could support or oppose any of them.

In 1944 Teodoro Picado, a friend of Calderón Guardia, won the presidency after a violent campaign in which at least nine were killed and many wounded in various riots. In a small country with a peaceful tradition, this is a large number of deaths. The opposition, which supported former President León Cortés, claimed that their candidate had won the election but the votes were fraudulently counted.

The political forces of the country maintained the alignment first formed for this electoral campaign of 1944. Various individuals were to change sides, but basically the political struggle in Costa Rica found Calderón Guardia and his personal following allied with the richest landowners in the country and the Communist Party. Each of these three groups had a different objective, but they managed to cooperate for more than twenty years. Against this alignment were the students and most of their professors, the majority of the members of the newly emerging middle class, the small farmers and farm workers, and those moneyed people who were interested in developing manufacturing and improving the economy. The struggle between these two factions became increasingly sharp as time went on.

José Figueres returned to Costa Rica after Picado was elected president. Living as an exile in Mexico, Figueres had decided to devote his full energies to politics, and had sharpened his ideas in discussions with the Mexicans and by extensive reading. On March 11, 1945, he and his friends succeeded in uniting Democratic Action and the Center for the Study of National Problems into a new organization, the Social Democratic Party. Led by Figueres, the Social Democrats organized the opposition to the incumbent government. Attempts were made to secure arms for a revolution, but these failed. The opposition to the government grew, however, until the 1948 election campaign ended in a civil war.

The 1948 presidential election was the great turning point in Costa Rican politics. The National Republican Party nominated former President Calderón Guardia. The Social Democratic Party combined with all other opponents of the Picado regime behind the candidacy of a conservative newspaper publisher, Otilio Ulate. The government made little effort to preserve law and order during the campaign. The Communists demonstrated their support of Calderón Guardia by breaking up the campaign meetings of the united opposition, and the police also interfered with Ulate's campaigning. Tension grew until a protest strike against the government brought almost all business and other activity to a halt. The strike was called off only when the government agreed to have the police guard the polls under the direction of a commander selected by the Supreme Tribunal of Elections, the body that controlled the election machinery.

When the votes were counted on February 8, 1948, Ulate had won a majority, but on March 1 the holdover legislature, by a vote of 27 to 19, canceled the election, and the police arrested Ulate, killing one of the leaders of the Social Democratic Party during the arrest. José Figueres abandoned the capital city and with nine others raised the banner of revolt at his farm in a mountain valley to the south of Cartago. In the short but bitter civil war that followed, about 2,000 persons were killed. On one side were the government of Picado, the army, Calderón Guardia and his friends, and the Communist Party. Against them were united the democratic-minded people of Costa Rica. Over a portable broadcasting station, Figueres appealed to the people to join him in a fight for liberty and honest elections. Intellectuals, students, teachers, businessmen, farmers, people of all sorts, many of whom had never fired a gun, joined the revolution. Commercial planes were commandeered to create an air force. To complicate the issue, the then dictatorial governments of Nicaragua and Honduras aided the Picado–Calderón Guardia–Communist forces, and the then democratic governments of Guatemala and Cuba and the democratic exiles of the Dominican Republic aided the revolutionary forces. The civilian army led by Figueres defeated the government army within a few weeks, and Picado, Calderón Guardia, Manuel Mora, and many other leaders of the defeated government left the country.

Figueres became the president of the founding junta of the Second Republic of Costa Rica on May 8, 1948. Under his leadership an election was held to create a constituent assembly which wrote a new constitution, and the army of Costa Rica was abolished. Other measures helped to enrage Figueres' opponents: the Communist Party was outlawed; all the banks in the country were nationalized; a small levy was assessed against the rich to raise the funds needed to repair the damage caused by the civil war; the machinery of government was overhauled and the beginning of a merit system for government employees was introduced. This reorganization of the government's personnel policies was one of the most important actions of the junta and led to the creation, in 1953, of a modern personnel system controlled by an independent agency. By 1967 a career service for government employees was an accepted feature of Costa Rican life, although the civil service system did not cover all government employees. The new constitution also enfranchised women for the first time.

The junta that governed Costa Rica from May 1948 to November 1949 was supported by the majority of the population. The elements defeated in the civil war of 1948, however, never reconciled themselves to their defeat. After the Costa Rican army was disbanded, on December 10, 1948, about 300 armed men invaded Costa Rica from Nicaragua. In two weeks the armyless country, infuriated at the connivance of Nicaragua's dictator, General Somoza, with Figueres' opponents, defeated the invaders. On April 2, 1949, there was another armed revolt, this time in San José. This was put down in one day. These events are worthy of notice because they illustrate one of the chief difficulties in the establishment of stable constitutional government in Latin America: the defenders of the status quo apparently cannot visualize a world in which they do not preserve their privileged position, and refuse to give up and recognize a reorganization of their countries no matter how many times they are outvoted or defeated in civil wars.

On November 8, 1949, Figueres turned his office over to Ulate, who had been elected in 1948, and retired from office, taking his cabinet ministers with him into private life. As Figueres explained: "The health of democracy in Latin America demands that men who have seized power by force go home when normalcy is restored. We restored normalcy and we went home."[6]

The period during which the junta controlled Costa Rica demonstrated that the Social Democratic Party's alliance with President Ulate and his supporters could not endure. The Social Democratic Party wanted to revolutionize Costa Rica; all Ulate and his friends apparently wanted was an electoral system that would enable them to win power. As a result, by 1953 Ulate and Calderón Guardia were united against Figueres and his followers.

During the years from 1949 to 1953, while Ulate was president, Calderón Guardia, Picado, and most of their closest associates remained outside of Costa Rica, although Manuel Mora and the other Communist leaders returned and became active in politics again. During Ulate's years as president coffee was bringing a good price on the world market and the country was fairly peaceful, although the Calderón Guardia supporters and the Communists did attempt two revolts during the Ulate presidency—on August 12, 1950, and again in February 1951. The President was a traditional politician who had opposed Calderón Guardia because he could not get elected under the election system used in 1944 and 1948. His sympathies, however, were not in favor of the radical reforms sponsored by Figueres and his friends.

When Figueres retired from office, he did not retire from politics. With his friends he created a new organization, the National Liberation Party, and set out to win support. The new party's program was simple but ambitious: it proposed to strengthen democratic government and to abolish poverty in Costa Rica. By 1952, when it became evident that the new party would probably elect Figueres president in 1953, all the opponents of its program united in an attempt to prevent Figueres' victory. Thus the supporters of Calderón Guardia, the Communists, and the supporters of Ulate, who had been allied with Figueres in the 1948 civil war, all supported the same candidate. As a result the election campaign of 1953 was a very bitter struggle. Although much of the turmoil turned on false issues, there was a clear division in the population. Figueres was trying to win power for a reformist movement that proposed to transform Costa Rica. His program was popular and he was popular with the people. His opposition, therefore, simply ignored the Figueres program and talked in contradictory generalities, claiming that Figueres was a Communist, a Fascist, a would-be dictator. How a group supported by

6 José Figueres, "Peaceful Costa Rica, the First Battleground" (address delivered at Rollins College, Winter Park, Florida, 1952), p. 10.

the Communist Party expected to gain votes by accusing its opponents of being Communists cannot be explained. Each group opposing Figueres had its own reasons for its position, but each was able to concentrate upon its opposition to Figueres and to forget its differences with its allies. When the votes were counted, José Figueres was the winner by a two-to-one majority and his party had won thirty of the forty-five seats in the Legislative Assembly as well as control of most of the local government machinery.

The years between 1953 and 1958 saw much change in Costa Rica. Figueres wanted to diversify the country's agriculture, spur industrialization, improve and extend social security, improve housing, and build public works. At the same time, he wanted to transform the governmental machinery so that it would continue to function democratically even if his own party were to lose an election in the future. Although he did not succeed in accomplishing everything he set out to do, his administration did succeed in so stimulating economic activity that the national income rose from $216,667,000 in 1953 to $287,879,000 in 1957, an increase of 33 percent. So much construction took place that the appearance of almost every city was changed. Highways were built, the most important being the completion, with the help of a grant from the United States government, of the Inter-American Highway from the Nicaraguan border to south of San José, thus making possible land communication between Costa Rica and its northern neighbors. The tax upon the United Fruit Company's profits was raised from 15 to 30 percent and the additional income was devoted to public works; one of the most important of them doubled the amount of electricity produced in the country. Additional agricultural experimental stations were set up and the production of beef cattle, rice, and sugar jumped until they were being exported, whereas before they had been imported. The merit system for government employees was strengthened and extended. Several autonomous organizations were created to handle some of the nonpolitical functions undertaken by the government.

Yet despite the improvement in the country's economic system and the consequent raising of the standard of living for the entire population, the opposition to Figueres continued. A vicious newspaper campaign conducted by former President Ulate in his *Diario de Costa Rica* culminated in the invasion of the country on January 11, 1955. This was a well-organized and well-financed project, the money apparently having been supplied by the then dictator of Venezuela, Marcos Pérez Jiménez, and the leadership coming from ex-Presidents Calderón Guardia and Picado. The son of ex-President Picado, who had been graduated from the United States Military Academy at West Point, was the field commander of the invading army. The Costa Rican National Guard, with the support of the Organization of American States, was able to smash the invasion in a short time.

By 1957, when it became time to prepare for the presidential election of February 1958, the National Liberation Party had split over the issue of continued reforms. Figueres and the majority of the party believed that more reforms were needed. The richer businessmen among those who had been supporting Figueres thought that the time had come to stop introducing innovations and let the country settle down. This group formed the Independent Party and nominated Jorge Rossi, who had been a minister in Figueres' cabinet, for president. The Calderón Guardia forces under the name of the National Republican Party combined with ex-President Ulate and his National Union Party and the Communist Party behind the candidacy of Mario Echandi, a rich landowner. The National Liberation Party nominated Francisco Orlich.

The campaign for the presidency was an extremely bitter one, although it was peaceful. Figueres was accused of being a dictator, a Communist, and a traitor to Costa Rica. Most of his opposition apparently wanted to go back to the "good old days" when politics was a gentleman's game and the bulk of the population did not participate. Figueres and his friends presented a platform of additional reforms needed by the country and promised to continue their efforts to abolish poverty. To prevent any charge of stealing an election it confidently expected to win, the Figueres government asked the United Nations to recommend a team of observers to witness that the election was fair.

To everyone's surprise, Echandi was elected president by a small plurality, receiving 104,500 votes. Orlich received 98,400 and Rossi 23,910. No party had a majority in the Legislative Assembly. The National Liberation Party had twenty seats, the National Republicans had eleven, the National Union had ten, the Independent Party had three, and the Civic Revolutionary Party, a minor splinter group, had one seat. Two of the Independents and the Civic Revolutionary representative voted with the National Liberation Party to give control of the legislature to the followers of Figueres.

Various factors contributed to the National Liberation Party's defeat in the election. An economic recession in the United States contributed to a drastic fall in the price of coffee and slowed down Costa Rica's economy, and the Liberation Party was blamed. The split in the party drained off votes, and the party suffered from overconfidence, probably as a result of the large majority Figueres had won in 1953. In addition, the party's candidate, Francisco Orlich, did not have the charismatic attraction for voters that Figueres had had in the previous election.

President Echandi took office faced by a legislature in which his party held only ten of the forty-five seats and his faction of the party had only five seats. His program, therefore, had little chance of being accepted, nor would he accept the program of the legislative majority. As a result, by March 3, 1961, he had vetoed sixty-five bills passed by the legislature, more than all the previous Costa Rican presidents combined had vetoed. The President was overridden on only seven of these vetoes, and Costa Rica had to learn to live with opposing parties controlling the executive and legislative branches of government.

When President Echandi's term expired the coalition he had organized fell apart, and four candidates ran for the presidency with nine parties offering candidates for the Legislative Assembly. After a hectic campaign, Francisco Orlich was elected, with the votes divided as follows: Orlich (National Liberation Party), 177,681; Calderón Guardia (National Republican Party), 122,534; Otilio Ulate (National Union Party), 46,909; Obregón (Popular Democratic Action Party), 2,977. The National Liberation Party elected twenty-nine deputies to gain a majority in the Legislative Assembly.

President Orlich took office on May 8, 1962. He was faced with a great crisis when the volcano Irazú erupted in March 1963 and began to rain ashes on some of the country's most fertile land. By January 1964 the almost continuous stream of ashes had created a most serious situation in and around San José. Yet the economy of the country continued to grow. President Orlich announced Costa Rica's adherence to the treaties setting up the Central American Common Market on July 23, 1962, and energetically pushed the movement for union.

When the new elections took place in February 1966, the opposition to the National Liberation Party once again united, this time behind the candidacy of a university professor, José Joaquín Trejos Fernández. The National Liberation Party nominated Daniel Oduber Quirós. Just as in the 1953, 1958, and 1962 elections, the campaign was bitter. The various factions supporting Trejos ran on a platform that consisted of calling Oduber a Communist. The National Liberation Party advocated increased development of the country and spent most of its energy in refighting the 1948 civil war. To the surprise of the National Liberation leaders, Trejos won with 222,012 votes against 217,514 votes for Daniel Oduber. It is interesting to note that in every election in Costa Rica from 1948 to 1966, the candidate supported by the incumbent president has lost. This may demonstrate an unusual facet of the Costa Rican personality, but it also demonstrates that the country has developed a political system that truly can be called democratic.

The Formal Constitutional Framework

Costa Rica is governed under the constitution of November 7, 1949, which describes Costa Rica as a free, independent, democratic republic. This constitution, Costa Rica's ninth, was a product of the 1948 civil war. The victors in that struggle wanted a new constitution for two reasons: it was to be a symbol of the new regime, and it was to create a governmental system that would not permit the usurpation of power the older document had allowed. A determined effort was made by the Constituent Assembly, therefore, to incorporate within the new document every possible safeguard to preserve democracy in Costa Rica and limit the power of the president. Yet Costa Rica's 1949 constitution is not a true reflection of the thinking of the victors in the 1948 civil war, because the election of the members of the Constituent Assembly gave the supporters of Ulate a majority. Figueres and his closest associates were all involved in the administration of the government and did not compete in the elections. In addition, the *Figueristas* at that time had not yet constructed a political party strong enough to elect many members of the assembly. As a result, they won only three of the forty-five seats in the assembly that wrote the new constitution. The Constituent Assembly discarded the draft constitution prepared by the revolutionary junta government headed by Figueres and used the 1871 constitution as the basis for the new document.

As the years went by, many of the leaders of the National Liberation Party attributed their failure to achieve all they wished to the legal framework created by the 1949 constitution. Their most important criticism is that it preserved the traditional rights of property by requiring a two-thirds vote of the legislature in order to pass laws affecting property. This makes it very difficult for the legislature to pass the kind of advanced social legislation the National Liberation Party favors, even when the party has a majority in the legislature.

The 1949 constitution sets up a presidential type of government that is popular, representative, alternative, and responsible. It is divided into three distinct and independent parts, the legislative, the executive, and the judicial. Although there is a clear division of powers, the Supreme Court can declare the acts of the legislative and executive powers unconstitutional by a two-thirds majority.

An interesting feature of the governmental system is the constitutional status given to autonomous institutions, which thus in effect become a fourth branch of government. The autonomous institutions are self-governing organizations, each of which directs an activity the constitution or Legislative Assembly sought to remove from the vagaries of political strife. Among them are an organization to regulate and control elections, the state banking monopoly, the state insurance monopoly, a land-reform organization, and various economic enterprises, the most important of which are a railroad, a housing corporation, an electricity company, and a tourist-promotion corporation. New autonomous institutions can be created by a vote of two-thirds of the total membership of the Legislative Assembly. Each is controlled by a board of directors, who are, except for the Electoral Tribunal, appointed by the Council of Government for staggered terms. Most boards have five directors serving for five years with one director's term expiring each year. In many of the autonomous institutions, a cabinet minister is an ex-officio member of the board of directors to coordinate the activity of the agency with the policies of the government.

Costa Rica's constitution is in the spirit of Latin-American constitutionalism. A decided fear of dictatorship results in the inclusion of clauses that seek to bar perpetuation in office of an individual, a family, or a group. All of the high officials of the government are barred while in office from running for legislative positions or for the presidency. At the same time, there is a staggered system of officeholding, which makes it more difficult for a party or a group to gain control of all of the branches of the government at the same time. The president and the members of the legislature serve four-year terms; most of the directors of the autonomous institutions have either four- or five-year terms; the budget director and the members of the Supreme Tribunal of Elections serve six-year terms; the Supreme Court justices, the comptroller general, and the assistant comptroller general are elected for eight-year terms. Although the president and members of the legislature cannot be immediately reelected, the others can.

Several other attempts are made in the constitution to prevent the development of a dictatorship. The president, his ministers, and all government employees are barred from interfering with or participating in election campaigns. Any government employee found participating in partisan political activity is, by constitutional mandate, to be removed from his position at once and is subject to whatever additional penalties the courts may decide. If the president, a minister, a diplomat, the comptroller general, the assistant comptroller general, or a justice of the Supreme Court is discovered to be politically partial during an election, he is not removed from office, but the case is submitted to the Legislative

Assembly. A permanent army is outlawed; the only armed force permitted is a police force of 2,700 men (the National Guard). Foreigners are not permitted to participate in political affairs, and no one may raise religious issues in political campaigns or claim to be discussing religion when discussing politics.

How the Constitution Is Amended

The Costa Rican constitution can be amended if the Legislative Assembly favors the change by a two-thirds vote in two consecutive sessions. A proposed amendment must be submitted to the Assembly with the signatures of at least ten deputies. It is then read to the Assembly three times with the readings six days apart. If the majority then thinks the proposal has merit, it goes to a committee that brings in a report within eight days. If the Assembly then favors the proposal by a two-thirds vote, it is submitted to the president of the republic for his recommendation. In the next session of the Assembly, if the proposed amendment—after again being debated three times—passes by a two-thirds vote, it becomes part of the constitution. A general revision of the entire constitution follows the same procedure, but in addition a constitutional convention is called to vote on the general revision.

Although this may seem to be a discouragingly involved procedure, the constitution has been amended a number of times. The most important changes affected Article 96, dealing with the financing of political parties; Articles 157 and 159, dealing with the Supreme Court; Article 171, dealing with local government; Article 177, dealing with the budget; and Article 106, dealing with the term in office of the members of the legislature. The basic responsibility for amending the constitution rests with the Legislative Assembly and the executive cannot veto amendments passed by the legislature. When Articles 93, 95, 100, and 177 were amended on May 20, 1959, the Council of Government stated that it was proclaiming the new amendments only because it had to; the council was of the opinion that the Legislative Assembly had not followed the constitutional procedure set forth in Article 195 in adopting these amendments. Nevertheless, the new amendments were incorporated into the constitution.

Who Participates in Politics

A majority of Costa Rica's adult population participates in the political life of the country. Since 1959 voting has been compulsory, and failure to vote is punished by a fine of C5 (about $0.75 in United States money).

The number of voters has risen rapidly, from 197,489 in 1953 to 439,526 in 1966. About 579,000 were registered in 1966, out of a population of around 1,450,000, or almost 40 percent. Since more than 50 percent of Costa Rica's population is below voting age, the 40 percent who voted in 1966 represent an overwhelming majority of the country's voting-age population.

To vote one must be a citizen more than twenty years of age and inscribed in the Civil Register. There are no literacy or property qualifications. Naturalized citizens can vote twelve months after naturalization. A few persons have lost their right to vote by judicial decree, but the overwhelming majority of the adult population is eligible to vote and most of them have been listed in the electoral rolls during the 1950's and 1960's.

The Electoral Machinery

In an attempt to take the electoral machinery out of the hands of partisan politicians, the Costa Rican constitution of 1949 placed control of elections in the hands of an autonomous organization, the Supreme Tribunal of Elections. This body consists of three persons who are elected by a two-thirds vote of the Supreme Court. To qualify for election, candidates for the tribunal must possess the same qualifications as Supreme Court justices: they must be citizens, laymen, older than thirty-five years, and lawyers who have practiced their profession for at least ten years. Three substitute members are also elected by the Supreme Court. The members and substitute members of the Supreme Tribunal of Elections are chosen for six-year terms, one member and one substitute every two years. The members of the electoral tribunal can be reelected and are subject to the same responsibilities and enjoy the same immunities and prerogatives as the president, the members of the Legislative Assembly, and the justices of the Supreme Court.

The constitution assigns the following duties to the Supreme Tribunal of Elections:

1. To organize elections.
2. To appoint the members of the electoral board who administer electoral machinery.
3. To have the exclusive right to interpret all constitutional provisions and legislative acts dealing with electoral matters.
4. To act upon appeals from the decisions of the Civil Register and the various electoral boards.
5. To investigate charges by the political parties that government employees to whom such activities are forbidden are active in politics, and to decide such cases.

6. To give the armed forces the instructions necessary to ensure a free election.
7. To check the election returns and to make the decision as to who have been elected president, vice-president, deputies, and members of the municipal councils.

There is no appeal from the decisions of the Supreme Tribunal of Elections except in those cases where there has been a betrayal of trust. Another activity of the electoral tribunal is to supervise the Civil Register, an agency assigned the task of making up the lists of voters, handling requests for the acquisition and regaining of citizenship, and issuing the identification booklets all citizens are required to have.

As is evident from their duties, the three members of the Supreme Tribunal of Elections supervise a large organization. Elections are held every four years, but the work of the tribunal is continuous, especially that of the Civil Register, which is actually the department of vital statistics of Costa Rica, since it keeps records of all births, marriages, and deaths within the country. The issuance of identification booklets is also a continuous process, as they must be renewed every ten years. This office also handles the paperwork connected with naturalization and other citizenship matters.

The constitutional principles that govern the exercise of the suffrage in Costa Rica are these: the electoral function is to be autonomous, i.e., independent of the executive branch of the government; the governmental authorities are to guarantee liberty, order, purity, and impartiality in the law governing elections; each voter is to be identified by an identification booklet containing his photograph; a citizen cannot vote except in the district in which his home is located at the time he receives his identification booklet; and minorities are to be guaranteed representation.

One other constitutional provision is designed to make it difficult for the legislature or the executive to interfere with a free election. All legislation dealing with elections is referred to the electoral tribunal, and its opinion must be followed unless at least two-thirds of the membership of the Legislative Assembly votes otherwise. During the six months prior to and the four months after an election, the Legislative Assembly cannot vote any law dealing with elections to which the electoral tribunal has not given its assent.

Elections are governed by carefully drawn rules adopted by the Legislative Assembly, and severe penalties are provided for any infraction of these rules. One can register at any time except just before an election. The election takes place on the first Sunday in February of an election year. All places selling liquor are closed and sealed the day before, the day of, and the day after an election. Most voting places are in schools and voting hours are from five A.M. to six P.M. When the polls close, the votes are counted and reported to the electoral tribunal, which scrutinizes the returns and announces the official results. To prevent the election of a minority president, the winner must have obtained at least 40 percent of the votes cast; otherwise a run-off election is held on the first Sunday in April between the two front-running candidates. Another unusual provision in the Costa Rican constitution requires that when two candidates receive a tie vote, if this is over 40 percent of the votes cast, the oldest will be declared elected.

Campaigning for Office

Election campaigns are colored by the country's customs, but they are not too different from campaigns in other democratic countries. The press, radio, and television are utilized, literature is distributed in large quantities, and demonstrations and mass meetings are organized to rouse the enthusiasm of the faithful and impress the opposition. And just as happens in many other countries, straw men are set up as targets of each political party's campaign activity.

The most popular campaign device used in Costa Rica is sheer repetition. One advertisement never suffices. Every radio speech is announced in newspaper advertisements for days before its delivery. Sometimes the same advertisement appears two, three, four times on different pages of one issue of a newspaper. And the advertisements, leaflets, and booklets are all similar, driving home the same point over and over again. With the repetition comes an effort to convince the public that the party is sure to win. The most common method is to print long lists of "adhesions"; that is, names of persons who support the party. In the United States such testimonials usually come from persons with some kind of public reputation, but in Costa Rica sheer quantity seems to be the idea. Adherence to a party is also demonstrated by posting a picture of a candidate on the wall or window of one's home facing the street or highway. The more enthusiastic partisans fly the party flag in front of their homes or completely cover the front of the building with posters and pictures. Lapel buttons and bumper signs on automobiles are also popular.

Another technique used to impress voters is to print the pictures of the party mass meetings in newspapers as advertisements. This is necessary because each newspaper reports the activities only of the candidates it supports; other candidates and parties can reach the newspaper's readers only by inserting advertisements. This type of propaganda is continuous. Each time a party runs a meeting, one or more pictures appear in all newspapers as paid advertisements to demonstrate that Heredia is with Figueres, or that Puntarenas joyously acclaims Echandi, or that Filadelfia supports Orlich.

As a result, much of the effort of the political parties goes into organizing meetings. The climate permits these meetings to be held out of doors, and all of them follow the same pattern. The candidate drives or flies or takes the train to a point near the site of the meeting, where a group of party stalwarts awaits him. Then the candidate gets on a horse or enters an open jeep or car, or sometimes perches on the shoulders of two brawny party supporters, and the group (the size varies in accordance with the population of the town), preceded by a band, parades to the square or park where the meeting is to be held. The parade is very noisy, with many cries of *"Viva!"* and exploding firecrackers. The paraders carry banners, party flags, slogans, and the more enthusiastic wear shirts or dresses made of the party colors. At the square or park, speeches are made; then the candidate and the local party leaders go to a nearby house or garden where a reception is held. Food is served and the local people have a chance to speak to the candidate.

Great care is taken to see that the campaign meetings do not end in clashes between the rival party supporters. Only one party is permitted to hold a meeting in any locality on any one day. All establishments selling liquor in the town and the headquarters of all rival parties are closed. The police are on hand to prevent violence.[7]

One feature of political campaigns not very common in most other countries is the traveling demonstration. In order to swell the crowd at meetings, some parties transport the party faithful in trucks, buses, and cars to wherever a meeting is being held. Many of those who go along on these outings are below the voting age, but they can make a fine racket and throw leaflets at people as the vehicles move along.

A great deal of money is spent for electoral campaigns in Costa Rica, but, just as in other countries, where it all comes from is difficult to discover. A part comes from the government, which appropriates for this purpose not more than 2 percent of the ordinary budget during the three years prior to the year in which an election is held. This is distributed among the parties in proportion to the number of votes each party re-

---

[7] I attended one such meeting in 1953 in San José, in a public park that was completely surrounded by police. Within the ring of police, two to three hundred persons listened as the leaders of the Communist Party tried to make themselves heard while outside the circle of police four to five hundred supporters of the National Liberation Party yelled, booed, and let off steam. This was an extreme case, but it demonstrates the effort the Costa Rican police make to prevent violence during campaign meetings.

ceives, but no party getting less than 10 percent of the votes receives any of the money. In the 1958 campaign, the amount distributed among the four largest parties was C7 million. This government money never covers all the costs of campaigns, particularly for the losing parties; yet each party tries to finance its campaign by selling bonds with the hope of redeeming them with the money it will receive from the government. After the 1958 campaign the National Union Party was able to pay back only 3 percent on the bonds it had sold because of the low vote it received. Who, then, puts up the money? Since the introduction of an effective personnel system for the hiring of governmental employees, the victorious parties can no longer pay their bills with collections from government employees. The money, therefore, comes—as it does in all countries—from the candidates and their rich supporters, supplemented by the money the government gives the parties.

There has been some criticism of the manner in which the government finances election campaigns. The Organization of American States observers of the 1966 election, in their report to the government, suggested that the amount given the parties was too much. The observers thought there was a danger of tying the means of publicity to the political parties. All observers of Costa Rican elections seem to agree that there is a tremendous duplication and repetition of propaganda, and that there is too much of it. The style of campaigning is certainly determined by the expected government grant to finance the campaign.

A much more serious criticism of Costa Rica's electoral system is that the constitutional rules forbidding practically all officeholders and government employees from running for office or campaigning tends to favor the opposition. It is a tribute to Costa Rica's democracy that in every election from 1948 to 1966 the presidential candidate opposed by the incumbent won the election. At the same time, the rotation in the executive has led to a fluctuation in policy, as each new administration followed a different course. In 1960, for example, the president canceled the national census for which the previous administration had invested a great deal of time and money, thus upsetting the orderly compilation of the statistics so necessary in planning sound government policy.

Political Parties

Permanently organized political parties are relatively new in Costa Rica, and as yet there really are only two permanent ideological parties: the Popular Vanguard Party, which was organized as the Communist Party in 1929 (and is not permitted to present candidates in elections), and the

National Liberation Party, organized in the early 1950's. All of the other organizations that call themselves political parties are either fronts for the Communist Party or in the tradition of Costa Rica's past; that is, they are either temporary organizations created to win a specific election or the personal followings of popular politicians.

Costa Rica, like most of the other Latin-American states, has had too many political parties. From 1948 to 1966, eighteen different "parties" were legally registered with the Supreme Tribunal of Elections, and nine different organizations presented candidates in the 1962 election. During the 1950's and 1960's, the strength of the National Liberation Party led its opponents to unite their forces, so that by the 1966 election there were only four main political parties, which between them had the support of almost all the voters.

Political parties are permitted to participate in elections only when they are officially registered with the Supreme Tribunal of Elections. Any group of electors is permitted to organize a party. All that is required is that at least twenty-five persons register such intention before a notary public, compile a list of names of the persons involved, and draw up the statutes of the party. The only parties not permitted to function are those that threaten the democratic organization or sovereignty of the country. This constitutional rule has been interpreted to ban the activities of the Communist Party, but in fact the Communist Party functions and enjoys all the guarantees of civil liberty enjoyed by the rest of the population, except that it cannot offer candidates under its own name in the elections and is not recognized as a political party by the Supreme Tribunal of Elections.

Costa Rican parties can be regional or national in their organization. They can be inscribed on the rolls of the electoral tribunal at any time except during the six months immediately prior to an election. To register his party as a national party, the president of the party's executive committee presents a request accompanied by the notorized statement drawn up at the founding of the party and the supporting signatures of 3,000 registered voters. To be a provincial or cantonal party, the organization must present the signatures of a number of voters equal to 1 percent of the registered voters in the province or canton. Each four years the party must present a new list of names and register again.

The largest and most important political party today is the National Liberation Party (PLN), led by ex-President José Figueres. The PLN won the presidency in 1953 and 1962 and the majority of the legislative seats in all the national legislatures since 1953, except that of 1958.

In the 1966–70 legislature it holds twenty-nine of the fifty-seven seats. Founded in the early 1950's, the PLN is an indigenous reformist party dedicated to abolishing poverty in Costa Rica by modernizing its economy and strengthening democracy. It favors maximum budgets for education, health, and housing, diversification and improvement of production, closer cooperation between the Central American states, and friendship with the United States and support of the United States in the cold war. It supports government operations upon modern administrative lines, with a career service for government employees, and strongly favors social planning as a means to improve the lot of the average Costa Rican. The National Liberation Party describes its program as an attempt to fuse the ideas of modern democracy with the traditional values of western Christianity. The PLN greatly resembles and cooperates closely with Venezuela's Democratic Action Party, Peru's *Aprista* Party, and Puerto Rico's Popular Democratic Party, through the Coordinating Committee of Popular Parties. In 1964 it became an affiliate of the Socialist International as an "observer" member.

The party that won the presidency in 1966 was the Party of National Unification (PUN), but this was not a true political party. Rather it was a fusion of the opponents of the PLN, who combined their efforts behind a joint slate and received the support of the Communists to win the presidency by about 5,000 votes. Although efforts have been made to make the PUN a permanent organization, it remains a coalition of the Republican Party, the National Union Party, and the Authentic Republican Union Party. Of these, the largest is the Republican Party (PR).

The PR is a curious sort of personalistic party made up of the followers of ex-President Rafael Calderón Guardia. After controlling the Costa Rican government from 1940 to 1948 in alliance with the Communists, the PR leaders went into exile following their defeat in the 1948 civil war. Since then, Calderón Guardia and his followers have been trying to regain power in any way possible. The party led invasions into Costa Rica in 1948 and 1955 and attempted to seize the government through revolts in 1950 and 1951, but all these attempts failed. In 1953 the party ran candidates on the Independent National Republican Party ticket and elected three deputies to the Assembly. In 1958 Calderón Guardia returned to Costa Rica after ten years of exile, and the party won 20 percent of the legislative vote and Calderón Guardia himself was elected a deputy. In 1962 Calderón Guardia ran for the presidency and received 35 percent of the votes cast, the PR winning eighteen seats in the Assembly.

Calderón Guardia is a demagogue of the Perón type, and it is difficult to say whether the PR will continue after he dies. Its members range from persons whose views are indistinguishable from the Communists' to rich, conservative landowners. It is suspected that some of the PR leaders are actually members of the Communist Party running on the PR ticket because the Communist Party is banned from the ballot. At the same time, the PR manages to run united campaigns with the National Union Party, the organization of the landowners and the traditional aristocracy.

The National Union Party (PUN) consists of most of the Costa Rican rich, particularly the landowners. It is dedicated to the preservation of the traditional organization of Costa Rican society, favors free enterprise, and opposes most of the reforms sponsored by the PLN. Although a PUN leader, Mario Echandi, was elected president in 1958, the party won only ten of the forty-five seats in the legislature in that election. After the 1962 election, ex-President Echandi left the PUN and created his own party, the Authentic Republican Union Party (PURA), but PURA joined the coalition to support Trejos for president in 1966.

The last of the important parties is that of the Communists, known as the Popular Vanguard Party (PVP) since 1943. Like most other Soviet-oriented Communist parties, the PVP claims to be for a more equitable organization of society, but always subordinates itself to the Moscow party line, is completely unscrupulous, and finds it easy to cooperate with the PUN and PR to fight the reformist PLN. The PVP is estimated to have about 300 members, but it exercises more influence than this small membership would allow by functioning through front organizations and by its alliance with the landowners in the PR and PUN.

In the 1962 and 1966 elections, the Communists tried to get on the ballot by using a new name. In 1962 it was the Popular Democratic Action Party, which received 3,339 votes for its presidential candidate. With 2 percent of the legislative vote, it elected one deputy to the Assembly. By 1966 the Communists had a new front party organized, the Popular Socialist Alliance Party, but the Legislative Assembly voted to keep this organization off the ballot. Strong in the United Fruit Company area around Golfito, the Communists supported the PUN and probably gave Professor Trejos his margin of victory.

One small party, a personalistic split from the PLN led by Frank Marshall Jiménez, has managed to elect one or two deputies to the Assembly in each of the elections from 1958 on. It has a conservative program, but is basically the shadow of Frank Marshall, a rich man who can afford to keep it going.

It is possible that Costa Rica will develop a two-party system in the future.[8] The voters are so evenly divided that no group except the National Liberation Party can win an election by itself, and its opponents are forced to unite in order to have any hope of winning. Eventually, perhaps the Communists, the landowners, the followers of Calderón Guardia, and all the rest who for various reasons do not want to vote for the PLN will be forced to create one party.

The National Liberation Party is the only one that maintains permanent headquarters in various parts of the country and tries to carry on continuous activity. The Communists are also permanently active. All the other parties are active only during election campaigns, except for those that have members in the Legislative Assembly, which function through legislative caucuses. Yet even these parties do not carry on any other activity between elections.

Nominations for Office

Candidates for office have traditionally been self-appointed or selected by the leader or leaders of the parties. Sometimes mass conventions have been organized to nominate a presidential candidate, but in very few cases were these more than prearranged shows staged to impress the public. In 1961 the National Liberation Party did something new to nominate its candidate. The party organized a primary election in which about 1,500 of the party's leaders were given votes. Two precandidates competed for the nomination. Francisco Orlich won the primary with 921 votes to 639 for his opponent, Daniel Oduber. This was a real competition for the nomination, with two points of view presented: Orlich represented the section of the party which put major emphasis upon the economic development of the country, and Oduber represented the section of the party which put major emphasis upon reforms that would help the underprivileged. The other parties continued to nominate their candidates in the old way. The National Union Party, for example, in 1960 announced the nomination of Otilio Ulate for president three months before a convention held in accordance with the country's electoral laws unanimously nominated him.

---

[8] In a study of San José's community power structure in the early 1960's it was discovered that there seemed to be two definite groups of top influentials, and that the members of one group tended to belong to one political party while the members of the other group claimed membership in another. See Harold T. Edwards, "Power Structure and Its Communication Behavior in San José, Costa Rica," *Journal of Inter-American Studies,* 9 (April 1967): 236–47.

Public Opinion and Pressure Groups

As Costa Rica's population is small, political life becomes very informal; almost everyone active in politics knows almost everyone else active in politics. The public is alert and aware of what is happening at all times. Three daily newspapers are issued in San José, all with a national circulation. *La Nación*, with a circulation of around 55,000, is the largest. The concentration of the majority of the population on the *meseta central* makes it easy for anything that happens to become known quickly. When an important debate takes place in the Legislative Assembly it is common for hundreds of ordinary citizens to crowd into the visitors' gallery to observe the proceedings.

Most of the professions are organized, and the professional organizations serve their memberships as pressure groups by publicizing the groups' opinions. The trade unions are weak in Costa Rica, as most workers are engaged in agriculture. In 1964 there were 23,708 members in 268 trade unions. To weaken organized labor further, these trade unions belonged to six different confederations. The Popular Vanguard and National Liberation Parties have tried to organize trade unions, but neither has had much success, although practically all the unions in existence support one of these two parties. Not many farm workers or small farmers are organized, but the larger landowners are.

The Catholic church sponsors a series of organizations that have a sizable membership. The government has stimulated the creation of cooperative organizations, but the movement is not strong, since most of the cooperatives are under the administrative control of the government banks that finance their activities. A chamber of commerce and some fifty employers' organizations of various kinds function. A country club and the Union Club serve as centers for the rich.

The common method of making an organized group's wishes known is to publish a letter in a newspaper, either as an advertisement or as a news story. Access to the Legislative Assembly and to the executive is readily available, and committees representing various groups make their wishes known to the president, the ministers, and the members of the Legislative Assembly in formal meetings.

Civil Liberties

The Costa Rican constitution guarantees all of the civil rights usually found in the most democratic countries, including the right to free speech, assembly, press, and organization. To guarantee these rights further, the constitution also includes the right to *habeas corpus* and *amparo*, a writ that enables the courts to aid any person whose constitutional rights have been violated by the government.

As is customary in Latin America, certain individual rights guaranteed by the constitution can be suspended in time of emergency. For a period of up to thirty days, the legislature by a two-thirds vote can suspend the rights to move freely, to be protected from invasion of the home and correspondence, to meet, to exercise freedom of speech, to have access to the government, and not to be detained by the police without a warrant. If the legislature is not in session, the president and his ministers can declare an emergency and suspend these rights also, but the Legislative Assembly must then be called into session within forty-eight hours.

Since the adoption of the 1949 constitution, the government has shown commendable restraint in exercising its power to suspend individual rights. The people of Costa Rica go about their business freely, and it is a common thing in Costa Rica to see the president of the republic, a Supreme Court justice, or a cabinet minister walking down the street alone or with a friend, almost completely unnoticed or ignored by the general public.

The Executive

One of the aims of the writers of the 1949 constitution was to weaken the relative power of the president. The constitution provides, therefore, that the executive power is to be exercised by a president and his ministers acting together. It also sets down in specific terms the powers that are exercised exclusively by the president, those he must exercise jointly with one of his ministers, and those that must be exercised in the name of the Council of Government, which consists of the president and his ministers meeting formally.

The president is elected for a four-year term and cannot be reelected until eight years after his term has expired. He must be a Costa Rican by birth, in full possession of all rights, a layman, and more than thirty years of age. Not eligible to be president, in addition to anyone who has been president during the previous eight years, are a person who has been vice-president during the twelve months previous to the election, relatives of the incumbent president, all ministers of government, justices of the Supreme Court, members of the Supreme Electoral Tribunal, the director of the Civil Register, the directors and managers of the autonomous institutions, and the comptroller general and assistant comptroller general of the republic. All these officials, except for the president and his relatives, can be candidates if they resign their positions at least twelve months before the date of the election in which they seek office.

The powers that the president of Costa Rica exercises alone include appointing and dismissing the ministers of government, acting as the titular head of the nation, and serving as supreme commander of the armed forces. (Although there is officially no army, there is a *fuerza pública* [public force], and it is armed.) The only other specific action required of him by the constitution is that he submit an annual "State of the Nation" message to the Legislative Assembly. Together with the responsible minister, the president enforces the law, maintains order, appoints and removes governmental employees in accordance with the civil service law, decrees the suspension of individual rights if necessary, supervises government funds, supervises the general administration, negotiates treaties subject to the approval of the Legislative Assembly, initiates and vetoes legislation, directs international relations, convenes special sessions of the Legislative Assembly, prepares the budget, supervises the armed forces, and executes and enforces the decisions of the judicial power and the electoral tribunal. The Council of Government is given the power to ask the Legislative Assembly to decree a state of national defense and to authorize the Council of Government to mobilize an armed force and to negotiate peace. The Council of Government also exercises the power to pardon, to appoint and remove diplomatic personnel, to appoint the directors of the autonomous organizations, and to consider all other matters placed before it by the president.

Whatever the intentions of the constitution, the president remains a strong executive. President Figueres made a deliberate attempt to strengthen the Council of Government by refusing at times to make his opinion known until the council had made a decision, but he did not have much success. The tradition of having the president make all important decisions was too strong to be overcome in one presidential term. As a result, generally speaking, the Council of Government waits for the president to speak his mind. No change in the wording of a constitution will ever change the situation as long as the essential features of the presidential system are preserved and the president has the exclusive power to appoint and discharge ministers.

Two vice-presidents are elected on the same ballot as the president, and succeed to the office in turn if the president leaves office. If the president and both of the vice-presidents are unable to function, the succession goes to the president of the Legislative Assembly. When the president temporarily leaves office, he can designate either of the two vice-presidents to act as president until he returns to duty. The vice-presidents and the members of the Legislative Assembly are eligible to serve as ministers. When a member of the legislature is appointed to the cabinet, his seat in the Assembly is filled by his substitute.

The president of Costa Rica receives a salary of C6,000 a month (about $900 U.S.) and the use of a presidential house, which is a modest wooden building largely devoted to offices. After he leaves office he is eligible for a pension of C3,000 a month, and in 1961 almost all of Costa Rica's living ex-presidents were receiving their pensions. The widows and children of ex-presidents also receive pensions from the government.

The Civil Service

In 1960 there were about 50,000 persons employed by the various branches of the Costa Rican government and by the autonomous and semi-autonomous organizations controlled by the government. Only about 20,000 of these employees were included in the classified civil service system, however, because the constitutional clause and the laws governing public employees have been interpreted as exempting all employees, except those directly under the executive, from control by the civil service system. Many of the autonomous organizations, the legislature, and the judicial system have, however, adopted policies that for all practical purposes provide a modern administrative organization.

Government employees in Costa Rica function at a rather high rate of efficiency and there is very little graft. There is much interest in the general problems of public administration, stimulated, perhaps, by the presence in San José of the United Nations Graduate School of Public Administration for Central America and Panama. A National School for Public Administration also functions as part of the University of Costa Rica.

Costa Rica's civil service system has its origins in the reforms instituted by the junta of government after the 1948 civil war. After some years of work, aided by a public administration specialist sent by the United States Technical Assistance Program, a comprehensive civil service system was created. Headed by a director general, the Civil Service Commission is attached to the office of the president. It selects employees, sponsors classification systems, and stimulates training in the field of management. A Civil Service Tribunal functions as an appeal agency for the complaints of employees. There is some sentiment for broadening the scope of the civil service system to include all government employees within its framework. Many of the government employees are unionized.

The Legislative Power

The legislative power resides in the people, who delegate their power to a unicameral Legislative Assembly (the *Asamblea Legislativa*) by means of the suffrage. The Legislative Assembly consists of fifty-seven deputies elected on a basis of proportional representation by provinces for four-year terms, at the same time that the president is elected. For every three deputies elected, one substitute deputy (*suplente*) is elected. After each census, the Supreme Tribunal of Elections assigns the number of deputies to which each province is entitled according to its population.

To be a deputy, one must be a citizen more than twenty-one years of age. The list of those not eligible to become members of the Legislative Assembly is long and includes the incumbent president of the republic, his ministers of government, justices of the Supreme Court, members of the Supreme Tribunal of Elections, the director of the Civil Register, members of the National Guard on active duty, those exercising civil or police authority over a province, the directors of the autonomous institutions, and relatives to the third degree of the incumbent president of the republic. The officials listed above can become candidates for election to the Legislative Assembly if they have resigned their positions at least six months before the date of an election.

There are further restrictions upon legislators. A deputy may not be elected to any other office or be an employee of any governmental bureau or autonomous institution. Exempted from this rule are members of the faculty of the University of Costa Rica and those holding posts in charitable institutions. A deputy can serve as a cabinet minister, but he gives up his seat while serving in that capacity. A deputy cannot do private business with any government agency. Deputies enjoy all of the privileges usually given to members of legislatures, including immunity from court action unless caught in the act or when the Assembly authorizes the court action. The salary of a deputy is C125 per diem (when the Assembly meets), or about $400 a month.

The Legislative Assembly meets in regular session twice a year, from May 1 to July 31 and from September 1 to November 30. The president may call special sessions, which can consider only the matters submitted by him. The principal powers of the Legislative Assembly are to enact all laws, to levy taxes, to investigate, approve, or disapprove treaties, to authorize declarations of war, and by a two-thirds vote to suspend certain civil liberties guaranteed by the constitution. The Assembly also elects certain officials, including the members and substitute members of the Supreme Court and the comptroller and subcomptroller general. Ministers can attend sessions of the Legislative Assembly with voice but without vote. They must attend the sessions if the Assembly requests their presence, and the Assembly can interrogate them and, by a two-thirds vote, censure them. The Assembly also has the power of impeaching the president, vice-president, and other members of the executive branch, as well as members of the diplomatic corps. If the Assembly votes against any of these by a two-thirds majority, the Supreme Court tries the case. The Legislative Assembly also makes the decision as to whether the president is physically incapable of exercising his office.

The Costa Rican Legislative Assembly functions as a truly deliberative body.[9] It follows a formal procedure in considering legislation, which includes debating each bill three times and consideration by committees. The Assembly ordinarily meets at three P.M. each weekday while it is in session and adjourns around six P.M. Although debate is formal, the atmosphere is informal. Until 1958, the Legislative Assembly met in a building on the busiest corner of San José, at Avenida Central and Calle Uno. The main door was always open, and anyone could enter the visitors' gallery and observe proceedings. Many of the members of the Assembly, like United States congressmen, spend a great deal of time and energy seeking public works for the provinces they represent.

The great weakness of the Costa Rican legislature is that it lacks continuity, since no member can be reelected until four years after his term expires. Every assembly usually has a small number of members who served in previous assemblies, but the overwhelming majority are new to their office.

The *Contraloría General*, an agency that audits the books of all government agencies, functions as an auxiliary agent of the Assembly, but has some functional autonomy. The comptroller general and the assistant comptroller general are appointed by the Assembly in the middle of a presidential term for eight-year terms and can be reelected. The position of this agency and the strict system of budget control gives the Assembly a great deal of control over financial matters.

The president of the republic can veto the bills passed by the legislature, but the Assembly can pass a bill over his veto by a two-thirds vote.

---

[9] The details of the legislative process are described in "Como se hacen las leyes," in *Memoria de labores de la Asamblea Legislativa, 1956–1957* (San José: Imprenta Nacional, 1957), pp. 9–14. The Assembly rules of procedure are described in Asamblea Legislativa, *Reglamento de orden, dirección y disciplina interior* (San José: Imprenta Nacional, 1962).

If the executive returns a bill with an amendment and the Assembly accepts the amendment, the president cannot then veto the amended bill. Nor can the president veto the budget as passed by the Assembly. If the president vetoes a bill because he thinks it is unconstitutional, the bill goes to the Supreme Court for its decision, which is binding.

Public Finance

Costa Rica's budget is presented to the Legislative Assembly by the president before the first of September and must be adopted before November 30. The executive budget must be in balance and the Assembly cannot increase the total amount to be spent without at the same time providing additional income. These rules lead to the use of extraordinary budgets, which are introduced during the year to allocate funds whose receipt was not foreseen and to appropriate funds for unexpected needs. Municipal budgets are of little importance, as a large part of the local government funds comes through grants from the national government.

The budget is drawn up by a special agency, the head of which is appointed by the president for a six-year term. This department has the authority to reduce or to delete items in the proposed budget drawn up by the heads of the executive departments and by the legislative and judicial officials. In the event of a dispute between the budget commission and an agency, the president makes the final decision. The budget from 1940 to 1948 had a deficit each year, but the level of government revenue has increased rapidly since the 1948 revolution. Budgets were in balance from 1948 to 1957, and much of the increased revenue was devoted to various development projects. With the drastic fall in the world market price of coffee since 1958, there have been deficits; in 1961 the deficit amounted to C42,651,991.

The budget adopted by the Legislative Assembly for 1964, shown in Tables 1 and 2, is typical of the pattern of receipts and expenditures during recent years, although the total amount is greater than ever before. These figures do not include the budgets of the autonomous and semi-autonomous organizations or those of the municipal governments. As the figures demonstrate, and as has been traditional in Costa Rica, the government spends its income wisely but gets it from the wrong sources. Almost one-fourth of all expenditures in 1964 were for education, and the amount spent for the armed forces, the police, and the other branches of public order totaled less than 10 percent of the budget. These proportions are all significantly different from the pattern in most of Latin America. On the other hand, about 57 percent of the government's

TABLE 1

ESTIMATED REVENUE OF COSTA RICA, 1964

Source	Amount in Colones	Percent of Total
Customs duties	C220,800,000	45.10%
Miscellaneous taxes	61,054,000	12.50
Total indirect taxes	C281,854,000	57.60%
Taxes on income and profits	62,919,000	12.85
Taxes on land, inheritances, and gifts	26,337,000	5.35
Total direct taxes	C89,256,000	18.20%
Total tax revenue	C371,110,000	75.80%
Public enterprises and services	35,125,000	7.20
Miscellaneous	83,148,000	17.00
Total budgeted revenue	C489,383,000	100.00%

TABLE 2

EXPENDITURES OF COSTA RICA, 1964

	Amount in Colones	Percent of Total
Legislature	C3,481,800	0.812%
General Auditing Office	1,539,656	0.359
Judiciary	19,460,000	4.540
Executive	216,901,746	50.607
President's office, including cost of administering civil service system and planning office	2,713,483	.633
Ministry of Agriculture and Livestock	8,900,000	2.076
Ministry of Economics and Finance	23,117,446	5.393
Ministry of Industry	1,338,000	0.312
Ministry of Public Education	106,364,700	24.817
Ministry of Government, Police, and Justice	21,784,400	5.082
Ministry of Transport	14,736,607	3.438
Ministry of Foreign Relations	5,137,110	1.198
Ministry of Public Health	12,391,200	2.891
Ministry of Public Security	15,418,800	3.597
Ministry of Labor and Social Welfare	5,000,000	1.166
Supreme Tribunal of Elections	4,651,719	1.085
Pensions, grants to autonomous organizations, quotas to international organizations, and miscellaneous grants	104,331,955	24.342
Debt service	78,416,124	18.296
Total estimated expenditures	C428,783,000	100.000%

revenues come from indirect taxes, which fall hardest on those least capable of paying. Import duties have been most important, but consumption and indirect taxes are significant, including taxes on coffee processing, cattle slaughter, liquor, beer, cigarettes, matches, soft drinks, and admissions to public spectacles, among others. A new law enacted in 1954 raised the level of taxes on income, and since then both the United Fruit Company, the largest enterprise in the country, and others with large incomes have paid higher taxes.

The Costa Rican income tax applies only to income obtained within the country, and applies equally to personal income and to the profits of all types of companies. The tax ranges from 1 percent on the first C3,000 of net taxable income to a maximum of 30 percent on incomes above C500,000. Exemptions on personal income amount to C5,000 for the taxpayer, C2,000 for the spouse, C1,500 for each child, and C1,000 for each other dependent. Various deductions from taxable income are permitted, including insurance premiums and part of the payment for professional services (medical, dental, legal, accounting, etc.). In 1957, 37,384 persons out of a population of 1,052,474 filed tax statements, but 10,054 of this number paid no taxes. Property taxes are low, amounting to C10,467,170 in 1957. All property valued at C10,000 or less is tax exempt. Property owners also pay a small tax to the municipality, and all employers pay a tax to the Social Security Institute.

Local Government

Costa Rica is a unitary republic that for administrative purposes is divided into seven provinces, sixty-eight cantons, and 326 districts. Each province has a governor who is appointed by the president and is responsible to the Minister of Government. There is no provincial assembly. Each canton, however, elects a council known as the *municipalidad*, which possesses legislative power within its jurisdiction and works with a *jefe político* appointed by the national executive. Each district has a police agent appointed by the national government. Representatives of its districts may participate in discussions within the *municipalidad* concerning their communities, but cannot vote. Local government does not have much vitality because of the limited finances available to the *municipalidad*, and most local public works are financed by the national government. There is some sentiment in favor of strengthening municipal government, and in recent years the League of Cost Rican Municipalities has been active in coordinating the efforts of the individual municipal governments to obtain more autonomy.

The Judicial Power

The judicial power of Costa Rica rests in a Supreme Court and subsidiary tribunals. The Supreme Court consists of seventeen justices elected for eight-year terms by the Legislative Assembly. The court is divided into chambers for different classes of business. Justices are automatically re-elected for an additional term of eight years unless the Legislative Assembly votes to the contrary by a two-thirds majority. Relatives of incumbent justices are ineligible for election. The Assembly also names twenty-five alternates from a list of fifty names submitted by the Supreme Court. Vacancies on the court are then filled by lot from the list of alternates. Judges of all lower courts are appointed by the Supreme Court, but justices of the peace are appointed by the Minister of Government acting for the president. The constitution bars capital punishment in Costa Rica.

The Costa Rican Supreme Court has the constitutional power to declare legislative and executive acts unconstitutional, and has done so various times.

The courts function freely in Costa Rica and the standard of justice is high. The average person gets a fair hearing and there is little complaint about the way the courts function. The Supreme Court has the power to give its opinion on all laws dealing with the judicial system. A two-thirds vote in the Legislative Assembly is needed to override the court's opinion on this type of legislation.

The Scope of Governmental Activity

Costa Rica has been compared to Uruguay and Denmark in that the government operates certain economic enterprises that in most democratic countries are privately owned. All of the country's banks are owned by the government, as is the only insurance company in Costa Rica. The government also operates a liquor-manufacturing monopoly, a railroad, a housing-construction agency, a construction organization that builds electric power plants, an electric company, and various other enterprises. In 1960 it was estimated that 35 percent of the country's production came from government-owned activities.

Costa Rica: A Last Word

At this writing Costa Rica is a functioning democracy in which civil liberties are well protected, elections are free and orderly, and the electoral victor, whoever he may be, takes office upon the appointed day. It is a country in which the executive, although powerful, is not a dictator; the legislature has genuine power and a personality of its own; the judiciary enjoys a high degree of independence; political parties tend more and more toward ideological groupings; and what armed forces exist appear to be without influence in determining public policy. Compared to its neighbors, Costa Rica is making great progress as the economy develops, the population increases rapidly, and education flourishes.

It is difficult to say with certainty just why Costa Rica has developed as it has. Three factors seem to have been most important. The lack of a military tradition and the poverty of the country helped to prevent the development of a strong army that could act as the guarantor of an outmoded status quo. The homogeneity of the population on the *meseta central* and the integrated society that developed there led to the strengthening of education. The undemocratic system of government that prevailed for a hundred years and the poverty due to the landholding system stimulated the growth of reformist movements. The way in which these movements developed led to the creation of a party system that came near to pitting two parties against each other. The opposing political groups have acted as checks upon each other, and politics has come close to being a struggle to win support for a program instead of a family affair in which the members of an aristocracy competed to see which individuals would exercise governmental power.

Costa Rica seems to demonstrate how important a factor education is in strengthening democracy. The first impetus to improve Costa Rica's political and economic system came because its people were at least partially educated. Since 1948, the funds devoted to education have greatly increased, a new university campus has been built, public administration has been strengthened, new agricultural experimental and demonstration stations have been developed, and all of these have further stimulated the growth of the economy and the strengthening of democratic institutions.

Costa Rica's experience also demonstrates that the struggle for democratic government is something that goes on eternally. It cannot be won in one battle. The various invasions of Costa Rica by the supporters of Calderón Guardia and the Communists and the splits that have taken place in the National Liberation Party are evidence that there can be no such thing as a status quo in political life. Costa Rica is developing differently today than it did in the past, and as this development unfolds, the relative power positions of the different groups and classes in the country are inevitably altered. Those who object to change fight with all their determination to preserve the status quo and are continuously being joined by those whose desire for reform has been satisfied and who believe that the time has come to call a halt to further change. Thus the struggle continues, against vested interests, tradition, and man's inhumanity to man, to achieve democracy and to keep it functioning once it has been introduced.

No one can say exactly what the future holds for Costa Rica, but if one can judge from its past, it faces a future in which its traditional economic and political institutions will have been so transformed that Costa Rica will become a modern state, the home of a prosperous, cultured, and happy people, and probably a part of a new Central American federation in which little Costa Rica will play an important role.

SELECTED READINGS

ALVERS-MONTALVO, M. "Cultural Change in a Costa Rican Village." *Human Organization* 15 (Winter 1957): 2–7.

BIESANZ, JOHN, and BIESANZ, MAVIS. *Costa Rican Life.* New York: Columbia University Press, 1944.

BLANDFORD, RUTH BROWNLOW. "The Women's Vote in Costa Rica." *Americas* 7 (June 1955): 3–7.

BOSCH, JUAN. *Apuntes para una interpretación de la historia costarricense.* San José: Editorial Eloy Morua Carrillo, 1963.

BUSEY, JAMES L. "Costa Rica: A Meaningful Democracy." In *Political Systems of Latin America*, edited by Martin C. Needler. Princeton, N.J.: D. Van Nostrand Co., Inc., 1964.

———. "Foundations of Political Contrast: Costa Rica and Nicaragua." *Western Political Quarterly* 11 (September 1958): 627–59.

———. *Notes on Costa Rican Democracy.* Boulder: University of Colorado Press, 1962.

———. "The Presidents of Costa Rica." *Americas* 18 (July 1961): 55–70.

CAÑAS, ALBERTO F. *Los ocho años.* San José: Editorial Liberación Nacional, 1955.

CASTRO ESQUIVEL, ARTURO. *José Figueres Ferrer: El Hombre y su obra.* San José: Imprenta Termo, 1955.

"Civil Service in Costa Rica." *Public Administration Review* 13 (Autumn 1953): 286.

COSTA RICA, OFICINA DEL PRESUPUESTO. *Manual de Organización de la Administración Pública de Costa Rica.* San José: Departamento de Publicaciones de la ESAPAC, 1962.

CREEDMAN, THEODORE S. "The Crisis in Costa Rican Politics." *South Eastern Latin Americanist* 10 (March 1967): 1–3.

EDWARDS, HAROLD T. "Power Structure and Its Communication Behavior in San José, Costa Rica." *Journal of Inter-American Studies* 9 (April 1967): 236–47.

FIGUERES FERRER, JOSÉ. *Cartas a un ciudadano.* San José: Imprenta Nacional, 1956.

———. "My Political Testament." *Socialist International Information* 15 (April 3, 1965): 63–65.

FOURNIER, FERNANDO. "Costa Rica: A Democratic Republic." *World Affairs* 119 (Spring 1956): 13–14.

GOLDRICH, DANIEL. *Sons of the Establishment: Elite Youth in Panama and Costa Rica.* Chicago: Rand McNally & Co., 1966.

JONES, CHESTER LLOYD. *Costa Rica and Civilization in the Caribbean*. Madison: University of Wisconsin Press, 1935.

KANTOR, HARRY. *The Costa Rica Election of 1953: A Case Study*. Gainesville: University of Florida Press, 1958.

KARSEN, SONJA. *Educational Development in Costa Rica with UNESCO's Technical Assistance, 1951–1954*. San José: Ministerio de Educación Pública, 1954.

LOOMIS, CHARLES PRICE, ed. *Turrialba: Social Systems and the Introduction of Change*. Glencoe, Ill.: Free Press, 1953.

MAY, STACY, *et al. Costa Rica: A Study in Economic Development*. New York: Twentieth Century Fund, 1952.

Memoria de labores de la Asamblea Legislativa. San José: Imprenta Nacional, annually.

NAVARRO BOLANDI, HUGO. *José Figueres en la evolución de Costa Rica*. Mexico City: Imprenta Quirós, 1953.

———. *La Generación del 48*. Mexico City: Ediciones Humanismo, 1957.

OBREGÓN LORIA, RAFAEL. *Conflictos militares y políticos de Costa Rica*. San José: Imprenta La Nación, 1951.

PACHECO, LEÓN. "Evolución del pensamiento democrático de Costa Rica." *Combate* 3 (March–April 1961): 31–43.

PERALTA, HERNÁN G. *Las Constituciones de Costa Rica*. Madrid: Instituto de Estudios Políticos, 1962.

QUIJANO QUESADA, ALBERTO. *Costa Rica ayer y hoy: 1800–1939*. San José: Editorial Borrasé Hnos., 1939.

RODRÍGUEZ VEGA, EUGENIO. *Apuntes para una sociología costarricense*. San José: Editorial Universitaria, 1953.

SARIOLA, SAKARI. *Social Class and Social Mobility in a Costa Rican Town*. Turrialba, C.R.: Inter-American Institute of Agricultural Sciences, 1954.

STEPHENSON, PAUL G. *Costa Rica Election Factbook, February 6, 1966*. Washington: Institute for the Comparative Study of Political Systems, 1965.

U.S. DEPARTMENT OF LABOR, Bureau of Labor Statistics. *Labor Law and Practice in Costa Rica*. Washington: U.S. Government Printing Office, 1962.

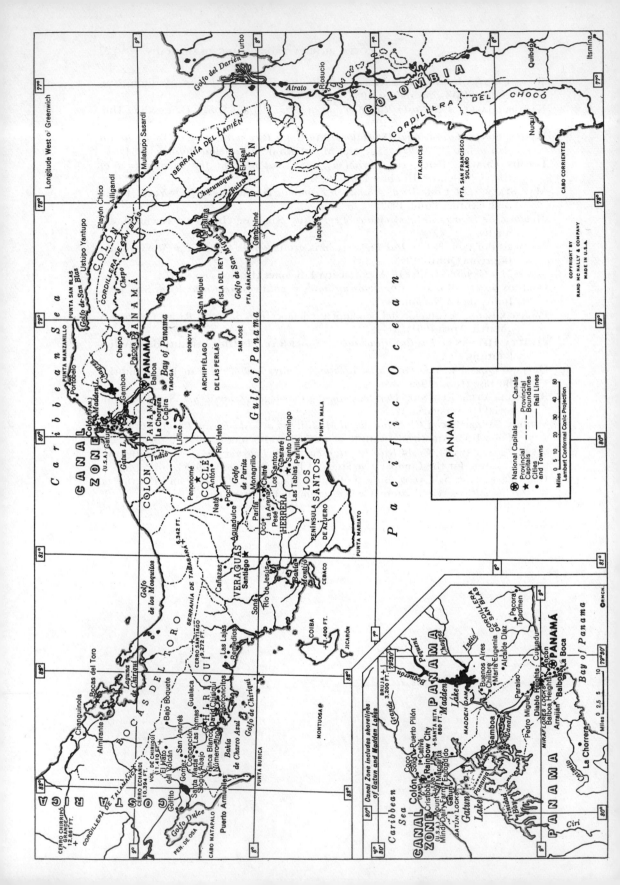

PANAMA

National Capitals
Provincial Capitals
Cities and Towns
Canals
Provincial Boundaries
Rail Lines

Miles 0 5 10 20 30 40 50
Lambert Conformal Conic Projection

COPYRIGHT BY RAND MC NALLY & COMPANY
MADE IN U.S.A.

Canal Zone includes shorelines of Gatun and Madden Lakes

─10─

PANAMA:

The Politics of the Canal

Panama is one of the small pieces of land which, because it is the site of an interoceanic canal, plays a far more important role in world affairs than its size or population warrant. Although an "independent" state since 1903, the republic of Panama has not been able as yet to develop into a viable political unit. Rather it has existed as the home of the Panama Canal, and its governmental activity and economic life have always revolved around the Canal. Two of the few scholars who have studied Panama write that "The Isthmus is a prime example of the way in which man has let his mastery of the physical world far outstrip that of the social world."[1] Anyone who studies the way Panama is governed quickly comes to the same conclusion, because alongside one of man's greatest engineering marvels, man has been unable to construct a home for a happy and prosperous people.

A National Profile

Located at the junction of the Central American isthmus and South America, Panama is an S-shaped strip of land about 480 miles long and from 37 to 110 miles wide. Its total area, excluding the Canal Zone, is 28,576 square miles. Two mountain chains run through Panama from northwest to southeast. In the west, near the Costa Rican border, the highest mountain reaches an altitude of over 11,000 feet. In the east

---

[1] John and Mavis Biesanz, *The People of Panama* (New York: Columbia University Press, 1955), p. 10.

229

the mountains are lower, reaching only 3,000 feet. Where the two chains meet, southwest of Panama City, the highest land is only about 285 feet above sea level, and here the Panama Canal was built.

The section of Panama west of the Canal has been somewhat developed, especially around David and near the Costa Rican border on the Pacific side, where the United Fruit Company operates extensive plantations. The section of Panama east of the Canal remains in large part unused jungle, impassable to man by ordinary means of transportation. Only about 16 percent of Panama's land area is developed for man's use, although many areas are capable of being used, and about 60 percent of the country's food supply is imported.

Panama's population at the census of July 1965 was 1,278,624. The population has been growing rapidly in recent years, at a rate of 3.3 percent from 1958 to 1962. The population is very mixed and very unevenly distributed. In 1960, 369,280, or 34.6 percent, lived in the province of Panamá, which includes the area around the Canal. There is only one large city in the country, Panama City, with 318,536 inhabitants in 1964. Other cities are Colón, with 62,756 in 1964, and David, with about 25,000. In 1960, 41.5 percent of the population was urban and 58.5 percent was rural.

Spanish is the country's official language, but many Panamanians use English and most members of the upper classes can speak it. At the 1960 census, 27,130 of the Indians over seven years of age knew no Spanish. Elementary education is compulsory for all children seven to fifteen years of age, but the 1960 census showed 25.1 percent of the total population illiterate; 21.7 percent of the non-Indian population over ten years of age and 86.1 percent of the Indians were illiterate.

About 93 percent of the population is considered to be of the Roman Catholic religion and about 6 percent are Protestants, but no really accurate figures are available on the population's religious affiliations. Church and state are constitutionally separate and there is freedom of worship. Clergymen may teach in schools, but may not hold public office.

Although Panama has a comparatively high per capita income, the figures are deceiving; basically Panama is a very poor and underdeveloped country. There are only two important industries: agriculture, which in 1960 occupied about 50 percent of the gainfully employed, and the interoceanic canal and all of the activities associated with it. Only about 3.1 percent of the land area is cultivated, 7.3 percent is in natural or artificial pasture, and 5 percent is fallow land; all the rest lies completely unused. Of those engaged in agriculture, the majority live from subsistence crops and the rest are paid laborers on the large haciendas and commercial farms.

Panama's most important export crop is bananas, produced by the United Fruit Company (59.7 percent of total exports in 1960). Rice is the most important crop grown for local consumption. Other products are maize, cocoa, abacá, sugar, coffee, and coconuts. Cattle raising is also important, and there are valuable timber resources. An active fishing fleet catches shrimp for export (25.6 percent of total exports in 1960). Little industry exists, but a flourishing free port at Colón brings in some revenue.

The Canal directly or indirectly provides a living for most of the people living alongside it, particularly in Panama City and Colón. Some are employed by the Canal Zone, but more make a living serving tourists and the crews of the ships passing through. The dependence of the country upon the Canal can be seen by the figures for the gross domestic product. In 1962, agricultural production amounted to $113.9 million, while income from services in general and services to the Canal amounted to $119.2 million. Income from industry amounted to only $56.3 million; construction, $25.2 million; electricity, gas, and water production, $7.8 million; transportation and communications, $27 million; commerce, $61.3 million; finance, $14 million; the ownership of dwellings, $38.7 million; and public administration and defense, $6.7 million, for a total gross domestic product of $470.1 million.

The result of the economic system is extreme poverty and poor health for the majority of the population. In 1960 there was no electricity in 52 percent of the homes in the country, 4 percent had no water supply, 36 percent had no plumbing for sanitary purposes. Undernourishment is common, and there is a great shortage of medical facilities in the rural areas. Panama City is surrounded by slums known as *barriadas brujas*, a collection of shacks thrown together.

As can readily be seen by this brief sketch, Panama is not an integrated economic unit. Underpopulated, dependent for prosperity upon the Canal, the country has never developed the habit of doing what needs to be done to build itself up economically. An economic system of this kind breeds poverty, and with the rise of extreme nationalism and *Fidelismo* in the years since World War II, the government and people have concentrated their energies upon getting a larger share of the revenue from the Canal rather than upon developing Panama. Political life has thus become very agitated, especially since the lack of economic opportunity drives many young Panamanians into politics as one of the few ways of making a living.

Yet it is fair to say that more progress has been made since World War II than in the forty years before that. From 1955 to 1960 the national income rose 33.2 percent, an annual economic growth rate of 5.9 percent. In the same period, the national per capita income rose from 305 balboas to B/350 (the balboa is equivalent to the dollar), an increase of 15.4 percent or an annual rate of 2.9 percent. But the gulf between the few rich and the many poor is still extremely sharp in Panama, thus making political life stormy as waves of nationalism sweep over the country.

The Development of Modern Panama

Panama was one of the first places on the American mainland visited by the Spanish *conquistadores*. Columbus himself tried to set up a colony in 1502 in what is now the province of Colón. Vasco Núñez de Balboa discovered the Pacific Ocean for the Spaniards in 1513 from a peak in Darién, and from that date on Panama became an important center from which other parts of the continent were attacked and conquered. Yet what is now the republic of Panama was never fully occupied during colonial days. Panama was merely the place where it was easiest to cross from the Atlantic to the Pacific and vice versa, so it never consisted of much more than a road connecting ports on each coast.

Panama became independent of Spain on November 28, 1821, but it immediately joined Bolívar's republic of Greater Colombia. When Greater Colombia fell apart in 1830, Panama became a part of the republic of New Granada, the ancestor of today's Colombia. During the nineteenth century there were many disputes about domination of Panama by faraway Bogotá, but the granting of extensive local power to Panama kept the territory within Colombia, although a movement to make Panama independent always had some support. Toward the middle of the century, when the discovery of gold in California increased traffic across Panama, the United States became an important force. Financial interests from the United States built a railroad across the isthmus, and United States troops were landed many times from 1857 to 1903 to protect the railroad or the lives and property of United States citizens. At the same time, a cosmopolitan population developed because people from all of the world's continents settled on the isthmus to make a living serving those who crossed from one ocean to the other.

During the last half of the nineteenth century, a French company began construction of an interocean canal in Panama, but the health conditions were so bad that the company went bankrupt before the canal was built. By 1900 the United States government had decided to build a canal somewhere in Central America, and a great conflict began in Washington as to its location: Nicaragua or Panama? There seems to be a great deal of evidence that the Nicaraguan route was technically better, and the U.S. House of Representatives voted to build the canal there, but the bankrupt French canal company succeeded in having Panama selected as the site for the United States canal by what has been called "one of the greatest and most effective campaigns of lobbying in the history of the Congress of the United States."[2] The French company wanted the Panama route chosen so it could sell its assets to the United States. The amount of cash that finally changed hands was $40 million, and for many decades there was a great mystery about who actually got the money. Many scholars now believe that United States financial interests had bought up most of the canal stock and the money went to them.[3]

When the United States made its decision to build a canal in Panama, it negotiated a treaty with Colombia under which the United States was to receive the right to build a canal in return for a payment of $10 million and an annual rental of $250,000. When the Colombian government procrastinated in ratifying the treaty, agents of the French canal company organized a plot to set Panama up as an independent republic. Utilizing the anti-Colombian sentiment that had always existed, and making arrangements in advance with President Theodore Roosevelt, the plotters launched a revolt on November 2, 1903. United States armed forces prevented Colombian troops from interfering.[4] On November 6, 1903, the United States recognized the rebels as the government of the new republic of Panama. An official of the bankrupt French canal company, Philippe Bunau-Varilla, became Panama's minister to the United States, and quickly a treaty was entered into under which the United States received the right to build its canal. The assets of the French company were purchased and the construction of the canal was begun. The first president of Panama was an employee of the French canal company.

Panama thus became an independent state, not because its people wanted a new status, but because someone was interested in $40 million.

---

[2] Jules Dubois, *Danger over Panama* (Indianapolis: Bobbs-Merrill Co., 1964), p. 25.

[3] For one version of who got the $40 million, see Earl Harding, *The Untold Story of Panama* (New York: Athene Press, 1959). For another description of the activities of Sullivan and Cromwell, the New York City law firm, in lobbying for the selection of the Panama Canal site, see Dubois, *Danger over Panama*, pp. 25–29.

[4] One scholar argues that President Roosevelt "believed his actions [in Panama] to be morally right." See Robert A. Friedlander, "A Reassessment of Roosevelt's Role in the Panamanian Revolution of 1903," *Western Political Quarterly*, 14 (June 1961): 535–43.

Much of the republic's difficulties in organizing a stable political system based upon a prosperous population can be traced to its original establishment. In 1903, what is now Panama had a population of about 200,000 to 300,000. About seven-eighths of the area was unpopulated and the little republic had none of the necessities for establishing a stable government of any kind. Until then, the Colombian government had sent officials to govern the area, and there were no trained political leaders or civil servants to take over the job. Much of the population was illiterate and diseased; economic development consisted of a little agriculture, a few enterprises catering to those crossing the isthmus or building the Canal, and the United States–owned railroad. The Colombian government would eventually have signed the treaty with the United States, but the United States was in a hurry, and so Panama entered the world as an independent state. For all practical purposes, however, from 1903 to 1936 Panama was a virtual protectorate of the United States.

Under the Hay–Bunau-Varilla treaty, the United States guaranteed the independence of Panama and in return was given the use, occupation, and control of a strip of territory ten miles wide, as well as "in perpetuity the use, occupation and control of *any other lands and waters outside of the zone*" which would be necessary for the "construction, maintenance, operation, sanitation and protection" of the Canal. In the Canal Zone and outside it the United States was to exercise all "rights, power and authority" as if "it were the sovereign of the territory within which said lands and waters are located to the entire exclusion of the exercise by the Republic of Panama of any such sovereign rights, power or authority." For these privileges, Panama received $10 million and an annual rental of $250,000 to begin nine years after the treaty was signed. Building of the Canal soon began, and in 1914 it was opened to world traffic.

Since 1903, the life of Panama has revolved around the Canal. Although President Roosevelt wrote in his biography, "We gave to the people of Panama self-government, and freed them from subjection to alien oppressors,"[5] the republic has witnessed little self-government. The first constitution of the republic, that of 1904, included Article VII of the Hay–Bunau-Varilla treaty of 1903, which permitted the United States to use its own armed forces to maintain order in the new republic "in case the Republic of Panama should not be, in the judgment of the United States, able to maintain such order."

---

[5] Quoted in Diógenes A. Arosemena, *Documentary Diplomatic History of the Panama Canal* (Panamá, n.p., 1961), p. 326.

Panama found itself dominated by the United States, with the economic and political machinery of the country in the hands of a few wealthy families. The exclusiveness of the oligarchy dominating Panama can be seen by looking at the names prominent throughout its history as a republic. The revolutionary junta that was Panama's first government included Federico Boyd, Carlos Constantino Arosemena, Tomás Arias, and Ricardo Arias. Ever since, the history of Panama has been full of presidents, cabinet ministers, and other political leaders named Boyd, Arosemena, and Arias; one presidential contest was between Harmodio Arias Madrid and Francisco Arias Paredes.

The United States supervised the elections in 1904, 1908, 1912, and 1920, but a stable electoral system never developed and politics became a struggle for power by the ambitious members of the upper classes. Education, transportation, settlement of empty lands, and economic development were fostered, but there were so few Panamanians that most development was financed by foreign capital. By 1929, $36 million from the United States and $7.5 million from Great Britain had been invested in railroads, agricultural developments, timberlands, minerals, banks, and public utilities. Panama always had an unfavorable balance of trade, which was made up by the money spent in Panama by Canal employees.

One other most important result of the construction of the Canal was that it changed the racial composition of Panama's population. The unhealthy conditions in Panama in 1903 led the United States to import many thousands of English-speaking Negroes from the British West Indies to do the common labor in the construction of the Canal. Many of the West Indians never returned to the islands from which they had been recruited, and today their descendants are Panamanians. The West Indians added a further complication to an already complex racial pattern, for Panama's cosmopolitan urbanites, rural farmers, and tribal Indians formed three completely unintegrated groups; the English-speaking West Indians became a fourth that would have to be assimilated before Panama could develop an integrated society.

As long as the Canal construction went on and the United States poured funds into the country, some kind of stability was maintained. But when the Canal was completed, most of the laborers were discharged to make their way as best they could. When the world depression of the 1930's hit Panama, the traditional system of government broke down, and in January 1931 the country experienced its first revolutionary change in government. About this time the former West Indian Negroes began to feel the race consciousness that was sweeping over the black people in all parts of the world. At the same time the Spanish-speaking Panamanians were beginning to feel the spirit of nationalism which has been so prominent a part of the history of Latin America in recent decades. From then on, this rising nationalism, which here had the Panama Canal as an object against which to protest, became a feature of Panamanian politics.

One other result of the Canal was the development of a segregation pattern for Negroes and other Panamanians in the Canal Zone, which created tension between the United States and Panama and was to lead to anti–United States riots in the 1950's and 1960's. As one study described the system, the United States "established gold and silver towns, gold and silver commissaries, gold and silver lavatories and drinking fountains, even gold and silver windows at the post office."[6] The "gold" payroll and facilities were for the United States citizens, the "silver" payroll and facilities for Panamanians. Officially segregation in the Canal Zone was abolished in 1947, but unofficially much of it remains.

When the political system broke down with the revolution of 1931, agitation began in Panama to revise the terms of the 1903 treaty between Panama and the United States. In 1936 the United States gave up its right to intervene in Panama's affairs and its pledge to guarantee Panama's sovereignty and independence. Certain economic complaints by Panama also were met, and the annual rental for the Canal was raised from $250,000 to $430,000. Meanwhile, in 1921, the United States and Colombia had signed a treaty concerning Panama, and in 1924, diplomatic relations between Panama and Colombia were instituted. The change in the United States–Panama treaty was formalized in the 1940 constitution.

Thus Panama really began its independent existence in 1936. Until World War II ended, political life continued much as before—a struggle between members of the upper-class families for control of the governmental apparatus. But by the time the war was over, Panama was greatly changed. The population had increased rapidly, education had produced a more alert public opinion, and health conditions were greatly improved. When the system of government by an entrenched oligarchy continued as before, riots and turmoil became an ever present part of Panama's political scene.

Panama had depended upon the United States to defend it from

---

[6] Biesanz and Biesanz, *People of Panama*, p. 56.

foreign enemies and had no army from 1903 to World War II. But by 1948, its police force of 2,500 was a well-trained, heavily armed body controlled by its chief, José Antonio Remón. In the postwar period he became the decisive force in selecting the president of the republic, and after installing and ejecting several chief executives, in 1952 Remón himself became a presidential candidate and easily won the election in May of that year. To the surprise of practically everyone, Remón became probably the best president the country had ever had until then.

He made a serious attempt to turn the country's attention away from the Canal and toward its undeveloped lands. He pushed public works (particularly roads), enforced and improved the tax laws, fought graft, moved toward cooperation with the other Central American states, set up a free zone in Colón which was very successful, reduced the country's internal debt, improved the agricultural system, changed the police force into an army, and succeeded in negotiating a new treaty with the United States under which, among other concessions to Panama, the United States increased its annual rental for the Canal to $1.93 million.

Under Remón, government was constitutional, political parties flourished, and Panama seemed about to enter a new period in its history. Unfortunately, on January 2, 1955, Remón was assassinated and chaos returned to the country. The first vice-president, who succeeded him, was accused of complicity in the assassination, impeached, and jailed. The second vice-president then became president and served until 1956, when Ernesto de la Guardia, Jr., was elected. During De la Guardia's term in office, virulent nationalism flared up. Anti–United States demonstrations were organized. There was great agitation to have the Panamanian flag flown over the Canal. A *Fidelista* movement became active in Panama. The United States finally agreed to fly the Panamanian flag over the Canal alongside the United States flag.

The 1960 election was thought to be the most honest ever held in Panama; a new electoral system had been created in 1956 and the government's opposition won, making Roberto F. Chiari president for the 1960–64 term. President Chiari found himself facing the perennial problem of Panama: relations with the United States and its canal. By the 1960's the Russians, working through Cuba, were agitating the Canal issue, and in January 1964 riots broke out and conditions became so bad that Panama broke relations with the United States. The riots began in a struggle between high school students over which flag was to fly in front of a Canal Zone school, but before it was over it resembled a minor war; rioting mobs destroyed considerable property, fifteen persons were killed, and many more were injured.[7]

The 1964 election saw seven candidates competing for the presidency. Since the elections came shortly after the January riots, the status of the Canal was the main issue. Marcos A. Robles, supported by eight different political parties and the outgoing president, won a plurality and took office. His problems were the same as his predecessors': the difficulties of developing a functioning economy and government in a country that had never really had either. To complicate the situation, the United States government announced that it was going to build a new, larger sea-level canal to supplement the Panama Canal. Panama, of course—despite all the problems the old canal had brought it—wanted to see the new one in its territory. Thus the life of Panama still revolved around a canal, just as it has done ever since canal politics created the republic.

In 1968, Robles, who could not succeed himself, backed former Finance Minister David Samudio for the presidency, but in a hotly contested election Samudio lost to former President Arnulfo Arias, who was elected for the 1968–72 term.

The Formal Constitutional Framework

Panama is governed under the constitution of March 1, 1946, which describes the republic of Panama as having a government that is "republican, democratic, and representative." This is Panama's third constitution. Like its predecessors of 1904 and 1941, the constitution of 1946 sets up a presidential type of government modeled on that of the United States. And like most other Latin-American constitutions, Panama's is a long document containing much extraneous matter, including long sections on the family, labor and culture, public health and social assistance. An extensive listing of individual rights and duties is followed by a clause permitting the government to suspend the most important individual rights "in the event of foreign war or domestic disturbance threatening the peace or public order." An unusual clause is Article XI, which states that naturalized citizens could lose their citizenship if they did not, within five years after the constitution went into force, "have a command of the Spanish language and an elementary knowledge of Panamanian geography, history, and political organization." Generally speaking, the 1946 constitution provides the framework of a democratic unitary state in which the rights of the people are well protected.

---

[7] See International Commission of Jurists, *Report on the Events in Panama, January 9–12, 1964* (Geneva, 1964).

How the Constitution Is Amended

Panama's constitution can be amended by a majority vote of the National Assembly in two sessions, but an election for new deputies must take place between the two votes. The president can object to an amendment, whereupon the Assembly can overrule his objection by a two-thirds vote. The process is not complicated, and amendments have been adopted since the constitution went into effect in 1946.

Who Participates in Politics

It is impossible to say what proportion of Panama's population meaningfully participates in the country's political life. The habit of voting is well developed among Panamanians, perhaps because the United States supervised several elections during the formative years of the republic, and failure to vote is punishable by a small fine, but this does not mean the votes are cast by an alert citizenry. All citizens over twenty-one can vote and run for office. All that is required is that one register and receive his certificate of personal identity (*cédula*). The *cédula*, in addition to being used for voting, is needed for any transaction with the government, and many people probably get their *cédulas* for this reason, and not because they want to vote.

Panama has a rather high percentage of voters in comparison with other Latin-American states. In 1952, 211,302 votes were cast; in 1960, 241,957; in 1964, 317,312. There are some reports that in the rural areas the votes are controlled by local landowners and "strong men." Real political participation seems to be confined to the urban area around the Canal, with Panama City dominating the political scene.

The Electoral Machinery

Because of dissatisfaction with the system previously used, elections since 1956 have been organized and controlled by a constitutionally created, independent Electoral Tribunal consisting of three members, one being selected by each of the three traditional powers, the executive, the legislative, and the judicial. The members of the Electoral Tribunal serve for twelve years and have complete control of all phases of the electoral process. Under this system, the Electoral Tribunal supervises the work of a pyramid of officials down to the committees to supervise the voting districts, each of which has a maximum of 425 voters. The Electoral Tribunal prepares a separate ballot for each party, but a voter can split his vote by choosing one party's presidential slate and another party's candidates for the legislature. Complaints still are made after each election, and since no thorough studies have been made of any Panamanian election, it cannot be said how good the system is. On paper it appears to be capable of producing fair elections.

Political Parties

Panama has never developed an effective party system or functioning political parties, and the best organized party is probably the Communist. Parties began in 1903 with the Panamanian sections of the Colombian Conservative and Liberal Parties, but these soon disappeared, and since then an uncountable number of "parties" have passed through the country's hectic political life. In 1964 there were nineteen national and seventeen municipal parties on the ballot with seven presidential candidates. For a country with a little over a million people, this is fantastic. Nearly all Panamanian parties are the reflections of individuals, and frequently an organization is known by its man's name with an *ista* at the end; e.g., *Jimenistas* or *Fabregistas*. Sometimes the man's first name is used, so that the followers of Arnulfo Arias, for example, become *Arnulfistas*.

To cut down the number of political parties, the number of members needed to found a party was raised to 50,000, but then almost all parties lost their ballot positions. At this writing a party needs 5,000 members to be registered nationally. A smaller number is needed to register as a municipal party (100 to 1,000). After registration a party must hold a national convention within thirty days. The party then receives certain privileges, the most important being that the government cannot interfere in the organization's internal affairs or make the party the defendant in a court case. The party must win a minimum of 5,000 votes in a national election to retain its position on the ballot.

The largest party in Panama at present is probably Arnulfo Arias' *Panameñista* Party, which has strong support from the urban poor. Arnulfo Arias has been president three times and was ejected from office twice, the second time after a minor civil war. He has been a sympathizer of the Nazis and has changed his political ideas several times, but he has managed to build support among the lower classes by being an extreme nationalist. Most of the other parties are little cliques revolving around one or two leaders, and their names are so similar it is difficult to keep track of them. Parties that participated in the 1964 election, for example, included the National Patriotic Coalition, the Renovating

Party, the National Civic Party, the Third Nationalist Party, the Dipal Party, the Liberal Civic Resistance, the National Liberal Party, the Republican Party, the National Liberation Movement, and the Independent Revolutionary Party.

The Liberal Party is split up into so many factions it does not have much importance. A Socialist party was founded in 1937 as a split-off of the Liberal Party and was strong from 1936 to 1940, but it has dwindled to a small group, although it is much more ideological than the other parties. In recent years a Christian Democratic party has been functioning, but in 1964 it received only 9,744 votes for its presidential candidate out of the more than 300,000 votes cast.

A Communist party has existed in Panama since the late 1920's, but it has never been very large. Its name at various times has been the Communist Party, the Party of the People, and the Leftist Socialist Party, but it has always followed the Moscow party line; in 1940, for example, it cooperated with Arnulfo Arias, since he was pro-Axis at the same time Stalin was allied with Hitler. In 1953 the Communist Party was made illegal, and since then the electoral law has contained a clause forbidding parties that advocate the destruction of the democratic form of government. After Fidel Castro became popular, the Communists grew in strength and vociferously cultivated anti–United States feeling, and they have participated in and helped organize the riots that have occurred since 1959. Various attempts to invade Panama from Cuba have been unsuccessful. The Communists continue to be a small group, but their organizational techniques and financial support make them look stronger than they really are.

Since the parties are all weak, they make alliances for the presidential elections. The victors in 1964 were a coalition of eight parties calling themselves the National Union of the Opposition, although they were supported by the incumbent president. Another group of parties was known as the Alliance of the Opposition. How the poor voter is expected to keep track of these groups is a mystery, but of course the campaigns revolve around the names of the presidential candidates.

Public Opinion and Pressure Groups

Public opinion is centralized in Panama City, and the population around the Canal is the only group able to affect public policy. The organized workers on the United Fruit Company plantation near the Costa Rican border are able to affect their wages and working conditions through strikes and other activities, but even this group plays a very minor role in the country's political life. Politics is made in the capital. The press and radio are centralized there, with ten of the country's twelve daily newspapers being published in the capital. Despite the high literacy rate in Panama, the circulation of newspapers is low. The most popular, though not the best, is *Panamá América*, with about 14,000 copies daily. *Estrella de Panamá*, a Spanish daily that circulates about 11,000, and its sister newspaper, the *Star and Herald* in English, with about 10,000 copies daily, are considered the best newspapers in Panama. Presidents, ex-presidents, and their families are conspicuous among newspaper owners and editors. Radio is probably the most important influence in the rural area; at last count about sixty-three radio stations were functioning.

Informal organizations, primarily the extended family, are the most important groups active in politics. John and Mavis Biesanz have reported that "many urban Panamanians profess complete indifference to politics. But there is not true indifference; it is disillusion with grafting politicians, rigged elections, and 'constitutionalized' *coups d'état*, and a determination to have nothing to do with such a dirty business."[8] There is some evidence that the spirit of nationalism which led to the riots of 1964 has awakened elements of the population which had not traditionally been active in politics. Much of the country's difficulty is due to the lack of well-organized, functioning secondary groups and strong political parties.

The most important group in Panama is what can roughly be called the aristocracy, the families that have dominated Panamanian politics since the country was organized. In addition to personal relationships among the members of this group, they utilize the various clubs and businessmen's organizations to keep contact with each other. There is some evidence that as the economy improves, this group is losing some of its dominance.

The leaders of the small armed forces have played an increasingly important role since the Second World War, and with Remón as president they became the dominant group in the country. Limited economic opportunities have always pushed the energetic educated middle-class youth toward positions in the government and the armed forces.

The students are one of the few groups able to demand change from the government. The size of the university helps to increase the students' leverage; in a city the size of Panama, some 5,000 students can make quite an impression. As Biesanz and Smith have pointed out, "the stu-

---

[8] Biesanz and Biesanz, *People of Panama,* p. 154.

dents dramatize political issues by strikes, parades, and rallies, calling on the president, marching on the assembly, printing and distributing handbills, writing for newspapers, getting jailed, setting up barricades, baring their breasts to the police and daring them to shoot, and sometimes getting injured or killed by the police."[9] The Communists have made great efforts to influence the students and at times have captured the student organizations, particularly the Panamanian Federation of Students. In 1961, when the struggle between Communists and their opponents for control of the student organizations became especially fierce, the university administration forced a university-wide election that saw the noncommunists winning with 64 percent of the votes.

The labor movement is weak because there are few industries and because the unions of workers in the Canal Zone are oriented toward the United States. In 1966 there were only 17,000 trade-union members in an estimated labor force of 370,000. The rural workers, except for those on the United Fruit Company plantations, have never been organized.

The politics of pressure groups is very distorted in Panama, as the largest employer is the Panama Canal Company and ordinary pressure politics cannot be applied. Perhaps this is the cause of the nationalist frenzy that led to the 1964 riots; Panamanian politics inevitably revolves not around what the country's government ought to do, but around how to get more income from the Canal.

Civil Liberties

The Panama constitution provides all of the standard civil liberties including equality before the law, no imprisonment for debt, the right to *habeas corpus,* the right to travel freely, freedom from search and seizure, and freedom of press, speech, and assembly. There is no death penalty. The constitution contains a provision for declaring a state of siege, but, generally speaking, Panamanians have had liberty to do as they please. Some observers attribute this to the Canal Zone, for anyone can avoid the Panamanian police by stepping into the Zone, but the reason for liberty probably goes deeper than this. Politics has developed in such a way that the aristocratic and middle classes, who have traditionally governed the country, have never seriously been threatened. Until the late 1930's the country was practically a protectorate of the United States, and it is only now beginning to get away from almost complete dependence upon the Canal and the United States govern-

---

[9] John Biesanz and Luke M. Smith, "Panamanian Politics," *Journal of Politics,* 14 (August 1962): 386–402.

ment. The record shows, however, that Panama has never had anything resembling the *caudillo* dictatorships of other Latin-American countries.

The Executive

Panama's executive is a president directly elected for a four-year term. He cannot be reelected until eight years after he has left office. With the president, a first and a second vice-president are elected to take his place when necessary, and it is common for a vice-president to substitute for a short time, then revert to the vice-presidency. To be elected president, one must be a Panamanian by birth and at least thirty-five years old. Not eligible is anyone who has held the presidency temporarily during the two years previous to the election or who is a relative of the incumbent president within the fourth degree by blood and the second degree of affinity. The president is not eligible to be a vice-president for the period after his term has expired, nor are his relatives.

The president is supposed to exercise his powers jointly with his ministers, and the wording of the constitution makes the Cabinet Council, consisting of the president and his ministers, the key agency in the executive. The president, however, has the power to appoint and remove his ministers freely, and he has the power to supervise the administration, to preserve public order, and to see that the National Assembly meets on the date set. He presents a message about the administration to the Assembly on the first day of its regular session. With his ministers individually, the Cabinet Council, or the Permanent Legislative Committee, the president sanctions and promulgates the laws; appoints and dismisses the governors of the provinces, officers of the armed forces, and other officials of the government; draws up and submits the budget; conducts foreign relations; and directs the armed forces.

The president of Panama is a strong executive who has traditionally dominated all aspects of political life. This is true even when a person who is not a member of the traditional aristocratic power group becomes president. The president's appointing power is large, and since the spoils system is used for most appointments, the members of the legislature and the judiciary usually do what the president wants so they can get their friends and relatives on the public payroll or keep them there. Local government also is completely dominated by the president. Most of Panama's presidents have utilized their power to make themselves rich or to preserve the wealth they already had.

Marco A. Robles, president from 1964 to 1968, is a typical Panamanian political leader who has been on the government payroll during most of his life. At one time or another he has been a member of Panama's diplomatic missions in London and Paris, secretary of the Electoral Tribunal, secretary of the national police force, first secretary to the Minister of Public Works, a deputy, president of the National Commission to Assess Real Estate, director of the National Bank of Panama, and Minister of Government and Justice.

The Civil Service

Panama has taken some weak, halting steps toward a formal merit system for its employees, but there are too many government employees and too few efficient ones. In August 1960 the national government had 23,884 employees and the fifteen autonomous organizations had 4,973. Practically all of them received their posts because of personal contact with someone in a position of power. The cabinet ministers cannot be relatives of the president within four degrees by blood and two degrees by affinity, but this rule has not helped matters. Panama has a tradition of peculation and graft in addition to overstaffing. In 1956 a gradual introduction of a career administrative system was begun, and in 1959 a General Office of Planning and Administration was created as a staff agency in the president's office. In 1963 an elaborate plan to reorganize the government was drawn up by the Department of Administrative Organization of the General Office of Planning and Administration, but most of its recommendations were never instituted.

The Legislative Power

Panama's legislature is a unicameral body of fifty-three members known as the National Assembly. One deputy is elected for each 25,000 persons plus an additional deputy for any remainder over 15,000. The deputies are allotted to the provinces in accordance with their population, the least populated provinces (Bocas del Toro, Darién) having one and the most populated province (Panamá) having seventeen. For each deputy, a first and a second alternate are elected, thus obviating the need for by-elections. Deputies serve four-year terms and are eligible for reelection. To be a deputy it is necessary only to be twenty-five years old and a citizen in possession of his rights.

A deputy cannot hold a paid position with the government of Panama except that of cabinet minister or head of a diplomatic mission, in which case he takes a leave of absence and an alternate temporarily holds his seat. Panama's National Assembly has all of the powers usually given a legislature, including enacting laws, organizing the public administration, approving or rejecting treaties and contracts signed by the executive, declaring war, fixing the number of the armed forces in time of peace, granting amnesty for political offenses, approving the budget, establishing taxes, impeaching the president, justices of the Supreme Court, and other officials, appointing various officials including the attorney general and the comptroller general, and approving or disapproving certain appointments made by the president. The Assembly meets annually on October 1 for four months in regular sessions, except in an election year, when the meeting adjourns on November 30. The executive can call the Assembly into special sessions, but in that case only the matters submitted can be dealt with.

When a legislative session ends, a Permanent Legislative Committee consisting of the president of the Assembly and six members (for each of whom a substitute is also elected) is chosen by proportional representation to handle legislative matters that come up while the Assembly is not in session. The Assembly elects a comptroller general who directs the agency that audits and supervises all of the government's accounts; his term is four years. The legislature has never played an important role and most legislation originates with the executive.

The relative importance and strength of the president and the National Assembly were demonstrated in 1968 when the Assembly voted to impeach President Robles, who immediately used the National Guard to prevent further meetings of the Assembly. The issue went to the Supreme Court, which, by a vote of 8 to 1, decided that the impeachment was illegal. The dispute between the Assembly and the President came during the campaign to elect a new president for the 1968–72 term.

Public Finance

The president presents the budget to the legislature for its approval each year and the comptroller general of the republic regulates, oversees, and controls the movement of funds out of the treasury. The total budget has been rising rapidly in recent years, total expenditures in 1964 being about double those of 1954 and four times as great as those of 1944. Per capita spending has also been rising, from B/28.69 in 1944 to B/45.31 in 1954 and B/66.81 in 1964. The budget for 1964, shown in Tables 1 and 2, is typical of the way Panama gets its money and spends it.

An exact breakdown of the taxes for 1964 is not available at this writing, but in 1963, of B/55,027,278 in taxes, B/35,389,753 came from indirect taxes, primarily on imports and consumption, and B/19,637,525

TABLE 1
REVENUE OF PANAMA, FISCAL YEAR 1964

Source	Amount in Balboas	Percent of Total
National wealth	B/335,000	0.4%
National services	4,584,000	5.6
Taxes	62,186,880	76.3
Income from government property	11,830,000	14.5
Miscellaneous	2,636,000	3.2
Total	B/81,571,880	100.0%

TABLE 2
EXPENDITURES OF PANAMA, FISCAL YEAR 1964

	Amount in Balboas	Percent of Total
National Assembly	B/1,166,650	1.4%
Auditing Bureau	1,571,681	1.9
President of the Republic	1,021,208	1.3
Ministry of Government and Justice (about half goes for the National Guard)	10,045,596	12.3
Ministry of Foreign Relations	1,404,136	1.7
Ministry of Finance	2,150,194	2.6
Ministry of Education	20,551,023	25.2
University of Panama	2,190,775	2.7
Ministry of Public Works	7,398,347	9.1
Ministry of Agriculture, Commerce, and Industry	3,391,062	4.2
Office of Price Regulation	112,535	0.1
Ministry of Labor, Social Security, and Public Health	12,200,848	15.0
Courts	851,628	1.1
Electoral system	1,400,000	1.7
External debt	5,032,614	6.2
Internal debt	5,982,341	7.3
Miscellaneous	5,101,242	6.2
Total	B/81,571,880	100.0%

from direct taxes, basically on income and property. Taxes are levied upon all income earned within the republic, ranging from 2 percent on incomes from B/900 to B/2,400 to 25.24 percent on incomes of B/1 million, with a maximum of 34 percent in all incomes over B/1 million. A 20 percent surtax applies only to income from business. Other important taxes are those on imports, real estate, tourists, and stamp taxes on legal papers and documents.

Local Government

For purposes of local government, Panama is divided into nine provinces and one territory, which contain sixty-three districts known as municipalities. The provinces play no real role in government; they serve merely as subdivisions of the national government. Each province is headed by a governor who is appointed by the president of the republic acting through the Ministry of Government and Justice. The governor is supposed to supervise the municipal governments and the agencies of the national government within his province and maintain law and order, but in actual practice the governors do little, as they have neither the funds nor the personnel to accomplish much.

Within the provinces, wherever a sufficient number of people is found, a municipal government is set up, consisting of a council elected for a four-year term and an *alcalde* who is appointed by the president. The municipal governments are autonomous, but they do not have the financial resources to enable them to do very much. Municipal taxes are limited by law to certain fields; the major income comes from license fees on businesses, annual auto and truck license plates, and fees for commercial signs and advertising posters. There is no clear division of duties between the *alcalde* and the council and there is little coordination between the activities of the municipal governments and those of the various national ministries. The provinces vary greatly in population, from 19,715 people in Darién in 1960 to 372,353 in the province of Panamá. The varying populations require varying services, but no provision is made for the differences. Both the provincial and the municipal governments are notoriously weak and inefficient.

The Judicial Power

Panama's court system is headed by a Supreme Court of Justice consisting of nine justices serving eighteen-year terms. The justices are appointed by the president with the approval of the Cabinet Council and of the National Assembly, one every two years. The Supreme Court is divided into panels of three justices each for transacting business, one panel each for civil, penal, and administrative cases, and a fourth panel consisting of one judge from each of the other three for transacting general business. Alternates are appointed at the same time as the regular justices. Below the Supreme Court of Justice ranges a hierarchy of lower courts consisting of superior courts, circuit courts, and municipal and special courts. The judges of each level of the court system are appointed by the court above, the Supreme Court appointing the judges of the superior courts and so on.

The Panama courts have the power of judicial review. If the president rejects a law sent to him by the legislature on the grounds that it is unconstitutional and the Assembly votes again that it is, the Supreme Court decides the question.

The Panama court system appears to work fairly well.

Panama: A Last Word

Panama is just now emerging as an independent political unit after living as an appendage to the Canal since it was organized in 1903. Perhaps this little country's dependence on the Canal was inevitable, since there really was no logical reason for an independent political unit to have been set up. The low population of the area, the primitive economy, and the overwhelming power of the United States forced the new country to become what it is.

Unfortunately, just as Panama turned its energies away from the Canal, particularly during the Remón administration, toward the stimulation of agriculture and industry, the development of the free port of Colón, and other economic innovations, the effects of the cold war and the rise of *Fidelismo* forced Panama back to the decades-old concentration upon the Canal. Both the United Arab Republic of Nasser and Castro's Cuba have been very active in Panama, trying to stir up demands for Panama to take over the Canal.[10] In Panama this is a relatively easy thing to do. But the United States government has never seriously considered this a workable solution to anyone's problems, and there is much evidence that the Panamanian government does not favor it either. The operation and safeguarding of an interocean route that is so important to so many countries of the world is a grave responsibility. Could little Panama run the Canal? Could it guarantee its safety? What if the Communists captured Panama?

It has also been suggested that the Canal be given to the Organization of American States. The OAS would then move its offices to the Zone, and it would give all the republics of America part ownership and part control of the Canal. All would defend it and all would use it. The Zone

---

[10] See, for example, Hanson W. Baldwin, "Cuban and Arab Activity in Panama," *New York Times*, March 13, 1960, p. 1.

would then be an international territory and the conflict between the United States and Panama would disappear. But would not Panama still focus its economy and energy upon the Canal?

Another proposed solution is that the United States invite the republic of Panama to join the Union as the fifty-first state or as an associated commonwealth with a status similar to that of Puerto Rico. This solution appeals to those who see no future for tiny nation-states.

It is impossible to say whether any of these solutions will be adopted. Meanwhile, Panama continues to be a weak country with a weak government because it does not control the most important economic activity within the country. The political parties and other secondary groups so essential in the modern world are all weak because the cultural pattern does not foster them. The economic system is backward because all eyes and energies are on the Canal. The only thing one can expect for Panama is that it will continue in the near future as it has continued in the past, as the home of an interocean route around which all economic and political activity will revolve.

As this book went to press, President Arnulfo Arias was deposed by the National Guard, Panama's army, only eleven days after his inauguration. Having been ousted by the military twice before, Arias began his third term in office with a shake-up of the officer corps, including the removal of the Guard's deputy chief, Colonel José M. Pinilla, and threatened further moves to weaken the Guard's political power. The officers responded by clearing the streets of Panama City and Colón, taking over the radio stations and the international airport, and installing a two-man junta, composed of Colonel Pinilla and Colonel Bolívar Urrutia, to rule the country. Their first governmental acts were to suspend constitutional guarantees and dissolve the National Assembly. New elections under a new electoral law were promised for the indefinite future. From the safety of the Canal Zone, Arias called for a general strike, a rush to the barricades, and United States military aid, none of which was forthcoming.

New elections will probably take place eventually, but there seems little reason to expect that they will bring stability to this unfortunate little country.

SELECTED READINGS

AROSEMENA, DIÓGENES A. *Documentary Diplomatic History of the Panama Canal.* Panama City, n.p., 1961.

ÁVILA, ENEIDA. *Looking into Panama.* Panama City: Impresora Panamá, 1953.

BIESANZ, JOHN. "Social Forces Retarding Development of Panama's Agricultural Resources." *Rural Sociology* 15 (June 1950): 148–55.

——— and BIESANZ, MAVIS. *The People of Panama.* New York: Columbia University Press, 1956.

DUBOIS, JULES. *Danger over Panama.* Indianapolis: Bobbs-Merrill Co., 1964.

GOLDRICH, DANIEL. "Panama." In *Political Systems of Latin America,* edited by Martin C. Needler. Princeton, N.J.: D. Van Nostrand Co., 1964.

———. *Radical Nationalism: The Political Orientation of Panamanian Law Students.* East Lansing: Michigan State University, 1961.

———. "Requisites for Political Legitimacy in Panama." *Public Opinion Quarterly* 26 (Winter 1962): 664–68.

——— and SCOTT, EDWARD W. "Developing Political Orientations of Panamanian Students." *Journal of Politics* 23 (February 1961): 84–107.

GOYTÍA, VÍCTOR F. *Las Constituciones de Panamá.* Madrid: Ediciones Cultura Hispánica, 1954.

INTERNATIONAL COMMISSION OF JURISTS. *Report on the Events in Panama, January 9–12, 1964.* Geneva, 1964.

JOINT TAX PROGRAM OF THE ORGANIZATION OF AMERICAN STATES AND THE INTER-AMERICAN DEVELOPMENT BANK, FISCAL MISSION TO PANAMA. *Fiscal Survey of Panama: Problems and Proposals for Reform.* Baltimore: Johns Hopkins Press, 1964.

MENDOZA, CARLOS ALBERTO. "La Constitución Panameña de 1946: Sus fundamentos sociales." *Lotería,* July 1959, pp. 65–79.

NICOLAU, ERNESTO J. "Cartilla electoral." *Lotería,* September 1959, pp. 52–62; October 1959, pp. 75–107; November 1959, pp. 126–59.

PANAMA, DIRECCIÓN GENERAL DE PLANIFICACIÓN Y ADMINISTRATIÓN. *Manual de Organización del Gobierno de Panamá.* Panama City, 1961.

———. *Reforma gubernamental del programa de desarrollo económico y social de la República de Panamá.* Panama City, 1963.

"Presidencia que es difícil." *Visión,* October 16, 1964, pp. 10–11.

"La Reforma va con Robles." *Visión,* May 29, 1964, pp. 10–11.

ROSA, DIÓGENES DE LA. "Ideas políticas y los partidos de la república." *Lotería,* July 1960, pp. 18–28.

TAYLOR, M. C., and RICHMAN, R. L. "Fiscal Reform and Development Needs in Panama." *National Tax Journal* 17 (June 1964): 173–86.

TURNER, DOMINGO H. "Apunta sociológica de la política panameña desde la república." *Lotería,* July 1960, pp. 14–17.

United States Army Area Handbook for Panama. Washington: Department of the Army (pamphlet no. 550–46), 1965.

——11——

THE CANAL ZONE

The Canal Zone of Panama, which includes 648 square miles of territory, has been governed as a colony ever since the United States took it over in 1903. At the 1960 census the Zone had a population of 41,683. Of this number, on June 30, 1962, 2,497 were full-time United States civilian employees and 8,677 were full-time employees of other nationalities, mostly Panamanians. The rest of the population consisted of the families of the employees and the military forces that guard the Canal.

The Canal Zone operates as a unit independent of Panama, with its own housing, stores, recreation, hospitals, schools, and other facilities. Much of Panama's ill feeling toward the United States is due to the position of the Canal Zone as a sort of enclave within Panama, living its own life. Little effort is made by many Zonians to learn Spanish, and the government of the Zone maintains two kinds of schools, one providing instruction in English for children of United States employees and the other teaching in Spanish for children of Panamanian employees. Spanish is taught in the English-language schools as a second language in the first to sixth grades for one hour a week. After that it is available only as an elective. The separation of the United States employees from the others is sharpened by a difference in the wages the two groups receive: United States citizens receive the benefit of a tax factor and a 25 percent tropical differential, so that their income is greater than that of Panamanian employees doing the same kind of work.

After the serious riots at the beginning of 1964, the Panama Canal Zone governor, Robert J. Fleming, testifying before a U.S. House of

Representatives committee, reported that the Zone's police force was composed entirely of United States citizens, although 86 percent of the contacts made by the police involved Panamanian citizens.

The Canal Zone is governed by a bifurcated bureaucracy headed by the governor of the Canal Zone, who at the same time is president of the Panama Canal Company. He is appointed by the president of the United States to a four-year term with the advice and consent of the Senate, and reports to the Secretary of the Army. Usually these positions are held by a military man with the rank of major general. As the governor of the Canal Zone, he supervises all government functions including police and fire protection, the postal service, schools, and hospitals. As president of the Panama Canal Company, a corporation whose stock is owned by the United States government, he supervises the operations of the Canal. An unpaid board of directors is appointed by the Secretary of the Army of the United States, but these men are all high government officials or businessmen who are occupied with their activities in the United States and leave the operation of the Canal to the president of the company.

There is no democratic machinery for legislative or local government activity; the United States Congress passes all needed legislation. The judicial system is headed by judges appointed by the president of the United States with the advice and consent of the Senate.

There is widespread belief that the Canal Zone's government should have been changed long ago. In 1967 President Lyndon B. Johnson made known his backing of proposals to revise the management of the Zone. It is to be hoped that a new system will eventually be forthcoming.

SELECTED READINGS

ARAGON, LEOPOLDO. "Has the Panama Canal a Future?" *New Republic* 147 (July 30, 1962): 16–17.

BIESANZ, JOHN, and BIESANZ, MAVIS. "Uncle Sam on the Isthmus of Panama—A Diplomatic Case History." In *The Caribbean: Contemporary Trends,* edited by A. Curtis Wilgus. Gainesville: University of Florida Press, 1953.

BUSEY, JAMES L. "Conflict in Panama." *New Leader* 43 (February 15, 1960): 16–19.

Canal Zone Code (U.S. Public Law 87–845, 87th Cong., H.R. 10931, approved October 18, 1962). Washington: U.S. Government Printing Office, 1962.

DIMOCK, MARSHALL E. *Government-Operated Enterprises in the Panama Canal Zone.* Chicago: University of Chicago Press, 1934.

MACK, GERSTLE. *The Land Divided.* New York: Alfred A. Knopf, Inc., 1944.

"More American than America: Americans in the Canal Zone." *Time,* January 24, 1964, p. 18.

PANAMA CANAL COMPANY. *Reports of the Panama Canal Company and the Canal Zone Government.* Washington: U.S. Government Printing Office, annually since 1951.

POOR, PEGGY. "A View from the Canal." *New Republic* 150 (February 22, 1964): 13–14.

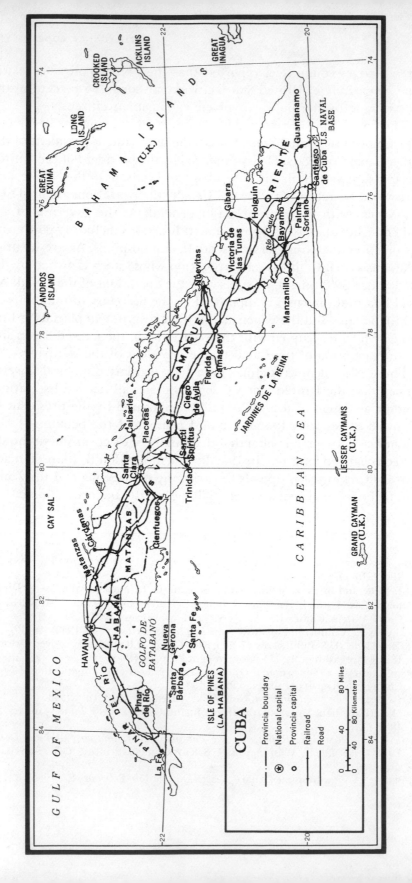

CUBA

- Provincia boundary
- ⊛ National capital
- ○ Provincia capital
- Railroad
- Road

0   40   80 Miles
0   40   80 Kilometers

—— 12 ——

CUBA:

The Revolution Betrayed

Cuba is the most talked-about country in Latin America—not because of its great size, large population, or strategic location, but because it has become the American symbol of one of the great ideologies struggling to dominate the people of the world. The group of adventurers headed by Fidel Castro who seized control of Cuba in 1959 have won the support and cooperation of all those in Latin America who favor a communist dictatorship. All who oppose this type of dictatorship have been forced to unite against Fidel Castro and his followers, who are constantly busy trying to establish their form of totalitarian government in other parts of America. At the same time, Cuba has become a pawn in the struggle between the world's superpowers, the United States, China, and the Soviet Union.

As a direct result of its symbolic position, the Cuban revolution quickly became enveloped in a mythology so extensive that it is almost impossible to study Cuba objectively. Students are discovering that George Orwell's prediction of a make-believe language has come true in Cuba long before 1984. The greatest myth is the one spread by Fidel Castro himself and echoed by such writers as C. Wright Mills, Jean Paul Sartre, Simone de Beauvoir, Leo Huberman, Paul M. Sweezy, and David Dellinger (the list could be greatly extended), who picture Cuba before January 1, 1959, as an island inhabited by a largely rural population living in misery and filth, illiteracy and exploitation, whose conditions of life were so abysmal that the country simply exploded under the leader-

255

ship of Fidel Castro to create a new social order. The facts are quite otherwise.

A National Profile

The republic of Cuba consists of Cuba, the largest island in the Caribbean, and a series of other islands ranging in size from specks of land to the Isle of Pines, with an area of 1,120 square miles. Its total area of 46,736 square miles makes Cuba larger than the Netherlands, Belgium, Switzerland, Austria, Hungary, or Denmark, although among Latin-American republics it is only fifteenth in size.

About 760 miles long and from 25 to 120 miles wide, the island consists mainly of plains (with much swampy area on the south coast), with three small areas of mountains not offering much of a barrier to the occupation of the land. Cuba's most important physical feature is its location: lying at the entrance to the Gulf of Mexico, just south of Florida, it is the Latin-American republic closest to the United States. Although the United States and Mexico share a common frontier, the main center of Mexico's population is hundreds of miles from this border, whereas many large cities on the United States' eastern seaboard and Gulf Coast are comparatively close to Cuba. And Cuba's location was of great strategic importance during the days when sea routes were of primary significance.

Located just inside the Tropic Zone, Cuba has a hot, humid climate, but temperatures are moderated by sea breezes. There are no frosts at any time and the only natural evil is wind—the hurricanes that now and then roar over the island. Rainfall is adequate and well distributed, and most of the island is well drained. The soil is fairly fertile, and it is computed that 52 percent of the area is at least potential cropland.

Cuba's population was estimated by the United Nations to be 7,833,000 in 1966. Although the original Indians were quickly exterminated in Cuba, the island has been a melting pot of Indians, Spaniards, Negroes (about a million slaves were brought to the island), British, French (many fled here from Haiti in the 1790's), and Chinese. It is impossible to give the exact racial composition, but the best estimates are that about 25 percent are basically Negro, about 50 percent are basically white, and the remaining 25 percent are a mixture of European, Negro, and Oriental.

No accurate figures are available for recent years, but the estimate for 1958 was that 57 percent of the population was urban and 43 percent rural, with 40 percent actually engaged in agriculture. Havana, the capital city, has always dominated the island. In 1953, when the last census was taken, 785,455 of the 5,829,029 population lived in Havana. Other cities and their 1953 population were Marianao, 219,278; Santiago, 163,237; Camagüey, 110,388; Santa Clara, 77,398; Guantánamo, 64,671; Matanzas, 63,916; Cienfuegos, 57,991; and Holguín, 57,573.

Spanish is the official language. Before 1959, education was compulsory between the ages of seven and fourteen, and the 1953 census showed that 76.4 percent of all those over ten years of age were literate; this was one of the highest literacy rates in Latin America. Most Cubans were nominally Catholic, but church and state were separated and all religions functioned freely.

Cuba has traditionally been an agricultural country producing crops for the world market, and in 1958 it was the world's largest exporter of sugar, which accounted for 79.1 percent in value of its total exports in that year. Yet farm production accounted for only a little more than one-third of the national income and furnished employment to only about two-fifths of the labor force. Much progress had been made, especially after World War II, in diversifying the economy and increasing nonagricultural sources of income, particularly tourism and manufacturing. In addition to sugar, tobacco, fruit, vegetables, cocoa, rice, henequen, and cedar (for cigar boxes) have been the chief agricultural products. Despite its fertile soil, which could have produced all that the population needed, the emphasis upon sugar led to the production of an insufficient amount of coffee, beans, potatoes, fats, oils, and dairy products, most of which, until 1959, were imported from the United States. Cuba's land ownership was very concentrated, although the situation was not as bad as in some of the other Latin-American countries. International corporations owned extensive areas devoted to sugar, and 894 farms (0.5 percent of all farms) over 1,000 *hectares* in 1958 contained 36.1 percent of all the farmland. Cuban capital, however, controlled 62.13 percent of sugar production.

An important beef and dairy-cattle industry flourished, especially in Camagüey and Oriente provinces. About half the country's farm area was in pasture, and meat ranked second, after sugar, in Cuban agriculture. A fishing industry employed about 13,000 men. Important mineral wealth includes manganese, chromium, copper, iron, and nickel, and 5 percent of the economically active population were in mining before 1959. Most of the mineral production was exported to the United States. Salt is produced from sea water. Cuba had a well-developed internal transportation system of roads and railroads and airports. After World War II Cuba had developed its industry at a rapid rate. Protected by a tariff, the country produced cigars, cigarettes, rope, dairy products, tinned fruit, cement, cotton and rayon textiles, footwear, paper, soap, flour, petroleum products, tires and tubes, paint, alcohol, rum and beer, soft drinks, fertilizers, and concrete. In industrial output Cuba was ranked fifth in Latin America, after Brazil, Argentina, Mexico, and Chile.

To sum up, Cuba in 1958 was emerging from a one-crop economy to become an industrial state, with agriculture moving to a minor position. The national income in 1954 was divided as follows: the sugar industry, 25 percent; other agriculture, 13 percent; other commerce and industry, 40 percent; services, etc., 21 percent.[1] Although the standard of living in Cuba was low in comparison with the United States, it was quite high by other standards. Only Venezuela, Argentina, and Chile in Latin America rated above Cuba in per capita income. Cuba had one auto for every 39 inhabitants (compared to one for every 60 in Argentina, for 91 in Mexico, and for 158 in Brazil), and had one radio for every five inhabitants. In fact, the Cubans were so prosperous that Cuban tourists spent more money in the United States than United States tourists spent in Cuba.

The great problems of Cuba were that it was still too dependent upon sugar and that its political institutions had not developed as fast as its economy. They failed to provide an orderly way of organizing political life, and violence, gangsterism, and graft were the common methods of seeking and keeping political power.

The Development of Modern Cuba

Cuba's location near the United States and athwart the Caribbean sea routes inevitably made it an object of international rivalry. Just as Cuba became a pawn in the cold war between the Soviet Union and the United States in the 1960's, so it was a coveted prize in the international wars of past centuries between England, France, and Spain. The result was a very mixed population and a pattern of violence which has been a conspicuous feature of Cuban history since the days of the Conquest. It was in Cuba that the famous Apostle of the Indies, Bartolomé de Las Casas, began his crusade for Indian rights after witnessing Spanish atrocities. "All of a sudden," Las Casas wrote in 1511, "the devil entered the bodies of the Christians [read "the Spaniards"], and in my presence they put to the sword without any motive whatsoever more than three thousand persons, men, women, and children, who were seated before us."[2]

---

[1] Percentages do not add to 100 because of rounding.

[2] Bartolomé de Las Casas, *Brevíssima Relación de la Destruyción de las Indias* (1552), reprinted in an English translation in Francis Augustus MacNutt, *Bartholomew de Las Casas, His Life, His Apostolate, and His Writings* (New York and London: G. P. Putnam's Sons, 1909), pp. 330–31.

Cuba's location made it a natural center from which the Spaniards could organize their conquest of the mainland, and the fine natural harbor at Havana was early fortified to make this city a key point on the route from Spain to America. By 1515 Havana was the headquarters of Spanish power in America. When the richer booty of Mexico and Peru was captured by the Spaniards, Cuba fell into neglect. Yet the importance of Havana was always recognized by Spain; as individual Spaniards left the island to seek their fortunes on the mainland, their places were taken by others, and as the Indians were killed, slaves were imported from Africa to replace them. Sugar early became an important crop, with slaves providing the labor. When the buccaneers and pirates of England, France, and the Netherlands became active in the Carribbean, Havana was one of the key points in Spain's defensive system. The almost continuous fighting to control this strategic point, however, did nothing to develop a peaceful, stable society in Cuba.

Because Cuba was primarily a military base and the home of many Spanish officials, the island never developed a strong independence movement in the early nineteenth century. The Spanish government, however, evidently learned nothing from the loss of its mainland colonies, and continued to govern Cuba in about the same way as it had in the past. Spanish *peninsulares* held almost all the important positions, and ultimate decision-making power rested in Spain. Since Spain had fewer colonies to exploit now, taxes in Cuba were increased to make up for the income lost from the other colonies. It has been estimated that Spain took $50 million in taxes out of Cuba between 1830 and 1850.

As Cuba developed its production of sugar and other crops, its trade with the growing United States increased. After 1826, the Spanish government tried to restrict trade between Cuba and the United States, thus provoking independence movements, smuggling, and revolts. Spain reacted by increasing its armed forces on the island until Cuba became a militarized colony. Forays led by Cubans seeking independence from Spain failed to expel the Spanish troops in 1849, 1850, and 1851. Movements to unite the island with the United States failed, although President Polk offered to buy Cuba for $100 million in 1848, and the administration of President Pierce was willing to pay $130 million.

By 1868 a civil war was being fought on the island, and Cubans and Spaniards went on killing each other for ten years. There was much brutality on both sides and a great deal of destruction of property, especially at the eastern end of the island. The civil war also ruined the coffee and cattle industries, thus pushing tobacco and sugar to new prominence and laying the basis for future economic difficulties. After the war, Spain granted some concessions to the Cubans, the most important being representation in Spain's parliament. But Spain never conceded enough to satisfy the Cubans, and the cost of the war meant newer and heavier taxes. Not until 1886 was slavery abolished.

As the nineteenth century wore on, Cuba advanced further and further into the economic orbit of the United States. Its sugar went there, and many of its imports came from there. In the 1890's, when the United States and Spain increased their taxes on each other's exports, Cuba lost most of its market for sugar. And so another revolution against Spain began, and from 1895 to 1898 a cruel and bitter military struggle went on. Both the government and the rebels used a scorched-earth policy. The Spaniards, commanded by General Valeriano Weyler, became famous for creating some of the world's first concentration camps, where perhaps 200,000 died from inadequate food and lack of sanitation.

United States investments in Cuba were jeopardized by the civil war, and the United States government sent a series of notes to the Spanish government in an attempt to stop the fighting. It is known that the Spanish government was about ready to give independence to Cuba when the United States battleship *Maine* was blown up in Havana Harbor on February 15, 1898. At that time, the *Journal* and the *World*, two New York newspapers, were carrying on a circulation war fueled by atrocity stories about Cuba. As a result of the incident, the United States declared war on Spain on April 24, 1898. The Spanish did little fighting and the United States soon was in control of what was left of Spain's empire, including Cuba. By the terms of the peace treaty, Cuba became an independent state, but nevertheless the United States army occupied the island and set up a military government that ruled Cuba until May 1902.

During the U.S. occupation there was some reconstruction of the economy, public health and education were improved, and roads and harbors were built. At the same time, United States corporations received large concessions of sugar and tobacco lands. In 1901 a constitution was promulgated which was a rough translation of the United States constitution. It was the typical liberal document of the nineteenth century, setting up a republic headed by a president, a two-house legislature, universal male suffrage, local autonomy for municipal and state governments, and separation of church and state. It had no relation to the political habits of the population, however, and two of its provisions were to plague the country in future years. By one, the president was given the power to intervene in local government. By another, the famous Platt Amendment, the United States was given the right to lease or buy Guantánamo Bay as a naval base and was given control over Cuba's foreign policy. The Cuban government was prohibited from making any treaties that might affect Cuba's independence, nor was it permitted to assume debts beyond the country's revenues. Finally, the United States was given the right to intervene at its own discretion to preserve order on the island. The provisions of the Platt Amendment were confirmed by a treaty signed in 1903.

An election was organized under the United States military government, and a government headed by Tomás Estrada Palma, one of the leaders of the revolution, took office on May 20, 1902. This government set up the machinery of Cuba's executive and presided over a flow of United States investments which transformed Cuba's economy. With the prosperity brought by this flow of money into sugar, tobacco, electrical power, cattle, real estate, and public utilities, men in the government could, if they desired, utilize their positions to enrich themselves. Thus, at the very beginning, the competition for positions in the government became a fierce rivalry in which success meant access to a large income.

Cuba was the only country in America whose liberation from colonialism was led by a political party, yet the Cuban Revolutionary Party (PRC) never developed into a stable modern political organization. The founder and theoretician of the PRC, José Martí, was killed during the struggle, and the United States occupation kept the lesser leaders out of office long enough for the PRC to fall apart. The Cubans who took power after 1902 were all men who had been engaged in guerrilla warfare for years, and none of them knew much about organizing a civil government. They were all big or little *caudillos*, used to violence and terror, and after getting posts in the government they used their positions for patronage and graft. Estrada Palma began the organization of a party to control the government, and his opponents organized themselves to oppose him. Until 1933 these two "parties" dominated the country's political life, but they never became modern political parties and there was little difference between them. Both were personalistic and led by *caudillos*.

When Estrada Palma was reelected in 1906, his opponents claimed fraud and revolted. Unable to put down the revolt, Estrada Palma appealed for help and the United States sent its Secretary of War, William Howard Taft, to Cuba, but he failed in his efforts to patch things up. Thereupon Estrada Palma resigned and the United States took over the government again from 1906 to 1909. This second intervention, under Charles E. Magoon, saw the Cuban treasury depleted, but again some roads were constructed, public health was improved, and some public works were built. Magoon presided over another election, and José Miguel Gómez, the leader of the 1906 revolt, was elected president. On

January 28, 1909, Magoon left Cuba, turning the presidency over to Gómez. From then until 1933, the political history of Cuba makes sorry reading. It is a record of graft, incompetence, and repeated intervention by the United States. Gómez is supposed to have become a millionaire during his term in office, while the Negro agricultural workers were staging revolts in eastern Cuba. The United States Marines and Gómez' army succeeded in curbing this protest against exploitation by killing about 3,000 rebels.

This became the pattern of government and economics in Cuba. Surplus money from the United States flowed into Cuban sugar production. World War I raised the price of sugar, and astronomical profits were made for some years as thousands of acres of good timber were burned to clear more land for the production of more sugar. The government received large amounts of taxes on the exported sugar, and a governmental position, especially on the higher levels, was a direct path to wealth. Very little of the money went for higher wages or social improvements. Cheap labor was brought from Haiti, from China, from any place it could be found. When elections took place, the losers invariably revolted, and during the fighting the habit of violence was strengthened. In 1916, for example, the rebels controlled the eastern end of the island, and to stall the government in Havana they destroyed the railroad and the telephone and telegraph lines connecting the eastern and western parts of Cuba. Fraudulent elections became the rule.

After World War I the sugar boom collapsed and Cuba practically went bankrupt. Many of the Cuban sugar producers went broke and were bought out by United States banks. It is reported that by 1927, United States companies owned about one-fifth of all the land in Cuba, and by 1929 total United States private investment in Cuba had reached $1.5 billion. Meanwhile, in 1920, to get the government financially solvent, the United States sent General Enoch Crowder as financial adviser to the Cuban president to control the government's finances. Crowder obtained a loan of $50 million from the House of Morgan to pay off the public debt and ran the government, although Alfredo Zayas remained as titular president. In 1923 Crowder's title was changed from financial adviser to ambassador, and the Cuban government immediately reverted to the style of government that had led to its bankruptcy in 1920.

The first really stable government independent Cuba had was that headed by Gerardo Machado, who became president in 1924 in a managed election. He was a typical Cuban *caudillo*, and his government was a tyrannical dictatorship that made him one of the most hated men in Latin America. Machado ruthlessly oppressed all who opposed him; he murdered, tortured, and exiled, and his terror was answered by terror from his oppressed people. The customary Cuban violence was intensified by an anarcho-sindicalist influence brought into Cuba during the first decades of the twentieth century by Spanish immigrants who had become anarchists in Spain.

Until 1933 the United States seemed to be supporting Machado. He had himself reelected and extended the president's term to six years. The opposition to Machado was composed of various elements, including many of the university professors and students, but the most publicized was a secret society, the ABC, composed of middle-class intellectuals. The ABC was not a political party; it was a terroristic organization in the familiar Cuban pattern.

Despite his opposition, Machado managed to cling to power until the middle of 1933. Then, weakened by the world depression, he lost the support of the new administration in Washington, headed by Franklin D. Roosevelt. Roosevelt sent a new ambassador, Sumner Welles, to Cuba in 1933, with instructions to tell Machado that he had to reach an agreement with his opposition and end the violence. Machado and most of the leaders of the opposition immediately began negotiations, with Welles acting as mediator. In August, however, the National Confederation of Workers declared a general strike and the situation deteriorated, whereupon Welles met with officers of the Cuban army and told them the United States would intervene in Cuba again unless the army forced Machado out of office. The army officers agreed, and on August 12, 1933, Machado left Cuba and a new period began, the era of Fulgencio Batista.

In 1933 Fulgencio Batista was an army sergeant whose work as a stenographer had taught him how the officers ran the army. When Machado was overthrown, a government headed by Dr. Carlos Manuel de Céspedes tried to dominate the situation. It had little success, and when the ABC, the university students and professors, the Communist Party, and the labor movement all organized strikes and riots against the new government, a group of army sergeants headed by Batista revolted, discharged all of the officers of the army, and on September 4 set up a new government headed by a five-man civilian junta. The United States refused to recognize the junta set up by the military and sent a fleet of battleships to Cuba. The junta then turned the government over to a professor of the National University, Dr. Ramón Grau San Martín, who had been active in the struggle against Machado.

With the support of the most important groups active in politics at that time—the army rebels, university professors, intellectuals, students, and labor leaders—Grau's government enacted the first progressive legislation in Cuba's history. Efforts were made to help the unemployed. Labor was encouraged to organize itself and a minimum wage was set for sugar workers higher than any paid until then. The National University was given complete autonomy.

This probably was the moment at which Cuba's future difficulties were predetermined. Grau San Martín and his followers were then young, unspoiled idealists. Those were the years of the world depression, when Roosevelt and his New Deal were reshaping the United States and Cárdenas and the PRI were determining the future course of the Mexican Revolution. Cuba might have gone the same way, but Sumner Welles, the United States representative in Cuba, refused to recognize the Grau government, and it finally fell on January 18, 1934.

After Grau left office, Batista was the dominant figure in Cuba until 1944, although until 1940 the presidency was held by a series of seven men. The United States, on January 23, 1934, recognized the new government and helped it by abrogating the Platt Amendment and by signing a reciprocal trade agreement which gave a subsidy to Cuban sugar. The new government, following a conservative program, tried to reverse the reforms begun by the Grau administration. When the schoolteachers, government employees, and labor organized a general strike in March 1935, Batista's army smashed it. After that, during much of the period until 1940, the government ruled as a dictatorship.

One of Batista's actions during this period was to have important consequences in the future: he strengthened the Communist Party. A small Communist party had been organized in Cuba in 1925, but it never had much support and was kept to illegal activity by the Machado dictatorship. When Grau San Martín held the presidency for four months at the end of 1933, the Communists were among his most vigorous opponents. Professor Robert Alexander believes this opposition

> was one of the principal factors bringing about the downfall of the Grau San Martín regime and the substitution for it of a conservative military dictatorship. The continuous Communist activities in the cities and the countryside gave the United States, which did not like the Grau San Martín government, ample opportunity to maintain that that government did not have effective control of the country, and that therefore the United States could not recognize it.[3]

It is interesting to note that after the fall of the Grau government the Communists continued to attack it instead of opposing the more conserv-

---

[3] Robert Alexander, *Communism in Latin America* (New Brunswick, N.J.: Rutgers University Press, 1957), p. 275.

ative government that had replaced it. And Batista allowed the Communists to begin legal activity under the name *Partido Unión Revolucionario*. On May 1, 1938, Batista allowed the Communists to begin publishing a daily paper, *Hoy*. In July 1938 Batista met at his Camp Columbia fortress with two Communist leaders, Blas Roca[4] and Joaquín Ordoqui. Soon after this meeting, rather close cooperation began between Batista and the Communists. They supported him in the 1940 presidential election and continued to work with him until just before he was overthrown on January 1, 1959, when they transferred their support to Fidel Castro. For his part, Batista helped the Communists take over the leadership of the Cuban trade unions and in 1943 appointed the first Communist cabinet minister in America, Juan Marinello. In 1944 he appointed another Communist, Carlos Rodríguez, to the cabinet.[5]

In 1940, although Batista won the presidency with the support of the Communists, the forces supporting Dr. Grau San Martín, by then organized as the Authentic (*Auténtico*) Cuban Revolutionary Party, elected a majority of the Constituent Assembly. After much bitter wrangling, a progressive constitution was drawn up and Batista became constitutional president for a four-year term.

The 1940 constitution was an interesting document. It provided for a president and a bicameral legislature, but it added a prime minister appointed by the president with a cabinet responsible to the Assembly. Thus a semiparliamentary system was set up, but it never received a fair trial. Other progressive features of the constitution included a very liberal labor code, government encouragement of cooperative organizations, a legal basis for agrarian reform, and an extensive list of civil rights.

Batista's official term in office coincided with World War II and he had little need to reinstitute dictatorship. The United States gave him a $25 million loan in 1941, and other financial aid whenever he needed it. In return, Batista gave the United States air, naval, and army bases. The United States stimulated the production of minerals needed for the war effort: nickel, manganese, copper, antimony, tungsten, chromium.

Batista became a multimillionaire during his years in power and one of the largest owners of real estate in and around Daytona Beach, Florida. He evidently thought he had Cuba so well under control that he could permit a fair election in 1944. To Batista's surprise, the candidate he and the Communists backed was defeated by Dr. Grau San Martín.

Democratic constitutional government finally came to Cuba with

---

[4] In the 1960's Blas Roca was one of Fidel Castro's closest collaborators and a member of the six-man secretariat of the Communist Party.

[5] Both Marinello and Rodríguez hold important positions in the Castro government.

Grau, but the eight years that followed were stormy and ended with Batista back in power as dictator. When Grau took office, Batista and his friends held a majority in the Assembly and the Communists were in control of the organized labor movement and certain government offices, especially the Department of Labor. Grau inherited a poorly administered government riddled with graft and nepotism, and during his years in office he constantly faced violence, gangsterism, and a refusal by the military, the Communists, the traditional landowning oligarchy, and foreign economic interests to cooperate with him.

The *Auténtico* administration headed by Dr. Grau made a determined effort to industrialize Cuba, to diversify agriculture, to combat illiteracy, to improve public health, and to lay the institutional basis for a functioning democratic governmental apparatus. Dr. Grau presided over a free society, and during his term in office political parties flourished. He shifted army officers and retired many until the army was brought under civilian control for the first time since the 1933 revolution.

The chief criticism made against Dr. Grau was that there was graft in his regime. Undoubtedly there was, but where has there ever been a government completely free of graft? The Grau government was so much better than all previous Cuban governments, as far as civil liberty and an impulse to social reform are concerned, that, on the balance, he was probably one of the best presidents Cuba has ever had. In 1948 he presided over an honest election, which the *Auténticos* won over a field of four candidates, putting Carlos Prío Socarrás in as president.

Prío Socarrás continued the progressive *Auténtico* program started by Dr. Grau. He pushed the building of luxury hotels to attract tourists and he helped the labor movement to strengthen itself. He cooperated with the liberal governments of Figueres in Costa Rica and Arévalo in Guatemala, and in 1950 he sponsored the Havana meeting of the liberals and noncommunist radicals of America which organized the Inter-American Association for Liberty and Democracy. Charges of graft were made against Prío, of course, and during his term Dr. Grau was accused of having stolen $174 million when he was president. Gangsterism was rife in the streets of Havana and politicians took frequent potshots at each other. But Prío preserved constitutional government and presided over democratic elections whenever they were due. Prío's brother was a candidate for mayor of Havana on the *Auténtico* ticket in 1950, but lost to an opposing candidate supported by the old-fashioned conservatives, Batista, Grau San Martín's faction of the *Auténticos*, and the Communists.

In 1952, democratic government disappeared in Cuba when Batista organized a coup d'état and took over the government. This was an election year and Batista was a candidate for the presidency. He was, according to all competent observers, running a poor third when on the night of March 10 he took control of the armed forces and captured the government.

He had been forced to it, he proclaimed, by the *pistolerismo* and gang-style killings that had punctuated the Prío administration. All that would have to be stopped, and he was the man to do it. The Prío government was leading Cuba toward a "savage dictatorship," according to Batista, and therefore he had come forward to save the country.

Batista saved the country from dictatorship by suspending the 1940 constitution, by canceling the elections scheduled for June 1, by abolishing the Assembly, by abrogating all of the constitutional guarantees of civil liberty, and by becoming the dictator of Cuba and exercising all legislative and executive power as chief of state. Batista's coup was relatively peaceful. Only three persons lost their lives. A few others were wounded. Many persons were exiled from the country, including all of the important government officials. The political refugees from Venezuela, Peru, and the Dominican Republic, then dictatorships, took refuge in various embassies and soon left the country.

Why did the Prío Socarrás government and the people of Cuba permit the reintroduction of dictatorship in Cuba? Was it because the Prío government was so bad? The only answer that seems to fit the facts is that eight years of constitutional government, after more than 400 years of dictatorship, are not enough to transform a people. In addition, Prío and his *Auténtico* Party were faced with the dilemma all democrats face when they come to power: shall they give complete freedom to the whole population of the country? If they do, the Communists, Fascists, and other totalitarians will use their freedom to sabotage everything the government is doing and make every effort to destroy it. Yet if the democratic government clamps controls on the Communists and Fascists, it may itself degenerate into dictatorship. It is to the credit of Grau San Martín and Prío Socarrás that, although they failed to institutionalize constitutional government, they gave Cuba the freest eight years its people had ever enjoyed.

Under Batista, from 1952 to the end of 1958, Cuba lived under a dictatorship that became progressively more tyrannical and brutal. Interestingly enough, these were prosperous years for Cuba. The Korean War kept the price of sugar high and the measures begun by the Grau and Prío governments continued to bear effect, especially in a building boom that saw many fine hotels rise in Havana to house the increasing number of tourists. As one historian describes the period: "Never were the Cubans richer—at least, those Cubans who held office, who were granted concessions, who owned land and fine businesses—and the richest of them all was ex-sergeant Fulgencio Batista. In fact under Batista Cuba had everything—except liberty."[6]

Opposition to the Batista regime began as soon as he took office and grew until he fled the country the night of January 1, 1959. Unfortunately, the various opposition political parties never could combine their forces for unified action. Batista was a clever politician and he was able to keep the support of the armed forces and organized labor. And he had the support of the Communists and the most important business groups, particularly the foreign interests. His main opposition came from students, intellectuals, professional men, and the two large reformist political parties, the *Auténticos* and the *Ortodoxos*. By alternating a state of siege and constitutional liberties, Batista was able to stay in power. In 1955 he permitted Prío to return to Cuba, but when negotiations for a fair election broke down, Prío once again was exiled.

Meanwhile, a young middle-class university student named Fidel Castro began to organize a revolutionary army that was to achieve what the other Cuban organizations could not. When Batista took power in 1952, Castro was a member of the *Ortodoxo* Party. Outraged by Batista's coup, he filed a brief with the Urgency Court of Havana asking the court to declare Batista's government unconstitutional. When nothing happened, Castro organized a group of students into a fighting organization and on July 26, 1953, 165 young people attacked the Moncada army post at Santiago de Cuba. Most of the students were killed. Castro and some others escaped, but later they surrendered and were sentenced to fifteen-year prison terms. Eleven months later, Batista pardoned all of his political prisoners, including Castro.

Fidel Castro went to Mexico and organized another army, which was trained in military techniques by a Spanish general. On December 2, 1956, eighty-two revolutionists led by Castro landed in Cuba. Most of them were killed in the first days, but Fidel Castro, his brother Raúl, the Argentine physician Ernesto (Che) Guevara, and some others escaped to the Sierra Maestra Mountains. Then began a most peculiar civil war. Castro used propaganda and terror to weaken Batista and win recruits. He fought on a program of restoring constitutional government, instituting the reforms Cuba needed to become a progressive democracy, and ending graft and corruption in government. Slowly he won recruits for his organization, called the 26th of July Movement, and as his attacks on

---

[6] Hubert Herring, *A History of Latin America from the Beginnings to the Present,* 2nd ed. (New York: Alfred A. Knopf, Inc., 1961), p. 414.

isolated army posts succeeded he was able to build up a fairly sizable army. Meanwhile, in Havana, the 26th of July Movement functioned as a secret terrorist organization, bombing and attacking Batista's police and soldiers. Other groups were also active, among them the *Auténticos* and the Triple A's, a group that had begun military action against Batista as early as 1952. The university students' *Directorio Revolucionario* attacked the National Palace and almost succeeded in killing Batista. All of these revolutionary groups tormented Batista so much that he seems to have lost his head; he allowed himself to be provoked into bloody reprisals, and for two years bombs burst, shots rang out, and many innocent people were killed. The navy revolted in Cienfuegos and army troops crushed the rebellion. The 26th of July Movement set fire to sugar fields. The government began indiscriminate bombing of the Sierra Maestra. How different is this from Bartolomé de Las Casas' eyewitness account in 1511, or the scorched-earth policies and concentration camps of the nineteenth century?

By the end of 1958, Batista's position was hopeless. The violence of his opponents provoked the army into savage reprisals that only aroused more opposition until the whole country was against Batista. The overthrow of the Pérez Jiménez regime in Venezuela encouraged the Cubans, and the Venezuelan government allowed a radio station in Caracas to beam anti-Batista propaganda to Cuba. Finally, on the night of January 1, 1959, Batista and his closest collaborators fled from Cuba in a fleet of airplanes and ships. The people of Cuba erupted in a delirious demonstration in which they destroyed some of the homes of hated Batista officials. But in a few days the rebel army led by Fidel Castro had taken control of the country and set up a new government to begin a new era in the life of Cuba.

Fidel Castro came to power with an unusual opportunity to solve most of Cuba's perennial problems. The flight of Batista left a vacuum in which Castro could insert any kind of government following any kind of program. His army was in undisputed control of the nation. He had won the adulation of the great majority of the people. At the same time, because of recent events, the United States government was in the process of changing its Latin-American policy and introducing the Alliance for Progress. The United States would have done nothing to interfere with any reforms, no matter how radical, in Cuba's economic and political structure.

During the years since 1952, Fidel Castro had advocated a program little different from the programs of other groups ranged against Batista: constitutional government under the 1940 constitution, fair elections, agricultural reform, an end to dependence on sugar, industrialization, and social reforms including better housing, public health, and education. The tragedy of Cuba is that Castro came to power in the name of one kind of revolution and used his power to institute another. Since the Cubans, by and large, wanted the kind of revolution Castro had been talking about since 1952, they objected to the kind he did introduce, and as a result Castro had to rely more and more on force to stay in power until his government was more dictatorial than Batista's had been.

By decree, Castro set up a government headed by Dr. Manuel Urrutia, a provincial judge who had voted to free persons involved in one of the revolts against Batista. A cabinet representing the various groups that had fought against Batista took over the work of reorganizing the governmental machinery and Fidel Castro became the commander in chief of the armed forces. A new Fundamental Law of the Revolutionary Government was promulgated on February 7, 1959, to take the place of the 1940 constitution. The legislature was dissolved and the courts were purged of judges who had supported Batista. The death penalty, banned in the 1940 constitution, was reintroduced, and the new revolutionary government set out to remake Cuba.

Unfortunately for Cuba, no sooner did the new government begin to function than it was discovered that there were two governments in Cuba, one headed by Dr. Urrutia and another by Fidel Castro. Castro began to speak over the radio and television daily for four, five, six hours; he issued orders; he appointed people to office; he did whatever he thought needed to be done without any reference to the cabinet that ostensibly was governing Cuba. At the same time, a series of show trials was conducted in which officials of Batista's army and government were tried by *ad hoc* military courts and usually punished by imprisonment or death within a few hours after the trial ended.

Another event of the first days of January 1959, one that went unnoticed at the time, was the prominent place the Cuban Communists assumed as soon as Fidel Castro's army took control of the country. They took over offices in all parts of the country; they took over a radio station; they resumed publication of their daily newspaper, *Hoy;* and they yelled *"Viva Fidel!"* at every opportunity.

Within a few months, disputes arose within the government and within the 26th of July Movement. By February 15, José Miró Cardona, the prime minister, had resigned and been replaced by Fidel Castro. By June 12, five cabinet ministers had resigned to be replaced by others more in harmony with Fidel Castro. By July 16, Fidel Castro was ready to fire the president he had hand-picked and replace him with a Communist by the name of Dr. Osvaldo Dorticós.

As these things were happening, the Cuban government began to confiscate the property of foreign corporations and Cuban and foreign residents. At first the confiscations were made in the name of agrarian reform, but as the years went by, practically everything of economic value in Cuba was taken over by the government. At the same time, an intensive campaign was begun against the United States. When the noncommunist members of the 26th of July Movement protested, they were either executed, jailed, or exiled. Hubert Matos, for example, one of the leaders of the 26th of July armed forces, sent a letter to Castro resigning his position because of his opposition to communism. For sending this letter he was jailed under a thirty-year sentence. Another of Castro's early colleagues, Camilio Cienfuegos, simply disappeared. The official story is that his plane crashed in some unknown place; no one really knows what happened to him, but most competent observers believe he was murdered.

The government of Cuba became a one-man operation. Fidel Castro became the government, and elections and constitutional government were no longer mentioned. More and more Communists received important positions, and the power of the government was used to take over or illegalize all other organizations functioning in the country. By the middle of 1960, for all practical purposes, a totalitarian state had been created. All opposition newspapers and other periodicals were silenced. All opposing political parties were forced underground, including those that had fought Batista. As property belonging to United States citizens was confiscated piece by piece and as Castro kept blaming the United States for all of Cuba's ills, the United States cut off Cuba's sugar quota. Cuba then began to turn the Cuban economy toward the Soviet Union and the other countries behind the iron curtain. The United States and Cuba broke relations January 4, 1961, and Cuba separated itself from the Organization of American States. By April 1961 the United States Central Intelligence Agency had organized an army of 1,500 Cubans for an invasion of Cuba, but they were defeated by Fidel's army.

By October 1962 Cuba had become a fortress in which the Soviet government was installing nuclear projectiles. In a dramatic confrontation the United States blockaded the island in that month, and the Soviet government removed its rockets. Today Cuba is a completely totalitarian state under the control of an army estimated to be the largest of any in the twenty Latin-American republics. The country is governed in the same way other totalitarian states are governed. At the top is a small group, headed by Fidel Castro, with control over the government, the armed forces, and the Communist Party. Under them stretches the apparatus of the government and the party, down to the police spy in each block. There is no freedom of the press, of speech, or of assembly. No trade unions function. There are no legal rules or an independent judiciary. The economy is in ruin and rationing distributes the food and clothing available. The agricultural crisis that caused rationing produced a situation in which per capita food consumption went down about one-fifth from 1958 to 1963. The crisis was caused by a drop in agricultural output, resulting primarily from mismanagement and a shift in trade patterns from the nearby United States to the faraway Soviet-bloc countries, which cuts down imports.[7]

How did a revolution that began under such auspicious circumstances in only a few years become a Cuban copy of Stalin's Russia or Hitler's Germany? Many explanations have been offered, but the only one that makes any sense is that Fidel Castro is a megalomaniac driven by the idea that only he can solve Cuba's problems, that he is the indispensable man. The Communists soon discovered this, and by yelling *"Viva Fidel!"* louder than anyone else, they were able to convince him that he needed them. Then as opposition arose, terror was needed to keep Fidel in power, until he became only another *caudillo*, forcing his people to follow him toward a paradise he envisioned for them.

The Formal Constitutional Framework

Cuba is ostensibly governed under the document known as the Fundamental Law of February 7, 1959, as amended, which basically is the country's 1940 constitution with important changes. The constitution of 1940 was a progressive document providing a semiparliamentary system of government, a series of advanced guarantees to the individual, and the legal basis for land reform. The revolution against Batista was fought to reintroduce this constitution, which Batista was ignoring, but after the revolution triumphed, the constitution was changed to create a legal basis for totalitarian dictatorship. The new document abolished elections and centralized legislative, executive, and judicial power into a self-perpetuating council that, in addition to all its other powers, was given the power to amend the Fundamental Law by a two-thirds vote. The

---

[7] See Leon G. Mears, "Cuba's Agriculture: Four Years under the Revolutionary Regime," *Foreign Agriculture*, 1 (January 7, 1963): 4–6.

spirit of the two documents can best be appreciated by comparing the clauses introducing them. In the 1940 constitution the preamble read:

> We the delegates of the people of Cuba, assembled in Constituent Convention, for the purposes of establishing a new fundamental law to consolidate our organization as an independent and sovereign state, capable of assuring freedom and justice, maintaining order and promoting the general welfare, do hereby, invoking the favor of God, set forth the following Constitution. . . .

The 1959 document begins:

> The Revolutionary Government, complying with its duty to the people of Cuba, interpreting their will and opinion, and in the presence of the immediate need of authorizing and carrying out adequate legislation in order to make possible the realization of the Revolution, using the full powers invested in it, agrees unanimously to approve, sanction, and promulgate the following. . . .

One document was thus intended to assure freedom and justice, maintain order, and promote the general welfare; the other was intended to "make possible the realization of the Revolution." One was written by the "delegates of the people of Cuba," the other talks of the "Revolutionary Government, complying with its duty to the people of Cuba, *interpreting their will and opinion.*" This is an accurate description of what Fidel Castro thinks: that he interprets the will and opinion of the Cuban people. No democratic representation, elections, or constitutional framework apparently are needed.

Since the 1959 document was adopted, practically none of its provisions have been followed except those giving the Council of Ministers the executive and legislative power. Article 24 prohibits the confiscation of property except for "justifiable reason of public benefit or social interest and *always after payment of appropriate compensation in cash.*" Article 33 provides that "Every person can, without prior censorship, freely express his thoughts orally or in writing," and Article 34 provides that "the domicile is inviolable." Article 37 provides that "the inhabitants of the Republic have the right to assemble peacefully and without arms, and to parade and associate themselves for all lawful purposes of life, in accordance with corresponding legal standards, without other limitations than are necessary to ensure public order." These are only examples; one finds many other constitutional provisions that have been completely ignored. If there are any formal rules being observed in Cuba, no one knows what they are.

Ironically enough, Fidel Castro, in his speech known as "History Will Absolve Me," probably described the government he heads better than anyone else has been able to do. In discussing the 1940 constitution, Castro said:

Article 1 says: "Cuba is a sovereign and independent state organized as a democratic republic . . ." Article 2 says: "Sovereignty resides in the people, and all powers originate in them." But then comes Article 118 and says: "The President of the Republic will be named by the Council of Ministers . . ." So it is not the people, now it's the Council of Ministers . . . And who chooses the Council of Ministers? Article 120, section 13: "The President may freely appoint and change ministers, replacing them as the occasion arises." Who chooses whom, after all? Isn't this the classic problem of the chicken and the egg, which no one has solved yet?

Castro then continues:

One day eighteen adventurers got together. The plan was to attack the Republic with its 350-million-peso budget. With treachery and underhandedness they achieved their purpose. "And what do we do now?" One of them said to the others: "You make me Prime Minister and I'll make you generals." This done, he rounded up a claque of twenty men and told them: "I'll name you my ministers and you name me President." And they took over the treasury of the Republic.

And it is not simply a matter of the usurpation of sovereignty on a single occasion to name ministers, generals, and president; but a man declared himself by statute absolute master, not only of sovereignty, but of the life and death of every citizen and of the very existence of the nation. . . .

There is in the statutes [of Batista] one article that has passed almost unnoticed, but it is the one that furnishes the key to this situation and from which we shall draw decisive conclusions. I refer to the modifying clause contained in Article 257, which says: "This constitutional law can be amended by the Council of Ministers with a quorum of two-thirds of its members." Here the hoax reached its height. Not only did they exercise sovereignty to impose upon the people a constitution without obtaining their consent and to install a government that concentrates all powers in their own hands; but also, through Article 257, they assume conclusively the most essential attribute of sovereignty, which is the power to amend the supreme and basic law of the nation, something they have already done several times since the tenth of March, although they assert with the greatest cynicism in the world in Article 2 that sovereignty resides in the people and all powers originate in them.

If all that is needed to bring about these changes is a two-thirds quorum of the Council of Ministers, and the President is the one who names the Council of Ministers, then the right to make and break the Republic is in the hands of one man, a man who is, moreover, the most unworthy of those born in this land. . . .

Such a power recognizes no limits. Under its aegis, any article, any chapter, any clause, the whole law can be modified. Article 1, for example, which I have just mentioned, says that Cuba is a sovereign and independent state organized as a democratic republic—although today it is in fact a bloody satrapy. . . .

Batista and his Council of Ministers, under the provisions of Article 257, can modify all those articles, can say that Cuba is no longer a republic, but a hereditary monarchy, and he, Batista, can anoint himself king. He can dismember the national territory and sell a province to a foreign country, as Napoleon did with Louisiana. He can suspend the right to life and, like Herod, order newborn children beheaded. All these measures would be legal, and you would have to throw in prison all those who opposed them, just as you intend to do to me right now.[8]

In this long quotation one only needs to substitute the name of Castro for that of Batista to read an exact description of the constitutional position of Cuba under Castro. Under the Fundamental Law of 1959, Article 129, clause m, the president of the republic is given the power "freely to appoint and remove the Ministers of Government," and Article 134 states that "In case of absence, incapacity or death of the President of the Republic, he shall be replaced temporarily or permanently, as the case may be, by the person designated by the Council of Ministers by agreement of two-thirds of its members." One can only ask with Castro: "Who chooses whom, after all?"

Even more striking to the scholar reading this fantastic document, Title 10, "The Executive Power," contains ten articles and occupies three pages, but nowhere does it state how the original president is supposed to get his position. Article 134 only describes the way in which vacancies are to be filled. Thus the Cuban constitution under Fidel Castro's leadership sets up a mysterious president who, having myste-

---

[8] *Pensamiento político, económico y social de Fidel Castro* (Havana: Editorial Lex, 1959), pp. 68–70.

riously obtained the position, appoints a cabinet of ministers who then appoint other presidents when necessary.

Beginning in 1961, Fidel Castro began to drop hints that a new, "socialist" constitution would someday be created. In the summer of 1965 Castro said: "We have not hurried in creating a socialist constitution. When we create our socialist constitution we want it to be, not a formal constitution, but one that has a realistic context which will juridically express revolutionary thinking: only then will our constitution and state be socialistic."[9] Castro then went on to describe what the constitution ought to contain, pointing out that it would define the role of the Communist Party and its relationship to the government. A few months later, in one of the reorganizations of the totalitarian party, a three-member commission on constitutional studies was set up with Blas Roca, one of the long-time leaders of the Communist Party, as president of the commission.

The only conclusion one can draw from tracing the course of Fidel Castro's verbiage is that another formal document will probably emerge someday, and that until then he is the constitution of Cuba. When the new document emerges, according to Castro, it will be a reflection of the system now functioning in Cuba.

Who Participates in Politics

Osvaldo Dorticós, the "president" of the dictatorial government, in a speech said that "the economic power and the political power are for the first time in the history of Cuba in the hands of the Cuban people."[10] No Cuban official, however, has ever explained how the people exercise this economic and political power. No elections are held, there is no freedom of speech, press, or assembly, and no organization of any kind not controlled by the dictatorship is permitted to exist. Political life, therefore, is entirely in the hands of the dictatorship.

It is impossible to state what proportion of the population supports the Cuban government or voluntarily participates in its work. Tremendous crowds are regularly assembled on command to hear Fidel Castro and others make speeches, but there is no way of knowing how many of them attend voluntarily. All kinds of numbers have been bandied about as to the proportion of Cuba's population that supports what the government is doing—from 10 to 90 percent—but all these

---

[9] "Discurso del Primer Ministro del Gobierno Revolucionario, comandante Fidel Castro, pronunciado el 26 de Julio de 1965, en el XII Aniversario del asalto al 'Moncada' celebrado en la ciudad de Santa Clara," *Política Internacional* (Havana), 3 (1965): 194.

[10] Osvaldo Dorticós Torrado, *Relación entre los cambios económicos y políticos en la sociedad cubana* (Havana: Imprenta Nacional de Cuba, n.d.), p. 16.

figures are mere guesses. It can be said that the majority of Cubans probably supported Fidel Castro in January 1959 and the majority probably does not today.

The government has created a series of "mass" organizations that are supposed to represent various strata of the population, but there is no evidence that any of these is anything but a mechanism set up to control the people. The most important of these organizations have been the armed militia (but in recent years this has seemed to be disappearing, to be replaced by a regular army based on conscription), the Communist Party of Cuba, the Revolutionary Confederation of Labor, the Committees for the Defense of the Revolution, the Union of Communist Youth, and the Federation of Cuban Women. In addition, all kinds of student and professional organizations carry on extensive activities, but all are controlled from the top by government officials.

The way decisions are made in Cuba and the way newspapers, magazines, radio, and television function point to a society so rigidly controlled that people are considered only as subjects to be manipulated by the small group in power. When a Stalin or a Hitler or a Mao Tze-tung runs a country in this way, it is called totalitarianism, but when Fidel Castro does it, many starry-eyed innocents mystifyingly see something new and progressive in it.

Political Parties

Cuban political life has always been fragmented, and until 1959 there never was a party that had the support of the majority of the population or a stable organization democratically controlled. Just before the 1952 elections (which were never held), the official register of parties showed just under two million voters in nine political parties: Authentic Cuban Revolutionary Party, 621,000; Orthodox Cuban People's Party, 330,000; Unitary Action (Batista's organization), 204,000; Democratic Party, 195,000; Cuban National Party, 189,000; Liberal Party, 185,000; Cuban Party, 94,000; Popular Socialist Party (Communist), 53,000; and Republican Party, 40,000.

All these organizations had disappeared by the 1960's and the Cuban government permitted only one political party to function legally, a newly constituted Communist party. When Castro came to power in 1959, he discovered that he had no organized group behind him capable of operating the machinery of government. His organization, the 26th of July Movement, was an amorphous action group that had attracted all kinds of supporters in the struggle to overthrow the Batista regime. To the consternation of many of its devoted members, after Fidel Castro took control of Cuba, the Popular Socialist Party (PSP) was the only political organization permitted to function freely. All other parties, including the 26th of July Movement and the *Auténtico*, whose members had also been very active in the struggle against Batista, found obstacles placed in their path. By 1960 it was clear that Cuba was to be a one-party state, and the Popular Socialist was the party.

Since Castro came to power, the party has had its name changed three times. From January 1959 to mid-1961 it continued to be called the Popular Socialist Party, the name it had assumed in 1944 when the word Communist had become extremely unpopular because of the party's cooperation with Batista. In 1961 Castro united what was left of the 26th of July Movement, the remnants of the student Revolutionary Directorate, and the Popular Socialist Party into an organization named the Integrated Revolutionary Organizations (ORI). By March 1962 Fidel Castro became alarmed because the old militants of the traditional Communist party, the PSP, seemed to be dominating the ORI. Aníbal Escalante, who had been secretary general of the PSP, had become secretary general of the ORI, and he put his old comrades into key positions in the new party and the government. A fierce internal struggle then took place which was won by Fidel Castro, and when the National Executive Committee of the ORI was announced in March 1962, it contained only ten former members of the PSP and fifteen devoted *Fidelistas*, and the six-member secretariat contained five *Fidelistas* (Fidel Castro, Raúl Castro, Che Guevara, Osvaldo Dorticós, and Emilio Aragonés) and only one PSP member (Blas Roca). To make clear who was number one in the new setup, Escalante was publicly purged and sent off to the Soviet Union.

By 1963 a new name was given the ORI. Now it was referred to as the United Party of the Socialist Revolution (PURS). Just as with the creation of the ORI, there was no public discussion of how the PURS was created or why. Suddenly it was there. In the same way, for unknown reasons on October 1, 1965, the name was again changed. Now the government's one party was to be the Communist Party of Cuba (PCC).

The PCC is the typical government party found in all totalitarian regimes. Herbert Matthews writes that "the PURS is therefore a carefully chosen elite, dedicated to the Revolution. I asked Fidel Castro if it were not similar in conception to the Communist Party in the Soviet Union, the Fascist Party in Italy and the Nazi Party in Germany, and he said that roughly it was."[11] The PCC is organized as a pyramid. At the base in

---

[11] Herbert L. Matthews, *Return to Cuba* (Stanford, Calif.: Institute of Hispanic-American and Luso-Brazilian Studies, Stanford University, 1964), p. 8.

farms, factories, and other centers are party groups that are supposed to
select seven persons as an executive committee. The various executive
committees in each municipality are combined into councils, each headed
by a seven-man executive. Then come regional councils and provincial
councils, culminating in the National Political Bureau, headed by Fidel
Castro. Theoretically, all of this is democratic, but in practice the bureau
headed by Fidel Castro makes all decisions.

Just as in other totalitarian regimes, the PCC acts as one of the arms
of the dictatorship in controlling the population. "Its functions are to
carry out the economic and political policies of the Government at every
level, to be an amalgam, to act as a channel between people and Government, to serve in emergencies, to defend the Revolution, to set an example to all others."[12]

Whether the PCC ought to be called a political party is debatable.
Rather it is another mechanism used to control the population, and as
such should be considered as part of the governmental machinery.

Public Opinion and Pressure Groups

Public opinion is strictly controlled by the Cuban government. No independent publication is allowed and all periodicals still appearing are
organs of the government. The only daily is *Gramma,* the organ of the
Communist Party, with a circulation of 372,000; *Verde Olivo* is a weekly
with a circulation of 67,000 which acts as a house organ for the military
forces. The only other important publication is *Bohemia,* a weekly
magazine that publishes 275,000 copies. A series of other organs with
small circulations appear, but all are under the control of the government and are propaganda bulletins aimed at youth, women, and other
special groups. There really is no way to measure public opinion in
Cuba as there are no legal pressure groups. The only way to influence
the government is through personal contact with someone who has access
to Fidel Castro. Not much is known about how this is done, but two
important routes to Castro are through his personal physician and his
secretary, Celia Sánchez.

The Executive

The society developed by the Castro dictatorship makes it very difficult
to know exactly how the government functions, but what little is known
seems to point to a sort of feudal autocracy with all power centralized in

---

[12] *Ibid.*

a small group around Fidel Castro. The formal organization set up by the 1959 "Fundamental Law" is completely ignored. When the government was taken over, all elective offices were abolished, and officers of Castro's army and members of the Popular Socialist Party were designated by Castro to take over the national, provincial, and municipal offices. There has been a great turnover in personnel, but the system continues.

The key group in Cuba since October 1965 seems to be the Political Bureau of the Communist Party, which consists of eight persons: Fidel Castro, Raúl Castro, Osvaldo Dorticós, Juan Almeida, Ramiro Valdés, Armando Hart, Sergio del Valle, and Guillermo García. Another important center of power, although apparently less important than the Political Bureau, is the Secretariat of the Communist Party, consisting of Fidel Castro, Raúl Castro, Osvaldo Dorticós, Fauré Chamón, Blas Roca, and Carlos Rafael Rodríguez. Armando Hart has the title of organizational secretary of the secretariat. In addition, there is a 104-member central committee, which functions through six committees: education, the armed forces and state security, economics, foreign relations, constitutional studies, and labor.

No matter what the name of the formal organizations Castro creates or how they are reorganized, he remains the key person in all committees and is the active head of the Cuban dictatorship in typical *caudillo* style. He holds the titles of prime minister of the formal government, first secretary of the Communist Party, and commander in chief of the armed forces, but he prefers to style himself simply the Maximum Leader. During the first years of his dictatorship, Castro seemed to govern by instinct, issuing orders wherever he happened to be: in his office, talking on television, traveling. Since then, the system has apparently become more formalized, but the orders continue to come from him.

With the army now based on a universal compulsory draft and the government owner of about 60 percent of all farmland and of almost all other economic activities, the Political Bureau holds a virtual monopoly of all economic, military, and governmental power in Cuba. Since no independent organization of any kind is permitted and since all educational and communication media are strictly controlled, the population has been completely atomized. No person can do anything except what the government permits him to do and there are no legal channels through which one can criticize the government.

One of the important results of this attempt by Fidel and his associates to monopolize all power has been economic chaos. This is best seen in the fantastic drop in food and sugar production, which has led to the introduction of rationing of most necessities. There are continuous campaigns to persuade the Cubans to work harder and to shift their efforts to agriculture, but these appeals have failed to produce any noticeable improvement.

The Judicial Power

In the English translation of the Fundamental Law of 1959 published by the Pan American Union, the description of judicial power takes twelve and a third pages, but there is no independent judicial power in Cuba. The cabinet has the power to change the Fundamental Law, and it did so a number of times until the judiciary was completely transformed into a branch of the executive. Among the rules governing the judiciary are one legalizing retroactive legislation by the cabinet, one introducing the death penalty for a long list of offenses, one giving complete power to appoint and control promotions and assignments of judges to the executive, and one (temporarily introduced a number of times) suspending the irremovability of judges. Under these rules the courts have been purged several times, and the chief justice of the Supreme Court who was appointed by Fidel Castro in January 1959 had to take refuge in the Argentine embassy on November 15, 1960, to save his life.

There is no legal system in Cuba except the whim of the dictatorship. The International Commission of Jurists, a nongovernmental organization with consultative status, Category B, with the United Nations Economic and Social Council, which was created to foster understanding and respect for the rule of law, after conducting an exhaustive study came to this conclusion:

> The Rule of Law has been violated in Cuba in a number of different but correlated ways. The first such method consisted of adding new concepts to the principles incorporated either in the Constitution of 1940 or in the Fundamental Law of 1959, or in any subsequent constitutional amendment . . . The second violation of the Rule of Law in Cuba consists in implementing the decisions of the responsible leaders of the Cuban regime without regard to existing legal provisions, including those of their own special legislation. The so-called "revolutionary legislation" has been brushed aside by the Castro regime whenever it suited their needs. . . . By subjecting the country to the rule of a totalitarian machine based on alien

ideology, the regime of Fidel Castro suppressed by violence the very principles which it promised to uphold. Foremost among them, the Rule of Law has disappeared from the Cuban scene.[13]

The state of the courts in Cuba under Fidel Castro can probably best be understood by a statement made in September 1961 by the public prosecutor of the Supreme Court, Dr. Santiago Cuba, during a speech opening the 1961–62 judicial term. After stating that the Supreme Court and other courts had been making counterrevolutionary decisions (i.e., ones he did not agree with), the prosecutor said:

> "The second way of counterrevolutionary activity by the Cuban Judiciary was the support given by most of its members to ancient theories about the separation of powers, and about independence and political neutrality of the judicial branch. This theory was also diffused among the members of the administration of justice and, in some cases, among the people. It was an attempt to oppose the old conception of the Judicial Power to the Revolutionary Power."[14]

Public Finance

With the Cuban government including most of the nation's economic activity in its budget, the total amount has risen astronomically during the 1960's and it is practically impossible to compare the pre- and post-Castro budgets. Before 1959, the legislature had little effect upon the country's budget, despite constitutional provisions for legislative approval; the 1949–50 budget was the first one actually approved by the Assembly since 1937. The executive simply extended his budget from year to year, modifying it as he saw fit. From 1940 to 1958, the budget usually was in balance; in only five years was there a deficit. During this period, the proportion of the total expenditures which went to the military decreased regularly, going from 24.2 percent of the total in 1940 to 17.4 percent in 1949–50, and to only 13 percent in 1958 despite the civil war. Education usually received a good proportion of the total, 23 percent in 1958. The Cuban tax system from 1940 to 1958 was very regressive. Until 1941 there was no tax on personal income, and when an income tax was finally instituted it was not very heavy. In 1958, when the

---

[13] International Commission of Jurists, *Cuba and the Rule of Law* (Geneva, 1962), pp. 266–67.

[14] *Ibid.*, p. 65. The complete speech can be found in *Boletín Oficial del Colegio de Abogados de La Habana*, 16, 2nd ser., nos. 2, 3, 4, 6, 7 (June–November 1961).

government's total income was 387 million pesos (equal to the U.S. dollar and designated by the same sign), the proportion of income from various sources was as follows: from indirect taxes, 38 percent; from custom duties, 29 percent; from taxes on income and real estate, 29 percent; miscellaneous, 4 percent.

Under Fidel Castro, the entire budgetary system was reorganized and the income and expenditures of the central government, the provinces, the municipalities, and the government-owned economic enterprises were all combined. The budget for 1962, shown in Tables 1 and 2, is typical of budgets under the Castro government. The figures demonstrate that in Cuba under Fidel taxation continues much as before. Only 17.39 percent of the income comes from income taxes while 56.32 percent comes from profits on government-owned enterprises. At the same time, military expenditures are about three times as high as in any year before Castro came to power, so high that the amount, $247 million, is equal to more than 60 percent of the government's total budget in 1958.

Local Government

Cuba's 1940 constitution gave autonomy to democratically elected provincial and municipal governmental bodies, and this worked fairly well except when the dictatorship interfered with local actions. When Castro's army took over the country in January 1959, all of the elected governors of provinces, mayors, and city councilmen were expelled from their positions and commissions appointed by the Minister of the Interior took

TABLE 1
REVENUE OF CUBA, 1962

Source	Amount in Pesos	Percent of Total
Income tax	$322,386,700	17.39%
Government enterprises	1,043,933,319	56.32
Social security tax	211,112,700	11.39
Tax on land transportation	6,500,000	0.35
Tax on transfer of real estate property, business firms, and inheritance	1,400,000	0.07
Tax on documents	7,500,000	0.40
Tax on consumer goods	19,600,000	1.05
Other taxes	75,888,000	4.10
Other revenues	165,411,000	8.93
Total	$1,853,731,719	100.00%

TABLE 2
EXPENDITURES OF CUBA, 1962

	Amount in Pesos	Percent of Total
Development of national economy		
Agriculture, forestry, cattle, fisheries	$111,574,700	6.02%
Industry	208,279,328	11.24
Commerce	14,567,701	0.78
Communications	48,070,732	2.59
Transportation	87,989,600	4.75
Basic services to community	232,727,314	12.55
Total national economy	$703,209,375	37.93%
Financing of culture and social service		
Education	237,645,425	12.85
Sciences and culture	32,710,692	1.80
Public health	89,031,472	4.84
Social security	174,689,830	9.34
Social assistance	20,484,324	1.10
Sports and recreation	14,373,793	0.77
Total social service	$568,935,536	30.70%
Financing of public administration		
Central administration	166,627,255	8.99
Provincial administration	28,377,181	1.53
Total public administration	$195,004,436	10.52%
National defense and internal order	247,000,000	13.33
Public debt	116,078,206	6.26
Reserve	23,504,166	1.26
Total expenditures	$1,853,731,719	100.00%

control of the provincial and municipal governments. When the government began to expropriate the means of production in Cuba, the system of commissions faded away and a new organization, the *Junta de Coordinación, Ejecución e Inspección* (JUCEI), was set up. Originally the functionaries of JUCEI received their instructions from the various ministries; after the ORI was set up in 1961, they took orders from the ORI provincial and local delegates.

By 1965, the attempt to control all local activity from Havana was recognized as a failure by the dictatorship. In a speech on July 26, 1965, Castro blamed the failure, of course, not on his dictatorship, but on the lack of experience and training among the officials he had appointed, and announced that JUCEI would be abolished. In its stead a system of provincial, regional, and municipal administrative agencies would be set up. The officials in this hierarchy are appointed by the provincial, regional, and local officials of the Communist Party.

Cuba thus has a three-level bureaucracy to handle local affairs. The provincial officials have only supervisory duties, while the planning and administration are done by the 52 regional and 294 municipal entities (in pre-Castro Cuba there were 126 *municipalidades*). Basically, this is the French system of local government, without elected councils to advise and control the officials. Castro refers to this as democracy, since the party that names the officials in the administration represents the workers' best interests.

Alongside the bureaucratic system described above, an organization known as the Committees for the Defense of the Revolution (CDR) spreads its tentacles all over the country. These committees were first organized in 1960 as a spy mechanism to keep track of the opposition to Castro. Their first task was to report on suspicious meetings, persons who had or who distributed "counterrevolutionary" propaganda, men who did not work, and suspicious conversations. The CDR proved so useful during the 1961 invasion, when they caused the arrest of 300,000 people in a few days, that they became the chief agency of government control and grew until in 1964 the government reported there were 1,544,762 members of these committees out of a total population of 7,203,000.

The CDR's are set up in each city block, large apartment house, factory, farm, and rural community. In the cities, especially in Havana, they have become formally organized, each CDR having a president, a vice-president, a secretary, and a coordinator, as well as eight delegates for indoctrination, the recovery of wealth, voluntary labor, culture, finance, public health, education, and sports.

The delegate for indoctrination passes out the leaflets and pamphlets issued by the government and organizes study circles where they are read. This position has become progressively more important as the years have passed, and the government has organized schools to train these delegates to be more effective. The delegate for voluntary labor sees that the persons in his district "volunteer" their services on demand. The delegate for the recovery of wealth keeps track of the property of those Cubans who legally leave the country. The delegate for finance raises the money to finance the CDR. There are no formal dues; the CDR is financed by the sale of stamps valued from five to twenty-five cents to the people in the districts. It is understood that persons with a "revolutionary attitude" will buy their quota regularly. Of the money collected in this manner, 75 percent is sent to the national office of the CDR and

25 percent remains to finance the local committees' work. The delegate for finance also handles collections for public improvements, such as fixing the street or putting up decorations for holidays. The delegate for public health keeps records of children, inoculations, and illnesses, and leads sanitation drives. The delegate for education sees that all children attend school. The delegate for culture organizes "cultural" meetings and the delegate for sports organizes athletic activity. The coordinator-secretary, the most important member of each CDR, directs the work of the committee.

In addition to all this, the CDR's issue and control ration cards and mobilize the crowds needed to swell the frequent mass meetings at which the leaders of Cuba are so fond of making speeches. Fidel Castro, in talking of the CDR, once said that

> we are going to establish a system of collective revolutionary vigilance and we are going to see how the lackeys of imperialism are able to move around because we definitely live in all the city; there is no block, no acre, no neighborhood, which is not represented here . . . and all the world will know who is who and what he who lives here does and what relations he has with the tyranny and to what he dedicates himself, with whom he associates, in what activities he participates . . . we are going to plant a Committee of Revolutionary Vigilance in each area so that the people can watch, so the people can observe . . .[15]

It is possible that the CDR may someday be merged into the system of local government of the French type which now functions, but it is also possible that the committees might be infiltrated by the opponents of the regime and become the framework of the opposition. So far as can be known now, however, this has not happened yet.

Cuba: A Last Word

Cuba is a totalitarian state kept from degenerating into anarchic civil war by tremendous subsidies in money, equipment, and manpower sent from the Soviet Union and other iron-curtain dictatorships. The high hopes born of a desperate and violent struggle against Batista have been completely crushed. As Juanita Castro Ruz has so well said, "My brother Fidel Castro filled the Cuban people with hope, promising to eliminate forever injustice, terror, and military domination. He guar-

---

[15] *Revolución* (Havana), September 28, 1960, p. 2.

anteed free elections and, in short, everything that people desire to be happy."[16] What the Cuban people actually got after Fidel Castro and his friends consolidated their power Juanita Castro calls "a prison surrounded by water."

Why did a revolution born with such high hopes become, in a few short years, only another totalitarian prison camp? Of the many explanations that have been offered, none completely satisfies and some are false. Fidel Castro and the international Communist publicity agencies claim the actions of the United States government forced Castro to become a dictator, but there is no evidence to justify this claim and much evidence against it. The only logical explanation seems to be that the political habits developed by the Cuban people during the past 400 years were not such as to encourage the growth of democratic institutions. It must always be remembered that Spain dominated Cuba until 1898; that the United States dominated Cuba until after World War I; and Soviet domination is not something really new. The Cubans simply never learned how to develop the strong trade unions, political parties, and other social organizations without which democracy cannot function. Thus when Batista was overthrown by an enraged people and the government disappeared, the only strong, well-organized force present to fill the power vacuum in Cuba was the Communist Party.

The Communist Party had the advantage, during all of the decades since it was founded in 1925, of not having to worry about a policy or money to finance its activities. Both came from Moscow. The money enabled the party to keep functioning whether it had members or not, and its cynical policy of expediency enabled it to cooperate with Machado and Batista. This cooperation tended to weaken the democratic trade unions and political parties.

When it became evident in the latter part of 1958 that the Batista regime was going to collapse, the Cuban Communist Party shifted its support to Fidel Castro's 26th of July Movement, after having made arrangements with Castro about the sharing of power. Thus, when Batista fled on January 1, 1959, and Castro became the dominant personality in the country, the Communists were at his side ready to insert their members into every key position. Since the Cuban people had not made a revolution to create another dictatorship or to see Communists in all the key posts, opposition began to be expressed quickly, and as the opposition grew stronger, Castro turned to more and more repressive measures. Opposition to communism became opposition to the "revolu-

---

[16] Juanita Castro Ruz, "A Prison Surrounded by Water," *AFL–CIO Free Trade Union News*, 19 (August 1964): 1.

tion." Freedom of speech, of the press, of organization, and all the other rights for which the people of the world have struggled for centuries became counterrevolutionary activities until, as Herbert L. Matthews, one of Fidel Castro's great admirers, writes: "It has long been obvious that the economy virtually collapsed; that there have been many injustices; that there are no civic freedoms such as freedom of the press, free trade unionism, habeas corpus, an independent judiciary."[17]

The great tragedy of the Cuban revolution is not that it became a dictatorship, or even that it became a Communist totalitarian dictatorship. Latin Americans have survived religious dictators like García Moreno, demagogic dictators like Juan Perón, illiterate peasant dictators like Juan Vicente Gómez, and a great many others, including Gerardo Machado and Fulgencio Batista. What is tragic in today's Cuba is that the Communists persuaded Fidel Castro to turn Cuba into a dependency of the Soviet Union and then permit the Soviet government to try to transform the island into a base for nuclear projectiles with which to threaten the United States and a training camp for guerrillas being prepared to conquer the rest of America. Thus Cuba became a pawn in the cold war between the great world powers, with less control over its own destiny than in many of the dark days of the past.

What are the prospects for Cuba? It is dangerous to guess, since the decisions affecting its future will increasingly be made outside of Cuba, but its past history seems to point to an eruption in which the Cuban people will turn on their masters and physically destroy them. The leaders of this new revolution will come from the armed forces, the government bureaucracy, and the illegal opposition groups that continue to exist. All democratic-minded friends of the Cuban people hope that when this happens, the Soviet, Chinese, and other Communist governments will keep their troops out and not try to save their base there. As for Fidel Castro, he will probably go down in history as the Cuban who could have been the country's greatest hero, but who, through megalomania, became its greatest betrayer. And Castro will join Quisling and McCarthy as a noun denoting something evil.

SELECTED READINGS

Acuña, Juan Antonio. *Cuba: Revolución traicionada.* Montevideo: Editorial Goes, 1962.
Alexander, Robert. "Stalinism in the Pearl of the Antilles," *Communism in Latin America*, pp. 270–94. New Brunswick, N.J.: Rutgers University Press, 1957.

---

[17] Matthews, *Return to Cuba*, p. 1.

ALISKY, MARVIN. "The Disappearing Cuban Daily." *Nieman Reports* 15 (April 1961): 5–6.

ÁLVAREZ DÍAZ, JOSÉ R., *et al. Cuba, geopolítica y pensamiento económico.* Miami: Colegio de Economistas de Cuba en el Exilio, 1964.

———, chairman, and CUBAN ECONOMIC RESEARCH PROJECT. *A Study on Cuba.* Miami: University of Miami Press, 1965.

BACIU, STEFAN. *Cortina de hierro sobre Cuba.* Buenos Aires: Editorial San Isidro, 1961.

BAEZA FLORES, ALBERTO. *Las Cadenas vienen de lejos.* Mexico City: Editorial Letras, 1960.

BURKS, DAVID D. *Cuba under Castro.* Headline Series, no. 165. New York: Foreign Policy Association, 1964.

———. "The Future of Castroism." *Current History* 44 (February 1963): 78–83, 116.

CAMERON, JAMES. "Cuba's Fumbling Marxism." *Atlantic* 214 (September 1964): 92–102.

CASTRO, FIDEL. *La Revolución cubana.* Buenos Aires: Editorial Palestra, 1960.

CASUSO, TERESA. *Cuba and Castro.* New York: Random House, 1961.

DARÍO RUMBAUT, RUBÉN. *La Revolución traicionada.* N.p.: Frente Revolucionario Democrático, 1962.

DRAPER, THEODORE. *Castro's Revolution: Myths and Reality.* New York: Frederick A. Praeger, Inc., 1962.

———. *Castroism, Theory and Practice.* New York: Frederick A. Praeger, Inc., 1965.

FITZGIBBON, RUSSELL H. "The Revolution Next Door." *Annals of the American Academy of Political and Social Sciences* 334 (March 1961): 123–32.

FRANCO, VICTOR. *The Morning After: A French Journalist's Impression of Cuba under Castro.* New York: Frederick A. Praeger, Inc., 1963.

GOLDENBERG, BORIS. "Análisis de la revolución cubana." *Problemas de Comunismo* 10 (1963): 1–9.

HALPERIN, ERNST. "The Castro Regime in Cuba." *Current History* 51 (December 1966): 354–59.

HENNESSY, C. A. M. "Cuba: The Politics of Frustrated Nationalism." In *Political Systems of Latin America*, edited by Martin C. Needler. Princeton, N.J.: D. Van Nostrand Co., 1964.

INTERNATIONAL COMMISSION OF JURISTS. *Cuba and the Rule of Law.* Geneva, 1962.

JAMES, DANIEL. *Cuba: The First Soviet Satellite in the Americas.* New York: Avon Books, 1961.

KLING, MERLE. "Cuba: A Case Study of a Successful Attempt to Seize Political Power by the Application of Unconventional Warfare." *Annals of the American Academy of Political and Social Science* 341 (May 1962): 42–52 .

MACDONALD, AUSTIN F. "Cuba," *Latin American Politics and Government*, pp. 550–79. 2nd ed. New York: Thomas Y. Crowell Co., 1954.

MACGAFFEY, WYATT, and BARNETT, C. R. *Cuba: The People, Its Society, Its Culture.* New Haven, Conn.: HRAF Press, 1962.

MASÓ, CALIXTO. "El Movimiento obrero cubano." *Panoramas* 2 (May–June 1964): 69–94.

MATTHEWS, HERBERT. *Cuba.* New York: Macmillan Co., 1964.

MONAHAN, JAMES, and GILMORE, KENNETH O. *The Great Deception: The Inside Story of How the Kremlin Took Over Cuba.* New York: Farrar, Straus, 1963.

PHILLIPS, R. HART. *The Cuban Dilemma.* New York: Ivan Obolensky, Inc., 1962.

———. *Cuba: Island of Paradox.* New York: McDowell, Obolensky, 1959.

RIVERO, NICOLÁS. *Castro's Cuba: An American Dilemma.* Washington: Luce, 1962.

SEERS, DUDLEY, *et al. Cuba: Its Economic and Social Revolution.* Chapel Hill: University of North Carolina Press, 1964.

STOKES, WILLIAM S. "National and Local Violence in Cuban Politics." *Southwestern Social Science Quarterly* 31 (September 1953): 57–63.

———. "The Cuban Parliamentary System in Action, 1940–1947." *Journal of Politics* 11 (May 1949): 335–64.

SUÁREZ, ANDRÉS. *Cuba: Castroism and Communism, 1959–1966.* Cambridge: M.I.T. Press, 1967.

TANNENBAUM, F. "Castro and Social Change." *Political Science Quarterly* 77 (June 1962): 178–204.

THOMAS, H. "Five Years of Cuban Revolution." *Current History* 46 (January 1964): 26–33.

URRUTIA LLEO, MANUEL. *Fidel Castro and Company, Inc.* New York: Frederick A. Praeger, Inc., 1964.

WILKERSON, LOREE. *Fidel Castro's Political Programs from Reformism to Marxism-Leninism.* Gainesville: University of Florida Press, 1965.

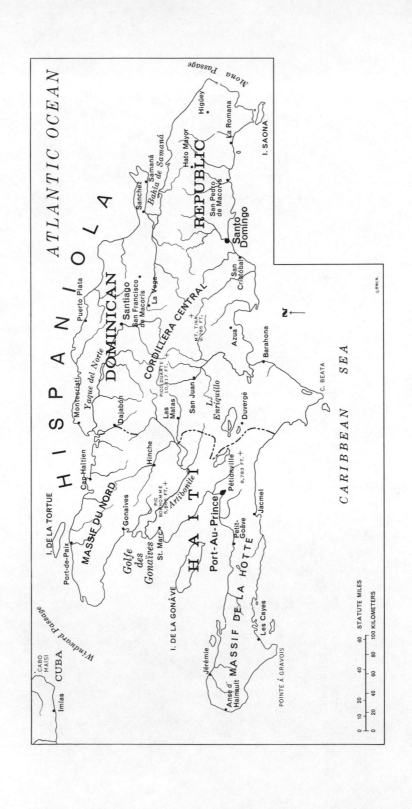

ATLANTIC OCEAN

Mona Passage

HISPANIOLA

DOMINICAN REPUBLIC

Higüey
La Romana
I. SAONA

Hato Mayor
San Pedro
de Macorís
Santo Domingo

Sánchez
Samaná
Bahía de Samaná

Puerto Plata
Santiago
San Francisco
de Macorís
La Vega
San Cristóbal

Montecristi
Yaque del Norte
Dajabón

CORDILLERA CENTRAL

MT. TINA
9,285 FT. +

Azua
Barahona

PICO DUARTE
10,417 FT. +

San Juan
L.
Enriquillo
Duvergé
C. BEATA

Las
Matas

CARIBBEAN SEA

Cap-Haïtien
MASSIF DU NORD
Hinche

I. DE LA TORTUE

Port-de-Paix

Gonaïves
PICO
BONHOMME
5,800 FT. +
St. Marc
Artibonite

HAITI
Port-Au-Prince
Pétionville
8,783 FT. +
Petit-
Goâve
Jacmel

Golfe
des
Gonaïves

I. DE LA GONÂVE

MASSIF DE LA HOTTE

Jérémie

Ansé d'
Hainault
POINTE À GRAVOIS
Les Cayes

Windward Passage

CABO
MAISI
CUBA

Imías

©RMCN

N

STATUTE MILES
0   10   20   40   60
0   20   40   60   80   100 KILOMETERS

THE ISLAND OF HISPANIOLA

Hispaniola was one of the places Columbus visited on his first trip to the New World in 1492, which means that this island has been subjected to European influence longer than any other part of the hemisphere. Yet it remains about as non-European in its culture as any part of the Western Hemisphere, certainly no bright example of how well the Spaniards and the other Europeans built stable cultures and societies of happy, prosperous people. It is divided into two tiny "sovereign" states, Haiti and the Dominican Republic, each trying to maintain itself in a world where much larger states have trouble existing. Haiti occupies the western third of the island. Its population is Negro; its languages are French and Creole. Most Haitians lead a primitive agricultural life on small farms, using hoe cultivation and producing mainly subsistence crops. The eastern two-thirds of the island is the Dominican Republic. Here the people are mostly mulatto, the language is Spanish, and the agriculture is plantation style, producing commercial crops for the world market. How a small island was split in this way makes an interesting story. Despite the existence of two governments, the island is a geographic unit and the two parts have always affected each other's development.

The first Spaniards settled the eastern section because that was where the Indians lived and because they found gold in the gravel streams there. The Indian population in 1492 has been estimated at 100,000. The Spaniards soon enslaved the Indians and used them to collect gold, to clear the forests, to build towns, and to work in the fields. The rapid destruction of the Indians by epidemics and wars undermined the economic system the Spaniards had set up just as the discovery of more profitable areas (Mexico and Peru) drained most of the Spaniards out of the island. By 1550 it was estimated that only 5,000 Indians remained. Then began a period of almost complete isolation and neglect for the small number of remaining Spaniards, the surviving Indians, the new *mestizos*, and the Negro slaves brought from Africa. The main occupation was raising cattle on large ranches owned by the Spaniards. By 1794, 300 years after Columbus first visited the island, the Spanish colony contained only about 100,000 people.

Meanwhile, a different kind of settler had occupied the western end of the island. The island of Tortuga, off the northwest coast of Hispaniola, now part of Haiti, became one of the headquarters of English and French pirates around 1625. The pirates began to visit the western end of Hispaniola to kill the wild hogs and cattle that had escaped from the Spanish ranches at the eastern end of the island. Through the years the French, the English, and the Spanish disputed possession of Tortuga and western Hispaniola until in 1697 Spain recognized France's claim to the western third of the island, which the French named Saint-Domingue (Santo Domingo).

Saint-Domingue became one of the richest colonies the world has known. Utilizing Negro slaves from Africa for labor and exploitative methods that eventually ruined the productive capacity of the soil, the French turned Saint-Domingue into a well-organized and temporarily extremely productive area. For a century the colony was noted for its large estates, good roads, aqueducts, cities, and extensive production of sugar, bananas, yams, manioc, cacao, coconuts, cotton, and coffee.

The French colony came to have about five times as many people as the larger Spanish colony. In 1794 the Spanish section of the island contained about 35,000 whites, about 38,000 free Negroes and mulattoes, and about 30,000 Negro slaves, a total of about 103,000 persons. In 1789 the French third of the island contained 30,826 whites, 27,548 free Negroes and mulattoes, and 465,429 slaves, a total of 523,803 persons.

When the ideas of the French Revolution became known in Saint-Domingue, many of the mulattoes and freed ex-slaves who had been educated in Paris took literally its slogan, "Liberty, Equality, Fraternity." Slowly unrest began to spread until it exploded into revolution. The revolt began in 1791 and the years that followed saw chaos spread over the island. In the destruction that accompanied the fighting, the roads and the plantations built up over a century were destroyed. The Spanish and the English invaded the island. The blacks and the mulattoes fought each other and the French tried to reconquer the area.

The remarkable fact is that the ex-slaves killed nearly all the white people and expelled the few survivors from the island. Under the leadership of one of the most interesting characters of the Western Hemisphere, Toussaint L'Ouverture, who had been born a slave, the people of Saint-Domingue even defeated Napoleon's troops in the years when those troops were invincible in Europe. Of course, the climate and disease helped them, but the ex-slaves fighting for freedom must be recognized as pioneers in the struggle for a free world. Saint-Domingue was the second colony in America to free itself from European domination, and it did so long before the Spanish, Portuguese, French, Dutch, and all of the English colonies except the thirteen that became the United States of America.

The problem facing the inhabitants now was how to set up a functioning government in an area that had gone through years of international and civil wars, an area in which the masses of the population had recently gone from illiterate slavery to illiterate freedom, an area in which the population was split into two groups, one French-orientated, the other Spanish-orientated, each group speaking a different language. To complicate matters, the ex-slaves had to organize their new government at a moment in history in which no other country would come to their aid. Neither France, Spain, nor England was willing to help the new state, for to do so might stimulate revolt in their colonies. The new United States could offer no help because it had its own slaves to worry about. So for over a hundred years the history of the island was one of war and chaos. During part of that time, all of the island was under one government, at other times under two, three, or more. Empires and republics were proclaimed, but nothing seemed to work. No one knows whether the result could have been different, but being America's only independent Negro state in a world dominated by white men at a time when they were enslaving millions of Negroes did not help the little island.

After 1844, the island was definitely divided into two separate states, Haiti and the Dominican Republic. Yet neither achieved any more stability than the combined country had known before 1844. The culmination to this epoch came when the United States armed forces took over the island and governed it virtually as a colony, remaining in Haiti for nineteen years and in the Dominican Republic for eight years. With the withdrawal of United States troops during the 1920's, the modern history of the island begins. Perhaps there has been a little less violence on the island in the twentieth century than in the previous centuries, but the difference has been one of degree, not of kind. At this writing, Haiti is governed by one of the most brutal dictatorships it has ever suffered, and the Dominican Republic, after being occupied by the troops of the United States, Brazil, El Salvador, Nicaragua, Honduras, and Costa Rica, is struggling to establish a functioning government with the help of the United Nations, the Organization of American States, and the United States. Why the island has had so much difficulty will become clearer as we look at the development of each of its parts.

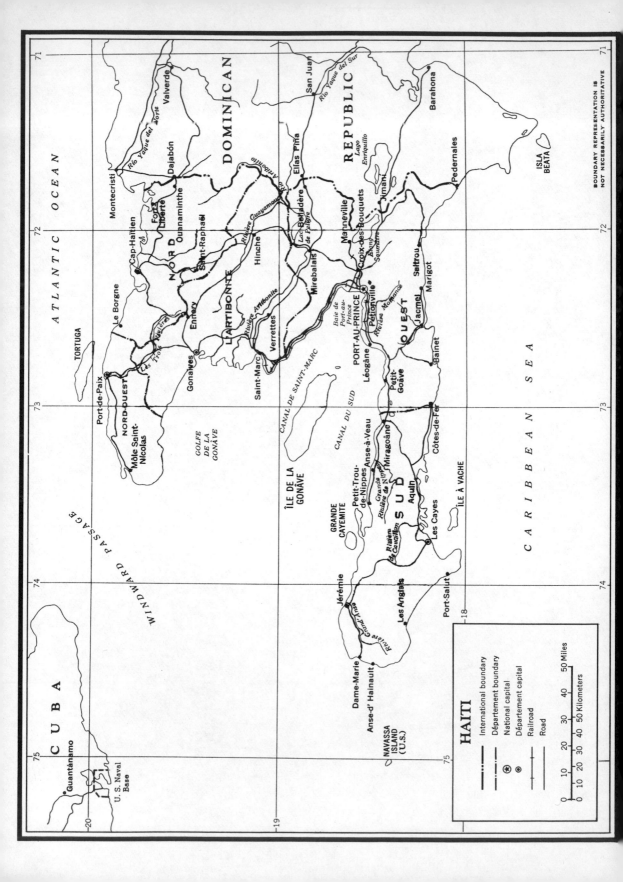

HAITI

International boundary	
Département boundary	
⊛	National capital
◉	Département capital
	Railroad
	Road

Miles: 0 10 20 30 40 50 Miles
Kilometers: 0 10 20 30 40 50 Kilometers

BOUNDARY REPRESENTATION IS
NOT NECESSARILY AUTHORITATIVE

CUBA

Guantánamo

U. S. Naval Base

WINDWARD PASSAGE

ATLANTIC OCEAN

TORTUGA

Port-de-Paix

NORD-OUEST

Môle Saint-Nicolas

Le Borgne

Cap-Haïtien

Montecristi

NORD

Fort-Liberté

Ouanaminthe

Dajabón

Valverde

Rio Yaque del Norte

DOMINICAN

REPUBLIC

San Juan

Rio Yaque del Sur

Saint-Raphaël

Ennery

Gonaïves

Les Trois Rivières

L'ARTIBONITE

Hinche

Rivière Cuayamouc

Rivière Artibonite

Río Artibonito

Elías Piña

Lac de Péligre

Belladère

Mirebalais

Verrettes

Saint-Marc

CANAL DE SAINT-MARC

GOLFE DE LA GONÂVE

ÎLE DE LA GONÂVE

GRANDE CAYEMITE

CANAL DU SUD

Anse-à-Veau

Petit-Trou-de-Nippes

Grande Rivière de Nippes

Miragoâne

Jérémie

Grand'Anse

Dame-Marie

Anse-d'Hainault

NAVASSA ISLAND (U.S.)

Les Anglais

Rivières de Cavaillon

SUD

Aquin

Les Cayes

Port-Salut

ÎLE À VACHE

Côtes-de-Fer

Bainet

Jacmel

Marigot

Seltrou

OUEST

Léogâne

Petit-Goâve

PORT-AU-PRINCE

Baie de Port-au-Prince

Pétionville

Rivière Momance

Croix-des-Bouquets

Mirabouquets

Étang Saumâtre

Manneville

Jimaní

Lago Enriquillo

Pedernales

Barahona

ISLA BEATA

CARIBBEAN SEA

—14—

HAITI:

The Tragic Land

A National Profile

With an area of about 10,700 square miles, Haiti is the second smallest of the twenty Latin-American republics. Located about 700 miles southeast of Florida, Haiti is shaped like a horseshoe with two westward-jutting peninsulas that enclose the Gulf of Gonaïves. To the northwest is Cuba, to the west is Jamaica, and on the east Haiti has a 170-mile border with the Dominican Republic. Four important mountain ranges and many smaller ones divide the country into a series of coastal plains and upland valleys. Transportation is poorly developed and most produce is carried on people's backs or heads or by mules over little trails and dirt roads. Although the climate varies with the altitude and the direction in which the mountains slope, most of the valleys are inhabited and no part of the country has a cold climate. The crops vary, but rainfall is plentiful in many parts of the country. Nature's great scourges in Haiti are the hurricanes that smash into the island almost regularly and recurrent regional droughts.

Statistics for Haiti are very inaccurate, but it is supposed to be the most densely populated of the American republics, with about 4,485,000 people in 1966, or about 419 inhabitants per square mile. The rate of population growth from 1953 to 1962 was 2 percent per year. More than 80 percent of the population is rural and the only large city is the capital, Port-au-Prince, with 250,000. The next largest city, Cap-Haïtien, has 24,423 inhabitants. Practically all Haitians are Negroes, with a very small minority of various shades of mulatto. The mulattoes were a privileged class until 1946, but since then they have lost much of their power, although the richer people still tend to be a little lighter than the rest. Yet color differences have little to do with a person's social status. Education, family position, and financial status set off about 10 percent of the population into a dominant elite. Within this 10 percent there is a smaller group that is Roman Catholic in religion and French in culture. The gulf between the well-to-do upper class and the poor, illiterate masses is very wide and social mobility is minimal.

French is the official language, but only about 10 percent use it. The rest use Haitian Creole, a combination of the Dahomey and Arawak languages with Norman French. Education is poor in Haiti and only 20 percent of those over fifteen years of age are literate, even though the constitution provides that elementary education shall be free and compulsory for all children from seven to fourteen. The university in Port-au-Prince usually has about a thousand students. The children of the rich are educated in private schools and sent overseas for their university training. Although the rich are usually Roman Catholic in religion, the poor have combined Catholicism with a heavy layer of Vodun (or voodoo), a folk religion traceable to Africa. From 1804 to 1860 there was a schism between the Vatican and Haiti, and it is thought this helped to strengthen Vodun. A concordat signed in 1860 established formal relations between Haiti and the Roman Catholic church, and under Duvalier a new *modus vivendi* has been worked out between the Haitian government and the Vatican under which Haiti's government preserves its control of the nomination of bishops. The Protestant denominations are fairly strong, with about 12.5 percent of the population in 1955 belonging to their 1,344 churches.

Haiti is an agricultural country with about 87 percent of its population engaged in farming, forestry, hunting, and fishing; 2.7 percent are in manufacturing, 3.6 percent work for the government, and the rest are mainly engaged in services. Most of the farm workers are self-employed or unpaid family laborers. Agriculture, in large part, is based on small plots that produce both family subsistence and cash crops for the market. One writer claims the Haitian system ought to be called horticulture, for it is based on tree crops that the Haitians harvest and get to market through a devious system.[1]

Coffee, sugar, and sisal have been the most important crops exported. Cassava, sweet potatoes, rice, cotton, and many kinds of fruits are pro-

---

[1] Maurice de Young, *Man and Land in the Haitian Economy* (Gainesville: University of Florida Press, 1958).

duced for local consumption. Bauxite and copper are mined by foreign firms. Some handicrafts are produced and a small tourist industry contributes to the economy. But as can be expected, the Haitians are desperately poor, undernourished, and in ill health. The gross national product in 1961 was estimated to be abut $280 million U.S. and per capita income in 1965 was estimated to be about $63, the lowest in the Western Hemisphere. Haiti is at the bottom of the list in practically all statistics for Latin America and there seems to be no prospect that conditions will improve in the near future.

The Development of Modern Haiti

When Haiti was declared an independant republic on January 1, 1804, by Jean Jacques Dessalines, the people of the island faced an almost impossible task. Almost every person who had gained some experience in the colonial government had been killed or expelled from Haiti. The only result possible was for the generals of the victorious armies to institute dictatorship as a means of reviving the economy and developing some kind of normal life. For the next hundred years, nearly every chief executive was to be a military man. There was always more than one candidate for the top position, however, and whoever became president, or emperor, had to struggle against his ambitious rivals. The pattern that emerged was one of a period of dictatorship followed by chaotic struggles until a new strong man arose to set up a dictatorship which eventually was overthrown in its turn.

To complicate matters, attempts by France, Spain, and England to reconquer the island produced a deep fear that European troops would someday return, and this necessitated the constant maintenance of a large army. Inevitably, the army developed traditions and ambitious officers. Since the army was composed largely of illiterates, some of the officers who rose from the ranks were also illiterates. Often their rank brought them important political posts and power. The army was therefore able to demand the use of the country's resources for its own development, leaving sanitation, education, highways, and economic development totally neglected. Since the government never had enough money to pay its soldiers, it developed the habit of having the troops live off the land, either cultivating their own crops or collecting food from the civilians. It is readily apparent how the army soon became an exploiting and parasitic group in Haiti.

Even more important, Haiti in 1804 did not have a unified population. In addition to the split between those who lived in the former

French colony and those of the former Spanish colony, Haiti was divided into two social strata. The first group was composed of educated mulattoes and a small number of blacks, all of whom were former freedmen. A few of these had even become slaveowners themselves. The vast majority were illiterate black ex-slaves. The two groups could cooperate in the struggle to expel the French, but once independence was achieved they found themselves in conflict. The former freedmen looked upon themselves as a natural ruling class. They spoke French, practiced Catholicism, and educated their sons for business and the professions. Between them and the mass of illiterate, Creole-speaking, Vodun-worshiping peasants there was and there remains a wide cultural gap.

Thus there arose a perennial struggle for power between the elite and the black generals who emerged as military leaders. In the early years the mulatto elite grouped themselves around Alexandre Pétion and Jean Pierre Boyer; the Negro generals were represented by Dessalines and Henri Christophe. It must be emphasized that this was not a racial struggle, for all were one shade or another of black, but rather a struggle between the educated former slaveowners and the illiterate former slaves who had become generals during the revolution. The tragedy of Haiti was that neither group had any preparation for governing the new republic. From 1804 to 1915, twenty-six chief executives were in office. This is an average of a little more than four years for each one, but the figure is deceiving. Actually, six men dominated Haiti during most of the period. Christophe was in power for 13 years, Alexandre Pétion for 11, Jean Pierre Boyer for 25, Faustin Soulouque for about 12, Nicholas Fabre Geffrard for 8, Louis Étienne Félicité Saloman for about 9: a total of about 78 years out of 111. In the chaotic intervals between strong-man rule there was little opportunity for the governments to sponsor developmental programs or to improve education, health, or transportation. The efforts of each government were devoted to staying in power.

During the century of struggle to stabilize a government in Haiti, politics became the leading career for all who wanted to become rich. The land had been divided into small plots during the early years and no extensive landowning aristocracy could emerge. Commerce was a difficult path to wealth, for the country produced little and foreigners dominated the field. Since the French type of classical education inclined the Haitian intellectuals to the law, they turned to government as the place to forge careers. But there were never enough opportunities open to the large number of job seekers; politics became a vicious struggle and graft was commonplace. The willingness of European bankers to loan money at very high rates of interest complicated matters, for many loans were defaulted or repudiated and the European governments became involved in helping their bankers collect the bills. The situation was further complicated when, in 1844, two-thirds of the island to the east was split off to become the Dominican Republic.

The United States began to take a great interest in what was happening in the Caribbean when the Panama Canal was built. The chaos in Haiti and the attempts of European powers to collect their debts there led the United States to land troops in 1915. Theoretically, the troops were there to maintain order, but in fact the United States ran the government through puppets it selected. (Franklin D. Roosevelt, then Assistant Secretary of the Navy, claimed in 1920 that he wrote most of the constitution promulgated by the United States troops.) Naturally, the United States occupation was unpopular with the Haitians. The occupation stabilized the country's finances, improved sanitation and education, saw some roads built, maintained peace in the country, and gave the United States corporations an opportunity to begin operations. This helped to increase production and so to increase the national income. But the United States troops failed miserably as teachers of democracy and as builders of the kind of social institutions a functioning democracy needs. Just as in Nicaragua and the Dominican Republic, the United States created a new armed force, here called the Garde d'Haïti, after disarming the population. When the United States troops were withdrawn in 1934, the pattern of politics returned to the style customary before the occupation, except that now the Garde d'Haïti became one of the leading contenders for power.[2]

The United States left Sténio Vincent as president of the republic when it withdrew, but kept control of the country's finances until 1947. Vincent, a mulatto politician, conducted himself as all previous presidents had done before him: he prolonged his stay in office for ten years and then he installed a hand-picked successor, Élie Lescot. When Lescot tried to prolong his own legal term in office, the army officers overthrew him in 1946 and installed Dumarsais Estimé, a former schoolteacher, as president. This was the period just after the Second World War, when a movement for democracy was sweeping Latin America, and its effects

---

[2] How little the United States Marine officers understood Haiti can be seen in the following statement written by the commandant of the Marine Corps in 1955: "When the last Marine unit departed from Haiti, 20 years later, it left behind a country which had once again resumed its place in the community of nations as a solvent, responsible democracy, a bulwark to the peace and security of the Western Hemisphere" (General Lemuel C. Shepherd, Jr., in the Foreword to *Garde d'Haïti, 1915–1934*, compiled by James H. McCrocklin [Annapolis: U.S. Naval Institute, 1956], p. v). For one scholar's summary of what United States intervention really accomplished, see Rayford W. Logan, "The United States Mission in Haiti," *Inter-American Economic Affairs*, 6 (Spring 1953): 18–28.

were felt in Haiti. During Estimé's term in office, the first halting steps were taken to improve the country's archaic social structure and end the domination by the mulatto elite. Democracy was encouraged and trade unions and political parties began to function. The press was allowed freedom, the first social legislation was adopted, and an attempt was made to create a Haitian nationalism based on the African heritage of the population. The French culture of the mulatto upper class was denigrated; Vodun was openly practiced; scholars began to study Creole; and an artistic upsurge took place. But Estimé, like all his predecessors, ran a one-man government, and when his term was about to expire he tried to prolong it. A new military junta expelled him from power. Estimé is important because he stirred up the Haitian people so effectively that after that all political leaders had to appeal to the masses; the traditional system of elite government no longer was possible.

Paul Magloire, an army officer, succeeded Estimé. When he in his turn tried to prolong his stay in office beyond the set term, he was overthrown and a new strong man emerged in 1957, "Papa Doc," François Duvalier, who is still in power. Duvalier succeeded where his recent predecessors failed by reorganizing the Garde d'Haïti and adding another armed force, the militia, under his personal control. In addition he created a secret police force, the Tonton Macoute, which has succeeded in terrorizing the population and keeping Duvalier in power. Yet Duvalier continues to appeal to the masses; he fosters Vodun, and he operates more as a modern demagogue (in the manner of Perón, for example) than as the traditional Latin-American strong man.

In many ways Duvalier is typical of the political leaders who have saddled Haiti throughout its history. He had himself proclaimed president for life in 1964, and in 1965 he began preparations to become "emperor" someday. Meanwhile, he spends his time hidden in his presidential palace while many of the Haitian intellectuals and trained professionals remain outside Haiti, working for the United Nations and various new African governments.

The Formal Constitutional Framework

Although Haiti has had more than twenty constitutions, none of its governments has ever paid much attention to any of them. The separation of powers, municipal administration, civil liberties, and other constitutional rules have traditionally been only window dressing for the government in power. In the twentieth century, clauses providing for improvements in the health and welfare of the nation's people have been added to the constitution, but little or no attention has been paid to them, either. One perennial clause in these constitutions provides that the president appoint practically all governmental officials. This is one clause that has been observed. In actual practice, there really is no formal constitution in Haiti, as Duvalier is demonstrating once again with the document he promulgated in 1964.

Who Participates in Politics

Politics in Haiti has been an activity confined to the 10 percent or less of the population that speak French and have a monopoly on education and financial power. When elections are held, they are controlled by whoever is in power, and until 1950 the president was elected by the legislature. Since then the president has been "elected" by universal suffrage, but the elections held in 1950, 1957, 1961, and 1964 were all fraudulent. Most Haitians try to scratch a living out of the soil in isolated rural communities, and for all practical purposes we can say they never participate in politics. The urban workers and commercial interests that have developed in the twentieth century have tried, especially since the Second World War, to make their weight felt, but without much success. Since the economy is so underdeveloped, a government position is one of the few ways to make money. Politics becomes a factional struggle for power among the members of the small elite. As each group attains power, it raids the treasury. The gap between the illiterate and Creole-speaking majority and the literate and French-speaking elite is as great or greater than the split between the Indians and the whites in such countries as Guatemala, Ecuador, and Peru.

Political Parties

Haiti has never had true political parties. The names Liberal and Nationalist were used for a long time, but these were coalitions of factions within the elite group. The first real attempt to found parties with mass support took place from 1946 to 1950. The Christian Social Party and the Workers' and Peasants' Movement were the most important. A small Communist party also began to function. When Magloire set up his dictatorship, all party activity was banned. During the interval between Magloire and Duvalier, parties again functioned, but Duvalier quickly destroyed all opposition, and since he consolidated his dictatorship the only political parties functioning are exile groups in Cuba, New York, Caracas, Santo Domingo, and San Juan. These groups have attempted invasions of Haiti and have carried on propaganda campaigns against the government, but none has any substantial support. Haitian society does not yet provide the basis upon which a modern party could be built. Duvalier has created an organization called the "Movement of National Renovation," but this is not a political party; it is one of the mechanisms Duvalier uses to stay in power.

Public Opinion and Pressure Groups

There is no way for public opinion to express itself in Haiti. The 90 percent of the population that speaks Creole cannot read the newspapers, which are all published in French and all controlled by the government. Press and radio are strictly controlled; even the periodical of the Catholic church was shut down by the government in 1961.

No independent organizations of any kind are permitted to function. From time to time Duvalier organizes demonstrations to which large numbers of peasants and workers are herded, but their only role is to cheer for Duvalier. Traditionally, the country has been split between the rural majority that did not participate in political life and the urban minority that did. Since Duvalier, even the urban population has been forced out of politics.

The most important group in Haiti during the twentieth century has been the armed forces, and they continue to be the main support of the Duvalier government. Duvalier has changed the original organization of the armed forces by retiring or expelling most of the professional officers and by relying more on his militia and his secret police (the Tonton Macoute). Controlling the telegraph and telephone system as well as the national airline and radio, the armed forces are spread all over the country. With their monopoly on military equipment, the leaders of the armed forces control and supervise what amounts to an army of occupation, and until the period of Duvalier were able to determine who was to control Haiti's government. Duvalier's militia (the Volunteers for National Security) has served as a check on the military, but in a conflict the regular army would probably win because it controls the heavy armament.

The Catholic and Protestant clergy as well as the leaders of the Vodun cult have always played an important role because they are among the few organized groups in Haiti. Duvalier's struggle with the Catholic hierarchy led to the expulsion of many French priests from the country and Duvalier's excommunication, but the church still remains a powerful force, despite the fact that it has been weakened by the paucity of Haitian priests. In 1964, only 138 of 400 priests in Haiti had been born in that country.

Urban businessmen, whether in commerce, banking, or manufacturing, have always been an important factor in Haiti's power struggle. Duvalier has succeeded in dominating this group by the use of brute force and confiscatory taxes. After the Second World War, it appeared as if the urban business and professional men might gain control of the government, but their traditional isolation from the rural majority and their relatively small size (perhaps 2 to 5 percent of the population) prevented their winning power.

The government employees in Haiti have never played an independent role as a pressure group. Since all positions are filled by favoritism, each new president reorganizes the entire civil service and government employees are always the agents of the man in power.

Throughout the twentieth century, the United States embassy has usually been able to influence the course of events in Haiti by means of loans, military missions, technical assistance, and social contacts. Since the early 1960's, however, the United States embassy has been rather cool to Duvalier and his regime, and has had little effect on his actions.

There never have been strong labor unions in Haiti. In 1966 there probably were not more that 10,000 to 15,000 workers organized in unions, all of them dominated by the government. The ORIT recognizes the leaders of the National Union of Workers of Haiti, who were exiled in 1958 and have functioned out of New York City since then.

Civil Liberties

As would be expected, civil liberty has never been a reality in Haiti, and none exists there today. So many complaints were made about the infraction of human rights under Duvalier's rule that the Inter-American Commission on Human Rights, an organ of the Organization of American States, investigated conditions and issued a report on October 21, 1963, supporting the charges. This had no effect, however, on conditions in Haiti.

The Executive

Haiti's executive is a president "for life," François Duvalier, who came to power through a controlled election in 1957 and has stayed in power by physically destroying all open opposition. Duvalier operates a one-man dictatorship that differs from the traditional strong-man government of Haiti only in his attempt to create a mass base for his regime by utilizing demogogic nationalism and Africanism as an ideology. He is constantly surrounded by bodyguards and keeps out of sight most of the time. The Haitian government traditionally does so little and has so little money at its disposal that it is relatively easy for one man to dominate its machinery. All positions, including those in local government, are filled by the president's appointees. Duvalier's government, as one Haitian has so well pointed out, "has abandoned all pretense of existing for any purpose except to perpetuate itself in power. The inherent evils of the system itself are rendered the more vivid because of the paranoid personality of Duvalier."[3]

The Legislative Power

Although Haiti's constitutions have all set up legislative bodies, the executive has always controlled their activities. Today there is no legislature for all practical purposes. Duvalier dissolved the bicameral legislative body in 1961 and organized a managed election to install a unicameral body that acts as a rubber stamp for his desires. The fifty-eight members of the Assembly were all unopposed in the "election." The Assembly regularly, by unanimous vote, grants Duvalier the power to take whatever measures he deems necessary by issuing decrees with the power of law, "to preserve the national territory, the sovereignty of the State, the preservation of order and of peace, and the defense of the interests of the Republic."

Public Finance

Even if Haiti had a government desirous of doing something for its people, its present economy is so backward and weak that there could never be enough money to do much. Since anywhere from one-third to one-half of the government's income goes to finance the armed forces, there is practically nothing left after the government's employees are paid and the graft is doled out. Recent budgets have run about 175 to 200 million gourdes a year. This comes to about $35 to $40 million U.S. a year, a sum so small as to be ridiculous were it not so tragic for a country with more than 4 million people. The budget shown in Tables 1 and 2 is typical of recent Haitian budgets in the proportionate distribution of income and expenditures.

---

[3] Leslie F. Manigat, *Haiti of the Sixties, Object of International Concern* (Washington: Center of Foreign Policy Research, 1964), p. 5.

TABLE 1

REVENUE OF HAITI, DECEMBER 1960–SEPTEMBER 1961

(10 Months)

Source	Amount in Gourdes	Percent of Total
Customs duties		
Taxes on imports	G36,300,000	31.57%
Taxes on exports	18,800,000	16.35
Other customs taxes	875,000	0.76
Total customs duties	G55,975,000	48.68%
Internal taxes		
On whiskey and other alcoholic beverages	897,450	0.78
On tobacco products	2,034,100	1.77
On flour	8,186,000	7.12
On income	9,000,000	7.83
Miscellaneous	17,507,450	15.23
Total internal taxes	G37,625,000	32.73%
Other taxes	3,225,000	2.81
Internal and other loans	18,140,000	15.78
Total revenue	G114,965,000	100.00%

TABLE 2

EXPENDITURES OF HAITI, DECEMBER 1960–SEPTEMBER 1961

(10 Months)

	Amount in Gourdes	Percent of Total
Public debt	G2,383,626	2.10%
International institutions	13,380,520	11.78
Department of Finance and Economic Affairs	11,669,200	10.27
Department of Agriculture, National Resources, and Rural Development	7,627,490	6.71
Department of Public Works, Transport, and Communications	7,263,310	6.39
Department of Public Health and Population	12,875,800	11.33
Department of Interior and National Defense	31,727,510	27.92
Department of Foreign Affairs	5,112,020	4.50
Department of National Education	11,985,650	10.55
Department of Labor and Public Welfare	1,500,470	1.32
Department of Commerce and Industry	1,658,270	1.46
Department of Tourism	1,000,000	0.88
Department of Justice	2,930,675	2.58
Department of Coordination and Information	1,373,100	1.20
Department of Religion	1,156,029	1.01
Total	G113,643,670	100.00%

Local Government

No local government exists in Haiti. For administrative purposes the country is divided into departments, which are divided into *arrondissements*, which in turn are divided into communes. In each department and *arrondissement* there is a prefect, who administers the area as the personal representative of the president. In each *arrondissement* there is a council appointed by the president, which supervises the communal councils, which also are appointed by the president. In the purely rural areas the government is represented by a *chef de section*, an officer of the police who is the link between the rural area and the district military authority in the nearest urban area. All decisions on all levels are made in the capital and practically no services are provided in most areas. The prefects, councils, and *chefs de section* are the representatives of the central power and police officials.

Haiti: A Last Word

Haiti is a total dictatorship controlled by one man, François Duvalier, who, using terror and intimidation, has made a mockery of constitutional government and driven many of the country's best educated and trained professionals into exile. There are no civil liberties; people disappear or are found murdered regularly; the legislature is a rubber stamp for Duvalier; the courts are designed to sanction whatever Duvalier does; and there is no local government. The entire governmental system revolves around "Papa Doc" as the country's population ekes out a miserable existence; the economy stagnates; and Duvalier spends his time trying to prolong his stay in the presidential palace.

Is the outlook for Haiti hopeless? Yes, probably, because the country is caught in a vicious circle. Poor communications and transportation facilities combine with mass illiteracy, poor health, and the political habits of the population to prevent the creation of the kind of political parties, trade unions, and other secondary organizations so important to a developing society. The national income is so low that there is no substantial sum available for development, and when money comes in from the United States or international organizations, it disappears before anything is accomplished. To improve matters, the economy, the government, education, public health—everything must be overhauled. But how does one get the process started? Until some group captures power with the will to effect complete change, and vast sums at its disposal over a long period of time, Haiti seems doomed to continue as it has for over 150 years.

SELECTED READINGS

ARMBRISTER, TREVOR. "Is There Any Hope for Haiti?" *Saturday Evening Post,* June 15, 1963, pp. 78–81.

CAREY, ALIDA L. "Our Choice in Haiti: Duvalier or the People." *Commonweal* 75 (March 2, 1962): 587–90.

DAVIS, H. P. *Black Democracy, The Story of Haiti.* Rev. ed. New York: Dodge Publishing Co., 1936.

DRAPER, THEODORE. "Return of the Elite." *Reporter,* October 2, 1951, pp. 17–21.

FARRELL, BARRY. "It's Hell to Live in Haiti with Papa Doc." *Life,* March 8, 1963, pp. 28–35.

GOLD, HERBERT. "Haiti, Hatred without Hope." *Saturday Evening Post,* April 24, 1965, pp. 74–81.

"Haiti, The Black Republic: A Snake Pit." *Newsweek,* January 21, 1963, pp. 51–52.

"Haiti: The Perón of Voodooism." *New Republic,* June 1, 1963, pp. 10–11.

HEINL, ROBERT DEBS, JR. "Haiti: A Case Study in Freedom." *New Republic,* May 16, 1964, pp. 15–21.

LATORTUE, GÉRARD R. "Tyranny in Haiti." *Current History* 51 (December 1966): 349–53.

LEYBURN, JAMES G. *The Haitian People.* New Haven: Yale University Press, 1941.

LOGAN, RAYFORD W. "Education in Haiti." *Journal of Negro History* 15 (July 1930): 401–60.

———. "The United States Mission in Haiti." *Inter-American Economic Affairs* 6 (Spring 1953): 18–28.

——— and NEEDLER, MARTIN C. "Haiti." In *Political Systems of Latin America,* edited by Martin C. Needler. Princeton, N.J.: D. Van Nostrand Co., 1964.

MACDONALD, AUSTIN F. "The Pattern of Haitian Politics," *Latin American Politics and Government,* pp. 587–98. 2nd ed. New York: Thomas Y. Crowell Co., 1954.

MANIGAT, LESLIE F. *Haiti of the Sixties, Object of International Concern.* Washington: Center of Foreign Policy Research, 1964.

MOORE, O. ERNEST. "Is Haiti Next?" *Yale Review* 51 (December 1961): 254–63.

UNIÓN PANAMERICANA, COMISIÓN INTERAMERICANA DE DERECHOS HUMANOS. *Informe sobre la situación de los derechos humanos en Haiti.* OEA/ser. L/V/11.8. Washington, December 5, 1963.

U.S. DEPARTMENT OF LABOR. *Labor Law and Practice in Haiti.* Bureau of Labor Statistics report no. 244. Washington: U.S. Government Printing Office, 1963.

YOUNG, MAURICE DE. *Man and Land in the Haitian Economy.* Gainesville: University of Florida Press, 1958.

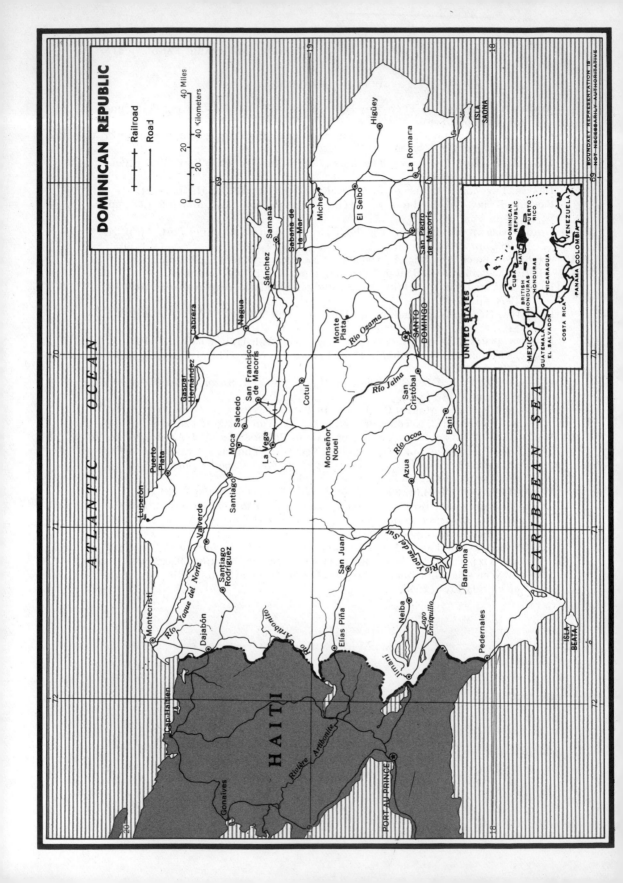

DOMINICAN REPUBLIC

Railroad
Road

40 Miles
40 Kilometers
20
20
0
0

ATLANTIC OCEAN

CARIBBEAN SEA

HAITI

UNITED STATES

DOMINICAN REPUBLIC
PUERTO RICO
CUBA
HAITI
MEXICO
BRITISH HONDURAS
HONDURAS
GUATEMALA
EL SALVADOR
NICARAGUA
COSTA RICA
PANAMA
COLOMBIA
VENEZUELA

BOUNDARY REPRESENTATION IS
NOT NECESSARILY AUTHORITATIVE

ISLA
SAONA

Higüey
La Romana
San Pedro de Macorís
El Seibo
Miches
SANTO DOMINGO
Monte Plata
Río Ozama
Río Jaina
San Cristóbal
Río Ocoa
Baní
Azua
Sabana de la Mar
Sánchez
Samana
Cabrera
Nagua
San Francisco de Macorís
Gaspar Hernández
Cotui
Monseñor Nouel
Salcedo
Moca
La Vega
Puerto Plata
Luperón
Santiago
Valverde
San Juan
Río Yaque del Sur
Neiba
Lago Enriquillo
Jimaní
Barahona
Pedernales
Elías Piña
Río Artibonite
Santiago Rodríguez
Río Yaque del Norte
Dajabón
Montecristi
Cap-Haïtien
Gonaïves
Rivière Artibonite
PORT-AU-PRINCE

ISLA
BEATA

19
18
69
70
71
72
18

THE DOMINICAN REPUBLIC:

Politics after Totalitarianism

The Dominican Republic has great symbolic importance to the United States because the United States Marines were largely responsible for the development of the Trujillo dictatorship, one of the most vicious and corrupt ever to rule in America. The Dominican Republic has even more important lessons for the student, for in this little country a battle is being fought to determine whether it is possible to develop constitutional government in a country after a totalitarian government is overthrown. As this is written, seven years have passed since the tyrant Trujillo was assassinated, but stable constitutional government has not yet been created.

A National Profile

The Dominican Republic includes the eastern two-thirds of the island of Hispaniola and has an area of 19,000 square miles. Bounded on the north by the Atlantic Ocean and on the south by the Caribbean Sea, the republic has always been isolated from the mainstream of life in the Caribbean. Four parallel mountain ranges cross the republic from southeast to northwest, creating a series of fertile valleys in which the bulk of the population lives. The largest concentration of people is in the Cibao Valley, between Santiago and San Francisco, and on the north coast, where about half the population is found. Another third lives in and around the capital city and on the southern coastal plain stretching from

San Cristóbal to La Romana. Despite the mountains, about 54.4 percent of the total area consists of arable land.

The population of the Dominican Republic was estimated to be 3,754,284 on July 1, 1966. No accurate figures are available as to racial composition, but a realistic estimate is that about 10 percent are white, about 20 percent are Negro, and about 70 percent mulattoes or *mestizos* of varying shades. The upper classes are white or near white, while the lower classes are much darker. Japanese and Spanish colonies have been established, and the Chinese are very prominent in the operation of restaurants and bars. About 70 percent of the population is rural; the remainder live in towns and cities over 1,000 in population. The only really large city in the country is the capital, Santo Domingo, with 560,636 inhabitants in 1966. The second city is Santiago de los Caballeros, which had 127,026 in 1966. There are no other cities with more than 35,000 persons.

Spanish is the official language and practically everyone uses it. Most of the population (98.2 percent) is considered to be Roman Catholic. Other religions have freedom to function. Education has been greatly neglected, and although the official figures place illiteracy at 60 percent, in some of the rural areas it runs up to 90 percent. A good guess would be that about 75 percent are illiterate overall. There is a great shortage of schools and teachers, and the schools that exist are short of equipment and the teachers short on training.

The Dominican Republic is primarily an agricultural country, but basic foodstuffs must be imported to feed the population. This is because the most fertile lands have been devoted to crops for the world market, which could bring a cash return to the landowners, of whom the dictator Trujillo was the largest in his time. Sugar is the most important crop, supplying about half by value of all exports. Cacao, coffee, rice, and tobacco are also produced for the world market. In addition to the food imported, a great deal is grown on the less fertile soils, particularly in out-of-the-way places, by subsistence farmers. Some minerals are produced —bauxite, iron ore, marble, nickel, gold, sulfur, copper, and salt—but no thorough surveys have ever been made with a view to exploiting the country's minerals efficiently. Some industrialization has developed, mainly in the processing of the country's agricultural products. The main manufactures are refined sugar, rum, chocolate, cigarettes, shoes, textiles, flour, cement, and beer.

The economy is greatly distorted because during the thirty-one years of Trujillo's regime he followed the rule of doing only those things that would swell his bank accounts in the United States and Switzerland.

Poverty is overwhelming in the Dominican Republic. In 1963, when the per capita income for all Latin America was about $325 a year, estimates for the Dominican Republic were between $189 and $235. What income there is is distributed so that a tiny upper class receives most of it and the bulk of the population lives almost on an animal level. In Santo Domingo one sees prostitutes as young as eight and nine years old looking for clients; one sees children up to ten or so naked in the streets; large numbers live without adequate food, water, or housing, with no medical or sanitation facilities, no educational or recreational facilities, no electricity, no roads, and no hope.

The Dominican Republic was not exceptional in its backwardness and poverty during the nineteenth century, when communications were less well developed than they are in the twentieth century, but the crime of Trujillo's regime is that he distorted the country's development during a period when other countries were modernizing their economies and developing their educational systems. As we shall see, Trujillo turned the republic into a sort of private estate that served to produce money so the Trujillos and their associates could enjoy life in Paris, Hollywood, and other glamour spots. When Trujillo disappeared, the governments that followed him were left with a country with a distorted economy, a bankrupt treasury, mass illiteracy, and widespread unemployment. It is not surprising that it proved difficult to set up any kind of government the people would accept.

The Development of the Modern Dominican Republic

As has been pointed out, the two parts of the island of Hispaniola were not definitely separated into two political units until 1844, although by 1821 sufficient consciousness of nationality had developed so that an independent Dominican Republic was proclaimed. It was able to function only a short time; the following year the Haitian army once again conquered the eastern section of the island, and until 1844 it was again united under one government. In 1844 the Haitians were at last expelled and the Dominican Republic tried for seventeen years to establish some kind of stable system. When none was successful, the president reunited the country with Spain in 1861, and until 1865 the country was again a colony. A new independence brought more chaos, and in 1870 an attempt was made to unite the Dominican Republic with the United States, but the treaty formalizing this union was not ratified by the United States Senate. Then followed more decades of chaos. From 1844 to 1914, the history of the Dominican Republic consists of a series of revolutions, counterrevolutions, dictatorships, invasions from and wars with Haiti, and much intervention from other foreign countries.

Why did the Dominican Republic have so much difficulty getting established? The only logical explanation is that the people of the "republic" were not prepared by their past experiences for self-government of any kind. Government became, therefore, a method of exploiting the population, and the spoils of office were savagely fought for. Hubert Herring has called the rule of Ulises Heureaux from 1882 to 1899 "perhaps the most pitiless tyranny in the history of Latin America."[1] Between 1844 and 1930 the Dominican Republic had fifty presidents, thirty revolutions, and twenty-eight constitutions.

The chaos came to an end with United States military occupation. The government was bankrupt, for each successive tyrant floated a loan in Europe which future tyrants never repaid. In 1905, when European creditors became insistent and the United States government thought one of the European powers might take over the country, the United States took charge of the administration of the customs in the hope of stabilizing the country. Part of the customs receipts were given to the foreign creditors, part to the government. This drastic measure did nothing to solve the country's problems, and finally, because of the crisis provoked by the First World War, the United States militarily took over the Dominican Republic on November 29, 1916, and kept control of the country until 1924. During that period the Congress was suspended, the Supreme Court was stripped of authority, and the executive consisted of a United States military governor who ruled by decree. Some roads were built and sanitation, communications, and education were improved, but the material progress was accompanied by the stifling of whatever political forces had been active in the country. All arms were confiscated, local government was abolished, and all policing was done by the United States armed forces.

In their concern for law and order, the United States organized an armed force, the Dominican Constabulary Guard, by means of which America's first totalitarian state was to be created after the United States troops left in 1924. The new Dominican armed force was doomed to be an antidemocratic force by its very composition. Although the country had been in chaos before United States intervention, at least it was Dominican chaos; there was virtual unanimity of opposition to the United States intervention among all educated and politically active groups. Therefore, when the new constabulary was organized, no re-

---

[1] Hubert Herring, *A History of Latin America*, 1st ed. (New York: Alfred A. Knopf, Inc., 1957), p. 426.

spectable Dominican would have anything to do with it. Every opportunist, gangster, and would-be strong man looking for a road to power, however, was eager to join up. Since most of these people had no military experience, the United States created a military academy to train them. Of course, all this cost a great deal of money; one estimate is that in 1919, 26.3 percent of the nation's income went to the support of the constabulary.

Before the United States troops left the country in 1924, a new constitution was drawn up and a government headed by President Horacio Vásquez was installed. The name of the constabulary was changed to the Dominican National Police, and in a decree of September 15, 1922, it was declared to be "the only national armed force encharged with the maintenance of public order." The Vásquez government was typical of traditional Dominican government, based on friendship and the spoils system. By 1929 Vásquez was a sick old man, and when the country's economic life declined with the onset of the world depression, a revolution soon ejected him from office. The commander in chief of the U.S.-created armed forces, Rafael Leonidas Trujillo, became president through a managed election in May 1930 and began a one-man rule that was to last until he was assassinated on May 30, 1961. The rise of Trujillo marked a change in the composition of the ruling class in the Dominican Republic, for the armed forces, which had put Trujillo into power, had been boycotted by the traditional upper classes of the country. Thus the United States created a centralized, unified, modern armed force enjoying a monopoly of armaments and controlled by elements traditionally out of favor who used their new position to capture power.

Trujillo's system of government was unique in the history of the Western Hemisphere and it probably lasted as long as it did only because the Dominicans were on an island, isolated from contact with anyone except the Haitians, their traditional enemies. It was a one-man operation with all power centralized in the hands of Trujillo. If this were all it was, it would not be significant, for there have been many one-man dictatorships in Latin America. What distinguished the rule of Trujillo was that it actually succeeded in encompassing every aspect of life, although its raw power was masked by an elaborate façade of constitutional apparatus. Legislatures, courts, elections, and all the other mechanisms of a constitutional state were there, but none functioned as it would have been expected to.

The most conspicuous feature of Trujillo's system was the constant fluctuation in the personnel of the military, political, economic, and other control centers. No person, no matter who he was, was permitted to remain in any position long enough to win a following that would enable him to become a threat to Trujillo's monopoly of power. Cabinet ministers, senators, army officers, secretaries, newspaper editors, all were continuously shuffled and reshuffled. Even personal friendships were not permitted. As soon as two persons became too friendly, something was done to drive a wedge between them.

The technique was simplicity itself: every "elected" or appointed official had to deposit a signed, undated resignation with Trujillo before taking office. Whenever Trujillo felt the need to do so, he filled in the date and accepted the resignation. Vacancies in the executive branch of the government or in economic enterprises were then filled by a normal appointive process; vacancies in elective positions, such as membership in the national legislature, were, by law, filled by the nominee of the political party to which the individual belonged. And the only political party functioning in the country was the Dominican Party, controlled by Trujillo. From 1947 to 1952, a regular legislative period, the Senate of the Dominican Republic, with a membership of twenty-one, had forty-one resignations. Even Trujillo's relatives were not immune. It was not unusual for a man to be unaware he had resigned until he heard the announcement on his car radio as he drove to work.

The armed forces, the tool Trujillo used to seize power originally, remained the ultimate source of his authority until his death. All male Dominicans between sixteen and fifty-five were subject to the draft, and at eighteen a year of military service was mandatory. It is impossible to say how large a force was maintained, but Trujillo often talked about fielding an army of 100,000. In 1957 *Jane's Fighting Ships* estimated the Dominican navy at 4,000 men and 39 combat and auxiliary vessels. This was a larger navy than that of Mexico or any other country in the Caribbean area, with the possible exception of Venezuela, and of course the United States. In addition there was an air force of around 3,000 men with 16 airports and 132 combat and training planes in 1952. Factories to make armaments were set up. By 1957, about 25 percent of the government's budget went to the support of the armed forces, but this amount of close to $29 million, fantastic for a poor country, did not include $1 million in military aid from the United States or the funds used to buy heavy equipment such as planes, ships, tanks, etc., or other funds that passed through governmental departments other than the Ministry of the Armed Forces. It is needless to say that the size of the armed forces Trujillo maintained had no relationship to the needs of the country for defense against aggressors. Their purpose was to keep Trujillo in power.

Trujillo kept personal control over all aspects of the military. When he was the president, he was automatically commander in chief of the armed forces. When he put a stooge in as president, he retained the position of commander in chief of the armed forces. In 1938 he had his puppet Congress pass a law conferring upon the commander in chief the same rights and privileges the president received. Trujillo always kept his office in the national capitol whether he was president or not, and always took precedence over the nominal president. Trujillo pampered the officer corps of the armed forces, but he constantly moved the individuals around so that they would have no opportunity to win popularity with their troops. At the same time, he made all of his friends and relatives officers in the armed forces. He permitted members of the armed forces to enrich themselves at the expense of the general public with all kinds of protection rackets, particularly in connection with gambling houses and houses of prostitution. It is thought that these illegal activities were condoned by Trujillo so that he could use the evidence collected by his secret police as a club over the heads of the army people engaged in them.

How did Trujillo utilize the armed forces? They were an army of occupation, a terror organization ever watchful to keep the population under control. Espionage, torture, and brutality were all commonplace. No freedom was permitted to anyone, and this terror was extended outside of the republic; Trujillo's secret police murdered many Dominican exiles, other Latin-American opponents, and even residents of the United States.

No political party was allowed to function but the Dominican Party, controlled by Trujillo. With one exception (1947), all presidential elections after 1930 were unanimous. All other elections were likewise formalities, for they were always unanimous. They had to be, for there was only one candidate for each office and he was selected by Trujillo.

Once Trujillo had won control of the governmental machinery, he used it to legalize whatever he did. That is, he would decide to do something and his puppet Congress would then pass a law giving him the power to do it. The classic example was the time he decided to take a new wife. Congress obligingly passed a law giving any married person the right to divorce his or her mate if there had been five years of childless marriage. As soon as the law was passed, Trujillo divorced his wife and married his mistress.

The basic tool to control the government machinery was his one-party system. All government employees were required to join his Dominican Party and 10 percent of their salaries were automatically deducted as dues. With this money, party offices were maintained all over the country, and in most of the small towns the Dominican Party club-house was the biggest and best building in town. The party rules stated that the "Dominican Party acclaims and recognizes as its chief and director Generalissimo Rafael L. Trujillo Molina, whose program and political creed of national renovation and of patriotic aggrandizement must be realized and fulfilled." Trujillo appointed the party chairman and all paid employees, he authorized all party expenditures, and he had the right to veto party resolutions and to eliminate "traitors" to the party.

The Dominican Party was a mechanism through which Trujillo kept track of the government officials and a channel for propagandizing the people. In each of the fifty-four party headquarters in the country a meeting was held weekly. The party kept files on the total population, thus acting as another spy organization.

Thus Trujillo had a monopoly of all physical power through control of the armed forces and a monopoly of all political power through his single-party system. Using these two, Trujillo then took over most of the country's economy and became one of the world's richest men, with a fortune of close to $750 million. He was the owner of all important economic enterprises in the country: farms, factories, stores, transportation lines, everything. As proprietor of so much wealth, he used the government as the legal mechanism to safeguard it. The armed forces were his security guards and the people were the consumers and producers. Whenever one of Trujillo's enterprises was losing money, he sold it to the government. Whenever any enterprise owned by another individual or the government showed a substantial profit, Trujillo sooner or later became the owner or part owner. Sometimes he simply jailed or exiled the owner of a property he coveted; other times he made an arrangement whereby the original owner became a minor partner and had a job in the business. It is estimated that eventually Trujillo and his family and friends controlled 75 percent of all economic activity in the country.

It was this control over the country's economy which helped to keep the country quiet and prevented revolutions. Such a large proportion of the population was on his payroll that he could control people by economic pressure or bribe them with offers of better jobs. It is estimated that about 80 percent of the employed population of the country was on his payroll, 45 percent in his economic enterprises and 35 percent on the government payroll.

As if this were not enough, Trujillo made the Dominican Republic one of the most graft-ridden places in the world. On practically every transaction by the government Trujillo got a 10 percent cut. This was brought into the open in 1957, when a committee of the United States Senate was investigating a corporation that deducted a $1.8-million bribe to Trujillo as a legitimate expense from its taxable income. The United States Internal Revenue Commissioner, justifying the allowance of the deduction, stated, "Bribes are an ordinary and necessary business expense to do work in the Dominican Republic."

A last prop of the Trujillo regime was his control of all socio-economic groups in the country. No organization could function independently of Trujillo's control. This included businessmen's organizations, social groups, trade unions, and the schools and educational organizations. He also controlled the press, all radio and television, the printing companies, and every other entrée to public opinion.

A constant stream of propaganda was issued to convince the Dominicans of the grandeur of their country and its glorious leader. Nor was this propaganda purely for local consumption. Millions of dollars were spent annually to create a favorable public opinion, particularly in the United States. In 1959 Trujillo paid the board chairman and the president of the Mutual Broadcasting System in the United States $750,000 to slant their news programs in favor of Trujillo. The bribe became public knowledge when Trujillo was stupid enough to file suit in a United States court to recover his $750,000 when he became dissatisfied with Mutual's propaganda. He also had half a dozen public relations firms on his payroll in the United States.

It must be pointed out that Trujillo was an uneducated megalomaniac and a sadist. How did he ever manage to dominate a country with more than two million people? The answer is that he was a very shrewd politician with an instinct for managing people. He was an extremely hard worker, the first one to the office in the morning and the last one home. His personal life was like something out of the Arabian Nights, and he fathered countless children. In his craving for adulation he was a close rival of Stalin. He changed the name of the oldest Spanish-founded city in the Western Hemisphere from Santo Domingo to Ciudad Trujillo. He named mountains, provinces, streets, parks, plazas, and anything else he could think of after himself and members of his family. His picture hung in almost every home in the country. Statues and busts of him were everywhere. Time was measured from his rise to power: this was the "Era of Trujillo." He collected decorations and medals by the dozen from Spain, the Vatican, Cuba, Haiti, Peru, Chile, Mexico, Colombia, Venezuela, Bolivia, Lebanon, Ecuador, Panama, France, China, and on and on. His title, which was repeated on every possible occasion, was "His Excellency Dr. Rafael Leonidas Trujillo Molina, Honorable President of the Republic, Benefactor of the Nation, Restorer of the Financial Independence of the Country, and Commander in Chief of the Armed Forces."

To the casual observer, Trujillo was at the apex of his power in the late 1950's. When he sent his son to the United States to be educated at an army school in Fort Leavenworth, Kansas, the son's adventures chasing and catching Hollywood screen stars were on the front pages of every paper. In the United States Trujillo was the friend of senators and Supreme Court justices, and he certainly seemed to be omnipotent in the Dominican Republic. But on May 30, 1961, he was shot dead and his imposing structure collapsed.

Trujillo's decline began when a wave of sentiment for democratic government swept Latin America in the 1950's. In short order, the dictators of Bolivia, Argentina, Colombia, Venezuela, and Cuba were overthrown. These events strengthened the morale of the Dominican opposition to Trujillo and stimulated a current of public opinion all over the Western Hemisphere against Trujillo, Somoza, and Stroessner, the three dictators then remaining.

This criticism of Trujillo seems to have stung him, and he reacted in a way typical of him: he murdered one of his critics. This was Jesús de Galíndez, a Spanish Republican refugee who had come to the Dominican Republic after the Spanish Civil War because it was the only place that would give him a visa. Trujillo at that time was trying to lighten the skin color of the Dominicans by establishing colonies of Spanish farmers, particularly on the Haitian frontier. Galíndez never was a farmer, but he found work in a government office and a teaching post at the university, and lived in the Dominican Republic for six years, ample time to learn how the regime operated. He left the Dominican Republic in 1946 and moved to New York, where he taught at Columbia University and became the representative of the Basque government in exile to the United Nations. He was a prolific writer whose work appeared in many periodicals, and in 1956 he presented as his doctoral dissertation a work entitled *"La Era de Trujillo,"* a thoroughly documented study of the Trujillo dictatorship based on his personal observations and library research.

When news of *"La Era de Trujillo"* became public, Trujillo became so enraged that merely silencing Galíndez was not enough: he wanted revenge. Galíndez was kidnapped off the streets of New York City on March 12, 1956, drugged, loaded aboard an airplane, and flown to the Dominican Republic, where Trujillo personally tortured him until he died. Soon after this, the pilot of the plane and several other persons connected with the case were murdered or disappeared under suspicious circumstances.

This was the great turning point in the career of Trujillo, for Galíndez was an international figure, a scholar and writer with many friends. His disappearance (the details were not known until later) created a furore all over Latin America and the United States, and opposition to Trujillo became more and more vocal. Much of this opposition began to center in Venezuela, especially after Juan Bosch, the president of the Dominican Revolutionary Party, made his headquarters there after leaving Cuba when Castro came to power. In addition, Rómulo Betancourt, one of the leading spokesmen for democracy in America, became president of Venezuela in February 1959 and used his office to press the issue of human rights in the Dominican Republic before the Organization of American States. In reaction, Trujillo, who evidently felt supremely confident of his power, began to finance and help organize campaigns to overthrow the Betancourt government. Venezuela broke relations with the Dominican Republic on June 12, 1959. In August the foreign ministers of the American republics met in Chile to consider the political tensions in the Caribbean and voted a resolution that the governments of America "should be derived from free elections and that perpetuation in power, or the exercise of power without fixed term, and with the manifest intent of perpetuation, is incompatible with the effective exercise of democracy." This resolution, of course, had no effect upon Trujillo.

An attempt was made to invade the Dominican Republic from Cuba and Trujillo arrested and killed a large number of people. On February 5, 1960, Betancourt brought charges in the Organization of American States that the Trujillo government was committing "flagrant violations of human rights." These charges were investigated by the Inter-American Peace Committee, a branch of the Organization of American States, and on June 8, 1960, the committee published a report supporting the charges.

While the Inter-American Peace Committee was investigating him, Trujillo again tried to overthrow the Betancourt government on April 30, 1960. A group led by a militaristic Venezuelan by the name of Castro León entered Colombia on Dominican diplomatic passports and invaded Venezuela, captured a border town, and announced over the radio that they had overthrown the Betancourt government and appealed to the Venezuelans to support a new government headed by Castro León. The peasants and the National Guard soon polished off Mr. Castro León and his army.

When all of these attempts to overthrow Betancourt failed, Trujillo organized a clever attempt to assassinate him. Using highly technical equipment flown in from the Dominican Republic, a group of assassins blew up the auto in which President Betancourt was riding, killing two people and wounding several others, including Betancourt. The police soon identified the criminals involved, and in their rooms found maps and other material prepared in the Dominican Republic to help the assassins which left no doubt that Trujillo and his secret police had organized the assassination attempt.

Venezuela immediately raised the issue in the Organization of American States and demanded action. Trujillo reacted with a great show of shuffling his puppet government. His brother, Héctor Trujillo, resigned the presidency on August 3, 1960, after having held the office since 1952. The vice-president, Dr. Joaquín Balaguer, took his place and announced that free government was now at hand. He said free elections would be held, he reorganized the cabinet, he permitted all refugees in the various embassies in Santo Domingo to leave the country, and he introduced a bill in Congress to provide for a general amnesty for all political prisoners.

None of these steps convinced anyone that Trujillo was reforming. The foreign ministers of the American states met again in San José, Costa Rica, from August 16 to 20, 1960, to decide what ought to be done about him. It was finally decided to condemn the government of the Dominican Republic and to apply sanctions including the breaking of diplomatic relations between all of the American republics and the government of the Dominican Republic, the partial interruption of commerce between the American states and the Dominican Republic, and the complete suspension of all arms shipments.

Trujillo thought he was being treated extremely unfairly. He began to make approaches to Castro and to the Soviet Union, he spent large sums for armaments in Europe, and he redoubled his propaganda campaign in the United States. Soon the United States put a special tax of two cents a pound on Dominican sugar, which penalized the Dominican producers, primarily Trujillo himself, about $30 million a year. There have been many rumors that in those days Trujillo became irrational. On January 4, 1961, the Organization of American States voted further sanctions against Trujillo: the cutting off of petroleum, trucks, and parts for trucks. The United States adopted this measure on January 20, 1961.

These measures stimulated opposition to Trujillo among his closest collaborators. Evidently those who had managed to live well under Trujillo—that is, his upper-class supporters—were afraid the whole edifice so carefully built up over three decades would collapse. When the United States and the Organization of American States began to talk of further sanctions, a group of Trujillo's intimate collaborators organized an ambush and killed him on May 30, 1961. Those thought to be implicated in the plot were immediately killed in revenge for the old man's death, including a brigadier general, a former army captain, a lieutenant, two engineers, and the nephew of an army officer, among others.

With Trujillo dead, the strongest groups in the country were the armed forces, the business-professional-landowning elite, and the Catholic church hierarchy. All had been controlled by Trujillo and all cooperated with his dictatorship. None suddenly became democratic or any more interested in the fate of the bulk of the population than they had been before the tyrant died. The army was accustomed to being a privileged class and it tried to preserve its privileges. The Catholic church had no intention of giving up its special status. The rich, who had played a secondary role to Trujillo, now saw a chance to become the dominant force in the republic. Thus it would have been a miracle if anything resembling popular government had emerged in the Dominican Republic. José Figueres, the perspicacious former president of Costa Rica, had foreseen the problem in 1958, when he wrote an article suggesting that the best way to create a political system based on the wishes of the Dominican people would be to set up a United Nations trusteeship when Trujillo and his government disappeared.[2]

Unfortunately, President Figueres' idea was never tried. With Trujillo dead, the *Trujillistas* tried to take over the power the old man had held and continue the regime as before. Fortunately for the Dominican people, none of Trujillo's associates was capable of assuming the tyrant's role. A few concessions were made to public opinion. The much-hated head of the secret police was fired and left the country. A few political prisoners were released. The troops became a little less arrogant, prices were cut on many consumer staples, the Trujillo monopolies on coffee and cacao were liquidated. But basically the regime was unchanged. Joaquín Balaguer, a long-time collaborator of the dead tyrant, was still president, and the Trujillo family, headed now by Rafael, Jr., continued to own the lion's share of the country's economic assets and to control the armed forces.

The exiled opposition returned home and began to organize political parties. The censorship and the terror relaxed, but no steps were taken to set up a government with popular support. The heirs of Tru-

---

[2] José Figueres, "Mandato de las Naciones Unidas en la República Dominicana," *Combate*, 1 (September–October 1958): 67–70.

jillo's wealth and power were faced with a real dilemma. The continuation of the OAS sanctions was forcing the country—of which they
owned 75 percent of the economic assets—closer toward bankruptcy
every day. The only way to get the sanctions lifted was to democratize,
but democratization would mean the end of power and wealth for the
relatives and friends of Trujillo.

For about five months an uneasy balance prevailed. The most hated
of Trujillo's gangsters left the country and much of the country's trans-
ferable wealth was shifted to the United States and Europe. The opposition kept growing and perfecting its organization. The businessmen kept
pressuring President Balaguer and the army officers to make concessions
so that the sanctions would be lifted, while the opposition political parties
kept insisting that the sanctions remain in force until all members of
the Trujillo family had left the country.

In November 1961 an agreement was finally reached between the
government of the United States and the Balaguer government which
provided that all members of the Trujillo family would leave the country
except Rafael, Jr., the commander in chief of the armed forces. In return,
the United States promised to sponsor a motion in the Organization of
American States to end some of the sanctions that were so harmful to
the country's economy. Some of Trujillo's relatives actually left the
country, but after a week two of the dead tyrant's brothers returned and
tried to organize a coup d'état to recapture the government machinery.
They persuaded Rafael, Jr., to leave the country, but Balaguer and the
commander of the air force opposed their move. The United States government gave its support to the Balaguer government and at last the
Trujillos gave up. On November 19, 1961, around midnight, about two
dozen Trujillos left the country.

During the next few days, a tumultuous mass of happy Dominicans
demonstrated their true feelings about the great "Benefactor" as they
rioted, looted the luxurious homes of the Trujillos, and tore down all the
statues put up by the megalomaniac. Finally the armed forces declared a
curfew to restore order, but the people refused to be repressed. By
November 28 they were carrying on a general strike. For eleven days
the majority of the population refused to carry on normal activities. The
strike was eventually lost, but it so shocked the armed forces officers that
on January 1, 1962, a Council of Government was created, headed by
Balaguer and consisting of businessmen. One of its first acts was to confiscate all the Trujillo property remaining in the country. In response, the
Organization of American States lifted its sanctions on January 4, 1962.

The real power in the country, however, remained in the hands of the armed forces, now headed by General Rodríguez Echevarría. At this time he began to put all of the members of his family into key positions and to take other actions that convinced many people that he wanted to become the new Trujillo. On January 14 the armed forces fired at a meeting of the opposition and the decisive battle began. By midnight Rodríguez Echevarría was attempting a coup d'état. Four council members were jailed and Balaguer resigned. For two days a minor civil war was waged between the people and the armed forces. The forces of the people had the help of the United States, which made it clear to the armed forces officers that it wanted no new dictatorship. By January 18 the officers of the air force accepted the United States' point of view, freed the arrested council members, and arrested General Rodríguez Echevarría instead. With the creation of a new Council of Government, headed by Dr. Rafael Bonnelly and without Balaguer, we can say a new stage began.

But the Dominican people were as unprepared for stable constitutional government as they had been in the past. All the remaining Trujillo properties were now the trust of the government, but the money to operate them was gone with the Trujillos. And since Trujillo had concentrated the country's agricultural effort on the production of sugar for sale abroad to fatten his Swiss bank accounts, not enough food was produced to feed the population.

The new Council of Government, faced as it was by an almost hopeless situation, tried to govern with the aid of the United States and a long list of international organizations. Freedom of speech and association was permitted. A beginning was made on agrarian reform. Political parties and trade unions functioned freely. Trujillo's constitution was changed to eliminate some of its most glaring infringements of democratic rights. The council had a great deal of difficulty in accomplishing very much, however, for it represented basically only the country's small commercial class. The two largest political parties that had emerged refused to participate in the government. And the entire Trujillo apparatus remained to burden the country with its swollen bureaucracy and its special privileges, including a work week of twenty-eight and one-half to thirty-two and one-half hours.[3] This short week was enjoyed by the employees of an almost bankrupt government faced with the fantastic amount of work needed to create a viable economic, social, and political system. Yet it was all but impossible to replace these government employees because of the country's high illiteracy rate. Thus the Council of

---

[3] Contrast this with the forty-hour work week of government employees in the affluent United States.

Government accomplished very little, but it carried out its promise to preside over free elections, which were held on December 20, 1962.

When the Dominican people began the construction of a democratic political system in 1962, they had had practically no experience with political parties. Trujillo's Dominican Party had been a party in name only. A few Dominicans had been trained by Communist schools to organize Communist parties, but these people were not interested in constructing a democratic political system. And so, although dozens of so-called political parties appeared in the years after Trujillo's death, no functioning political party system developed.

The Dominican Revolutionary Party (PRD), originally an exile group, won a sweeping victory in the election of December 20, 1962, and its leader, Juan Bosch, was inaugurated on February 27, 1963, as the first democratically elected president the country had ever had. He was faced with a superhuman task. The entire apparatus created by Trujillo remained in being. To disband the swollen armed force would only swell the army of unemployed and invite the ex-soldiers, particularly the officers, to organize revolutions. The government bureaucracy was the same one Trujillo had organized: inefficient, corrupt, and incapable of managing the needed reforms the government was about to adopt. The business-professional-landowning elite remained what it had been under Trujillo: a privileged class interested only in preserving its privileges. As President Bosch once said to me, "The trouble is the PRD is strong only on election day, when the votes are counted. At all other times the country's small upper class has all the financial, military, economic, and educational power."

Bosch had his strongest support among the illiterate peasants and workers, none of whom could become cabinet ministers or staff the government bureaucracy without extensive training. A small part of the educated professional and business group supported the new government, but it was not a large enough group to dominate the country. Bosch tried to get some of the other parties to join his cabinet to create a coalition government, but all the other political parties refused to co-operate with him. Thus President Bosch had to introduce democratic government to a country that had never had any, a country in which the economy was stagnant, with up to 40 percent of the work force unemployed, a country with the most important economic enterprises in the hands of the government, a country in which he could not find the manpower to staff the government with persons he could trust because most of the educated were opposed to everything he wanted to do.

Thus President Bosch could not accomplish very much, but he tried.

Full freedom was enjoyed by all Dominicans, but this only led Bosch's opponents to call him soft on communism. When the legislature adopted a new constitution that did not recognize Catholicism as the country's official religion, the Catholic hierarchy was further alienated. Not surprisingly, unemployment, illiteracy, poverty, and backwardness were not abolished in a day. Bosch's government worked, but planning the future of an underdeveloped country, staffing the government, and organizing an administration take time. This time Bosch was not given.

Juan Bosch lasted as president just seven months. Bosch himself implies that the organizers of the coup d'état against him began their work to overthrow his government before he even took office. On the day after Bosch was inaugurated, one of the defeated presidential candidates told me that his party's campaign against Bosch would begin in a day or two. When I asked why Bosch could not at least be given enough time to settle down in the Presidential Palace, he replied that Bosch was appointing "gangsters" as ministers and they had to be exposed.

The plots came to a head in September 1963, when the army, backed by the Catholic hierarchy and most of the business-professional-landowning upper class, expelled President Bosch from the country, disbanded the legislature, threw out the new constitution, and set up a military government consisting of members of the same small upper class that had prospered under Trujillo. Many of the men who received important positions were the same ones who had served the government that had handed over power to Bosch seven months previously. Since nothing united the aristocracy, the armed forces officers, and the Catholic hierarchy except a dislike for Bosch and his program, the new government was unable to work out a stable program and staggered from crisis to crisis as the economy became weaker than it had been. Eventually Donald Reid Cabral, a businessman, emerged as the dominant figure in the new regime. Under his leadership, the government began to take some halting steps to stabilize the regime, for by 1964 the situation had become completely chaotic. In addition to everything else wrong in the Dominican Republic, the commercial groups found themselves going bankrupt because the military were bringing in consumer products without paying duty and selling them on the black market. Many who had supported the overthrow of President Bosch now looked back upon his seven months in office as a time of peace and prosperity. At the same time, the PRD, Bosch's party, had grown stronger than it had ever been before.

Now preparations began for a revolution to restore Bosch to the presidency. It must be understood that by this time the Dominican people had had two years of political freedom. Trujillo's totalitarianism had disappeared into history. Yet for the average person life had changed very little. Therefore, as conditions continued to get worse, the PRD and the Revolutionary Social Christian Party signed a pact on January 30, 1965, to cooperate to restore constitutional order in the republic. These two parties combined had won 62 percent of the votes cast in the 1962 election and probably represented the majority of the country's population in January 1965.

The spark that set off revolution came when Reid Cabral tried to fire some of the armed forces officers and the armed forces split. On April 24, 1965, when the shooting began, one group of officers, mainly younger men, cooperated with the PRD and its allied parties to restore Juan Bosch to the presidency. The revolutionary forces had great success in Santo Domingo and soon controlled most of the city. Unfortunately, the policy-makers in the U.S. State Department around Under Secretary Thomas Mann, who at that time evidently made policy for the United States in the Dominican Republic, decided that Bosch ought not to be allowed to return to the Dominican Republic, nor should his followers be allowed to win the revolution.[4] Suddenly a new military junta headed by General Wessin y Wessin sprang up, calling itself the government of the Dominican Republic. The junta's airplanes and battleships began to bombard Santo Domingo, but the rebel forces continued to fight and Wessin y Wessin's forces began to disintegrate.

Just at that moment, on April 28, the United States began to land troops on the island. It is still not known why, but two explanations have been offered. One is that "hundreds" of United States citizens were in danger of being killed. The other is that there was a danger that the Dominican Republic would become another Cuba because the Communists were taking over the revolutionary army. Neither of these explanations coincides with what actually was happening in Santo Domingo. The most likely explanation is that Thomas Mann and Tapley Bennett, the United States ambassador in the Dominican Republic, favored the military junta and convinced President Johnson of the advisability of intervening. Although the U.S. troops were sent ashore ostensibly to evacuate U.S. citizens in danger, eventually over 22,000 were landed, and they interposed themselves between the revolutionary forces and the troops loyal to the military junta at a time when it looked as if the revolutionary forces would win.

For some time the situation was almost chaotic, with fighting con-

---

[4] See Theodore Draper, "A Case of Defamation: U.S. Intelligence versus Juan Bosch," *New Republic,* February 19, 1966, pp. 13–19; February 26, 1966, pp. 15–18.

tinuing as negotiations went on between the United States government, Juan Bosch in Puerto Rico, General Wessin y Wessin, Colonel Caamaño Deno, and others.[5] This phase ended when the United States emissaries set up a new *de facto* government, known as the Government of National Restoration, headed by an old *Trujillista*, General Antonio Imbert. This "government" was completely unacceptable to the revolutionary forces, which had elected Colonel Francisco Caamaño Deno as president of the "constitutional" forces. Thus the Dominican Republic had one government, which had been set up by the United States and was protected by United States troops, in control of all of the country except the capital city, and another government that controlled the heart of Santo Domingo.

Then began a period of struggle and negotiation in which the United Nations, the Organization of American States, and the United States, sometimes cooperating and sometimes working at cross-purposes, tried to get the two Dominican governments to stop fighting and permit the creation of a provisional government that would be recognized by both sides. After months of negotiations, a provisional government headed by Héctor García Godoy, who had been foreign minister in Juan Bosch's cabinet, was set up in September 1965 and the Imbert and Caamaño governments were disbanded.

Under the García Godoy government some of the tensions eased, some of the leading military men on both sides were persuaded to leave the country, and an election was organized for June 1, 1966, which was to return the country to constitutional government. Three candidates sought the presidency in the 1966 election. Juan Bosch was nominated by the PRD and supported by the Revolutionary Social Christian Party and the 14th of June Party; Joaquín Balaguer was nominated by the Reformist Party; and Rafael Bonnelly was nominated by the National Integration Movement, a coalition of five parties, of which the most important was the National Civic Union. A hectic campaign followed, and to the surprise of most observers Joaquín Balaguer won the presidency with 769,265 votes and his party gained a majority in both houses of the legislature. Bosch received 525,230 votes and Bonnelly 39,535.

President Balaguer began his term in office by announcing an austerity program and appointing a coalition cabinet that included representatives of all shades of opinion, including the PRD. The foreign troops were withdrawn from the country, but violence continued to be

___

[5] The full story of the confused fighting and negotiating is best told in Tad Szulc's *Dominican Diary* (New York: Delacorte Press, Dial Press, 1965) and Dan Kurzman's *Santo Domingo: Revolt of the Damned* (New York: G. P. Putnam's Sons, 1965).

a normal part of life. Many persons were killed, arrested, and disappeared as the *Trujillistas* among the military officers used their positions to take revenge upon their opponents in the civil war. It soon became apparent that Balaguer was not strong enough to dominate the situation. Juan Bosch left the country and the PRD split over its future course.

The country remains unstable. Radio, television, and all the other modern means of communication have aroused the underprivileged masses from their acquiescence in exploitation. The small middle class demands a share in the control of the country. But the bureaucracy and the military machine built by Trujillo remain. The great hope in the Dominican Republic at the time of the 1966 election was that the death and destruction of the 1965 civil war had taught something to the political leaders, so that this time they would devote their energies to building their country by strengthening its political institutions. This hope has not been realized. The Dominican Republic needs a strong government devoted to tackling the country's problems, but it has one so weak it cannot even prevent the almost daily murder of the opponents of the *Trujillista* military men. The country needs a strong healthy opposition to keep the government working as it should, but the military and the *Trujillistas* keep killing and mutilating activists of the PRD, the only healthy opposition party available. As this is written there were few signs that any kind of stable political system will emerge in the foreseeable future.

The Formal Constitutional Framework

The Dominican Republic is governed under the constitution that took effect on November 28, 1966. This greatly resembles the Institutional Act of August 31, 1965, which ended the civil war. The Institutional Act, in turn, incorporates into the structure of the government sections of the 1962 and 1963 constitutions.

It is difficult to say much about the Dominican Republic's formal constitution, as it has not been in force long enough for an observer to see whether it will be observed any better than the long stream of constitutions that preceded it. With the possible exception of the government headed by Juan Bosch, no Dominican government ever paid much attention to the constitution. The habit early developed of writing a new constitution every time a new government appeared or the power holders wanted to make a change. Trujillo, for example, introduced new constitutions in 1934, 1942, 1947, and 1955, but all his constitutions resembled each other and he never paid attention to any of them.

The 1966 constitution provides for a civil, republican, democratic, and representative government divided into the traditional executive, legislative, and judicial branches.

How the Constitution Is Amended

To amend the constitution two steps are necessary. Amendments can be presented by one-third of the members of either house or by the executive. If the Congress supports the amendment, it votes by a majority for the National Assembly (the two houses meeting together) to meet, and that body must assemble within fifteen days. If a quorum of a majority of the members of the Assembly is present, they can approve the amendment by a two-thirds majority, whereupon it immediately goes into effect. This appears to be a rapid way of amending a constitution; the only difficult part appears to be the need for a two-thirds majority.

Who Participates in Politics

Until 1930, politics was a game played by the members of the upper classes. Under Trujillo no political activity was permitted. The sudden change to participation by anyone who wanted to enter politics after Trujillo's death made political life very hectic. Under the rules adopted under international pressure, all Dominicans over eighteen, or younger if married, were allowed to vote in the 1961 and 1966 elections. The only exceptions were the members of the armed forces and the police and those who had lost their citizenship rights by law, which excluded comparatively few persons.

In 1962, 1,054,944 voted, and in 1966, 1,334,030 ballots were cast for the three presidential candidates. When one considers the masses of Santo Domingo who participated in the street fighting in 1965, one must conclude that a substantial majority of the adult population is now participating in some way in the country's political life.

The Electoral Machinery

For a country that has experienced only two fair elections in its history, the Dominican Republic has a rather modern electoral system. This is due to international pressure, which led the government in August 1961 to ask the Organization of American States to send a technical assistance mission to Santo Domingo to help set up a system of free elections. This was done, and a modern electoral system was prepared before the December 1962 elections.[6] Another three-man mission was sent to Santo Domingo by the Organization of American States in 1966.

Under the system used in the Dominican Republic, elections are administered by a central election board, provincial and municipal electoral boards, and electoral committees in each polling place. The three members of the central election board are supposed to be elected by a two-thirds vote of the Congress, but in 1966 the board was appointed by the provisional president of the republic. The central election board appoints the members of the provincial and municipal electoral boards; the municipal boards appoint the members of the local election committees.

The central electoral board prints separate ballots for each party. Each party's ballot is a different color and bears the emblem of the party. When the voter presents himself at the polling place, he is given a ballot for each party and an envelope. He selects the ballot he prefers in privacy, puts it in the envelope, and deposits the envelope in the ballot box. The voter must cast his ballot for all nominees of the party he selects. In the 1966 election, nine different ballots were available, although there were only three candidates for the presidency. Although the electoral law requires that voters must register in advance, in the 1962 and 1966 elections registration was omitted and anyone could vote with his *cédula* of identification, and women over twenty-five were allowed to vote even if they had no *cédula*.

Polls are open from six A.M. to six P.M. No liquor is sold on election day, which is a legal holiday. Regulations governing the twenty-four-hour period before and during the election prevent voters' being arrested except for serious crimes and under judicial order; no political rallies can be held and no political propaganda can be distributed or broadcast. The armed forces remain in their barracks and only the police guarding the polls can carry arms. The many foreign observers who witnessed the 1962 and 1966 elections all agreed that the elections had been fairly conducted.

Political Parties

No political parties existed in the Dominican Republic during the nineteenth century. Politics then was a struggle for power among members of the small upper class. The outs opposed the ins, but these groupings

---

[6] See *Report of the Technical Assistance Mission of the Organization of American States to the Dominican Republic on Electoral Matters* (Washington: Pan American Union, 1961).

were never formalized into political parties. As the twentieth century began, rudimentary parties developed, the following of individual leaders, but moving in the direction of true political parties. This development was slowed by the United States occupation. When the Marines left the country in 1924, it appeared as if real political parties might emerge, but Trujillo's dictatorship ended all hope of that. When he was assassinated, the Dominicans had to construct political parties without actually knowing from experience what they were. As a result, in the years after Trujillo's death dozens of organizations called parties appeared, but a well-functioning party system did not develop.

The most important political parties that did emerge in the early 1960's had their roots in the opposition to Trujillo. The largest political organization in the country from 1961 to 1965 was the Dominican Revolutionary Party (PRD), headed by Juan Bosch. During its years of exile, the PRD had been associated with the League of Popular Parties. Like its sister parties, it advocated democracy, economic development, a fairer distribution of the national income, and government regulation and/or ownership of the economy. In the 1961 election campaign it became known as the party of the poor, and most of its following came from workers, peasants, small shopkeepers, and intellectuals. Since 1961 it has lost some of its leaders through factional strife, but one man, Juan Bosch, has remained its chief leader and spokesman.[7] In 1966 it received 494,570 votes. It is impossible to forecast the future of the PRD. Juan Bosch left the country in late 1966 and a new president was elected, a young student at the university, José Francisco Peña Gómez. Factionalism was racking the party. The two members who joined Balaguer's cabinet were expelled. The terror in the streets made it difficult for the party to function, and outside of Santo Domingo its organization was shattered. Whether it can continue to function without Juan Bosch's charismatic presence cannot be said.

The *Partido Reformista* (PR) was probably the country's largest in 1966, as evidenced by the 759,887 votes it received in its electoral victory, but it is difficult to say whether it is anything more than the personal following of Joaquín Balaguer, who was elected president for reasons that had nothing to do with the party. Founded in 1963, the PR was first legally recognized in 1964. Its program is similar to that of the PRD and some of its organizers were once members of the PRD.

---

[7] The PRD history demonstrates how important a problem factionalism is in Latin-American parties. When Trujillo was assassinated, the committee sent to the Dominican Republic by the PRD consisted of Ramón Castillo, Nicolás Silfa, and Ángel Miolán. By 1966 none of the three was still a member of the PRD; all three had been expelled, although they had been important leaders of the party for decades.

The National Civic Union (UCN) was important in the Dominican Republic from 1961 until after it lost the election in 1962. At its origin it had the support of most of the business and professional men in the country, particularly those who never went into exile. It won the second highest vote in the 1962 election, and after Bosch was overthrown it supplied many of the figures of the *de facto* government. By 1966 it had shriveled away to another little group, so small it did not even run a candidate for president, but supported Rafael Bonnelly, who ran as the candidate of a coalition of small parties. The UCN received 16,152 votes in 1966.

If all the Communists and their fellow travelers could unite their forces, they would represent an important minority, but they are split among themselves, as are the rest of the Dominicans. The 14th of June Movement (14J) was organized in 1959, soon after an invasion to overthrow Trujillo on that date failed and most of the invaders were killed. Operating as an underground resistance movement, the 14J soon attracted many of the younger members of the upper classes, particularly university students. For a time after Trujillo was killed, the 14J became one of the country's largest political groups, but it had no program except anti-*Trujillismo,* and it included within its ranks both Communists and anticommunists. As a result, it soon began to lose its noncommunist members, and by the time of the 1962 election it was so weak it did not even run a candidate. The 14J supported the Bosch government and tried to start a guerrilla movement after his overthrow. Illegalized by the junta in December 1963, the 14J participated in the civil war on the side of the constitutionalist forces and was again legalized on April 7, 1966. It supported Bosch in the election, although Bosch publicly rejected its support. Basically a Marxist group looking to Castro's Cuba for inspiration, the 14J has both Soviet and Chinese factions within its ranks.

The Soviet-oriented Dominican Communist Party (PCD) was known as the Popular Socialist Party until August 9, 1965. Organized with Trujillo's help in the 1940's, it soon lost his support and functioned as an underground organization until his death. Very anti–United States, the PCD cooperates with the 14J and the Dominican Popular Movement (MPD), the Chinese-oriented Communist party. The MPD is a small organization of perhaps 500 persons, but its militancy gives it some importance. It was used by Trujillo in 1960, when he allowed it to function when no other opposition group could, so he could point to the "freedom" he permitted. Another small Marxist and Soviet-oriented group is the Nationalist Revolutionary Party (PNR).

In addition, there are dozens of minor parties that come and go.

Most are the personal followings of individuals and their efforts are concentrated within the capital city. Of the minor parties, the Liberal Evolutionist (PLE, 6,540 votes in 1966), the Dominican Revolutionary Vanguard (VRD, 13,855 votes in 1966), and the Revolutionary Social Christian Party (PRSC, 30,660 votes in 1966) have some support and play a role in the country's political life. Other groups of less importance are the Christian Democratic Party (PDC, 9,378 votes), a split-off of the PRSC; the Progressive Democratic Christian Party (PPDC), a split-off of the PRD; the Nationalist Democratic Revolutionary Party (PNRD, 4,039 votes in 1966), the personal following of General Miguel Ángel Ramírez Alcántara, which has some importance because its strength is concentrated in San Juan and Elías Piña provinces; the Revolutionary Action Party (PAR, 5,489 votes in 1966); the Workers' and Peasants' Democratic Party (PDOC); the 24th of April Movement, led by Héctor Aristy, who was an important leader in the 1965 civil war; and the Social Democratic Alliance (ASD), the personal following of Juan Isidro Jiménes Grullón.

It cannot be said that there is a real party system in the country. For a party to keep its registration under the present rules it must win 3 percent of the votes cast or elect one member of the Congress. This rule automatically eliminates most of the parties, but after the 1962 election many continued functioning despite their poor showing at the polls, and the same happened in 1966. The PRD, the PR, and the various Communist groups probably will continue to function unless another dictatorship is created; in that case, most of the small parties would probably disappear.

Pressure Groups and Public Opinion

Public opinion in the Dominican Republic centers in Santo Domingo. Santiago, the second largest city, sometimes makes itself heard, but basically the newspapers, radio stations, and political leaders of the capital city are the only ones that count. The uneducated agricultural population is inarticulate except for the sugar workers on the large plantations who have been organized into trade unions.

The groups that play important roles in the Dominican political system are the armed forces, the Catholic church, the business-professional-landowning elite, the government employees, the labor unions, and the communications media. Much of the difficulty in establishing a stable political system since the death of Trujillo is due to the weakness of some of these groups in comparison with others. With this lack of balance, the military, aided by the church hierarchy and the wealthy elite, has been able to dominate the government.

The armed forces officers have been the single most powerful group in Dominican society since the death of Trujillo. It was they who destroyed Bosch's government, and it was they who were the leaders of both sides in the 1965 civil war. There have been only about 30,000 men in the armed forces during recent years, but the weakness of all other groups gave them dominance. In 1963 about 37 percent of the national budget went to the armed forces, and even in 1966, after the United States intervention, 26.3 percent of the government's expenditures went to the armed forces. To establish any kind of constitutional government the armed forces ought to be abolished, but none of the governments since Trujillo has even tried to do this.

The second most important group in Dominican society is the business-professional-landholding elite. Juan Bosch estimates that this consists of perhaps 5,000 families with about 15,000 adult members, but despite its small size the members of this group hold most of the important positions in whatever government is in power. There seems to be some evidence that a feeling of aggressiveness has developed among them since Trujillo's death. After being in a subordinate position for so long, at last they saw an opportunity to occupy the dominant position to which they felt their family names and money entitled them. As members of an elite, these people have more sustained face-to-face contact with each other than the rest of the population. Since Trujillo's death they have become organized into a series of social, fraternal, and professional organizations, which enable them to channel their influence more effectively. Most of the members of this group seem to have supported Balaguer in the 1966 election.

Because Trujillo came to an agreement with the Vatican formalized in a concordat, the Catholic church hierarchy supported his government almost to the end. Since then it has been particularly active in fighting "communism" and was important in the movement that overthrew Juan Bosch. Yet the Catholic church organization is relatively small in the Dominican Republic. In 1963 there were only 390 priests in the country, one for every 7,800 persons, and of the 390 only 50, or 14 percent, had been born in the Dominican Republic. Through many subsidiary organizations such as Catholic Action, the Legion of Merit, the Apostles of Prayer, the Marianos, schools, hospitals, social centers, etc., the Catholic church influences a large number of Dominicans.

Government employees are important in the Dominican Republic because there are so many of them. If one includes the workers in the autonomous agencies, they comprise a rather high proportion of the labor force. Despite efforts to organize these workers, no unified organization has emerged, but government employees have played an important role in determining whether political leaders could carry out their programs.

Organized labor has emerged as an active force since Trujillo's death, but it has been weakened by splits and by the struggles by the various political parties to capture the movement. There are independent unions, Catholic unions, democratic unions, and Communist unions. The United States embassy, through its labor attaché, and the Inter-American Confederation (ORIT) have had a dominant influence over the development of the labor movement because they have the funds to supply organizers and subsidies. The largest federation, with about 125,000 members, is the National Confederation of Free Workers (CONATRAL), affiliated with the ORIT.

The weakness of the pressure-group system is that the peasants are practically unorganized, although they form the largest group in the country. The mass illiteracy also contributes to making large groups inarticulate. The only real newspapers are in Santo Domingo and Santiago and have small circulations. Radio and television have helped to keep people informed, but the comparative strength of the armed forces, the church hierarchy, and the upper class has prevented a balance of power.

Civil Liberties

The 1966 constitution contains all of the civil rights usually found in democratic constitutions, but this has been true in the past and no one's rights were protected. It is impossible, therefore, to forecast how much civil liberty the Dominicans will enjoy. All during the past few years bombs went off, people were killed, and individual rights were largely ignored.

Until mass illiteracy, a swollen bureaucracy, and a useless army are all drastically reduced, it is impossible to be optimistic about the status of civil liberty in the Dominican Republic. A spirit of equality has never moved the upper classes or the bureaucracy or the armed forces. Who then is to protect the illiterate peon's civil rights?

The Executive

The Dominican Republic's executive power is exercised by a president elected for a four-year term. To be elected president one must be a Dominican by birth, at least thirty years old, and in possession of all

political and civil rights. A vice-president who must have the same qualifications is elected at the same time as the president and succeeds to the
office when the president is unable to perform his duties. If there is a
vacancy in the presidency and there is no vice-president available, the
president of the Senate succeeds to the office, followed by the president
of the Chamber of Deputies, but within fifteen days the National Assembly must be called into session to elect a new president, who must be a
member of the political party that nominated the president chosen in the
last election.

The president of the Dominican Republic is a strong executive, and
if he controls the armed forces he dominates the entire government.
Constitutionally he controls the whole administration and is commander
in chief of the armed forces. The president has the power to appoint
and remove cabinet ministers and many other officials, including members of the diplomatic corps, whose appointment must be approved by
the Senate. He also fills vacancies on the Supreme Court if Congress is
not in session, subject to its approval when it meets. As is so common in
Latin America, the president, when the Congress is not in session, can
declare a state of siege and suspend the exercise of civil liberties in times
of calamity or of disturbance of the peace. In case of grave national threat,
he can declare a state of national emergency and again suspend civil
rights, except that the death penalty cannot be invoked. In either case,
the president must inform Congress of his actions. There are few limitations upon the powers of the president except the provisions for congressional approval for certain of his appointments and other actions. The
great limitation upon the president since Trujillo's death has been the
power of the armed forces.

The Legislative Power

The Dominican Republic has had so little experience with a true legislature that it is difficult to describe the power of the Congress. Under
Trujillo, the legislature was a formal law-approving body that did whatever the dictator asked it to do. From 1961 to February 1963 and from
September 1963 to July 1, 1966, there was no legislature. During the
Bosch period, the legislature did not function long enough to develop
any kind of independent activity.

The legislature set up by the Institutional Act of 1965 and the
constitution of 1966 consists of a twenty-seven-member Senate and a
seventy-four-member Chamber of Deputies elected for four-year terms.
Together the two bodies are known as the Congress, and all legislative

power resides in it. One senator is elected from each of the twenty-six provinces and one from the National District. Deputies are elected by the D'Hondt system of proportional representation, with one deputy being elected for each 50,000 persons or fraction of more than 25,000. Each province receives a minimum of two deputies. Senators and deputies must be at least twenty-five years old, Dominican citizens in possession of their full political and civil rights, and natives of the province in which they seek election or residents for at least five years. In case of vacancy, the political party that elected the missing member submits a list of three names to the house in which the vacancy exists, which then elects one of the three. If the party does not submit names, the Chamber of Deputies or Senate can elect anyone it chooses.

The two houses of Congress meet together as the National Assembly to receive the annual message of the president and on other special occasions. Meeting separately, the two houses handle the business normal to a legislature: levying taxes; creating and abolishing provinces, municipalities, and other political divisions; declaring a state of national emergency or state of siege; regulating immigration, setting up and revising the court system, approving treaties and legislating in all matters over which the constitution gives it jurisdiction. The Congress can interrogate ministers, but they are responsible to the executive and not to the Congress. The executive can veto the bills passed by the Congress, but the legislature can repass a bill by a two-thirds vote, and it then becomes law.

The legislature meets biannually on February 27 and August 16 for ninety-day sessions that can be extended for sixty days more. The Senate, in addition to its other powers, has important appointment powers, which include electing all the country's judges, the members of the auditing bureau, and the central electoral council.

Public Finance

The Dominican Republic has been in a financial crisis ever since the Trujillos left with their booty, and only subsidies from the United States and a host of international organizations have kept the people from starving and the government functioning. In 1966, for example, the budget adopted by the government of President García Godoy showed a deficit of 113,525,349 pesos (the Dominican peso is equal to the dollar). This deficit will be covered by grants and loans from the United States. Tables 1 and 2 show where the Dominican government expected to get its money and how it proposed to spend it in 1966.

TABLE 1

ESTIMATED REVENUE OF THE DOMINICAN REPUBLIC, 1966

Source	Amount in Pesos	Percent of Total
Profits on national lottery	P5,890,000	4.21%
Profits on state-owned businesses	2,059,000	1.46
Motor-vehicles taxes	3,250,000	2.32
Stamps for documents, titles, etc.	2,223,185	1.58
Direct income tax	20,000,000	14.28
Taxes on immigration, transportation tickets, patents, etc.	3,365,000	2.40
Customs duties on imports	60,000,000	42.82
Customs duties on exports	3,500,000	2.49
Sales and production taxes	30,675,000	21.90
Inheritance and business taxes	4,703,500	3.35
Miscellaneous taxes	4,473,600	3.19
Total	P140,139,285	100.00%

TABLE 2

ESTIMATED EXPENDITURES OF THE DOMINICAN REPUBLIC, 1966

	Amount in Pesos	Percent of Total
Legislative branch		
National Congress	P594,774	0.2%
Auditing Bureau	59,220	0.0002
Executive branch		
Presidency	13,433,712	5.3
Ministry of the Interior and Police	30,547,476	12.2
Ministry of the Armed Forces	36,083,629	14.3
Ministry of Foreign Relations	3,063,372	1.2
Ministry of Finance	27,927,293	11.0
National debt	27,390,000	10.9
Ministry of Education, Fine Arts, and Religion	37,135,561	14.7
Ministry of Health and Social Welfare	20,621,001	8.1
Ministry of Labor	611,952	0.2
Ministry of Agriculture	19,715,115	7.3
Ministry of Public Works and Communications	30,011,825	12.0
Judicial branch		
Supreme Court	1,925,540	0.8
Attorney General	2,127,500	0.8
Electoral Commission	2,416,664	1.0
Total	P253,664,634	100.0002%*

* Figures do not add to 100 because of rounding.

Like so much else in the Dominican Republic, its financial system ought to be reorganized. As can be seen in Table 1, in 1966 only 14.28 percent of the total income came from income taxes and 64.72 percent came from taxes on imports, sales, and production. This helps to explain why prices are so high in the republic. Nor is the money spent very wisely. In 1966, police and the armed forces were allotted 26.5 percent of the total expenditures, while education received 14.7 percent and health and social welfare 8.1 percent.

Local Government

For administrative purposes, the Dominican Republic is divided into twenty-six provinces and a National District. The provinces are further divided into seventy-six municipalities. Each province has at its head a governor appointed by the president. Each municipality and the National District is governed by a mayor and a council elected for two-year terms. The mayor is elected by a plurality vote, the council by proportional representation. Each council has at least five members. President Balaguer appointed twenty-six women as governors of provinces in an attempt to change the traditional way of operating the office of governor. Since there are only two large cities in the country, Santo Domingo and Santiago, local government really is not very important, and the governors, acting for the president, are the dominant figures in the countryside.

The Judicial Power

The judicial system is headed by a Supreme Court of Justice and subordinate courts. All the judges are elected by the Senate. The country has had so little experience with a court system functioning under constitutional government that any evaluation of it would be premature.

The Dominican Republic: A Last Word

The Dominican Republic demonstrates how difficult it is to construct a constitutional democracy on the ruins of a totalitarian state. In 1966 the republic began a new attempt with an elected president and legislature, but it is difficult to forecast how long this will continue. The armed forces left behind by the dictatorship, the illiteracy, and the poverty continue as before. The habits ingrained by generations of undemocratic government will not easily disappear, nor will the almost institutionalized graft. Yet the Dominican Republic is not overpopulated, it has great untapped resources in soil and minerals, and it has been receiving the help of the United States and the Organization of American States. Whether this will be enough only the future can tell. Meanwhile, the Dominican Republic remains what it was at the death of Trujillo: a country trying to arrive at a consensus.

SELECTED READINGS

ALBA, VÍCTOR. "Why Bosch Fell." *New Republic,* October 12, 1963, pp. 12–14.

ALEXANDER, ROBERT J. "Dominican Republic," *Communism in Latin America,* pp. 298–303. New Brunswick, N.J.: Rutgers University Press, 1957.

BOSCH, JUAN. *Trujillo: Causas de una tiranía sin ejemplo.* 2nd ed. Caracas: n.p., 1961.

———. *The Unfinished Experiment: Democracy in the Dominican Republic.* New York: Frederick A. Praeger, Inc., 1965.

———. "Why I Was Overthrown." *New Leader* 46 (October 14, 1963): 3–4.

CRASSWELLER, ROBERT D. *Trujillo: The Life and Times of a Caribbean Dictator.* New York: Macmillan Co., 1966.

DRAPER, THEODORE. "A Case of Defamation: U.S. Intelligence versus Juan Bosch." *New Republic,* February 19, 1966, pp. 13–19; February 26, 1966, pp. 15–18.

——— et al. *Dominican Republic: A Study in the New Imperialism.* New York: Institute for International Labor Research, n.d.

GALÍNDEZ, JESÚS DE. *La Era de Trujillo.* Santiago de Chile: Editorial del Pacífico, 1956.

KANTOR, HARRY. "Ascenso y caída de Rafael Trujillo." *Cuadernos,* no. 72 (May 1963), pp. 47–54.

KURZMAN, DAN. *Santo Domingo: Revolt of the Damned.* New York: G. P. Putnam's Sons, 1965.

MACDONALD, AUSTIN F. "The Pattern of Dominican Politics," *Latin American Politics and Government,* pp. 598–609. 2nd ed. New York: Thomas Y. Crowell Co., 1954.

ORNES, GERMAN E. *Trujillo, Little Caesar of the Caribbean.* New York: Thomas Nelson & Sons, 1958.

RODMAN, SELDEN. "Balaguer: The First Nine Months: An Interim Report on the Dominican Republic." *New Republic,* March 25, 1967, pp. 19–23.

———. "Why Balaguer Won: Anatomy of a Revolution That Failed." *New Republic,* June 18, 1966, pp. 17–21.

SLATER, JEROME. "The United States, the Organization of American States, and the Dominican Republic, 1961–1963." *International Organization* 18 (Spring 1964): 268–91.

SZULC, TAD. *Dominican Diary.* New York: Delacorte Press, Dial Press, 1965.

WELLS, HENRY. "The Dominican Search for Stability." *Current History* 51 (December 1966): 328–32, 364–65.

———. "The O.A.S. and the Dominican Elections." *Orbis* 7 (Spring 1963): 150–63.

WIARDA, HOWARD. "The Aftermath of the Trujillo Dictatorship: The Emergence of a Pluralistic Political System in the Dominican Republic." Ph.D. dissertation, University of Florida, 1965.

———. "The Development of the Labor Movement in the Dominican Republic." *Inter-American Economic Affairs* 20 (Summer 1966): 41–63.

———, ed. *Dominican Republic Election Factbook, June 1, 1966.* Washington: Institute for the Comparative Study of Political Systems, 1966.

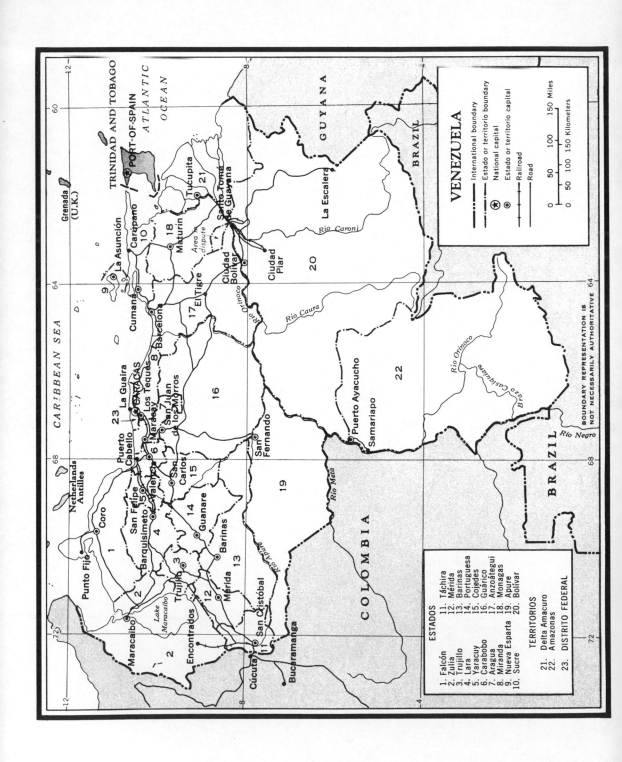

CARIBBEAN SEA

ATLANTIC OCEAN

TRINIDAD AND TOBAGO

PORT-OF-SPAIN

Grenada (U.K.)

Netherlands Antilles

Punto Fijo

Coro

Maracaibo

Lake Maracaibo

Encontrados

Cúcuta

Bucaramanga

San Cristóbal

Mérida

Trujillo

Barquisimeto

San Felipe

Valencia

Puerto Cabello

La Guaira

CARACAS

Los Teques

Maracay

San Juan de los Morros

Guanare

Barinas

San Carlos

San Fernando

Rio Apure

Rio Meta

COLOMBIA

La Asunción

Cumaná

Barcelona

El Tigre

Carúpano

Maturín

Tucupita

Santo Tomé de Guayana

Ciudad Bolívar

Ciudad Piar

Rio Orinoco

Rio Caura

Rio Caroni

La Escalera

Puerto Ayacucho

Samariapo

Rio Orinoco

Rio Negro

Brazo Casiquiare

Area en disputa

GUYANA

BRAZIL

BRAZIL

1
2
3
4
5
6
7
8
9
10
11
12
13
14
15
16
17
18
19
20
21
22
23

VENEZUELA

International boundary
Estado or territorio boundary
National capital
Estado or territorio capital
Railroad
Road

0   50   100   150 Miles
0 50 100 150 Kilometers

BOUNDARY REPRESENTATION IS
NOT NECESSARILY AUTHORITATIVE

ESTADOS
1. Falcón
2. Zulia
3. Trujillo
4. Lara
5. Yaracuy
6. Carabobo
7. Aragua
8. Miranda
9. Nueva Esparta
10. Sucre
11. Táchira
12. Mérida
13. Barinas
14. Portuguesa
15. Cojedes
16. Guárico
17. Anzoátegui
18. Monagas
19. Apure
20. Bolívar

TERRITORIOS
21. Delta Amacuro
22. Amazonas
23. DISTRITO FEDERAL

—16—

VENEZUELA:

Struggling to Achieve Democracy

Venezuela is one of the most important of the Latin-American countries, not because of its size or tremendous population, but because it is the scene of a desperate struggle to implant democratic constitutional government in a country that has never had any. At the same time, Venezuela is trying to demonstrate that democracy can do more to help people than dictatorship can. In a way, there is a competition going on between the dictatorship in Cuba and the constitutional democracy in Venezuela to see which can achieve a more rapid economic development, and the outcome of this rivalry will greatly influence the other Latin-American republics during the next few years.

Venezuela is the largest oil exporter in the world and is second only to the United States as a crude-oil producer. It is a vivid demonstration that economic development by itself does not necessarily bring liberty and prosperity. On the other hand, Venezuela also demonstrates that economic development, no matter under what auspices it begins, sets in motion forces that inevitably transform every aspect of society and make it impossible for the traditional patterns of social organization to be preserved. The changes produced by the development of the oil industry in Venezuela brought the country closer to constitutional government than it had ever been before. Whether stable democracy will become the rule depends on the events of the next few years.

A National Profile

Venezuela is located on the north coast of South America, bounded on the east by Guyana, on the south by Brazil, and on the west by Colombia.

Its area is 352,051 square miles, including about seventy-two islands along the coast.

Rivers and mountains divide Venezuela into five regions, each very different from the others in climate, topography, vegetation, and economy. The coastal highlands, ranging from about 1,000 to 4,000 feet above sea level, include eight states and the national capital. Here, on about 8.7 percent of the country's territory, live about 53 percent of the population, particularly in the Lake Valencia basin and the Caracas valley. This is the country's most important agricultural area and manufacturing center, and the home of the most important economic, educational, military, and cultural leaders of the country. To the west, in the three Andean states of Táchira, Mérida, and Trujillo, live about 13.2 percent of the population on about 3.3 percent of the country's area. This is an important agricultural area with some industrial activity, but 64 percent of the population is rural.

To the south of the mountains lies the Orinoco River basin, an area known as the *llanos*. Here, in seven states and one territory, about 35.5 percent of the country's area is inhabited by about 18 percent of the population. In this area a very dry season follows a very wet season. Little of it is cultivated; most of the land is in natural grasses used for grazing cattle. In the northwestern part of the country is the coastal lowland around Lake Maracaibo, a narrow strip of land between the mountains and the sea. This is the state of Zulia, with 6.9 percent of the country's area and about 12 percent of the population. It is a highly urbanized area of tropical lowland, which contains some agriculture and three-fourths of the Venezuelan oil industry. About 45.1 percent of the country's area lies south of the Orinoco basin. Known as the Guiana Highlands, this is an almost unpopulated and unexploited area, some parts of which have never been fully explored. The only development is on its northern border, where the iron-ore deposits near Ciudad Bolívar are now being exploited. There is evidence that there are large reserves of coal, iron, and other minerals here. Gold and diamonds are now produced, but most of the area is populated only by Indians, who live their traditional life.

Venezuela's population in December 1966 was estimated to be 9,189,282 and increasing at the rate of 3.3 percent annually. It is estimated the country possesses the resources and room to support a population of around 50 million persons. Average density was about twenty-six per square mile. Venezuela's population has grown rapidly in recent years, from 5.03 million in 1950 to over 9 million in 1966. The increase can be attributed to the fostering of immigration and a high birth rate combined with a low death rate.

Venezuela is an overurbanized country with more than one-sixth of the total population (an estimated 1.6 million in December 1965) living in the Caracas metropolitan area. Other important cities are Maracaibo, with a population of 421,166 at the time of the census of 1961; Barquisimeto, with 199,691; Valencia, with 163,601; and Maracay, with 135,353. At the census of 1950, 53.8 percent of the population was urban; by 1963, it was estimated that this figure had grown to about 62.5 percent, with 5 percent living in an intermediate zone of towns with populations from 1,000 to 2,499.

The population of Venezuela is fairly homogeneous, although no really accurate figures are available. The majority of Venezuelans are *mestizos*—from 65 to 90 percent, depending upon whose figures one uses. Europeans are estimated to total between 10 and 20 percent. Perhaps 8 percent are Negroes; about 4 percent are mulattoes and *zambos* (a mixture of Negro and Indian); and about 2 to 11 percent are Indians, with 50,000 to 100,000 of these tribal Indians, including certain tribes with no contact with the rest of the population. The bulk of the white and near-white population lives in and around Caracas, Maracaibo, and Valencia; the bulk of the Negro population lives along the coast; the Indians are found mostly in the south and in the far west of the country. About 8 percent of the population are foreigners, including many from the United States, concentrated in the oil industry and in business in Caracas.

The majority of the population are Roman Catholics and Catholicism is the official religion; the government exercises patronage over the upper echelons of the hierarchy and helps to subsidize the church. At the same time, there is freedom for all other religious groups, and it is estimated there are at least 20,000 organized Protestants.

Spanish is Venezuela's national language. Illiteracy was an important problem in past years; about 48.7 percent of those ten years and older were unable to read or write in 1950. Since then there has been tremendous improvement, and only 10.9 percent of the total population over fifteen years of age was illiterate in 1965.

During most of its history, Venezuela's economy was based upon agriculture. The chief export products were coffee, cocoa, and cattle. There was the typical agricultural pattern of the Spanish heritage, with vast latifundia. It is estimated that before the land-reform law of the Betancourt administration, about 82 percent of the arable land was owned by 2.5 percent of the population. Oil became important during World War I and increased in production until the industry dominated the country's economy. Oil provides more than 90 percent of the country's foreign exchange and about 63 percent of the government's revenues. After World

War II, iron-ore deposits developed around Ciudad Bolívar helped to lessen the country's dependence upon oil.

The most important crops produced are coffee, cocoa, sugar cane, wheat, rice, tobacco, maize, cotton, and beans. But because of the emphasis upon oil, the overurbanization of the country, and the backwardness of most of the agricultural areas, Venezuela has not produced enough food to feed its population in recent years. About $4 million a year has been spent to import food, which helps to make the cost of living exceedingly high. Since most wages are low, poverty is widespread.

Venezuela contains large deposits of minerals and other natural resources and abundant potential water power, but many of the minerals and most of the potential water power have never been exploited. The known minerals include oil, gold, diamonds, coal of poor quality, copper, manganese, bauxite, nickel, marble, sulfur, phosphate, salt, tin, asbestos, and mica. Pearl fisheries off the islands once formed a thriving industry, but they have declined in importance with the competition of Japanese cultured pearls. The pastoral zone of the country produces cattle, horses, and hogs. The tropical forest zone supplies many useful products: *cautchouc*, balata gum, tonka beans, divi-divi, copaiba, vanilla, lumber.

Manufacturing has been of minor importance in Venezuela, but strenuous efforts have been made since World War II to foster its development. Until World War II, none of the petroleum produced was refined in the country, but since then some refineries have been built. Millions of dollars are being invested in an integrated development to produce steel, aluminum, and electricity at Caroní, and a petrochemical industry is being developed. Caracas and Valencia are the main centers for what industry exists. The main articles produced are cotton and rayon textiles, wood products, cement, glass, cigarettes, food and dairy products, edible oils, canned fish, beverages, tires and tubes, soap, shoes, clothing, and paper. Airlines are in operation and the government operates a shipping company.

Venezuela's main problem is that it is not yet an integrated, well-organized country, but an aggregate of diverse elements. During most of its history it was held together by military dictatorship. Transportation is poorly developed and the population is very unevenly distributed, with vast areas almost completely unpopulated. This population pattern and the character of the economic system result in poverty and backwardness for a large portion of the population. In addition, there is a sharp split between city and country. Caracas, Maracaibo, and certain parts of Valencia and Maracay have some of the characteristics of cosmopolitan cities. Here the concentration of wealth and the importation of ideas and products from Europe and the United States have produced a modern atmosphere, with country clubs, golf courses, paved highways, modern hotels, office buildings, homes, and factories. Yet at the same time, at least until the end of the Pérez Jiménez regime in 1958, in the rural areas life went on much as it had in the past, with the remnants of a rigid two-class system, large latifundia, and the old customary ways of doing things. The prosperity that came with oil affected only a small group, since the oil industry does not need a large labor force. The cream of the profits went to foreign interests. In 1949 the Venezuelan Central Bank estimated that the petroleum industry was netting an annual profit equal to about 27 percent of its investment. At the same time, the city and the oil industry kept attracting the rural population, which could only swell the slum areas of Caracas.

Venezuela has made tremendous progress since World War II, but it still has a long way to go. About 10 percent of the population continued to receive about 50 percent of the national income as the 1960's began.

The Development of Modern Venezuela

What is now Venezuela was one of Spain's less important colonies during the sixteenth and seventeenth centuries. The area had no easily discovered mineral wealth, nor was it inhabited by sedentary Indians who could be exploited. It therefore became an agricultural colony based on slave labor. More than 250 years of Spanish rule left the country with vast areas empty of human population. Illiteracy, poverty, and disease were almost universal. Nor did Spain's system of colonial administration do anything to prepare the colony for self-government.

But Venezuela's location made it more easily accessible to non-Spanish traders than most other Spanish colonial ports, and its distance from the authorities outside of the colony promoted a spirit of independence among the Creole landowners. Thus Venezuela produced the most important leaders of the movement for independence from Spain, men who became the fathers of independence for what were to become five South American republics: Venezuela, Colombia, Ecuador, Peru, and Bolivia. Yet Venezuela paid a terrible price for its leadership. For thirteen years battles raged. It has been estimated that Venezuela lost between a quarter and a third of its male population in the wars of independence. At the same time, the seeds of militarism were sown, and for more than a century Venezuela's history consisted of civil wars, *caudillos*, epidemics, and inefficient administrations that left most of the people miserably poor and the country's enormous natural resources untouched. Twenty-one different constitutions were adopted between independence and 1936, but none brought stability. A landowning aristocracy lived well in the cities, supported by the labor of a landless peasantry. Politics was a struggle for power among the members of a small upper class. When the masses converted the civil wars into social wars, the widespread illiteracy and backwardness kept a more liberal society from being organized. Simón Bolívar, the great independence leader, tried to unite Venezuela with its neighbors in Gran Colombia, but the Venezuelan landowners defeated the attempt.

Three men dominated Venezuela during its first century of history: General José Antonio Páez (1790–1873), Antonio Guzmán Blanco (1829–99), and Juan Vicente Gómez (1857–1935). Conservative and Liberal Parties were early organized, but they soon became mechanisms to further the personal ambitions of the *caudillos,* and it made little difference whether those in power called themselves Liberals or Conservatives, Federalists or Unitarians.

Páez was typical of the Latin-American *caudillos* of the nineteenth century. He came from the Orinoco *llanos* and became one of Bolívar's chief lieutenants in the war against Spain. When Gran Colombia was set up, Páez became vice-president of Venezuela. When Gran Colombia broke up in 1830, he was elected president of the new republic for the 1831–35 term, and he continued to rule Venezuela, sometimes as president, at other times from behind a puppet, until 1846. Páez began as a great national hero but he soon became the leader of the Conservative Party, consisting of the large landowners. In opposition to the Páez Conservatives, the Liberal Party was organized by Antonio Leocadio Guzmán.

Páez installed General José Tadeo Mónagas as president in 1846. Mónagas, trying to act independently, cooperated with the Liberal Party leaders, whereupon Páez revolted. This time the old *caudillo* was defeated and exiled from the country. Mónagas and his brother managed to control the country until 1858, ruling as benevolent dictators. From 1858 to 1863 civil war raged. This was the famous "Federal War," with Páez leading the Conservative forces and General Falcón leading the Liberal armies, which favored a federalist organization of the country and some limitation upon the privileges of the oligarchy and the Catholic church. The Liberals won the war but were unable to set up a stable regime, and for nine more years the struggle continued.

Antonio Guzmán Blanco came to power in 1872 and controlled the country until 1887. He was one of the most famous *caudillos* in Latin America, if only for his self-imposed title: "The Illustrious American."

Although he was a liberal and animated by the ideology of the French Revolution, democracy was not one of his objectives. There was some economic progress during his rule and the power of the church was curbed, but administrative corruption led Venezuela toward bankruptcy.

During Guzmán Blanco's rule, political parties completely disappeared, and after his overthrow the generals fought continuously until 1908, when Juan Vicente Gómez came to power. This period saw Venezuela at its lowest point; England, Germany, and Italy blockaded the coast to force payment of the country's debts, and there were constant boundary disputes with England over Guiana.

Juan Vicente Gómez, who ruled Venezuela from December 20, 1908, to December 17, 1935, was without doubt one of the cruelest and most bloodthirsty tyrants Latin America has ever produced. There is some doubt as to whether Gómez was a Venezuelan, for he probably was born in Colombia, but he succeeded in so dominating the country that he could govern as if Venezuela were his private estate and its population his slaves. A reign of terror kept the jails full. Gómez never differentiated between his private property and government income. If there were a farm or an enterprise that he wanted, he used the power of the government to take it. Thus he became one of the richest men in the world, with a fortune estimated at his death at $200 million. He maintained homes in various parts of the country, all completely staffed at all times, and his harem produced children in large quantities; estimates vary between ninety and several hundred. Gómez, who never married any of his concubines, put all of his children, as well as his brothers and other relatives, into official positions. This was an absolute monarchy in peasant style.

Gómez is supposed to have brought Venezuela peace and some development of natural resources. But it was the peace of the penitentiary, and the development, especially in the petroleum industry, was by foreign interests who drained the oil out and left little behind. Roads were usually built from Gómez' home to someplace he wanted to go. This sort of peace was not relished, and it took full jails, an army of spies, another army of police, and continuous vigilance for Gómez to stay in power. Yet he died in bed in 1935, at the age of seventy-eight.

The greatest harm done to Venezuela by the Gómez regime was his stifling of all political activity. Although the people of Venezuela had had no experience in self-government on any level since the Spanish conquered the area, Gómez complicated the picture by forcibly preventing any political activity at a time when democratic ideologies were spreading throughout the world and most of the modern democratic systems were being organized. At the same time Gómez was stifling all political activity, the development of the oil industry was creating an industrial proletariat and a middle class, which, although small in numbers, were to play an ever increasing role in Venezuela, for workers and white-collar people cannot be treated in the same way as an illiterate peasantry toiling on the latifundia.

World War I, the Mexican and Russian Revolutions, and the Argentine student movement of 1919 all combined to set off a wave of reform that pushed into political activity what is now known as the generation of 1928, a group of young Venezuelans who in that year began their struggle for a freer society in their country. Gómez managed to keep these reformists from overthrowing his regime by jailing and exiling them, but during the last years of his rule the political and economic climate produced the leaders of the main political groups active in Venezuelan politics in the 1940's, 1950's, and 1960's.

Because of the political inexperience of the Venezuelan people, very little change came when Gómez died. His cabinet elected the Minister of War, General Eleázar López Contreras, as provisional president, and except for minor rioting in the streets to celebrate the death of the hated tyrant, all went on about as before. There was some relaxation of government interference with political activity; the political prisoners were freed; the exiles were invited to return home. But the pace toward a freer society was very slow. Political parties and trade unions began to function, but by 1937 some of the returned political exiles were once again in exile or in jail. The government continued to be organized in the traditional manner; conservatives continued to hold the most important positions.

Under the constitution of 1936, adopted to replace the last one introduced by Gómez, the people were excluded from direct participation in the national government just as completely as they had been in the past. Again the Congress was to elect the president, and the Congress was to be elected by the state legislatures and the municipal councils. Judges were to be elected by the Congress. It was a continuation of the old system, and as a result, López Contreras was soon in conflict with the masses. Strikes broke out. The new political parties protested. But López Contreras never really permitted freedom, and Rómulo Betancourt, the young leader who was to play so important a role in Venezuela's future, was exiled by López, just as he had been exiled by Gómez.

General López Contreras did push economic development, including an improvement in shipping facilities, the promotion of tourism and immigration, and improvements in public health and education. And most important, political parties got their start in the country. The most important was the party that eventually became known as Democratic Action (AD), which included most of Venezuela's liberals, socialists, intellectuals, and labor leaders, and some of the younger army officers. The president created a sort of party consisting mainly of officeholders.

For the election of 1940, AD put up as its candidate Rómulo Gallegos, one of Latin America's greatest writers, but since the voting was done by the members of the Congress, López Contreras was able to use his governmental machinery to dictate the election of another army officer, General Isaías Medina Angarita. Although Medina Angarita was a professional soldier who had been put into office by López Contreras, he accelerated the movement toward democracy by permitting freedom of speech and of the press and by giving preference in appointments to civilians rather than to military officers. Medina Angarita even put into effect an income tax, which lost him the support of the rich. And he permitted the exiles to return home to organize political parties and trade unions.

The Second World War had given a tremendous impulse to the development of the oil industry. The resultant inflow of dollars led to the growth of light industries. New classes began to develop as insurance, transportation, construction, and the professions were stimulated. The old landowning aristocracy was transformed into an urban commercial, industrial, and financial aristocracy. The middle class and the working class grew rapidly. The war prosperity slightly relaxed the political tensions as the national income rose rapidly, and as a result, political parties were permitted to function freely.

During the war, Democratic Action became a powerful organization as it won the support of the overwhelming majority of the country's workers, peasants, intellectuals, and middle class. To consolidate his position, Medina organized an official party, the Venezuelan Democratic Party, composed of government employees, who were requested to join. During this period, members of Democratic Action began to get elected to the municipal councils, and an intense political struggle was launched to gain the presidency in 1945.

Under the constitutional system, the municipal councilmen elected the deputies of the lower house of Congress and the state assemblymen elected the senators. The National Congress elected the president. Under this indirect system, with a limited franchise and controlled elections, it was impossible for Democratic Action's presidential candidate to win.

López Contreras organized a "party" to sponsor his candidacy for another term. Medina threw his support to Diógenes Escalante, and since

Escalante had a reputation as a liberal, AD also supported him. Unfortunately, Escalante suffered a nervous breakdown and withdrew from the race. Medina then threw his support to an extreme conservative and AD found itself unable to support either of the two candidates. Its leaders proposed, therefore, that Medina, López Contreras, and AD agree upon a neutral candidate who would be elected for one year. During that year, a constitutional convention would write a constitution that would provide for the direct election of the next president. The parties could then compete in a fair election.

This was Venezuela's chance to establish constitutional government and to save itself more years of dictatorship and turmoil. That this opportunity was not taken demonstrates what Latin America's aristocracy really wants.

And so AD and a group of young army officers plotted revolution. It is difficult to say whether the leaders of AD made a mistake by cooperating with the army officers. The original overtures were made by the officers, and they convinced the AD leaders that they were in favor of democracy. AD had the alternative of continuing to educate and agitate until it could win an election with the indirect system in use or of cooperating with the army officers, and it took the second alternative. After some bloody fighting in October 1945, the revolution triumphed. Medina and López Contreras were expelled from the country and power was assumed by a seven-man junta consisting of two army officers and five civilians under the presidency of Rómulo Betancourt, the secretary general of AD. Betancourt was the first civilian president of Venezuela since José M. Vargas in 1835.

The three years during which Democratic Action led Venezuela's government saw many changes in the country. One of the most democratic constitutions in the world was adopted and put into force after fair elections. Universal secret suffrage was introduced for the first time in the country's history. The tax on the oil companies' profits was raised to 50 percent and the money was devoted to public works. A new University City was begun as part of the far-reaching plan to improve all education. Public lands were distributed to landless peasants. Immigration was stimulated; between 1946 and 1955, 711,100 immigrants entered Venezuela, mostly from Europe. A government-owned merchant fleet was set up in cooperation with the governments of Colombia and Ecuador. Public housing, highways, and other public works were built, and plans were formulated for many more such projects. An attempt was made to control inflation by setting maximum prices on foodstuffs and other necessities. The formation of democratic trade unions was encouraged and the number in existence grew rapidly. The social insurance system was revised and improved. Planning for the future was encouraged. Public health was improved by greatly increasing the amounts spent for hospitals, health education, and the training of medical personnel. Democracy came to Venezuela and political parties flourished.

The junta headed by Betancourt came to an end after it presided over Venezuela's first honest popular election of a president and Congress. On January 6, 1948, 1,225,470 votes were cast, with 871,752 going to Rómulo Gallegos, the AD candidate—over twice as many as the other three candidates combined received. AD also elected a majority of the members of both houses of the Congress.

On February 15, 1948, Rómulo Gallegos took office as the first directly elected president Venezuela ever had. Most observers believed the country was about to enter a new stage in its political development. The army officers and the conservative elements of Venezuela, however, were becoming restless under so much reform, and they evidently became fearful that their privileges would be completely abolished. Encouraged by the Odría coup d'état in Peru in October 1948, on November 24, 1948, less than a year after Gallegos was inaugurated, basically the same group of army officers that had cooperated with AD in 1945 turned against the government it had helped to create and set up a new military dictatorship. And the Venezuelan people, who so short a time ago had enthusiastically voted for the government, stood quietly by and let them do it.

It is interesting to read the demagogic statement issued by the president of the new military junta, Lieutenant Colonel Carlos Delgado Chalbaud:

> We want to state categorically that this movement is in no way intended to install a military dictatorship. When the army had to do what it did, it was not to act against democratic principles, but on the contrary, to save those principles, which are the fundamental objects of all Venezuelans, and to prepare as soon as possible elections at which the Venezuelan people can choose the government they wish.

The junta then proceeded to suspend constitutional guarantees "relative to the inviolability of correspondence, of the home, of liberty of thought, of travel, of changing address, of leaving the country and returning to it, of public assembly, and of individual security." A few days later, the military dictatorship dissolved the National Congress and all state legislatures, the municipal councils and the Supreme Court, declared the constitution void, and until 1952 governed without a constitution. Most of the leaders of the democratic political parties were exiled or jailed, President Gallegos was expelled from the country, and the army took control of all aspects of life.

The only ones who seemed to believe that the militarists meant to hold elections were the functionaries of the U.S. State Department, for the United States recognized the military junta as the government of Venezuela on January 21, 1949, and issued the following statement through the United States ambassador in Venezuela:

> My government has noted Your Excellency's statement that the new administration will strictly fulfill its international obligations. It has also noted a passage in an address delivered on November 26, 1948, by His Excellency, the President of the Junta, in which it is stated that the Junta will prepare for elections in which all citizens will participate under conditions of equality.[1]

Despite the expectations of the U.S. State Department, the years from 1948 to 1958 were tragic ones for the people of Venezuela. Freedom was ended; the trade unions were not permitted to function freely; the jails were full and concentration camps were set up in the jungle to hold the overflow. Two consecutive national secretaries of *Acción Democrática* were killed by the police. Graft and embezzlement wasted hundreds of millions of dollars in taxes on oil companies' profits, which rose rapidly because of the Korean War and the closing of the Iranian oil refinery at Abadan in 1951. Controlled elections were organized in 1952 and in 1957, but the dictatorship never gained any wide support.

On November 13, 1950, the president of the military junta, Delgado Chalbaud, was assassinated by a fellow officer who did not think he was getting his share of the spoils. There is much evidence that Marcos Pérez Jiménez, one of the other officers in the junta, had something to do with this murder, but the killing was never properly investigated, so it is impossible to know what happened. What is known is that soon afterward the junta was abolished and Pérez Jiménez emerged as the dictator of Venezuela.

Pérez Jiménez tried to legalize his position in 1952 by organizing an election he felt sure he could win, since he had outlawed the country's largest political party, Democratic Action. The parties permitted to participate were the Republican Democratic Union (URD), the Copei Party, and Pérez Jiménez' official party, the Independent Electoral Front. AD's underground leadership instructed its followers to vote for the URD and

---

[1] *New York Times*, January 22, 1949, p. 5. © 1949 by The New York Times Company. Reprinted by permission.

Copei, and to Pérez Jiménez' surprise, when the votes were counted the URD had won. Censorship was immediately imposed, and after two days of secret recounting Pérez Jiménez announced that his party had won and that he had been named provisional president of the republic.

Pérez Jiménez developed into a sort of junior-grade Juan Vicente Gómez. He transformed the public works program begun by the 1945–48 governments into a lavish display of useless monuments. What is probably the world's most expensive highway in cost per mile was built from La Guaira to Caracas. The most expensive and luxurious officers' club in the world was built at a cost of over $8 million. Caracas was transformed with skyscrapers and broad avenues. University City, planned by the previous government, was completed, but during much of Pérez Jiménez' rule the university buildings were kept closed in an attempt to prevent the students from organizing an opposition. The most competent estimates are that at least 50 to 60 percent of the government's income was either stolen or wasted. Lavish drunken orgies consumed part of the wasted money, and after Pérez Jiménez was overthrown it was discovered that he had organized a sort of private resort on an island where he had women flown in from Cuba and other countries to entertain him and his friends. An Indian government official who attended an international conference in Caracas in 1956 reported that Pérez Jiménez reminded him of the beleaguered feudal maharajas in western India just before independence.

Pérez Jiménez may not have impressed the visitor from India, but he did impress General Eisenhower, who in 1954 gave the Venezuelan dictator the highest military decoration the United States confers on foreigners, the Legion of Merit, degree of chief commander. In his statement Eisenhower said:

"The sound economic, financial and foreign investment policies advocated and pursued by his administration have contributed to the economic well-being of his country and to the rapid development of its tremendous resources. These policies, judiciously combined with a far-reaching public works program, have remarkably improved its education, sanitation, transportation, housing and other basic facilities. All of these developments have advanced the general welfare of the Venezuelan people."[2]

That the people of Venezuela did not agree with General Eisenhower is evident, for all during the decade from 1948 to 1958 a well-

---

[2] *Venezuela Up-to-Date,* 5 (December 1954): 7.

financed and constantly expanding military force and a vigilant secret police were necessary to keep the government from being overthrown.

The dictatorship looked imposing in 1958, but its fate was settled in that year when the four Venezuelan political parties agreed to stop fighting each other and to cooperate to overthrow it. A four-man committee coordinated the efforts, but each of the parties operated through its own apparatus.

According to the 1952 constitution, Pérez Jiménez' term ran out in 1958, and he decided to organize an election, as he said, "in a manner befitting our recent economic, social, and political evolution." He interpreted this to mean that each voter should be given two cards, a blue one to vote yes and a red one to vote no on the question of whether Pérez Jiménez should continue in office. Needless to say, the vote was four to one in favor of Pérez Jiménez. But this so enraged the long-suffering Venezuelans that soon afterward a revolution broke out and the unarmed people overthrew the imposing military dictatorship. Rioting became common in January of 1958; demonstrations were organized daily. Finally, on January 20, the opposition called a general strike that paralyzed all economic activity and closed all schools. Hundreds were killed and wounded in the fighting that followed, and thousands were jailed as the Venezuelan people took to the streets to rid themselves of the dictator and his army. By January 22 Pérez Jiménez was on a plane bound for the Dominican Republic. A junta led by Rear Admiral Wolfgang Larrazábal took control of the country. The jails were emptied of political prisoners and exiles came flocking home.

The leaders of the political parties were determined that this time they would succeed in their efforts to create a modern nation-state based on democratic government. The three largest parties (AD, URD, and Copei) signed a pact of cooperation and tried to agree upon a joint candidate to run for the presidency. They were fearful that a political campaign would disrupt the cooperation between the parties, thus permitting the supporters of dictatorship to regain control of the country. No agreement could be reached, however, and three candidates were presented by four parties. Democratic Action nominated its leader, Rómulo Betancourt. Copei nominated its leader, Rafael Caldera. The URD and the Communist Party nominated the head of the temporary junta, Wolfgang Larrazábal. After a heated campaign, the voters gave Betancourt 49.2 percent of the votes, Larrazábal 34.6 percent, and Caldera 16.2 percent. Rómulo Betancourt therefore became constitutional president for the 1959–64 term. AD also won a majority of the seats in both houses of the National Congress. To strengthen the government, President Betancourt appointed a cabinet that included members of all important parties except the Communist.

A feverish program of reorganization and development began. Rómulo Betancourt and his party associates were determined that this time they would change Venezuela so much that dictatorship would never return. Great emphasis was put upon investing as much money as possible in industrialization, roads, schools, and other public works. The education budget for 1959–60 was 390 percent higher than for the 1957–58 fiscal year. From 1957–58 to 1962–63 the number of primary schools in Venezuela went up from 6,676 to 12,599. The number of students enrolled in the various schools (from primary to university) rose from 886,397 in the 1957–58 school year to 1,704,682 in the 1962–63 school year, an increase of 92.3 percent. The number of university students in that period rose 237 percent, from 10,270 to 34,656. The budget for health in 1959–60 was 385 percent higher than it had been in 1957–58. Great efforts were made to decrease the number of unemployed. New industrial installations were pushed to completion, the most important being the integrated project at Caroní on the Orinoco River in eastern Venezuela, where a hydroelectric power project, a steel mill, and a petrochemical plant were constructed. This project had tremendous significance in helping to turn the country's attention toward its unexploited and almost empty east and south. A land-reform law was passed to enable the government to supply tracts of land to the landless rural population and to help them become self-sufficient by supplying them with loans, seeds, implements, and technical advice. A determined effort was made to increase the production of foodstuffs in order to lower the cost of living by ending the need to import expensive food from the United States. At the same time, Venezuela became a leader in the attempt to democratize the Organization of American States and to have that organization do something about eliminating the remaining dictatorships in America.

Yet the new government of Venezuela faced almost insurmountable problems. The overemphasis on petroleum production in the past combined with the robbery of the public treasury by the militarists had created an extreme inflation and given Caracas one of the highest living costs in the world. The dictatorship's spending of millions for showy public works in Caracas had turned the country into a sort of city-state as people poured into Caracas until it had about one-fifth of the country's total. And as Caracas grew, the rest of the country, with certain exceptions, vegetated.

To complicate matters, the Betancourt government was unable to devote its full attention to the country's problems because the totalitarians, both the conservative and the Communist varieties, were constantly attacking the government and attempting to overthrow it. An almost continuous series of invasions, street riots, attempted coups, and attempted and successful assassinations was financed by the Soviet Union, Cuba, and the Dominican Republic.[3] The high points in this struggle came in June 1960, when Rafael Trujillo, the dictator then in control of the Dominican Republic, financed a bombing attack that almost killed President Betancourt,[4] and in October 1960, when the Russians, through Castro, financed an armed revolt that left hundreds dead and many more wounded.

This series of insurrections made Venezuela a testing ground to determine whether democratic institutions could be firmly established in a country in which a minority of the population refused to accept democracy. The old beneficiaries of power, including the aristocracy and some of the military officers, continued to plot revolts because they could not visualize a world in which they did not have special privileges. But even more dangerous than the remnants of the old ruling class in Venezuela were the followers of the Soviet government who operated in Venezuela under the name of the Communist Party and a host of front organizations. These people fought the Betancourt government because it is not in the interests of the Soviet Union to permit a successful reformist government to function in any part of the world, since this would help destroy the myth, so assiduously cultivated, that the Communists and their followers hold a monopoly on progress in the world and that all other political movements are reactionary.

The Communists have always fought the AD. They cooperated with Pérez Jiménez, since he too was interested in destroying AD, and they benefited greatly from the aid they received from the dictatorship.[5] In the 1958 election campaign the Communists supported Admiral Larrazábal, and when he was defeated they began an attack upon the government and upon Democratic Action. The Communists were aided in their project of sowing confusion by the participation of the other three parties in the coalition government. These parties were so busy trying to orga-

---

[3] These attacks upon the government ranged from the violent to the ridiculous. Probably the silliest took place in November 1959, when two Cuban pilots took off from one of Trujillo's air bases and dropped millions of leaflets on Curaçao, a Dutch island off the coast of Venezuela, urging the population to revolt against Betancourt. When they landed their plane on the neighboring island of Aruba after running out of gas, the authorities arrested and fined them. See the *New York Times*, November 25, 1959, p. 26.

[4] See the Organization of American States' report *Los Hechos según los elementos de juicio reunidos por la comisión*, issued on August 8, 1960.

[5] See, for example, *Inter-American Labor Bulletin*, 3 (December 1953): 5–6, for a specific example of Pérez Jiménez–Communist cooperation to fight the AD-controlled trade unions.

nize the government, staff it, and repair the chaos caused by ten years of dictatorship that they tended to neglect their party machinery. The Communists, having no government responsibility, well supplied with money, and enjoying the propaganda advantage of their capture of the Castro revolution in Cuba, were able to make important gains among the masses, particularly in Caracas, and almost succeeded in taking over control of the country.

The Communists organized a faction within AD, which, under the name of AD of the Left, grew to sizable significance. At the same time, they infiltrated the URD so well that they captured the party apparatus. The Communists obtained important positions in the trade unions, in the university and student organizations, and in the newspapers and radio stations. Soon they were dominating the streets of Caracas by organizing the numerous unemployed in almost continuous demonstrations.

While this was going on, the Soviet government began to sell petroleum on the world market in larger quantities than it ever had in the past.[6] When Fidel Castro took over the Cuban refineries and began to use Soviet oil, Venezuela's exports were decreased by 20,000 barrels a day. This had serious consequences in Venezuela; wells were closed and the general economy slowed down. It was just at this moment that the *Fidelistas* and Communists in Venezuela began an aggressive campaign against the Betancourt government, accusing it of not doing enough about the country's problems. It is difficult to believe that all these events were mere coincidences.

The Communist campaign came to a climax during 1960. In the spring AD finally decided to expel all of its members who were Communists, including several members of the National Congress. This group organized a new party, the Revolutionary Leftist Movement (MIR), which cooperated closely with the Communist Party. In June, after Trujillo had financed a bomb attack that left President Betancourt wounded and unable to devote full time to his duties, the Communists, the MIR, and the URD organized continual demonstrations that culminated in a minor civil war. This was defeated only after many deaths, much destruction, and days of terror in Caracas. Betancourt fired the URD members of his cabinet. The trade unions began a drive to expel the Communists

---

[6] The Soviet government also helped ruin Bolivia's economy after the MNR revolution by dumping tin on the world market. See Haya de la Torre's forecast in the 1920's, when he wrote, "Latin American sugar, cotton, petroleum, and other products compete in the world market with the Russian products. To contribute to their nonproduction in countries like ours is to help Russian production" (Víctor Raúl Haya de la Torre, *Impresiones de la Inglaterra imperialista y la Rusia Soviética*" [Buenos Aires: Colección Claridad, Acción y Crítica, 1932], pp. 127–28).

from membership. By 1961 things had quieted down and the Communists were isolated.

Nineteen-sixty-three was an important year for Venezuela. If an election were held as scheduled that year and Rómulo Betancourt turned over his office to the victor, it would mark the first time in the republic's history that a popularly elected president had completed his term. To prevent this from happening, all the enemies of Venezuelan democracy united their forces in an organization known as the Armed Forces of National Liberation (FALN) and renewed their attacks. Plentifully supplied with arms and money from Cuba and the Soviet Union, the FALN murdered, bombed, kidnapped, and otherwise disrupted Venezuela, but the more aggressive it became, the less popular support it seemed to win. In October 1963, after a particularly brutal attack on unarmed passengers on a railroad train, President Betancourt finally ordered the arrest of the Communist members of Congress, because they were directing the terrorist campaign behind their shield of parliamentary immunity.[7]

The Associated Press described the Communist activity in Venezuela in 1962 as follows:

> Like the Bolshevik bandits of Czarist Russia under Stalin and others, bands of wild-eyed young Communist thugs, each anywhere from six to a dozen strong, storm into country banks, nervous fingers on the triggers of Czechoslovak tommy guns smuggled to them from Cuba. Openly they announce to cowed victims that this raid is for the party. The party needs the money. . . . Others carry out swift, senseless assassinations of ordinary policemen.[8]

The violence of the Communists failed to destroy Venezuelan constitutional government. The election of December 1, 1963, was the great milestone in Venezuela's democratic development. Seven candidates were nominated for the presidency and vigorous campaigns were conducted by all of them. The Communist Party and the MIR had lost their ballot positions by court order as a result of their terroristic tactics, but

---

[7] In May 1962 the police arrested Eloy Torres, a member of the Congress, among the defeated rebels following a revolt at Carúpano. He was wearing a naval officer's uniform and was identified as one of the leaders of the revolt. The Congress suspended his parliamentary immunity and he was convicted and sentenced to eight years in prison for his part in the Carúpano revolt. After another revolt was suppressed at Puerto Cabello, the police arrested two other members of the Chamber of Deputies, one a member of the Communist Party and one a member of the MIR, who had participated in that attempt. There was much additional evidence that the supporters of the FALN in the Congress were involved in the terroristic campaign, but until 1963 President Betancourt could not get a vote to lift the parliamentary immunity of the Communists and their friends in Congress.

[8] *Gainesville* (Florida) *Daily Sun*, September 30, 1962, p. 4.

the Communists participated in the campaign by supporting some of the minor candidates. To complicate matters, the FALN announced that it would kill any Venezuelan who left his home on election day and unleashed a last-ditch campaign of terror. On November 19, for example, fifteen to twenty were killed by snipers and hundreds were arrested in what the *New York Times* called Caracas' "worst day in years."[9]

It is to the eternal credit of the Venezuelan people that they ignored the threats of the Communist terrorists on election day: over 95 percent of the registered voters, 2,917,896 persons, voted for a new president. AD and the Social Christian Party (Copei) between them won a majority of the votes cast, and Dr. Raúl Leoni, the AD candidate, was elected president. The AD vote had declined from what it had been in 1958, but it was a remarkable showing for a party that had had two important splits in the years before the election.

The Social Christians had made a strong showing at the polls, and they decided that their chances in the next election would be even better if they left the coalition government. When Raúl Leoni was inaugurated as president, therefore, the AD–Social Christian coalition government was dissolved. But since AD had polled only 32.8 percent of the votes cast, the new president was forced to work out a new coalition. After much negotiation, the new arrangement was announced in November of 1964. The new coalition government consisted of AD, the URD, and the National Democratic Front. Each of the three parties was assigned three ministries and four governorships, and their members were appointed to the boards of directors of various government corporations. On March 14, 1966, the National Democratic Front left the coalition to join the opposition.

Under the leadership of President Leoni, the Venezuelan government continued the program of the previous administration. Its greatest success probably was in finally crushing the activities of the guerrillas. Leoni even allowed many of those in jail to leave the country upon promising not to renew their terrorist activities. A few fanatics continued to roam the mountain forests, but the widespread violence of the past had been stopped.

Venezuela adopted a new democratic constitution in 1961. An agrarian-reform law had gone into effect in 1960, and in the next seven years 131,250 families were settled on their new farms. An elaborate four-year plan to cost $8 billion was adopted to complete the industrialization of the country and finish the land-reform program. One can only

[9] Richard Eder, "Terrorists Give Caracas Worst Day in Years," *New York Times*, November 20, 1963, p. 13. © 1963 The New York Times Company. Reprinted by permission.

be optimistic when looking at Venezuela, for the transformation in the economic, political, and social structures of the country during the years since 1945 has been startling. The exceptionally rapid growth in popula- tion (it has more than doubled in the past twenty years), the rise in national income, the development of new economic enterprises, the im- proved transportation, education, and health are all changing the country so much that neither those who dream of a return to the past nor the Soviet-, Cuban-, and Chinese-oriented adventurers would find it easy now to turn the Venezuelans from the construction of a modern nation-state, the home of a prosperous, cultured people.

The Formal Constitutional Framework

Venezuela is governed under the constitution of January 23, 1961, which sets up a federal, democratic, representative, responsible government. "Sovereignty resides in the people," who exercise it by means of suffrage, through the branches of the government created by the constitution. This is the twenty-fourth constitution the country has had, and the mere fact that so many have been needed demonstrates how little attention has been paid to them during most of Venezuela's history.

The government elected in 1958 followed constitutional rules in cre- ating its new document, which was finally inaugurated on January 23, 1961. It took so long because those in power wanted to make sure that this time they had included everything that could possibly strengthen democracy, but basically the new document was a rewrite of the 1947 charter. It provides for a federal republic in which there is a clear division of power. The rights of individuals are clearly spelled out and the death penalty is abolished. As is customary, individual rights may be suspended during "internal or external conflict," but even in this case the death penalty is banned.

Like the constitution of Mexico, Venezuela's contains a clause pro- viding that the constitution will remain in force even if a revolution over- throws the government, thus legalizing opposition to any successor gov- ernment. An interesting article provides for territories to join Venezuela with the approval of the Congress. These additions to Venezuela may be ruled by a special juridical system set up by law.

How the Constitution Is Amended

Amendments to the Venezuelan constitution can be proposed by one- fourth of the members of one of the houses of the National Congress or by one-fourth of the state legislatures after two debates. After being approved by a majority vote in both houses of the Congress, the proposed amendment is sent to the state legislatures, where the proposal must be discussed twice before being voted upon. If two-thirds of the state legislatures approve the amendment, it becomes part of the constitution.

General revisions of the constitution can be proposed by one-third of the members of the Congress or by a majority of the state legislatures. The president of the Congress then convokes a joint session of the two houses. If that body votes by a two-thirds majority that a constitutional revision is needed, it designates which house is to begin the discussion. After both houses have approved a new draft constitution, it is submitted to a referendum of the country's registered voters and, if approved by a majority, is then proclaimed by the Congress.

This constitution has not been in force long enough, as this is written, to justify any opinion about how the amending process will work.

Who Participates in Politics

The majority of Venezuela's adult population has been participating in political life and voting since 1946, when the Democratic Action government abolished indirect elections and the literacy requirement for voting. In the 1958 election, when the population was about 6 million, there were slightly more than 2.9 million registered voters, of whom 2.7 million, or 90 percent, cast their ballots for president. By 1963 the number of registered voters had gone up to 3.37 million, and 3.06 million actually voted. Thus 91 percent of the total registered participated in the election. In both elections the voters turned out in the same proportions in urban and rural areas.

Both voting and registration are obligatory for all Venezuelans over eighteen except those disqualified for criminal activities and those on active military duty. No literacy or property qualifications are required, although one must be literate to be elected. The penalties for not registering or voting are severe, except for those over sixty-five or under twenty-one, or who have good reason not to do so. All citizens have to present evidence of having voted or an exemption when applying for a government job, when making a contract with the government, when enrolling in a university, and when applying for trade-marks, patents, and licenses.

The Electoral Machinery

All electoral matters are controlled by a Supreme Electoral Council, composed of thirteen members elected for two-year terms by the National

Congress during the first thirty days of its ordinary session. No political party can have a "preeminent representation" on the Supreme Electoral Council or on any of the lower electoral councils. In each state there is a principal electoral board of seven members, appointed by the Supreme Electoral Council. In the electoral districts into which the states are divided there are district electoral boards of five members, appointed by the principal electoral board of the state. In each municipality there is a municipal electoral board of five members, appointed by the district electoral board. In each local polling place there are a three-man committee appointed by the district electoral board and watchers for each political party. For the 1963 election, 12,400 polling places functioned, one for each 300 voters.

Ballots of different sizes, colors, and combinations of colors make voting easier for the illiterate. The president is elected by a simple plurality of the votes cast and the Congress is elected by a system of proportional representation which combines the D'Hondt system with a national quotient system for those parties underrepresented in the distribution of seats under the D'Hondt system. All elections—national, state, and local—take place at the same time, with the voter using two ballots, one for the president and the other for all other positions. Voters do not vote for individuals, except for the president, as proportional representation requires a list which is drawn up by the party.

An attempt is made to keep the polling places free of all who would influence voters. Liquor is not sold on election day, nor can meetings or public spectacles be held then. The elections of 1958 and 1963 were fairly conducted, and the only criticism of the electoral machinery comes from the Communist terrorists, who have been banned from the ballot.

Political Parties

Modern political parties emerged in Venezuela after the death of Juan Vicente Gómez. Dozens of organizations calling themselves political parties have appeared on the scene, but only four have had any important support since the end of World War II. Some commentators think the Venezuelan system of proportional representation stimulates the creation of small parties, as even a tiny party can hope to accumulate enough votes to win one or two seats in the Congress. Yet the D'Hondt system gives so accurate a reflection of the voters' wishes that the majority parties have no difficulty in winning most of the seats in the two houses.

For the 1963 election, thirteen political parties were registered with the Supreme Electoral Council and seven candidates were nominated for the presidency. In order to nominate a presidential candidate, a party must be registered in any seven of the country's electoral districts, or must have at least 200 literate members in each of at least seven electoral districts. To nominate candidates for the Senate, the Chamber of Deputies, and the state legislative assemblies, a political party or independent group must have five literate members over twenty-one years of age for each 100 voters in the electoral jurisdiction for which the group wants to nominate a candidate.

Venezuela's largest and most important political party in 1964 was Democratic Action (AD), founded in 1941. AD received 80 percent of the votes cast in 1946, 74 percent of the votes cast in 1947, 49.2 percent of the votes cast in 1958, and 32.8 percent of the votes cast in 1963. Thus its vote has decreased in each successive election, but it remains the largest party in the country, and its nominees were elected to the presidency in 1947, 1958, and 1963. It has suffered three important splits, but it remains the country's most important party. In 1963, when Raúl Leoni was elected president with 957,699 votes, AD won 24 of the 48 seats in the Senate and 65 of the 177 in the Chamber of Deputies.

Democratic Action is an indigenous multiclass party dedicated to transforming Venezuela into a modern democratic state. AD has worked for democratic government, agrarian reform, mass education, industrialization, strict control of foreign economic enterprises, national planning, and a policy oriented toward improving the conditions of life of the lower classes. Since the party is strongly anticommunist, the international Communist propaganda machine has worked hard to convince people that AD has forgotten its democratic philosophy and that Rómulo Betancourt, its leader, has betrayed the Venezuelan people. Meanwhile, the John Birch Society and various similar organizations in the United States have tried to paint Betancourt and AD as Communist. AD favors cooperation among the continent's democratic political parties and is affiliated with the League of Popular Parties and is an observer member of the Socialist International. Its youth section is affiliated with the International Union of Socialist Youth. Democratic Action is particularly strong among the organized workers, the peasants, and the middle class. It is weakest in Caracas, which it failed to carry in the 1958 election. In 1963 it claimed 903,000 registered members. The 1963 election results demonstrate that this was an accurate count.

The Democratic Republican Union is a personalistic party founded in 1945 by Jovito Villalba, a former member of AD who did not like to take second place to Rómulo Betancourt. It has always been an opportunistic party with no clear program. In 1958 it was allied with the Communist Party in support of Admiral Larrazábal, and after that date its ranks were greatly infiltrated by Communists and fellow travelers. In 1963 it had two factions, one led by Villalba, the other by Luis Miquelena, whose views were indistinguishable from those of the Communist Party. In the 1958–64 Congress it had eleven senators and thirty-four deputies. It was estimated to have 300,000 members in 1963, when Villalba won 551,120 votes, and it elected seven senators and twenty-nine deputies. After the 1963 election Villalba offered the cooperation of the URD congressmen to the new government and began to expel the Communists from the party. Eventually the URD entered President Leoni's coalition government.

The Social Christian Party began life in 1946 as the Committee for Independent Political and Electoral Institutions (its popular name, Copei, comes from the first letters of the Spanish words). When it was organized, Copei included in its ranks many of the conservative elements in Venezuela, but through the years, and especially after 1958, it became more and more a reformist Christian democratic organization and the conservative members left the party. Copei is animated by Catholic social philosophy, but it has no formal connection with the Catholic church. It is estimated to have about 300,000 members and is strongest among practicing Catholics, the middle class, and the rural population of the Andean states. In the 1958–64 Congress it had six senators and twenty deputies. In the 1964–69 Congress it had nine senators and forty deputies.

The Venezuelan Communist Party was founded in the 1920's and has led a life typical of Latin-American Communist parties. Strictly following the Soviet line, at times it has cooperated with dictatorial governments to fight against AD. Permitted to participate in the 1958 elections because it had been part of the united front that overthrew the Pérez Jiménez government,[10] it began a terroristic campaign to destroy democracy after the Venezuelan masses refused to accept its leadership. It has cooperated with dissident conservative army officers in several attempts at coups, but has grown consistently weaker as the country loses patience with its terrorism. The party has been banned since 1962. In the 1958 election the Communist Party elected two senators and seven deputies by polling 160,791 votes (6.2 percent). It is estimated that the party had about 50,000 members and about 200,000 sympathizers. It functions through a host of front organizations, the most important of

---

[10] For a description of the Communist Party when it was at the height of its influence in Venezuela, see Tad Szulc, "Venezuelan Reds Attain Influence," *New York Times*, September 23, 1958, p. 14.

which has been the Armed Forces of National Liberation (FALN).

It is difficult to say which of the many minor parties has permanent significance. The Revolutionary Leftist Movement (MIR), now outlawed because of its terroristic activities, began as a faction within AD, led by Domingo Alberto Rangel, then national political secretary of AD. The MIR apparently included many Communists, who had joined AD in an attempt to capture its machinery, and since its expulsion from AD the MIR has become almost indistinguishable from the Communist Party. At the time the MIR was expelled from AD, it had two senators and fourteen deputies in its ranks.

Another split-off from AD, led by Raúl Ramos Jiménez, was known as Democratic Action of the Opposition at first, and then as the Nationalist Revolutionary Party. In the 1963 election, when it ran Ramos Jiménez for the presidency, it received 66,837 votes. This was a very small vote, for the group included four senators and twenty-two deputies when it split from the AD. The party may well disappear sooner or later, for its parliamentary faction went down to one senator and six deputies in the 1964–69 legislature.

Of the minor parties, the most important is the *Frente Nacional Democrático* (FND), which developed out of the organization known as Independent Venezuelan Action (AVI), founded in 1962. AVI included within its ranks many of the richest businessmen in the country. In its first years it functioned as a pressure group, trying to persuade AD and other parties to nominate the kind of candidates AVI could support. After one of its members, Arturo Uslar Pietri, running as an independent, did well in the 1963 election, AVI changed its name to *Frente Nacional Democrático* and began to act more like a political party. With its entrance into President Leoni's coalition government it became the most important of the minor parties.

Other minor parties functioning during the 1963 election included the Popular Democratic Force (FDP), founded in 1963, which ran Admiral Larrazábal for president and received 274,304 votes, 9.4 percent of the total cast, electing four senators and sixteen deputies. The National Action Movement (MAN) was founded in 1960 and won 9,324 votes, 0.3 percent of the total, for its presidential candidate. Other groups that did not present presidential candidates were the Independent National Electoral Front (MENI), founded in 1958, which elected one deputy; the Progressive Republican Movement (MRP), a conservative party founded in 1961; the Nationalist Socialist Movement (MSN), founded in 1962; the Popular Social Grouping Electoral Committee (CEPAS), founded in 1962; the Independent Democratic Electoral Bloc (BEDI), founded in 1962; and the Authentic Nationalist Party (PAN), founded in July 1963. The Independents for the National Front elected three senators and twenty deputies and the Venezuelan Socialist Party elected one deputy. Venezuela has too many small political parties that come and go, but most of them will probably disappear eventually as the large parties become institutionalized.

Pressure Groups and Public Opinion

The dominant position of Caracas in Venezuela's life centralizes public opinion there. The radio and press are most important in spreading information, with radio most effective because of the high illiteracy rate in past years. About half the homes in Venezuela were thought to have radios in 1959. Fifty-seven noncommunist newspapers were being published in 1959, thirty-three of them dailies with a combined circulation of around 550,000. In addition, 115 noncommunist magazines appeared. The Communists published sixteen periodicals, including *Tribuna Popular*, the official organ of the Communist Party. *Últimas Noticias* is the largest daily, with a circulation of 85,000 copies. All newspapers are partisan in their coverage of political news, giving proportionally more space to the candidates they favor.

The officer corps of the armed forces has been the country's most important power group ever since independence. It is only since 1945 that any groups capable of challenging its position have emerged, and it is still too soon to state categorically that the armed forces of Venezuela are no longer the most important social group in the country. The Venezuelan army has about 10,000 officers and men, the navy about 2,500, the air force about 5,000. The governments since 1958 have succeeded in keeping the officers under control. It is thought that Betancourt and Leoni had some kind of agreement with the officer corps, under which the officers helped defend the government in return for the preservation of their privileges. In 1962, for example, the national budget provided 582.8 million bolívares for national defense, only B36.2 million less than the amount spent for education. It may be that as weapons become more complex, a greater degree of professionalization takes place, and the officers are more willing to remain out of politics. It is too soon to tell.

The second most important group in Venezuela is probably the newly emerged upper middle class, the industrialists, professionals, and businessmen. Functioning through a series of formal organizations, including the Federation of Industrial Chambers, the Association of Commerce, and associations of bankers, engineers, lawyers, and other professional men, these people want stable constitutional government so they can proceed with their activities without the chaos and turmoil of dictatorship and civil war. Independent Venezuelan Action, which was a sort of political party that never ran candidates, was organized by this group and included within its membership many of the richest industrialists in the country. It has been estimated that from 1953 to 1963 the Venezuelan middle class grew from about 8 percent to nearly 20 percent of the population. Educated, articulate, and with a financial stake in the preservation of orderly government, the middle class has been one of the strong supports of AD.

The Catholic church was a most important group during the early years of the republic. The anticlerical laws adopted in the second half of the nineteenth century, when Guzmán Blanco dominated the country, greatly weakened the church, but in recent years it has recovered some of its influence. It operates a series of educational institutions. The government continues to appoint the higher officials of the church, but in recent years there have been good relations between the church and the government.

The large landowners have been losing their power in recent decades, but it was one of the dominant groups in Venezuela until oil, iron ore, and manufacturing transformed the economy.. With the 1960 land-reform law, the beginning of the end is in sight for this group, which, although composed of only 2 percent of the rural population, owned about 75 percent of the agricultural land. In recent years this group has tended to support the Social Christian Party during elections.

The university students have played an important role as an action group since World War I. Rómulo Betancourt, Raúl Leoni, and many of the other most prominent political leaders began their political careers as student leaders. The capture of the Central University student organization by the Communists in recent years and their utilization of the university as a base for terrorist activity have tended to lessen the influence of the student groups. In addition, the Betancourt government followed a deliberate policy of weakening the Central University in Caracas by strengthening other universities and organizing new ones. Until mass literacy becomes the rule, however, the university students will play an important role, and all of the political parties have functioning organizations among students. Political activity is forbidden by law in primary and secondary schools, but even here the parties are active.

Organized labor is a recently developed pressure group whose importance grows yearly as industrialization increases. Since January 1962 the 1.2-million-member Venezuelan Confederation of Labor (CTV) has been affiliated with the International Confederation of Free Trade Unions and the Inter-American Regional Organization of Labor (ORIT). About 400,000 to 500,000 of the CTV members are agricultural workers organized into the Peasants' Federation (FCV), which has its own apparatus but is affiliated with the CTV. The CTV has been one of the most important factors contributing to AD's electoral success. Both city and rural workers are able to influence policy through union officials who hold important positions within AD, Copei, and the government. Many labor leaders have been elected to the state legislatures and the National Congress.

The Venezuelan pressure groups make use of all the methods utilized by similar groups in other democratic countries. Propaganda, strikes, and demonstrations are most important. The strength of the labor unions and other economic interest groups may have been decisive in preserving constitutional government in recent years. By 1964 the activities of the Soviet- and Cuban-financed terrorist organizations had created a realignment of the traditional pressure groups. In earlier decades the large landowners and merchants were aligned with the military and ecclesiastical elite against organized labor, the white-collar workers, and the small farmers. Since the buildup of Communist pressure, those groups interested in constitutional government, including the labor movement, the middle classes, the industrialists, the peasants, and the government bureaucracy, have formed an overwhelming majority, supported by the army and the Catholic church hierarchy. In opposition are those inspired by a fanatical communism, remnants of the old military and government elite, and the large landowners. This oddly assorted opposition has supported the FALN and other terrorist organizations, and has seemed to have no program beyond destroying constitutional government.

Civil Liberties

Venezuela's constitution guarantees all the liberties traditional in democratic political systems: respect for the individual, equality before the law, access to the courts, due process of law, habeas corpus, inviolability of the home and correspondence, freedom of movement, liberty of conscience, opinion, and speech, freedom of association. Propaganda for war, speech offensive to public morality, and utterances designed to provoke disobedience of the laws are forbidden. In addition, the constitution includes a series of social rights dealing with the family, education, culture, work, and social security. Economic rights are listed, but these place the welfare of the group over that of the individual. Monopolies are banned, and a wish is expressed for the disappearance of latifundia. These constitutional clauses are only general principles expressing the sentiment of the constitutional convention; special legislation would be needed to make them operative.

The executive, as has been customary in Venezuela, is given the right to suspend almost all of the civil rights listed in the constitution "in case of emergency or disorder that may disturb the peace." During the Communist uprisings, constitutional guarantees were suspended and restored and suspended again several times as the tide of terrorism rose and fell. The government of President Betancourt was reluctant to restrict civil rights, which was what the Communist terrorists wanted, but was forced to do so regularly. President Betancourt finally broke the ability of the Communists to start riots at will by staging a rally in the Plaza de Silencio, one of Caracas' largest squares, and organizing a "self-defense corps" consisting of burly workers trucked in from the industrial areas. When the President began to speak and the Communists started their anticipated tumult, the "self-defense corps" quickly silenced them. After that episode, the Communists found it harder to create public disturbances, and turned more and more to bombs and armed terrorism.

President Leoni was able to govern without resorting to a state of siege until December 13, 1966, when he declared an emergency after terrorists murdered an army major and wounded the chief of the General Staff. The President also ordered the police onto the university campus because it had been used as a base by the terrorists. The condition of civil liberty is not perfect in Venezuela, but it is about as good as can be expected in a country under continuous attack by terrorists financed and organized by foreign governments. A committee of the Organization of American States investigated Venezuelan charges that Cuba was involved in the terrorism after a shipment of Cuban arms was discovered in Venezuela in 1964, and substantiated the charges.

The average citizen enjoys complete liberty in Venezuela. He moves about as he pleases, the press is free and outspoken, all kinds of ideas are freely propagated. Trade unions are flourishing and all political parties function freely except those engaged in terrorism.

The Executive

Venezuela's executive is a president elected for a five-year term by direct popular vote who cannot be reelected until ten years after he has completed his term in office. There is no vice-president. If the office of the president becomes temporarily vacant because the president has left the country or is sick, his position is filled by a minister appointed by the president. If the president dies, his position is filled temporarily by the president of the Congress; if he is not available, by the vice-president of the Congress; following him, by the president of the Supreme Court. Meanwhile, by secret vote within thirty days, the Congress elects a new president, to complete the unexpired term.

To be president one must be a Venezuelan by birth, over thirty years of age, and a layman. Not eligible to be president, in addition to anyone who has been president during the nine years before an election, are the relatives of the incumbent president within the third degree of consanguinity and the second degree by affinity. Nor can a minister, a state governor, or the secretary to the president be a candidate unless he has resigned his position before becoming a candidate.

Venezuela's executive power is divided so that part is exercised by the president acting alone, part by the president acting together with his council of ministers, and part by the president countersigned by a minister. This is not much of a check on the president, however, as he alone has the power to appoint and remove his ministers. The president has the title of chief of state and of the national executive.

Acting alone, the president enforces the constitution and the laws and appoints and removes ministers. With his ministers he is the commander in chief of the armed forces; he fixes the size of the armed forces, directs foreign affairs, makes and ratifies international treaties, administers the national finances, appoints and removes certain officials (some with the authorization of the Senate and some without), and grants pardons. With his council of ministers the president has the power to declare a state of emergency and order the restriction or suspension of certain constitutional guarantees, to take action to defend the republic, to take such extraordinary measures in economic and financial matters as the law authorizes, to convoke special sessions of Congress, to negotiate loans, and to make those contracts permitted by the constitution and the laws.

The president of Venezuela is a strong executive. His powers are wide and the restrictions upon his actions have not yet been tried because of the unsettled times. President Betancourt seemed to lean over backward to do everything constitutionally, but it is impossible to say how the powers of the president will be exercised until the country has had a prolonged period of peace. The president has the power to veto laws within ten days, but the Congress can override his veto by a two-thirds majority of those present.

The Venezuelan executive power is divided among thirteen ministers, each of whom by law is assigned the control of various activities. The president of the republic has his office in the Palace of Miraflores and has an extensive staff to assist him in his work. In addition to the regular clerks, administrative assistants, and guards, the president has a Central Office of Coordination and Planning (Cordiplan) and a Public Administration Commission (CAP) to help him. Cordiplan advises the president on investments, program budgeting, and long-range planning; the CAP studies the organization, methods, and procedures of the public administration to suggest ways of making it more efficient, especially in regard to the training of personnel for the public service.

During recent years a determined effort has been made to improve government efficiency by creating an effective public administration. The CAP played a leading role in this effort, particularly in drafting five basic laws: a civil service merit system, a reorganization of the office of the comptroller general, an organic law for the budget, an organic law for the government's autonomous institutions, and an organic law for the national treasury. The CAP has also pushed for a better recruitment system, in-service training, and classification of employees. The Venezuelan public administration is one of the better ones in Latin America. Through the School of Public Administration attached to the Public Administration Commission, in-service training has been given to public employees since 1962.

The Legislative Power

Venezuela's legislative power rests in a bicameral Congress, consisting of the Senate and the Chamber of Deputies. The Senate is made up of two members from each state and the Federal District, plus those members who receive their seats through proportional representation, plus all ex-presidents. In 1963 the Senate had fifty-one members, forty-two from the states and the Federal District and nine from the national quotient in the proportional election. At the time senators are elected, alternates are also elected; thus no by-elections are needed. The Chamber of Deputies consists of one deputy for every 50,000 inhabitants and one for a fraction over 25,000, plus those who receive seats by proportional representation. In 1963 it consisted of 133 members, 127 members allotted on a proportional basis to the states and 6 from the national quotient. Alternates are also elected to the Chamber of Deputies. Each state receives at least two deputies and each territory at least one.

To be a senator one must be a Venezuelan by birth and more than thirty years old. To be a deputy one must be a Venezuelan by birth and at least twenty-one years old. The law bans as candidates for Congress cabinet ministers, the president's secretary, federal judges, the attorney general, the comptroller and his assistant, directors or managers of autonomous government institutions, governors, government employees, and representatives of business firms having contracts with the national government. The only exceptions are teachers and employees of the electoral department.

The Congress meets in regular session from March 2 to July 6 and from October 1 to November 30, except in the last year of a constitutional period, when it meets from March 2 to August 15. In either case, the Congress has the power to prolong its session. The powers of the legislature are divided, with the Senate being given certain exclusive powers, the Chamber others, and both together exercising others jointly. When the two houses disagree, they meet in joint session and decide the issue by an absolute majority of those present. The exclusive powers of the Senate include initiating all discussions of treaties, authorizing the executive to alienate real property from the private domain of the nation, authorizing public officials and employees to accept posts, honors, or recompense from foreign governments, authorizing promotion of officers of the armed forces higher than colonel or naval captain, authorizing the president to leave the country, authorizing certain appointments, and authorizing by a majority vote the trial of the president after the Supreme Court has ruled there are grounds for this action. When the Senate votes to try the president, he is immediately suspended from office.

Exclusive powers of the Chamber include initiating all financial measures and voting censure of ministers. Each house controls its internal organization and both houses have the power to investigate all public employees. Bills can be introduced into the legislature by committees of Congress, the national executive, three or more senators or deputies, the Supreme Court (on matters dealing with judicial organization or procedure), or 20,000 registered voters. All bills passed by the Congress become law unless the president sends them back within ten days, but the Supreme Court has the power to declare all laws and acts of the legislature unconstitutional.

When the Congress is not in session, a delegated committee, consisting of its president, vice-president, and twenty-one members who are elected to reflect the strength of the various parties in the Congress, represents the Congress and can, in addition to other actions, call the Congress into special session.

Members of the Congress can serve as ministers, secretary to the president of the republic, governor, chief of a diplomatic mission, or president of a government autonomous institute, but must give their seats up to their alternates while doing so. They can return to Congress after giving up their executive posts.

The legislature has functioned freely since 1959.

Public Finance

Venezuela's fabulous wealth in petroleum and iron gives the government a large regular income, which can be utilized for developing the country. This income has also enabled the government to improve the technical efficiency of the public service. The country's budget is presented to the Congress by the Minister of Finance for its approval, but the Congress may not authorize expenditures that exceed the amount of estimated revenue.

Tables 1 and 2 show Venezuela's income and expenses in 1966. As the figures show, Venezuela has a much healthier budget than most of the other Latin-American republics. Its tax system is much broader than is usual in Latin America and its income taxes bring in a substantial amount. Its expenditures are also made with a view to building up the country. In the 1966 budget, defense received B778 million, but education received B914 million, despite the need for troops to fight the Communist terrorists.

TABLE 1

REVENUE OF VENEZUELA, 1966

(000,000 Omitted)

Source	Amount in Bolivares	Percent of Total
Royalties and oil taxes	B2,590	...
Income tax from oil industry	2,335	...
Total oil revenue	B4,925	63%
Customs duties	515	7
Income tax from iron industry	295	4
Foreign exchange	37	...
Bond issue	212	2
Income and inheritance taxes	954	12
Excise taxes (liquor, cigarettes, etc.)	616	8
Other taxes	296	4
Total revenue	B7,850	100%

TABLE 2
EXPENDITURES OF VENEZUELA, 1966
(000,000 Omitted)

	Amount in Bolívares	Percent of Total
Interior relations, including subsidies to states for health, education, and public works	B1,593	20.3%
Foreign affairs	61	0.8
Treasury	732	9.3
Defense	778	10.0
Development	177	2.1
Public works (schools, roads)	1,614	20.6
Education	914	11.7
Health and social welfare	685	8.7
Agriculture and cattle	540	6.9
Labor	61	0.8
Communications	281	3.4
Justice	211	2.7
Mines and hydrocarbons	155	2.0
Adjustments	50	0.7
Total	B7,852	100.0%

Local Government

Venezuela's constitution sets up a federal republic divided into twenty states, the Federal District, two federal territories, and the federal dependencies, which are the seventy-two offshore islands. Until the constitution of 1961, Venezuela never actually had true federal government, no matter what the constitution supposed to be in force at the time provided. Since that time, the government has tried to increase the power of the states, but they remain in a weak position. In part, this is due to the great variations in area and population of the states.

The Venezuelan states have the power to merge, alter their boundaries, or cede parts of their territories to other states or the federal government with the consent of the national Senate. Each state is autonomous and equal to every other state, but it must give faith and credit to the public acts of the national government, the other states, and the municipalities.

The states are given the power to set up their governmental machinery and local subdivisions in accordance with the general rules of the national constitution. The states also exercise residual powers—anything that, in conformity with the constitution, does not pertain to national or municipal jurisdiction. In addition, the National Congress, by a two-thirds vote, can give the state or the municipality control over national matters in order to promote administrative decentralization. The states are forbidden to tax imports or exports or other revenue items under national or municipal jurisdiction. They cannot discriminate against goods produced outside their territories, nor can they tax livestock or their products or by-products. Each state must set up a democratically elected legislature. A governor is the head of each state.

The constitution gives the national legislature the power to set up a method of electing the governors, but that has never been done; the governors are appointed by the president. The governor is both the executive head of the state and the agent of the national executive. The governor can be removed by a two-thirds vote of the state legislature.

The states are divided into 156 districts and 613 municipalities. The districts are arbitrary areas for administration, but the muncipalities are endowed with self-governing powers by the constitution. Municipalities are empowered to act in "all matters proper to local life," including urban development, traffic, culture, health, social assistance, tourist travel, and municipal police. They have the power to levy taxes on certain property and to receive state or national subsidies and donations.

Under Betancourt and Leoni, yearly conventions of governors have been held to improve the functioning of state governments. All territories and federal dependencies are administered by the Ministry of Interior Relations. Both the states and the municipalities have limited taxing power and receive most of their income from the national government.[11] The traditional centralization of the national government in Caracas helps to keep local government unimportant, as practically all of the central administration is located in the capital city and the regional offices with which local government units would deal are limited in their powers. Thus practically all decisions are made in Caracas.

The Judicial Power

The Venezuelan judicial power is centralized with the states having no part in the judicial process. At the top of the judicial hierarchy is a nine-

---

[11] In 1958–59, when total government expenditures were about B6 billion, the three levels of government spent as follows: national government, B5.813 billion, of which B513 million were grants to the states, leaving B5.3 billion as total national expenditures; states and territories, B570 million, of which B40 million were grants to municipalities and districts, leaving B530 million as total state and territorial expenditures; districts and municipalities, B170 million. See Carl S. Shoup *et al.*, *The Fiscal System of Venezuela* (Baltimore: Johns Hopkins Press, 1959), p. 313.

member Supreme Court of Justice, whose members and their alternates are elected for nine-year terms, one-third every three years, by the National Congress. All other judges are selected by the Supreme Court from lists of names submitted by the Minister of Justice. The Supreme Court conducts most of its business through three divisions (*salas*), one each to hear political, civil, and criminal cases. The Supreme Court also supervises the organization and conduct of the lower courts. Under the Supreme Court of Justice is a hierarchy of regular and special courts. Regular courts include superior courts, courts of instruction, municipal courts, district courts, and courts of first instance. The most important special courts are those dealing with juvenile, labor, military, tax, and traffic cases.

The judicial power in Venezuela has traditionally been weaker than the executive and the legislature. The new system created by the 1961 constitution was intended to strengthen the court system, but not enough experience has been gained to warrant any conclusion. The Supreme Court now has the right to decide whether the president of the republic, the members of the Congress, the Supreme Court justices, and other high officials should be tried. For the president and the members of the Congress, the court needs the consent of Congress, but for the other officials the court can try and punish as it sees fit. The Venezuelan courts also have the power of judicial review and can declare null in part or wholly all national, state, and municipal laws and ordinances, as well as the acts of the executive.

The courts of Venezuela have been functioning well under the new system. In criminal cases, the findings of the court are automatically sent for review to the next higher court, which can order the case retried if the review suggests this step. There is no death penalty under the 1961 constitution; the highest penalty the courts can give is thirty years' imprisonment.

To see that the constitutional rights and guarantees are respected and that justice is administered properly, the Congress elects a prosecutor general, who supervises the Public Ministry.

Venezuela: A Last Word

Venezuela is on the verge of institutionalizing a democratic political system. If this happens, the country will have given the other republics of Latin America a most important example. Venezuela and Cuba have been the two great rivals since 1959, for both emerged about the same time from a period of military dictatorship, both set out to reorganize their economies, social systems, and government machinery, but each set about it in a different manner. Cuba's new leaders tried to use dictatorship and guidance from the Soviet Union; Venezuela tried to use democratic government and cooperation with the other republics of America, especially the United States. Whichever country produces the better life for its people will inevitably be imitated by most of the other Latin-American republics.

Venezuela is not yet a 100 percent functioning democracy, but it has almost reached that goal. The results of elections are respected and those of 1958 and 1963 were fairly conducted. The president remains a strong executive, but the legislature and the courts function independently, sometimes in disagreement with the president. The great infractions of democracy have been the occasional usage of the state of siege and the outlawing of the Communist Party and some of its front organizations, particularly the FALN and the MIR. Yet both of these actions can be justified as defensive, since the Communists and their friends, although a tiny minority, insist upon using terror as a means of gaining power.

Democracy requires an alert citizenry, and Venezuela has demonstrated that attacks upon democracy can strengthen it. The example the Venezuelan voters gave the world when they went to the polls on December 1, 1963, despite the threats of the Communists to shoot any person on the streets, is evidence of that.

A second most important lesson Venezuela has given the world is that underdeveloped nations can change their economic structures rapidly if they will devote their energies and resources to the task. Venezuela is lucky in having a very high income in taxes from the oil and iron-ore industries, but the Pérez Jiménez government showed that large amounts of money need not necessarily bring prosperity to a country. In six years the Betancourt government, by investing its income wisely, was able to improve education and health tremendously, increase manufacturing, improve communications and transportation, and organize a well-functioning government by using the techniques of modern public administration. Most striking, in 1958 two-thirds of all consumer goods were imported, and by 1964 two-thirds were being produced within Venezuela. If Venezuela has been able to do this much in a few years, the hope is held out to other Latin-American republics that they also can transform themselves. Venezuela's change has been the result of social engineering of a high order led by a political party, Democratic Action. Since similar parties are in existence in other countries, they should be able to achieve similar results. It must be emphasized that Venezuela's development also shows that when economic development takes place, it produces new classes and groups whose interests must be taken into account.

The government headed by President Raúl Leoni faces many difficulties. The Communists continue their disruptive activities, but if Venezuela progress as much in the next twenty years as it has in the past twenty, it will become a modern nation-state, democratically governed, the home of a progressive people.

SELECTED READINGS

ACCIÓN DEMOCRÁTICA. *Bases programáticas de Acción Democrática*. Caracas: Editorial Antonio Pinto Salinas, 1958.

ALEXANDER, ROBERT J. "Communism in Venezuela," *Communism in Latin America*, pp. 253–69. New Brunswick, N.J.: Rutgers University Press, 1957.

———. "Rómulo Betancourt, the Statesman of the Andes," *Prophets of the Revolution*, pp. 109–43. New York: Macmillan Co., 1962.

———. "Two Revolutions." *Progressive* 24 (October 1960): 34–36.

———. *The Venezuelan Democratic Revolution*. New Bruswick, N.J.: Rutgers University Press, 1964.

"The Atlantic Report: Venezuela." *Atlantic* 211 (May 1963): 31–35.

BERLE, A. A. "Venezuela: The Achievement of Don Rómulo." *Reporter*, November 7, 1963, pp. 33–34.

BETANCOURT, RÓMULO. *Posición y doctrina*. Caracas: Editorial Cordillera, 1958.

———. *Trayectoria democrática de una revolución*. Caracas: Imprenta Nacional, 1948.

———. *Tres años de gobierno democrático: 1959–1962*. Caracas: Imprenta Nacional, 1962.

———. *Venezuela, político y petróleo*. Mexico City: Fondo de Cultura Económica, 1956.

DRAYTON, GEOFFREY. "Venezuela's Uneasy Revolution." *Listener* 66 (September 28, 1961): 453–55.

FORREST, ALAN. "La revolución democrática de Venezuela." *Mundo del Trabajo Libre* 13 (October–November 1962): 18–22.

INTERNATIONAL BANK FOR RECONSTRUCTION AND DEVELOPMENT. *The Economic Development of Venezuela*. Baltimore: Johns Hopkins Press, 1961.

"It's Hot in Venezuela." *Fortune*, May 1949, pp. 100–7, 150–64.

KANTOR, HARRY. "The Development of Acción Democrática de Venezuela." *Journal of Inter-American Studies* 1 (April 1959): 237–51.

———. "The Development of a Democratic Venezuela." *Vital Speeches of the Day* 26 (December 1, 1959): 102–5.

KUEBLER, JEANNE. "Venezuela: Target for Reds." *Editorial Research Reports* 1 (1963): 189–206.

LANDER, LUIS. "La doctrina venezolana de Acción Democrática." *Cuadernos Americanos* 9 (July–August 1950): 20–39.

LAVIN, JOHN. *A Halo for Gomez*. New York: Pageant Press, 1954.

LEONI, RAÚL. "Un Nacionalismo firme y sensato." *Política* (Caracas) 4 (April 1966): 93–104.

LIEUWEN, EDWIN. *Petroleum in Venezuela*. Berkeley: University of California Press, 1954.

———. "Political Forces in Venezuela." *World Today* 16 (August 1960): 345–55.

————. *Venezuela*. London: Oxford University Press, 1961.

LOTT, LEO B. "The Nationalization of Justice in Venezuela." *Inter-American Economic Affairs* 13 (Summer 1959): 2–20.

MACDONALD, AUSTIN F. "Venezuela," *Latin American Politics and Government*, pp. 419–33. 2nd ed. New York: Thomas Y. Crowell Co., 1954.

MARTZ, JOHN D. *Acción Democrática: Evolution of a Modern Political Party in Venezuela*. Princeton, N.J.: Princeton University Press, 1966.

PAREJA DIEZCANSECO, ALFREDO. "Venezuela: Una Revolución en marcha." *Cuadernos*, no. 86 (July 1964): pp. 28–36.

PÉREZ, CARLOS ANDRÉS, *et al. La Subversión extremista en Venezuela*. Caracas: Publicaciones de la Fracción Parlamentaria de Acción Democrática, n.d.

PORTER, CHARLES O., and ALEXANDER, ROBERT J. "The End of the Pérez Jiménez Regime," *The Struggle for Democracy in Latin America*, pp. 111–24. New York: Macmillan Co., 1961.

POWELL, JOHN D. *Preliminary Report on the Federación Campesina de Venezuela: Origins, Organization, Leadership, and Role in the Agrarian Reform Program*. Research paper no. 9. Madison: University of Wisconsin Land Tenure Center, 1964.

RICHARDSON, DAVID B. "Where U.S. Won and Castro Lost in Latin America." *U.S. News and World Report* 55 (December 16, 1963): 92–94.

RIPPY, J. FRED. "Venezuelan Vicissitudes, 1945–1956." *Inter-American Economic Affairs* 11 (Winter 1957): 73–82.

"The Rooster That Cannot Crow." *Newsweek*, August 12, 1963, pp. 40–45.

ROUCEK, JOSEPH S. "Venezuela in Geopolitics." *Contemporary Review*, February 1963, pp. 84–87; March 1963, pp. 126–32, 140.

SCHOUP, CARL S., *et al. The Fiscal System of Venezuela*. Baltimore: Johns Hopkins Press, 1959.

SERXNER, S. J. *Acción Democrática of Venezuela, Its Origin and Development*. Gainesville: University of Florida Press, 1959.

STUCKI, LORENY: "Venezuela's Alternative to Castroism." *Atlas* 2 (July 1961): 22–26.

TUGWELL, FRANKLIN. "The Christian Democrats of Venezuela." *Journal of Inter-American Studies* 7 (April 1965): 245–67.

VELIE, LESTER. "The Latin American the Communists Most Fear." *Reader's Digest*, February 1961, pp. 65–70.

VENEZUELA, COMISIÓN DE ADMINISTRACIÓN PÚBLICA. *Manual de organización, base legal, atribuciones, estructura, y funciones del poder ejecutivo*. Caracas: Comisión de Administración Pública, 1963.

Venezuela Election Factbook, Elections: December, 1963. Washington: Institute for the Comparative Study of Political Systems, 1963.

The Venezuelan Elections of December 1, 1963. Part I, *An Analysis*, by John D. Martz. Part II, *Candidate Biographies and Candidate and Party Platforms*. Part III, *Final Provisional Election Returns, Presidential and Legislative, Broken Down by Region and State*. Washington: Institute for the Comparative Study of Political Systems, 1964.

"Visit of Former President Betancourt of Venezuela." *Congressional Record* 110 (April 21, 1964): 8346–49, 8361–63.

WASHINGTON, S. WALTER. "Student Politics in Latin America, The Venezuelan Example." *Foreign Affairs* 37 (April 1959): 463–73.

CARIBBEAN

SEA

Certain Islands of the
Archipiélago de San Andrés
y Providencia (13°00'N
81°30'W) and the Isla de
Malpelo (3°58'N 81°35'W)
belonging to Colombia are
not shown on this map.

NETHERLANDS
ANTILLES

WILLEMSTAD

Santa
Marta
Ríohacha
LA
GUAJIRA
Barranquilla
ATLÁNTICO
Maracaibo
La Guaira
CARACAS
Cartagena
Valledupar
LAKE
MARACAIBO
Valencia

CANAL
ZONE

PANAMA

PANAMA

Sincelejo

Montería
SUCRE
CÓRDOBA
BOLÍVAR
NORTE
DE
SANTANDER

VENEZUELA

Turbo
Cúcuta

ANTIOQUIA
Bucaramanga
SANTANDER
Arauca
ARAUCA

Río Arauca

Río Orinoco

PACIFIC

OCEAN

Quibdó
CHOCÓ
Medellín

CALDAS
RISARALDA
Manizales
Pereira
Armenia
QUINDÍO
Ibagué
Tunja
BOYACÁ
Puerto
Carreño

Río Meta

VICHADA

CUNDINAMARCA

BOGOTÁ
Villavicencio
Puerto López
Río Upía

Buenaventura
VALLE
DEL
CAUCA
DISTRITO
ESPECIAL

TOLIMA
META
Río Guaviare

Cali
GUAINÍA

CAUCA
Popayán
Neiva
HUILA
Río Guainía
San
Felipe

VAUPÉS

Tumaco
NARIÑO
Florencia
Río Vaupés
Mitú
Río Orinoco

Pasto
Mocoa
CAQUETÁ

Ipiales
PUTUMAYO

Río

Neg

QUITO

ECUADOR

Río Caquetá

BRAZIL

Río Japurá
AMAZONAS

COLOMBIA
——— International boundary
—·–·— Internal administrative
boundary
⊛ National capital
○ Internal administrative
capital
+++++ Railroad
——— Road

Río Napo
Río Putumayo
AMAZON

PERU
Río
AMAZON

0 50 100 150 Miles
0 50 100 150 Kilometers

Iquitos

Leticia

PERU
Río Marañón
Río Javari

BOUNDARY REPRESENTATION IS
NOT NECESSARILY AUTHORITATIVE

—— 17 ——

COLOMBIA:

Violence in Politics

Colombia is one of the most difficult of all the Latin-American republics to understand. For a long time the myth persisted, as Professor Lewis Hanke put it, "that Colombia represented Latin American democracy at its best."[1] Or as another writer put it, "Colombia is one of the few countries of Latin America that can fairly be called a democracy. Its differences of opinion are settled at the ballot box instead of on the field of battle. Its elections are reasonably honest."[2] This was a widely held opinion, but the "democracy" was terribly fragile, for no sooner was the book containing the second statement published than a terrible civil war began which left more than 200,000 Colombians dead. To try to stop the senseless slaughter, the country's two most important political parties won support for the novel idea that all governmental power should be shared equally by the two large political parties, and some stability has since returned to the country. But its problems are far from solved and violence continues to plague Colombia.

---

[1] Lewis Hanke, *Mexico and the Caribbean* (Princeton, N.J.: D. Van Nostrand Co., 1959), p. 48.

[2] Austin F. MacDonald, *Latin American Politics and Government* (New York: Thomas Y. Crowell Co., 1949), p. 377. One can find innumerable statements of this type. For another example, "Colombia more consistently and over a longer period than any other L.A. republic has made relatively democratic institutions work" ("The Atlantic Report on the World Today: Colombia," *Atlantic*, 185 [January 1950]: 13. Copyright © *1949* by The Atlantic Monthly Company, Boston, Mass. Reprinted with permission.)

A National Profile

Colombia is Latin America's fifth largest country; its 447,536 square miles make it bigger than Texas and California combined. Occupying the northwest corner of South America, Colombia has the Pacific Ocean, Panama, and the Caribbean Sea to the west, Venezuela to the north and east, Ecuador and Peru to the south, and Brazil to the east and south. Roughly diamond-shaped, Colombia consists of two distinct sections. An eastern plain, largely uninhabited, makes up two-thirds of the republic. Its northern part is an area known as the *llanos*, a dry plain used mainly for cattle raising. To the south the plain becomes *selva*, unexplored rainforest jungle, which is part of the Orinoco and Amazon River basins, inhabited by tribal Indians. The western third of Colombia is divided into three distinct parts, a coastal plain, upland valleys, and mountains. The coastal plain on the Caribbean and the Pacific includes areas used for tropical crops and cattle. The rest of Colombia is dominated by three ranges of the Andes Mountains running north from Ecuador. Between the mountains are two river valleys, one formed by the thousand-mile Magdalena, flowing into the Caribbean, and the other formed by the Cauca River, the principal tributary of the Magdalena. A number of islands in the Pacific and Caribbean complete Colombia's area.

Although the equator passes through Colombia, most of the population lives from 4,000 to 9,000 feet above sea level, where it is not too hot. The highest peaks reach more than 19,000 feet and create great obstacles to transportation. As a result, the bulk of the population lives in fourteen clusters, each of which has developed an almost independent life. This isolation is so pronounced that one writer calls Colombia "a nation of city states."[3] The people in the various clusters range from pure European in some to pure Negro and pure Indian in others. The economy varies from region to region. This is one reason the republic has had so much difficulty becoming an integrated nation-state. Yet the variations in the altitudes of the various settled areas permit the production of different kinds of crops which can move in internal trade: cotton from the lowlands to the highland textile factories, etc.

Colombia's population in 1967 was estimated to be 18,700,000, about 60 percent urban. There is a high birth rate and a rather low death rate, which has led to a population increase of about 3.2 percent in recent years. Bogotá is the capital and largest city with a population of 1.98 million. Other important cities are Medellín, 925,000; Cali, 767,000;

---

[3] Arthur P. Whitaker, *The United States and South America: The Northern Republics* (Cambridge: Harvard University Press, 1948), p. 45.

Barranquilla, 547,000; Cartagena, 285,000; and Bucaramanga, 272,000.

Colombia's population is extremely varied, ranging, as Kathleen Romoli wrote, "from sophisticates to savages . . . It is impossible to establish a type by mixing the whole population and dividing the result by nine millions [the population at that time], because they don't mix; you cannot make a composite picture by adding a Motilone Indian to a professor of political economy."[4]

No really accurate figures are available on Colombia's population, but the best estimates are 33 to 58 percent *mestizo*, 10 to 25 percent white, 4 to 10 percent Negro, 17 to 30 percent mulatto or *zambo* (a mixture of Negro and Indian), and 1 to 15 percent Indian.

Perhaps 200,000 aboriginal Indians live in the *selva* and other out-of-the-way areas, completely separated from the rest of the population. Most of the Negroes are found on the coasts, most of the whites in the cities.

Spanish is the official language and is used by all except the aboriginal Indians and some isolated islanders who use English. Roman Catholicism is the national religion and the church claims 90 percent of the population. About 6 percent are Protestant and 2 percent are Jewish.

Colombia has a reputation for being a nation of culture, but the culture is the property of the small upper class. In 1961 about 43 percent of the population were supposed to be illiterate. This is probably too low a figure, because in 1960 at least 1.1 million school-age children were not attending school. Of those over school age, 72 percent had no education or had attended school less than five years; 23 percent had completed five years of primary school; 4 percent had completed six years of secondary schooling; and 1 percent had graduated from secondary school.

Colombia's traditional social structure consisted of a small high-income aristocracy basically of Spanish descent, a small middle class, and a large lower class. By the 1960's the middle class included about 15 percent of the population, with 80 percent in the lower class.

Traditionally Colombia had an agricultural and mineral-producing economy, but since World War I great advances have been made in industrialization. The most important crops in recent years have been coffee, cotton, bananas, cattle, and foodstuffs for local consumption. The mineral production includes petroleum, gold, silver, copper, lead, mercury, manganese, emeralds, platinum, coal, and iron. The country has extraordinary capacity for producing hydroelectrical power and has supplies of natural gas which are utilized. Industrialization was stimulated

---

[4] Kathleen Romoli, *Colombia: Gateway to South America* (Garden City, N.Y.: Doubleday, Doran & Co., 1941), p. 20.

by the income from the export of coffee and petroleum and by foreign investments. By 1964 about 18 percent of the national product came from manufacturing. The most important products are textiles, foodstuffs, cement, tires, steel, leather and leather goods, chemicals, and electrical equipment.

Colombia's production is localized, with each of the clusters of population producing something different. Because of the concentration upon market crops such as coffee, not enough food is produced, and maize, rice, beans, wheat, sugar, and vegetables are imported. Transportation is poor, although there has been much improvement in recent years. Some of the valleys contain people who live from subsistence agriculture; others produce coffee or other crops for the world market. Certain areas are divided into small landholdings; others contain latifundia. Industry is concentrated in and around Medellín; Bogotá monopolizes political power and culture.

Colombia's population has never enjoyed a high standard of living, but the development of industry has improved conditions in some areas. This has made it even more difficult than it had been in the past to achieve political unity, for the differences between the various parts of Colombia were accentuated. Colombia's great problem has always been the difficulty of unifying the area into a functioning economic unit. The modern means of communication have awakened the population, but not all the roads, railroads, schools, hospitals, and other modern conveniences the people demand have yet been built. In addition, the dependence of the economy on the foreign exchange earned by coffee exports has made Colombia vulnerable to the fluctuations of the world market. The development of labor unions and Communist organizations has contributed to the development of much unrest. Basically, Colombia has the possibility of being a rich country. It has many untapped resources. It has vast empty areas capable of being developed, and it has an economy that has been growing during recent decades. Why Colombia has had so much difficulty taking its place among modern nations will be clearer after its historical development has been reviewed.

The Development of Modern Colombia

Political institutions in all countries reflect their historical development, but this is especially true in Colombia, which appears to be the most tradition-bound country in Latin America. Geography in large part explains why this is so. Enclosed by their mountains, the Colombians developed their civilization with little direct contact with other peoples. Ideas came in from time to time from the United States, France, and other places, but in a country with a majority of illiterates new ideas spread slowly and were never completely assimilated.

When the Spaniards first came to what is now Colombia they found a number of Indian tribes in the area. The Indians varied in their cultural patterns from hunting and fishing wanderers to settled agricultural peoples, and because each group had its own system of organization, the conquest of the area took a long time. There was sufficient wealth, however—particularly gold and precious and semiprecious stones—to make the area valuable to the Spanish conquerors. In addition, the highlands were inhabited by sedentary Indians who could be forced to work in the mines and on the farms. Thus a typically Spanish type of semifeudal society developed. On the coasts, where the Indians could not be forced to work, Negro slaves from Africa were introduced, thus adding a new racial strain to the population.

The colony of New Granada, as it came to be called, included the ports of Cartagena and Santa Marta. These were attacked and occasionally captured by pirates or English fleets of warships. It appears as if these attacks strengthened the grip of Spanish Catholicism on the ruling class, for its enemies not only spoke a different language, but were Protestants.

The wars between England and Spain led the government of the colony to impose exorbitant taxes and use brutal methods to collect them. The result was the famous revolt of the *Comuneros* in 1781, when an army of 20,000 enraged Creoles, *mestizos*, and Indians rose in protest. Its location also put New Granada into contact with smugglers and traders from England, France, and the Netherlands, who brought with them the new ideas set adrift by the French and American Revolutions. New Granada's liberal citizens soon joined with Bolívar and his Venezuelans in a desperate struggle for independence from Spain, which was finally won by the rebels in 1819.

New Granada began its independent life as a part of Bolívar's Gran Colombia, which included what are now Panama, Venezuela, Colombia, and Ecuador, but the localism of the landowners soon destroyed this effort to set up a viable political unit, and by 1830 Colombia, including the area that is now the republic of Panama, began its existence as a nation-state. As in other parts of Latin America, independence meant the substitution of Creoles in the seats of power formerly held by Spaniards. The first constitutional structure of the new country therefore provided an aristocratic government. A president and a senate were to be indirectly elected and suffrage was restricted to males over twenty-one who could meet certain property qualifications. Slavery, of course, continued, and life in general proceeded as before. The population at that time was close to 2 million, yet the total vote cast in the presidential election of 1833 was only 1,263, and in 1837 only 1,623.[5] This was to be expected, for the area was completely unprepared for self-government. No flourishing economic system existed; the population consisted of a tiny educated class of landowners and a mass of illiterate peasants and slaves; a crop of ambitious generals had been produced by the long war of independence; and the upper classes were divided between those who wanted a continuation of their special privileges and those who, stimulated by the revolutions in the United States and France, wanted reforms.

Surprisingly enough, the first governments of Colombia were fairly liberal by the standards of the nineteenth century. They fostered education and economic development, and in the term of José Hilario López (1849–53) slavery and the death penalty were abolished, liberty of the press was allowed, and education was made free and compulsory. At the same time, the Jesuits were expelled from the country, ecclesiastical privileges were canceled, and other restrictions were put upon the Catholic church. This early period culminated during the presidency of José María Obando, when a new constitution was adopted in 1853 providing for the separation of church and state, religious liberty, freedom of the press and association, direct elections by universal secret male suffrage, and a decentralization of governmental power, including the direct election of the governors of the provinces and the strengthening of local government on all levels.

But the social system inherited from the Spanish colony could not assimilate so progressive a constitution. By the 1850's two distinct political parties had developed, the Conservative and the Liberal. The Conservatives, animated by Catholic ideology, looked to a continuation of the Spanish social system. They favored centralized government, special privileges for the Catholic church and the landowning aristocracy, intolerance of non-Catholics, limited suffrage, and the continuation of an agricultural society. The Liberals, influenced by the French Revolution and English utilitarianism, especially the writings of Jeremy Bentham, opposed most of these measures and favored federalism, the disestablishment of the church, religious toleration, and curtailment of the special privileges of the church and the upper classes. There seems to have been some regional differentiation also; the southern provinces tended to be devoted to the Catholic church while the areas around Bogotá and the coast were more liberal.

---

[5] Jesús María Henao and Gerardo Arrubla, *History of Colombia* (Chapel Hill: University of North Carolina Press, 1958), pp. 435–41.

After the 1853 constitution was adopted, the Liberal Party split into two factions: a radical group, the Draconians, which vigorously supported the separation of church and state, and a more moderate group, the Golgothans, which opposed this measure. As the Golgothans became more conservative, constitutional government broke down in 1854. After a short civil war, Conservatives and Golgothan Liberals defeated the Draconian Liberals and more conservative government became the rule. In 1858 another new constitution was introduced, reuniting church and state and creating a form of federalism. In 1860 the Liberals returned to power after an armed revolt, and in 1863 another new constitution was introduced. This too was federalist, but it attempted again to weaken the Catholic church and separate church and state. In 1867 a series of civil wars began which lasted until 1877. The type of federalism that prevailed during this period prevented a strong central government from developing, and there was much lawlessness as regional *caudillos* struggled for power.

By 1880 Rafael Núñez, a staunch supporter of the Catholic church, was president. He began political activity as a Liberal but eventually became a Conservative and a dictator who restored the church to all its traditional power. The constitution of 1886, which was introduced during his period in office, has lasted, with amendments, to the present time. In its original form it was a conservative document. All federalism was dropped and Colombia became a unitary state headed by an all-powerful president. The vote was restricted to males over twenty-one who had an income of 500 pesos or owned real estate valued at 1,500 pesos. At the same time, the Catholic church became the official religion and was given control of education. By a concordat with the Vatican signed in 1887 the church was also compensated for all losses suffered under Liberal governments, the clergy was exempted from the country's laws, and ecclesiastical courts were permitted. Thus began a period in which Liberals were exiled, imprisoned, and executed. This led to another savage civil war that continued from 1899 to 1903 and left perhaps 100,000 Colombians dead.

About the time the civil war was coming to an end, the United States began to negotiate with the Colombian government for the right to construct a canal in Panama. Because the negotiations did not proceed as smoothly as certain groups wanted them to, the United States government cooperated with certain financial interests and Panamanian politicians to set up the independent republic of Panama, and Colombia lost one of its provinces. The shock of losing Panama combined with the reaction to the chaos of the civil war so affected the Colombian oligarchy that it stopped its internal fighting and some stability came to the government. As Germán Arciniegas, a Colombian leader, put it, "The two traditional parties reached an understanding whereby they would henceforth discuss their respective programs and personalities without the bitterness characteristic of the romantic and aggressive Nineteenth Century. Further civil wars were ruled out."[6]

With some stability in Colombia's government, a period of rapid economic development began. The government, however, continued to be the traditional type the country had had for a hundred years. Phanor Eder, writing in 1913, stated that in the president's office "Democratic simplicity reigns: a secretary, a chief clerk, and three subordinates are all that are provided by law. In addition, the President makes use of messengers and a soldier or two attached to the palace, but his chief assistance comes through the various Ministries."[7] The government, of course, was not democratic, nor was it equipped to handle the tasks the development of the economy was thrusting upon it.

Although the government and the society were unprepared for the great changes that came to Colombia, outside forces stimulated these changes. The First World War caused a demand for petroleum, coffee, bananas, forest products, and minerals, and millions of dollars of British and United States capital helped to develop their production in Colombia. The opening of the Panama Canal at the same time that a railroad was built from Cali to the port of Buenaventura made it easier to export Colombian products and helped to break down the country's isolation. Scadta, the first commercial airline in the world, was organized in Colombia by German pilots in 1919, and this too aided greatly in knitting the country together.

It was during this period that the myth developed that Colombia was a democratic country. Actually, the country continued to be governed by a small aristocracy, with only a limited electorate participating in the selection of the president. In 1914, for example, 229,003 votes were cast in the presidential election when the population was more than 5 million. In 1918, only 407,258 voted out of a population of 5,855,777. But the relative peacefulness of Colombia at a time when dictatorships and chaos were the rule in neighboring countries deceived many unsophisticated observers. Perhaps, compared with the United States Marines, who during this period ruled Nicaragua, Haiti, and the Dominican Republic, and such characters as Juan Vicente Gómez in Ven-

---

[6] Germán Arciniegas, "Colombia under the New Order," *Current History*, 32 (April 1957): 200.

[7] Phanor James Eder, *Colombia* (London: T. Fisher Unwin, Ltd., 1913), p. 65.

ezuela and Maximiliano Hernández Martínez in El Salvador, Colombia's governments were better, but they certainly were not democratically created nor were they animated by a democratic ideology.

By 1900 the Colombian upper classes had become so firmly divided between the Liberal and Conservative parties that the two organizations had become rigid. Practically all of the Colombians active in politics were either Conservatives or Liberals. One was born into a family affiliated with one or the other, and one accepted the political label as one accepted one's name. It must be remembered, however, that both political parties consisted predominantly of members of the upper classes, and the majority of the population, which was illiterate, had no say in what was happening.

At the same time, the development of manufacturing and the growth of the coffee and petroleum industries started a period of rapid urban growth. As the cities grew, modern means of communication and transportation were growing too, and a mass of uneducated former peasants was available in the growing city slums to be won for the new revolutionary ideologies released by events in other parts of the world. The Mexican and Russian Revolutions and the Latin-American student movement stimulated the organization of socialist and Communist movements and the growth of labor unions. Violent strikes and riots swept the country. One strike in particular seems to have greatly affected public opinion and crystallized opposition to the Conservative Party government: a strike against the United Fruit Company on its banana plantations, which was broken when the army was sent against the workers. This caused great resentment, particularly since United Fruit was a foreign corporation. When the world depression began to affect Colombia's economy and the flow of foreign investments dried up in 1930, the Liberal Party was able to win the election for the first time in the twentieth century.

Unfortunately, the Liberals did not win a clear-cut victory, for they combined their efforts with those of the moderate Conservatives to present a joint candidate, Enrique Olaya Herrera. By this time the two traditional political parties had developed factions so dissimilar that Colombia's party system began to resemble that of the United States. From then on there really were four groups functioning in the two parties. Olaya Herrera represented what can be called the conservative or traditional Liberals, supporters of laissez-faire economics and a states'-rights philosophy that resembled that of the United States Dixiecrats. The progressive Liberals, on the other hand, were in the style of the New Deal. They favored social reform and welfare measures to improve the conditions of the poor, and they were strongly anticlerical. Mixed in with them were trade unionists and various kinds of socialists who wanted radical reforms.

The Conservatives had a progressive faction that favored gradual economic and social reforms through manipulation of controlled labor unions and farmers' organizations. The reactionary Conservatives favored strong centralized government to keep control of city workers and peasants, a Catholic church closely associated with the government as an educational and disciplinary group, and no reforms at all. Thus the lines were being drawn for the intense political struggles that began in 1934 with the election of President Alfonso López, leader of the progressive Liberals.

There were signs as early as 1930 that constitutional government was about to break down. When the Liberals took control of the government in that year, there was sporadic violence from ousted Conservatives. Little attention was paid to it at the time—just some disgruntled Conservatives and hotheaded Liberals taking potshots at each other in some out-of-the-way place—but it was a symptom of what was to come. Another symptom came in 1934 when the Conservative Party officially boycotted the election, claiming that the Liberals were about to steal it anyway. About that time, Laureano Gómez, who was to play an important role in the country's political life from the 1930's to the 1960's, became the leader of the reactionary Conservatives and the dominant figure in his party. Gómez was an extremist of the fascist persuasion, a great admirer of Franco's Spain, and was responsible for much of the bloodshed to come. A minority must act as a responsible opposition if democracy is to function, and Gómez, by encouraging the Conservative boycott of the 1934 and other elections when his party was definitely in the minority, helped destroy constitutional government.

Not much change came to Colombia during the term of Olaya Herrera (1930–34). As a result, the progressive Liberals grew stronger and won the presidential nomination for their leader, Alfonso López, who was elected president for the 1934–38 term. During these four years, extensive reform legislation was passed by the legislature. The constitution was amended to put the government instead of the Catholic church in charge of education, to give labor the right to strike, to declare that private property had a social function, and to give the government the right to intervene in economic affairs by directing production, distribution, and consumption. At the same time a system of direct elections was introduced, income taxes were levied for the first time, and an agrarian-reform law was adopted. The López government encouraged the organization of trade unions and improved education. The policies sponsored by López were not really revolutionary, but they frightened the Conservatives and alienated the traditional Liberals. Thus, when it came time for the Liberal Party to nominate a candidate for president in 1938, the traditional Liberals won the majority at the party convention and nominated Eduardo Santos, who was elected for the 1938–42 term. The Conservatives again did not participate in the election.

President Santos slowed down the wave of reform begun by the López administration, but he did not try to repeal any of the measures adopted during the previous term. The Second World War began in his term and the country had new problems to face. The Axis and Allied powers both had their sympathizers in Colombia, and the struggle between the various political groups grew more hectic. There is much evidence that the German embassy was financing the most reactionary Conservatives, who were vociferously against the United States.

The division in the Liberal Party became so wide that when López was nominated for a second term in 1942, the traditional Liberals split the party and nominated Arango Vélez, a prominent attorney. The Conservative Party, seeing an opportunity to widen the split in the Liberal Party, supported Arango Vélez, but López won just the same.

Opposition to López during his second term was virulent and continuous. The Nazi sympathizers and Spanish Falangists redoubled their efforts when President López declared war on the Axis powers in November 1943. By then López had lost some of his fire for reform. The war had slowed the economy. Shipping was scarce and coffee could not be exported. The shortage of imports created black markets in scarce goods. Graft and corruption flourished. All kinds of personal attacks were made against López. Riots and other disturbances broke out. On July 10, 1944, some army officers arrested López and tried to start a revolution, but when no one supported them they released him. The struggle became so chaotic that López finally broke down and resigned his office in July 1945. The *designado*, Alberto Lleras Camargo, finished his term in office as head of a coalition cabinet that included conservative Liberals and liberal Conservatives.

The 1946 election campaign again saw the Liberal Party present two candidates, Jorge Gaitán, representing the radical Liberals, and Gabriel Turbay, representing the more conservative Liberals. This time the Conservative Party saw its opportunity and nominated a candidate of its own, and the split in the Liberal Party gave victory to the Conservative candidate with 42 percent of the total vote. At the same time the Liberals won a majority of both houses of Congress. The new president,

Mariano Ospina Pérez, continued the coalition government started by Lleras Camargo and continued the same basic policies.

As the minority party, the Conservatives could look forward only to defeat in 1950 if the two Liberal factions were to reunite their forces. They therefore apparently began to use extralegal methods to weaken the Liberal Party. In 1947, however, the Liberals again won a majority in the congressional by-elections as well as a majority of the municipal governments. The Conservative government took even more extreme measures against them. Meanwhile, Turbay, the leader of the more conservative Liberals, had died and Jorge Gaitán became the leader of the united Liberal Party and its probable candidate for president in 1950.

In April 1948 the pseudo-democratic aristocratic government of Colombia broke down completely. The Ninth Conference of the American States was being held in Bogotá and apparently all was peaceful when someone assassinated Gaitán. The assassination so inflamed the working classes of Bogotá that they erupted in a city-wide riot, known as the *Bogotazo*, during which about 160 buildings were destroyed or seriously damaged, including Catholic churches, the National Palace, Conservative newspaper offices, and the homes of Conservative leaders, including that of Laureano Gómez, who had to take refuge in an embassy and then leave the country to escape being lynched by the mob. This was probably the most violent and destructive riot ever to take place in Latin America.

It has frequently been alleged that the riot was a revolutionary attempt by Communists to grab control of the country, but there is little evidence that the Communists, foreign or Colombian, did more than participate in the mob's activities and try to keep the riots going. There is evidence that some of the police joined the mobs, but the army did not. What seems to have happened is that all of the disappointment and resentment by Bogotá's poor, which had been building during years of government inaction, exploded at the murder of Gaitán. Jorge Gaitán was the idol of Bogotá's poor. He was killed at noon on the street in a crowded section. The public killing set off the mob, and once it became inflamed it could not be stopped until its rage had been expended. Other, lesser riots took place in other cities when the news became known. Thus began what was to grow into a chaotic, senseless civil war during which more than 200,000 Colombians were to be killed and hundreds of millions of dollars' worth of property destroyed.

The *Bogotazo* was the great turning point in Colombia's modern political development. The Conservatives apparently were so thoroughly frightened that they stopped even pretending to favor constitutional government. President Ospina Pérez, of course, declared a state of siege and set up a new coalition government to try to pacify the country. But the hate had been set free and the killings went on. Soon it was noticed that the government, the church, and the army all seemed to be on the side of the Conservatives when an armed clash took place.

In May 1949 the Liberal members of the coalition cabinet and all Liberals holding important positions in the national and departmental governments resigned in protest at the failure of the government to preserve order to ensure free elections. When the Liberals won 920,718 votes to 788,662 for the Conservatives in the 1949 congressional elections, thus maintaining a majority in both houses of the Congress, the Conservatives redoubled their efforts to destroy the Liberal Party. Certain officials of the Catholic church helped exacerbate the conflict by continually associating the Liberals with Communists. People were killed daily. Conflict was intensified between Catholics and Protestants, either because of or as a part of the general conflict between Liberals and Conservatives. Protestant churches were prominent among buildings burned. The struggles grew into a civil war between armies as the months passed, especially on the eastern *llanos*.

As time for the 1950 presidential election drew near, it became evident that the Conservatives, although clearly a minority, were determined to remain in power. They presented as their candidate their most reactionary leader, Laureano Gómez, and refused to allow the Liberals to campaign freely. When the Liberal majority in the Congress began to talk of impeaching the President, Ospina Pérez used the army to dissolve the Congress before it could vote on the impeachment. He also dissolved all local governmental assemblies and councils, censored the radio and the press, and replaced all remaining Liberal officials. Finally he banned all Liberal Party meetings. The terror became so great that the Liberal Party withdrew from the election campaign, and on a day in which about ten were killed in clashes at the polls Laureano Gómez won the presidency in an uncontested "election." The government reported Gómez received 1,140,122 of the 1,140,646 votes cast. More than a thousand Colombians had been killed during the campaign.

With Gómez as president, the Conservatives made a determined attempt to wipe out Liberalism in Colombia and reorganize the country into a corporate state modeled on Franco's Spain. Gómez continued the state of siege, and constitutional rights were indefinitely suspended. As the dictatorship became tighter, the civil war became bloodier than

ever.[8] Conditions became so bad that finally practically the whole population opposed the government. When Gómez tried to arrest the chief of
staff of the army, the army took control of the government on June 13,
1953, and Gómez went into exile. Thus General Rojas Pinilla, head of
the armed forces, came to power.

This was the first time in almost a hundred years that the army had
interfered in politics. The people were so happy to see the Conservatives
out of power that they greeted Rojas Pinilla as a hero. He had great
popular support during his first months in office as he relaxed the
severity of the dictatorship, restored some freedom to the press, in-
duced some of the armed guerrilla bands to stop fighting, and relaxed
the pressure upon the Protestants. Unfortunately, Rojas Pinilla and his
associates proved to be extremely incompetent. He did nothing about
making the government more representative; he purged the judicial
system; he and his associates enriched themselves while in office; and
he renewed press censorship. He tried to create a popular base to perpetuate himself in office by imitating some of the measures of Juan
Perón in Argentina: a government-controlled political party and trade-
union movement, flashy economic developments, many of which were
failures, and an elaborate propaganda office. When the more moderate
Conservative leaders began to oppose him, he tried to have the controlled
legislature extend his term in office. The civil war flared up again as the
guerrillas took to the warpath.

At times the violence became so chaotic that the very basis of society
seemed in danger of destruction. Catholics opposed Protestants, Liberals
opposed Conservatives, factions of the Conservative Party fought each
other, and the number of Colombians killed rose to fantastic figures.
Instead of trying to solve the problem, the government spent its energies
devising ways of continuing itself in office. One commentator called the
years from 1946 to 1958 a "tragic period of twelve years of savage civil
violence."

During this period some 300,000 people lost their lives; entire
communities were destroyed and many of these, already separated

---

[8] One example of the kind of law and order produced by the state of siege was what
happened on September 6, 1952, when "mobs" in Bogotá wrecked the buildings in which the
Liberal newspapers *El Tiempo* and *El Espectador* were published and destroyed the homes
of Alfonzo López, the ex-president, and Carlos Lleras Restrepo, a Liberal leader who was to
be elected president in 1966. The home of former President López was two houses away from
the home of the acting president, Roberto Urdaneta Arbeláez, which was guarded by troops
who did nothing to prevent the "riot" some yards away. See, for example, "Colombia: Time
of Crisis," *Newsweek*, September 29, 1952, pp. 53–54, and "Colombia: The Wheel of Hate,"
Time, September 22, 1952, p. 40.

by geographic barriers and an inadequate system of communications, were torn out of the national fabric; thousands of acres of cultivated land were ravished and reverted to a state of wilderness; many untold millions of dollars worth of property were wantonly destroyed. A mere semblance of national life was precariously maintained by an irresponsible dictatorship. The national debt soared to unprecedented heights as a result of ill-conceived and ill-planned national capital investments and the decay of trade and production.[9]

At last a few intelligent political leaders began to meet to discuss ways of ending the chaos. Finally, in 1957, the Liberal and Conservative Parties, led by ex-Presidents Lleras Camargo and Laureano Gómez, came to an agreement to restore constitutional government and organized a "Civil Front" to expel Rojas Pinilla from office. Under the agreement the two parties were to share power equally, with a Conservative, Guillermo León Valencia, as president for the 1958–62 term. When Rojas Pinilla tried to arrest Valencia, a general strike closed most businesses in Bogotá and some other cities and street fighting and demonstrations broke out again. Rojas Pinilla had his tame Constituent Assembly extend his term in office until 1962 in an attempt to present the opposition with a *fait accompli*, but this impressed very few. The opposition was so determined and the chaos so great that the leaders of the armed forces presented an ultimatum to Rojas Pinilla. Faced by this united opposition, Rojas finally gave in and left the country on May 10, 1957.

With a temporary military government in power, the Liberal and Conservative leaders continued their negotiations and came up with an agreement to set up a "National Front" government for twelve years in which the presidency would rotate between the two parties and all other positions would be shared equally between them. This agreement was drawn up as a constitutional amendment, which was approved by an overwhelming vote of the electorate on December 1, 1957. The plebiscite introduced the principles of alternation and equality of the two parties, supported the creation of a modern civil service system, gave the vote to women, and directed the government to devote at least 10 percent of the national budget to education. Because the various Conservative Party factions were now in disagreement over Valencia, the candidate previously agreed upon, the agreement was amended to give the presidency to a Liberal Party leader, ex-President Alberto Lleras Camargo, and the life of the agreement was extended to sixteen years. Thus the new

---

[9] CARE, *Colombia Community Development: A Survey Report* (New York, 1960), p. 1.

system would be in use until 1974, and it was hoped that by that time passions would have died down, the government bureaucracy would be professionalized and strengthened, education and health would be improved, the economy would be developed, and the conditions of the poor would be improved enough so that the country could return to partisan politics without renewed civil war.

During this period of *convivencia* (living together), political life has been very confused as the proponents and opponents of the new system struggle for power. The supporters of the system have won the majority of the votes cast in each election, but the minority has had full scope for its opposition. Large numbers have abstained from voting both as a protest against the system and because of lack of interest. In the congressional elections, a system of proportional representation allows each of the factions in both parties to seat representatives. Naturally, all who belong to other political parties, particularly the Communists, oppose the system. There is some dissatisfaction among Liberals because the party has been winning a majority of the votes in most elections yet receiving only 50 percent of the seats in the two houses of the Congress, and of course receiving the presidency only in alternate terms.

Colombia's basic problem remains, as a government agency stated in 1960, that "Production is still not sufficient to assure even minimum welfare to the large majority of our people."[10] The *convivencia* governments have recognized this problem and created two organizations to deal with it, the Council for Economic Policy and Planning and the Administrative Department for Planning and Technical Services, under whose auspices a long-range plan has been drawn up. The Colombian planners are pushing land reform, economic development, educational improvement, community development, civil service reform, and other measures that it is hoped will resolve the country's crisis. The civil war has stopped, although sporadic violence continues and people are regularly killed by various armed bands.[11]

Some think the *convivencia* is Columbia's last chance to reform its antiquated social structure before a *Fidelista* revolution breaks out. Two fanatical groups, the Revolutionary Armed Forces of Colombia (FARC), led by a leader of the Communist Party, and the National

[10] Consejo Nacional de Política Económica y Planeación, *Economic Development and Social Welfare* (Bogotá: Imprenta Banco de la República, 1960), pp. 7–8.

[11] *The Atlantic* in 1963 reported that "the death toll from the banditry, blood revenge, and protection racketeering in many rural areas has decreased to an average of two hundred and fifty men, women and children a month" ("The Atlantic Report: Colombia," *Atlantic*, 212 [December 1963]: 10. Copyright © *1963* by The Atlantic Monthly Company, Boston, Mass. Reprinted with permission).

Liberation Army (ELN), together probably numbering less than 500 persons, receive support and inspiration from Cuba and other Communist states and are able to keep functioning in the jungle forests in isolated parts of the country.

The FARC and the ELN have some popular support because some Colombians regard the *convivencia* system as only a united front of the members of Colombia's oligarchy in both parties attempting to preserve the status quo. This opinion has also contributed to the development of anti-National Front factions in the Liberal and Conservative Parties.

Despite the opposition to the National Front government and the large number of Colombians who have abstained from voting since 1958, the majority of the votes cast in all elections since 1958 have gone to the factions of the Conservative and Liberal Parties favoring the continuation of the system. The United States and various international organizations have helped Colombia by financing economic development projects. The Peace Corps is very active in Colombia, and there is much ferment as new developments change the traditional pattern of life. On the other hand, the government is forced to resort to a state of siege regularly, and issues "decree laws" when it is unable to get a two-thirds vote in the legislature, as required by the *convivencia* system. Much of the difficulty during the 1960's was due to the low price of coffee on the world market. This led to a devaluation of the Colombian peso and many complaints that the pace of change was too slow. *Newsweek*, for example, claimed in 1964 that only 800 of 750,000 farm families had been resettled under the land-reform program.[12] Others are more optimistic in their assessment. A majority of the people seems to be happy with the system, primarily because it ended much of the violence of the civil war.

The inauguration of Carlos Lleras Restrepo as president in August 1966 gave the system of *convivencia* a new lease on life, for the new president was a much more capable executive than León Valencia, his predecessor. Soon after his inauguration Lleras Restrepo, a vigorous supporter of the Latin-American Common Market, met with the presidents of Venezuela and Chile to discuss measures to solve Colombia's most pressing problems. There seems to be a good possibility that the National Front may hold onto power until 1974. If enough economic and political development has taken place by then, a competitive political system should be able to function.

---

[12] *Newsweek*, July 20, 1964, p. 50.

404   PATTERNS OF POLITICS AND POLITICAL SYSTEMS IN LATIN AMERICA

The Formal Constitutional Framework

Colombia is governed under the constitution of August 4, 1886, as
amended. The amendments, particularly those of 1905, 1910, 1936,
1945, and 1957, have been so extensive that the old constitution is hardly
recognizable.

The 1886 constitution is typical of the idealistic constitutions produced in Latin America: instead of setting up a framework of government, it describes an ideal constitutional system which the constitutional
convention hoped to see develop. The constitution divides political
power among legislative, executive, and judicial branches, but it gives
the executive such great powers that the president becomes the dominant force in the government. The government is asked to respect the
rights of the individual, but the executive is empowered to abrogate
these clauses in time of emergency. Religious freedom is granted by the
constitution, but at the same time the Roman Catholic church is given
a special position.

How the Constitution Is Amended

The Colombia constitution is amended by a relatively simple process,
the Congress being the only body involved. Congress must vote for an
amendment by a two-thirds majority in two consecutive sessions. The
1886 constitution has been amended many times, with regular codifica-
tions in 1936 and 1945. The 1957 amendments were submitted to the
voters for their approval, but this was done because of the delicate situation the country was in, not because the constitution required this
procedure.

Who Participates in Politics

Until the late 1950's, most Colombians did not vote or take active part
in political affairs, and even today most of the population is represented
in governmental bodies by members of the small oligarchy. In the first
century of the republic, various kinds of restrictions were placed upon
the right to vote, particularly the need to be a literate male and to own
property or have an income. The granting of universal male suffrage in
the 1853 constitution brought no real change. As late as 1942, only
1,147,806 voted when the population was about 9,540,000. The great
jump in voting came in the 1957 plebiscite, when 72.3 percent of those
eligible, 4,397,090 out of a population of 14,223,000, cast ballots. Since

then the percentage of those eligible who vote has fallen to a low of 36.9 in March 1964. (It rose slightly, to about 40 percent, in the presidential election of 1966.) Opponents of the National Front claim this is a sign of opposition; other observers think it is a sign of indifference, since the results are predetermined.

All citizens over twenty-one are eligible to vote except the members of the national police, members of the armed forces on active duty, and those disqualified by a court. Women did not have the suffrage until 1957, but since then they have been eligible to vote, and a few women have been elected to the Congress and other governmental bodies. It is hoped that by 1974, when elections become truly competitive, the electorate will have been trained so that the overwhelming majority of the population will vote.

The Electoral Machinery

Colombia has devised one of the world's most unusual electoral systems in an attempt to calm the passions that led to the civil war of the 1950's. Until 1974 all positions in the government service and the legislative bodies are to be shared equally by the two traditional political parties, the Liberal and Conservative, and all executive positions, including the presidency and governorships, alternate between them. No member of any other political party can be elected to office during that period. If the traditional parties develop factions (as they have), each faction can present a list of candidates and the 50 percent of the seats to which the party is entitled is divided among the factions in proportion to the votes cast for each.

Great care was taken to draw up a set of rules governing elections which would give an accurate reflection of the wishes of the electorate. This is not 100 percent democracy, since the Communists and members of all other minority parties are ineligible for election, but since the system was approved by the largest number of voters who ever participated in an election, it must be assumed that the articulate Colombians favored this temporary restriction upon democracy. The votes are counted for ineligible candidates, but none has won a majority since the system was introduced.

The electoral system is intended to be nonpartisan. It is headed by an independent Electoral Court, which must have an equal number of Liberals and Conservatives. The six members are the oldest living Liberal and Conservative ex-presidents capable of serving, the Liberal and Conservative Supreme Court justices of longest service, the rector of the National University, and the manager of the Bank of the Republic. The Electoral Court is the supreme authority in all matters pertaining to elections. It appoints its own staff and canvasses the votes for the president, the Congress, and the department assemblies, and declares the winner for each position.

The chief executive officer of the system, who serves as secretary to the Electoral Court, is the national registrar of voters, who is appointed by the Electoral Court every two years. Under him there is a system of subregistrars leading down to the locality.

Great care is taken to make the system impartial. The electoral officials have free use of the post office and the telegraph system. Voters are divided into groups of not more than 400 (known as a *mesa*). On election day the polls remain open for eight hours and no one is permitted to travel from one precinct to another while the polls are open. After voting, the voter dips his index finger into indelible ink as a further safeguard against multiple voting. Elections are financed by all three levels of Colombian government. The national government supplies office space and services for the Electoral Court and the office of the national registrar. The department governments provide office space, furniture, and office supplies for the department electoral delegation. The municipality supplies a place in which to vote, furniture, office supplies, ballot boxes, and whatever else is needed at the polling place. Each party or faction prints and distributes its own ballots, but all look alike. Elections have been fairly conducted since 1958.

Political Parties

In the tradition-ruled oligarchic society of Colombia, the dominance of the Liberal and Conservative Parties made it all but impossible to organize a third political party. Many attempts have been made through the years, but the only third party that has endured has been the Communist Party, which was able to survive because its motive power came from outside the country. The many factions in the Liberal and Conservative parties may foreshadow the development of a new type of party system, but to date the traditional parties maintain the support of the overwhelming majority of the voters.

Neither of the parties has had a very clear program, since none was necessary. One was born a Liberal or a Conservative and then looked for reasons to uphold the position. This tended to make politics extremely rigid, as it was almost impossible to persuade a follower of one party to switch to its opponent. Generally, the Liberals emphasized liberty and the Conservatives stressed order. Both political parties have appealed to persons in all social classes, and until recent decades there was little difference in their composition. In recent years, however, the Liberal Party seems to have attracted the support of the majority of the workers and peasants. The leaders of both parties have come from the educated and aristocratic classes, with names traditionally associated with political leadership. There have been Llerases, Restrepos, Valencias, and Ospinas in positions of leadership throughout the nineteenth and twentieth centuries.

During the 1960's the Liberal Party has been divided into two contending factions. One, which receives about two-thirds of the votes cast for the party, is known as the "official" group. The official Liberals support the National Front and have been decisive in preventing the collapse of the system. In 1966 the official Liberals held forty-seven Senate seats and seventy-one House seats. Led by Carlos Lleras Restrepo and Alberto Lleras Camargo, this faction has tried to broaden the appeal of the Liberal Party. The official Liberals favor agrarian reform, educational improvement, economic development, and modern public administration. They have been accused of being in favor of reform at so slow a pace that it will never come, but they have succeeded in maintaining the support of the majority of Colombia's voters since about 1930.

The section of the Liberal Party opposed to the continuation of the National Front is known as the Liberal Revolutionary Movement (MRL), but is itself split into two factions over the issue of whether to allow Communists into its ranks. The majority group, which opposes Communist membership, is led by Alfonso López Michelsen, the son of ex-President López. He pushes for quicker reform and tries to be the spokesman for the lower classes. In 1962 the MRL received 19.5 percent of the votes cast in the presidential election. In the 1966–68 legislature, the MRL had six seats in the Senate and twenty-one in the House. The minority faction of the MRL appears to be dying as its members join new extremist organizations. This group, a conglomeration of Communists, *Fidelistas*, and other impatient radicals, calls itself the hard-line faction of the MRL (*Acción Revolucionaria, Línea Dura del MRL*). The hard-liners call for a revolution to liquidate the economic and political power of the ruling class in order to pave the way for radical transformation of the social structure. They refuse to admit that they are members of the Communist Party trying to capture the MRL, but their program is indistinguishable from that of the Communist Party and the only advertisements printed in the group's periodical, *La Calle*, are for Communist propaganda.

The Conservative Party, although it controlled the government from 1946 to 1957, has had the support of a minority of Colombia's voters since about 1930. It is composed of so many factions that it is almost impossible to keep track of them. In the 1962 election, there were three main factions: the Unionists, led by ex-President Ospina Pérez, received 25.7 percent of the votes; the Doctrinaires, led by ex-President Laureano Gómez and his son Álvaro, received 15.8 percent; and the Conservative Popular National Alliance (Anapo), led by the ex-dictator Rojas Pinilla, won 3.7 percent. By the time of the 1966 elections, Rojas Pinilla's movement had grown so much that some observers thought it ought to classify as a new third party. But if it sought to do so, of course, it would be disfranchised under the present electoral system. In 1966 it won seventeen seats in the Senate and thirty-six in the House. Its candidate for president, José Jaramillo Giraldo, received 712,193 votes, 28.3 percent of the total. The Anapo has gained the support of those seeking a rapid solution to the country's problems, including conservative nationalistic extremists and fanatic radicals. General Rojas Pinilla is a demagogue who advocates abolishing the National Front system and the "oligarchy," and ending United States influence in Colombian affairs.

The largest faction in the Conservative Party is the Unionist, which, although it opposed the National Front in 1958, has been supporting the coalition government since about 1960. In the 1966–68 legislature, this group had nineteen seats in the Senate and thirty-five in the House. The Unionist group contains all the moderate Conservatives, advocates of modern capitalism, and a group that advocates the social doctrine of the Catholic church.

The other main factions of the Conservative Party in 1966 were the *Alvaristas*, the *Alzatistas*, and the *Leyvistas*. All opposed the National Front system and combined their votes to elect seventeen senators and twenty-six members of the House. All are extremely conservative and nationalistic. They seem to be shrinking in size, especially as the Anapo gains in strength.

Of the minor parties, the most important is the Communist, which has been functioning in Colombia since the 1920's. It made little progress until the period of violence after 1948 gave it an opportunity to infiltrate some of the guerrilla bands. When Fidel Castro came to power in Cuba, the Communist Party was strengthened by the support of those Castro attracted. In the late sixties the Communist Party split into two groups. One, the Communist Party of Colombia, is pro-Moscow and participates in elections. The other, called the Communist Party of Colombia–Marxist-Leninist, is pro-Chinese and opposes participation in elections. And just as there are two Communist parties, there are two guerrilla armies with Communist programs, the National Revolutionary Army and the Revolutionary Armed Forces. The Communists operate through various front organizations and have some support in the organized labor movement, among university students, and among the professionals and intellectuals of the aristocratic families, but do not play a really important role in Colombia's political life.

Other minor parties include a small Christian Social Democratic Party, which was formed in 1959. The National Democratic Movement was created to foster the political ambitions of General Alberto Ruiz Novoa, onetime Minister of War, but split into two small groups, Popular Nationalist and National Purpose. Ruiz Novoa is the leader of National Purpose. The Popular Nationalist Movement was founded in 1964 by some of the leaders of the hard-line faction of the MRL, but it has no important support.

The Liberal and Conservative Parties will probably continue to hold the support of most Colombians in the foreseeable future. Especially if President Lleras Restrepo is able to make the government function well enough to begin solving the country's most pressing problems, there seems to be no future for the little radical parties. Both the Liberal and the Conservative Parties are well organized, with structures similar to those of parties in the United States. The Liberal Party seems to have the better organization, but both parties function all year round. Local organizations operate in each city, district, and department, and in the larger cities the parties have permanent offices. Candidates are nominated at city, district, and department conventions, which are held regularly. A national convention selects the national leadership and nominates the presidential candidate. The national executive committees have a great deal of power, but have been unable to prevent the continuous creation of factions.

Public Opinion and Pressure Groups

Because real political power has been monopolized by a relatively small aristocracy for centuries in Colombia, public opinion is not the expression of the whole population. The mass illiteracy and poor means of communication have isolated a large number of people, and it has been only in recent decades, with the spread of radio, television, motion pictures, and urbanization, that public opinion has come to be made by a larger group than the small aristocracy. The total circulation of daily newspapers in 1961, when the population was about 13.2 million, was 1,024,830 daily. Colombia's newspapers have a reputation for quality, but the largest and best known, *El Tiempo* of Bogotá, circulates only 280,000 copies. The second highest daily circulation is 174,942 daily for *El Espectador* of Bogotá, and *El País* of Cali is third with 80,000. About 122 magazines of various types are published in Colombia with a total circulation of about 1,072,500 copies. The highest circulation for a Communist periodical is 12,000 to 15,000 for *Voz de la Democracia*, published in Bogotá.

The traditional way to influence the political process in Colombia was through personal contact. The political parties never really succeeded in articulating the wishes of the various groups in society, and the breakdown of constitutional government in the 1940's was due in large part to the fact that the Liberal Party became the spokesman for the urban and rural lower classes at a time when the Conservative Party refused to admit that the lower classes had any right to participate in the decision-making process.

The most important group in Colombia remains the aristocracy. But it is beginning to lose some of its power, and the political process is changing. Formal pressure groups are now taking the place of discussions in clubs and at social affairs, and most of them have been organized by the members of the aristocracy. Prominent are the National Association of Industrialists, the Economic Association of the Friends of the Country, the National Federation of Coffee Growers, the Agricultural Society, the Colombian Association of Cattlemen, the Bankers Association, and the National Federation of Merchants. The social clubs, such as the Jockey Club in Bogotá, remain important, however. The *Centro de Estudio y Acción Sociales* (CEAS) is an educational and action group organized by industrialists, bankers, and intellectuals associated with the moderate factions of the Liberal and Conservative Parties. Primarily a propaganda group, the CEAS pushes the idea that Colombia needs change and fights the Communist Party. It also is involved in action projects, such as the construction of low-cost housing.[13]

The most widely diffused of all groups in Colombia is the Catholic church, which one observer thinks is "much stronger than either political party and most likely commands more respect and loyalty than any past government."[14] Colombia is one of the most Catholic countries in Latin America. The hierarchy has always had a middle- or upper-class

---

[13] See Norman A. Bailey, "The Black Hand," *Inter-American Economic Affairs*, 16 (Autumn 1962): 79–85.

[14] John M. Hunter, *Emerging Colombia* (Washington: Public Affairs Press, 1962), p. 70.

background and the church has always had close connections with the government. The 1942 concordat with the Vatican requires that all archbishops and bishops shall be Colombian citizens, that the president of the republic shall approve their selection, and that they take an oath before him that they will be faithful to the state, respect its laws, and neither undertake anything prejudicial to public order nor allow their clergy to do so. The church is particularly important in the field of education. As Professor Orlando Fals Borda put it:

> The Roman Catholic Church is still, by a Concordat with the Vatican signed in 1888, the moral overseer of national education. This position of predominance has been utilized by the Church: (a) to control whenever possible the content of what is taught, establishing official textbooks for the primary and secondary schools, many of which are authored by clerics; (b) to quell competitors, both lay and ecclesiastical, who might diminish the Church's influence, especially in the rural areas and in the great portion of national territory classified as "Missionary," although the same may happen in urban areas; for example, the severe restrictive campaigns during the Gómez-Urdaneta regime (1950–1953); (c) to exercise influence on educational policy-making through government agencies and councils.[15]

In recent years the Catholic church has become active in efforts to improve life for the people through such organizations as Cultural Popular Action. The church is also influential in the Colombian Workers' Union (UTC), one of the country's national labor federations.

The armed forces, which are so important in most Latin-American countries, have almost always played a minor role in Colombia. Civilians have dominated the government even when the president held the title of general, for the civil wars of the nineteenth century were fought by armies of peasants led by civilian *caudillos*. It is estimated that as late as 1922 there were only 139 officers and 1,500 enlisted men in the entire Colombian army. The Leticia Dispute, provoked by the Peruvian dictator in 1932, stimulated the growth of the armed forces. World War II helped to enlarge them further, and the civil war of the late 1940's and 1950's saw the armed forces assume importance for the first time in the history of the republic. The Rojas Pinilla government, from 1953 to 1957, was the first in more than a century in which military men held the

---

[15] Orlando Fals Borda, "Bases for a Sociological Interpretation of Education in Colombia," in *The Caribbean: Contemporary Colombia*, edited by A. Curtis Wilgus (Gainesville: University of Florida Press, 1962), pp. 187–88.

important decision-making positions. The rapidity with which civilian government returned seems to indicate that the military are still only a minor force in Colombian life. Under the National Front government, the armed forces have been participating in what is known as *acción cívica-militar,* a system of utilizing military men and skills to build schools, roads, and wells, to supply medical services in out-of-the-way places, and to operate an airline in the eastern low-populated areas.[16]

The lower classes generally have been Indian, Negro, *mestizo,* and mulatto, and until the First World War did not vote, knew little about the government, and had practically nothing to say about public policy. In the 1920's, with the development of the economy and the rise of labor unions and revolutionary political movements, the lower classes began to have some influence. Jorge Gaitán was the most prominent spokesman they ever had. Many attempts have been made, especially by Communist leaders, to utilize Gaitán's name as a means of mobilizing the poor of the country, but until now none of these efforts has been very successful. Alfonso López Michelsen has some lower-class support, but it is impossible to say whether this is due to his father's reputation or to his own efforts.

The organized labor movement has never played an important role in Colombian life. The slowness of industrialization, combined with the efforts of political and other groups to use labor for their own ends, kept the movement weak. During the 1960's the unions have been divided into two national federations and a group of unaffiliated unions. The larger of the federations is the Colombian Confederation of Workers (CTC), which is dominated by the Liberal Party. After a long history of struggle with Communists for control, most of the Communist-led unions were expelled in the 1960's. The CTC claims about 200,000 members and is affiliated with the ORIT and the International Confederation of Free Trade Unions. The Union of Colombian Workers (UTC) is also affiliated with the ORIT and the ICFTU, but has been strongly influenced by the Catholic church ever since it was created by church and Conservative leaders in 1946. It claims about 120,000 members. All labor unions combined probably do not have within their ranks more than 10 to 15 percent of the labor force. Most of the members are urban; very few agricultural workers are organized, except for the United Fruit Company employees. It is only in recent years, when the National Front accepted labor unions, that labor leaders have been able to exert significant pressure. Unions are subject to much government pressure and control.

Organized university students are very active in politics, especially

---

[16] See "Colombia: The New Look," *Newsweek,* August 17, 1964, p. 47.

those influenced by the Communists and the Catholic church. Strikes that prevent the universities from functioning are frequent, and most political leaders begin their political activities as students. Regionalism remains an important element in the political struggle, with the more heavily populated areas the most important. All kinds of new organizations have developed in recent years as Colombia develops a more pluralistic society. One interesting group is the Union of Women Citizens of Colombia, patterned after the League of Women Voters in the United States. This is one of the very few organizations in which women of all classes come together to work on their problems.

Civil Liberties

The Colombian constitution contains all of the civil liberties and personal guarantees usually found in modern constitutions, but it also contains a clause permitting the president to declare a state of siege. The country lived under a state of siege from April 9, 1948, to August 7, 1958, and certain areas remained under the state of siege even after that. Generally speaking, the rights of the individual have been respected since 1958, and freedom of speech and of the press has been observed. The history of Colombia contains many infractions of the rights of individuals, and it is too soon to say whether freedom has come to stay in Colombia.

The Executive

Colombia's executive is a president elected for a four-year term who cannot succeed himself. There is no vice-president. Every two years Congress elects a president designate (*designado*), who must be a member of the same party as the president, who fills out the president's term if necessary and serves temporarily when the president leaves the country or is ill. If Congress has failed to select a *designado*, the last one elected continues to serve until it does. If there are no *designados* available when the presidency becomes vacant, the executive power is exercised by the ministers in their order of precedence; if there are no ministers available, by the governors in the order of their proximity to the capital. The *designado* has no duties unless he becomes president.

To be president one must be a native-born Colombian, more than thirty years old and in full possession of political rights, who has practiced a liberal profession that requires a university degree, or who has been a university professor for at least five years, or who has held one of the following offices: president of the republic, *designado*, member of Congress, cabinet minister, chief of a diplomatic mission, governor of a department, judge of a superior court or tribunal, councillor of state, attorney general, or comptroller general of the republic. But no person may be elected president who during the six months prior to the election has served as a minister, justice of the Supreme Court, councillor of state, attorney general, or comptroller general.

In actual practice under the present system, the party whose turn it is to have the presidency sends to the other party a list of several names. The other party decides which individual is most acceptable to it and he is formally nominated. The president for the 1966–70 term is Carlos Lleras Restrepo, a member of the Liberal Party. He receives a salary of 5,000 pesos monthly plus an expense account of 2,000 pesos a month. (There are 16.3 Colombian pesos to the dollar. As in Mexico and Cuba, the peso is symbolized by the "dollar" sign.)

The Colombian president is a strong executive who is granted extensive powers by the constitution. In addition to those powers held by all executives of democratic states, the Colombian president appoints the governors of all the departments and many other officials, and with the countersignature of his ministers, whom he also appoints, can issue ordinances, decrees, and the resolutions necessary for the execution of the laws.

The two great limitations upon the president are the legislature and the necessity to give half his appointments to members of the opposition party. When the president declares a state of siege he must immediately call Congress into session if it is in recess, and the Congress stays in session as long as the state of siege continues. During this period, Congress may ask the Supreme Court to pass on the constitutionality of any decree issued by the president under his emergency powers. The president must have the signature of a minister or the head of an administrative department for all of his acts except the appointment of ministers and heads of administrative departments.

There are thirteen ministers in the president's cabinet, six from each party plus a Minister of War, who is always a military officer and is considered to be nonpartisan. In 1960 a standard form of structure was decreed for all ministries and a beginning was made on the creation of a career nonpartisan civil service. Ministers must present themselves at the sessions of the Congress upon request.

The office of the president is divided into a presidential staff and a general secretariat. The staff consists of a private secretariat of advisers who make studies and suggest actions: a secretariat for organization and inspection of the public administration, which deals with the improvement of the civil service, and a military group to protect the president and keep him in contact with the Ministry of War. The general secretariat handles correspondence and other communications, maintains the archives and a library, provides legal opinions, handles relations with the press and the public, draws up the budget, and takes care of all house-keeping affairs for the president's office.

Not exactly a part of the executive is the Council of State, composed of ten members, five from each party elected every four years by the Congress from a list of names presented by the president. The Council of State must be consulted by the president in certain situations when the Congress is not in session, and the advice of the council is binding in certain matters. A section of the Council of State also acts as the highest court for cases of administrative law. The full council has certain supervisory responsibilities in connection with new public-service reforms.

Until 1958, all government positions were considered to be political patronage, and the new party in power always dismissed most of the old employees. As a result, government employees were extremely inefficient, and a sort of collective irresponsibility was the rule. As one observer described the Colombian government employees at the beginning of the 1950's: "Conspicuous numbers of employees do not appear to be engaged at useful tasks with sufficient regularity to justify the present organization of their duties. Their days are passed in intra-office visiting, reading newspapers, drinking coffee, and looking out of windows."[17]

One result of the poor quality of public administration in Colombia was a general distrust of government. This led the legislature to set up through the years a number of semipublic agencies that function outside of the ministerial structure of government. Many of these, although financed by taxes, function as completely independent agencies, and all are little controlled by the government. In the early 1950's Caldwell found nineteen of these semi-autonomous agencies, including financial organizations, banks, economic development agencies, and agricultural agencies. By 1961 the number had grown to forty-eight.[18]

To improve the public service, under the 1957 constitutional amendment for parity of the two parties, Conservatives were discharged until each party had 50 percent of the jobs. In 1958 a law was finally passed setting up a career civil service and a start was made in professionalizing the governmental bureaucracy. Specialists in public administration were supplied by the United Nations and a national Civil

---

[17] Lynton K. Caldwell, "Technical Assistance and Administrative Reform in Colombia," *American Political Science Review*, 47 (June 1953): 503.

[18] A list of the "public corporations" can be found in *Manual de organización de la rama ejecutiva del poder público nacional* (Bogotá: Imprenta Nacional, 1961), pp. 4–6.

Service Commission was set up to recruit, classify, train, and control the civil service. Under the new system all government employees are chosen by examination, and no employee is permitted to participate in partisan political activity.

The 1963 budget provided 4,205,506 pesos to finance the Civil Service Commission. This sum paid for ninety-six employees and allowed 1.5 million pesos to finance and develop the Higher School of Public Administration, which opened its doors in 1961. There is much hope the new school will, through in-service training, help to improve the public administration. Early in 1960 it was estimated there were 240,000 employees of the national, departmental, and municipal governments, excluding police and the military. By 1962 only a small proportion of the personnel had been brought into the career service. Most of the employees are organized into the Federation of Government Employees.

The Legislative Power

Colombia's legislative power rests in the Congress, consisting of the Senate and the House of Representatives, both directly elected by the voters. The Senate is composed of one member for each 190,000 inhabitants plus one for any fraction of not less than 95,000. The department is used as the administrative unit in electing senators, but no department is to have less than three. To give each of the parties half of the senators in each department, one is added whenever the quota of senators is an odd number; thus in 1966 there were 106 senators, with the smallest departments having 4 and the largest 12. If more than one list is presented from the same party in a department in which the party gets more than two seats in the Senate, the seats are shared by the competing factions by a system of proportional representation. Thus, in the Senate sitting in 1964, of the 53 Liberals about one-fourth belonged to the MRL faction; of the 53 Conservatives, the majority were from the Ospina faction and the minority from the party's other two factions. The senators serve four-year terms and can be reelected indefinitely.

To be a senator one must be a Colombian by birth with full citizenship rights, over thirty years old, who has previously held one of the following offices: president of the republic, designate to the presidency, member of Congress, cabinet minister, head of a diplomatic mission, governor of a department, magistrate of a superior court or tribunal, member of the Council of State, attorney general, or comptroller general, or have been a university professor for at least five years or have practiced a liberal profession for which a university degree is needed.

The House of Representatives consists of 190 members elected for two years by direct election from the departments. They can be reelected indefinitely. One representative is allowed for each 90,000 persons plus one for a fraction over 45,000, except that each department gets at least three. Whenever the department quota is odd, one is added to give each party 50 percent. As in the Senate, the various party factions can present lists and the seats are divided among the several factions. To be a member of the House of Representatives one must be a citizen, never convicted of certain crimes, and more than twenty-five years old. At the same time the senators and representatives are elected, alternates are chosen; thus no by-elections are ever needed.

Together the two houses of Congress make and repeal laws, issue the law codes, and do all those things a legislature in a democratic state usually does. During the period of emergency slated to end in 1974, the majority needed to pass all legislation, both in committees and in the houses, is two-thirds of the votes cast. This can be changed to a simple majority by a two-thirds vote for specific purposes. With the growth of the Liberal and Conservative factions opposed to the National Front system, it became very difficult for the government to get a two-thirds majority. This was especially so during Guillermo León Valencia's term in office, from 1962 to 1966. To avoid the complete paralysis of the government, the president at times has resorted to rule by decree under a state of siege. Of all the arrangements made in the 1957 constitutional amendments, this provision for a two-thirds majority is probably the most unworkable.

Bills can be introduced into either house by any member or by a cabinet minister. Bills passed by the Congress can be vetoed by the president, but the Congress can override the veto by a two-thirds majority in each house except in such cases as are exempt from the two-thirds rule, when an absolute majority can override. If the president vetoes a bill on constitutional grounds, the Congress cannot override the veto, but can refer the bill to the Supreme Court, which must render a decision within six days. If the Supreme Court upholds the Congress, the president cannot veto the bill again.

Congress meets regularly on July 20 for 150 days, but the president can call extra sessions, in which only those matters submitted by the executive can be considered. Each house elects its own officers every two months while in session, a president and two vice-presidents in each house. Ministers, justices of the Supreme Court, members of the Council of State, the comptroller general, and the attorney general may participate in the discussions in both houses and their committees.

A member of Congress has the usual parliamentary immunity. He receives a per diem for each session. He cannot accept any other government post without giving up his seat, nor can he enter into a contract with the government.

Public Finance

Colombia's budget is drawn up in the president's secretariat and is presented to the Congress for its approval. The budget must be in balance and regular revenues proposed cannot be more than 10 percent higher than they were in the previous year. These rules are negated by the use of supplementary budgets. For about twenty years before 1959 there was a deficit each year, but a small surplus of 72 million pesos appeared in 1959.

The income and expenditures of the Colombian government have risen rapidly in recent decades, especially since the Second World War. In 1950, for example, income was 514 million pesos and expenditures 519 million. By 1964 the projected income and expenditures were 2,810 million pesos, more than five times what they were in 1950.

Tables 1 and 2 show the 1961 budget as adopted. It is typical of Colombia's public finance in recent years. As the figures demonstrate,

TABLE 1
REVENUE OF COLOMBIA, 1961
(000,000 Omitted)

Source	Amount in Pesos	Percent of Total
Direct taxes		
On income and property	$1,086	40.8%
On inheritance	55	2.1
On lottery prizes	10	0.4
On land registration and titles	11	0.4
Others	1	0.1
Total direct taxes	$1,163	43.8%
Indirect taxes		
Customs duties	703	26.3
Others	324	12.2
Total indirect taxes	$1,027	38.5%
Fees and fines, including post office and ports	127	4.8
National enterprises (salt, petroleum, etc.)	118	4.3
Financing (loans, etc.)	178	6.7
Irregular income	50	1.9
Total revenue	$2,663	100.0%

TABLE 2
EXPENDITURES OF COLOMBIA, 1961
(000,000 Omitted)

	Amount in Pesos	Percent of Total
Executive		
President's office	$2.9	0.1%
Planning office	3.0	0.1
Statistical office	13.5	0.5
Civil service	4.7	0.2
National security	27.9	1.0
General services	11.4	0.5
Civil aeronautics	5.6	0.2
Police	119.4	4.5
Ministry of Government	32.4	1.2
Ministry of Foreign Affairs	34.6	1.3
Ministry of Justice	53.1	2.1
Ministry of the Treasury	128.1	4.8
Public debt	290.2	10.9
Ministry of War	351.8	13.2
Ministry of Agriculture	80.1	3.0
Ministry of Labor	69.3	2.6
Ministry of Public Health	157.6	5.9
Ministry of Development	146.3	5.5
Ministry of Mines and Petroleum	52.9	2.0
Ministry of Education	300.7	11.3
Ministry of Communications	72.8	2.7
Ministry of Public Works	603.5	22.7
Total executive expenditures	$2,561.8	96.3%
Legislature	8.2	0.3
Judiciary	72.2	2.7
Comptroller general	18.2	0.7
Total expenditures	$2,660.4	100.0%

much of the government's revenue goes into investments, but until comparatively recently no long-range planning was done. Even with the improvements instituted by the new governments of national unity, almost one-fourth of the budget goes for police, defense, and courts. There has been much improvement in recent years, for in the years before World War II only 7 percent of the budget went for education and public health. By 1961 this had gone up to 17.2 percent.

Traditionally, Colombia's tax structure depended upon customs duties. Since coffee was the great income source, there was much fluctuation in the government's income. Before the First World War about 75 percent of the revenue came from this source. Slowly direct taxes were introduced until in 1961 they produced 43.8 percent of the total income. By the 1960's a fairly equitable tax structure had been developed, but there has been much tax evasion by the rich. Landowners traditionally pay little, as they set their own valuation upon their property. The direct tax upon low-income groups is relatively light, with progressive increases in the tax as income goes up.

The Judicial Power

Colombia's judicial power rests in a Supreme Court and a series of lower courts, in all of which half of the judges are Liberals and half are Conservatives. The Supreme Court consists of twenty members, ten elected by the House of Representatives and ten by the Senate from lists submitted to the houses by the president. At the same time, alternates are elected to fill temporary vacancies. In case of a permanent vacancy, new elections are held. The justices of the Supreme Court serve on good behavior until retirement. To be a justice of the Supreme Court one must be a citizen by birth, in full possession of legal rights, at least thirty-five years old, and licensed as a lawyer. In addition, one must have previously been a judge of a superior district court, a prosecuting attorney in a superior district court, a member of the Council of State, a practicing attorney for at least four years, or the attorney general for last three years.

The Supreme Court meets as a body to vote on constitutional questions and to hear cases involving the president and other high officials. It also appoints the judges of superior courts. For other matters it divides itself into sections: one to hear civil cases with six justices; one to hear criminal cases with six justices; one to hear general cases of a certain type with four justices; and one to hear labor cases with four justices. A governing board consisting of the chief justice (the president of the court) and the presiding justice of each section handles the administrative functions of the Supreme Court.

Below the Supreme Court are twenty judicial districts in which there are superior district tribunals, whose members are appointed by the Supreme Court for four-year terms. In each of the twenty districts there are several superior judges, appointed by the supreme district tribunal for two-year terms. Below these superior judges are the circuit judges, who serve in 157 different circuits and are appointed for two-year terms by the superior district tribunal. Below them are the municipal judges, also appointed by the superior district tribunal for two-year terms. In addition, there are special courts for minors, labor cases, and military matters.

The Public Ministry handles the prosecution of those brought before the courts. Headed by the attorney general, the Public Ministry has representatives before each court. The attorney general is elected by the House of Representatives for a four-year term. All other prosecutors are appointed by the president from lists of nominations made up by the attorney general.

The Colombian courts have the power to declare legislation unconstitutional and have exercised this power regularly.[19] As Professor J. A. C. Grant has pointed out, the justices have even shown a willingness to declare invalid statutes they found to be " 'contrary to the democratic spirit of Colombian institutions,' or to interfere with certain 'inalienable rights' said to be 'older than and superior to the state' and hence requiring no specific recognition in its fundamental law to give them a higher place in the legal hierarchy than statutes or administrative decrees."[20]

In actual practice, the Colombian legal system more closely resembles that of France than that of the United States. All cases dealing with administrative law are handled by a separate system culminating in the Council of State. During the 1940's and 1950's the executive "packed" the Supreme Court several times because it did not agree with its decisions, but under the new system of parity for the two parties, relations between the executive and the courts have returned to normal.

Local Government

Colombia is a unitary republic divided for purposes of local government into departments and national territories. The departments are further subdivided into municipalities, which in turn may be divided into *corregimientos* by the individual municipalities, but most have not done this. All local government is centralized, with the most self-government at the municipality level.

Departmental status has been given to nineteen areas, which include about half the national territory. A geographical unit may be granted department status if it has a population of at least 250,000 and has an annual

[19] See, for example, P. J. Eder, "Confiscation of Enemy Alien Property Held Unconstitutional by Colombian Supreme Court," *American Journal of International Law*, 54 (January 1960): 159–160.

[20] J. A. C. Grant, "Judicial Control of the Constitutionality of Statutes and Administrative Leglislation in Colombia: Nature and Evolution of the Present System," *Southern California Law Review*, 23 (July 1950): 484–85.

revenue of at least 500,000 pesos. Departments are headed by a governor appointed by the president for an indefinite term. The governor supervises municipal activities, is responsible for law enforcement, and serves as the link between municipal and national officials. He appoints and supervises the staff of the department. A provincial council elected for a two-year term has limited ordinance-making authority, but the governor can veto its action. Because the poor transportation system in the past made communication with Bogotá difficult, the department officials came to handle many details themselves, but all decisions of any importance are made in the national capital. Table 3 gives an idea of the kinds of things a department government did in 1951, in comparison with the government of the state of New York. As the table shows, departments do spend

TABLE 3

DISTRIBUTION OF EXPENDITURES OF THE GOVERNMENTS OF
CALDAS DEPARTMENT AND NEW YORK STATE

	Caldas Department	New York State
Legislature	0.0%	0.6%
Chief executive	3.3	1.0
Law enforcement	14.8	7.2
Finance administration, including debt service	35.1	9.8
Audit and control	1.3	2.3
Education	23.9	32.0
Health and hygiene	4.3	27.5
Agriculture	1.5	1.3
Public works	9.1	3.9
Public services and general aid to local government	6.7	14.2
Total expenditures	100.0%	100.0%
Per capita expenditures	U.S. $9	U.S. $67

SOURCE: Horst Mendershausen, "Economic and Fiscal Problems of a Colombian Department," *Inter-American Economic Affairs*, 6 (Spring 1953): 79.

large amounts of money. In 1960, all of the departmental governments combined took in 681,519,036 pesos and spent 656,000,668 pesos. This is about a fourth of what the national government was spending at the time. Only 19,855,045 pesos came from direct taxes, the balance from indirect taxes and other sources.

Each municipality is headed by an *alcalde*, who is appointed by the department governor for a one-year term, but is usually reappointed indefinitely. The *alcalde* serves as head of the municipal administration and as agent of the central government. He is also the chief of police. A municipal council is elected for a two-year term, but the *alcalde* must approve or disapprove its acts. The council and the *alcalde* supervise such things as roads, water supply, local schools, and municipal courts and prisons. There is strict control over the municipalities by the central government.

In important villages municipal councils have the power to set up submunicipal units known as *corregimientos*, headed by a *corregidor*, who is appointed by the *alcalde*. All of his actions must be approved by the *alcalde*.

The national territories are divided into two kinds of units, three *intendencias* and five *comisarías especiales*. The officials in both are appointed by the president and there is no local participation. The national territories include the eastern underpopulated areas.

The ineffectiveness of the local government system led to the development of a movement known as community development, a sort of self-help project sponsored by the President's Special Commission on Rehabilitation, which was set up on September 3, 1958. The commission sends into areas a team of specialists—medical doctors, agronomists, engineers, nurses, etc.—whose task it is to stimulate local community projects. Local committees for community action are entrusted with carrying out the projects. In addition, the local committees act as pressure groups to secure aid from the formal structure of local government.[21]

Colombia: A Last Word

Colombia is not now a democracy, nor has it ever been one. The terrible civil war that the Colombian people endured from 1948 to 1957 seems to have frightened enough people so that some real efforts have been made during recent years to solve the country's problems. Yet the situation remains grave, and the Communists and those whom General Rojas Pinilla has won to his banner seem determined to destroy the system of joint government now in force.

Colombia demonstrates how the political habits developed through centuries continue to affect the political system of a country long after the conditions that produced them have disappeared. Colombia today is a far different country from the Colombia of the years before World War II. It has become urbanized, it is rapidly industrializing, and its population has risen so sharply that it no longer is a "small" country. At the same time, the traditional oligarchy clings to its power, illiteracy

---

[21] See E. Gordon Alderfer, "The People, Sí: Colombian Communities Build a New Life," *Americas*, 13 (May 1961): 2–9.

remains a major problem, transportation is still poor, and the eastern two-thirds of the nation's territory remain undeveloped.

The best hope for Colombia lies in the continuance of the *convivencia* system until its scheduled retirement in 1974. If the system can last out its appointed term, the country will have taken its first steps toward constitutional democracy. The incompetence of President Guillermo León Valencia during the 1962–66 period helped to aggravate Colombia's crisis, but the man who succeeded him, Carlos Lleras Restrepo, apparently is much more effective and has more popular support. Meanwhile, the Colombian people continue to live through a period of crisis in their political system as the struggle goes on between the unfulfilled expectations of the masses and the slow development being pushed by the government.

SELECTED READINGS

ALDERFER, E. GORDON. "The People, Sí: Colombian Communities Build a New Life." *Americas* 13 (May 1961): 2–9.

ALEXANDER, ROBERT J. "Communism in Colombia," *Communism in Latin America*, pp. 243–53. New Brunswick, N.J.: Rutgers University Press, 1957.

"The Atlantic Report: Colombia." *Atlantic* 212 (December 1963): 10, 13, 14, 16, 18.

"The Atlantic Report on the World Today: Colombia." *Atlantic* 185 (January 1950): 13, 15–16.

BAILEY, NORMAN A. "The Black Hand." *Inter-American Economic Affairs* 16 (Autumn 1962): 79–85.

CALDWELL, LYNTON K. "Technical Assistance and Administrative Reform in Colombia." *American Political Science Review* 47 (June 1953): 494–510.

CÁRDENAS GARCÍA, JORGE. *El Frente Nacional y los partidos políticos.* Tunja, Col.: Imprenta Deptal, 1958.

CARE. *Colombia Community Development: A Survey Report.* New York, 1960.

COLOMBIA, SECRETARÍA DE ORGANIZACIÓN E INSPECCIÓN DE LA ADMINISTRACIÓN PÚBLICA, OFICINA DE ORGANIZACIÓN Y MÉTODOS. *Manual de Organización de la Rama Ejecutiva del Poder Público Nacional.* Bogotá: Imprenta Nacional, 1961.

"Colombia Stamping Out la Violencia." *Time*, March 13, 1964, pp. 40–42.

DIX, ROBERT H. *Colombia: The Political Dimensions of Change.* New Haven: Yale University Press, 1967.

ELÍAS DE TEJADA, FRANCISCO. "Trayectoria del pensamiento político colombiano." *Revista de la Universidad del Cauca* (Popayán, Col.) 13 (May 1950): 39–65.

FALS BORDA, ORLANDO. "Violence and the Break-up of Tradition in Colombia." In *Obstacles to Change in Latin America*, edited by Claudio Veliz. New York: Oxford University Press, 1965.

FOREIGN AREAS STUDIES DIVISION, SPECIAL OPERATIONS RESEARCH OFFICE, THE AMERICAN UNIVERSITY. *U.S. Army Area Handbook for Colombia.* Department of the Army pamphlet no. 550–26, 2nd ed. Washington: U.S. Government Printing Office, 1964.

FRIEDE, JUAN. "El Problema indígena en Colombia." *América Indígena* (Mexico) 17 (October 1957): 293–318.

GIBSON, WILLIAM MARION. *The Constitutions of Colombia.* Durham, N.C.: Duke University Press, 1948.

GRANT, J. A. C. "Judicial Control of the Constitutionality of Statutes and Administrative Legislation in Colombia: Nature and Evolution of the Present System." *Southern California Law Review* 23 (July 1950): 484–504.

GUZMÁN CAMPOS, GERMÁN; FALS BORDA, ORLANDO; and UMAÑA LUNA, EDUARDO. *La Violencia en Colombia*, vol. 1. Bogotá: Ediciones Tercer Mundo, 1962.

HELGUERA, J. LEON. "The Changing Role of the Military in Colombia." *Journal of Inter-American Studies* 3 (July 1961): 351–58.

HOBSBAWM, E. J. "The Revolutionary Situation in Colombia." *World Today*, 19 (June 1963): 248–58.

HOLT, PAT M. *Colombia Today—And Tomorrow*. New York: Frederick A. Praeger, Inc., 1964.

HUMES, SAMUEL, and MARTIN, EILEEN M. "Colombia," *The Structure of Local Governments throughout the World*, pp. 351–55. The Hague: Martinus Nijhoff, 1961.

HUNTER, JOHN M. *Emerging Colombia*. Washington: Public Affairs Press, 1962.

———. "Colombia: A Tarnished Showcase." *Current History* 51 (November 1966): 276–83, 309.

JOINT TAX PROGRAM. *Fiscal Survey of Colombia*. Baltimore: Johns Hopkins Press, 1965.

MacDONALD, AUSTIN F. "Colombia," *Latin American Politics and Government*, pp. 384–418. 2nd ed. New York: Thomas Y. Crowell Co., 1954.

MENDERSHAUSEN, HORST. "Economic and Fiscal Problems of a Colombian Department." *Inter-American Economic Affairs* 6 (Spring 1953): 49–89.

SANTA, EDUARDO. *Nos duele Colombia*. Bogotá: Ediciones Tercer Mundo, 1962.

———. *Sociología política de Colombia*. Bogotá: Ediciones Tercer Mundo, 1964.

TOTH, CSANAD. *Colombian Election Factbook March–May, 1966*. Washington: Institute for the Comparative Study of Political Systems, 1966.

U.S. DEPARTMENT OF LABOR. *Labor in Colombia*. Bureau of Labor Statistics report no. 222. Washington: U.S. Government Printing Office, 1962.

WHITAKER, ARTHUR P. "Colombia: A Nation of City States," *The United States and South America: The Northern Republics*, pp. 45–58, 85–91, 197–202. Cambridge: Harvard University Press, 1948.

WILLIAMSON, ROBERT C. "Toward a Theory of Political Violence: The Case of Rural Colombia." *Western Political Quarterly* 18 (March 1965): 35–44.

GALAPAGOS ISLANDS
0   50   100 Miles
0 50 100 Kilometers
Pacific Ocean

Fernandina
I. San Salvador
Santa Cruz
Isla Isabela
I. Santa María
I. San Cristóbal

92   90   89

COLOMBIA

Pasto

Pan American Highway

San Lorenzo

Esmeraldas

ESMERALDAS

Río Mira

CARCHI

Tulcán

Río Esmeraldas

Río Putumayo

Río San Miguel

IMBABURA

Ibarra

Río Güepi

PACIFIC

OCEAN

PICHINCHA

QUITO

Papallacta

NAPO

Río Napo

Río Aguarico

Flavio Alfaro

Santo Domingo

Río Chinchipe

Río Daule

MANABÍ

Bahía de Caráquez

Chone

Tena

Nuevo Rocafuerte

Río Cononaco

Manta

COTOPAXI

Latacunga

ISLA LA PLATA

Portoviejo

Quevedo

Jipijapa

Ambato

TUNGURAHUA

Río Nushino

Puyo

Río Curaray

LOS RÍOS

BOLÍVAR

Guaranda

PASTAZA

Babahoyo

Riobamba

CHIMBORAZO

Daule

GUAYAS

Santa Elena

Guayaquil

Alfaro

Macas

Salinas

Río Pastaza

PERU

Playas

CAÑAR

MORONA-SANTIAGO

ISLA PUNÁ

Azogues

GULF OF GUAYAQUIL

Cuenca

Río Tigre

AZUAY

Río Santiago

Machala

Río Zamora

Pasaje

Pan American Hwy.

EL ORO

Tumbes

Piedras

Río Tumbes

Río Chira

LOJA

Loja

Zamora

PERU

Macará

ZAMORA-CHINCHIPE

Talara

Río Marañón

Sullana

Río Zanchipe

ECUADOR
—— International boundary
—·— Provincia boundary
⊛ National capital
○ Provincia capital
+++ Railroad
—— Road

0   50   100 Miles
0   50   100 Kilometers

──18──

ECUADOR:

The Politics of Regionalism

Ecuador emerged as an independent state in 1830. Since in its previous history it had never been an integrated political unit, it did not become one by assuming the status of an independent republic. Split by its mountains into varied geographical sections, populated by groups of people who had never had any unifying factor to knit them together, Ecuador grew continuously smaller as its neighbors took control of parts of the territory it claimed, and at least half its population lived a self-sufficient life untouched by Ecuadorian nationality. Since World War I great strides have been taken, but Ecuador still has a long way to go before it becomes an integrated nation-state.

A National Profile

Ecuador, South America's second smallest country, is located on the west coast of the continent between Colombia and Peru. Its 111,168 square miles include many contrasting varieties of topography and climate. Two chains of the Andes Mountains run from north to south, demarcating three distinct zones. On the coast an extremely fertile alluvial plain from 12 to 100 miles wide includes just over a quarter of the territory and about 46 percent of the population. Cut by numerous rivers flowing down from the mountains, the coastal region produces oil and many crops for the world market. Here is located the country's largest city, Guayaquil. Running parallel to the coast are two Andean chains with peaks reaching more than 20,000 feet above sea level. Between the two

427

ranges of mountains, which are twenty-five to forty miles apart, are valleys from 7,800 to 9,500 feet above sea level. This area, known in Ecuador as the sierra, makes up about a third of the country's area and is inhabited by about 51 percent of the population. It produces Temperate Zone crops for domestic consumption and contains Quito, the capital of the republic. To the east of the mountains lies Ecuador's *oriente*, about half of the country's territory, containing 0.017 percent of the population, a tropical jungle where many of the tributaries of the Amazon River have their origin. This area is not under the effective control of Ecuador. The fourth part of the country is the archipelago of Colón, more commonly known as the Galápagos Islands, lying about 580 miles off the coast, with a total area of about 3,000 square miles and 0.0005 percent of the population.

The differences between the four parts of Ecuador are enormous. Each has a different kind of population, a different kind of economic system, a different kind of climate, even a different kind of flora and fauna. It is these differences that have made it so difficult to transform Ecuador into an integrated nation-state. One observer writes:

> I found the counterpart of the Dyaks of Borneo in the Ecuadorian *Oriente*; the music-loving, voodoo-invoking Negroes of Africa in Esmeraldas; Tibetan-like herders, sitting at the foot of Chimborazo; and Spanish monks praying in the Quito churches; in fact I found in Ecuador a replica in miniature of many of the things I have seen in my years of travel.[1]

For all practical purposes, however, Ecuador consists only of the coast and the sierra. The total population in mid-1966 was 5,110,000. Only about 80,000 lived in the *oriente*, most of them indigenous Indians, and in the Galápagos Islands the census takers counted only 2,412 inhabitants in 1962. In the same year 2,362,678 lived in the sierra, 2,138,347 on the coast. The majority of the Ecuadorians are rural; only a trifle more than 35 percent live in the urban areas. Guayaquil, the chief port, had a population estimated at 680,000 in 1962; Quito, the capital, had 420,000; Cuenca, 64,000; Ambato, 43,000; Riobamba, 40,000. The population has grown rapidly in recent years, from 3,202,757 at the country's first census in 1950 to the 4,581,476 counted at the second census in 1962 to the 5,326,000 estimated by the United Nations in 1966. The density is 25.12 persons per square kilometer on the coast and 35.39 persons per square kilometer in the sierra.

No really accurate figures are available on ethnic composition, but it

---

[1] Rolf Blomberg, ed., *Ecuador, Andean Mosaic* (Stockholm: Hugo Gebers Förlag, 1952), p. 5.

is estimated that about 10 percent are white, 41 percent *mestizo*, 39 percent Indian, and 10 percent Negro, mulatto, and Oriental. Many of the people of the coast, called *Montuvios*, are a mixture of Indian, Negro, and white. They speak Spanish, dress in European-style clothes, and share more fully in the national culture than the Indians of the sierra and the *oriente*. Many of the highland Indians speak Quechua, and the jungle Indians use their indigenous languages.

The majority of the Ecuadorians are Roman Catholic and Ecuador has been one of the more devoutly Catholic countries of Latin America since colonial days. Church and state have been separated, however, since the end of the nineteenth century, and all religions operate freely. There are only a few Protestants, but Protestant missionaries operate one of the world's most powerful radio stations, *La Voz de los Andes* (The Voice of the Andes), near Quito. Despite their activity over many decades, the various Protestant sects have won few recruits.

Ecuador is basically an agricultural country, but its economy, like everything else, is bifurcated. Generally speaking, the coastal agriculture is of the plantation type, with a chronic shortage of labor and much good soil, while the sierra agriculture is semifeudal and still shows the influence of the Spanish latifundia. (The Catholic church and the national goverment are the two largest landowners in the country.) Ecuador's agricultural system has traditionally been backward, and it is estimated that less than 5 percent of the total area is under cultivation with another 5 percent used for natural or artificial pasture. In 1954 almost 82 percent of Ecuador's farms included within their boundaries only 14.4 percent of the farmland, while 0.66 percent of the farms, the large ones, contained 54.4 percent of the farmland. Another computation based on the government's figures showed that in 1959 there were 344,234 farms in Ecuador, of which 1,369 (0.4 percent) were larger than 500 *hectares* each and contained 45.1 percent of the agricultural land. This situation creates terrific pressure for a change in the system of landownership.

The most important crops are maize, barley, wheat, rye, potatoes, lentils, and kidney beans in the sierra, and rice, sugar, coffee, cacao, castor beans, bananas, and cotton on the coast. Another important coastal crop is the *toquilla* palm, which supplies the straw from which the famous "Panama" hats are made. The most important exports are bananas, coffee, cacao, and tropical products such as balsa wood and cinchona bark. Agricultural methods are generally primitive, and many projects have been started to teach the farmers modern methods of cultivation.

Ecuador has never been an important mineral-producing country, despite its mountains. Some gold, silver, and petroleum have been exploited, and it is known that there are some coal, manganese, copper, sulfur, and other minerals. Manufacturing is limited and most things are made in small workshops or the home. Hats and certain medicines are exported, but almost all other manufactured products are consumed by the internal market. The most important products, in addition to hats and medicine, are textiles (the leading industry, which utilized about 70 percent of all industrial workers), cement, beer, flour, sugar, edible fats, and soft drinks.

One of Ecuador's problems all through its history has been the difficulty of joining its various parts together. The mountains and river gorges make the construction of good roads and railroads very expensive and difficult. Guayaquil and Quito were united by rail in 1908, and a railroad from Quito to a port at San Lorenzo on the north coast was completed in 1957. It is hoped that the railroad will eventually open up much new land for settlement.

Ecuador's per capita income in 1961 was computed to be only $222.70 U.S. a year, slightly over half the average for all of Latin America. Fifty-three percent of the labor force was in agriculture and only 19 percent in industry in 1960. The annual average gross domestic product rose about 4.7 percent from 1950 to 1960, and 4.2 percent from 1960 to 1965. From 1950 to 1962 the average population growth was 3.2 percent.

In 1957 the Central Bank of Ecuador computed that 1 percent of the population was in the upper class and received 51 percent of the country's total personal income; about 24 percent of the population was in the middle class and received about 32 percent of the total personal income; the rest of the population, 75 percent, was considered to be in the lower class and received 17 percent of the country's total personal income. What this means in real money is that the small farmers, fishermen, miners, and industrial workers and their families had a per capita annual income of 1,615 sucres ($106.59 U.S. at the 1957 rate of exchange) while the white-collar workers, merchants, small manufacturers, and medium-sized farmers and their dependents had a per capita income of about S3,133 ($206.78 U.S.) and the small upper class had a per capita income of S33,156 ($2,188.30 U.S.).

Ecuador's great problem is that progress toward a better life for the masses has been infinitesimal at a time when the population has been roused from its acceptance of the traditional organization of society by the modern means of transportation and communication. Ecuador is basically a rich country and would have great prospects if it could only reorganize its economic and political systems. That it has made a tiny bit of progress during the years since 1948 gives at least faint hope that it may eventually be able to overcome its past.

The Development of Modern Ecuador

Ecuador has had tremendous difficulty in establishing a stable governmental system of any kind because the country is an artificial aggregate of varied elements, both physical and human, which no one has ever been able to unify. When the Spaniards arrived in what is now Ecuador, they found it inhabited by a number of Indian tribes, many of which had no relations with the others. Not much is known about the original inhabitants of the area, but interesting objects made of gold, stone, and other materials have been found which demonstrate some cultural advancement by some of the tribes. Yet these Indians never reached the cultural levels of the Incas to the south and the Mayas to the north. Sometime after 1000 A.D. the highland area of present-day Ecuador seems to have become organized into two political units. Some writers have given the name "Kingdom of Quito" to the northern area, but there is little information about its political system and there is great doubt that the Kingdom of Quito ever controlled all of what is now Ecuador, or even all of what is now Ecuador's sierra.

About the middle of the fifteenth century the Inca armies began to move into the area of present-day Ecuador, and by the end of the century had incorporated the sierra and part of the coastal region into their empire of Tahuantínsuyu. The Inca armies never completely subjugated all of the Indians, particularly those on the eastern plains and some of the coastal tribes, and Inca rule did not continue long enough to implant Inca culture firmly. The Incas did give those who lived in the sierra some feeling of unity, however. This was accentuated when, in 1526, Huaina Capac, the Inca emporer, died and divided his empire, leaving the Ecuadorian part to his son Atahualpa and the area to the south to his son Huáscar.

A war between Atahualpa and Huáscar ended with victory for the armies of Atahualpa, but weakened both sides just as the Spanish *conquistadores* arrived in Peru. Pizarro and his soldiers murdered Atahualpa in 1533, and his centralized empire was quickly taken over by the Spanish. The northern region was conquered in a series of ruthless expeditions. In 1534 the city of Quito was established, in 1535 Guayaquil was founded, and in 1563 the area now known as Ecuador became a royal *audiencia*, usually subject to the viceroy in Lima, but at other times subject to the viceroy in Bogotá. The differences among the Indians of the area were early manifested. On the sierra the Indians were traditionally agricultural and proved to be docile. The climate was mild here, so this became the center of Spanish power. In the present-day *oriente*, as one writer put it, "time and again the Indians burnt down the houses and killed every single inhabitant, until in many regions of the *oriente* all efforts at colonization were finally abandoned. Along the coast, the Indians showed no greater willingness to be subjugated by and work for the white men."[2] And so the *oriente* was abandoned to its Indian owners, and basically it has remained outside the effective control of Quito ever since. On the coast, however, the development was different. Guayaquil was the best harbor in western South America and the Spaniards needed it. When the coastal Indians refused to work for the Spaniards, they were killed or pushed into the coastal jungles and Negroes from Africa were imported to work the plantations that were being developed. Thus on the coast a new human type developed, the *Montuvio*, a mixture of white, Indian, and Negro.

The sierra with its docile Indians permitted the establishment of the typical semifeudal system of the Spaniards, with a small ruling class of whites and a mass of Indian serfs. Catholicism seems to have been deeply impregnated into this society, and Quito became the home of elaborate churches.

> By the end of the seventeenth century Quito counted ten huge churches, about an equal number of convents and monasteries, and two big educational establishments, all built by the various religious orders so solidly that they are still in use, and within an area of only about half a square mile. In addition numerous chapels were constructed by private initiative. The town's population was then estimated at 25,000.[3]

The population of what is now Ecuador was probably very low during colonial days, as it is estimated that the total number of inhabitants in 1825 was only 558,000. The isolation of the area seems to have contributed to the development of a rather stable society, and the most exciting events of colonial days were probably the earthquakes and volcanic eruptions that occurred from time to time. After 1770 there were some Indian uprisings in parts of the sierra, but these were always put down, although they caused much loss of life and property destruction. Quito was one of the first places in which opposition to Spanish domination appeared, but it was not until 1822, when Venezuelan, Colombian, and Peruvian troops commanded by General Sucre joined the struggle, that independence came. For eight years after that Ecuador was part of Bolívar's Gran Colombia. It seceded in 1830 to become an independent republic.

[2] Lilo Linke, *Ecuador, Country of Contrasts*, 3rd ed. (London: Oxford University Press, 1960), p. 19.
[3] *Ibid.*, p. 18.

Independence was the beginning of a century of chaotic struggles during which the country changed little. The Spanish colonial society had done nothing to prepare Ecuador for self-government. The first constitution adopted, as in the other Latin-American republics, created a presidential system with a division of powers among the three traditional branches of government. In addition, it provided for decentralization into a confederation of the departments of Quito, Guayaquil, and Cuenca. Since no one wanted to or had any idea of how to operate a government under this constitution, the result was a dictatorship under the first president, General Juan José Flores, an almost illiterate Venezuelan who had come to Ecuador in 1824 as Bolívar's military representative.

During the 138 years from 1830 to 1968 Ecuador had seventeen constitutions, at least twenty-three unconstitutional changes in the government, including three revolutions, and an uncounted number of attempted coups d'état. One computation puts the number of executives (presidents and juntas) during the 138 years at 69, or an average of 2 years for each executive. During these years there were only seven honest elections, those of 1875, 1931, 1933, 1948, 1952, 1956, and 1960. The social structure continued about as it was during colonial days, with a small group of rich and educated holding all power and the masses illiterate, agricultural, indifferent to what the political leaders were doing. Until 1861 elections were indirect; after that date the suffrage was reserved to the literate, and the overwhelming majority were thus disfranchised. In 1933, for example, in what is considered to be one of the few really free elections ever held in Ecuador, about 52,500 votes were cast when the country's population was close to 3 million.

In addition to all the problems the other former colonies of Spain had in establishing stable government, Ecuador's ruling class, a tiny fraction of the total population, was itself split between those who lived on the coast and those who lived in the sierra. The coastal ruling class, based in Guayaquil, was more in contact with the world. But because the capital was located in Quito, the coastal group was completely cut off from the seat of power whenever the sierra group controlled the government.

Curiously enough, one of the best presidents the country had before 1895 was a fanatical Catholic, Gabriel García Moreno, who tried to turn Ecuador into a theocracy in which only Catholics could be citizens. He fostered the construction of roads, schools, barracks, prisons, railroads. But his greatest contribution lay in his effort to unify the country. As his unifier he tried to use the Catholic church. He brought the Jesuits back to Ecuador, and in 1873 he had Ecuador dedicated to the Sacred Heart of Jesus. But the church failed to serve as the unifying factor he thought it could be, and in 1875 García Moreno was assassinated. He had been dictator for fifteen years.

By the last quarter of the nineteenth century the articulate minority that ruled Ecuador had become divided into two groups, the Liberal and Conservative Parties. The Liberals were strongest in Guayaquil; they were mainly exporters and importers, and strongly anticlerical. They were in favor of free trade and wanted to build up the country's economic system. They were greatly influenced by ideas from France, England, and the United States. The Conservatives were strongest in the sierra and dominated the government until 1895. They looked to Catholicism and tradition for stability and expected the country to continue as it was forever. They were the owners of the great latifundia. After García Moreno's death the Liberals kept growing stronger, and for twenty years they made renewed attempts to overthrow the Conservative governments in Quito. In 1896, led by their great *caudillo*, Eloy Alfaro, they finally won control of the government and made the first serious attempt to organize a modern state. The Liberal governments granted religious freedom, abolished certain of the privileges of the Catholic church, expropriated some of the church's vast landholdings, introduced one of the first divorce laws in America, abolished the death penalty, and completed the railroad from Guayaquil to Quito.

Unfortunately, the Liberal governments failed to do anything to introduced democracy into Ecuador or to revise the semifeudal system of landownership. Elections continued to be based on a small electorate and were strictly controlled. The church lands were not distributed to the Indians who worked them, but continued as latifundia under government ownership; their profits were used for charity and the Indians continued to live as before. Nothing was done about the privately owned latifundia. Economic development was fostered, but the main result was simply to increase the production of cacao on the coastal plantations. Ecuador became the world's largest producer of cacao, but little of the income went to the peasants. Several landowners, however, became millionaires. And so the Liberal Party declined in popularity just as the Conservative Party had done. Eloy Alfaro himself was actually lynched by a howling mob in 1912, and politics in Ecuador continued about as before, with the government the prize that the members of the small ruling class struggled to capture.

The First World War marks the beginning of real change for Ecuador. With the opening of the Panama Canal, the country's isolation was lessened. Cacao and sugar production increased, a petroleum industry was developed, and the new ideas let loose by the war and the Mexican and Russian Revolutions began to enter the country. The first trade unions appeared. In 1926 a Socialist party was organized, which then spawned a Communist party. All these events threw the country into greater confusion than ever. The world depression severely affected the country's economy. From 1925 to 1948 Ecuador knew even greater political turbulence than in the past. During the twenty-four years from September 1, 1924, to September 1, 1948, Ecuador had twenty-three presidents or provisional juntas. For a time it appeared as if the country would descend into complete anarchy as the presidents came and went, ministers were changed with great rapidity, new constitutions were produced. It was at the end of this period that Professor George Blanksten was making his study of Ecuadorian government, and he came to the conclusion that:

> The government of Ecuador since 1830 . . . has been strikingly similar to its predecessor. The institution of divine-right monarchy was modified but not abolished. "Kings with the names of presidents" succeeded kings with the names of kings. The principal "republican" reforms centered around the abolition of the hereditary method of selecting successors to defunct monarchs. The government in Ecuador since 1830 has been something less than monarchy in the sense that no formalized vehicle of succession has effectively replaced the hereditary principle underlying the stable legitimacy of the older monarchy. The resultant chaos is known as political instability, and the monarch in republican dress answers to the name of caudillo.
>
> The "national life" of Ecuador has continued to be dominated by a small ruling class. These "whites" constitute approximately 20 percent of the population of the republic. The Ecuadorean political process rests on a brand of anarchy or chaos within the ruling class. This condition is occasionally referred to by Ecuadorians as "democracy in the Greek sense": a considerable degree of liberty and equality has developed within the "white" group so far as intra-class behavior is concerned. The nation's rigid class system imposes an impressively strong barrier between the "whites" and the overwhelming mass of the people of the country.
>
> Ecuador's "democracy in the Greek sense" has meant a chaotic intra-class struggle conducted by the "whites," an anarchical contest in which the lower classes do not participate and in which they normally exhibit little or no interest. The battle of the "whites" among themselves frequently crystallizes along personal and re-

gional lines, ideological differences usually being a distinctly minor factor. Victory in the contest is typically brief, and the victors preside over unstable and uncertain governments.[4]

To the surprise of most observers, however, the election of Galo Plaza in 1948 ushered in thirteen years of constitutional government. Changes had come slowly to Ecuador, but they had come, and now their effects could be felt. Health had been greatly improved, especially on the coast, and the population had increased rapidly. The cities swelled as peasants flocked in from the countryside. The Second World War had stimulated a demand for certain Ecuadorian products—balsa wood, for example, which was valuable in the construction of airplanes. The spirit of democracy, which spread around the world with the victory of the Allies, found its way to Ecuador. And the man elected in 1948, although a member of the aristocracy, happened to have a sincere desire to prove that Ecuador could be governed constitutionally. As he put it, "I put my ear to the ground and listened to what the people for a long time had been saying and hoping in vain, and made up my mind to act according to their wishes."[5]

Galo Plaza invited foreign specialists to Ecuador to help plan the future of the country. He presided over the first census the country had ever had, public health was improved, roads and schools were built, and the economy flourished. Probably most important in the long run was an increase in the production of bananas until Ecuador became the world's largest exporter; the country took in over $20 million from bananas in 1952. Galo Plaza made one mistake: he had been the candidate of an *ad hoc* group known as the National Civic Democratic Movement, and he failed to turn it into a political party. When his term ended, therefore, he could not himself run for reelection and there was no party to continue his work. The election over which he presided saw Dr. José María Velasco Ibarra, a rabble-rousing demagogue, elected to succeed him.

Velasco Ibarra had been president twice before, and both times he had been expelled from office. He was a marvelous public speaker and the masses adored him, but he never seemed to know what he wanted to do beyond being elected. In 1952 he received 150,000 votes out of 351,000 cast for the four candidates, demonstrating once again how fragmented public opinion was. This time, to everyone's surprise, he was able to serve out his four years without being expelled from office, although he failed to continue most of Galo Plaza's projects.

---

[4] George I. Blanksten, *Ecuador: Constitutions and Caudillos* (Berkeley and Los Angeles: University of California Press, 1951), pp. 169–70.

[5] Galo Plaza, *Problems of Democracy in Latin America* (Chapel Hill: University of North Carolina Press, 1955), p. 31.

In 1956 the voters were again divided into many factions, and again no one received a majority. The new president, Dr. Camilo Ponce Enríquez, was the first candidate supported by the Conservative Party to be elected president since 1896. He received 178,424 of the 614,423 votes cast, and with this tiny plurality took office. Dr. Ponce too served his four years in office, and in the 1960 election Dr. Velasco Ibarra was again elected. The great impetus given to stable constitutional government by Galo Plaza had died by then; in fact, Galo Plaza was one of the candidates defeated by Velasco Ibarra. And again the poor electoral system put into office a president not supported by the majority of the voters, for Velasco received only 373,585 of the 766,834 votes cast.

Velasco Ibarra was no better as president this time than he had been the other three times he had held the office. To get everyone excited, in his inaugural address he denounced the 1942 agreement between Ecuador and Peru and stated that he would refuse to recognize the boundary then agreed upon. He discharged many government employees and replaced them with his followers, despite a civil service career law that had gone into effect. He retired forty-eight top-ranking army officers. In fourteen months in office he had two Ministers each of Defense, Foreign Affairs, Economics, and the Treasury, and eight Ministers of the Interior. And between firings he traveled around the country promising heaven on earth to the masses.

Toward the end of 1961 the government broke down completely. This was the period when the influence of Fidel Castro was at its height in Latin America, and his supporters and opponents organized demonstrations. Riots broke out. Velasco lost so much support that his vice-president, Carlos Julio Arosemena, began to speak out publicly against him. Velasco had Arosemena arrested and jailed. Finally, on November 7, 1961, the army expelled President Velasco. The leaders of the army did not trust Arosemena, who had just returned from a trip to China, and tried to install Dr. Camilo Gallegos, the chief justice of the Supreme Court, as president. The Congress and the air force refused to accept this. Air-force planes strafed army tanks. Dr. Gallegos then decided that he would not take the presidency, the army officers accepted Arosemena, and the Vice-President was sworn in as president to finish Velasco's term on November 8, 1961.

Arosemena proved to be as bad a president as most of his predecessors had been. At his inauguration he announced that he would renew relations with Fidel Castro's government (Velasco Ibarra had broken them), but almost as soon as he had done so he changed his mind under pressure from the armed forces and again broke relations with Cuba, and with two of the east-European dictatorships besides. The Communists began to or-

ganize guerrilla groups in the mountains. President Arosemena seemed to
have no consistent policy. At times he talked like another Castro, an
apostle of instant reform; at others he sounded like a traditional Conservative. To complicate matters, it turned out that he was a chronic alcoholic. His frequent inability to handle routine matters tied up the administration completely. As chaos became confounded, the military
officers plotted a new revolution. The end came when President Arosemena attended a state banquet drunk and attacked the United States government. That night, July 11, 1963, to clear the "besmirched honor" of
Ecuador, the military expelled Arosemena from the country and installed
a junta of four officers to exercise the government's powers. Why could
not the Congress have impeached Arosemena to save the country's honor?
This had been attempted, but although the motion was twice introduced,
a majority could not be achieved either time. There was little opposition
to the military take-over. Three were killed and seventeen injured when
troops dispersed demonstrations the day of the coup, but the vast majority
of the population took the change in government calmly.

The military junta that took office on July 11, 1963, began as all
military governments do. It declared a state of siege, abrogated the
constitution, disbanded the legislature, postponed all scheduled elections, canceled all guarantees of civil liberties, illegalized the Communist
Party, and arrested many Communists. But most unusual for a military
junta, it appointed one of the best cabinets the country had ever had,
consisting of six civilians and three military officers. The Minister of
Development, for example, was a high official of the Inter-American
Bank who was asked to return from Washington to push economic development. Evidently the more intelligent among Ecuador's leaders had
come to the conclusion that only the introduction of basic structural
reforms would prevent a *Fidelista* take-over or a return to the kind of
turbulence the country had suffered from 1924 to 1948. Since the legislatures and presidents from 1952 to 1963 had proved incapable of introducing the reforms the country needed so badly, the junta proposed to
introduce them by unconstitutional means, and with this, apparently, a
majority of the traditional political leaders agreed.

Under the junta the economy improved; the sucre rose in value;
international organizations, including the United States government,
loaned Ecuador millions of dollars for various projects; and the budget
was increased, especially for education and investments. The 1964 budget
was $1,100 million higher than the 1963 budget. Education received 10
percent more, public works 135 percent more, development investments 233 percent more. The tax system was revised and a new income-

tax law was introduced in January 1964. On July 11, 1964, the first anniversary of the revolution, a well-planned extensive agrarian-reform law was adopted. A modern merit system for public employees was instituted. A law regulating corporations was adopted, under which, for the first time in Ecuador's history, a government agency was created to supervise corporations in order to facilitate the accumulation of capital, which would be protected by the regulatory agency. Other programs of the government included a massive drive to eradicate illiteracy, a broadening of the social security system, an improvement of the highway system, and the reorganization of the university system (for this a group of professors from the University of Pittsburgh, financed by the USAID, was brought to Ecuador).

Despite all its efforts, the junta did not succeed in transforming the country. Every reform aroused opposition from small but powerful groups. And since change could not come instantaneously, as time passed, more and more Ecuadorians began to feel cheated. A movement for elections grew. In 1965 prices fell on many of the country's exports. As the government's income from export taxes fell, the junta raised the rate to compensate for the lower collections. This provoked a general shutdown of business in Ecuador as businessmen refused to pay the new tax. The labor unions and the radical students united with the businessmen. The junta managed to survive the 1965 businessmen's strikes by canceling the raise in taxes, but the crisis was on.

The problem was the same one all Ecuadorian governments face. Political, economic, and social development costs money. As the new reform laws were adopted, money was needed to finance them. Some came from international loans, but not enough. The united opposition of the businessmen made further reform impossible. During 1965 and the first part of 1966 the junta tried all kinds of measures, but nothing helped. The junta was finally overthrown on March 29, 1966.

This time the armed forces leadership asked the political parties to suggest a temporary president, and they settled on Clemente Yerovi Indaburu, a wealthy Guayaquil businessman who had been associated with Galo Plaza and was considered a liberal. A *New York Times* editorial described the new government as "a small business, landowning, military elite."[6] Of course this was correct. It was the businessmen who overthrew the junta, and they now took over the government to organize it in a way that would not conflict with their interests.

The Yerovi administration organized an election to create a con-

---

[6] *New York Times,* March 30, 1966, p. 44.

stituent assembly that would elect a president and adopt a constitution. Meanwhile, the 1946 constitution was restored. The members of the deposed junta were stripped of their citizenship for three years and criminal charges were placed against them. Six generals were discharged from the armed forces. Velasco Ibarra came home to be greeted by 15,000 cheering supporters.

Conservative political forces won a majority of the seats in the constituent assembly. This was due in part to a rule requiring citizens to have a new identification card (*cédula única*) in order to vote. It is estimated that about 140,000 people were disfranchised because they failed to get their new *cédulas* on time. In addition, Ecuador has a system in which certain functional deputies are always elected, and nine of the twelve elected in this group were Conservative businessmen and landowners. The Conservatives in the Assembly elected Otto Arosemena Gómez interim president pending general elections in 1968, and he took office on November 16, 1966. A new constitution went into effect on May 25, 1967.

On June 2, 1968, Ecuador's voters went to the polls and again elected José María Velasco Ibarra, by that time seventy-five years old, for his fifth term as president. In his victory statement Velasco promised to "strengthen democracy" and to increase the production of bananas. One of his nameless supporters offered this explanation of Velasco's popularity, and incidentally of the popular mood that is so disheartening to those who hope for progress in Ecuador: "You see, unless you belong to the group that has always run things, you don't have much of a chance in Ecuador. The poor people know that it doesn't really matter who the president is. But they know that Velasco makes the people up there uncomfortable. So they vote for him. It is the only way they have to protest."[7]

But despite Velasco's latest victory, it is doubtful that the country will be able to go back to its traditional political system. The events since 1948 have brought new groups into activity who will never go back to being passive observers. The new laws passed by the various governments, especially some of the measures introduced by the last junta, cannot be repealed. One small sign of the continuing effects of change was the paralysis of the government's operations for forty-eight hours by a strike of the government employees' union on April 27, 1967. The strike began when the Constituent Assembly decided to discharge 4,000 civil servants to balance the budget. In the past all new governments

---

[7] *New York Times*, June 4, 1968, p. 8.

discharged employees and replaced them with their friends. The junta, however, had instituted a modern civil service system, and the civil servants struck to force the observance of the law protecting their status. In the same way the new tax laws, the agrarian-reform law, and all the others are on the books, and pressure will come to make the government carry them out. Ecuador remains at a crossroad. The junta failed and Velasco is once again making the businessmen "uncomfortable." It would be unrealistic to expect stability from such a situation.

The Formal Constitutional Framework

Ecuador is governed under the constitution of May 5, 1967. This is the seventeenth formal constitution Ecuador has had since 1830, when it began its existence as an independent state. All the constitutions were very similar. All set up a presidential system with the three traditional powers in a unitary state and all were more ignored than observed. Lilo Linke, who lived in Ecuador for many years, wrote that "the question arises whether there really can be unconditional respect for the law and the Constitution in a country lacking almost entirely basic civil and political organization."[8] The question can also be asked whether Ecuador needs a written constitution when it was able to function as well as it did during the years from July 1963 to March 1966 without one in effect.

All of Ecuador's formal constitutions have been of considerable length and have included many minor details. That of 1967, for example, needs sixty-two articles to list all the individual, family, education, property, labor, social security, and political rights, duties, and guarantees Ecuadorians are to have. This long list includes practically every progressive measure found in the most democratic and developed prosperous states. At the same time, however, Articles 185, 186, 187, 188, and 189 provide for the suspension of practically all civil liberties "in case of internal commotion or international war." Whether the constitution of 1967 will last longer than most of its predecessors only time will tell.

How the Constitution Is Amended

Ecuador's constitution can be amended relatively easily. The Congress or the president can suggest amendments, the president by sending a message to the Congress, the Congress by passing a resolution in the same way it passes a law. After the Congress has passed the resolution, the president publishes the proposed amendment with his opinion of

---

[8] Linke, *Ecuador*, p. 56.

it. If he favors the amendment, the Congress meets in special session with the members of the Supreme Court of Justice participating with voice and vote An absolute majority vote in this session puts the amendment into the constitution. If the president and the Congress are in disagreement about a proposed amendment, the decision is made by a plebiscite of the country's voters. The constitution forbids the consideration of amendments that abolish the republican or democratic form of government.

Who Participates in Politics

Until the post–World War II period, the overwhelming majority of the population had no formal role in the political process. Voting has always been restricted to those who could read and write, and only a minority could meet this qualification before the Second World War. Even in the 1960's it is estimated that at least 32 percent of the population is illiterate, and many believe that the figure is really much higher. Voting for those eighteen years or older is compulsory, but the right to vote can be lost upon conviction for certain crimes. In addition, members of the armed forces may not vote or be elected to office.

Those who participated in politics during the first century of Ecuador's independent life were the members of the "white" group, the rich landowners, businessmen, and professionals who were generally of Spanish descent. In 1948, in one of the freest elections ever held, slightly less than 8 percent of the estimated population voted on the coast, slightly more than 9 percent in the sierra, and less than 2 percent in the *oriente*. Voting participation increased from then on, with 766,834 ballots being cast in 1960, the largest election until that date. This number, however, still represented a minority of the population, which by 1960 was more than 4 million. If we use 4 million as the population, then 19 percent voted. The increased participation has broken the absolute monopoly of the upper class on political power, but only in the cities do the masses play an important role. Punishment for not voting includes dismissal from a government position, disqualification from public employment for one year, and small fines. In the past this tended to force the educated whites in the government bureaucracy to vote, and thus to increase the control of the small upper class.

The Electoral Machinery

Since 1946, elections have been conducted by an independent Supreme Electoral Tribunal (TSE), seventeen provincial electoral tribunals, and local electoral boards. Of the seven members of the TSE, three are elected by the Congress, two are appointed by the president of the republic, and two are appointed by the Supreme Court. The members of the TSE may not resign without the permission of the organ of government that selected them; they serve four-year terms. The TSE handles all matters dealing with elections and counts the votes for president and vice-president. It also appoints the members of the provincial electoral tribunals and supervises their functioning. A provincial electoral tribunal has five members with two-year terms and is located in the capital of each province. It handles all matters dealing with elections in its province and appoints the local electoral boards, which conduct the elections.

The local polling places, known as *mesas,* are often located in the open air. The polls are open from seven A.M. to five P.M., and each voter has his hand stamped with indelible ink to prevent repeated voting. After the votes are counted in each *mesa,* they are sent to the provincial electoral tribunal, where all votes are checked. For the Chamber of Deputies and for provincial councils, members are elected by proportional representation from party lists. It is thought that this system tends to lessen interest in these elections and fasten attention upon the president, as it takes weeks for the results to be announced.

Since 1948 elections have been fairly honestly conducted, but the system in use to elect the president produces victors who may have only minority support, thus producing weak government, and it is possible for the president to be of one party and the vice-president of another.

Political Parties

Ecuador's two major political parties, the Conservative and the Liberal, developed toward the end of the nineteenth century. Because of the small number of voters and the mass illiteracy, personality played the greatest role in determining which party was to control the government, and when a charismatic individual was not attached to one of the political parties, he would be elected president by an *ad hoc* group set up for the election.

The electoral law makes it relatively easy for a political party to be recognized. All one must do is submit an application signed by 2,000 members and a program that is not opposed to morality or the republican institutions guaranteed by the constitution. The registration is good for six years and entitles the party to nominate candidates for office.

The Conservative Party is the country's oldest, although it was not formally organized until 1883, in response to the formation of the Liberal Party, which had been organized to fight the political power of the Conservatives. Its great hero is Gabriel García Moreno. Conservative elements dominated Ecuador's governments from 1830 to 1895, and the party has always been an important force, even though a Conservative did not reach the presidency from 1895 to 1956. The Conservative Party has always been especially strong in the sierra. Its leaders are rich landowners or professional men, though it has always had the support of some workers and other groups, especially those influenced by the Catholic church. It does not really have a distinct ideology, but in recent years it has reemphasized its devotion to Catholicism and been able to count on the bloc vote of nuns and priests.

The dominant party from 1895 to 1944 was the Liberal Party, founded in 1878. Its great hero is Eloy Alfaro, the *caudillo* who led it to victory in the revolution of 1895. Now known as the Radical Liberal Party, it is especially strong on the coast and among industrialists, bankers, and those involved in the export and import trade. It has the following of many workers, especially those organized into trade unions. The Liberal Party began as an ideological party, strongly anticlerical, pushing for the liberal reforms common at the end of the nineteenth century, but in recent years, as the church issue died, it has had little to say about religion. The party's programs through the years have contained planks for land reform, improving the lot of the Indian, better education, housing for workers, and many other similar demands, but the party never vigorously pushed these measures when it was in power. By the 1950's there was little except tradition and regionalism to distinguish the Liberal Party from the Conservative. Both have national organizations based on the political units into which the country is divided. National conventions elect a general directorate for the Conservative Party and a supreme junta for the Liberal Party. Below these bodies are assemblies and directorates in each province, canton, and parish. Neither party has canton and parish organizations in all parts of the country, the Conservatives being weakest on the coast and the Liberals in the sierra.

During the 1920's a group of young intellectuals and some student and labor leaders organized the Socialist Party of Ecuador, which joined the Third International as a fraternal member in 1928. A split soon developed between those who were impressed by the Russian Revolution but were basically romantic Ecuadorians and those who became Communists in the full meaning of the term, and two parties emerged: the Socialist Party (PSE) and the Communist Party (PCE). Through the years the Communists have usually been successful in manipulating both the labor movement and the Socialist Party, probably because they always had more money and the backing of the Soviet Union. At times the Socialist Party has combined its efforts with the Communist Party, at times with the Liberal Party, and at times all three have cooperated, especially in the *Alianza Democrática,* which was important in the 1940's. The Socialist Party has always had a very radical program, which its members have done little to implement when they served as ministers or as members of the Congress. In the 1960's the Socialist Party split into democratic and *Fidelista* factions. Soon three different Socialist parties were functioning: the Ecuadorean Socialist Party, the Unified Socialist Party, and the Revolutionary Socialist Party. All of the Socialist Party leaders are from the middle and upper classes, although they have always had some support among the organized workers.

The Communist Party was very weak during the 1930's and 1940's, but always managed to keep functioning; the victory of Fidel Castro strengthened it, and today it is fairly strong among students, intellectuals, and organized workers. Both Velasco Ibarra and Carlos Julio Arosemena at times seemed to be cooperating with the Communist Party, which became more prominent around 1961 and 1962. When President Arosemena broke relations with Cuba, the Communists began to organize guerrilla groups in the mountains, and when this effort was smashed they were greatly weakened. The junta outlawed the PCE and arrested many of its leaders in 1963. The PCE traditionally has operated through front organizations, the most important of which in recent years has been the *Unión Revolucionaria de Juventudes Ecuatorianas* (URJE). The PCE is believed to have from 5,000 to 6,000 members. A split between those Communists who support the Soviet Union and those who support China occurred in the early 1960's, and the pro-Chinese took the name Social Revolutionary Party.

During the 1950's the *Movimiento Social-Cristiano* became active and assumed some importance when its leader, Dr. Camilo Ponce, was elected president in 1956 by the Conservative Party. It remains a small organization. Another minor party is the *Concentración de Fuerzas Populares* (CFP), which is the personal following of a Guayaquil *caudillo,* Dr. Carlos Guevara Moreno. The CFP apparently has no program and supports anyone who offers cooperation. *Acción Revolucionaria Nacionalista Ecuatoriana* (ARNE) is an extremely conservative group inspired by the Spanish Falangist movement. Its following is small, but includes many young students and government employees. It has cooperated at times with the *Velasquista* movement and the Conservative Party.

The *Velasquista* committees make up one of the largest political parties, but it will probably never be anything more than the personal following of Velasco Ibarra. The committees have no program except support of Velasco. They are organized only in Guayaquil, Quito, and a few other cities, and function only when Velasco returns to Ecuador to run for president again.

All Ecuadorian political parties are personalistic. The electoral system, which gives the presidency to the candidate who wins a plurality, no matter how small a proportion of the total vote this represents, has probably helped to weaken the parties. As this is written, all of Ecuador's parties are in crisis and trying to reorganize themselves.

Public Opinion and Pressure Groups

Until the First World War, public opinion was a reflection of the small ruling class. The mass illiteracy and the Indian character of so much of the population combined effectively to exclude all but a small number from participation in the country's political life. The circulation of newspapers was small, and before the advent of radio and television, news was passed by word of mouth. Pressure was a form of interpersonal relationships. If one wanted a job or a favor from the government, one looked for a friend or a relative who held an important position. To a large extent, one still does.

With modern means of communication and the development of trade unions and other mass organizations, some change came to Ecuador, but the press has never been widely read. In 1961 there were 25 daily newspapers with a combined circulation of about 148,000, or only 48 copies for each 1,000 inhabitants of Ecuador. (Radio was more important; in 1961 there were about 125 radio broadcasting stations with about 110 radio receivers for each 1,000 inhabitants.) *El Universo* of Guayaquil, with a daily circulation of about 50,000, and *El Comercio* of Quito, with a circulation of about 30,000, are the largest newspapers. Much Communist propaganda printed in China, the Soviet Union, and Cuba is brought into the country because the weak Communist Party can produce little by itself; the largest Communist periodical is *El Pueblo* of Quito, the official organ of the Communist Party, with a circulation of 4,000.

The army in Ecuador must be counted as one of the country's strongest groups. Military service is compulsory for two years and the system functions fairly well, but some of the sons of the rich manage not to serve by paying a fine. Since 1946 the officers have been assigned one senator as part of the system of functional representation, and are thus represented in the Congress.

The Catholic church is probably the most widespread organization in Ecuador, although all constitutions since 1897 have guaranteed freedom of religion. The Catholic church operates many schools, including a teacher-training institute, a university, and a seminary to train priests. It also operates a radio station. The Social Christian Movement, led by ex-President Ponce, and the Conservative Party have favored the church. Professor Blanksten in his 1951 study of Ecuador claimed the Catholic church was one of the seven instruments used by the small ruling class at that time to dominate the country.[9]

Employers, large landowners, and industrialists have always been very influential in determining public policy because almost all are members of the small upper class. They are organized into various associations, including chambers of commerce in the larger cities and agricultural and industrial organizations. Two of the more important are the National Association of Banana Growers and the Ecuadorian Textile Industry Association. Most professionals belong to national professional organizations.

Labor is very weak in Ecuador. There are fewer than 100,000 organized workers, and they represent a minority of all workers in all sectors of employment. Most of the functioning trade unions are located in Guayaquil and Quito. Contributing to the weakness of the labor movement is the rivalry between Communists, democrats, and Catholics. The largest organization is probably the Confederation of Ecuadorian Workers (CTE), in which the Communists for some years have been very influential. The CTE is affiliated with the World Federation of Trade Unions and has about 50,000 to 60,000 members. The Ecuadorian Confederation of Free Trade Union Organizations (CEOSL) is affiliated with the ORIT and the International Confederation of Free Trade Unions. The CEOSL was set up to oppose Communist control of the labor movement and has about 50,000 members. A third organization, with about 4,000 members, is the Ecuador Confederation of Catholic Workers. In addition, independent of all three federations, there are a number of unions with perhaps 10,000 to 15,000 members. All unions are weak and depend a great deal upon the government for assistance. The ORIT has been operating a school to train labor leaders in order to strengthen the unions.

Civil Liberties

Until about the time of World War II, the majority of Ecuador's population practically never enjoyed true civil liberty. With the rise of urban-

---

[9] Blanksten, *Ecuador*, pp. 37, 39, 170.

ism a more alert public opinion developed, and in recent years city workers have made frequent use of strikes, demonstrations, and petitions for relief in support of liberties their parents never dreamed of.

All of Ecuador's constitutions have contained elaborate lists of constitutional rights, but these are generally ignored. The freest period for Ecuador probably came during the years from 1948 to 1963, but even then the executive at times resorted to a state of siege to maintain "law and order." It is impossible to state whether the new constitutional system being created will allow complete liberty for all Ecuadorians.

The Executive

Under the 1967 constitution, the president is elected by direct secret vote for a four-year term and is not eligible for reelection. As is common in Latin America, many officials, relatives of the incumbent president, members of the clergy, and those who hold certain contracts or concessions from the government are not eligible to become president. A vice-president is elected at the same time as the president. One of the great weaknesses of the presidency in the past was that a candidate did not need a majority of the votes to be elected. Any plurality sufficed, and at times the president was elected by a very small minority of the total vote—29 percent in 1956, for example. This manner of election complicated relations with the Congress. And since the vice-president did not have to be a member of the same party as the president, violent fluctuations in government policy could occur, as in 1961, when Arosemena replaced Velasco Ibarra. Nothing was done about correcting these weaknesses in the new constitution.

In the past, the president had the power to appoint and remove practically all government employees and could dominate the Congress through his patronage and control of the budget. To weaken the president, past legislatures developed the custom of setting up what were known as decentralized organizations, whose budgets were not under the control of the president. From 1952 to 1956 these agencies spent from 34 to 44 percent of the total budget, thus severely limiting the control exercised by the president. There apparently was no logical reason why one organization was independent and another was not. Civil aviation, radio, telegraph and telephones, and the post office, for example, were directly under the Ministry of Public Works, but roads in the province of Guayas, many ports, the state railroads, drinking water in Manta, and various other kinds of public works were controlled by decentralized agencies. The president was strengthened, however, by his control of the armed forces, by the system of local government, and by his power to declare a state of siege. As long as he had the support of the officer corps of the armed forces, he usually could do about as he wanted to do.

The great hope of the military junta and those who supported its activity was that the government of Ecuador could be institutionalized. To that end, improvements were made in the public service by strengthening the law regulating public employees to create a career civil service, and modern methods of accounting, control, and organization were introduced. It was hoped that when constitutional government was reintroduced, the public service would be able to manage the government's business in a more efficient way than had been the rule in the past. How much of this will be retained by the new government cannot be forecast, but the new constitution contains provisions creating a career public service based upon a system of competitive examinations. Nepotism is banned, conflict of interest is banned, and all government officials and employees must file declarations of wealth upon entering and upon leaving the public service. Another interesting item in the new constitution provides for a plebiscite when the Congress refuses to adopt a law proposed by the president.

Another check upon the president created by the new constitution is the Court of Constitutional Guarantees. This takes the place of the Council of State in previous constitutions, a body that knit the legislative, executive, and judicial powers together and acted as an advisory body whose approval was needed for certain actions by the president. The new Court of Constitutional Guarantees is composed of a senator elected by the Senate, two deputies elected by the Chamber of Deputies, the president of the Supreme Court of Justice, a representative of the president of the republic, the attorney general, the president of the Supreme Electoral Tribunal, and three citizens elected by the Congress. This body is to watch for the observance of the constitution and the laws, particularly the constitutional guarantees; to make suggestions about these matters; to hear complaints; when the Congress is not in session, to make temporary nominations to fill offices that should be filled by vote of Congress; to advise the president of the republic; and to do whatever else the laws provide. Whether this body will be any more effective than the old Council of State cannot be forecast. In 1963 the junta simply disbanded the Council of State, just as it abolished the Congress. Whether a stable functioning government can be created by tinkering with the constitution is doubtful as long as illiterates cannot vote, the legislature is weak, and the French system of centralized local government continues.

The Legislative Power

The legislature has always been relatively unimportant in Ecuador. The 1843 constitution, for example, had it meeting only once every four years, and that of 1861 provided meetings every two years. Attempts were made in the twentieth century to strengthen the Congress, but without much success, as no well-functioning political party system existed upon which a legislature could be based. The 1946 constitution provided for only one session of sixty days annually, though it could be prolonged for thirty days more and special sessions could be called. The 1967 constitution doubles the number of days of congressional sessions by calling for Congress to sit from March 6 to May 4 and again from August 10 to October 9.

The 1967 constitution continues Ecuador's traditional bicameral legislature, consisting of the Senate and the Chamber of Deputies. The Senate's fifty-two members are elected for four-year terms with the right to be reelected indefinitely. Senators are elected both territorially and functionally. The eighteen provinces elect two senators each and the Galápagos Islands one. Fifteen functional senators are elected by special electoral colleges with the representation as follows: one senator each for public education, private education, the armed forces, the national police, and the communications industries and scientific and literary societies; commerce, industry, and agriculture each elect two senators, one representing the sierra and the *oriente* and one representing the coast and the Galápagos Islands; and four senators are elected to represent labor, two from the *oriente* and sierra and two to represent the coast and the Galápagos Islands.

The Chamber of Deputies is elected from the provinces with one member for each 80,000 persons or fraction over 40,000. Each province has a minimum of two deputies, and the Galápagos Islands have one. Deputies serve two-year terms and can be reelected indefinitely. When a province has more than two deputies, they are elected by a system of proportional representation.

When the Congress is not in session, it is represented by a permanent legislative commission composed of four senators and five deputies. This body studies proposed legislation and constitutional amendments, and codifies and edits law codes.

The Ecuadorian legislature always was an ineffective body. This was in part due to its unrepresentative character: only "whites" ever seemed to get elected. Even the Communist functional senator who represented coastal labor in the early 1960's was the son of a rich Guayaquil businessman. In addition, the political parties have always been weak, and none of them ever had a majority in either house. When Professor Blanksten made his study of Ecuador in 1948, in the Senate the Radical Liberal Party had 38 percent of the membership, 31 percent represented the Conservative Party, 18 percent were from the Socialist Party, 2 percent were Communist, and 11 percent were independent. In that year in the Chamber of Deputies 36 percent were Conservatives, 31 percent were Radical Liberals, 14 percent were Socialists, 3 percent were Communists, and 16 percent were independent.[10] In 1961, just before constitutional government broke down, the composition of the houses was as follows: in the Senate, 17 *Arosemenistas*, 11 Conservatives, 10 from the Independent Center, 4 *Velasquistas*, 4 Liberals elected by the FDN, 3 independent rightists, and 2 independents elected by the FDN; the Chamber had 6 *Arosemenistas*, 16 Conservatives, 5 from the Independent Center, 4 *Velasquistas*, 16 Liberals elected on the FDN ticket, 2 from ARNE, 12 independent rightists, 4 from the CFP, 3 independents elected by the FDN, 2 Socialists elected on the FDN ticket, and 3 independents. With a legislature as fragmented as this it never was possible to get anything done. One of the main reasons the junta refused to call new elections for so long was that the political parties had done nothing to unify their forces, so only the same kind of legislature would have been produced by a new election. It is too soon to forecast how the legislature created by the new constitution will function.

Public Finance

"The year 1961 was characterized by an accentuation of the financial disorder which has affected the country for so many years," wrote the general manager of the Central Bank of Ecuador as he began his report on the country's fiscal situation.[11] As a poor and underdeveloped country, Ecuador always had financial difficulties, but the problem grew greater after the Second World War as the demand increased for better roads, schools, and other public facilities. Under the 1946 constitution, Ecuador's budget was drawn up by a special Budget Commission (*Comisión Técnica del Presupuesto*), which consisted of the Minister of Finance, the Minister of Economy, one congressman who was a member of the Budget Committee, and one member of the National Economic Council. The budget was presented to the Congress when it met and had to be approved before Congress adjourned or it went into effect as submitted. The 1946 constitution included fourteen articles that laid down detailed rules

[10] *Ibid.*, pp. 109, 112–13.
[11] *Memoria del Gerente General del Banco Central del Ecuador correspondiente al ejercicio de 1961* (Quito: Imprenta del Banco Central, 1962), p. 285.

about how the budget was to be handled. The 1967 constitution continues this system. The president sends the budget to the Congress on August 10. If by September 10 it has not been passed, it is considered passed as presented.

A most interesting provision of the new constitution requires that not less than 30 percent of the ordinary income shall be appropriated for education beginning five years after the adoption of the constitution, and that meanwhile the amount for education shall be raised each year. It will be interesting to see how well this constitutional provision is followed.

TABLE 1

REVENUE OF ECUADOR, 1961

(000 Omitted)

Source	Amount in Sucres	Percent of Total
Taxes		
On imports	S653,292	28.87%
On exports	93,297	4.12
On transport	16,114	0.71
On sales and consumption	216,432	9.58
On production (industry)	26,180	1.16
On capital	27,963	1.24
On income	206,762	9.13
On state monopolies	84,212	3.72
Total taxes	S1,324,252	58.53%
Fees		
For services	101,686	4.50
Tax stamps	73,042	3.22
Total fees	S174,728	7.72%
Other revenue		
From state property	20,770	0.92
Miscellaneous	43,358	1.92
Reimbursements and surplus of previous years	15,502	0.68
Total other revenue	S79,630	3.52%
Total regular income	S1,578,610	69.77%
Loans		
Internal	240,182	10.62
External	287,190	12.70
From previous years	156,435	6.91
Total loans	S683,807	30.23%
Total revenue	S2,262,417	100.00%

The income and expenses of the government have risen very rapidly since the First World War. Even if one takes into consideration the cheapening of the monetary unit, the sucre (there are 18.18 to the dollar), the rise of government expenditures has been rapid. In 1920, only S22,874,900 were spent. By 1930 expenditures had more than doubled, rising to S60,177,700; in 1940 the total was S114,050,700; in 1950 it was S425,557,400; and by 1961 it had reached S2,262,417,000.

Tables 1 and 2 show the income and expenditures for 1961. As the

TABLE 2

EXPENDITURES OF ECUADOR, 1961

(000 Omitted)

	Amount in Sucres	Percent of Total
Legislature	S16,913	0.75%
Judiciary	17,361	0.77
Executive		
President and vice-president	25,997	1.15
Ministry of Government	86,366	3.82
Ministry of Foreign Relations	35,797	1.58
Ministry of Education	242,624	10.72
Ministry of Defense	381,665	16.87
Ministry of Public Works	381,060	16.84
Ministry of Social Welfare	70,647	3.12
Ministry of Economy	13,178	0.58
Ministry of Development	21,658	0.96
Ministry of Finance	53,130	2.35
Miscellaneous	20,231	0.89
State monopolies	85,697	3.79
Emergency funds	37,484	1.66
Pensions	55,325	2.45
Capital funds for autonomous agencies	78,035	3.45
Subsidies for autonomous agencies	210,727	9.31
Quotas due to international organizations	35,508	1.57
Total regular expenditures	S1,869,403	82.63%
Public debt (internal)		
For capital	112,017	4.95
For interest	75,634	3.34
Public debt (external)		
For capital	77,105	3.41
For interest	37,504	1.66
Miscellaneous	90,754	4.01
Total public debt	S393,014	17.37%
Total expenditures	S2,262,417	100.00%

figures demonstrate, Ecuador has a serious budget deficit, and it has had one regularly since 1950 except for 1951, 1952, 1957, and 1958. In 1962 there was a S236-million deficit, which was again covered by internal borrowing and a S126-million loan from the United States government, and in 1963 the deficit was about S250 million. The bulk of the government's tax revenue comes from taxes on business transactions and capital; only a small part comes from the income business activity produces. Howard P. Morrison, who participated in a field survey in Ecuador, reported that "we estimate conservatively that efficient collection of income taxes, without rate increases, could more than double the present government revenues from this source."[12]

Ecuador has never spent enough money for education, health, and development, and it has spent too much for its armed forces, as the 1961 budget demonstrates. Another great weakness is that the 800 or so autonomous institutions handle large amounts of money not under the control of the executive. In 1961 the national government seemed to be handling only about 55 percent of the money received and spent by all public bodies. Table 3 shows the Central Bank's estimate of expenditures

TABLE 3

ESTIMATED REVENUE AND EXPENDITURES OF ECUADOR, 1961
(000 Omitted)

	Revenue	Expenditures
National government	S1,529,601	S1,661,415
Autonomous agencies	1,890,961	1,677,787
Provincial councils	45,447	42,490
Municipal councils	600,498	684,815
Total	S4,066,507	S4,066,507

and income in 1961. The difference between the bank's figures and the total shown in the budget is one more symptom of the general confusion. As Lilo Linke once wrote:

> Whenever money was needed for some new health campaign, some institution or local construction, Congress simply established another tax, increased an existing one, or allocated a percentage of some government income. . . . Owing to these constant additions, there are now altogether about 500 different taxes in force: fiscal, municipal, additional provincial, regional, and others. Some were

---

[12] Howard P. Morrison, "Recommended Reforms: Corporation Laws, Taxes and Customs in Ecuador," *International Development Review*, 4 (December 1962): 21.

so ill conceived that they were completely insufficient to finance whatever project they were intended for, others yielded so insignificant an amount that they were not even worth the collecting. Chaos has been the result.[13]

The military junta turned its attention to this problem and adopted a comprehensive law revising the tax system and introducing a new income-tax law in January 1964. At the same time, an accelerated effort was made to improve the technical efficiency of the tax-collection office. Modern office machinery and methods were introduced in Guayaquil, and the plan was to use the same methods in Quito and other cities after the efficiency of the Guayaquil office had been improved. It was this attempt to collect taxes efficiently that was largely responsible for the junta's overthrow. What will happen under the new government cannot be forecast.

Local Government

Ecuador has always used the French system of local government, with authority centralized in the Ministry of Government. The new constitution sets up a double system that may transform the traditional pattern, but only experience can show how the new system will work. For purposes of local government the country is divided into eighteen provinces. In each one there is a governor appointed by the president, an elected provincial council, and an elected provincial prefect. The provinces are divided into ninety-five cantons. Each has a political chief (*jefe político*) appointed by the president and an elected municipal council. The cantons are divided into 767 parishes, each of which has a political lieutenant appointed by the president and an elected parish junta.

In the past, the governor controlled all government authorities under him and coordinated their activities. The provincial council promoted the progress of the province and had certain supervisory powers over the acts of the municipal councils. On the canton level, the municipal council established the budget, set taxes, and passed ordinances dealing with such services as planning, roads, prisons, public health, schools, local police, and other matters. In those cantons that are provincial capitals, an additional official is the *alcalde*, who is elected for a two-year term and presides over the council. In the parish, the political lieutenant has always been the most important figure.

To make sure the new system will really strengthen local govern-

---

[13] Linke, *Ecuador*, p. 175.

456 PATTERNS OF POLITICS AND POLITICAL SYSTEMS IN LATIN AMERICA

ment, the constitution provides a source of income for each of its three levels. Each provincial council gets 10 percent of the income tax collected in the province. Each municipal council gets the income from taxes on urban real estate and on sales within the canton. The parish gets the income from the tax on rural land. The tax-collecting agencies turn these moneys over to the parish, canton, or province within thirty days of their receipt. If the new system works, it may transform Ecuador, for the local governments may then be strong enough to become the building blocks for a firm governmental structure that will no longer need to be propped up by the charismatic sort of presidents Ecuador has leaned on in the past.

The Judicial Power

Ecuador's judicial hierarchy was the only part of the constitutional system left untouched by the military junta that took control of the government in 1963. Under the 1946 constitution the judicial power was exercised by the Supreme Court, under which were eight superior courts and a number of provincial and cantonal courts. This system is continued under the 1967 constitution. The composition of the Supreme Court is determined by the Congress, not by the constitution. In recent years it has consisted of three chambers, each of which has three members. The nine justices are elected by the Congress for six-year terms and are eligible for continuous reelection. The Supreme Court is headed by a president who is elected for a one-year term by the nine justices. To be elected a Supreme Court justice, one must be at least forty years old and have been a judge of a superior court for twelve years or have practiced law for at least fifteen years. The judges of the superior courts are elected by the Supreme Court for five-year terms and may be reelected indefinitely. To be a judge of a superior court one must be thirty-five years old and have been a judge or have taught in a law school for at least eight years or have practiced law for ten years. The superior courts appoint the judges of the lower courts.

The Ecuadorian courts function well, although apparently with an upper-class bias because of their composition. The Supreme Court introduces chance into the system, as its three panels handle all kinds of cases, and a decision may be affected by the panel that receives the case. The Ecuadorian courts have the power to declare laws unconstitutional.

Ecuador: A Last Word

The military government of Ecuador in 1963 presented the country with a chance to begin the modernization of its political, social, and economic institutions without having to live through a period of violent civil war. The great awakening of the Andean Indians after World War II, stimulated by the modern means of communication, was not translated into a strengthening of democracy in Ecuador because, unfortunately, the country turned to a charismatic *caudillo*, Velasco Ibarra, who had one great talent: he could get elected. In his five occupancies of the presidency he has demonstrated over and over that he is incapable of functioning as a constitutional president, and three times he was expelled from office before his term expired, but his failures as a chief executive never prevented his getting elected again.

Ecuador is fortunate that it is not overpopulated, has large areas capable of development, and possesses many untapped resources. A race is on, however, to see whether economic and political development can take place before the pressure of population growth brings renewed chaos. By improving the organization of the civil service, the collection of taxes, education, and transportation, the junta seemed to be on the right track, but as we have seen, the opposition these measures aroused pushed the junta out of office, and in 1968 the voters turned again to the old demagogue Velasco Ibarra.

What seems to be missing in Ecuador is a modern political party or parties to serve as an effective mechanism to organize the people. Nothing resembling a modern political party has yet emerged in Ecuador. It was this lack that forced the military officers into taking control of the country's destiny. With the installation of President Arosemena in 1966, the traditional political parties all began to reorganize themselves for the 1968 elections, but again they were unable to woo the voters from Velasco. There is nothing on the horizon to show that new political parties better than those of the past will appear. It is to be hoped that the improvements in education and transportation of the 1960's will help trade unions, political parties, and other organizations to grow stronger so that some kind of balance against the power of the upper classes can be created. Until that happens, Ecuador will probably face continued instability in its political system.

SELECTED READINGS

ALEXANDER, ROBERT J. "Ecuador," *Communism in Latin America*, pp. 234–42. New Brunswick, N.J.: Rutgers University Press, 1957.
BLANKSTEN, GEORGE I. *Ecuador: Constitutions and Caudillos*. Berkeley and Los Angeles: University of California Press, 1951.
BORJA C., RODRIGO. "Panorama de la política ecuatoriana." *Combate* 4 (November–December 1961): 16–22.
BORJA Y BORJA, RAMIRO. *Las constituciones del Ecuador*. Madrid: Ediciones Cultura Hispánica, 1951.

BOWEN, J. DAVID. "Ecuador on a Tightrope." *Reporter* 26 (March 29, 1962): 30–33.

DÍAZ, ANTONIO. "Ecuador: Entre la revolución y el miedo." *Política* (Caracas) 4 (January 1965): 115–34.

"Ecuador: A Case Study in Politics." *Latin American Report* 1 (July 1956): 24–29.

FERNÁNDEZ Y FERNÁNDEZ, RAMÓN. "Reforma agraria en el Ecuador." *El Trimestre Económico* 28 (October–December 1961): 569–94.

HUMES, SAMUEL, and MARTIN, EILEEN M. "Ecuador," *The Structure of Local Governments throughout the World*, pp. 346–51. The Hague: Martinus Nijhoff, 1961.

LINKE, LILO. *Ecuador, Country of Contrasts.* 3rd ed. London: Oxford University Press, 1960.

———. "Ecuador's Politics: President Velasco's Fourth Exit." *World Today* 18 (February 1962): 57–69.

MACDONALD, AUSTIN F. "Ecuador," *Latin American Politics and Government*, pp. 454–75. 2nd ed. New York: Thomas Y. Crowell Co., 1954.

MORRISON, HOWARD P. "Recommended Reforms: Corporation Laws, Taxes and Customs in Ecuador." *International Development Review* 4 (December 1962): 18–24.

NEEDLER, MARTIN C. *Anatomy of a Coup d'État: Ecuador 1963.* Washington: Institute for the Comparative Study of Political Systems, 1964.

PAREJA DIEZCANSECO, ALFREDO. *La Lucha por la democracia en el Ecuador.* Quito: Editorial Ruminahui, 1956.

———. "Teoría y práctica del conductor conducido." *Combate* 4 (January–February 1962): 9–23.

PLAZA, GALO. "Ecuador—An Experiment in Democracy," *Problems of Democracy in Latin America*, pp. 20–42. Chapel Hill: University of North Carolina Press, 1955.

ROUCEK, JOSEPH S. "Ecuador in Geopolitics." *Contemporary Review* 205 (February 1964): 74–82.

U.S. DEPARTMENT OF LABOR. *Labor Law and Practice in Ecuador.* Bureau of Labor Statistics report no. 242. Washington: U.S. Government Printing Office, 1963.

UNIVERSIDAD CENTRAL DEL ECUADOR, INSTITUTO DE ESTUDIOS ADMINISTRATIVOS. *Manual de gobierno de la República del Ecuador.* Quito: División de Administración Pública del Punto IV, 1962.

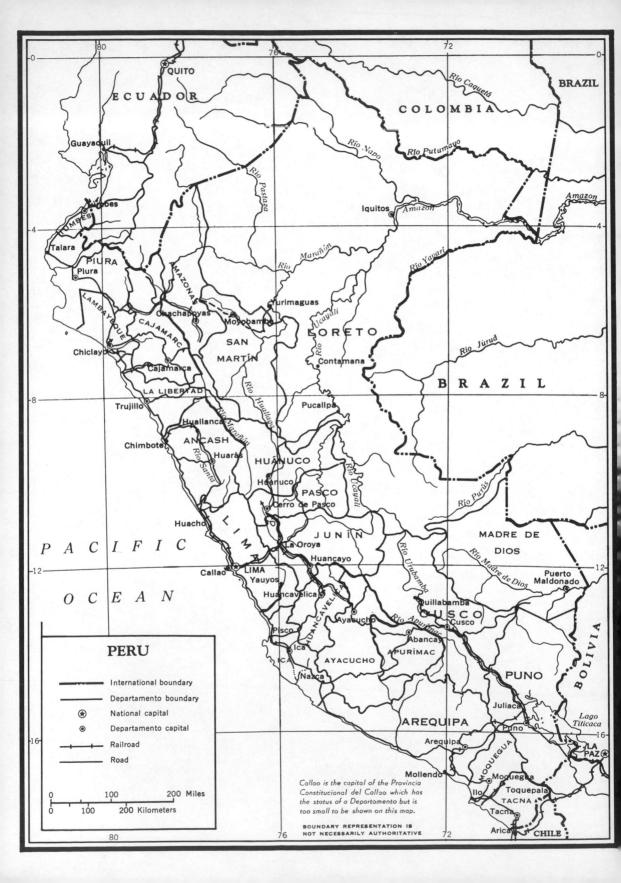

PERU

	International boundary
	Departamento boundary
✪	National capital
⊙	Departamento capital
	Railroad
	Road

0   100   200 Miles
0   100   200 Kilometers

Callao is the capital of the Provincia
Constitucional del Callao which has
the status of a Departamento but is
too small to be shown on this map.

BOUNDARY REPRESENTATION IS
NOT NECESSARILY AUTHORITATIVE

ECUADOR

QUITO

Guayaquil

Tumbes

Talara

PIURA
Piura

LAMBAYEQUE

Chiclayo

CAJAMARCA

Cajamarca

LA LIBERTAD

Trujillo

Huallanca

Chimbote

ANCASH
Huarás

HUÁNUCO

Huánuco

Huacho

LIMA

Callao   LIMA
Yauyos

PACIFIC

OCEAN

AMAZONAS

Chachapoyas

Moyobamba

SAN
MARTÍN

Río Huallaga

Río Marañón

Río Santa

PASCO
Cerro de Pasco

La Oroya
Huancayo

JUNÍN

Huancavelica

HUANCAVELICA

Pisco

Ica

ICA

Nazca

AYACUCHO

Ayacucho

Río Pastaza

Río Napo

Río Marañón

Yurimaguas

LORETO

Contamana

Río Ucayali

Río Huallaga

Pucallpa

Río Ucayali

Iquitos   Amazon

Río Caquetá

COLOMBIA

Río Putumayo

BRAZIL

Amazon

Río Yavarí

BRAZIL

Río Juruá

Río Purús

MADRE DE
DIOS

Río Urubamba

Río Madre de Dios

Puerto
Maldonado

Quillabamba

CUSCO

Cusco

Río Apurímac

Abancay

APURÍMAC

PUNO

Juliaca

Puno

Lago
Titicaca

BOLIVIA

LA
PAZ

AREQUIPA

Arequipa

MOQUEGUA

Moquegua

Mollendo

Ilo

Toquepala

TACNA

Tacna

Arica   CHILE

——19——

PERU:

Entrenched Oligarchy versus Reform

Peru has been called with justice a land of beggars sitting on a golden throne. Once the home of the great Inca empire, then the dazzling star in the Spanish colonial empire, Peru during most of its history has been a backward, stagnant land in which foreigners controlled nearly all important enterprises while the majority of the population lived in squalor. Peru's history since World War I has been largely the story of Apra, one of the first strong, nationalistic, indigenous reform movements to emerge in Latin America. Apra's struggle to establish a progressive modern state against the determined opposition of the defenders of an antiquated past is not yet over, but Peru has changed so dramatically during the decades since World War I that it may become a modern state within a relatively short time.

A National Profile

With an area of 495,853 square miles, Peru is Latin America's fourth largest state. Stretching along the west coast of South America for 1,410 miles, Peru is bounded on the west and southwest by the Pacific Ocean, on the north by Ecuador, on the northeast by Colombia, on the east by Brazil, on the southeast by Bolivia, and on the south by Chile. The extreme width from east to west is about 800 miles. Despite its size, Peru's presently used territory is only a small portion of its total area. About 1.2 percent is used for cropland, 9 percent for pastoral purposes, 53 percent is

461

covered with forests, and 37 percent is either useless or occupied by the few urban areas.

The towering Andes Mountains divide Peru into three distinct areas, each having a different climate, economy, and cultural pattern: the coastal region, the intermountain plateaus, and the jungle east of the mountains. One of Peru's major problems has always been the difficulty of unifying these three sections into a functioning whole, and this has not yet been achieved. So different are the ways of life in each of Peru's areas that one anthropologist writes of a "stratification of culture in Peru."[1]

Between the ocean and the western slopes of the Andes is a narrow strip of land 10 to 40 miles in width and 1,410 miles long. Containing about 12 percent of the country's total land area, this coastal belt varies in altitude from sea level to 5,000 feet. Earthquakes are frequent here, and it rains so seldom that the region is a desert of sand and rock except where rivers flowing down from the mountains have deposited alluvial soil to make about forty little oases where about 1.25 million acres are being cultivated. In and around these oases live about 27 percent of Peru's population. This is Peru's principal wealth-producing area, for it contains Peru's ports, its capital city, important petroleum fields, what industry exists, and irrigated lands where the chief export crops are grown. Off the coast are thirty islands, fifty-four keys, and miscellaneous rocks that supply Peru with guano, a valuable fertilizer, as well as fishing grounds that have made Peru the world's largest producer of fish products in recent years. The bulk of Peru's coastal population consists of European whites, *mestizos*, Negroes, and Orientals who are within the mainstream of Western culture. The language here is Spanish, the economics capitalistic, the religion overwhelmingly Roman Catholic. The inhabitants of the coastal plain hold a monopoly of political, military, economic, religious, and cultural power in Peru.

Peru's mountainous region, known as the sierra, has within it three main elements: a high-level plateau of gentle slopes; towering groups and ranges of peaks; and canyons with sides so steep that ascent and descent are extremely difficult. Some of these canyons are twice as deep as the Grand Canyon of the Colorado in the United States. The westernmost rim of high ranges forms the continental divide. The eastern slopes are such a maze of narrow ridges and ravines that they, rather than the high mountains, are the main barrier to travel between east and west. The sierra is from 200 to 250 miles wide and from 5,000 to more than

---

[1] Harry Tschopik, *Highland Communities of Central Peru: A Regional Survey* (Washington: U.S. Government Printing Office, 1947), p. 55.

20,000 feet above sea level, with an average elevation of about 12,000 feet. The sierra includes about 27 percent of Peru's area and about 60 percent of the population, concentrated in valleys and on certain hospitable slopes. Here are located the principal mineral deposits being exploited in Peru, with the exception of the oilfields.

Most of the sierra population consists of Quechua and Aymará Indians. The majority do not speak Spanish and cling tenaciously to their traditional culture. Their songs, dances, dress, land-tenure systems, agricultural practices, and religious habits are all distinctly their own. Certain features of European culture have been incorporated into their life, but after 400 years the cultural abyss between the Indians and the Europeans is almost as far from being bridged as it was the day Pizarro led his troops into Cajamarca. Some Indians have settled in Lima and as workers on the coastal farms, but the vast majority remain in the sierra.

Peru's *montaña* comprises the lower eastern slopes of the Andes and the jungle-covered plains of the upper Amazon basin. It includes about 61 percent of the total area and only about 13 percent of the population. The western sector contains fertile valleys and rolling hills of great agricultural potential, but forest products are the chief present source of wealth, since the mountains and canyons isolate the area from Peru's main centers of population and transportation facilities are poor or nonexistent. Vast areas remain unexplored and are inhabited only by the sizable portion of the *montaña's* population (estimated at 439,700) which consists of about a hundred jungle tribes, only twenty-five of which are generally known. These people remain almost completely out of contact with the rest of the population, living by hunting, fishing, and primitive agriculture. The most important Westernized city in the *montaña* is the port of Iquitos, which has become the trading and financial center for the entire upper Amazon valley.

This tripartite division extends to all aspects of Peruvian life. Its economy is three different economies. The coast produces the bulk of the country's export crops on irrigated lands, cotton and sugar cane being the most important. The sierra produces mainly minerals and food crops and livestock. The eastern *montaña* supplies many kinds of forest products, which are exported through Iquitos. New agricultural developments on the eastern slopes of the mountains, especially in the Perené valley east of Cerro de Pasco and in the Huallaga valley near Tingo María, produce tea, coffee, cocoa, and tobacco. Some petroleum is being exploited and refined in and around Pucallpa, but the most important petroleum areas are on the north coastal plain. Most of the country's manufacturing is located on the coast, and of course the important fishing industry has its headquarters on the coast.

Peru has had a poor transportation system ever since the Inca roads were destroyed. Most of the roads and railroads were built from a mine, farm, or city to the nearest point on the coast; roads connecting points within the country were few and inadequate. The completion of the trans-Andean highway in 1943 at last connected east and west Peru, and there is now an integrated railroad system around Lima. A determined road-building effort continues.

Peru's population in 1966 was estimated to be 12,012,000. No accurate statistics on ethnic composition are available, but the best estimates divide Peru's population as follows: whites, 13 percent; *mestizos*, 37 percent; Indians, 49 percent; Negroes and Orientals, 1 percent. The population has been increasing at a rate of about 3.19 percent a year, although there is practically no immigration. In 1961, only 566 entered as immigrants while 1,430 emigrated to other countries. Although Spanish is the official language, probably 40 percent of the total population cannot speak it. In 1961, 52.94 percent of the population was rural and there was only one large metropolitan center, Lima, the capital, with a population of 1,715,971. The next largest cities in that year were Callao, Lima's port, with 161,268 people; Arequipa, the regional center of the south, with 156,657; Chiclayo, a northern center, 74,885; Cuzco, the old Indian capital in the highlands, 69,681; Trujillo, the regional center on the north coast, 62,230; and Iquitos, the trading center for the upper Amazon area, 55,600.

Peru's population is very unevenly distributed. The population density varies from a low of 0.44 persons per square kilometer in Madre de Dios department in the east to 2,446.32 per square kilometer in Callao; there are 49.5 per square kilometer in the department of Lima.

A majority of Peru's population is illiterate, although strenuous efforts have been made in recent years to improve the educational system. Until recent years, primary education was compulsory and free for only three years. Education was free but not compulsory for the fourth and fifth years. Students with high grades were admitted to the secondary schools with a minimum fee. This system produced an illiteracy rate of around 60 percent; Lima and a few other cities were the only places where the majority was not illiterate. Many children never attended school at all. In 1958, for example, the *Peruvian Statistical Bulletin* reported that the country had 2,413,135 children between five and fourteen years old, while the total enrollment in all primary and secondary schools that year was 1,464,867. The number of private schools in Peru is high. Most are operated by Catholic religious orders and most of their students are from the middle and upper classes. A new education law was passed in 1963, making all education from kindergarten to the university free of cost, but strenuous efforts will have to be continued for decades to raise Peru's educational level significantly.

The government helps to finance the Catholic church, and all high officials of the church are nominated by the government. Freedom is permitted for other religions.

Peru has done much to develop its economy since World War II, but it remains poor and backward. Traditionally the country has been an exporter of agricultural and mineral raw materials and an importer of manufactured products and food. Slightly less than 4,000,000 of Peru's 10,524,000 inhabitants in 1959 were economically active: 2,225,923 (57.94 percent) in agriculture and 1,637,628 (42.06 percent) in nonagricultural activities.

Peru's economic and class systems produce extreme poverty for the majority of the population.[2] Landownership is extremely concentrated; 4.6 percent of the farms are larger than 1,000 *hectares* each and together contain 66.5 percent of the country's farmland. Ninety-two percent of the landowners, about 233,000 persons, own less than five *hectares* each. The poverty is most extreme among the highland Indians. One observer reported: "In Vicos, the Indians have barely, if at all, attained the status of human beings, much less 'Peruvians' or 'citizens.' They are chattels."[3] Good housing is in very short supply in all parts of the country. One observer reported that in Arequipa, of 120,000 people, about 80,000 lived in substandard housing. He is of the opinion that proper housing is the biggest problem the country faces.[4]

Thus split into three distinct sections, with a population speaking a variety of languages and living in various stages of cultural evolution ranging from primitive barbarism to modern capitalism, with most of the valuable natural resources exploited by foreign financial groups or being produced for the world market, Peru has had great difficulty establishing a stable governmental system. The number of Peruvians has risen rapidly in recent decades (from 7,023,111 in 1940 to 12,012,000 in 1966), but economic development has not kept pace. The average Peruvian has an ex-

---

[2] The gulf between rich and poor is fantastic. On December 29, 1964, the Peruvian Senate approved a law limiting the salary of government officials to 30,000 soles per month ($1,110 U.S.). On the same day a Lima worker informed me his salary was S25 a day. If he worked thirty days a month, he would have an income of S750 ($27.75).

[3] Richard W. Patch, "Life in a Peruvian Indian Community," *American Universities Field Staff Reports Service*, West Coast South America series, 9 (January 1962): 4.

[4] William H. MacLeish, "Vivienda I" (letter to the Institute of Current World Affairs, March 13, 1955), mimeographed.

tremely low living standard: his diet is starchy and low in nutritional value, his housing and clothing are poor, and he lacks most of the amenities of modern civilization, including good schools, roads, and health facilities.

It is only in recent years that a start has been made on solving Peru's perennial problems. The conditions of life created so much social dynamite that the traditional political system broke down and constitutional government emerged in the 1960's. Whether the changes being introduced are coming fast enough to prevent a chaotic revolution cannot be said, but Peru today is living through a period of rapid change and development, and the outlook seems reasonably bright.

The Development of Modern Peru

Peru is one of the few places in the world where topography, climate, natural resources, and an energetic people combined to develop a civilization. Although controversy continues about the length of time man has inhabited Peru, archaeological investigations have brought to light vast treasures of textiles, pottery, and metal objects dating from thousands of years in the past. Sometime before the Christian Era (500 to 15,000 B.C., according to which authority is consulted), migratory peoples settled in what is now Peru and began to develop the civilizations whose artifacts are now found in the world's museums. These early people settled mainly around Lake Titicaca and on the north and south coastal plains. Between the eleventh and fifteenth centuries A.D. a tribe of Quechua Indians who have gone down in history as the Incas consolidated the area from northern Ecuador to central Chile into the empire of Tahuantínsuyu, which endured until the Spanish conquest and forged the region into a political, economic, cultural, and religious unit. The Incas took most of their culture from the peoples they conquered; their contribution seems to have been an unusual organizational ability. The empire ruled by the Incas was notable for its social organization, agriculture, pottery, weaving, engineering, metalwork, and medical knowledge.

The Inca civilization was respectful of the lives of strangers, and it proved unable to cope with the gold-hungry Spanish *conquistadores* when 180 of them, led by Francisco Pizarro, arrived in Peru in 1532, soon after a civil war had split the empire into two quarreling halves. This coincidence, plus the terror inspired by guns and horses, neither of which had been known before in Peru, permitted a handful of adventurers to conquer an empire of millions. In completing their conquest, the Spaniards destroyed many of the country's irrigation systems and the roads that had knit the empire together. As a result of this destruction and of the diseases the Spaniards brought with them, to which the Indians had no immunity, the native population rapidly declined in numbers.

The great achievement of the Inca civilization had been to unify what is now Peru into a functioning integrated society by developing a manner of living suitable to the area. The Spanish conquest stopped the orderly development of the Peruvian people, for the Spaniards' monetary and religious attitudes were completely foreign to them. In addition, Pizarro, fearing the natives and needing a base near the sea, founded Lima as his capital in 1535, thus physically separating Peru's rulers from the ruled, most of whom continued to live in the highlands. At the same time the energy of the population was directed toward producing minerals and crops needed in Spain.

Despite the efforts by the Spanish rulers of Peru, the bulk of the Indians never adopted the Spanish culture or language. Catholicism remains the state religion, but the majority of the Indians are only imperfectly Christianized. The Spanish system of land tenure was introduced, but the Indians never really understood or accepted it. Colonial rule solidly established an aristocracy of wealth and privilege, but communications were poor and wealth and privilege were to be found only in and around Lima. Little was done to educate the Indians. During the years of Spanish rule Peruvian society consisted of a small upper class, which monopolized the land, education, and political, military, and religious power, and a large mass of Indians, comprising about 90 percent of the population, mostly landless, illiterate, and exploited. This two-class system contained certain feudal features that gave it great stability.

As the headquarters of Spanish power in South America, Peru had proportionally more monarchists and supporters of Spain than did the other Spanish colonies. Independence, therefore, came late to Peru, and was won not by the Peruvians, but by armies brought to Peru by an Argentinian and a Venezuelan. Sporadic revolts by Indians and Creoles had taken place in Peru from 1808 to 1815, but they were easily crushed by the royalist army. In September 1820, however, the Argentine revolutionary leader José de San Martín landed an army of Chileans, Argentines, and various soldiers of fortune in Peru. They captured Lima and proclaimed Peru's independence on July 28, 1821. After the famous conference of Guayaquil between San Martín and Simón Bolívar in 1822, San Martín left Peru, and Bolívar's troops, led by General Antonio José de Sucre, defeated the last Spanish troops holding out in Peru in 1824 at the battle of Ayacucho, which marked the end of Spanish rule in South America.

Thus a new independent state came into being because others willed it. For 300 years the people of Peru had been ruled by a centralized bureaucracy directed from Spain. Now that their symbol of authority, the crown, had been abolished, they drifted from crisis to crisis as a series of military and civilian *caudillos* competed for the right to misgovern them. The only *caudillo* who even partially pacified the country was Ramón Castilla, who, although he had the title of president only from 1845 to 1851 and from 1855 to 1862, continuously dominated the country from 1845 to his death in 1867. Castilla stimulated some economic development, abolished Negro slavery, freed the Indians from the payment of tribute, introduced the telegraph and railway, and began the development of Peru's guano and nitrate resources. In 1860 he introduced a constitution that remained in force until 1920, although it was seldom completely observed. All the other governments of Peru during its first century of independence were incompetent, graft-ridden, and disruptive.

Until World War I, Peru's economy was based upon the export of products that could be used by the more developed countries of the world: minerals, guano, cotton, and so on. The government financed itself by export taxes. When it was short of money because fluctuations in the world market cut its income, it borrowed from bankers in England or the United States. To pay the bankers it gave them liberal economic concessions; thus foreign groups took control of the country's most valuable resources. One historian has called Peru's history from 1822 to 1920 a period of "feudal anarchy."[5] Dominated by a series of corrupt and incompetent generals and rich landowners, the country vegetated. One general, Andrés Santa Cruz, set up a Bolivian-Peruvian confederation, but the Chilean and Argentine armies defeated Santa Cruz and in 1839 the confederation was ended. In 1864, Spain tried to reconquer the country, but an alliance between Peru and its neighbors thwarted this attempt. In 1879 Peru became involved in the War of the Pacific on Bolivia's side against Chile. The Chilean army soon invaded Peru and took control of Lima. As spoils of war Chile took for itself Peru's section of the Atacama desert and left the country in a state of financial and economic collapse. The development of the rubber industry in the Amazon area led in 1903 to a treaty between Brazil and Peru giving Brazil control of 442,000 square kilometers claimed by Peru in the Acre River basin.

During Peru's first century as an independent republic, its government was completely undemocratic. Although a large number of constitutions was adopted, none was ever observed. Suffrage was limited to a

---

[5] Alfred Barnaby Thomas, *Latin America: A History* (New York: Macmillan Co., 1956), p. 447.

tiny minority. The president was an uncrowned king, all-powerful until he was overthrown. Government was a road to riches, and the vast majority of the population had no contact with it. In fact, toward the end of the century about 90,000 Chinese were brought in to do the work the Indians were untrained or unwilling to do.

The opening of the Panama Canal in 1914 and the First World War shook the traditional patterns of life into new forms. Entering the war period bankrupt, corrupt, and backward, Peru found its exports rapidly declining, its customs receipts decreasing, and unemployment rising. When the United States entered the war, Peru's products again were valuable, and a slight boom developed. The bust came soon after the war ended, but by this time the new currents of the twentieth century had entered the country and a movement arose to reform Peru. From then until the 1960's, the history of Peru is the story of the oligarchy's attempt to prevent the destruction of its favored position by the reformers.

Supported by the military, Augusto B. Leguía, who had been president from 1908 to 1912, organized a coup d'état in 1919, set up a dictatorship, and ruled Peru until the world depression of the 1930's destroyed his financial base. Leguía was representative of the new upper middle class that emerged in Peru as a result of the foreign-controlled economic developments. He was an insurance salesman, and he seemed to see the need for the economic development of the country. He invited foreign capital to come to Peru under very favorable conditions for profit, and he floated many bond issues and foreign loans. Although he increased the national debt to a new high, the economic developments began to transform the country. New roads, railroads, and irrigation projects were most important, but the production of petroleum, sugar, coffee, rubber, cotton, and other products was also pushed.

Ruling as a harsh dictator, Leguía soon stimulated an opposition, but this opposition differed from all previous political groups in Peru. Economic development had created a small working class, and now it began to organize. The new intellectual currents stimulated by the Mexican Revolution, the First World War, and the Argentine student movement had created an aggressive reform-minded student organization in Peru. Out of the amalgamation of the new trade unions and the revolutionary student movement was to come the Peruvian *Aprista* movement.

The Peruvian student movement got its start in 1919, when, inspired by events at the University of Córdoba in Argentina, the students at Lima's University of San Marcos went on strike to win a modern reorganization of their university. They were supported by the workers of Lima, and after a four-month struggle they won most of their demands. This victory inspired the creation of a national student organization, whose first congress took place at Cuzco in March 1920. There students from Lima, Arequipa, and Cuzco came together to discuss their mutual problems. Most of the students wanted to see Peru reformed into a modern state, and an unusual idea was proposed: that the students should try to educate the rest of the people, since the government would not. The idea was accepted, and the students created "popular universities," night schools where university students were asked to give free service teaching courses in reading, writing, social problems, and the role of the Indian in Peruvian society to illiterate workers.

The remarkable thing was that the schools were a success, particularly in Cuzco and Lima. The contact between students and workers created, for the first time in Peru, a feeling of solidarity between these two groups. Unfortunately, the government was not very enthusiastic about this new educational development, and soon found a way to destroy it.

In May 1923 President Leguía proposed a ceremony to dedicate the country to the Sacred Heart of Jesus. He evidently thought this would increase his popularity and so prolong his stay in office. But the students objected and organized a demonstration against him. On May 23, 1923, the government attacked the demonstrators and the university buildings became a battle scene. One student and one worker were killed in the fighting. At that the archbishop of Lima suspended the ceremony, but the government clamped down on the students: the university was closed, the night schools were closed, many of the student leaders were jailed or exiled. This was the turning point in the student movement. Until then, the students had relied on education to renovate the country. Now they began to see that education alone was not enough; if any real reform was to come to Peru, political action was needed.

The president of the Peruvian Student Federation was Víctor Raúl Haya de la Torre. He was one of those exiled, and he was invited to Mexico by José Vasconcelos, then Minister of Education. There, on May 7, 1924, Haya de la Torre founded the *Alianza Popular Revolucionaria Americana*, which was destined to become Peru's most important political party. From the first letters of this name new words were to be coined: Apra, a short name for the organization; *Aprismo*, the philosophy of Apra; *Aprista*, a member of the organization.

From the beginning Apra was meant to be an organization for all of Latin America, and the founders spread their ideas by writing for periodicals all over America. Yet the movement made its greatest progress in Peru—naturally enough, since its leaders were Peruvians. They were Peruvians in exile, however, and were unable to function freely in their own country. In 1928 the *Apristas* who were Communists split off to found their own organization, and since then the Peruvian Communist Party has cooperated with the oligarchy in its campaign to destroy the *Aprista* movement.

Meanwhile, Leguía was able to remain in power. The world depression of the 1930's, however, cut off his flow of foreign loans and decreased Peru's income so severely that the government had to repudiate payments on its external debt. In August 1930 the army put Leguía in jail and a Colonel Sánchez Cerro became acting president. An election was organized and Sánchez Cerro and Víctor Raúl Haya de la Torre became candidates for president. Then for the first time in the history of Peru a political party presented a carefully drawn-up program to the voters. More freedom prevailed during the election campaign than had been customary for many years. The *Aprista* Party's membership lists grew long. But when the election took place on October 11, 1931, widespread fraud gave the official victory to Sánchez Cerro. Nearly all impartial observers are convinced the *Apristas* really won the election.

The election of 1931 was Peru's golden opportunity to reform its archaic political and social institutions. The *Apristas'* program called for democracy in government, the assimilation of the Indians into the mainstream of the nation's life by means of education and an end to their exploitation by the semifeudal land-tenure system, the abolition of illiteracy by reorganizing the educational system, an attack upon alcoholism and coca chewing, agrarian reform, industrialization, and the improvement of public health. Its international program called for the political and economic unification of Latin America, cooperation between Latin America and the United States, and overall planning for Latin America. Most controversial was the idea that Peru ought to concentrate on production for consumption rather than for export, and that the state ought to intervene in production to this end as well as foster the cooperative form of organization for productive enterprises.

Most unusual for a Latin-American political group, the Apra leadership refused to lead a revolt against Sánchez Cerro, even though the majority of the population apparently supported them. The *Apristas* had elected twenty-seven members of the Congress, and they decided to support constitutional government in the hope of winning the next election. But Sánchez Cerro refused to govern constitutionally. By December of 1931, two months after the election, the *Aprista* headquarters were closed by the army; by February 1932 the *Aprista* congressmen had been deported and most of the *Aprista* leaders were jailed, among them Haya de la Torre. Sánchez Cerro almost provoked an international war when, to turn the country's attention away from his failures, he had his troops seize the useless, unknown Amazon town of Leticia in Colombia. On April 30, 1933, just as the threat of war was greatest, Sánchez Cerro was shot dead.

What was left of the Congress elected another general, Oscar Benavides, to succeed him. Benavides continued the military dictatorship, but he moderated its severity. In August 1933 Benavides had two laws passed by his rump Congress: one was an amnesty freeing political prisoners; the other was a law barring persons affiliated with international organizations from running for office. The latter measure was a new attempt to suppress the *Apristas*, but it did not succeed. Within a few months the *Apristas* had rebuilt their organization. Elections had been scheduled to complete the Congress, but now the government canceled them and abolished all civil liberty. The *Apristas* were driven underground. This was to be the continuing pattern for the next decades. Whenever liberty was permitted, the *Aprista* Party flourished, whereupon dictatorship was reintroduced. When the dictator slackened his grip, the *Apristas* revived and grew stronger until they were driven underground again.

On October 11, 1936, Benavides arranged to hold a new presidential election after banning the *Apristas* from the ballot. The *Apristas* therefore supported an unknown candidate, Dr. Luis Antonio Eguiguren. When the votes were counted, to General Benavides' surprise, Dr. Eguiguren had been elected. Benavides immediately canceled the election, had his term extended, and abolished what was left of the Congress.

The *Aprista* movement continued to function underground after 1936. In 1939 the government organized a controlled election that put Manuel Prado Ugarteche in the presidency. President Prado served during World War II, when a modicum of prosperity came to Peru and political tensions died down. There was no democracy, but relations between the government and the people relaxed. A great deal of industrial development was begun and road building was pushed. The United States helped in many of these projects. Education was improved, labor unions grew stronger, and when the general enthusiasm for democracy generated by the victory of the Allies came to Peru, President Prado organized the first free election the country had ever had. This is not to say it was a democratic election, for the *Apristas* were not permitted to run a candidate and the majority of the population was not permitted to vote, but the votes were counted fairly, and on May 20, 1945, forty days before the election, the *Apristas* were legalized and permitted to vote.

In 1944 the *Apristas* had organized the National Democratic Front (FDN), which combined everyone active in Peruvian politics who favored constitutional government. The two chief engineers of the FDN were ex-President Benavides and Haya de la Torre. Their nominee for the presidency was a conservative university professor, José Bustamante y Rivero. They were so eager to establish constitutional government that they were willing to help elect a conservative when he promised to govern constitutionally. This, as future events proved, was a mistake.

Bustamante y Rivero won over his opponent by two to one and the FDN elected a majority of both houses of Congress, with the majority of the FDN congressmen *Apristas*. The *Apristas* sponsored laws to end all censorship and limitations on the liberty of the individual, to free political prisoners, to increase the pay of teachers, to improve education, to foster industrial development, to raise workers' wages. At the same time they began to push their long-range plans for Peru: to reorganize Peru into a federal democracy; to set up machinery for overall planning; to permit exploitation of the Sechura area by foreign oil companies; to build tunnels through the Andes to supply Amazon water to the coastal desert.

These activities frightened the oligarchs. Organizing a united front with the Communists, who traditionally opposed Apra, they unleashed a barrage of propaganda meant to convince the people that the *Apristas* were gangsters, totalitarians, and fascists. To combat this campaign, the *Apristas* pushed a bill through Congress making it necessary for each newspaper to print the names of its owners and to publish financial reports. During the struggle over the bill to regulate newspapers, the *Apristas* discovered that the President was more in sympathy with the oligarchy than with the congressional majority that had been elected with him. Cabinet crisis followed cabinet crisis. From January 23, 1946, to January 12, 1947, three *Apristas* were named to the cabinet, but this did not help, as they were given the less important ministries.

When the *Apristas* gained more congressional seats in the 1946 by-elections, the oligarchy became fearful of completely losing its power. Conservative political leaders abandoned all pretense of supporting constitutional government and organized a boycott of the congressional session due to open on July 28, 1947. An unusual constitutional provision required a 55 percent attendance in each house to open the first session of Congress, and the Chamber of Deputies could not meet without the Senate. The 46 percent of the senators in the conservative minority simply stayed away, thus preventing the Congress from functioning. President Bustamante did nothing to get the recalcitrant senators to attend the session. The *Apristas* tried to pressure the minority by organizing a strike in Lima and Callao on August 28, 1947. When the strike seriously interfered with commerce and industry, the President proclaimed a state of siege, suspended the constitutional guarantees of civil liberty, and arrested forty-eight trade-union leaders.

In this deadlock, Bustamante ruled by decree. On February 28, 1948, he appointed a new cabinet consisting entirely of military officers. He abolished all municipal councils because *Apristas* were members of most of them. He again postponed the congressional by-elections. Strikes turned into riots. Finally, on October 3, 1948, a revolt broke out in Callao and in the navy. There was bitter fighting, including the aerial bombing of naval vessels captured by the rebels. After the army put down the revolt, Bustamante accused the *Apristas* of having instigated it, ordered the army to occupy all *Aprista* headquarters, outlawed the party by decree, and arrested more than a thousand *Aprista* leaders. Apra officially denied complicity in the revolt, although some of its members did take part in it. The state of siege, however, prevented any open discussion of what had happened.

With the political party that had supplied the votes to elect him outlawed, Bustamante had no substantial support in the country. Three weeks after the Callao revolt, the army, under the leadership of General Manuel Odría, an unknown colonel whom Bustamante had promoted and named Minister of the Interior, deposed Bustamante and exiled him from the country.

General Odría set up a provisional government consisting of military men and disbanded the Congress. He made strenuous efforts to destroy Apra and capture its leaders, but many of them managed to escape the country. Víctor Raúl Haya de la Torre, the *jefe* of the party, took refuge in the Colombian embassy in Lima on January 2, 1949. Odría refused to give him safe-conduct out of the country for five years, and finally gave in only under pressure from the Organization of American States.

Odría scheduled a presidential election for July 1950, in which the only name on the ballot was his. Two other candidates had declared their candidacy, but Odría's hand-picked electoral jury ruled their nominations void. The jury did not hesitate to rule Odría's name eligible for the ballot, however, even though Article 137 of the Peruvian constitution declares that members of the armed forces on active service and any citizen exercising the presidency, by any title, are ineligible. Odría was disqualified on both grounds. He "resigned" as acting president one month before the July 2 "election," and simply disregarded the military clause. The news that Odría had barred all names but his from the ballot caused a revolt in Arequipa, which Odría's troops crushed ruthlessly; hundreds were killed and wounded. With troops patrolling the polling places, Odría was then "elected" as constitutional president. "My election," he stated in his inaugural address, "is the unquestionable product of the popular vote, expressed overwhelmingly."[6]

Adopting the *Aprista* ideas on industrialization, Odría combined the stimulation of production, patricularly of raw materials, with Peronist tactics to keep control in the hands of the oligarchy. As a result of this policy, foreign trade increased, all exchange controls were abolished, and partial payments were started on the defaulted Peruvian bonds. There was much construction of new plants, highways, irrigation projects, railroads, smelters, and other works financed by private capital, the Peruvian government, various International Bank loans, and the United States Point Four Program. When the first oil well in the Sechura desert brought in 420 barrels a day, fifty oil companies obtained concessions in the area. As *Business Week* put it at the time, "Peru is looking better and better to United States investors with a yen to do business in Latin America." Odría's time in power also coincided with the Korean War, which raised the prices of many of Peru's exports and thus kept the economy flourishing. Odría signed a military-assistance agreement with the United States in 1952, and received military aid including three warships at a cost of 10 percent of their value. He increased the size of the armed forces, raised the pay of military personnel, and spent millions of dollars building air bases, army barracks, and munitions factories.

With the expansion of production and military power came a tightening of controls over the population. Liberty was choked off. The opposition press was banned. To make sure that it could not function secretly, the importation, sale, and possession of all duplicating machines were restricted, and permission was needed before such machines were either imported or sold. The death penalty was restored and made applicable to a series of political crimes. Odría took a leaf from Perón's book and tried to identify himself as labor's best friend by issuing decrees granting workers higher pay and other benefits. Unions were barely tolerated, however, and the International Confederation of Free Trade Unions filed a complaint with the International Labor Organization on April 16, 1951, claiming that Peru's government violated trade-union rights. Odría's regime was also criticized by the International League for the Rights of Man and the Inter-American Press Association.

Odría's policy of economic development combined with restrictions on liberty did not please the mass of Peruvians, although it was popular with the oligarchy. The *Aprista* movement continued to function underground, distributing leaflets and newspapers in Peru. Apra leaders were

---

[6] Manuel A. Odría, *A Program of Action* (Lima: Dirección General de Informaciones del Perú, 1950), p. 4.

arrested regularly, and several were killed by the police while "resisting arrest." Thousands of political prisoners were in jail, many of whom were never tried. But despite all this, General Odría never succeeded in stabilizing his regime, and in 1956 the pressure for constitutional government became so great that he permitted a fair election and handed over his office to the victor.

Three candidates presented their names to the voters: Dr. Hernando de Lavalle, Fernando Belaúnde Terry, and Manuel Prado. The *Apristas* asked each of the candidates to promise them freedom to function, and threw their support to ex-President Prado when he promised to govern constitutionally with liberty for all. With the support of the *Apristas*, Prado was elected (Prado, 568,057 votes; Belaúnde, 458,248; Lavalle, 222,618), and he kept his promise. All political prisoners were freed, the exiles returned, and liberty for all was the rule in Peru. The Peruvian Federation of Labor and the *Aprista* Party were allowed to function freely, and both grew rapidly.

To the *Apristas*, the Prado administration was a transitional regime that would govern until 1962, when they expected to win power in a free election. They therefore supported the Prado government against those who wanted to overthrow it, claiming that Peru's great need was constitutional government. The rise of Castroism during this period, the general do-nothing policy of the Prado administration, and the fall in the prices of most of Peru's exports on the world market beginning in 1956 combined to bring inflation and turmoil to Peru. All during Prado's administration, economic conditions were bad. An unusual drought in the southern highlands and United States quota restrictons on lead and zinc, two important Peruvian exports, made matters worse. President Prado kept juggling his cabinet, but he never succeeded in accomplishing much, although the term in office of Prime Minister Pedro Beltrán (1959–61) saw an attempt at developing a policy that would improve conditions.

The election of 1962 was therefore of great importance. By then it was clear to everyone in Peru that something drastic had to be done or the masses of Indians would rise up in violent rebellion. All of the seven candidates for the presidency, therefore, talked about reform. The *Apristas* organized a democratic front with their friends and presented Haya de la Torre as their presidential candidate. General Odría organized a personalistic party, the National *Odriista* Union, to sponsor his candidacy. Fernando Belaúnde Terry, who had been defeated in 1956, was again nominated by the Popular Action Party and again supported by the Communist Party. Four minor candidates also ran: Héctor Cornejo Chávez for the Christian Democratic Movement, Luciano C. Castillo for the Socialist Party, Alberto Ruiz Eldridge for the Social Progess Party, and General César Pando Egusquiza for the National Liberation Front.

The results of the election were a surprise to many people, including the *Apristas*, for although Haya de la Torre received more votes than any other candidate, he failed to receive a majority of the total vote. The official results gave Haya de la Torre 557,047, 32.95 percent; Belaúnde Terry, 544,180, 32.19 percent; Odría, 480,798, 28.43 percent; Cornejo Chávez, 48,792, 2.85 percent; Pando, 33,941, 2.01 percent; Castillo, 16,658, 0.99 percent; and Ruiz, 9,202, 0.54 percent; 8,869 votes were blank, 8,073 were void, and 29,578 were annulled.

Under the Peruvian constitution, if no candidate receives at least one-third of the votes cast, the Congress elects the president from among the three candidates receiving the most votes. The *Apristas* had elected more members of the Congress than any other party, and they attempted to come to an understanding with Belaúnde Terry and Odría to organize a coalition government. They were unable to reach any understanding with Belaúnde Terry, but succeeded in coming to an agreement with their old persecutor, General Odría. Under the terms of this agreement the *Aprista* and *Odriista* congressmen, who together made up a majority of the newly elected Congress, would elect Odría president and an *Aprista* vice-president, and the *Apristas* would get a majority of the cabinet posts.

When the agreement was made known, the officers in control of the armed forces accused the *Apristas* of fraud and asked President Prado to cancel the elections. When he refused, the generals and admirals used tanks to break down the gate of the Presidential Palace, overthrew the government, and set up a military junta to rule Peru. The old routine began all over again as Apra was declared illegal and the armed forces took over its headquarters and prevented its daily newspaper from appearing. But the reaction of the Peruvian people and most foreign governments, including that of the United States, apparently convinced the generals it was impossible to go back to the old ways, and they promised to permit another election in June 1963, to remove their troops from *Aprista* headquarters, and to permit the party to function again.

Since no party had won a majority in the election, this arrangement was accepted and peace returned to Peru. From July 1962 to June 1963 the country was involved in a continuous electoral campaign. This time only four presidential candidates were on the ballot: Haya de la Torre for the *Aprista* Party, Odría for the National *Odriista* Union (UNO), Belaúnde Terry for a coalition of Popular Action and the Christian Democrats, and a Señor Samame who had no important support. The

Communist Party officially supported Belaúnde Terry, although he claimed he did not want their support. With a great deal of fraud and chicanery the election took place as scheduled, and all political parties accepted the results. Belaúnde Terry won the presidency with 708,931 votes, 39.06 percent. Haya de la Torre received 623,532, 34.35 percent; Odría had 463,325, 25.53 percent; and Samame, 19,279, 1.06 percent. Belaúnde could attribute his election to the votes the Christian Democrats and Communists brought him, for his plurality was only about 85,000 votes.

No party won a majority of the seats in either house of the Congress, but the *Apristas* elected the largest bloc of congressmen. After much negotiation between the political party leaders, the *Apristas* and the *Odriistas* agreed to elect an *Odriista* president of the Senate and an *Aprista* president of the Chamber of Deputies for the sessions of the first year. Thus Peru began a new experiment in constitutional government with leaders of the country's four most important parties holding key positions in the legislature and the executive.

During the years following 1963 Peru progressed at a faster rate than it had ever done before. The legislature passed hundreds of laws that changed Peru almost beyond recognition. In December 1963 the first municipal elections ever held introduced local self-government to the cities, and in 1966 another set of local elections took place. Laws were passed to make education free from kindergarten to university. The social security system was liberalized. Trade unions grew in number and in size. A housing agency was set up to foster home building and thousands of housing units were built. An agrarian-reform law was adopted and a beginning was made in satisfying the land hunger of the Indians. Tax rates were increased. A start was made on improving public service. A program known as Popular Cooperation, similar to the Peace Corps, mobilized university students to go to the rural areas to stimulate community development. Industrialization was pushed, the most important development being the creation of automobile assembly plants. Hundreds of millions of dollars in loans came from the Inter-American Development Bank, the United States AID, the Export-Import Bank, and other international agencies for programs in public health, roadbuilding, education, port improvement, housing, irrigation projects, electricity, airports, and other developments.

Most important, constitutional government functioned and something approaching a two-party system emerged. The *Apristas* and the UNO coalition controlled the legislature and ran joint candidates in the local elections of 1963 and 1966. The coalition, of course, tried to take credit for all the laws passed by the legislature. Disputes arose between the coalition and the Popular Action–Christian Democratic Alliance, which also claimed credit for the developments taking place. The congressional majority was much more anticommunist than the Alliance, which had received Communist support in the elections. When the Communists organized a guerrilla force in the jungles, the Congress accused the executive of not taking aggressive action to fight the guerrillas and set up a congressional committee to investigate Communist activities. In addition, the congressional majority opposed deficit financing and voted heavy raises for schoolteachers. This decreased the amount of money available for other developments, and President Belaúnde claimed the *Apristas* were trying to sabotage his programs.

Several times the legislature voted no confidence in Belaúnde's cabinet ministers, and several were forced to resign. Once the Senate refused to confirm the promotion of a general which had been recommended by the President. Despite the disputes, however, both the legislature and the executive were able to function constitutionally, and perhaps it was all to the good to have members of the country's four most important political parties sharing in the control of the government. The only ones not happy with the functioning of the government were the Communists and other absolutists who demanded an instantaneous revolution to introduce utopia. Powerful radio stations in Cuba, the Soviet Union, China, and elsewhere bombarded Peru with programs in Spanish and Quechua, urging the Indians to revolt. A few fanatical university students left Lima and began guerrilla activity in isolated jungles, but they never received support from the Indians and the army defeated all such efforts. Bombs were set off in Lima and other cities.[7] At times the government had to declare a state of siege, but it never developed into dictatorship. The Communists had so small a following in Peru that they were never more than nuisances.

Peru is changing so fast that it is impossible to forecast its future. It is such a rich country that it is little short of tragedy that what has been accomplished in recent years was not begun a long time ago. The country's mineral resources are enormous. Vast areas of land can be developed for agriculture. But until recent years the oligarchy prevented the development of this potential. Even today, except for a small area on the Pacific coast and the Lima metropolitan district, much of the country is still living as it did a hundred years ago. The majority of the population re-

---

[7] See, for example, "Peru: Shock of Recognition," *Newsweek*, July 19, 1965, pp. 39, 42, which reports the activities of a guerrilla group on the eastern slope of the Andes and the bombs set off at the Club Nacional and Hotel Crillon in Lima.

mains illiterate, and since only literates vote, elections are determined by a minority.

The class structure of the country has been changed by the recent developments in industry, agriculture, and transportation, and by a tremendous increase in population. The highland Indians are awakening from their centuries of passive acceptance of an outdated status quo. With the entry of the Peruvian masses into a more active part in the country's life, Peru becomes one of the lands of the future, for its large area and tremendous resources give it the means to support many more millions of people. The decisive moment for Peru will probably come at the 1969 elections. If progress continues until then and a fair election takes place, and if the victor is permitted to take office, perhaps Peru will begin to be the kind of country it has the potential to become.

The Formal Constitutional Framework

Peru is supposed to be governed under the constitution of April 9, 1933, as amended, which states that "Peru is a democratic republic." Yet until a very few years ago true democracy was as far from flourishing in Peru as it had been all through the republic's history. Although Peru has produced seventeen different provisional regulations and constitutions, none has ever been completely observed by those in control of the government, and for long periods the formal constitution has been completely ignored.

Peru's first formal constitution, that of 1823, was drawn up by a convention that, in reaction to General San Martín's dictatorship, tried to limit the executive. But Peru was not ready in 1823 for a complicated system of constitutional government, and by September of that year General Simón Bolívar had been given full authority to lead the war against Spain. This first constitution of Peru was typical of practically all the country's later organic laws. In spite of the unreadiness of the people for self-government and the chaos of war and a collapsing empire, the constitution pictured an ideal state based upon the rights of man and governed by a very complicated system of checks and balances. It was doomed to failure and soon was abolished by the "practical" men of power. Then followed a whole stream of new constitutional "plans." By 1933 Peru had had thirteen constitutions.

The 1933 constitution resembles all of its predecessors, and like them has seldom been observed. It provides for a unitary, democratic, republican system of government divided into executive, legislative, and judicial branches. It has an interesting background. It was written by a constituent assembly that was elected in one of the very few free elections Peru has ever had (although a majority of the population was not permitted to vote). As a result, Peru's constitution contains many clauses that, if they had ever been enforced, might have produced interesting results. For one thing, the president is to be elected by the voters and he appoints his cabinet, but the Congress has the authority to force the resignation of a minister by a vote of no confidence. In addition, Article 166 requires that "The Acts of Government and Administration of the President of the Republic are countersigned by the Minister of the respective department. Without this requisite they are null." If these clauses were enforced, they would result in a parliamentary form of government, since the Congress could continue to censure ministers until those were appointed who had its confidence. As a French scholar wrote in 1934:

> If these articles do not remain a dead letter, if they are honestly applied, it can be held that the presidential system has suffered a defeat in Peru. The possibility of defeating the ministry and compelling it to resign puts an end to presidential autocracy. The President—if, let me say again, the constitution is sincerely applied—will have the character of a parliamentary head of state.[8]

But these clauses were never enforced, and the president continues to be the dominant figure of the government. Until 1963, whenever a dispute arose the executive either abolished or ignored the legislature.

Another interesting section of the constitution provides for a "council of national economy, formed by representatives of the consumer population, capital, labor, and the liberal professions." Such a council has never been established.

The 1933 constitution has on various occasions been superseded by "statutes" issued by military dictatorships. The junta headed by General Odría, for example, issued a decree stating that the junta was "assuming all the attributes which the constitution conferred upon the Executive and the Legislative Powers." Peru's constitution is fairly short, as Latin-American constitutions go, and provides a framework within which constitutional government could function if those in power wanted it to function. Since many of its provisions have never been enforced, it is impossible to say how they would work out in practice, although the experience since 1963 seems to demonstrate that this is a workable constitution.

How the Constitution Is Amended

Peru's constitution can be formally amended by the vote of the majority of the legal membership of each house of Congress. This vote must be

---

8 Boris Mirkine-Guetzevitch, "Presidential System in Peru," *Political Quarterly,* 5 (April 1934): 271.

taken in two different ordinary legislative sessions. Amendments can be introduced for consideration by the members of either house or by the president of the republic with the approval of the Council of Ministers.

The 1933 constitution has been formally amended several times, and the process is fairly responsive to the wishes of a majority of both houses.

Who Participates in Politics

The majority of Peru's population has never participated in the political life of the country, and it was not until 1955 that the constitution was amended to permit women to vote. Although the number of voters has progressively increased since the end of World War II, the constitutional provision that illiterates cannot vote bans the majority from participating in elections. In the 1924 election, when the population was around 5 million, only 288,124 voted. In 1931, the number that voted increased to 299,643. By 1945 the number had risen to 456,310, and by 1956, in the first election in which women voted, 1,249,015 votes were cast, but by then the population was nearly 10 million. By 1963 the number registered to vote had increased to 2,071,117, or 19.1 percent of the total population of 10,838,500 at the census of 1961: 1,815,067 valid votes were cast, 16.47 percent of the total population and 87.63 percent of the number registered.

There are great geographical variations in the proportion of the population which votes, with the smallest percentages in the highland rural areas and the highest in the larger coastal cities. In 1963 only 5.46 percent of the 1961 population was registered to vote in the department of Apurímac, and 8.80 percent in the department of Puno. In Callao, however, 39.62 percent were registered, and 34.61 percent in Lima. The vote in Peru is compulsory for all literate citizens over eighteen if married and over twenty-one if not married. All over sixty are allowed to vote, but for them the vote is not compulsory.

The illiterate generally fail to participate in political life in any way, except for the few enrolled in trade unions in Lima and a few other cities. One investigator reported that in a study of a group of poverty-stricken and largely illiterate adults, 70 percent had never voted in a general election or participated in an official public position, commission, or political party.[9]

Although conditions have improved, it used to be the custom for the government to use its power to prevent the people's participation in

---

[9] Wells M. Allred, "System of Government in Peru," *Philippine Journal of Public Administration*, 4 (January 1960): 59.

political life. In 1944 Professor John Gillin, in his study of the coastal community of Moche, discovered that

> In Moche individuals are not molested in their daily private activities (unless they are suspected of belonging to the suppressed *Aprista* Party), but they are definitely discouraged from attempting to participate on their own initiative in any way in decisions affecting the community as a whole. . . . A considerable amount of grumbling is current, however, and the complaint is common that "Moche is neglected" and has no effective way of making its wants and needs known to the higher administrative centers. . . . In Moche, as elsewhere in Peru, no public meeting may legally take place without the previous issuance of a police permit,[10] which is obtainable only after full explanation of the purposes and expected constituency of the gathering, its place, time, and program. The objective of this regulation is to prevent the formation of disorderly mobs or subversive organizations.[11]

After being prevented from participating in politics for so long, the majority of Peruvians continue to stay outside of political life. The *Aprista* and Communist Parties are the only political organizations that have made any systematic efforts to politicize the illiterate, the rural, and the poverty-stricken.

The Electoral Machinery

Peru has had so few elections in which the votes were fairly counted that it is difficult to speak seriously of the electoral machinery during most of its history; the present system was created only in 1962 by the military junta in preparation for the 1963 election. Graham Stuart writes that "Up until 1896 the election procedure might almost have been termed scandalous."[12] It was in 1896 that direct open voting was introduced, but at the same time the enforcement of the literacy requirement began. The first fairly honestly conducted election came in 1945, but even then the *Aprista* Party, the largest in the country, was not permitted to run its own candidates. In 1956 also a fairly honestly conducted election took place, but again the *Apristas* were not permitted to present candidates.

---

[10] This rule was still being enforced in 1963. I was there when the *Aprista* Party was refused a permit to hold a meeting in a rural area north of Trujillo that year.

[11] John Gillin, *Moche, A Peruvian Coastal Community* (Washington: U.S. Government Printing Office, 1945), p. 93.

[12] Graham H. Stuart, *The Governmental System of Peru* (Washington: Carnegie Institution, 1925), p. 119.

The first really fair election ever held in the country was that of 1962, and when the *Apristas* won the largest plurality, as we have seen, the armed forces canceled the election and took control of the government. The popular reaction was so overwhelmingly opposed to these develop ments that the military junta then permitted another election in 1963, which created the government headed by Belaúnde. Under the system set up by the junta, the election machinery consists of a series of election courts headed by a National Court of Elections, which consists of seven members. The chairman is elected by the Supreme Court of Justice; three members are elected by various university bodies; and three members are chosen by lot from a panel of names submitted by departmental electoral courts. The lower electoral courts are selected in a similar manner.

Elaborate rules have been drawn up to govern the voting. The polls are open from eight A.M. to four P.M. All electoral propaganda ceases two days before election day. All sales of alcoholic beverages cease. No electoral official, candidate, or party official can be arrested except *in flagrante delicto*. The government supplies the ballots. Despite all the elaborate rules and machinery, the 1963 election was marked by many irregularities. In one department where the *Apristas* were very strong, the packages supposed to contain ballots were found to contain blank pieces of paper. In addition, the Communist Party was not permitted to present candidates under a rule that in the past had been used to keep the *Apristas* off the ballot. With the introduction of constitutional government under President Belaúnde, the legislature began efforts to purify the electoral law.

Political Parties

Peru has only recently begun to develop modern political parties to take the place of the personalistic cliques that were known as political parties during most of the country's history. When Professor Stuart made his study of the Peruvian government in 1925, he wrote, "Peru at the present time presents the curious picture of a South American republic without political parties."[13] Since this was written, dozens of political parties have been announced, but nearly all of them died as quickly as they were created. From 1930 to 1963 there were the Syndicalist Party, Peruvian Action, Peruvian Democratic Action, Independent Youth, the National Agrarian Party, the National Party, the Nationalist Party, the Labor

---

[13] *Ibid.*, p. 112.

Party, the Popular Nationalist Party, the Social Democratic Party, the Progressive Party, the Workers' Party, the Social Republican Party, the Authentic Socialist Party, the Decentralist Party, the Social Christian Party, the Social Republican Party, the Radical Party, the Democratic Union, the Federalist Party, and on and on. All parties like these are formed by some person who wants to run for office, not necessarily the presidency. Most of them die as soon as the election for which they were formed has taken place; those that survive do so because a political leader plans to run again or believes that a functioning party will give him political leverage. Dozens of organizations participate in each election campaign, and each of the presidential candidates is sponsored by a coalition of many parties.[14]

Despite the multiplicity of party names, Peru in recent decades has had only two real political parties, one a small Communist party kept going by the international Communist movement and the other the Peruvian *Aprista* Party. Apra is a multiclass party that tries to unite all those who agree with its program. The *Aprista* thinkers believe that the country's colonial past has so conditioned most of the upper classes that they continuously look outside of Peru for ideas, just as they look to more modern countries for markets and for products that Peru could produce for itself. To the *Apristas*, Peru's problem is simple: it needs to discover how to organize its political and social institutions so that they will reflect the needs and aspirations of the Peruvian people. This will mean revolutionary changes in the economic, social, and political organizations of Peru. Some of the specific changes the *Apristas* advocate are universal adult suffrage, an effort to incorporate the Indians within the mainstream of the country's life, and emphasis upon education, health, housing, and social welfare instead of upon militarism and the preservation of the status quo. The *Apristas* favor land reform, industrialization, democratic local government, and decentralization of the national government. On the international scene, they support the free world against Communist expansion and more cooperation among the Latin Americans. The *Aprista* Party cooperates with similar parties in Latin America and has been a member of the League of Popular Parties since 1960 and an observer member of the Socialist International since 1964. In the 1963–69 Congress its members had fifteen seats in the Senate and fifty-seven seats in the Chamber of Deputies.

---

[14] See, for example, the article "Diversos partidos políticos proclaman la candidatura presidencial del Doctor Hernando de Lavalle," *El Comercio*, April 16, 1956, p. 3, which reports that in one day the *Partido Unión Revolucionaria*, the *Partido Descentralista*, and the *Partido Demócrata* all endorsed De Lavalle.

During the 1950's and 1960's, new parties have been organized to oppose the *Apristas*, and many of the old personalistic groups continue to function. The party that received the most votes after the *Apristas* in the 1962 and 1963 elections was the Popular Action Party (AP), headed by Fernando Belaúnde Terry. This is a personalistic grouping that was organized by Belaúnde after the 1956 election as a permanent electoral machine to further his interests. It is difficult to say whether AP is more than a temporary organization. As we have noted, Belaúnde was elected by a coalition of AP and the Christian Democratic Party, supported by the Communist Party and the armed forces. Since taking office, Belaúnde has made some effort to build up his party, but it is impossible to forecast the future of AP. Its program is very similar to that of the *Apristas*, and Belaúnde has talked a great deal of development and of incorporating the Indians into Peru's life. In the 1963–69 legislature, AP had thirty-nine seats in the Chamber of Deputies and fourteen in the Senate. AP has the support of most of the middle class, many of the landowners, and the bulk of the military officers. It is strong in Lima and in the southern part of the country.

The third largest party in Peru is the National *Odriista* Union (UNO), which is composed of the following of General Odría. It is doubtful that this will survive the death of the General. It attracts many of the businessmen and has some support in the slums of Lima and Callao. As the junior partner in the *Aprista*-UNO coalition in the Congress, it has not had to enunciate a clear program. In the 1963–69 legislature it had six senators and twenty-six deputies.

The Christian Democratic Party, although the country's fourth largest in 1963, is a small organization. After receiving a very small vote in 1962, it made an electoral front with the Popular Action Party for the 1963 elections. Its program is similar to that of other Christian Democratic parties, but it contains a faction that has always cooperated with the extremists affiliated with the Communist organizations. In December 1966 the PCD finally split apart and the anticommunist faction, led by Luis Bedoya Reyes, the mayor of Lima, took the name Christian Popular Party (PPC). The other faction continued to use the name Christian Democratic Party. In the 1963–69 legislature, the two factions had thirteen seats in the Chamber and five in the Senate.

Peru's Communist Party (PCP) began life in 1928 as the Peruvian Socialist Party. In 1930 it joined the Third International and changed its name at the request of that body. The success of the *Aprista* Party has kept the PCP small, and has led it to cooperate with anyone who opposed the *Apristas*. Thus at times the PCP has been legal when the *Aprista*

Party was outlawed. It was helped by various dictators who tried to use it to fight *Aprista* influence, especially in the trade unions. Today the Communist Party is split into a series of small groups, each oriented to another "fatherland." One group looks to Moscow, another to Peiping, another to Havana, and still another is Trotskyite. These groups split, unite, and adopt new names so rapidly it is almost impossible to keep track of them. In the 1963–69 legislature, two deputies were elected as candidates of the National Liberation Front, which is a Communist front. Other Communist groups currently use the names Communist Party, the Progressive Social Party, and the Revolutionary Workers' Party (the Trotskyites).

Many other small parties function in Peru, but none is of significance. The Peruvian Democratic Movement had one member in the 1963–69 legislature. The Revolutionary Union at times elects a member. There is a small Socialist party, whose program resembles that of the Communist Party.

Under the rules in force in 1963, parties had to register with the Electoral Court and present a list of 60,000 members to nominate a presidential candidate and 20,000 to nominate candidates for Congress. When a party nominates a candidate, the nominee, in addition to fulfilling all requirements for the office, must file a list of names and a deposit varying from 30,000 soles for presidential candidates to S2,000 for senatorial candidates and S1,000 for candidates to the Chamber of Deputies. Smaller amounts of signatures and money are required for Madre de Dios, the most thinly populated department.

The competition of the AP-CD Alliance with the *Aprista*-UNO coalition gives Peru something resembling a two-party system. If this can continue for a few years, Peru may develop a viable party system at last.

Public Opinion and Pressure Groups

Public opinion is centralized in Lima, as is everything else in the country. The illiterate Indians do not make themselves heard except when a riot occurs in some isolated community. In 1959, when the population was estimated at 10 million, there were 56 newspapers in Peru with a total circulation of about 575,000. The principal dailies were published in Lima but circulated nationally; the provincial newspapers had circulations ranging from 500 to 7,500. The largest circulation was that of *La Crónica*, 80,000 daily. Other large newspapers were *El Comercio* with 75,000, *Última Hora* with 60,000, and *La Prensa* with 55,000. *La Tribuna*, the *Aprista* newspaper, had a circulation of 8,000. Various Communist, Trotskyite and other small political groups issued periodicals, but their circulation was negligible.

The best organized and most important pressure group in Peru is the armed forces, which have either dominated the government or run it outright during most of the republican period. The armed forces act as a sort of state within a state; they have their own schools, hospitals, housing projects, and other privileges that set the officers and enlisted men apart from the rest of the population. Military service is theoretically compulsory and universal, but not everyone is called up for the two years of servce to which all males twenty to twenty-five are liable. In addition to the army, Peru has a national police force of 18,000, an air force with 209 planes (in the early 1960's), and a navy with 54 vessels, including 2 cruisers, 2 destroyers, and 4 submarines. It is thought that much of the armed forces' opposition to a government headed by the *Apristas* is not based on ideology, but is caused by fear of a reduction in their budgets and the loss of their special privileges.

The Catholic church is probably the most nearly universal group in the country and has always been intimately connected with the government. The constitution gives the Catholic church a preferred position, and various constitutional provisions and laws regulate relations between the government and the church. The bishops and archbishops are appointed by the Pope after nomination by the government. The salaries of archbishops, bishops, and priests are a part of the national budget, which also provides funds yearly for the erection and repair of church buildings. The intimate connection between church and state almost inevitably makes the church a defender of the status quo in Peru.

Business groups are well organized in Peru and make their opinions known on all issues affecting them. Every provincial capital has its chamber of commerce and landowners' association. Arequipa, for example, has a Chamber of Commerce, an Association of Commerce and Industry, an Agricultural Society, an Association of Woolgrowers of the South, a Bus Owners' Association, and an Association of Retailers. Professional groups are also well organized.

The labor movement is fairly strong, especially in and around Lima. The Peruvian Confederation of Labor claims about 800,000 members. The National Federation of Farm Workers was organized in 1956 and now claims one to two million members. Many of the large industrialized coastal farms, such as Casa Grande, now have strong unions of their workers pushing for better wages and working conditions. The trade unions have been weakened by the competition between political parties over their control. During General Odría's dictatorship, the government helped the Communists take over some of the trade unions in order to weaken the *Apristas*. Since constitutional government was restored, the *Apristas* have regained control of most of the trade unions, and they hold almost all the offices in the Confederation of Labor.

The organized university students play a special role, as they are articulate and devote much of their time to political activity. The political parties all maintain student organizations, and competition between the various political groups is keen in student elections.

Civil Liberties

The majority of Peru's population seldom enjoyed true civil liberty until the 1960's. With the development of the *Aprista* movement after World War I, a great struggle began to introduce constitutional government and civil liberty. In 1931, when the Leguía dictatorship was overthrown, there was a short period of freedom for the country. This ended in December 1931. From August 1933 to the end of 1934 and from May 1945 to October 1948 there was freedom again in Peru. Except for these short periods, it was not until May 1956 that a Peruvian was able to speak, organize, and travel freely. Since 1956, except for a short time in 1962 just after the military coup d'état, civil liberties have been upheld.

The constitution of 1933, of course, contains all the individual guarantees usually found in modern constitutions. Unfortunately, Article 70 reads, "When the security of the State may require it, the Executive may suspend, completely or partially, in all or in a part of the national territory, the guarantees stated in Articles 56, 61, 62, 67, and 68." (Article 56 sets down the rules governing arrest; Article 61 states, "The domicile is inviolable"; Article 62 gives the right to assemble peacefully; Article 67 covers the right to enter, leave, and travel in Peru; and Article 68 outlaws exile.) Under Article 70, during most of the time since 1933 these rights could not be exercised. It was during these years of dictatorship that about 6,000 *Apristas* were killed, and thousands more were jailed and exiled. It probably was this persecution that steeled the *Apristas* and helped to create the public opinion that insisted upon a freer society in the 1960's.

Since 1963 civil liberty has been the rule in Peru, and there is little evidence that dictatorship any longer has the strength and support it had during so much of Peru's past.

The Executive

The Peruvian executive is headed by a president elected for a six-year term by a simple majority vote, which must consist of at least 33.33

percent of the votes cast. If no candidate receives at least one-third of the votes cast, the Congress chooses from among the three highest candidates. No president has been fairly elected and allowed to complete his term since the constitution was adopted in 1933. Manuel Prado has come closest to doing this. Elected in a managed election by the Benavides dictatorship in 1938, he served until July 28, 1945, when he turned his office over to the candidate regularly elected in that year. In 1956 Prado was elected in a fair election by getting the *Apristas* to support him, but he was expelled from the country by a military junta in 1962, shortly before he would have completed his term.

The president is supposed to serve a six-year term and is not eligible for the following term, although he can become a candidate after an interval of six years. Elaborate constitutional provisions outline who is not eligible to be president, but these have seldom been observed. Two vice-presidents are elected at the same time, in the same manner, with the same qualifications, and for the same term as the president. Since the constitutional amendment setting forth these provisions was adopted in 1936, no vice-president has succeeded to the presidency. The vice-presidents have no power except to serve the unexpired term and to substitute for the president temporarily when he leaves the country, takes command of the armed forces, or is incapacitated. The president can appoint the vice-presidents to other positions, and in the Belaúnde administration the first vice-president is in charge of the agrarian-reform program.

Whoever exercises the presidency in Peru is a strong executive if he can control the armed forces, for the limitations upon his actions, especially the power of Congress to vote no confidence in his cabinet ministers, have not operated as intended. In addition, the failure for so many years to institute the type of local government outlined by the constituion further strengthened the president. The constitution gives the president extensive powers, the most important of which are the power to issue decrees and regulations, to suspend certain guarantees of individual liberties, to appoint most officials including those of the Catholic church, to make up the budget, and to command the armed forces and police. If the president has control of the armed forces he can do almost anything he wants to do, including extending his term in office, as General Odría did from 1948 to 1956. Although all acts of the government and administration must be countersigned by a cabinet minister, this does not seriously limit the president, as he appoints and removes the ministers on the proposal and with the agreement of the president of the Council of Ministers, and he alone appoints and removes the president of the Council of Ministers.

The president of Peru receives a salary of S600,000 a year (about $22,370 U.S.) plus S120,000 for official entertaining ($4,475). Each of his twelve ministers receives S120,000 a year. In 1965 there were 114,595 permanent civilian positions in the Peruvian government plus 421 Catholic archbishops, bishops, and other church functionaries. The budget supplied no figures on the armed services. Generally speaking, the public service is overstaffed, inefficient, and tied down by a multiplicity of forms requiring signatures. There seems to be a very large number of clerical and stenographic employees and minor functionaries, but there do not appear to be adequate funds for travel or modern office equipment. Many complicated regulations and internal controls have created a seemingly endless stream of papers passed from desk to desk. Very few formal public administration techniques are used, and hiring, firing, promotion, and classification are done on the basis of patronage and friendship. The poor quality of administration is particularly noticeable outside Lima, as everything is centralized in the capital. In 1963 President Belaúnde set up an agency to improve the public administration. A substantial part of the government's work is handled by various kinds of independent agencies not too well controlled by the president.

The Legislative Power

The Peruvian legislature is a bicameral body consisting of a Senate and a Chamber of Deputies. The membership of the legislature is set by law, roughly in proportion to the population of the various departments. In the 1963–69 term the Senate had 45 members and the Chamber of Deputies 140. The members of both houses serve the same six-year term as the president and are elected by proportional representation. The retiring president becomes a part of the Senate for one senatorial term. To be a deputy one must be a Peruvian by birth, enjoy the right of suffrage, and be twenty-five years old and a native of the department from which elected or have had three years of consecutive residence in the department. To be a senator one must be Peruvian by birth, enjoy the right of suffrage, and be thirty-five years old. Not eligible to be a deputy or a senator, unless they have resigned their positions six months before the election, are the president of the republic, ministers of state, prefects, subprefects, governors, all judges, members of the departmental councils or of the municipal councils of the district where one is a candidate, the clergy, members of the armed forces, and all public employees directly removable by the executive power, including those of the departmental or municipal councils, public benevolent societies, and institutions or corporations subordinate to the executive or subject to its veto. This disqualifies a tremendous number of persons and perhaps helps to explain why the legislature has generally been of such poor quality in Peru. Members of the legislature cannot hold any other public office or be employees of any level of government, including the public charitable societies or corporations subordinate to the executive power. The only exception to this constitutional rule is that members of the Congress can be ministers of state or heads of international delegations. They also can accept unremunerated commissions from the executive with the permission of the house of which they are members.

Peruvian legislators receive substantial salaries, but practically all of them continue to work at their professions while the legislature is in session. Although reelection is allowed, the irregular life of the legislature in the past and its relative unimportance in comparison with the executive tended to prevent individuals from making a career of the Senate or the Chamber. Deputies and senators receive S7,000 ($261) monthly plus S8,000 ($298) for secretarial help and certain other perquisites including medical services, certain free transportation, mail, telegraph, and telephone service, and the use of offices. The president of each house is provided with a car and a chauffeur as well as a sum for entertainment of guests to the Congress.

The Peruvian legislature has traditionally been subservient to the executive, but since 1963 it has tried to act like the legislatures in other democratic countries.[15] Since the 1963 election, the legislative majority has consisted of members of the *Aprista* and UNO parties and their allies, while the minority has consisted of the AP and Christian Democratic Party members and their allies. The congressional majority has made a determined effort to have the legislature function effectively and the results have been good. Thus a balance of power has been set up in which the executive is continuously faced by a legislature controlled by the opposition. In the United States such a situation is accepted as not unusual, but it is a new experience for Peru.

Peru's legislature has all the powers a legislature usually has in a democratic state. Its main work consists of passing laws, and for this purpose it has a system of committees that handle the preparation of the bills. The legislature can amend the constitution and has certain pardoning powers. The president of the republic can veto the bills passed by the

---

[15] The lineup in the Peruvian legislature elected in 1963 was as follows: Senate: *Acción Popular*, 14; *Partido Demócrata Cristiano*, 5; *Movimiento Democrático Peruano*, 2; *Partido Aprista Peruano*, 15; *Unión Nacional Odriista*, 6; independents, 3. Chamber of Deputies: *Acción Popular*, 39; *Partido Demócrata Cristiano*, 10; *Movimiento Democrático Peruano*, 1; *Partido Aprista Peruano*, 57; *Partido Socialista*, 1; *Unión Nacional Odriista*, 24; *Frente de Liberación Nacional*, 2; and independents, 6.

Congress, but the Congress can override his veto by a three-fifths vote of the total membership of both houses. If the president does not sign or veto a bill passed by the Congress, Congress can publish it after ten days, and the executive branch must then comply with and administer the provisions of the law.

Most competent observers believe the present legislature is the best one the country has ever had, and the balance between the legislature and the executive is doing more to strengthen constitutional government than anything else that has happened in Peru in recent years. It is becoming accepted that a government can have an opposition yet continue to function. At the same time, all the political parties are exceedingly careful not to upset the constitutional system.

Twice from 1963 to 1965 the legislature voted no confidence in a minister, and in each case the minister resigned. These actions stimulated much antagonism between the legislature and the executive, but the long-run effect was good in that each side has learned to try to cooperate with the other. In December 1964 the Senate refused to agree to the promotion of an air-force general when the promotion was submitted by the president, but in this case also, since the legislature was acting constitutionally, a crisis was avoided. If the present situation can be continued until 1969, when a new election is scheduled, the spirit of compromise may be so strengthened that constitutional government will become the normal procedure in Peru.[16]

Public Finance

Peru's budget is prepared by the Office of the Budget in the Ministry of Finance. After the proposed budget has been discussed and approved by the Council of Ministers, it is sent to the Chamber of Deputies before August 31, with a copy to the Senate. The Chamber and Senate budget committees have the power to revise, but must keep the budget in balance.

Both income and expenditures of the Peruvian government have risen rapidly since World War II. Income in 1949 was less than S1 billion. By 1951 it was S1.94 billion; in 1955 it was S3.36 billion; in 1961 is was S9.89 billion; and by 1963 it had reached S14,021,167,700. The 1963 budget as approved by the military junta then in control of the government, shown in Tables 1 and 2, is representative of the recent revenues

---

[16] In July 1967, when the legislature was supposed to meet, President Belaúnde's supporters in the Senate refused to attend sessions, thus preventing the legislature from functioning. Under the rule that requires 55 percent of the senators for a quorum, the minority was able to create a constitutional crisis similar to that of the 1940's which ended with military dicatorship and the disbanding of the legislature by force.

TABLE 1
ESTIMATED REVENUE OF PERU, 1963

Source	Amount in Soles	Percent of Total
Direct taxes on income and profits	S3,735,000,000	26.63%
Indirect taxes (imports, exports, etc.)	3,901,150,000	27.82
Government monopolies (alcohol, coca, guano, salt, tobacco, imported wines and liquors)	725,000,000	5.18
Government property	98,988,716	0.71
Various taxes and fees, postage stamps, etc.	298,133,984	2.13
Extraordinary income	625,720,000	4.46
Special-account income (national fund for economic development, special taxes on public works)	4,637,175,000	33.07
Total	S14,021,167,700	100.00%

TABLE 2
ESTIMATED EXPENDITURES OF PERU, 1963

	Amount in Soles	Percent of Total
Legislature	S58,989,000	0.42%
Judiciary	113,036,000	0.80
National election jury	48,619,000	0.35
Executive		
President's office	67,927,000	0.48
Ministry of Government, Police, Post Office, and Telecommunications	1,676,090,000	11.95
Ministry of Foreign Relations	119,000,000	0.85
Ministry of Justice and Religion	161,725,000	1.15
Ministry of Labor and Indian Affairs	42,600,075	0.30
Ministry of Public Education	2,579,206,100	18.39
Ministry of Finance and Commerce	1,678,548,716	11.97
Ministry of War	1,268,225,500	9.04
Ministry of the Navy	667,651,000	4.76
Ministry of the Air Force	678,583,000	4.83
Ministry of Development and Public Works	2,428,696,100	17.32
Ministry of Public Health and Social Welfare	2,042,085,900	14.56
Ministry of Agriculture	382,880,025	2.73
Controller General	7,305,284	0.10
Total	S14,021,167,700	100.00%

and expenditures of Peru. As the figures demonstrate, and as has been traditional in Peru, not enough revenue comes from those best able to pay taxes; most comes from indirect taxes, charges for services, and profits on government monopolies (73.37 percent in 1963).

Peru utilizes a privately owned but government-supervised tax collecting agency to collect most taxes, the *Caja de Depósitos y Consignaciones*. This agency also makes payments to certain government employees and agencies. The *Caja* receives a commission on money collected as payment for its services. There is much complaint about the way the *Caja* functions, particularly its slowness in sending tax notices and in making collections. These deficiencies are reported to contribute to a high rate of tax delinquency. Complaints are also voiced against the *Caja* for the high commissions it charges various governmental units for its services. These charges, one study reported, amounted to 5, 8, and 10 percent of the total annual expense for three local governmental units.

The Peruvian income tax is progressive, from 7 percent to a maximum of 30 percent. Certain taxes are based on the source of the income, however, and it is possible to be taxed more than 30 percent. There are, in addition, taxes on profits and excess profits which range from 7 to 20 percent.

Local Government

For administrative purposes the republic of Peru is divided into 23 departments, which are divided into 144 provinces, which are divided into 1,499 districts. The system of local government is extremely centralized and has continued almost without change since it was created by the 1828 constitution. Many of the boundaries of the local subdivisions were set hundreds of years ago and have no relation to the geographical features of the areas. Some units include a part of the coast, a part of the sierra, and a part of the Amazon jungle.

Each department is headed by a prefect who is appointed by the president. Each province is headed by a subprefect who is responsible to the prefect and is appointed by the president. Each district is under a governor appointed by the prefect upon recommendation of the subprefect. In each part of a district where there is a population group needing special attention, there is a lieutenant governor appointed by the subprefect upon recommendation by the governor.

This system provides a very inefficient way of doing things, as all decisions of any importance are made in the office of the Ministry of Government in Lima. Prefects and subprefects have low budgets, small staffs, and low salaries.[17] They are powerful officials, not because of the financial and material resources at their command, but because of their close connection with the national executive and the police and armed forces. The powers and responsibilities of the prefects, subprefects, governors, and lieutenant governors include representing the president, maintaining law and order, publicizing and enforcing decrees and laws, supervising all government officials and employees in their jurisdictions, receiving complaints from citizens and organized groups, levying and collecting fines for some kinds of illegal acts, policing price controls, enforcing court orders, and carrying out orders from higher officials. Prefects and subprefects are usually not natives of the departments or provinces they supervise. Governors usually are residents of their districts and lieutenant governors always are natives of their communities; neither of them receives a salary for his work.

The 1933 constitution provides for democratically elected councils in the departments and in the urban municipalities, but this was not the practice until 1963. Before that all departmental and municipal councils were appointed from above, either by the Ministry of Government in Lima or by the prefect. There are really three levels of local government in Peru. Internal security and the wishes of the central government are under the chain of command which goes from the ministry to the prefect to the subprefect to the governor and the lieutenant governor.

In the capital cities of the 144 provinces, municipal governments have been set up under an *alcalde* and a council. Until 1963 the *alcalde* and the council were appointed by the ministry or the prefect, depending on the importance of the city. The municipal government concerns itself with health, water supply, streets, supervision of the market, public spectacles, electricity, lighting of streets, public transportation, sewers, and such things. Since they have little independent taxing power, until 1963 the municipal officials were agents of the central government in providing whatever services the central government wanted to finance in each locality. In 1964 the central government began a system of subsidies to local governments which has about doubled the income of most municipalities.

A third level of local government is found in the Indian communities: about 1,500 Indian communities are legally recognized, 800

---

[17] In 1958 the department of Cuzco, with a population estimated at 782,000, had a budget of S247,500 and ten employees in addition to the prefect. In that year the province of Chachis had a budget of S33,750 and two employees in addition to the subprefect. See the study made by the Plan Regional para el Desarrollo del Sur del Perú, *Informe*, vol. 23, *Funciones y medios del gobierno local* (Lima, 1959), pp. ii–iii, 34.

are going through the legal process to acquire recognition, and about 2,000 have made no attempt to be legally recognized. The Indian communities handle the distribution and redistribution of the lands owned by the group, settle disputes, and maintain public order. Theoretically they are supervised by the Ministry of Labor and Indian Affairs, but in practice almost all Indian communities are dominated by the governor or lieutenant governor of the area. The national ministries are supposed to provide services such as education, public health, roads, and police, but in practice such services are either nonexistent or of very poor quality in most small rural communities.

All observers agree that until 1963 there was almost no local self-government in Peru, despite the elaborate provisions for it in the constitution. The four parties that won most of the votes in the 1963 election all pledged their efforts to democratize the local government system, and the newly created national organization for the improvement of public administration is carrying on studies to lay the basis for a reorganization of the system of local government.

The Judicial Power

Peru's judicial power is exercised by a Supreme Court of eleven members, nineteen superior courts, and various lower courts. Justices of the Supreme Court are chosen by the Congress from a list of ten names proposed by the executive. The executive appoints the members of the superior courts from lists of names presented to it by the Supreme Court, and the members of the minor courts from lists of names presented by the superior courts. The military operates its own military tribunals.

Justice in Peru is slow and the judicial system is dominated by the executive power, which participates in the appointment of all judges and other judicial officials.

Peru: A Last Word

At this writing Peru is living under the most democratic political system it has enjoyed since it became a republic. The executive is governing constitutionally, the legislature and the courts function freely, and the ordinary Peruvian is free to come and go as he pleases. The economic system is growing, education and transportation are improving, and there is much optimism about Peru's future.

Peru appears to be on the verge of institutionalizing constitutional government. In all of the country's history as an independent republic, no freely elected president has ever completed his term and handed over his sash of office to another freely elected president. If Fernando Belaúnde can do this in 1969, it will be time to say a new day has dawned in Peru.

Peru demonstrates that a country may need a good, responsible opposition as much as or even more than it needs a good, responsible government. Much of the difficulty in Peru has been due to the refusal of the oligarchy to permit *any* opposition to its method of governing. When the *Aprista* movement developed into the country's first modern political party in the 1920's, the oligarchy for the first time in its history was faced by an opposition interested in more than simply gaining power. Perhaps the most important speech Haya de la Torre ever made was the one he delivered in Trujillo after a falsified vote count had deprived him of the presidency of the republic. He appealed to the *Apristas* not to revolt, because it was not their sole mission to win political power. "Anyone," he said, "can arrive at the palace because the road that leads to it may be bought with gold or conquered with guns."[18] But the *Aprista* movement was to be a responsible educational organization. Thus began the historic struggle out of which the new Peru was to emerge.

The Peruvian experience demonstrates how important modern political parties are to the creation of constitutional government. The mere presence of the *Aprista* Party forced its opposition to found competing political parties, and thus a stable party system seems to be emerging. In the years since 1963 there have been regular party caucuses in the legislature, and all political groups try to function in imitation of the *Apristas*, with permanent headquarters and formal organizations. Not all the groups that call themselves political parties in Peru are modern political parties, but the presence of one strong permanent party has had a polarizing effect, and in 1965 four parties between them gained almost all the votes cast.

Peru still has a long way to go. Its five million or so Indians still must be brought into the mainstream of events. The electoral system must be democratized so that all Peruvians can participate in politics. Illiteracy remains high, transportation still must be developed, agrarian reform is just beginning; but starts have been made in all these areas. The Communists try to rouse the Indians to violent revolt, but the economy is booming, the Peruvians seem to have a new feeling of confidence, and regardless of party all except those who admire the Soviet or Chinese system are optimistic about the future. Success for Peru will mean another nail in communism's coffin in Latin America, for if revolutionary changes

----

[18] Víctor Raúl Haya de la Torre, "Discurso post-electoral en la ciudad de Trujillo," *Política Aprista* (Lima: Editorial Cooperativa Aprista Atahualpa, 1933), p. 82.

can come to a country with all the problems of Peru, then violent revolution is unnecessary anywhere in Latin America.

As this book went to press, news came that Belaúnde had been deposed in a bloodless coup by the military leaders who had helped to install him in the presidency five years earlier. At two o'clock one October morning in 1968, army tanks moved on the Presidential Palace and a force of Peruvian Rangers burst in to hustle Belaúnde unceremoniously to the airport, where he was put aboard a plane for exile in Argentina.

The ostensible reason for the coup was Belaúnde's failure to make good on an old campaign promise to expropriate the International Petroleum Company, a subsidiary of Standard Oil of New Jersey. He did take over the company's La Brea y Pariñas oilfield, but the terms of the settlement, permitting the company to continue to refine and market Peruvian oil, aroused the military to nationalistic rage.

Belaúnde's own Popular Action Party was split over the oilfield affair, as over much else, and the rest of Peru's traditional political parties had grown increasingly fragmented and factionalized. The outlook for the *Apristas* in the elections scheduled for 1969 had seemed very good indeed. But with the October coup the picture changed literally overnight.

With Belaúnde gone, the commander of Peru's army, General Juan Velasco Alvarado, installed himself as president, appointed an all-military cabinet, closed the Congress, and canceled the government's agreement with the United States-owned oil company. For the moment, at least, he had nothing to say on the subject of elections.

And so once again the military has intervened to depose a duly elected president and prevent the orderly processes of democratic government in Latin America.

SELECTED READINGS

ALEXANDER, ROBERT J. "Communism in Peru," *Communism in Latin America*, pp. 220–34. New Brunswick, N.J.: Rutgers University Press, 1957.
———. "Víctor Raúl Haya de la Torre and 'Indo-America,'" *Prophets of the Revolution*, pp. 75–108. New York: Macmillan Co., 1962.
ALLRED, WELLS M. "System of Government in Peru," *Philippine Journal of Public Administration* 4 (January 1960): 46–60.
ARCINIEGAS, GERMÁN DE. "The Military vs. Aprismo in Peru," *The State of Latin America*, pp. 79–94. New York: Alfred A. Knopf, Inc., 1952.
"The Atlantic Report: Peru." *Atlantic* 205 (April 1960): 26–33.
BEALS, CARLETON. "Aprismo: The Rise of Haya de la Torre." *Foreign Affairs* 13 (January 1935): 236–46.

BEATTY, W. D. "Peru's Growth toward Stability." *Current History* 40 (April 1960): 225–31.

BELAÚNDE TERRY, FERNANDO. *La Conquista del Perú por los peruanos.* Lima: Ediciones Tawantínsuyu, 1959.

BOURRICAULD, FRANÇOIS. "Remarques sur l'oligarchie peruvienne." *Revue française de science politique* 14 (August 1964): 675–708.

CAREY, JAMES C. *Peru and the United States, 1900–1962.* Notre Dame, Ind.: University of Notre Dame Press, 1964.

GÓMEZ, ROSENDO A. "Peru: The Politics of Military Guardianship." In *Political Systems of Latin America*, edited by Martin C. Needler. Princeton, N.J.: D. Van Nostrand Co., 1964.

HAYA DE LA TORRE, VÍCTOR RAÚL. *Pensamiento político.* 5 vols. Lima: Ediciones Pueblo, 1961.

HOLMBERG, ALLAN R. "Changing Community Attitudes and Values in Peru: A Case Study in Guided Change." In Richard N. Adams *et al., Social Change in Latin America Today: Its Implications for United States Policy.* New York: Harper & Bros., 1960.

"How to Win an Election." *Newsweek,* July 15, 1950, p. 40.

HUME, SAMUEL, and MARTIN, EILEEN M. "Peru," *The Structure of Local Governments throughout the World,* pp. 428–32. The Hague: Martinus Nijhoff, 1961.

KANTOR, HARRY. "Aprismo: Peru's Indigenous Political Theory." *South Atlantic Quarterly* 53 (January 1954): 1–9.

———. *The Ideology and Program of the Peruvian Aprista Movement.* Berkeley: University of California Press, 1953. 2nd ed. Washington: Savile Book Shop, 1966. In Spanish as *El Movimiento Aprista Peruano.* Buenos Aires: Pleamar, 1964.

———. "Las Lecciones del movimiento aprista para la América Latina." *Presente* (Lima) 7 (August–September 1964): 21–24.

LEÓN DE VIVERO, FERNANDO. *El Tirano quedó atrás.* Mexico City: Editorial Cultural, 1951.

MACDONALD, AUSTIN F. "Peru," *Latin American Politics and Government,* pp. 344–83. 2nd ed. New York: Thomas Y. Crowell Co., 1954.

MCNICOLL, ROBERT E. "Recent Political Developments in Peru." *Inter-American Economic Affairs* 18 (Summer 1964): 77–86.

MARIÁTEGUI, JOSÉ CARLOS. *Siete ensayos de interpretación de la realidad peruana.* Santiago de Chile: Editorial Universitaria, 1955.

OWENS, R. J. *Peru.* London: Oxford University Press, 1963.

PAYNE, JAMES L. *Labor and Politics in Peru.* New Haven: Yale University Press, 1965.

PAZ-SOLDÁN, JOSÉ. *Las Constituciones del Perú.* Madrid: Ediciones Cultura Hispánica, 1954.

"Peru: The New Conquest." *Time,* March 12, 1965, pp. 32–42.

PLAN REGIONAL PARA EL DESARROLLO DEL SUR DEL PERÚ. *Informe.* Vol. 23, *Funciones y medios del gobierno local.* Lima, 1959.

QUIJANO O., ANÍBAL. "El Movimiento campesino del Perú y sus líderes." *América Latina,* October–December 1965, pp. 43–65.

SOUTHERN PERU REGIONAL DEVELOPMENT PROJECT. *Report.* Vol. 5, *The Political System* [in Puno], pp. 39–42; vol. 12, *The Political System from the Parcialidad to the Department,* pp. 2–25. Lima, 1959.

STUART, GRAHAM H. *The Governmental System of Peru.* Washington: Carnegie Institution, 1925.

U.S. Department of Labor. *Labor in Peru.* Bureau of Labor Statistics report no. 262. Washington: U.S. Government Printing Office, 1964.

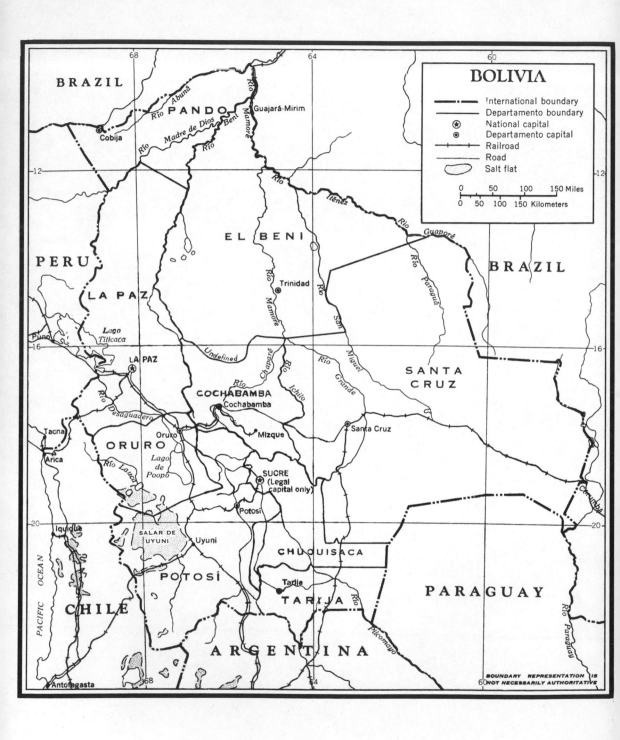

BRAZIL

PANDO

Río Abuná

Río Madre de Dios

Río

Río Beni

Río Mamoré

Guajará-Mirim

Cobija

PERU

LA PAZ

EL BENI

Río Mamoré

Trinidad

Río Iténez

Río Guaporé

Río Paraguá

BRAZIL

Puno

Lago Titicaca

Undefined

Río Chaparé

Río Ichilo

Río San Miguel

Río Grande

SANTA CRUZ

Tacna

Arica

LA PAZ

Río Desaguadero

ORURO

Lago de Poopó

COCHABAMBA

Cochabamba

Oruro

Mizque

Santa Cruz

Corumbá

SUCRE
(Legal
capital only)

Río Lauca

Potosí

IQUIQUE

SALAR DE UYUNI

Uyuni

CHUQUISACA

PARAGUAY

PACIFIC OCEAN

CHILE

POTOSÍ

Tarija

TARIJA

Río

Río Pilcomayo

Río Paraguay

Antofagasta

ARGENTINA

BOLIVIA

International boundary
Departamento boundary
National capital
Departamento capital
Railroad
Road
Salt flat

0   50   100   150 Miles
0   50 100 150 Kilometers

——20——

BOLIVIA:

The Struggling Revolution

Bolivia, probably because it was one of the main sources of wealth for the Spanish government during colonial days, had fastened upon it in extreme form an exploitive, reactionary, semifeudal social system that prevented its people from developing a modern state after independence. The Chaco War of the 1930's unleashed new forces that culminated in the revolution of 1952. Since then Bolivia has been the scene of a tremendous struggle to create a modern nation-state. It is still too soon to say what the final result will be, but great advances have been made toward setting up viable political institutions. The country probably has changed more in the years since 1952 than it did in all the decades since independence, and it is doubtful that it could ever go back to what it was.

A National Profile

Bolivia, located in the west-central part of South America, is one of the continent's two republics without a seacoast. Measuring 950 miles at its greatest length and about 900 miles at its greatest width, with an area of about 424,162 square miles, Bolivia is one of the larger Latin-American countries, even though it has lost about 492,165 square miles of territory through chronic misgovernment that led to wars and border disputes with more powerful neighbors. Bounded by Peru and Chile on the west, by Brazil on the north and east, by Paraguay and Argentina on the south, Bolivia has vast expanses of territory that are virtually uninhabited. The

503

bulk of the population lives on a high plateau between the parallel chains of the Andes, which are most widely separated as they pass through Bolivia.

Bolivia's mountains divide the country into three main regions. The upland plateau, known as the *altiplano,* includes about 27 percent of the country's territory and is inhabited by about 58 percent of the population. This is a cold, semiarid region from 12,000 to 14,000 feet above sea level, surrounded by Andes peaks reaching 20,000 feet. This is the political, educational, and economic heartland of the country. To the east and north of the mountains is a lowland area, much of which is unexplored and empty jungle, a part of the Amazon and La Plata valleys. This region includes 58 percent of the area and is inhabited by only 15 percent of the population. Between the *altiplano* and the lowlands is an area known as the *yungas,* semitropical valleys leading down from the mountains. Here are found 27 percent of the people living on 13 percent of the land area. This is a region of mild climate, fertile soil, and abundant rainfall. It could support many more people if the difficulty of building roads on the steep slopes did not keep it so isolated.

Bolivia has always been a land of great contrasts, and much of its difficulty in establishing a stable constitutional government originates in the difficulty of knitting these three areas together politically, economically, and socially. Never in history have these three areas been unified by anything except lines drawn on a map; until the development of modern means of communication and transportation, the three areas were strangers to each other.

Bolivia in mid-1966 had an estimated population of 4,136,400. About 55 to 60 percent of Bolivia's people are Indians, mostly Aymarás, Quechuas, and Guaranís. About 87,000 Indians live a tribal life in the lowland tropical forest. The highland Indians, from the Spanish conquest to 1952, were illiterate, exploited semiserfs working on the latifundia and in the mines owned by the "whites."[1] About 25 percent of the population are *mestizos* (known as *cholos* in Bolivia) and about 13 percent are white. There has always been a sharp differentiation between the three groups in Bolivian society, and it is only since the 1952 revolution that efforts have been made to integrate the Indians into the mainstream of Bolivian development. The most important measure was the land-reform program. Before 1953, it was estimated that about 4.5 percent of the farms contained about 70 percent of the total farmland. Less than 10

---

[1] For a picture of how these people lived before the 1952 revolution, see Frank L. Keller, "Finca Ingavi—A Medieval Survival on the Bolivian Altiplano," *Economic Geography,* 26 (January 1950): 37–50.

percent of the farmland was under intensive cultivation and 35 percent of the country's total imports consisted of farm products, almost all of which could have been grown in Bolivia. Most of the latifundia have been redistributed; the only large landholdings remaining are the few that were being efficiently operated before the land-reform program was initiated.

Only 35 percent of the population is urban and about half of the country's area is almost completely unpopulated. Although there is little prospect that the highland area can be developed, there are extensive areas on the eastern and northern plains susceptible of development. Spanish is the official language, but only about 40 percent use it.

About 95 percent of the population is supposed to be Roman Catholic, but there are many indigenous customs grafted onto Catholicism. Until 1961 church and state were united, with the government exercising the patronage, but this ended when the constitution of 1961 was adopted. Most of the Indian population has always been illiterate, and as late as 1957 only 28 percent of children from five to nineteen were enrolled in schools. Of those who attend school, about 70 percent drop out before completing the six-year primary course, although it is free and theoretically obligatory. As a result, only about 37 percent of those over fifteen years of age were literate in 1964. It is estimated that less than 2 percent of the population has the equivalent of a high school education. In recent years the government has increased the amounts spent on education, and in 1966 it devoted more than a fourth of the total budget to the schools.

In addition to being illiterate, most Bolivians are poor, ill fed, and ill housed. About 73 percent of all urban dwellers and 90 percent of the rural population are poorly housed, and it is estimated that there is a shortage of about 615,000 dwelling units. Good water and sewers are in short supply. In 1966 only 12 percent of the people had access to running water, and some of this was of doubtful purity. Less than 9 percent of the total population was served by a sewer system. As a result, many diseases are endemic. Most of the poor Indians habitually chew coca leaves, a mild narcotic, to make their hunger and misery bearable. Class lines are very sharply drawn. The best estimate is that until the 1952 revolution not more than 0.2 percent of the population constituted an aristocracy that controlled practically all wealth and power. Although most of the aristocracy was white, money was the distinguishing factor; the richest man in Bolivia was a full-blooded Indian, Simón Patiño, who accumulated one of the world's great fortunes from tin, Bolivia's most important export since the latter part of the nineteenth century.

As recently as 1965 the effective labor force was estimated to include only 41 percent of the population. About 3 percent of the labor force, those in mining and petroleum, produced most of the exports that earned foreign exchange. Agriculture utilized 48.7 percent of the economically active; industry, 5.6 percent; construction, 5.8 percent; trade and finance, 5.3 percent; transport, 2.9 percent; government, 2.8 percent; other services, 8.9 percent; and 17 percent were unemployed. Although almost 50 percent of the economically active were in agriculture and livestock production, they produced only 28 percent of the gross national product. From 1960 to 1965 the gross national product went up at an annual rate of about 5 percent, which was better than the average rate for all of Latin America. Yet it remains necessary to import food, especially wheat.

Bolivia has always been famous for its mines. In addition to tin, Bolivia produces lead, antimony, zinc, copper, gold, and silver. Since 1952 petroleum production has increased greatly, and minerals now account for about 95 percent of the total value of exports. Industry contributes 14.4 percent of the gross national product; textiles, foodstuffs, beverages, glass, ceramics, chemicals, cement, and leather goods are the most important products. The governments since 1952 have pushed economic development with the assistance of foreign aid.

As can be seen from this brief review, Bolivia is a backward, underdeveloped country, although there is much evidence that it contains extensive unexploited and in some cases unexplored natural resources. Only about 2 percent of the land is used for agriculture, and strangely enough, most of this is poor land, while much rich land lies unused. A poor communications system isolates the Bolivians, and their health, the level of their education, and their cultural patterns do not permit rapid development of the country's resources. Not only is Bolivia underpopulated; most of its people live in the wrong part of the territory. During the 1950's and 1960's there has been a flow of people from the *altiplano* and the *yungas* to the lowlands, where the economy has been growing, but the plains remain very underpopulated. The United States government, recognizing the importance of helping Bolivia's revolution to succeed, supplied $198,068,000 in aid (3.3 percent of total United States aid to Latin America and 0.2 percent of total world aid) from 1954 to 1963. Other assistance has come from the United Nations, Germany, Argentina, Japan, and Great Britain.

The Development of Modern Bolivia

What is now Bolivia never existed as a unit before the Spaniards came to America, and much of its difficulty in developing a viable political system can be traced to the Spanish custom of creating boundaries where there was no logical reason for them to be. Although the history of the area before the sixteenth century is practically unknown, it is now established that the area around Lake Titicaca has been inhabited for thousands of years. This is one of the places where America's first inhabitants began the development that culminated in the Inca empire. Long before the Incas rose to power, however, at a site eight miles southeast of Lake Titicaca, now known as Tiahuanaco, there existed a great stone city whose ruins have astonished all who have seen them.

When the Inca state developed, what is now the mountainous section of Bolivia became the southern part of Kollasuyu, one of the four major subdivisions of the empire of Tahuantínsuyu. Kollasuyu was inhabited by farmers who lived in the valleys of the Andean plateau, with Cuzco as their central city. The Inca troops never succeeded in conquering the lowland Indians of the Amazon and La Plata basins east of the mountains, but they impressed a unified culture on most of the highland area from Ecuador to Chile. Unfortunately, the Spaniards split the Inca empire into variously named political units, thus creating discrete colonies out of what had been a fairly well-integrated political, social, and economic unit.

The Spanish troops had little difficulty in conquering Kollasuyu and soon founded most of the cities that today are important in Bolivia. The area had the three things the Spanish most wanted: docile Indians, fertile soil, and minerals of value. Thus what was to be known as Charcas, later as Upper Peru, then as Bolivia, became a colony of great value to Spain. The Indians and the land were divided among the Spanish invaders by means of the systems of *encomienda* and *repartimiento*. Under the *encomienda* system, the crown made a Spaniard responsible for the protection, education, and religious training of a particular group of Indians, in return for which the Spaniard was entitled to their labor. The evils of the system became so notorious that attempts were made to replace it with the *repartimiento*, under which the Indians were still forced to work in agriculture, mining, and construction, but under contract, on a temporary basis, and for wages. Actually the *encomienda* system lingered on into the eighteenth century, and for a long period the two systems were employed simultaneously. When the Spaniards came to know of the richness of the mines in the area, particularly the hill of silver at Potosí, more Indians were drawn into the net by the *mita* system: it was decreed that the Indians owed the state taxes, which could be paid in labor in lieu of cash; the state then rented their labor to private individuals. The bleak mountain valley where Potosí was located was transformed into one of the most fabulous boom towns the world has ever known. By 1574 Potosí was the largest city in America, with a population of around 160,000.

The wealth of Charcas attracted more and greedier Spaniards than the average colony, and thus the rigid Spanish class system was fastened upon what is now Bolivia in an extreme degree and implemented with great severity. It is estimated, for example, that one-third of the conscripted miners died before their four-month service was over. The wealth of the mines also caused education (for the upper class only) to flourish, civil wars to be commonplace, and Indian revolts to be fierce and frequent. As a crossroad between the Atlantic and the Pacific, Charcas was an area in ferment, and many contemporary historians attribute most of Bolivia's twentieth-century problems to the heritage of the social system developed in the sixteenth century. The emphasis upon mining had one most important long-lasting effect: as farmers were forced to abandon their fields to toil in the mines, agricultural production went down, the terraces and irrigation systems built up over a long span of time fell into ruin, and what had been a very productive agricultural region eventually became an importer of food.

In 1559 the Spaniards set up the *Audiencia* of Charcas as the government of their new colony. At one time the *Audiencia* exercised jurisdiction over what is today Bolivia, Paraguay, Argentina, Uruguay, and parts of Peru, Brazil, and Chile. This system of colonial jurisdiction was to have lasting effects on future developments, for, as has been mentioned, what is now Bolivia never was a unified area in any sense of the term. Basically, Upper Peru, or the *Audiencia* of Charcas, was the mining and agricultural area on the Andean plateau, where most of Bolivia's population lives. Most of the rest of the territory governed by the *Audiencia* was separated from what is now Bolivia, some during colonial times and some during republican days.

Bolivia was one of the first places in America to experience revolts against Spain. Because Charcas was a long way from Lima and Buenos Aires, viceregal control over the local officials was light, and thus a feeling of self-sufficiency developed, which eventually was to grow into nationalism. By the late eighteenth century, Indian revolts were rocking the area and producing much death and destruction. In 1809 the Creoles succeeded in deposing the Spanish authorities and an independent state was created. This was smashed by Spanish troops sent from Peru, but the remnants of the rebel forces continued a guerrilla war for sixteen years. With the coming of the armies led by Bolívar and San Martín after the battle of Ayacucho, Upper Peru finally became independent of Spain in 1825.

Because Bolívar's troops had defeated the Spanish army, Upper Peru began life dominated by Bolívar, his lieutenants, and his troops. It was Bolívar who gave the new "republic" its name, Bolívar, later changed to Bolivia; its first president, General Antonio José de Sucre, a Venezuelan; and its first constitution. There has been much debate about whether Bolívar's constitution would have created a stable government, but this is only academic speculation, since it inevitably lasted only as long as Bolívar's troops remained in Bolivia.

The constitution was authoritarian in character. It provided for a lifetime president, who appointed his successor and the vice-president; recognized Catholicism as the state religion; and contained provisions for a three-house legislature based on suffrage restricted to property owners, which disfranchised at least 90 percent of the population. The French system of local government placed all power in the hands of the president, who appointed the local officials. When he assumed the presidency General Sucre began the organization of the political machinery, but he was driven out by Peruvian armies led by General Santa Cruz and General Gamarra.

Independence had changed nothing except the names of the office-holders, since Bolivia, like the other new Latin-American states, was completely unprepared for self-government. In addition, by making Lake Titicaca the boundary between Peru and Bolivia and adding to Bolivia vast sections of the Amazon and La Plata valleys as well as part of the Pacific coastal desert, the founders of the new country forced it to begin life as a collection of heterogeneous elements that could not be controlled from either Sucre, the capital of the old *Audiencia* and still the legal capital of Bolivia, or La Paz, more centrally located on the *altiplano* and the actual seat of government.

Thus there began a century of chaotic struggles over control of the new republic by various generals and *caudillos*, almost all of them from the small Spanish upper class. During this century Bolivia progressively shrank in size as its more stable neighbors took control of parts of the country that were economically valuable but were not integrated with the highland area around La Paz. Attempts were made to unite Peru and Bolivia, but the armies of Argentina and Chile prevented the confederation. As the twentieth century approached, Bolivia's most important economic assets, its minerals, were taken over by foreign interests that had the financial strength to develop the mines, whose products were needed by the industrial nations of Europe and North America. During the century before World War I, Bolivia's population became progressively poorer, and illiteracy and ill health were the lot of the overwhelming majority.

One estimate (probably exaggerated, but not very much) is that between 1825 and 1952 Bolivia's government was changed by coups d'état, civil wars, and illegal maneuvering 178 times. This is not a record to be proud of, but it was probably inevitable, given the social and political system colonial life had developed. General Mariano Melgarejo, president from 1865 to 1870, was probably the most notorious example of the kind of political leaders the social system produced. He was an almost illiterate *caudillo* who ruled through a personal army and spent his time drinking, gambling, enjoying women, and persecuting his enemies. Whenever he needed money, he sold Indian communal lands at auction, or mortgaged the wealth in nitrates newly discovered on the coastal desert. Harold Osborne calls him "a typical product of an age of violence and abuse, and only in such an age could such a man have risen to wield the reins of government."[2] Osborne quotes a Chilean diplomat who lived in La Paz during the rule of Melgarejo:

> The imprint of the sword is everywhere and the prostration of industry, the poverty of the Exchequer, charitable institutions suspended, education establishments closed, public offices in chaos, justice neglected, public officials unpaid and abuse rampant, all combine to condemn the administration.[3]

This period culminated in the War of the Pacific, 1879–83, in which Bolivia was both aggressor and victim. In 1877 President Hilarión Daza tried to get an extra ten-centavo tax per hundred pounds out of the owners of the Chilean Nitrate Company, who were Chilean nationals. When they refused to pay, President Daza seized the nitrate company's installations, whereupon Chile marched troops into Bolivian territory. Daza was soon overthrown and the Bolivian army was defeated. In the treaty ending the war, Peru and Chile divided the coastal plain between themselves, thus turning Bolivia into a country without a seacoast.

During the fifty years after 1883, Bolivia's governments were as bad as ever, but the need for minerals led to the entry of foreign interests that helped to stabilize the government and by the time of World War I transformed Bolivia into an important producer of tin, copper, wolfram, bismuth, and antimony. Unfortunately, while this prosperity made a few families rich, it never benefited the Indian miners, nor was it utilized to begin the modernization of Bolivia's archaic institutions. In fact, the development of mineral production distorted the economy further, because

---

[2] Harold Osborne, *Bolivia: A Land Divided*, 3rd ed. (London: Oxford University Press, 1964), p. 58.

[3] *Ibid.*, quoting R. Sotomayor Valdés, *La Legación de Chili en Bolivia* (Santiago de Chile, 1872).

by draining labor to the mines it lowered agricultural production and forced increased reliance on the importation of food to feed the city and mining populations. But since minerals are subject to the vagaries of the world market, Bolivia's ability to import food fluctuated as prices rose and fell. The most striking result of the mining economy was the stockpiling of wealth for the mine owners in European and United States banks while the country grew poorer.

When the world depression of the 1930's began, Bolivia's economy collapsed. An attempt to improve matters by securing an outlet to the sea via the Paraguay River led to a war with Paraguay. There is some evidence that certain Bolivian officials believed large quantities of petroleum could be found in the Chaco, as the disputed area was called. The Chaco War was the great turning point in Bolivia's modern history. It marked the end of the traditional organization of society and unleashed the forces that were to come to power in 1952.

The Chaco War was a tragedy for Bolivia. Fought in a lowland of jungle and desert, it cost over 60,000 Bolivian lives, and the highland Indians who were conscripted to fight it suffered severely from the tropical climate. The corruption of the government was so great that the troops often did not get supplies, while in La Paz the rich got richer. The war was a great eye-opener for many young Bolivians. Most of them were seeing for the first time what Bolivia was like outside the village or urban *barrio* where they were born; more important, educated, middle-class whites and *cholos* were for the first time engaging in common tasks and sharing a common life with rural, illiterate Indians, and finding them human after all. In troop encampments and Paraguayan prisoner-of-war barracks, friendships could be formed, ideas could be exchanged, and dreams could be dreamed. When the war was settled, with Paraguay retaining most of the Chaco, the country was swept by a great surge of dissatisfaction, out of which grew new forces and new organizations destined to play important roles in the future life of Bolivia.

One of the first of these organizations, founded in a prisoner-of-war camp, was the Marshal Santa Cruz Lodge, often known as Radepa after the first letters of the group's slogan, *Razón de Patria* (Cause of the Fatherland). Radepa was a secret society composed of army officers. By 1936 it was strong enough to participate in the revolution of May 19, which brought Colonel David Toro to the presidency. Toro tried to institute change by increasing the wages of the miners, encouraging the organization of trade unions, and nationalizing the property of the Standard Oil Company. In 1937 Toro was overthrown and Colonel Germán Busch became head of the government. Busch was an idealistic dreamer who organized a social security system, stimulated education, and tried to make the mine owners disclose details of their operations so that they could be fairly taxed. The large mine owners responded by cutting their production. In 1938 a democratic constitution was introduced. In August of that year Busch put Hochschild, one of the great tin barons, in jail. On August 23 Busch was found mysteriously dead, probably murdered. With Busch's death the oligarchy regained control of the government, and for five years they made liberal use of strong-arm tactics to stabilize their rule.

Meanwhile, modern political parties were forming. In 1937 a group of exiles in Chile, stimulated by the Franco movement in Spain, created the Bolivian Socialist Falange, a conservative political group. In 1940 various Marxist-oriented groups merged to found the *Partido de la Izquierda Revolucionaria* (PIR), led by José Antonio Arze. Many of the members of the PIR were to become members of Bolivia's Communist Party in later years. About the same time (1939–43) a Trotskyite organization, the Revolutionary Workers' Party (POR), developed. In 1941 was founded the most important of the new organizations, the National Revolutionary Movement (MNR), which was to grow into the country's dominant political party. All the new parties had two things in common: they were organized by men who were roused to political consciousness by the Chaco War, and they were opposed to a return to the old political, economic, and social ways that the war had disrupted.

With the aristocracy back in power just as the Second World War created a tremendous demand for tin and other minerals, a new period of superprofits began for the mine owners. But the miners benefited little, and when war shortages and inflation cut their already low standard of living, miners' strikes became common. All the new political parties actively supported the miners, although the government frequently illegalized the MNR, the PIR, and the POR. In 1942 scores of striking tin miners were massacred at Catavi. This aroused such a furore that by December 1943 a group of militarists led by Major Gualberto Villarroel, combining forces with the MNR, was able to capture control of the government. Because the Second World War was on and the overthrown government had cooperated with the United States, the new government was called Nazi-inspired, and the United States withheld recognition for six months.

The MNR was a minority faction in the Villarroel government, but it pushed reforms and some halting steps were taken. These roused such fears in the oligarchy that a right-wing revolt was organized, and on July 21, 1946, Villarroel was lynched and left hanging upside down from a lamppost.

In writing of those years, Víctor Paz Estenssoro, one of the prime movers of the MNR, has pointed out that as a result of the Chaco War the army was enlarged, the old parties were without prestige, and the new parties had not yet matured. Therefore, he writes, "The mine companies conspired with the Generals; we conspired with the Lieutenant Colonels."[4] In both cases the military dominated the government.

After the overthrow of the Villarroel government, the oligarchy tried to stabilize its rule for five years, but failed in its efforts. The revolutionary parties continued to grow, especially the MNR. Strikes by the miners were regular occurrences. The reopening of tin mines in Asia cut down the demand for Bolivia's most important export and contributed to budget deficits. Struggles were the order of the day; the MNR estimates that 5,000 of its members lost their lives during this period. In one revolt the MNR was able to capture the cities of Santa Cruz, Cochabamba, and Oruro and hold them for ten days, but the government, by use of a state of siege and violent reprisals, defeated the revolt. Conditions went from bad to worse.

The United Nations technical-assistance mission that made an investigation in Bolivia from April to August 1950 has given us a picture of the country at the time:

> Bolivia has within its boundaries all the resources necessary to provide a sound economic foundation for a national life distinguished by a wide diffusion of culture, by progress and prosperity. . . . [But] Bolivia has thus far failed to develop the kind of life that its national inheritance could reasonably be expected to produce. . . . The conditions of life for the great majority of the Bolivian people, heirs of more than one brilliant civilization and inhabiting a country of vast potential resources, are harsh, static and largely devoid of present satisfaction or future hope. Agriculture is stagnant, and foodstuffs and raw materials that could be produced at home are being imported. The mining industry has reached a point at which, unless confidence can be created and considerable capital invested, a period of serious decline seems imminent. Oil and hydro-electric energy cannot be adequately developed because the available resources have not even been surveyed. A large part of the population is illiterate and ill, and infant mortality is appallingly high.[5]

[4] Víctor Paz Estenssoro, "La Revolución Boliviana," in *La América Latina de hoy*, edited by Eugenio Chang-Rodríguez and Harry Kantor (New York: Ronald Press, 1961), p. 165.

[5] United Nations Technical Assistance Administration, *Report of the United Nations Mission of Technical Assistance to Bolivia* (New York: United Nations, 1951), p. 2.

The report also said that "there is neither economic nor political stability in Bolivia today,"[6] and "During the decade 1940–1949, the annual deficit [of the government] averaged around 150,000,000 bolivars . . . or approximately 10 percent of the total."[7]

In 1950 Bolivia's traditional system of economic, social, and political organization was archaic. The United Nations mission pointed out that

> *from one-half to two-thirds of its people still live practically outside the money economy on a more or less sulf-sustaining agricultural basis* . . . Perhaps the most difficult among the many difficult problems which Bolivia has to confront is the isolation of these groups, whose members continue to speak their own aboriginal languages and to maintain many of their pre-Columbian traditions and ways of life. They remain practically untouched by such organized activities as exist in the fields of education, sanitation, public health, labour legislation and social welfare in general.[8]

The mass of Bolivians may have escaped "education, sanitation, public health," etc., but the message of the revolutionary parties came to them. Before the United Nations mission could return to implement its recommendations to Bolivia's government, the revolution had destroyed both the government and the army that kept it in power.

By 1950 the MNR had won the support of the overwhelming majority of the population. Unfortunately, most of Bolivia's people were disfranchised, because to vote one had to be male and over twenty-one, have completed military service, possess a certain income, and be able to read and write Spanish. When the regular presidential election of May 1951 was scheduled, therefore, out of a population of 3,054,000 only about 213,700 were eligible to vote, and only 59 percent of that number, 126,123, actually voted. The government candidate received only 39,940 of the votes; Víctor Paz Estenssoro, the MNR candidate, received 54,049. Four other candidates received 31,613 votes. Under the constitution then in force, since no candidate had a majority, the Congress was to choose the new president. The oligarchy had so little confidence in what the Congress would do that the president resigned and turned his office over to a military junta, which immediately declared the elections invalid and instituted a state of siege in an attempt to preserve the traditional system. It managed to hang on to power for eleven months.

Unable to come to power legally, the MNR organized an armed re-

---

6 *Ibid.*, p. 3.
7 *Ibid.*, p. 19.
8 *Ibid.*, p. 106; emphasis added.

volt. It stated that since it had received the highest vote, it deserved to see its candidate in office as president. Paz Estenssoro was in exile in Argentina, but Hernán Siles Zuazo, who had been his vice-presidential running mate, negotiated with army officers and labor leaders and led the fighting when it began. On April 9, 1952, the shooting started; by April 11 the first true revolution in Latin America since that in Mexico was successful. More than 3,000 were killed in the fighting, but the tin miners, who were accustomed to handling dynamite, with some police and other groups were able to defeat the regular army.

The revolution of 1952 was a great shock to the oligarchy and the traditionalists. Their feeling was expressed by Alberto Ostria Gutiérrez, the author of the most widely distributed book opposing the revolution, who reported in tones of outrage that a few months after taking office the new president gave a ball to which he invited the public at large. Ostria quoted the newspaper *El Diario's* description of the scene: " 'Indians . . . dressed in their characteristic costumes, were sitting . . . glued to their chairs. Many of them had probably never until that moment sat on anything but the . . . ground.' Thus the man in the street began to see himself as an intimate of the man who lived in the presidential palace."[9]

One can only sympathize with anyone who sees the world coming to an end because the masses of Indians for the first time in more than 400 years were invited into the Palace of Government and treated as citizens and human beings.

The MNR was faced by almost insurmountable obstacles when it took power. Bolivia had no well-organized public service, and the new government had great difficulty in staffing its administration. Since many of the educated upper-class functionaries and foreign technicians abandoned the country, and most of the remaining Bolivians were illiterate, untrained loyal MNR members had to be assigned to fill difficult administrative positions.[10] Besides, the MNR was a typical nationalistic revolutionary movement that had been organized for only one purpose, to overthrow the government. Having achieved its purpose, it split into a large number of factions. For the next twelve years the MNR was continuously torn by dissension as various groups within the party struggled to capture control.

But reforms went forward. The old army was destroyed. Many of the

---

[9] Alberto Ostria Gutiérrez, *The Tragedy of Bolivia: A People Crucified* (New York: Devin-Adair Co., 1958), pp. 191–192.

[10] Richard W. Patch reports that José Rojas, one-time Minister of *Campesino* Affairs, spoke only a "halting Spanish" and "conducted interviews with foreign visitors in Quechua" ("Bolivia Today: An Assessment Nine Years after the Revolution," *American Universities Field Staff Reports Service*, West Coast South America series, 8, no. 4 [March 17, 1961], p. 15).

officers were dismissed or exiled, and a large proportion of the soldiers were sent home. After about a year and a half, a new army was created on a new basis. Access to the military academy had always been determined by the social background and political loyalties of the applicants and their parents, but it was a different background that was wanted now. In the first classes at the military academy under the MNR, 20 percent of the students were the sons of farmers, 30 percent the sons of workers and miners, and 50 percent the sons of middle-class MNR members who had belonged to the party at least six years. It was this reorganization of the army and the strengthening of the farmers' and workers' self-defense militia that helped the MNR government to stay in power as long as it did.

Under the MNR, for the first time in the history of the country, the vote was given to all over twenty-one years of age and to all over eighteen who were married. An agrarian-reform law gave agricultural land to the Indian farmers, and by January 1962, 178,384 properties covering 3,345,158 *hectares* had been redistributed to 106,510 farm families. The tin mines owned by the three dominant international corporations were nationalized, as were the British-owned railroads. The organization of labor unions and farmers' leagues was stimulated until almost all city and mine workers and a large proportion of the farmers were organized. Education was fostered and reorganized. A determined effort was made to shift some of the population from the *altiplano* to the eastern and northern plains. A most important step was the construction, with the help of the United States government, of a highway from Cochabamba to Santa Cruz, which opened the eastern plains to development and established a new transcontinental route: from Santos, Brazil, to Corumba to Santa Cruz to Cochabamba, and by railroad from there to Arica, Chile. Hundreds of thousands of Indians moved into the plains as a result of this road-building activity, and Dr. Paz Estenssoro has said that this was probably the one MNR accomplishment that would have the most far-reaching effect. Within thirty or forty years, he predicted, a majority of Bolivia's population would be living on the plains of the Beni or of Santa Cruz.[11] Another of the MNR's great successes was an increase in the production of petroleum; by 1955 Bolivia was exporting oil, whereas before then it had had to import it. Determined efforts were made to develop other new agricultural, mining, and industrial production.

This was a country that had been badly in need of change for centuries, where the people inhabited the less desirable parts of the territory, where the majority of the population consisted of illiterate agricultural Indians. The geography, both human and physical, remained the same

---

[11] In a private interview in Lima on January 2, 1965.

under the new government. The very conditions that cried out for change kept the country from taking full advantage of its opportunities. And so the economic situation grew worse instead of better, resulting in great unrest manifested in strikes, demonstrations, and attempts to overthrow the government. The government staggered from crisis to crisis, and many times survived only because of the money pumped into the country by the United States and international organizations.

Graft and dishonesty tormented the MNR governments. This was probably inevitable, especially in a country notorious for its corruption in the past. The same thing happened in Mexico during the 1920's, yet Mexico overcame the corruption. Trying to organize a government when the most loyal supporters of the party in power are either illiterate or not very well educated workers and farmers inevitably leads to graft. A more serious criticism of the MNR was that it jailed and exiled some of its opponents and closed down opposition newspapers, in particular *La Razón* of La Paz and *Los Tiempos* of Cochabamba.

A catastrophic result of the MNR policies was the terrible inflation the country suffered. From 190 *bolivianos* to the United States dollar on the day of the revolution, the country's monetary unit lost value until it stood at 16,000 to the dollar in October 1956, and tremendous efforts were needed to stabilize it at 12,000 to the dollar. Prices had been rising in Bolivia since about 1931, but after 1952 the rate of inflation soared out of control. The basic cause was probably the nationalization of three-fourths of the tin mines just at the time the price of tin fell drastically on the world market. At the same time, government ownership led to a sharp increase in expenses as the number of miners on the payroll rose rapidly and various social-welfare programs were introduced for the miners. The government mining corporation was soon showing a deficit of millions of dollars every year. In addition, the government used deficit financing to pay for many of its activities in development. The only way the deficit could be met was to print new money, and this fed the inflation. Only cash subsidies by the United States government kept the MNR government from collapsing. The worst of the inflation was finally halted by a stabilization program that produced the first serious split in the MNR.

Part of the problem was personality and ambition. All the MNR leaders wanted to be president. After Paz Estenssoro's term expired in 1956, Hernán Siles Zuazo, who had served as vice-president, was elected in what was probably the fairest election Bolivia has ever had. Under the constitution then in effect he could not succeed himself, and when his term expired in 1960 the nomination again went to Paz Estenssoro. This led to a serious split in the party as Walter Guevara Arze, who had been a cabinet minister since 1952 and had presidential ambitions, organized a new party, the Authentic Revolutionary Party, and declared himself a candidate. The party survived this split and Paz Estenssoro was elected for a second term, but when a new constitution was drawn up the following year it was deemed prudent to include a provision for the reelection of an incumbent president. By 1964 the situation had deteriorated further, and Paz Estenssoro considered himself the only man who could hold the revolutionary movement together. Paz obtained the nomination of the MNR against the opposition of his vice-president, Juan Lechín, and former president Hernán Siles Zuazo. Paz was reelected, but the election was boycotted by all of the opposition groups and his was the only name on the ballot. He had been forced to put the head of the air force, General René Barrientos Ortuño, on his ticket as vice-president.

After the "election," the opposition parties and the various political leaders who coveted the presidency refused to recognize the result and continuously organized strikes, demonstrations, and riots. By October an armed revolt was in full swing. During the first stage of the revolt, university students, led by Communists, Juan Lechín, and the Socialist Falange, were defeated by the army and the peasant militia. Then the miners, led by Communists, revolted and were also defeated by the army and militia. But by the end of the month the army officers themselves, led by Vice-President Barrientos, were demanding that Paz Estenssoro resign. When he refused, the army, with the help of the air force, defeated the militia, and Paz Estenssoro left the country without resigning. A military junta headed by General Barrientos took control of the government and a great experiment ended.

Militarism is thus still a powerful force. According to Paz Estenssoro, the only reason the military was able to topple his government was that the officers had modern equipment, supplied earlier by the United States. The next time he came to power, he said, the army would be permanently abolished.[12]

Paz Estenssoro and the MNR probably did more to enable all of the country's people to think of themselves as Bolivians than all previous governments combined. Before 1952, more than half the population lived outside the economy and the culture of the dominant minority. Giving land to the Indians and nationalizing most of the tin mines made most Bolivians feel that at last Bolivia was to belong to the Bolivians. And by giving the ballot to the illiterate and non-Spanish-speaking, the MNR made it possible for a large number of these Indians to become involved

---

[12] *Ibid.*

politically for the first time in the country's history. There have been reports that many illiterate Indians have been led to the polls by party workers and guided in casting their votes (for the MNR until 1964, for Barrientos in 1966). If this is true—and I have no reason to doubt it—at least they are participating in the electoral process more directly than they ever did before.

After 1964 the military junta continued in force all of the important changes instituted by the MNR while moving to improve the country's economic health. General Barrientos broke the power of the tin miners' union by military force in May 1965. Wages were reduced, the freedom of the unions was curtailed, the number of persons on the payroll was cut from 26,000 to 22,000, and by 1966 the government tin company was showing a profit and paying taxes. A new constitution was put into effect in February 1967. Paz Estenssoro remained in exile, and Juan Lechín and Siles Zuazo, who had helped Barrientos come to power, also found themselves in exile.

Running as the candidate of an *ad hoc* group known as the Bolivian Revolutionary Front, Barrientos was elected president in 1966 in an election that was controlled by the government. Barrientos' party was given eighteen Senate seats and eighty-two Chamber seats. The Christian Democratic Community, a united front of the Falange and the Christian Democratic Party, received eight seats in the Senate and nineteen seats in the Chamber. One faction of the MNR received one seat in the Senate and one in the Chamber.

The big event of 1966 and 1967 was the beginning of a guerrilla movement in the southeastern jungle, financed and organized by the Cuban Communists. This attracted international attention when Régis Debray, a French aristocrat, and Che Guevara, who had been prominent in Castro's Cuban government, were discovered to be involved. Guevara was killed; Debray was sentenced to a long term in jail. The guerrillas never won the support of many Bolivians and eventually, in 1968, the survivors left the country.

Bolivia continues to be a country in turmoil, with a military government trying to stabilize the situation and to get economic development going. Whether it can succeed cannot be predicted. What President Paz Estenssoro wrote about Latin America in 1960 applies well to Bolivia today:

> Latin America today is experiencing economic, political and social changes which, whatever their limitations, are really fundamental. This transformation, in its essence, implies development of na-

tional economies, a raising of the living standards of great masses of human beings and the creation of a basis for democratic government: and I cannot doubt that its results will be for the good of the peoples of Latin America and for their relations with the rest of the world. As for the temporary difficulties inevitably caused by these changes, perhaps I can borrow the English saying that in this new decade things must get worse before they can get better.[13]

The Formal Constitutional Framework

Bolivia is governed under the constitution of February 1967, which is basically similar to most of its fifteen predecessors. This constitution sets up a unitary government with a presidential system of the type traditional in most of Latin America. The powers of the president are wide, and the great reforms introduced by the 1952 revolution—agrarian reform, universal suffrage, and nationalization of the large mines—are all incorporated.

Bolivia has now had sixteen constitutions, but all have been more honored than observed. All were patterned on that of the United States, except that there has been no provision for federalism. Alcides Arguedas quotes President Melgarejo as once having said:

> "I want the gentleman who has just spoken and all the honorable deputies gathered here to know that I have put the Constitution of 1861, which was very good, in this pocket [pointing to his left trousers pocket] and that of 1868, which is even better in the opinion of these gentlemen, in this one [pointing to his right pocket], and that nobody is going to rule in Bolivia but me."[14]

This may or may not be an apocryphal story, but that was indeed the way the governments of Bolivia treated its constitutions until 1952.

The revolutionary government functioned without a congress from 1952 to 1956, but from the election of 1956 on it tried to observe the constitutional rules. In August 1961 the Congress followed the required procedure to produce a new document. There was some objection by the opposition, which claimed that a special constituent assembly should have been called to introduce the new constitution, but the old constitution did not require one. When Paz Estenssoro was overthrown, the 1961

[13] Paz Estenssoro, "Latin America's Revolution—A New Decade," *An Extract from the Statist's Economic Survey of South America* (London: March 26, 1960), p. 3.

[14] Alcides Arguedas, "Melgarejo," in *The Green Continent*, edited by Germán Arciniegas (New York: Alfred A. Knopf, Inc., 1945), p. 222.

constitution was abrogated and the new document of 1967 was prepared. Whether this will have a longer life than the other fifteen "basic documents" is doubtful; if one may judge by the past, it will probably soon join its predecessors in the history books.

How the Constitution Is Amended

The Bolivian constitution can be amended by a two-thirds vote of both houses of Congress, but that vote must be taken twice, with an election for the Chamber of Deputies between the two votes. If the constitutional term in office of the president is changed by an amendment, the change can become effective only in the next presidential term.

Who Participates in Politics

Until the Chaco War, the overwhelming majority of the Bolivian people did not participate in politics. The social structure effectively removed at least 90 percent of all Bolivians from any contact with the decision-making process, and legal provisions for voting disfranchised many more, so that no more than 1.5 or 2 percent ever voted. There were cases of deputies' being elected with less than a hundred votes; one was elected with seventeen votes. With the rise of the first labor unions, peasant organizations, and revolutionary parties after the Chaco War, a larger percentage of the population began to be politically active, but the electorate continued to be small until after the revolution. To vote before 1952, one had to be male, twenty-one years old, literate in Spanish, and have a minimum annual income of 200 bolivianos ($3.20 U.S. at the 1952 rate of exchange). Dr. Enrique Hertzog was elected president with 44,700 votes in 1947, when the population was over 3 million.

Under the present rules, all Bolivians over twenty-one must register and vote. Those over seventy and married persons between eighteen and twenty-one may vote if they are registered, but this is not compulsory. Excluded from registration and voting are the insane, those deaf and dumb who cannot make themselves understood by writing, those with overdue debts to the state, those who have been legally determined to have defrauded the public treasury, and those convicted of certain crimes. Fines are levied upon those eligible who fail to register or vote.

The number of voters reached 1,297,319 in 1964, or 36 percent of the total population. A substantial proportion of the population still does not vote, but it is estimated that at least 50 percent now influence the political system. The peasants and workers have organizations to speak for them and access to the decision-making process is much easier than it was before 1952, although peasant leagues and trade unions have lost much of the power they had in the first years of the revolution.

The Electoral Machinery

The 1961 and 1967 constitutions authorized a National Electoral Court whose membership consists of two members selected by the Congress, one by the Supreme Court, one by the president, and one by all of the recognized political parties. The court supervises all matters concerning elections, including the registration of candidates and political parties. In each of the departments into which Bolivia is divided, a departmental electoral court is set up, consisting of three members, one designated by the Congress, one by the Supreme Court, and one by the president. The departmental electoral courts supervise the registration of voters and count the votes cast in their departments. Under the departmental electoral courts are electoral judges who supervise and organize the many electoral notaries and juries and select the polling places. The electoral notaries are the men who register the voters and give them their *cédulas electorales*, the cards that allow citizens to vote. The electoral juries are the five persons who conduct affairs at the polling places. They are chosen by lot from among the literate voters registered in each polling place (*mesa*).

Each party's ballot has a distinctive color and symbol to make voting easier for the illiterate. The voter casts his vote for a party; nothing appears on the ballot except the party's initials and symbol. There is much dispute about how fair elections have been under this system. There is general agreement that the MNR won a majority in the 1956 election, but there is no agreement about the fairness of subsequent elections. The MNR and later President Barrientos' machine seem to have managed to control the illiterate vote, and the boycotting of the 1964 election by all opposition groups except the MNR did little to train the voters. Bolivia still has a long way to go before its electoral system will produce fair results.

Political Parties

Bolivia never had any real political parties until the Chaco War. During the nineteenth century there were groups calling themselves Liberals and Conservatives, and the names of many "political parties" appear in the history of Bolivia before the 1940's, but these were all personalistic cliques that revolved around the leading *caudillos*. One historian refers to an election in 1931 which "was a victory for the Patiño mine interests," and writes that "the true arbiters of Bolivian destiny were . . . [in the 1920's] the New York bankers."[15]

To participate in elections a political party must be registered with the National Electoral Court. To become registered, an organization must present a document that includes a list of 1,000 members, a summary of the party platform, a copy of its bylaws, and a list of its national and departmental officers. An organization with less than 1,000 members can be registered as a political group and participate in congressional elections if it represents a special interest or a distinct point of view.

The most important political party from the early 1940's to 1964 was the National Revolutionary Movement (*Movimiento Nacional Revolucionario*, or MNR), which probably had the support of about 75 percent of the population when it came to power and controlled the government from the 1952 revolution until November 1964. The MNR is one of the indigenous reform parties associated with the League of Popular Parties. Probably because it came to power so soon after it was organized, it never became a solidly knit organization with a well-developed program, but remained a loose aggregation, and consequently suffered greatly from factionalism.

The MNR favored industrialization, agricultural diversification, colonization, development of the northern and eastern lowlands, and cooperation with the United States. Until 1964 the MNR tried to keep its organization functioning on a permanent basis. The local units, known as *comandos*, were tied together into municipal and regional divisions with a national political command at the top. Candidates for president were nominated at a national convention.

The MNR remains a member of the League of Popular Parties and in the 1960's became a fraternal member of the Socialist International. In 1966 there were several MNR's functioning. One faction, led by Víctor Andrade, for many years Bolivia's ambassador to the United States and one of the founders of the MNR, was registered by the National Electoral Court. Another faction recognized Paz Estenssoro as its leader and was headed within Bolivia by Federico Álvarez Plata, at one time president of the Senate. A third was known as the *Movimiento Revolucionario Paz Estenssorista* and was based on the MNR youth movement. In June 1967 the three groups signed a unity pact, but it is difficult to forecast what the future of the MNR will be.

[15] Hubert Herring, *A History of Latin America from the Beginnings to the Present* (New York: Alfred A. Knopf, Inc., 1961), p. 557.

Until 1964 President Barrientos was an important member of the MNR. When the revolution took place in 1952, he was the pilot who was sent to fly Paz Estenssoro back to Bolivia, and in 1964, as we have seen, he was the party's candidate for vice-president. In the 1966 election he was the candidate of the Bolivian Revolutionary Front (FRB), a combination of four parties and the Chaco War Veterans Confederation. Of the four pro-Barrientos parties, the Popular Christian Movement (MCP) is probably closest to being a personal vehicle for Barrientos. The MCP was organized in 1965, and its program is similar to that of the MNR. The Authentic Revolutionary Party (PRA) consists of the following of Walter Guevara Arze, a former MNR leader who left the party in 1959, claiming the MNR had betrayed the revolution, when he was denied its nomination for the presidency. In 1960 the PRA received 140,000 votes, and in 1967 Guevara Arze was a member of President Barrientos' cabinet.

The Social Democratic Party (PSD) has been functioning since 1945, but it was always a small organization, and since it boycotted all elections after 1952 until 1966, it is impossible to estimate its strength. Its leader, Luis Adolfo Siles Salinas, was elected vice-president in 1966 as part of the Barrientos FRB. The PIR (*Partido de la Izquierda Revolucionaria*) originally was a Marxist group most of whose members eventually joined the Communist Party. Others joined the MNR. In 1956 the party was reorganized, but boycotted elections until 1966.

Another party that supported Barrientos in 1966 but did not join the FRB is the Revolutionary Socialist Party. This has some support among the military and is led by a former member of the Falange.

Of the parties that opposed Barrientos for president, next to the MNR, the Bolivian Socialist Falange (FSB) was the most important. The FSB has had a long and confusing career. Founded in the 1930's by admirers of Spain's Franco, through the years it has taken very contradictory positions, and today it is a moderate reformist organization supporting most of the reforms the other parties advocate: integration of the Indians, industrialization, development of agriculture and mining. The FSB actively supported Barrientos in overthrowing the MNR government, but broke with him when he ignored their claims to an important role in the new government. The FSB has been strong among the university students and the urban middle classes. In the 1966 election it ran a joint slate with the Democratic Revolutionary Alliance, a small organization based on the social doctrines of the Catholic church.

The Communists in Bolivia are split into pro-Soviet and pro-Chinese factions and several varieties of Trotskyites. They have always been strongest among the miners, in the universities, and among the middle-class intellectuals. It is difficult to keep track of the various factions, but the pro-Chinese group seemed to be strongest at last count. The Trotsky-ite organization is the Revolutionary Workers' Party (POR), which has been strong among the miners since the early 1940's. Another organization of some significance is the Revolutionary Party of the National Left. This is the personal following of Juan Lechín, who was an important leader of the MNR until 1964 and president of the miners' union for many years.

Bolivia has far too many parties, of course, and could get along without most of them. They are a reflection of the unintegrated character of Bolivian society and probably will come and go as long as Bolivia remains the kind of country it is.

Public Opinion and Pressure Groups

The extensive illiteracy in Bolivia tends to limit public opinion to a definite minority voice. The organized peasant movement articulates the needs of many of the illiterate agricultural Indians, but no interest group can transform them into the kind of effective citizens a democracy needs. La Paz, with a population of 347,394, tends to dominate the country, as there is no other urban center with as many as 100,000 inhabitants. Newspapers are consequently severely limited in circulation; the largest daily is *El Diario* of La Paz, with a circulation of about 36,000. In all, there are about twenty-three newspapers and magazines being published, with a combined daily circulation of around 100,000 copies.

The result of the civil war at the end of October 1964 demonstrates that the army remains the most powerful group in Bolivia. From 1952 to 1964 the army exercised little influence because in 1952 the old army was disbanded and replaced by a new army led by officers who were members of the MNR. This new army was kept small, and much of its energy went into civic action programs such as road building and the preparation of land for colonization. The workers and peasants were organized into militias and supplied much of the armed power needed to suppress revolts. With the election of General René Barrientos as vice-president in 1964, it was evident that the army officers were regaining their traditional strength, and when the army overthrew the government and set up a military junta headed by General Barrientos, the army once again was the most powerful group in Bolivia.

Although there are not very many industrial workers or miners, for all practical purposes the government was jointly controlled by the MNR and the *Central Obrera Boliviana* (COB), the central trade-union organization, from 1952 to about 1958. This came about because the miners and workers were strategically placed and organized and did much of the fighting in 1952. The MNR leaders favored the organized workers, and Juan Lechín was only one of many union leaders to hold high government posts. During the late 1950's, however, when the government introduced a system of price stabilization to fight inflation, it came into conflict with the organized labor movement. After years of struggle, Paz Estenssoro finally split the COB and gained control of the majority of the organized workers. When Barrientos came to power the labor movement was pushed into a subordinate role, and finally, in 1965, Barrientos used troops to take over the mines. Thereafter the organized labor movement was a minor factor in the determination of public policy.

The organized Indian farmers, known as *campesinos*, played an important role from 1952 to 1964. It was their votes that determined elections, and their armed militia several times was the decisive force in putting down rebellions. Their illiteracy makes it easy for their leaders to speak for them, and in many cases the leaders are able to translate their support into positions in local and national government. The *campesino* leadership was tied into the MNR political machine; at present General Barrientos seems to control this group.

Until 1952, the most important pressure group in Bolivia was a tiny aristocracy of mine and land owners, but the nationalization of the three biggest mining companies and the distribution of land to the peasants destroyed the economic base of this group. Organizations of businessmen still function, but because these groups have generally supported the opposition political parties, they have little political power.

The middle class and the intellectuals are important in all of the political parties, but they have not yet been able to function as a group. The university students, most of whom come from middle-class families, are important as articulators of their demands, often by demonstrations and violence. Many of the students are associated with the more ideological political parties, the Communists, the Falange, and the MNR, but there are not enough university students to play a really important role.

The Catholic church never was as important a force in Bolivia as it was in some of the other Latin-American countries. With the constitution of 1961 the government gave up its control of the *patronato*, the right to nominate officials of the church, and this should tend to remove the church further from politics. Yet the country's population is almost all Catholic, and church officials participate in government celebrations.

A rapidly developing force in Bolivia is the government bureaucracy. With the nationalization of oil, mines, railroads, and other economic enterprises and the attempt to improve the public administration, the government employees will inevitably play an increasingly important role in the future.

Pressure groups have a long way to go in Bolivia before they become important actors in politics. Perhaps not until literacy is more widespread will strong pressure groups become the rule.

Civil Liberties

All Bolivian constitutions have guaranteed to the people all the rights usually listed in a democratic constitution, yet true liberty has been rare in Bolivia. The period from 1952 to 1964 was probably the freest in the country's history, yet even then there were many claims that the MNR government was a dictatorship, that it refused liberty to its opponents. As is customary in Latin America, the president could (and still can), with the approval of the Council of Ministers, decree a state of siege, and this power has been utilized many times since 1952. Despite all the turmoil that accompanied the revolutionary changes, including armed revolts, violent strikes, and attempts to blackmail the government by kidnapping foreign citizens, the MNR never became a true dictatorship and always permitted an opposition, which published periodicals and sold them on the streets of all cities. The Barrientos government has followed a similar policy—that is, most Bolivians do as they please and say what they want to say—but some of the government's most powerful enemies still live in exile.

The Executive

The Bolivian executive is a president elected for a four-year term by direct suffrage and by a simple majority. He is ineligible for reelection until another term has passed. Many officials of the government are ineligible for the presidency, but they become eligible if they resign their positions at least six months before the election. Blood relatives of the president and vice-president, as well as relatives to the second degree by affinity, are also ineligible, and so are members of the clergy of any faith. A presidential candidate must be at least thirty-five years old, literate, a registered voter, and the nominee of a political party. A vice-president who meets the same requirements is elected with the president on a party ticket. The vice-president presides over the Senate, and succeeds to the presidency if the incumbent dies or is removed from office. If both the president and the vice-president are unable to serve, the succession goes to the president pro tem of the Senate, followed by the president of the Chamber of Deputies.

By tradition and constitutional law, the president is a strong executive. In addition to the powers granted to all executives—enforcing the law, negotiating treaties, appointing officials, conducting foreign affairs, administering the national revenues, enforcing the decisions of the courts, and commanding the armed forces—the Bolivian president controls all local government and has the power to declare a state of siege. The ministers of the president's cabinet, who serve as the heads of the various executive departments, are appointed and removed by the president. It has been claimed that Bolivia "blends the presidential and cabinet types" of government because the constitution gives the legislature the power to vote "a censure of the acts of the Executive addressing it against the Ministers of State"[16] and to command a minister to appear before the Congress for questioning; but this does not change the presidential type of government. The president is in charge of the executive power, and although he and his ministers are responsible for their actions, they can be removed from office only by impeachment by the legislature.

The basic problem all presidents face in Bolivia is the lack of an effective administrative apparatus. The public service remains rudimentary because of the mass illiteracy and general backwardness of the country. In 1962, the total number of government employees was only 35,774 (omitting the defense department, which in 1961 had 5,021 employees). This number has risen slightly in recent years. The largest number of employees are in education (10,785), the Department of Government, Justice, and Immigration, which includes local government (7,934), and the Peasant Affairs Ministry (6,645). Practically all employees are appointed on a patronage basis and only the first steps have been taken to set up a modern civil service system. The effectiveness of the administrative apparatus, therefore, is very low.

The president has assisting him a general secretary with cabinet rank who has only fifteen persons on his staff to supervise the office of the president. A military officer is in charge of the president's security, handles problems of protocol, and supervises the caretakers of the Palace of Government. The budget is prepared by twelve employees: six officials and six clerks. Professor Allan Richards points out that the lack of money leads to little efficiency. In Bolivia, he writes,

---

[16] Allan R. Richards, *Administration—Bolivia and the United States* (Albuquerque: University of New Mexico Press, 1961), p. 3.

cold, completely unheated, high-ceilinged gymnasium-like rooms often house thirty to forty employees and their equipment. Vintaged, unpainted, wobbly desks with inadequate drawer space, museum-relic typewriters, and aged cardboard boxes filled with only-the-employee-knows-what crowd offices so that elbow rubbing and back slapping compete for time consumption. Inadequate light, dirt, and stacks of unused materials and furniture are added burdens.[17]

And, Professor Richards adds: "Bolivian administration is overburdened with papers, seals, and signatures."[18]

Organizing a new administration is not a new problem in Bolivia. In 1949 the government asked the secretary general of the United Nations to send a mission to Bolivia to advise the government on drawing up and implementing a program of economic and social development. The result was the famous Keenlyside Report, which proposed a novel solution: that since Bolivia had the potential to produce enough for its people if it had a stable administration, the United Nations should send a group of advisers-administrators who would become integral members of the Bolivian civil service in order to strengthen the administration. Surprisingly, the Bolivian government agreed, but before the United Nations administrators could go to work the revolution took place. After a year had passed the revolutionary government accepted the United Nations advisers, but the UN personnel lost their powers in 1954 and soon left the country. Another attempt was made to improve public administration in the late 1950's when the United States AID gave the University of Tennessee a grant to set up a school of public administration at San Carlos University, but this too was a failure, probably because the wrong people were sent to Bolivia by the University of Tennessee.

The president of Bolivia, then, is a very strong executive who must do his work with inadequate administrative machinery. Much of the inefficiency, graft, and incompetence of the government can be attributed to a lack of trained personnel.

The Legislative Power

Bolivia's legislature is a bicameral Congress consisting of a Senate and a Chamber of Deputies, both elected under rules that guarantee representation for an opposition. The Senate consists of twenty-seven mem-

---

[17] *Ibid.,* p. 12.
[18] *Ibid.,* p. 15.

bers, three from each department, who are elected for six-year terms. The party winning the most votes in each department gets two senators; the party with the second highest vote gets the third. Ordinarily the twenty-seven senators are divided into three groups, with one-third elected every two years; but the entire Senate was elected in 1966 and divided into three groups by lot. The current Chamber of Deputies has 102 members elected by a system of proportional representation for four-year terms. Ordinarily half are elected every two years, but in 1966 the entire house was elected. Each department has five deputies plus one more for each 50,000 inhabitants or fraction over 30,000. Vacancies in the Congress are filled by alternates, who are the candidates who were not elected. To become a member of the Chamber of Deputies one must be at least twenty-five years old, a Bolivian by birth, a registered voter, and not a government employee, a clergyman, or a contractor for public works. To become a senator one must be at least thirty-five years old and meet all the requirements of a deputy.

The two houses of Bolivia's legislature function both separately and in joint sessions. The constitution lists the powers and duties of the houses in great detail. Disagreements between the two houses are settled in joint session. The president of the republic has the right to veto bills passed by the Congress, but the Congress can override the veto by a two-thirds majority of each house. According to the constitution, the Congress is a very powerful body, but in practice the president dominates the legislature. Since the revolution the various political parties and factions have developed the custom of having "watchers," mostly women, in the visitors' gallery when the Congress meets. These watchers make a great deal of noise and do little to encourage decorum on the floors of the houses.

When Congress is not in session, its place is taken by a Legislative Committee composed of five senators and nine deputies elected by their houses. The Legislative Committee is "to see that the Constitution and the laws are complied with" and in case of emergency to authorize the president, by a two-thirds vote, to issue decrees with the force of law. The Legislative Committee also has the power provisionally to approve a presidential decree of a state of siege.

Public Finance

Bolivia's budget is drawn up by a special agency and submitted to the Congress, which cannot increase the amounts requested, but can accept, reject, or decrease the overall amount for each program. Congress must make its decision within sixty days; if it has not approved the budget by then, it becomes law as submitted. The budget includes local and national government expenditures in the same document. The total of the budget has risen rapidly since the revolution, but the government is handicapped by the poverty of the country and its poor administrative system. As a result of improvements in income-tax and customs administration, tax revenues increased 30 percent from 1961 to 1963, but the government never has enough money for what it wants to do, and the United States has provided grants in recent years to balance the budget. This aid amounted to about $20 million from 1961 through 1963 and $5.8 million in 1964. The income and expenditures for 1962, shown in Tables 1 and 2, are typical of Bolivia's recent budgets, except for substantial increases in the amount spent for education in more recent years. (The boliviano is currently quoted at $0.084 U.S.)

The Judicial Power

Bolivia's judicial power rests in a Supreme Court of ten justices and a series of subsidiary tribunals. The members of the Supreme Court are elected by the Chamber of Deputies from a list proposed by the Senate for ten-year terms and cannot be reelected. The Supreme Court nominates the justices of the district courts, who are elected by the Senate for six-year terms. The Supreme Court selects the judges of the lower courts for four-year terms.

The court system is a weak third branch of government. The head-

TABLE 1
REVENUE OF BOLIVIA, 1962
(000 Omitted)

Source	Amount in Bolivianos	Percent of Total
National property	B1,006	0.0002
National services	24,902,400	5.38
Direct and indirect taxes	337,403,731	72.72
Miscellaneous	10,290,134	2.20
Extraordinary income	91,402,729	19.70
Total	B464,000,000	100.0002*

* Figures do not add to 100 because of rounding.

TABLE 2

EXPENDITURES OF BOLIVIA, 1962

(000 Omitted)

	Amount in Bolivianos	Percent of Total
Legislature	B6,296,000	1.36%
Judicial system	4,691,000	1.01
Electoral system	2,000,000	0.42
Executive departments		
President	1,889,000	0.41
National Commission of Coordination and Planning	2,000,000	0.42
National Office of Press, Information, and Culture	690,000	0.15
National Council of Monetary Stabilization	50,000	0.01
National Council of Agrarian Reform	2,298,000	0.50
National Tourism Service	289,000	0.06
Department of Religion	921,000	0.20
National Council of Cooperatives	912,000	0.20
Ministry of Foreign Relations	15,055,000	3.24
Ministry of Government, Justice, and Immigration	30,276,000	6.03
Ministry of Finance	7,600,000	1.64
Ministry of Defense	60,000,000	12.93
Ministry of Education and Fine Arts	66,000,000	14.22
Ministry of Peasant Affairs	32,088,670	6.92
Ministry of Public Works and Communications	25,241,200	5.44
Ministry of Labor and Social Security	17,300,000	3.73
Ministry of Public Health	16,265,000	3.51
Ministry of National Economy	1,300,000	0.28
Ministry of Mines and Petroleum	1,318,000	0.28
Ministry of Agriculture, Livestock, and Irrigation	4,342,000	0.94
Auditing Bureau	1,705,000	0.37
Debt service	156,297,130	33.68
Miscellaneous	7,176,000	1.55
Total	B464,000,000	100.00%

quarters of the Supreme Court are in the city of Sucre, the legal capital of the country, and thus physically separated from La Paz, where the executive and legislative powers are located. The courts tend to go along with whichever government is in power. To administer the land-reform laws a special series of agrarian courts was set up.

Local Government

Bolivia is a unitary republic divided for purposes of local administration into nine departments, which are divided into ninety-six provinces, which are divided into 940 cantons. Local government is based on the French system, with practically all powers vested in the president. In each department there is a prefect, appointed by the president for a four-year term, who directs all government activities except those of the army. In each province there is a subprefect appointed by the president upon recommendation by the prefect. In each canton there is a *corregidor* who is appointed by the prefect. The prefect supervises all subprefects and *corregidores* in his department.

The constitution grants autonomy to the municipalities, and in the capitals of the departments, provinces, and cantons there are councils and *alcaldes* (mayors). The councils are elected. Until 1966, the president of the republic appointed the *alcaldes* from among the members of the councils, but since 1966 they have been elected by and from the councils. Centralization in the system of municipal councils is just as rigid as in the rest of the local government system: the councils in the capitals of departments supervise and control provincial municipal councils, and the *alcaldes* of the departmental capitals supervise and control *alcaldes* in the provinces, who in turn supervise those in the cantons.

The national territories are divided into three *delegaciones*, each of which is governed by a delegate who is appointed by the president.

Bolivia: A Last Word

Bolivia is again trying to govern itself constitutionally, its president a general who has found himself facing all the problems the MNR governments were unable to solve. In the summer of 1967 General Barrientos, seeking support for his government, asked Paz Estenssoro, Siles Zuazo, and Juan Lechín to return to Bolivia, but all three refused. The basic problem facing General Barrientos is that the country's population remains largely illiterate, unproductive, and almost impervious to change.

The Bolivian revolution was a true revolution, whose leaders tried to destroy the country's traditional economic, social, and political systems. Time has demonstrated that this is not easily done, and even when the old is destroyed, the new that comes may not be what was expected. At the same time, Bolivia demonstrates that revolutionary changes impelled by the majority of the population do not disappear very easily when those who introduced the changes lose control of the government.

The most important measures taken by the revolutionary government—
redistribution of the large landowners' latifundia to the landless Indian
farmers, universal suffrage, and nationalization of the large tin mines—
remain in force, and almost no one suggests they ought to be ended.

Bolivia is very different today from what it was in 1950. Although
a revolution does not transform a people overnight or over a decade, it
so upsets traditional ways that change inevitably comes. Since people
everywhere are creatures of habit, the customs of centuries are abandoned
only slowly, and the significant changes are taking place gradually. Their
cumulative effect will be realized only after decades have passed. Of the
measures taken by the revolutionary government, those that will probably have the most far-reaching effects are the improvement and enlarg-
ment of the educational system and the building of roads into the northern and eastern plains. As a result of these measures, the literacy rate is
rising and the proportion of the population living on the *altiplano* is going down. Eventually the educated Bolivians living in the parts of the
country most susceptible of development will be able to create a more
stable political system. Until then, Bolivia will live from crisis to crisis.

The emergence in the southeastern jungles of a few dozen guerrillas
inspired and financed by the Soviet Union, China, and Cuba aroused
much publicity and created problems for the government of President
Barrientos, but they had no real importance. They showed the limitations of the Bolivian army and excited some of the Communists on the
altiplano, but they could not affect the functioning of the country's government or economy. To do that they would have to have mass support,
and this they do not have.

The Che Guevara affair had its greatest repercussion on the Bolivian
government in July 1968. The government was trying to sell Guevara's
diary to publishers for a large sum, when suddenly Fidel Castro turned
copies of the diary over to various periodicals. When it was discovered that
Barrientos' Minister of Government, Antonio Arguedas Mendieta, had
given a copy of the diary to Castro, he had to flee into exile in Chile. The
cabinet fell, and for a few days it appeared as if the government would be
overthrown. With the coalition government dead, Barrientos organized a
new cabinet consisting in its entirety of military men. The affair of the
diary is another demonstration of how chaotic political life is in Bolivia.
The revolutionary government of the MNR was overthrown by a coalition consisting of the armed forces, the Communists, and the dissident
ambitious MNR leaders. Four years later it is discovered that the Minister
of Government is an admirer of Fidel Castro.

What Bolivia needs most of all is a political party system capable of peacefully articulating the wishes of the various groups in the society. The experiences of exile and persecution may help the MNR to become that kind of party. Adversity always seems to strengthen healthy political movements with a mass base, and the leaders of the MNR may learn in exile what they were unable to learn in power: how to cooperate with each other and even disagree without disrupting the party organization.

SELECTED READINGS

ALEXANDER, ROBERT J. *The Bolivian National Revolution*. New Brunswick, N.J.: Rutgers University Press, 1958.

———. "Bolivia: The National Revolution." In *Political Systems of Latin America*, edited by Martin C. Needler. Princeton, N.J.: D. Van Nostrand Co., 1964.

———. "Organized Labor and the Bolivian National Revolution." In *National Labor Movements in the Postwar World,* edited by Everett M. Kassalow. Evanston, Ill.: Northwestern University Press, 1963.

ANDRADE, VÍCTOR. "Bolivia—Past and Future." *Vital Speeches of the Day* 23 (November 1, 1956): 61–64.

BOLIVIA, COMISIÓN DE LA REFORMA ADMINISTRATIVA. *Informe*. La Paz, 1963.

BOWEN, J. DAVID. "Bolivia's Revolution Comes of Age." *Reporter*, September 26, 1963, pp. 34–36.

CLEVEN, N. ANDREW N. *The Political Organization of Bolivia*. Washington: Carnegie Institution, 1940.

KARASZ, ARTHUR. "Experiment in Development: Bolivia since 1952." In *Freedom and Reform in Latin America*, edited by Frederick B. Pike. Notre Dame, Ind.: University of Notre Dame Press, 1959.

MACDONALD, AUSTIN F. "Bolivia," *Latin American Politics and Government*, pp. 525–49. 2nd ed. New York: Thomas Y. Crowell Co., 1954.

MACDONALD, N. P. "Bolivia's Revolution." *Quarterly Review* (London) 295 (January 1957): 46–59.

PATCH, RICHARD W. *American Universities Field Staff Reports*, West Coast South America series:
"Bolivian Background," October 10, 1958.
"Bolivia: The Seventh Year," February 3, 1959.
"Bolivia: Decision or Debacle," April 18, 1959.
"The Bolivian Falange," May 14, 1959.
"Bolivia Today: An Assessment Nine Years after the Revolution," March 17, 1961.
"The Pro and Anti-Castristas in La Paz," February 1962.
"Bolivia's Developing Interior," April 1962.
"Personalities and Politics in Bolivia," May 1962.
"Bolivia's Experiments in Development without Aid," June 1964.

———. "Bolivia, the Restrained Revolution." *Annals of the American Academy of Political and Social Sciences* 334 (March 1961): 123–32.

PAZ ESTENSSORO, VÍCTOR. "La Revolución boliviana." In *La América Latina de hoy*, edited by Eugenio Chang-Rodríguez and Harry Kantor. New York: Ronald Press, 1961.

———. *La Revolución boliviana*. La Paz: Dirección Nacional de Informaciones, 1964.

———. *La Presencia de la revolución nacional*. Antofagasta, Chile: Imprenta La Reforma, 1966.

RAND, CHRISTOPHER. "Letter from La Paz." *New Yorker*, December 31, 1966, pp. 35–56.

RICHARDS, ALLAN R. *Administration—Bolivia and the United States.* Albuquerque: University of New Mexico Press, 1961.

TRIGO, CIRO FÉLIX. *Las Constituciones de Bolivia.* Madrid: Instituto de Estudios Políticos, 1958.

UNITED NATIONS TECHNICAL ASSISTANCE ADMINSTRATION. *Report of the United Nations Mission of Technical Assistance to Bolivia.* New York: United Nations, 1951.

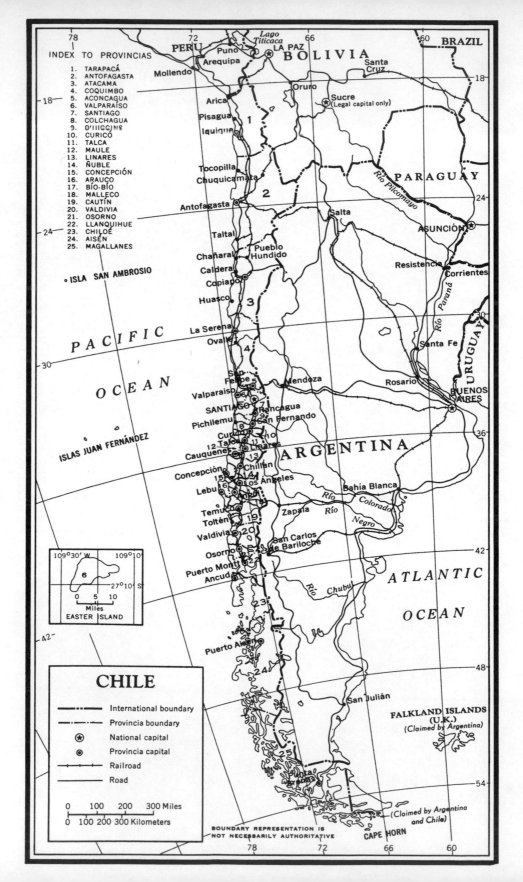

INDEX TO PROVINCIAS
1. TARAPACÁ
2. ANTOFAGASTA
3. ATACAMA
4. COQUIMBO
5. ACONCAGUA
6. VALPARAÍSO
7. SANTIAGO
8. COLCHAGUA
9. O'HIGGINS
10. CURICÓ
11. TALCA
12. MAULE
13. LINARES
14. ÑUBLE
15. CONCEPCIÓN
16. ARAUCO
17. BÍO-BÍO
18. MALLECO
19. CAUTÍN
20. VALDIVIA
21. OSORNO
22. LLANQUIHUE
23. CHILOÉ
24. AISÉN
25. MAGALLANES

PERU
BRAZIL
Lago Titicaca
Puno
LA PAZ
BOLIVIA
Santa Cruz
Mollendo
Arequipa
Oruro
Sucre
(Legal capital only)
Arica
PARAGUAY
Pisagua
Río Pilcomayo
Iquique
Tocopilla
Chuquicamata
Salta
ASUNCIÓN
Antofagasta
Taltal
Resistencia
Chañaral
Pueblo Hundido
Corrientes
Caldera
Copiapó
Río Paraná
Huasco
ISLA SAN AMBROSIO
PACIFIC
La Serena
Ovalle
Santa Fe
OCEAN
URUGUAY
Mendoza
Rosario
San Felipe
BUENOS AIRES
Valparaíso
SANTIAGO
Rancagua
Pichilemu
San Fernando
Curicó
ISLAS JUAN FERNÁNDEZ
Talca
Linares
Cauquenes
ARGENTINA
Chillán
Concepción
Los Ángeles
Lebu
Bahía Blanca
Río Colorado
Temuco
Zapala
Río
Toltén
Río Negro
Valdivia
San Carlos de Bariloche
Osorno
Puerto Montt
Ancud
ATLANTIC
Río Chubut
OCEAN
Puerto Aisén
San Julián
FALKLAND ISLANDS
(U.K.)
(Claimed by Argentina)
CAPE HORN
(Claimed by Argentina and Chile)

EASTER ISLAND
109°30'W   109°10'
6
27°10'S
0   5   10
Miles

CHILE

- - - International boundary
- - - Provincia boundary
⊛ National capital
◉ Provincia capital
Railroad
Road

0   100   200   300 Miles
0 100 200 300 Kilometers

BOUNDARY REPRESENTATION IS
NOT NECESSARILY AUTHORITATIVE

CHILE:

The Shoestring Democracy

Chile was one of the first Latin-American countries to achieve stability, and by the 1960's it had developed one of the area's more mature political systems. Despite its relatively small population and peculiar physical configuration, Chile's elections are meaningful, political conflict is conducted in a civilized manner, and some progress has been made in solving the country's problems. Yet the country suffers from extreme inflation, it is the home of one of the continent's strongest Soviet-oriented Communist parties, and poverty is widespread. Chile is also the home of Latin America's leading Christian Democratic party. These developments, seemingly contradictory, make Chile a most interesting country.

A National Profile

Chile occupies a strip of land on the west coast of South America stretching about 2,620 miles from the southern border of Peru to the continent's end in Tierra del Fuego. With an average width of 110 miles, Chile has often been called the "shoestring" republic. In every way that matters, Chile is an island isolated by geography. Its northern region is a desert separating its populated areas from Peru and Bolivia; to the east, the ranges of the Andes, reaching to more than 22,000 feet above sea level, effectively separate it from Argentina; to the west, the South Pacific stretches for thousands of miles before it reaches New Zealand and Australia; to the south there is Antarctica, of which Chile claims a slice between 53 and 90 degrees west longtitude, inhabited by 202 persons. With an area of 286,396 square miles (excluding its share of Antarctica), Chile is larger than Texas, although it is the fourth smallest of the ten South American republics.

Chile contains three distinct sections and some islands in the Pacific, the most important of which is Easter Island, more than 2,000 miles west of the mainland. About 60 percent of all Chileans live on 12.5 percent of the national territory, known as Mediterranean Chile, the area from 30°5′ to 37°5′, which includes Chile's famous central valley. This was all there was to Chile during colonial days and well into the nineteenth century, an isolated area of mild climate, much fertile soil, and a good harbor at Valparaíso. Today the country's most important industries are located here, and most of its agriculture, its commercial complexes, its cultural and educational centers, and the bulk of the governmental machinery. To the north is an almost waterless desert that contains rich deposits of sodium nitrate and iodine. The southern part of the northern zone is a transitional area in which some agriculture is carried on, but all of north Chile, about 40 percent of the nation's area, contains only about 10 percent of the population. Southern Chile is a region of forests, lakes, islands, and a narrow coastal strip. Inhabited by 29.1 percent of the total population, this part of Chile includes 46.9 percent of the country's total area.

In addition to its isolation, one other feature of Chile's geographical setting has affected its political system: in the twentieth century, frequent destructive quakes have forced heavy expenditures for relief and reconstruction which might otherwise have gone into development.

Chile's population in 1967 was estimated to be 9.2 million; 68.18 percent was urban, according to the census of 1960. The population has been increasing in recent years at a rate of 2.5 percent per year, about average for Latin America. The leading cities are Santiago, with a population of about 2.5 million; Valparaíso, with 300,000; and Concepción, with 250,000. Chile has a fairly homogeneous population;[1] only about 1.5 percent were registered as foreigners and about 2 percent as Indians in the 1952 census. Most Chileans are of *mestizo* stock, with the upper classes generally lighter in complexion than the lower classes.

Spanish is Chile's official language and practically everyone uses it. About 90 percent of the population is supposed to be affiliated with the

---

[1] Professor Earl Parker Hanson thinks that "to a greater extent than in any other American nation has the melting pot worked there to fuse various groups into a homogeneous, 'new,' and truly American race" (*Chile: Land of Progress* [New York: Reynal & Hitchcock, 1941], p. 47).

Roman Catholic church, but in many cases the affiliation is only nominal. The remaining 10 percent of the population consists of Protestants, Jews, Greek Orthodox, and freethinkers. About 75 to 80 percent of the population over fourteen is literate, but a very high portion of the population never goes beyond the elementary grades.

Economically Chile is one of the more developed nations of Latin America, but it has a long way to go before the economy provides all Chileans with an adequate standard of living. The agricultural system is very backward, and about $140 million worth of food must be imported annually. Most of the imported food could be produced in Chile, but the defenders of the antiquated land-tenure system prevented the modernization of the agricultural system until the 1960's, when a land-reform law was finally adopted. Chile's agricultural problem flows out of the preservation of the latifundia system of colonial days. In 1959, 2.2 percent of Chile's farms were larger than 1,000 *hectares* each and contained 73.2 percent of the country's total farmland. Since about 30.1 percent of the population depend upon agriculture and allied activities for their livelihood, poverty in the rural areas is widespread.

Another factor contributing to a distortion of the economic system is the high dependence upon foreign credits, earned by exporting minerals, especially copper. Although the mineral industry contributes only about 5 percent of the gross domestic product and in 1960 employed only 3.8 percent of the economically active population, it contributed about a fourth of all government revenue and two-thirds of the value of all exports. Manufacturing is the largest contributor to the gross national product, about 25 percent in recent years. Of the economically active, the largest numbers, 27.7 percent in 1960, were in agriculture, hunting, and fishing; 3.8 percent were in mining; 17.9 percent were in manufacturing; 5.6 percent were in construction; 10.9 percent were in commerce; 22.7 percent were in services; and 11.4 percent were in other fields. As these figures demonstrate, Chile has a developing economy, but for various reasons the country has had an almost permanent inflation, which has weakened the economic system and contributed to keeping most of the population in poverty.

One result of Chile's poverty is an ingrained habit of mind that accepts human affliction humbly, either as a sad but unavoidable accident or as the will of God. This may help to explain why Chile has had a relatively peaceful development, unmarked by any such bloodthirsty tyrants as Juan Vicente Gómez or Rafael Trujillo, or by chaotic civil wars.

Chile has a three-class society. Only about 25 percent of the popula-

tion participates with any real effectiveness in the country's political life
and enjoys a fairly good standard of living. The other 75 percent is alienated from the mainstream of Chilean life by lack of education, poverty,
and isolation from the large urban centers. The upper class is split between the landowning aristocracy, based on family and inherited wealth,
and the new rich, the industrialists, politicians, city businessmen, and
some military men. Many of the new rich are foreign-born or the children of foreign-born parents. Between the rich and the alienated poor is
a middle class, estimated by Professor Federico Gil to include about 1.1
million people, about 100,000 in the rural areas (small landowners and
their families) and about 1 million in the urban areas, including professionals, the university faculties, schoolteachers, the officer corps of the
armed forces, about two-thirds of the civil service, office employees, small
industrialists, merchants, and the owners of rental property.

Professor K. H. Silvert has written that

> about a fifth to a quarter of all Chileans live in what we think of as
> a modern society: they are educated; they can aspire to higher posi-
> tion for their children without being unrealistic; they can talk and
> gather and write and read freely; they can make a fairly wide occu-
> pational choice; they have access to government and can be assured
> of equality before the laws; they can enjoy a wide array of the
> material fruits of industrial life; they can belong to unions and
> political parties and pressure groups and professional societies; and
> they can assume that their vote has some real significance. This part
> of Chilean society is the effective nation. All public officials, mili-
> tary officers, intellectuals, professionals, bank clerks, storekeepers,
> industrialists, and large farmers are recruited from this limited but
> still significantly large segment.[2]

The poverty and alienation of about three-fourths of the population
during the decades after the Second World War created a political climate that tended to strengthen the reformist political parties. By the
middle of the 1960's, the overwhelming majority of the votes cast in each
election went to the parties pledged to institute radical changes in
Chile's political and economic organization. There was little dispute
about the need for change; the vast majority of Chileans recognized that
the country could not continue to develop peacefully without ending
the poverty and other social ills so many Chileans suffered. The only
arguments were about the ways in which change was to come about.

---

[2] K. H. Silvert, "Some Propositions on Chile," *American Universities Field Staff Reports
Service*, West Coast South America series, 11 (January 1964): 47.

The Development of Modern Chile

The Spanish colony of Chile was a neglected, far-off backwater. Hubert Herring estimated the population, at independence, at about one-half million, of whom some 100,000 were Indians in the south who did not recognize Spanish authority. Santiago was a city of about 30,000 and agriculture occupied almost the entire population. Isolation apparently bred an independent spirit among the Creoles of Chile, and independence came early, though San Martín's Argentine army had to cross the Andes to consolidate it by helping to defeat diehard forces loyal to the Spanish crown. Thus Chile's independence was not formally proclaimed until 1818, although the first local government had been set up in 1810.

From 1817 to 1830, Chile was torn by a series of struggles between factions of the aristocratic upper classes: those who wanted a liberal society versus those who wanted to continue the type of organization left behind by Spain. During this period two groups that were to dominate Chilean political life until the twentieth century developed among the aristocracy. One group, known as the *Pelucones* (the bigwigs), later to become the Conservative Party, had the support of most of the landowners, the Catholic hierarchy, and the army officers. Basically these groups wanted "law and order," centralized government, and a continuation of the semifeudal land-tenure system and colonial social organization. The other group, known as the *Pipiolos* (novices), later to become the Liberal Party, influenced by French and British ideas, sought a more liberal system, including state controls over the Catholic church, federalism, land reform, and economic development.

In 1830, at the battle of Lircay, the *Pelucón* army decisively defeated the *Pipiolo* army and a thirty-year period of political stability began. During these years, Chile's political system emerged as it was to continue for more than a century. A constitution was adopted in 1833 which remained in force until 1925, although it changed somewhat through the years. The constitution of 1833 set up a government in which the president and the legislature were elected by indirect vote, with only males over twenty-five who were literate and owned a certain amount of property eligible to vote. (This probably included 10 percent of the adult population in the first half of the nineteenth century.) Local government and the electoral system were dominated by the president, and the Catholic church retained many of the privileges it had in colonial days. It was the Spanish monarchy in republican dress. The economy flourished during these years as mining was developed. Settlement expanded to the south. Victory over Peru and Bolivia in the war of 1836–39 gave the Chileans a feeling of confidence. Education flourished.

By the 1850's, the liberals were strong enough to challenge the conservatives, and from then on the small portion of the population active in the country's political life began to separate into what were to become true political parties. Eventually a multiparty system developed which was to continue functioning for a hundred years. As early as the 1860's, three groups could be distinguished: the nationalists, the more traditional-minded conservatives; the coalitionists, the moderates of the old conservative and liberal groups who supported the presidents; and the radicals, the ex-liberals who wanted more democracy and less power for the Catholic church. These divisions were created by the economic development of the country. Railroads, mining, and commerce produced wealthy new aspirants for political power. Eventually the more liberal groups began to dominate the country and the political machinery was slightly democratized. In 1868 the president was forbidden reelection; in 1871 a new system of proportional election was introduced to give all political parties representation in the Congress; in 1885 the property requirement for voters was abolished; municipalities grew stronger and the Congress gained the power to override a presidential veto. Meanwhile, the economy continued to develop, the population increased, and education and culture flourished.

In 1864 Chile fought off attempts by Spain to reconquer its former colony, and in the War of the Pacific, from 1879 to 1883, Chile defeated Peru and Bolivia again and increased its area by more than a third as it incorporated into its territory the important Atacama desert and its great wealth in copper and mineral salts, from which nitrates and other valuable products could be extracted. The victorious armies returned from Peru to crush the last stand of the Araucanian Indians, who were driven to the far south, and treaties were signed to end the Indian wars.

Just when all should have been going well, Chile's political system broke down. The president, José Manuel Balmaceda, who was inaugurated in 1886, tried to push liberal ideas at a rapid pace. This aroused great opposition in the legislature, and he lost the support of the Liberal Party members in the Congress. The aristocrats were particularly incensed at some of his ideas about state intervention in the economy. A civil war broke out with one side led by the Congress, the other by the President. The congressional forces won after eight months of heavy fighting, in which about 10,000 were killed, and ushered in a period of parliamentary government which was to endure from 1891 to 1920. Now the aristocracy would govern the country directly, instead of using a president.

The period of parliamentary government saw the development of the Conservative, Liberal, and Radical parties in the forms they were to preserve for many decades. These were years of comparative prosperity and growth for the Chilean economy, but it was a prosperity based upon royalties collected on the export of nitrates and upon an agricultural system organized around the great latifundia, known in Chile as *fundos.* During this period the railroads finally connected northern and southern Chile, many public works were built, and industrialization flourished, aided by a protective tariff. But the class system gave perhaps nine-tenths of the population a bare existence while only 10 percent enjoyed a decent living and a tiny minority enjoyed all of the prerogatives of unlimited wealth. In addition, the parliamentary system never worked well.[3] Each aristocrat had his own ideas and the government was constantly unstable. From 1892 to 1920, about 120 cabinet changes took place, primarily because, in the proliferation of political parties, no one party ever received a majority. Politics became a chaotic struggle for power, and no government was able to work out or follow a consistent policy.

During the First World War, when the Allied blockade cut Germany off from its supply of Chilean nitrates, a chemist in Germany devised a way of fixing nitrates from the air. Thus, although Chilean nitrates and copper were in great demand during the war and prices were high, when the war ended Chile was no longer able to sell its nitrates and a depression set in. Unemployment bred strikes and riots, and the growth of a Socialist-Labor and a Communist party deepened the crisis. In 1920 a new charismatic figure appeared upon the scene, Arturo Alessandri, a lawyer who united behind his Liberal Alliance the Liberal, the Socialist-Labor, and other parties that had the support of most of the poor and dissatisfied. Advocating a program to come to grips with Chile's problems, he campaigned in all parts of the country and aroused great enthusiasm, which swept him to victory in the 1920 election.

Unfortunately, during the first four years of his term the majority in the Congress opposed Alessandri, and under the parliamentary system there was little he could do to further reform. The Congress simply refused to vote the funds the government needed. President Alessandri campaigned for congressmen who supported him, but when they won,

---

[3] On the crisis in Chile during the parliamentary regime, see the interesting quotations by Chilean writers in "What's Wrong with Chile?" in Fredrick B. Pike, *Chile and the United States, 1880–1960* (Notre Dame, Ind.: University of Notre Dame Press, 1963), pp. 94–99.

the new congressmen also failed to vote for his program. Meanwhile, the economic situation worsened until, in September 1924, the army persuaded Alessandri to set up a cabinet dominated by the military, whereupon he went into exile. The military junta that supplanted Alessandri then abolished the Congress, but it too proved unable to cope with the nation's problems, and in a few months it was expelled from office by a group of younger officers whose first action was to invite Alessandri to return. Assuming the presidency again on March 20, 1925, Alessandri acted vigorously. By decree he introduced a graduated income tax, expelled certain conservative political leaders, retired many generals and colonels from the army, and persuaded the Congress to write a new constitution that restored the strong presidential system to Chile. Under the new system, the president was to be elected by direct vote, and Congress could no longer vote no confidence in the cabinet and force it to resign. At the same time, the Catholic church lost its special status.

The new constitution, however, did nothing to lessen the effects of Chile's economic difficulties, and after six months Alessandri again went into exile. In a few months Colonel Carlos Ibáñez del Campo had control of the government, and he ruled as a dictator from 1925 to 1931. This was the period of Coolidge "prosperity" in the United States, during which New York bankers sold Chilean bonds worth over $300 million to unwary investors. With this money Ibáñez was able to finance public works, pay the army and the bureaucracy, and keep the government functioning. A synthetic prosperity developed, though most of the population still lived on the edge of starvation. But the dictatorship kept Congress quiet and the press noncommittal; prison and exile awaited all who protested.

By 1931 the bubble had burst. With the 1929 world depression the flow of money from Wall Street stopped as Chile defaulted on its bonds. World trade was almost at a standstill. The government could not pay its employees, especially the army, and the unemployed rioted in the streets. Finally the government broke down and Ibáñez fled to Argentina. These were chaotic years for Chile. Revolts and coups came one after another as nine different governments tried to stabilize the situation. Finally, at the end of 1932, an election brought Alessandri to the presidency once again for the 1932–38 term. By then Alessandri was no longer a radical reformer, but a traditional conservative who admired Mussolini. Conservative political leaders were appointed as his cabinet ministers. All efforts went into improving the country's economic situation, and in this the Alessandri government was successful. Trade was restored as markets were again found for nitrates. The British-owned

Trans-Andean railroad was purchased by the Chilean government. Industrial production was increased until most manufactured consumer products were being produced locally. But the improvement in the economy did little for the masses, and as Alessandri's term drew to a close, the Radical Party, the Socialist Party, and the Communist Party united in a popular front that elected Pedro Aguirre Cerda president by a margin of 4,000 votes in 1938.

The installation of the Popular Front government gave Chile another chance to reorganize its archaic economic and social systems, but again, as in 1920, nothing much was done. In the first place, a terrible earthquake hit southern Chile just after President Aguirre took office, killing thousands, leaving some 100,000 persons homeless, and causing about $50 million worth of damage. The energies of the government went to feeding and housing the victims of the earthquake instead of into reforms. In the second place, the Stalin-Hitler pact changed the Communist Party line, and on instructions from Moscow the Communists energetically opposed the government they had just helped elect. By January 1941 the Popular Front was formally disbanded. A development corporation was set up to stimulate production, education was expanded, social services were improved, wages of workers were raised, but no really fundamental changes took place. To complicate matters, President Aguirre died in 1941 before his term expired, bringing a new election to occupy the attention of the political leaders and the voters.

In 1942 and 1946 the Radical Party elected its candidates for president, Juan Antonio Ríos and Gabriel González Videla. This decade of Radical government, from 1942 to 1952, saw constitutional liberty observed, but again no important reforms were instituted. In this period a sort of semi-parliamentary system of government developed because no party ever elected a majority of either house of the Congress. In 1949, for example, fourteen parties were represented in the Congress. To get any support for his legislative program, President González was forced to appoint cabinet ministers from enough parties to enable him to get the support of a majority of the Congress. The style of government was similar to that used in the French Third Republic. One cabinet would incline to the conservative side, another to the liberal, but always the Radical Party was at the helm.

Since no real structural changes took place in Chile, in 1952 the demagogic ex-dictator Carlos Ibáñez, although not supported by any of the important political parties, was elected president by voters desperate for a solution to their problems. Ibáñez did as little as his predecessors. He was an old man with no solid political party backing and his course was eratic. In six years he appointed 135 cabinet ministers. This fluctuation prevented any consistent policy. To the accompaniment of much propaganda, he and Juan Perón signed a trade agreement to unite the Argentine and Chilean economies, but for various reasons neither country benefited and the unification ended. Meanwhile, inflation rocked the country and the feeble attempts to improve the economy failed when a drastic fall in the price of copper from 1956 to 1958 caused an even more serious economic crisis. To his credit, this time President Ibáñez governed constitutionally, but he was eighty-one by the time his term was up and nothing much had been accomplished.

Having had Radical Party presidents from 1938 to 1952 and having tried the demagogy of Ibáñez, the Chilean voters seemed at a loss as to how to vote in 1958. In the presidential election of that year, the four leading candidates all received substantial votes, with Jorge Alessandri, the candidate of the Conservative and Liberal Parties, receiving the largest number. This election demonstrated how divided the Chilean voters were. Alessandri received 389,909 votes, 31.6 percent; Salvador Allende, candidate of the FRAP (the coalition of the Communists and Socialists and their friends), received 356,493 votes, 28.9 percent; Eduardo Frei, candidate of the Christian Democratic Party, received 255,760 votes, 20.7 percent; Luis Bossay, candidate of the Radical Party, received 192,077 votes, 15.6 percent; and Antonio Zamorano, an independent revolutionary, received 41,304 votes, 3.3 percent of the total. The Congress elected Alessandri as president. He was the first conservative to take office in twenty years, but he too was unable to solve the country's problems. On January 1, 1960, he introduced a new monetary unit, the escudo, to take the place of the peso, which had sunk to 1,049 to the dollar. He tried to govern with a technical cabinet of nonpartisan specialists and made a serious attempt to stop the inflationary spiral, but in May and June 1960 a series of earthquakes accompanied by tidal waves, landslides, and volcanic eruptions devastated southern Chile, killing about 10,000, affecting about one-third of the population, and causing about $500 million worth of damage. Again the government's efforts had to turn toward relief and reconstruction instead of to reform.

By the time of the 1964 presidential election, the struggle to implant the needed reforms had polarized the Chilean population into two great blocs and the multiparty system seemed to be dying.

The group that was to win the presidency in 1964 was led by the Christian Democratic Party (PDC), whose leader, Eduardo Frei, became president. The PDC had begun as a split-off from the Conservative Party in 1938. By 1964 it was a vigorous organization with members in all parts of the country. Dedicated to reform by democratic means, it won the support of most of the liberal and conservative voters because they were frightened by the possibility that the other great bloc, the FRAP, which included the Chilean Communists, would win the election.

By 1964 the need for reform was so obvious that the Conservative and Liberal Parties did not even offer a presidential candidate. In 1963 these parties had combined with the Radical Party to support a Radical, Julio Durán, but the three-party combination never jelled and Durán finally ran as the candidate of only his own party.

The voters gave Frei 1,409,012 votes, 56.09 percent of the total, an unusual majority for Chile. Allende received 977,902 votes, 38.93 percent, and Durán 125,233 votes, 4.9 percent; 18,550 votes were blank or spoiled. Frei took office on November 3, 1964, but because his party did not have a majority in the Congress he was unable to begin the reforms he was pledged to institute. He and his party proposed constitutional reform, including the institution of a plebiscite system to be called upon when a government proposal was rejected by the Congress, and the expropriation of rented lands with an initial payment of 10 percent and the balance to be paid in twenty-five years. At the same time, a system of agricultural credit and technical assistance was to be set up. Exports were to be stimulated; an inheritance tax was proposed; a reorganization of the copper industry was to make the Chilean government a major partner in the industry; education and housing were to be pushed and measures were to be taken to control inflation. Industrial expansion would help to satisfy the demand for consumer goods and wages and salaries were to be adjusted to the cost of living. The Frei administration reestablished diplomatic and commercial relations with most of the Communist countries, proposed that the Organization of American States be reorganized, and pushed for Latin-American economic integration.

The reforms proposed by the Frei program were badly needed by Chile, but the congressional opposition led by the FRAP refused to pass the necessary legislation, maintaining that only an instantaneous revolution on the Cuban model could help Chile. As a result of the deadlock during 1964, the voters gave the PDC an astounding victory in the congressional election of 1965. For the first time in more than a hundred years, one party, the PDC, won a majority of the seats in the Chamber of Deputies and twelve of the twenty-one contested Senate seats, although it still lacked a majority in the Senate.

The remnants of the old traditional parties, by combining their votes in the Senate with those of the "rule or ruin" radicals of the Communist and Socialist Parties, were able to prevent the adoption of much of the legislation introduced by the government. In January 1967 the Senate demonstrated its sentiment by refusing, by a vote of 23 to 15, to give President Frei permission to leave Chile to make a state visit to the United States.[4]

In March 1966 President Frei finally lost his patience with the innumerable strikes the FRAP labor leaders were organizing and used troops to stop a wildcat strike in the copper region. Eight miners were killed and thiry-five wounded. The FRAP called a general strike four days later in protest, but this was a failure. Evidently the majority of the population still supports the Frei government, though the holdover senators have been able to prevent the complete adoption of his program. The next congressional elections will be of extreme importance, because if Frei's Christian Democrats gain a majority in the Senate, the last political obstacle to their reforms will have been removed.

The Formal Constitutional Framework

Chile is governed under the constitution of 1925, which sets up a unitary republican representative democracy in which the sovereignty is vested in the nation with the constitutional authorities exercising delegated powers. Despite the relatively recent date of its adoption, this is one of Latin America's older constitutions. Chile has had comparatively few constitutions in the course of its history. Five attempts were made to set up a constitutional system from 1812 to 1828, but none of these proved workable. Only when the conservatives under Diego Portales came to power in 1829 was a constitution created, in 1833, which proved able to survive a reasonable lifetime. This one lasted until 1925.

The political machinery under the 1833 constitution was oligarchic and greatly resembled colonial government, but it fitted the conditions of the country at that time. That this constitution could remain in force about ninety-two years demonstrates that its creators understood their country. During those years Chile developed its nationalism, extended its boundaries, and led a far more stable institutional life than any of its neighbors. The oligarchic character of the government suited the social conditions of the era and permitted the developments that led to the

---

[4] This cooperation between the so-called right and left is common in Chile, as it is in all of Latin America. Ernst Halperin says, "European political concepts and terminology evidently do not suffice to explain the intricacies of Chilean politics," after pointing out that Arturo Olavarria Bravo was campaign manager for the Popular Front in 1938, for Carlos Ibáñez in 1952, for Jorge Alessandri in 1958, and for Salvador Allende in 1964 (*Nationalism and Communism in Chile* [Cambridge: M.I.T. Press, 1965], p. 47).

creation of a more democratic constitution when the time was ripe for it.

When Alessandri was recalled to head the government in 1925, his first effort was to create a more modern constitution. The 1925 charter was written by an assembly of 122 persons appointed by the president. How oligarchic Chile remained in 1925 can be estimated by the vote to adopt the new constitution. Of a total vote of 132,421, 127,483 voted in favor of the draft submitted by Alessandri's assembly. The population of Chile at that time was about 4,073,000. Despite its oligarchic origin, this constitution was close enough to the realities of Chilean life that, with amendments, it has been able to democratize the political system. There is little objection today to the constitutional framework of the country by any political groups.

The 1925 constitution abolished the parliamentary system that had functioned since 1891 and substituted for it a presidential system. Individual rights were spelled out, the terms in office of the legislature and of the president were lengthened, and an independent electoral court was created to supervise elections. The elections of the president and the members of the legislature were separated, and a system of proportional representation was adopted for the selection of the members of the Congress. A strengthening of local government was included in the new constitution, but this has never been put into effect. Church and state were separated. The judiciary was given the power to nominate judges, who are appointed by the president. Most important for the future democratization of Chile, the right to vote was granted to all literate males over twenty-one. Women received the right to vote in 1949.

The 1925 constitution has been amended at times since its adoption and has proved flexible enough to permit Chile to develop in a constitutional manner. Since the difficulties that accompanied the economic recession of the post–World War I period, there have been no unconstitutional changes in Chile's political system. Whoever is elected president is inaugurated. When no candidate obtains a majority of the votes, the constitutional procedure set up to select the winner has worked as it is supposed to.

How the Constitution Is Amended

Amendments to the constitution begin in the same way as legislative bills. Introduced in one of the houses of Congress, the proposed amendment is voted upon by both houses. If it is approved by a majority of the members of both houses, a joint meeting of the two chambers is called sixty days later. Here, without debate, a vote is taken, and if a majority votes yes, the proposed amendment is submitted to the president. The president can suggest changes; if these are accepted by both chambers, the amendment is returned to him for his signature. If the legislature refuses to accept the president's changes by a two-thirds vote of those present, the proposed amendment is returned to him and he must either accept it or submit it to a plebiscite of the citizens. Any proposal approved by plebiscite must be promulgated as an amendment. Several amendments to the constitution have been approved since 1925, the most important being those of 1943 and 1959.

Who Participates in Politics

Under the 1833 constitution and the laws passed to implement its provisions, only males over twenty-five, if single, and over twenty-one, if married, who were literate and had a certain amount of income or property could vote. Only a small minority could meet these requirements. During the years from 1833 to 1925 the restrictions on the suffrage were slowly relaxed; the property restriction disappeared in 1874 and the voting age for single males was lowered to twenty-one in 1888. During these years the proportion of the literate population increased, but still only a tiny minority voted. During the twentieth century, as education, industrialization, and urbanization increased, the percentage of the voting population also increased. Since women received the right to vote in 1949, only the 20 to 25 percent of the population which is illiterate cannot vote.

The number of voters in Chile has gone up steadily since the 1940's. In 1938, only 10.4 percent of the population was registered to vote and 9.16 percent voted. In 1964, 36.40 percent of the population was registered and 31.82 percent voted, a greater proportion than in any previous election.

To vote in Chile, one must be a citizen, over twenty-one years old, able to read and write, and be listed on the Electoral Register. Voting and registering are compulsory in Chile. Those excepted include enlisted men in the armed forces and in the police, those who have been convicted of certain crimes or have been found to have physical or mental disabilities, and all men under twenty-five who have not fulfilled their military obligations. Penalties can be inflicted upon those who do not register or vote, and proof of registration must be presented when transacting business with banks and other credit agencies and with governmental agencies.

The Electoral Machinery

Chile has probably had more honestly conducted elections than any other Latin-American country. Through the years, the electoral system has been refined, additional groups have been given the franchise, and a tradition of respect for the results of elections has developed. The electoral process is administered by the Office of Electoral Registry, electoral boards in each department, and polling officials at the local voting places. The director of the national electoral office is traditionally nonpolitical, and is appointed by the president of the republic with the consent of the Senate. He cannot be removed from office without the consent of that body.

The Office of Electoral Registry handles the routine work involved in an election, including the preparation of ballots, storing the ballot boxes, keeping records, and preparing the alphabetical list of voters. In each department an electoral board selects the officials of the polling places, decides where the polling places will be located, and handles the routine work involved in elections. There also is a registration board in each department which handles the registration of the voters. At the polling places, the names of the registered voters are divided into groups of 300, and for each group an electoral table (*mesa receptora*) is created. From the 300 voters, five voters and five alternates are selected by lot to supervise the voting and count the ballots.

All candidates are listed on the same ballot. Most observers agree that elections in Chile are honestly conducted. The campaigns are rather hectic as the many parties bombard the voters with propaganda. The rules permit campaigning for only two months before congressional elections and six months before presidential elections, but these rules are disregarded and the presidential campaign unofficially begins more than a year before the votes are cast. Since the presidential, congressional, and local elections are held on different dates, the Chilean voter gets many opportunities to vote.

Political Parties

During the 1960's Chile's traditional multiparty system has been slowly transformed until, for all practical purposes, only four large groups are left, with one, the Christian Democratic Party, winning a majority of the votes cast in 1964. Until that year no one party in modern times ever won anything approaching a majority. In 1952, for example, the winning presidential candidate received 43 percent of the votes cast. In 1958, the candidate elected president received only 34.1 percent of the votes. As the inflationary crisis continued, however, the electorate coalesced into the present four large groups.

To participate in elections a party registers with the Office of Electoral Registry by presenting its statutes, the names of its executive committee members, and the signatures of 10,000 voters. At times the Communist Party has been outlawed, but since 1958 all parties that can obtain 10,000 signatures are registered, including the Communist. If a party does not elect at least one member of the Congress, it loses its registration and must reregister to participate in another election.

The most important party in recent years has been the Christian Democratic Party (PDC), which won a majority of the total vote in 1964 and 41.06 percent in 1965. In the 1965–69 Congress its members held 82 of the 147 Chamber of Deputies seats and 13 of the 45 Senate seats. Originating as a split-off from the Conservative Party in 1938, it was known until 1957 as the National Falange. Led by a group of brilliant young men, it grew slowly until the 1960's, when it captured the imagination of the majority of the voters. The PDC is a radical reformist group greatly influenced by the social doctrines of the Catholic church and such thinkers as Jacques Maritain. It advocates social pluralism, political democracy including universal suffrage, a mixed economy with the government playing an important role, agrarian reform, strengthening of the legislature, and decentralization of the national administration. The ideas of the faction of the party led by Radomir Tomic (ambassador to the United States in 1967) are practically indistinguishable from those of democratic socialists in other countries. The Chilean PDC has been described as an *Aprista*-type party whose members go to church. In international policy, the PDC looks upon itself as a third force opposing both Communist and capitalist ideologies. It is anti-imperialist and favors peace, universal disarmament, and a ban on nuclear weapons.

The PDC is particularly attractive to the Catholic members of the middle class, intellectuals, technicians, professionals, and women. In recent years it has won some support among organized workers. Many self-made financiers and industrialists, with no tradition of alliance with the old oligarchy, support the PDC. The PDC also has strong support among the new arrivals in the city shantytowns, known in Chile as *callampas*. And the PDC seems to be strong among young people. Its members in the Chamber of Deputies average 39.8 years, while the Radical Party deputies average 47.6 years, the Communist deputies 47.5, and the Socialists 44.6.[5] The PDC is a member of the International Organization of

[5] George W. Grayson, Jr., "Significance of the Frei Administration for Latin America," *Orbis*, 9 (Fall 1965): 764.

Christian Democratic Parties, and its organ, *Política y Espíritu,* is a sort of theoretical magazine for all of the Latin-American Christian Democratic parties.

The second largest political group in Chile is the *Frente de Acción Popular,* more commonly known as the FRAP, which is a coalition of the Communist, Socialist, National Democratic, and National Vanguard of the People Parties. Since 1958 these parties have been able to unite their voting power in the presidential elections, and both in 1958 and in 1964 their candidate came in second in the presidential race. Within the FRAP the Chilean Communist Party (PCCh) is the most important group. In the 1965–69 legislature it held eighteen Chamber seats and five Senate seats. It has more money and a larger number of full-time, paid functionaries than any of the other members of the FRAP, and its semireligious ideological connection with the Soviet government gives it a disciplined, hard-working group of activists unmatched by the other parties. In most respects it is similar to other Communist parties of Latin America, supporting the Soviet Union and its satellites, opposing the United States, and advocating violent revolution. What distinguishes the PCCh from other Latin-American Communist parties is the fact that it is one of Chile's oldest parties, having been founded in 1914 (as the Workers' Socialist Party), and has a great deal of support among organized workers. During most of the time since 1914, its members have probably controlled the majority of the Chilean trade unions. Its support for Fidel Castro helped the PCCh to gain additional support among agricultural workers. It has always had some of the intellectuals and university students among its supporters. In recent years, Chinese and Soviet factions have appeared. There is no way of assessing the strength of the Chinese faction, as the party, controlled by a self-perpetuating bureaucracy, consistently follows the Soviet line.

Although socialist ideas have been propagated in Chile since the middle of the nineteenth century, it was only in the 1930's that a Socialist party was founded. Since then the party has gone through a number of splits as those who favored and opposed cooperation with the Communists struggled for control. Eventually, in 1957, most of the Socialists united as the Socialist Party of Chile (PSCh) and voted to join the FRAP. The PSCh is a Marxist organization and its program is almost indistinguishable from that of the PCCh. It has no ties with the Soviet government, but it talks as violently of revolution, a workers' society, and the iniquities of the United States as does the PCCh. One of its leaders, Salvador Allende, has been the presidential candidate of the FRAP coalition twice and has been one of Fidel Castro's leading supporters in Latin America. The PSCh, like the PCCh, is organized on the principle of democratic centralism, with most of the power held by the leadership. The PSCh is strong among the workers, the intellectuals, and the middle class, and for historical reasons has always been very strong in Magallanes province. The PSCh is not affiliated with any international organization. In 1965–69 it held fifteen seats in the Chamber and seven in the Senate.

The third largest party is the Radical Party, founded in 1861. From about 1940 until the 1964 election, the Radicals consistently received more votes than any other party, but as the years passed it became more and more torn by factionalism and lost some of its support. Originally the Radical Party had been a typical nineteenth-century liberal group favoring such things as extension of the suffrage, freedom of the press and association, free secular education, and curtailment of church powers. As the years passed, however, it began to adopt a socialist position, and in the 1938 Popular Front it joined in an electoral bloc with the Socialist and Communist Parties. During the 1940's and 1950's it cooperated at times with the Liberal and Conservative Parties and at other times with the Socialists and Communists. After the 1964 election, the more socialistically inclined faction won the leadership of the party and adopted a completely socialist program for a peaceful transformation of Chile. In 1965 the Radical Party affiliated itself with the Socialist International. In the 1965–69 legislature its members held twenty seats in the Chamber and eight in the Senate.

The Radical Party has strength in all parts of the country, but it is especially strong among white-collar urban workers, government employees, and some of the upwardly mobile businessmen. It is the most democratic of Chile's political parties and thus offers the most opportunity for ambitious middle-class youth to rise in politics. It is difficult to forecast the future of the Radical Party, but if it maintains its present orientation, it may become the natural home for those who seek change in Chile but who are against totalitarian revolution and have an antipathy toward the Christian Democratic Party because of its church connections.

The two parties that governed Chile until after World War I, the United Conservative (PCU) and the Liberal (PL), have shrunk to tiny minorities. After Frei's electoral victory, the PCU and the PL united to create the National Party (PN). The PN represents the wealthy, the landed aristocracy, and some of the upper middle class. When the PCU and PL were stronger, they received many votes among agricultural laborers, but they have lost most of this support. In the 1965–69 Congress the PN had nine seats in the Chamber of Deputies and seven in the Senate.

Other minor parties of little importance are the National Democratic Party (Padena), a part of FRAP, with three seats in the Chamber and one in the Senate; the National Vanguard of the People, another affiliate of FRAP; and the Democratic Party.

Little is known about how the parties are financed, except that the Communist Party seems to have sources of support outside the country. It owns the most modern printing press in Santiago, one so large that it prints four daily newspapers, its own and three others.

Public Opinion and Pressure Groups

Public opinion is centralized in Santiago, where all the important opinion-forming agencies are located. The press is free and outspoken, and all political views are represented. In 1960 about 118 daily newspapers circulated for every 1,000 Chileans, which was the third highest circulation in Latin America. Most newspapers are associated with a political party. *El Mercurio*, a moderately conservative newspaper with a circulation of about 65,000 in 1961, is the country's largest daily. Many political magazines are published, including *Topaze*, a satirical review. Radio is important in reaching the rural areas; 187 radio receivers per 1,000 population make Chile sixth in this respect in Latin America. Television is growing in popularity but is still too expensive to be widely influential.

Very little is known about the organization and activities of pressure groups in Chile. The rich, who have their clubs and economic interest groups, were able to dominate political life until the 1960's. Most organized pressure groups have had close ties to one of the political parties, with the businessmen more closely associated with the Conservative and Liberal Parties and the trade unions with the Communist and Socialist Parties.

Organized labor gives the impression of being a strong force in Chile, but labor has never played as important a role in the country's political system as it could have. The first trade unions grew out of the workers' mutual aid societies that were organized in the middle of the nineteenth century. When the first national federation of trade unions was organized in 1909, it soon came under the control of the Workers' Socialist Party, which was to join the Third International and become the Communist Party of Chile. Ever since then, the trade unions have been the battleground for Communists, Socialists, Radicals, and Christian Democrats, and have been used for political purposes as much as to advance the workers' economic interests. The struggles by the political parties to control them have weakened the trade unions, and most of them during recent decades have been dominated by one of the political parties.[6]

Only about 30 percent of the workers are organized, the largest group of trade unions being affiliated with the Chilean Confederation of Labor (CUTCh). CUTCh has about 300,000 members and is dominated by the Socialist and Communist Parties. The National Confederation of Workers and the Maritime Confederation of Chile have about 100,000 members and are affiliated with ORIT. Another group of unions is affiliated with the Catholic trade-union international and has about 80,000 members.

The government is very much involved in labor relations. Until 1956 it set minimum wages; since then it has set practically all wages. The labor unions use violence at times, but strikes and demonstrations are their main weapons. In many cases, strikes are more political than economic. In the 1960's, as the Christian Democratic Party grew stronger, its influence in the trade unions grew. The poverty of most Chilean workers has helped the Communist Party, for it has always had more full-time organizers than any other political party.

All other groups in Chile play a less important role in the political system than business and labor. The Chilean Catholic church is probably the most enlightened Catholic church in Latin America. Completely separated from the state since 1925, the church has confined its efforts to educational and spiritual matters. Its followers are mainly the poor and the conservative wealthy; the middle class tends to ignore it. Since the Christian Democratic Party became a major force, some observers have believed the Catholic church is becoming more active politically, but there is little evidence of this. The Christian Democratic Party gets a higher proportion of the women's vote than of the men's vote, and the women are more religious than the men, but there has been little overt political activity by the church hierarchy in recent decades.

The military has played little political part in Chile. Of the seven chief executives since stability returned to Chile in 1932, only one was

---

[6] In one investigation of the opinions held by the presidents of local unions composed of blue-collar workers in Santiago, Valparaíso, and Concepción, 88 percent of the 294 presidents polled thought the condition of the trade unions was bad, and 38 percent of these thought that union weakness was due to disorganization as a result of party politics. When the trade-union leaders were asked, "Which party do you think is doing more for the working class?" 43 percent selected the FRAP, 23 percent named the Christian Democrats, 19 percent selected none, and 6 percent selected the Radical Party. See Henry A. Landsberger, Manuel Barrera, and Abel Toro, "The Chilean Labor Union Leader: A Preliminary Report on His Background and Attitudes," reprinted from *Industrial and Labor Relations Review,* 17 (April 1964), as no. 4 in the Cornell University Latin America Studies Program reprint series.

a military man, and he, Colonel Ibáñez, was more a political figure than a military man. The Chilean armed forces are highly professional, are based on a system of compulsory military service, and in large part are drawn from the middle and lower classes. Numbering about 45,000 in recent years, the armed forces act as a neutral defense organization and are respected by all groups in Chilean society.

University students have always played a role in the Chilean political system. All university students automatically become members of the Federation of Chilean Students, and the political parties make strong efforts to elect their followers as officers of the student federation. When the campus of the main university was in the center of town, near the Presidential Palace, it was very easy to organize a demonstration of students. Their small numbers, however, prevent them from being a major force. Student politics are the training ground for the recruitment of political leaders, and such important figures as President Frei and Salvador Allende began their careers as student leaders.

The agricultural laborers are completely unorganized and they are generally disregarded by the decision makers. In recent years the reformist political parties have begun attempts to organize them and have advocated agrarian-reform measures. With the passage of an agrarian-reform law in the 1960's, it is possible that this group may soon become a more active participant in the country's political life. The proposal by the Frei administration of a system of community development projects known as *Promoción Popular* was never accepted by the majority in the Senate, but something like this shows promise of finally waking the inert majority of Chile's people. Under President Frei's original proposal, the government would try to set up local organizations that would become pressure groups and problem-solving organizations.

Civil Liberties

Chile's constitution guarantees its people all the traditional liberties, including equality before the law, freedom of conscience, of speech, and of the press, and the right to assemble, to create organizations, to teach, to own property, and to have a fair trial. To protect these liberties, the Chilean constitution provides for a writ of *amparo*, under which anyone who thinks he is being illegally detained can appeal to the courts for protection. As is so common in Latin America, the Congress, and the President when Congress is not in session, can suspend certain rights by declaring a state of siege for up to six months. Although this power is exercised at times, Chileans generally live freely and civil rights are respected,

560 PATTERNS OF POLITICS AND POLITICAL SYSTEMS IN LATIN AMERICA

especially in the cities. For the one-fourth or so who are in the modernized section of the population, true liberty is a reality. It is poverty, illiteracy, and social backwardness that handicap the rest of the population.

The Executive

The Chilean executive is a president elected by direct vote who serves for six years and cannot be reelected for the next term. If no candidate receives a majority of the votes, then the Congress chooses from among the two candidates who have received the most votes. In all cases where this has been necessary, the Congress has chosen the candidate who won the largest plurality in the election. To be elected president, one must have been born in Chile, be at least thirty years old, never have been convicted of certain crimes, and not hold any of the following positions: minister of state, intendant, governor, magistrate of the superior courts, scholastic judge, or official of a public ministry; nor can the presidential candidate have any connection with a corporation doing business with the government. There is no vice-president in Chile, but a minister is given this title upon the death of the president and a new election is called within sixty days.

The Chilean president is a strong executive granted a wide range of powers by the constitution. The 1925 constitution was created to abolish parliamentary government, and the president was therefore put in a strong position. He controls the administration of the government and appoints the most important officials as he sees fit. The Senate must approve his ambassadorial appointments, but even here the constitution makes it clear the ambassadors are to be the president's choice, not the senators'. The president also has the power to "prescribe regulations, decrees, and instructions that he may deem suitable for the execution of the law." This ordinance is the base of the president's control, as the habit has developed of issuing rules that may affect both the form and the spirit of the laws passed by the Congress. The president controls the finances, appoints most of the judges, controls foreign relations, supervises the armed forces, and issues pardons. Yet despite his extensive powers, the president is not as dominant a figure as are most other Latin-American executives. His inability to get legislation passed when the Congress is controlled by the opposition, as has so often been the case, limits his ability to act.

The president freely appoints and removes his cabinet ministers. Although the Congress cannot vote no confidence in a minister, it has the power to impeach any of them, and it has exercised this power from time to time. When the president had to appoint a coalition cabinet in order to win party support in the legislature, as was the rule until 1964, he was limited in what he could do. The president is further limited, according to some writers, by his lack of a professional staff and by the demands of petty routine.[7] In the manual of organization of the government dated 1959, the president had a very small staff assigned to help him.

A check upon the president is the *Contraloría General,* an autonomous auditing agency headed by a comptroller general, who is appointed by the president with the consent of the Senate. It checks all governmental financial transactions, manages all the government's accounts, holds custody of all the nation's property, and has some jurisdiction over financial legislation. It can challenge the constitutionality of the decrees issued by the executive, and at times it has disagreed with the president and won its point.

The president controls the civil service. A formal merit system exists, but it does not work very well. Every branch of the administration seems to have its own rules governing its employees. By law the civil service is forbidden to organize trade unions, although the constitution contains a general clause granting all Chileans the right to organize unions; but from time to time strikes take place which demonstrate that at least some government employees are organized. The president has the exclusive power to introduce legislation regarding salaries of government employees. A School of Administrative Sciences was created in 1956, but its location in the College of Law has helped to keep the training of public administrators legalistic. The Chilean administrative system is bureaucratic and not too efficient. It is highly centralized in Santiago and tied to a formal legalism that becomes routine. Many of the employees are poorly qualified because they obtained their posts for reasons other than ability, usually political.

The Legislative Power

Chile's legislature is a bicameral Congress consisting of a Senate and a Chamber of Deputies. The Senate consists of forty-five members, five elected from each of nine districts. Senators serve for eight years, with about half being elected every four years. The Chamber of Deputies consists of 147 members serving four-year terms, one being elected for each

---

[7] Jorge Ahumada claims the president in the late fifties was signing 5,000 documents daily and being visited by "hundreds of persons who distracted him from more important problems" (*En vez de la miseria,* 3rd ed. [Santiago de Chile: Editorial del Pacífico, 1960], p. 36).

30,000 inhabitants or fraction over 15,000. The members of both houses are elected by a complicated system of proportional representation based on departments and groups of departments; the voter chooses the individual he prefers among those on the list presented by the party for which he votes. If there is a vacancy, a by-election is held to complete the regular term. Since the division of seats in both houses is based on the 1930 census, there is great inequality in the districts today.

To be a deputy one must be a citizen who has never been convicted of certain crimes, and must not be a minister of state, an intendant, a governor, a judge, or a member of a firm doing business with the government. A senator, in addition, must be at least thirty-five years old. These provisions do not keep anyone from running for Congress, as the victorious candidates are given fifteen days after the election to resign any conflicting positions. The only exception to this rule permits teachers in secondary schools and institutions of higher learning located in Santiago to continue teaching while serving in Congress.

The Chilean Congress meets as one body for certain purposes specified in the constitution, but ordinarily the two houses meet separately. A regular session meets each year from May 21 to September 18. Special sessions, which can deal only with the specific matters mentioned in the call, can be convened at the request of the president of the republic or the president of the Senate upon the request of a majority of the members of either house. Chile's Congress has most of the powers enjoyed by legislatures in democratic countries, but certain constitutional rules make it weaker than the executive, although it is one of the strongest legislatures in Latin America. The Congress cannot amend sections or items in the budget law; only the president can do this. And only the president can introduce laws to change the political or administrative divisions of the country, to create new services or salaried positions, or to grant or increase salaries of government employees. In all of these cases the Congress can only accept the president's suggestion, or decrease or reject the proposals. In addition, if the president declares a proposal urgent the Congress must act upon the matter within thirty days. The members of the president's cabinet, although they cannot be members of the Congress, can participate in its sessions, and they have precedence in debate although they cannot vote.

The president has the right to veto a bill in whole or in part. If the legislature accepts the president's changes, the bill goes to the president for his signature. If the president vetoes the bill, the legislature can override the veto by a two-thirds vote of the members of each house. If the two houses disagree, an elaborate process is provided to settle the matter.

Despite its constitutional limitations, the legislature is a powerful body. In recent years almost all presidential candidates have been senators who achieved prominence in the Congress. The members of the legislature have the parliamentary immunity customary in democratic countries. They receive 1,000 escudos a month salary (about $211 U.S.; there are 4.74 escudos to the dollar), free postage and telegrams within Chile, and stationery and other office supplies, including a typewriter. Each one gets a private office and free passage on railroads, airlines, and boats to visit his district. The salary of a secretary for each member is paid by the Senate.

The legislature follows a formal procedure in considering proposed legislation and is organized with its own officers and committee system. The parties have caucuses in each house, but party discipline is not as strong as it could be, and many legislators have changed their party affiliations while serving as members of the Congress, especially those belonging to the nonideological parties.

Public Finance

Chile's budget is drawn up by the executive and presented to the Congress, which must act upon it within four months or the bill introduced by the president goes into effect automatically. Chile's financial system has been characterized by the shifting of funds from one budgeted classification to another and the use of supplementary appropriation laws. Government income and expenditures have gone up a great deal since World War II. The budget for 1962, shown in Tables 1 and 2, is typical of the pattern of receipts and expenditures during recent years. As the figures demonstrate, Chile spends most of its income productively but gets it from the wrong places. Only 18.67 percent of the income in 1962 came from direct taxes, whereas 50.63 percent came from indirect taxes, including import taxes and sales taxes, which fell hardest on those least capable of paying. With only 5.68 percent coming from taxes on personal income, it is clear that the rich are not being overtaxed. Great efforts have been made to improve the tax system in recent years, but Chile still has a long way to go before its tax system will be equitable.

The Judicial Power

Chile's judicial power rests in a Supreme Court of thirteen justices and a series of subsidiary tribunals. The members of the Supreme Court are appointed by the president from a list of five names submitted by the

TABLE 1
REVENUE OF CHILE, 1962

Source	Amount in Escudos	Percent of Total
Direct taxes		
On personal income	E62,811,321	5.68%
On business income	88,410,584	8.00
On property	55,111,449	4.99
Total direct taxes	E206,333,354	18.67%
Indirect taxes		
On buying and selling	184,044,381	16.66
On production (liquor, tobacco, records, soft drinks, matches, etc.)	77,156,167	6.98
On services	56,156,692	5.08
On judicial proceedings (stamps, official papers, etc.)	54,148,229	4.90
On imports	184,293,451	16.68
Miscellaneous	3,608,506	0.33
Total indirect taxes	E559,407,426	50.63%
Total tax revenue	E765,740,780	69.30%
From government enterprises, services, and miscellaneous	79,898,998	7.23
Internal and external loans, other capital income	259,377,410	23.47
Total revenue	E1,105,017,188	100.00%

Supreme Court, with two of the five always being the judges who have longest been members of an appeals court. Below the Supreme Court are nine appeals courts, and below them are the local courts. Although all judges are appointed by the president, the various courts send him lists of names that always include judges of the court just below the one in which there is a vacancy. Until 1925 there was a great deal of political influence in the appointment of judges, and the present system was created to take the courts out of partisan politics.

Except for the judges of the lowest courts in rural areas, all judges must have legal training and be at least twenty-five years old. Departmental judges must have practiced law at least two years, and Supreme Court justices must have practiced law for at least fifteen years. All judges have life tenure pending good behavior, and, generally speaking, the Chilean courts are independent. The Supreme Court is the only body that can remove a judge, and it can do so only by a two-thirds vote. Judges

TABLE 2
EXPENDITURES OF CHILE, 1962

	Amount in Escudos	Percent of Total
Current operating expenses		
President's office	E373,636	0.03%
Congress	5,967,067	0.52
Court system	6,811,062	0.60
Accounting office	3,388,447	0.30
Ministry of Government	80,344,461	7.00
Ministry of Foreign Relations	1,509,433	0.13
Ministry of Economy, Development, and Reconstruction	94,164,674	8.20
Ministry of Finance	211,467,820	18.36
Ministry of Education	164,140,105	14.25
Ministry of Justice	14,150,696	1.23
Ministry of National Defense	121,055,184	10.51
Ministry of Public Works	19,720,901	1.63
Ministry of Agriculture	24,605,693	2.15
Ministry of Lands and Colonization	1,674,240	0.15
Ministry of Labor and Social Security	10,810,224	0.95
Ministry of Public Health	98,263,015	8.53
Ministry of Mining	10,364,493	0.90
Total current operating expenses	E868,811,151	75.44%
Capital expenditures		
Ministry of Government	1,761,667	0.15
Ministry of Economy, Development, and Reconstruction	158,551,719	13.77
Ministry of Finance	14,827,616	1.29
Ministry of Education	4,252,171	0.37
Ministry of Justice	189,612	0.02
Ministry of National Defense	2,949,270	0.26
Ministry of Public Works	88,343,009	7.67
Ministry of Agriculture	2,089,628	0.18
Ministry of Lands and Colonization	3,169,289	0.27
Ministry of Public Health	4,035,254	0.34
Ministry of Mining	2,733,039	0.24
Total capital expenditures	E282,902,274	24.56%
Total expenditures	E1,151,713,425	100.00%

are forbidden to participate in partisan political activities or to be remu-
nerated beyond their salaries by public funds for anything except teaching
law in the universities and secondary schools.

The Chilean constitution gives the Supreme Court the power to de-

clare the acts of the executive and laws passed by the legislature unconstitutional, but this power is limited because each decision applies only
to the case being considered; that is, the court can declare that in a certain
case the law or executive act does not apply, but not that it is invalid in
all cases. The Supreme Court also has certain supervisory and budgetary
control over the lower courts. Special courts dealing with electoral, Indian, juvenile, aeronautical, labor, military, land, and water law and
other matters have been set up, but all these special courts are under the
Supreme Court's supervision.

The Chilean court system works well, but the system of written procedures makes the courts function slowly. This is basically due to the
Roman law system, not to the way the courts are organized. Most Chileans
look upon the courts as neutral bodies that function effectively.

Local Government

Chile is divided for administrative purposes into twenty-five provinces,
which contain eighty-seven departments, which are divided into *subdelegaciones*, which are divided into districts. Each province is headed by an
intendente appointed by the president for a three-year term; each department by a governor appointed by the president for three years, on
the nomination of the *intendente*; each *subdelegación* by a subdelegate
appointed by the governor for a one-year term; and each district by an
inspector appointed by the subdelegate.

There are supposed to be local elective bodies at the provincial level
and in the *subdelegaciones*, which for this purpose are known as communes. The provincial councils have never been created, but at the com-
mune level there is a council known as the *municipalidad*, composed of
elected *regidores*. These *municipalidades* have very limited power and
the *intendente* can veto their actions. In addition, in those *municipalidades* that have populations of more than 100,000 and in certain strategic
cities (Santiago, Valparaíso, Concepción, and Viña del Mar) the *alcalde*,
the presiding officer, is appointed by the president of the republic. Two
hundred and sixty-three municipal councils have been functioning in
recent years, but for all practical purposes there is no true local self-
government. Chile has the French system of local government in an extreme degree, with the national executive completely dominating the
subdivisions of the country.

The Frei administration has proposed amending the constitution to
decentralize the bureaucratic system. Under the proposal, ten regions
would take the place of the present twenty-five provinces, and each region

would have an elected council that would handle some of the activities now centralized in Santiago. The proposal has not yet been acted upon, but something like this must inevitably come if real democracy is to be developed in Chile.

The Autonomous Organizations

The Chilean government is an important factor in the country's economic activity. Through a large number of independent autonomous agencies that have been created by legislative action, the government stimulates production, carries on activities that private business has for various reasons neglected, and provides many kinds of services. These autonomous organizations are controlled by boards of directors whose members include persons appointed by the president of Chile, but in many cases the president receives nominations from private organizations such as trade unions and businessmen's groups. The Chilean Development Corporation, which has been very important in introducing new economic enterprises to Chile, is governed by a board of directors that consists of two cabinet ministers, two senators, two deputies, ten representatives of various banks and such organizations as the Chamber of Commerce, five persons appointed by the president, and the comptroller general.

It is impossible to say how much of the country's economic activity is carried on by these autonomous agencies, but it is a substantial proportion. The 1959 manual of organization of the Chilean government listed forty-two autonomous agencies. Some are very important, such as the Chilean Development Corporation, the LAN Airline, the Central Bank of Chile, the University of Chile, and the National Health Service. Others are more limited in their activities—the Committee to Develop Arica, for example—but all are performing useful and necessary tasks. Through these autonomous agencies the Chilean government provides education and health services; operates banks, railroads, steamship lines, airlines, and surface transportation; produces steel, hydroelectric power, petroleum, sugar, munitions, airplanes; controls exports, imports, international exchange, domestic prices; operates the statistical and census machinery; sells insurance; amortizes the national debt; constructs housing; carries on agricultural research; and operates the social security system. The president's role in appointing so many of the directors of these autonomous agencies has helped to strengthen the executive, but in many cases he must appoint from a list of nominees presented to him by a private organization.

Chile: A Last Word

Chile is a functioning democracy in which civil liberties are well protected and elections are meaningful and orderly. The executive, although powerful, is no dictator; the legislature is a powerful formulator of public policy; and an independent judiciary functions without interference. Chile has a group of well-organized political parties, most of which have clearly worked-out ideological positions, and the struggle for political power is carried on peacefully. Not all of Chile's population is as yet participating meaningfully in its political system, but the proportion that does has increased with each decade.

The great weakness of Chile's political system has been the lack of sufficient well-organized pressure groups to speak for the various sectors within the population. No effective organization represents the interests of the agricultural laborers. The urban workers and miners are only partially organized, and there is even some doubt that many Chileans belong to political parties.[8] As has been pointed out, only about 25 percent of the population is really included in "modernized" Chile. The rest of the Chileans are too poverty-stricken to do much more than worry about making a living.

Despite its handicaps, Chile has many advantages. It is a true nation in which the people are unified enough to recognize and value their nationhood. The people believe many myths about themselves and their country which help to reinforce the political system. One belief is that Chile is a true democracy. Another is that education can accomplish wonders and that Chile has a good educational system. These myths help political development to proceed peacefully, and the progress made since World War I is truly notable.

Yet Chile cannot rest content with its accomplishments. The overwhelming vote given to the two reform candidates in the 1964 presidential election is a notice that change must come quickly. President Frei has pushed for a constitutional reform that will permit resolution of the frequent deadlocks between the legislature and the executive, including holding all elections at the same time instead of staggering them, and allowing a referendum of all voters to decide upon legislation demanded by the president and refused by the legislature. Whether these reforms will be adopted is still undecided, but slowly President Frei has been

---

[8] Federico G. Gil and Charles Parrish report that, according to one nationwide survey, more than 90 percent of all Chileans belong to no political party (*The Chilean Presidential Election of September 4, 1964*. Part I, "An Analysis" [Washington: Institute for the Comparative Study of Political Systems, 1965], pp. 15–17).

able to get some of his ideas through the legislature. He is one of the leading spokesmen in America for a Latin-American common market, and with the emphasis given this project by the Punte del Este meeting in April 1967, there is reason to hope that some of Chile's economic problems may be on the way to solution. Chile's people have made notable progress in developing a functioning democratic political system in what was once one of Spain's poorest, most isolated dependencies, and one ought to be hopeful that they will make as much progress in the future as they have in the past. If they do, Chile will become a modern democratic state.

Why has Chile developed so differently from its neighbors? Practically all observers rate Chile as one of the three most democratic political systems in Latin America (the others are Uruguay and Costa Rica).[9] If one tries to isolate what these three countries have in common, one is struck by the fact that all three are small and were rather isolated during their formative years, and that the Spanish cultural pattern was not instituted in as rigid a manner here as it was in all the rest of the colonies. Chile has probably also benefited from its location, which attracted many immigrants: before the opening of the Panama Canal, all ships going through the Straits of Magellan stopped in Chile. Thus an isolated group, not strongly dominated by Spain, was able to develop a political system that suited its needs. Having achieved unification long before its neighbors, Chile could expand at their expense. Today Chile has solved many of the problems its neighbors are still struggling with. What remains now is to develop the economic system so that the standard of living can be raised. Since the overwhelming majority of voters cast their ballots for the parties pledged to achieve just this, it probably will come within a relatively short time.

SELECTED READINGS

AHUMADA C., JORGE. *En vez de la miseria.* 3rd ed. Santiago de Chile: Editorial del Pacífico, 1960.

ALEXANDER, ROBERT J. "Chile," *Labor Relations in Argentina, Brazil, and Chile,* pp. 236–391. New York: McGraw-Hill Book Co., 1962.

————. "Communism in the Shoestring Republic," *Communism in Latin America,* pp. 177–210. New Brunswick, N.J.: Rutgers University Press, 1957.

ARMBRISTER, TREVOR. "Will Chile Go Communist?" *Saturday Evening Post,* September 5, 1964, pp. 69–73.

"The Atlantic Report: Chile." *Atlantic* 215 (June 1965): 22–31.

BARRÍA SERÓN, JORGE. *Trayectoria y estructura del movimiento sindical chileno 1946–1962.* Santiago de Chile: Editorial Insora, 1963.

[9] See Russell H. Fitzgibbon, "Measuring Democratic Change in Latin America," *Journal of Politics,* 29 (February 1967): 129–66.

BERNASCHINA G., MARIO. *Cartilla Electoral*. Santiago de Chile: Editorial Jurídica de Chile, 1958.

———. *La constitución chilena*. 2nd ed. Santiago de Chile: Editorial Jurídica de Chile, 1957.

BLASIER, S. COLE. "Chile, a Communist Battleground." *Political Science Quarterly* 65 (September 1950): 353–75.

BOWERS, CLAUDE G. *Chile through Embassy Windows: 1939–1953*. New York: Simon & Schuster, 1958.

BRIONES, GUILLERMO. "La Estructura social y la participación política: Un Estudio de sociología electoral en Santiago de Chile." *Revista Interamericana de Ciencias Sociales* 2 (1963): 376–404.

BUTLAND, GILBERT J. *Chile, an Outline of Its Geography, Economics, and Politics*. 3rd ed. London and New York: Royal Institute of International Affairs, 1956.

CAMPOS HARRIET, FERNANDO. *Historia constitucional de Chile*. Santiago de Chile: Editorial Jurídica de Chile, 1956.

CASTRO, JOSÉ LUIS. *El Sistema electoral chileno*. Santiago de Chile: Editorial Nascimento, 1951.

CHILE, DEPARTAMENTO DE ESTUDIOS FINANCIEROS. *Manual de la Organización del Gobierno de Chile*. Santiago de Chile: Imprenta El Imparcial, 1959.

CLISSOLD, STEPHEN. *Chilean Scrap-Book*. New York: Frederick A. Praeger, Inc., 1952.

CRUZ-COKE, RICARDO. *Geografía Electoral de Chile*. Santiago de Chile: Editorial del Pacífico, 1952.

DAUGHERTY, CHARLES H., ed. *Chile: Election Factbook, September 4, 1964*. Washington: Institute for the Comparative Study of Political Systems, 1963.

DONOSO, RICARDO. *Las Ideas políticas en Chile*. Mexico City: Fondo de Cultura Económica, 1946.

EDWARDS, ALBERTO. *Bosquejo histórico de los partidos políticos chilenos*. Santiago de Chile: Ediciones Ercilla, 1936.

———. *La Organización política de Chile*. Santiago de Chile: Editorial del Pacífico, 1955.

ESTÉVEZ GAZMURI, CARLOS. *Elementos de derecho constitucional*. Santiago de Chile: Editorial Jurídica de Chile, 1949.

FICHTER, JOSEPH H. *Cambio social en Chile: Un Estudio de actitudes*. Santiago de Chile: Editorial Universidad Católica, 1962.

GIL, FEDERICO G. "Chile, Society in Transition." In *Political Systems of Latin America*, edited by Martin C. Needler. Princeton, N.J.: D. Van Nostrand Co., 1964.

———. *Genesis and Modernization of Political Parties in Chile*. Latin American Monographs, no. 18. Gainesville: University of Florida Press, 1962.

———. *The Political System of Chile*. Boston: Houghton Mifflin Co., 1966.

——— and PARRISH, CHARLES J. *The Chilean Presidential Election of September 4, 1964*. Part I, "An Analysis." Washington: Institute for the Comparative Study of Political Systems, 1965.

GRAYSON, GEORGE W., JR. "Significance of the Frei Administration for Latin America." *Orbis* 9 (Fall 1965): 760–79.

HALPERIN, ERNST. *Nationalism and Communism in Chile*. Cambridge: M.I.T. Press, 1965.

JOBET, JULIO CÉSAR. "Acción e historia del socialismo chileno." *Combate* 2 (September–October 1960): 32–45; 3 (January–February 1961): 39–49.

KAUFMAN, ROBERT R. *The Chilean Political Right and Agrarian Reform: Resistance and Moderation*. Washington: Institute for the Comparative Study of Political Systems, 1967.

León Echaiz, René. *Evolución histórica de los partidos políticos chilenos.* Santiago de Chile: Editorial Ercilla, 1939.

Menges, Constantine C. "Public Policy and Organized Business in Chile: A Preliminary Analysis." *Journal of International Affairs* 20 (1966): 343–65.

Nunn, Frederick M. "Chile's Government in Perspective: Political Change or More of the Same?" *Inter-American Economic Affairs* 20 (Spring 1967): 73–89.

Pike, Fredrick B. *Chile and the United States, 1880–1962.* Notre Dame, Ind.: University of Notre Dame Press, 1963.

Serrano, Julio. "Como han votado los chilenos 1937–1961." *Política y Espíritu* 27 (February–March 1963): 24–36.

Silvert, K. H. "A Political-Economic Sketch of Chilean History from 1879," *The Conflict Society: Reaction and Revolution in Latin America,* pp. 50–75. New Orleans: Hauser Press, 1961.

———. *Chile, Yesterday and Today.* New York: Holt, Rinehart & Winston, 1965.

———. "Some Propositions on Chile." *American Universities Field Staff Reports Service,* West Coast South America series, 11 (January 1964): 43–57.

Stevenson, John Reese. *The Chilean Popular Front.* Philadelphia: University of Pennsylvania Press, 1942.

Sunkel, Osvaldo. "Change and Frustration in Chile." In *Obstacles to Change in Latin America,* edited by Claudio Véliz. New York: Oxford University Press, 1965.

U.S. Department of Labor. *Labor in Chile.* Bureau of Labor Statistics report no. 224. Washington: U.S. Government Printing Office, 1962.

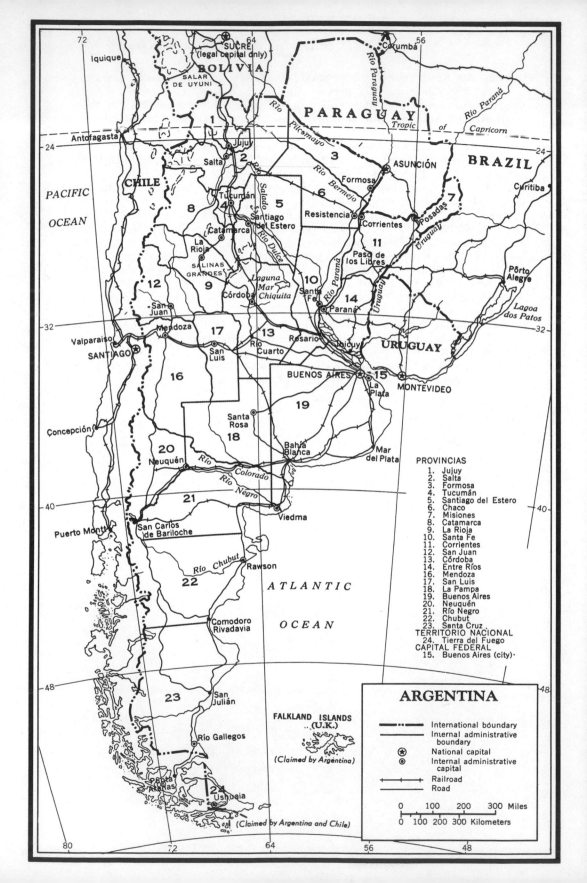

ARGENTINA

PROVINCIAS
1. Jujuy
2. Salta
3. Formosa
4. Tucumán
5. Santiago del Estero
6. Chaco
7. Misiones
8. Catamarca
9. La Rioja
10. Santa Fe
11. Corrientes
12. San Juan
13. Córdoba
14. Entre Ríos
16. Mendoza
17. San Luis
18. La Pampa
19. Buenos Aires
20. Neuquén
21. Río Negro
22. Chubut
23. Santa Cruz

TERRITORIO NACIONAL
24. Tierra del Fuego

CAPITAL FEDERAL
15. Buenos Aires (city)·

International boundary
Inernal administrative boundary
National capital
Internal administrative capital
Railroad
Road

0   100   200   300 Miles
0 100 200 300 Kilometers

FALKLAND ISLANDS
(U.K.)

(Claimed by Argentina)

(Claimed by Argentina and Chile)

ARGENTINA:

The Permanent Crisis

Argentina is a highly developed country compared with most of the other Latin-American republics, for it has an educated, urbanized population, its industrial production is higher than its agricultural output, and it has a good transportation system and good public health. Blessed with extremely fertile soil and a mild climate over most of its territory, Argentina, until about the time of the depression after World War I, was the leading nation of Latin America.

Despite its great lead in developing a modern society, since 1930 Argentina has been living through a permanent crisis that has uncovered the weaknesses of its economic, political, and social structures. During these years of crisis, it has proved impossible to create a stable constitutional system to manage the country's affairs. Dictatorships created by military coups are followed by short-lived constitutional governments that in turn are ushered out of office by new military juntas. The weakness of the country's political party system and the strength of its political militarists are the results of deep underlying social conditions.

A National Profile

Argentina is Latin America's second largest country; its 1,079,965 square miles make it larger than Great Britain, France, Germany, Italy, and Spain combined. More than 2,300 miles separate Argentina's northern and southern boundaries, and it is more than 800 miles across at the widest point in the north. Roughly triangular in shape, Argentina stretches from the tropical jungles of the Chaco to the cold waters of the Antarctic Ocean. Separated from Chile on the west by the high peaks of the Andes, Argentina is bounded on the north by Bolivia and Paraguay and on the east by Brazil and Uruguay. Below Uruguay the eastern and southeastern boundary is an Atlantic coastline that stretches 1,656 miles to the extreme southern tip of the country, Tierra del Fuego, which it shares with Chile. Argentina also owns a few small islands and claims ownership of part of Antarctica and the islands to the east known as the Malvinas in Argentina and the Falklands in Great Britain.

Within its boundaries are found many kinds of climate, soil, and mineral resources, but the country is generally considered to have six main regions. Surrounding Buenos Aires, the capital and largest city, is a plain known as the pampa, whose fertility, mild climate, and fairly evenly distributed rainfall make it ideal for agriculture and high-grade livestock. There are variations in the pampa: the southeast section is devoted almost exclusively to cattle and sheep; a western belt produces mainly alfalfa and wheat, and supports some cattle; a third section of the pampa, around Rosario, is known for its maize, flax, and cattle; closer to Buenos Aires, vegetables, fruits, and dairy products are most important. Although the pampa includes only about 22 percent of Argentina's territory, it contains about three-fourths of its population and the major part of the country's agricultural and industrial development.

To the north of Buenos Aires, lying between the Paraná and Uruguay Rivers, is an extremely fertile section with a mild climate producing linseed, rice, fruit, and cattle. South of Bolivia and Paraguay is the Argentine section of the Chaco. This is tropical country with a hot and humid climate. Hardwoods are produced in the northern part; in the south the forests have been cleared to produce subtropical crops including tobacco, rice, oranges, cotton, sugar, and *yerba mate*. The central part of Argentina is the wine section. Fruit is also grown here, and oil has been discovered.

In the west are the Andean provinces stretching along the mountains that extend south from the Bolivian border. This is a sparsely settled area, and although wine, sugar, and some minerals are produced, much of the region is unexploited. The sixth part of Argentina is Patagonia, a cold, semi-arid tableland greatly underpopulated and neglected. In the north there is some agriculture, in the province of Chubut oil is produced, and there are millions of sheep. Patagonia is inhabited by less than one person per square mile.

Argentina's population on July 1, 1966, was estimated to be 22,691,000. About 72 percent of the people lived in urban areas. Buenos

Aires, with a population close to 6 million in the metropolitan area, dominates the country; no other city has reached a million as yet. Argentina has a very low growth rate; the average annual increase from 1947 to 1960 was only 1.8 percent. The population is fairly homogeneous racially because large numbers of immigrants who came from Italy, Spain, and other parts of Europe between 1857 and 1940 mixed with the Indians, Negroes, mulattoes, and *mestizos* who composed about 98 percent of the population in 1810, when independence came, to create an integrated population. The surviving Indian population is estimated to be 20,000 to 30,000. Spanish is the official language and the Roman Catholic religion is supported by the state.

Education is free and compulsory for children from six to fourteen years of age, but not all children are in school, especially in the rural areas. In 1960 only 8.6 percent of those over fourteen were illiterate, a very low proportion for Latin America. Argentina's educational system is one of the best in Latin America, and in 1965 there were 195,169 students attending the country's nine public and sixteen private universities.

Until about 1900, Argentina was almost exclusively an agricultural country, producing meat and wheat for the world market. Since then, Argentina has become one of the most industrialized countries in Latin America, though it remains dependent upon meat and agricultural products to pay for its imports. Argentina is one of the world's leading meat exporters. Other important exports are cereals, hides, wool, dairy products, pastoral by-products, forest products, and oil seeds. Forty percent of the land is used for pasture for livestock; 10 percent produces crops; forests cover 30 percent; and 20 percent is unsuited for farming. Mining is of minor importance except for petroleum production during recent years. Other minerals found in Argentina are coal, gold, silver, copper, iron, tungsten, lead, zinc, barites, manganese, and limestone. The most important industrial products are textiles, cement, pig iron, steel and castings, chemicals, petroleum, and motor vehicles. Of the economically active population in 1960, 20 percent were in agriculture, 34 percent in manufacturing and construction, and the remaining 46 percent in services of various kinds.

Transportation and communications are well developed, the country ranking at or near the top among the Latin-American republics in miles of highways and railroad tracks, in the per capita number of daily newspapers sold, and in telephones, cars, and radios. The Río de la Plata is utilized for cargo vessels, and Buenos Aires is one of the world's leading ports. No part of the country is really isolated from the rest.

What is most puzzling about Argentina is that economic development does not seem to be helping to create a stable political system. In 1965 the gross domestic product increased, in real terms, by 7.8 percent. The distribution of income was considered to be more equitable than in most other Latin-American countries. Yet in 1966, constitutional government was destroyed by the army and a military dictatorship took control of the country's destinies.

Argentina's great crisis is generally attributed to two causes. Most important seems to be the very uneven distribution of population. Concentrated within 350 miles of Buenos Aires on only 20 percent of the country's area are found 67 percent of the population, 76 percent of the country's cereal-growing area, 63 percent of the cattle, almost half the country's sheep, 54 percent of the railway mileage, 71 percent of all telephones, 79 percent of all automobiles, and 78 percent of the capital invested in extractive and manufacturing industries. If one drew another semicircle around Buenos Aires with a radius of 700 miles, this would include only 40 percent of the country's area, but it would contain 92 percent of the total population and practically all of the country's developed agriculture and industry.

There is a great cultural difference between the people in and around Buenos Aires and the rest of the population. Buenos Aires has always looked to Europe or to the United States and ignored the rest of the country. At the same time, the city's position enabled it practically to monopolize the wealth, culture, and talent of the entire nation. Thus economic development has been concentrated in and around the capital city, and the Argentine federal system has been correspondingly distorted. The Buenos Aires metropolitan area of 255 square miles contains almost 30 percent of the country's total population. If one adds the population of Buenos Aires province to that of the city and its suburbs, the total is about 50 percent of the country's population in a small corner of the total area. Ever since independence the country has suffered from a lack of balance between the interests of Buenos Aires and those of the rest of Argentina.

A second factor contributing to Argentina's difficulties is the country's almost feudal land-tenure system. In 1959, 5.1 percent of the farms in Argentina were larger than 1,000 *hectares* each. These 28,834 farms included 74.8 percent of the country's agricultural and pastoral land. Naturally, this situation creates a large group of landless agricultural workers who move from one large farm to another as the need for labor changes.

As mechanization and fertilizers increase production, the need for farm workers goes down, and Buenos Aires has become surrounded by shack towns to which new arrivals swarm from the outlying regions in search of work. The wealthy landowners who draw their incomes from the rural areas also make their homes in Buenos Aires, where they can conveniently and effectively oppose any reorganization of the country's political and economic machinery.

Before 1930, when the population was about 10 million and a large proportion of the immigrants did not vote or participate in the country's political life, stability reigned. But as the population increased and the foreigners became Argentines, the old system broke down, and a new stable one has not yet been created. Perhaps Argentina has been suffering a crisis of overdevelopment; that is, the economic development came so quickly that the rest of the social machinery could not keep pace with it. In recent years Argentina, an important agricultural country, has been importing beef, potatoes, and eggs. Meatless days, which began during Juan Perón's misgovernment, were a regular feature of life by the 1960's. Inflation ran rampant, the government could not balance its budget, and there seemed to be no agreement among the most important groups as to what should be done. Political instability was the result. How this came about will be clearer after Argentina's historical development has been reviewed.

The Development of Modern Argentina

In the sixteenth and seventeenth centuries, what is now Argentina was a far-off, undeveloped subdivision of the Spanish empire in South America, administered as part of the viceroyalty of Peru. Because the Spaniards first entered the country from Peru, Chile, and Paraguay, Argentina's first Spanish settlements were inland: Santiago del Estero, founded in 1553; Tucumán, founded in 1564; Córdoba, founded in 1573; Mendoza, founded in 1561; and San Juan, founded in 1562. Buenos Aires, which has dominated the country in the twentieth century, although the scene of a short-lived settlement in 1536, was permanently established only in 1580 by an expedition that came from Asunción in Paraguay.

Argentina continued as a dependency of the Peruvian viceroyalty until 1777. Buenos Aires was not permitted to trade by the sea at its door, or even freely with its interior neighbors. All trade was strictly controlled, and what there was went by land to Lima, 3,000 miles way, from there to Panama, and so to Spain. Buenos Aires, at the end of this long trail, could only vegetate or resort to smuggling. It was not until 1777, when the vice-royalty of La Plata was created and the restrictions upon trade were relaxed, that Buenos Aires began to grow rapidly.

Buenos Aires' isolation led to the development of self reliance and independence among its population. At the same time, an antagonism grew between the people of Buenos Aires, called *porteños* (people of the port), and the inhabitants of the interior sections of Argentina. Thus even before the republic of Argentina had been founded, the people of Buenos Aires and those of the interior were developing two distinct ways of life, two contrary attitudes about the world, which were to become the foundations of Argentina's future political conflicts. And when the *porteños* unaided expelled English invaders in 1806 and 1807, they took the attitude that Buenos Aires was destined to be the leader of South America.

Buenos Aires' isolation and its independent struggle against the English helped to loosen its ties with Spain, and the *porteños* took the lead in the independence movement with a revolt in 1810 and a declaration of independence on July 9, 1816. Led by General José de San Martín, the Argentine troops also freed Chile and part of Peru, strengthening the *porteños'* confidence in the importance of their city's role in South America's future.

Independence came early to what is now Argentina, but many decades had to pass before the area became organized under a stable government accepted by the population. During the early years of independence, Buenos Aires struggled against the rest of the region in wars and periods of anarchy that resulted in the rise of an extreme degree of local *caudillismo*, and what had been the viceroyalty of La Plata, by then known as the United Provinces of South America, split into the disunited independent states of Paraguay, Bolivia, Uruguay, and Argentina. Governments came and went with great rapidity. In the year 1820 Buenos Aires province had twenty-four governors. Local *caudillos* came to dominate each province until in 1829 one of them, Juan Manuel de Rosas, became governor of Buenos Aires province and succeeded in dominating all of what is now Argentina.

Rosas succeeded in staying in power for seventeen years, but his rule compounded the country's problems. He governed through a secret police force that enforced his edicts and assassinated his opponents. Education languished, conflicts with France and England led to a blockade of Buenos Aires, military campaigns to crush the oppositon were common. And most important for the future of Argentina, there was a tremendous growth of large cattle ranches, the *estancias*, which concentrated the ownership of the land in the hands of a few thousand of Rosas' loyal supporters. Rosas himself, of course, was one of the country's biggest landowners. The Rosas dictatorship collapsed in 1852, but the land-ownership pattern has continued into the middle of the twentieth century, and its effects still influence political life.

After Rosas was overthrown, the political leaders succeeded in working out a compromise between Buenos Aires and the rest of the provinces, under which the city of Buenos Aires became a federal district and the home of the national government, thus ending the problems that came when two governments, the national and the provincial, tried to exist in the same territory. Since the final settlement in 1880, the problem has not been as acute as it was in the early years, but it remains. The basic problem has always been the disproportion between Buenos Aires and the other provinces. It is estimated that in the 1850's Buenos Aires province contained about two-thirds of the country's population and about three-fourths of the country's wealth. Since the city of Buenos Aires was the only important port in the country in that period and export and import taxes were the chief source of the government's income, it was inevitable that Buenos Aires would dominate the country, no matter what kind of government was set up. Even though the federal capital in Buenos Aires has been separated from Buenos Aires province, this province remains the largest in area, the largest in population, and by far the richest.

The contrast between Buenos Aires and the rest of Argentina has affected its political organization in many ways. The residents of Tucumán, Mendoza, Córdoba, and the other inland cities were molded by their past in a cultural pattern different from that of the people of Buenos Aires. The inlanders were more religious, more traditional-minded, and, after independence, poorer than the *porteños*. Buenos Aires had more foreigners, it had more contact with Europe, and it was far more prosperous. It was only in the twentieth century, when modern means of communication and transportation were introduced, that the vast gulf between the port and the interior began to be bridged. The traditional hero of Argentina is the gaucho, the man of the interior, whose life is different enough from most Argentines' experience to seem romantic.

It was during the period from the fall of Rosas to the First World War that the pampa's fertility and British capital transformed Argentina's economy and made it the producer of meat for the British population. The cattle and sheep were improved by importing breeding stock; the open range was fenced; the grass became alfalfa and other nourishing crops; and railroads improved transportation. At the same time, immigration was encouraged, and millions of Europeans, especially Italians and Spaniards, came to live and work in Argentina. The educational system was greatly improved. As the population increased and the railroad knit the country together, the parts of Argentina beyond the pampa were somewhat developed.

During most of the period from 1853 until the First World War, Argentina was governed by a fairly enlightened oligarchy of conservatives, a paternalistic, landholding artistocracy that developed some very capable leaders and functioned through a conservative political party that eventually assumed the name National Democratic Party. No opponents to the policies of the oligarchy were permitted to share in the work of government; federalism was negated by the practice of government "intervention" in the provinces; power was transmitted from one president to his successor in closed caucuses; and elections were controlled. The growth of the economy seemed to justify this kind of government, especially since the hard-working Italian and Spanish immigrants were not accustomed to participating in politics. During this period the Argentines occupied all of the national territory, killing most of the surviving Indians in campaigns similar to those waged in the United States' West during the same period.

Toward the end of the 1880's the rapid economic development culminated in a financial and economic crisis that stimulated the organization of the country's first true political parties. The country's prosperity had fostered the growth of a numerous middle class, and when the economic depression of that decade began to be felt, a group of young intellectuals founded the Civic Union of Youth.

Led by Leandro N. Além, the Civic Union won wide support, particularly in Buenos Aires. The new organization agitated for free suffrage and honest elections, and when it did not achieve them it attempted an armed revolt in 1890. After this revolt was defeated, the Civic Union became a political party, the Radical Civic Union, more commonly known as the Radical Party. In 1893 the Radical Party attempted another armed revolt, but again it was defeated. By this time Hipólito Irigoyen, a *caudillo* type, had become the party's leader, and he developed the pattern of boycotting elections. In 1894 Juan B. Justo and a group of more radical members broke away from the Radical Party and founded the Socialist Party. Both the Radical and the Socialist Parties grew to be mass organizations, the Radical in all parts of the country, the Socialist strongest in Buenos Aires.

Meanwhile, the population was steadily rising, the economy recovered from its depression of 1890–91, and the conservatives continued to keep a tight grip on the political machinery. George Pendle thinks that perhaps the oligarchic system was not as bad as its critics have painted it.

> Faced with a never-ending swarm of immigrants of many diverse nationalities and a locally-born population which for the most part was illiterate and quite inexperienced in public affairs, the ruling class perhaps acted wisely in retaining power in their own hands; and their rule, though selfish, was benign. Immigrants enjoyed personal liberty to come and go, to do and think as they pleased, and they were completely free from political or racial persecution.[1]

Yet the power of the urban middle class, the small farmers, and the developing working class could not be denied. The immigrants had brought syndicalist, anarchist, Marxist, and socialist ideas with them. The growth of the Radical and Socialist Parties was constant and the pressure finally convinced the conservatives that they had to reform the political system. In 1910, Roque Sáenz Peña became president in the typically fraudulent managed elections to which Argentina had become accustomed. To everyone's surprise, he pushed through a new election law that provided for universal compulsory male suffrage, a secret ballot, and the previous registration of voters. Sáenz Peña died before the new law could be tested, but the vice-president who succeeded him supervised Argentina's first free election in 1916 and the Radicals won, putting their leader, Hipólito Irigoyen, into the presidency.

Nineteen-sixteen was a decisive year for Argentina. Unfortunately, the First World War was on and Argentina's landowners were receiving fantastic profits from their sales of meat and hides to Britain and France. This deflected attention away from reform and created great inflation. At the same time, the war, by stimulating the growth of industry to supply the products that Europe and the United States could no longer send to Argentina, was changing the class composition of the population. Thus, instead of attacking Argentina's basic problems, the country was occupied feeding the European belligerents and developing new industries and social groups. Irigoyen had a chance to change Argentine history, but he failed to do so, and a political crisis began which has not been resolved yet.

Irigoyen's basic weakness was that he really had no clear policy, and so did not convert the general ideas of liberalism preached by the Radical Party into a program. He did nothing to change the system of large-scale landownership; his feeble attempts at social legislation did little to re-

---

[1] George Pendle, *Argentina*, 2nd ed. (London: Oxford University Press, 1963), p. 68.

organize the society; and he governed as autocratically as his predecessors had done before him. He used his powers of intervention to put his friends into control of the provincial governments, and to make matters worse, many of his associates and appointees were corrupt. Irigoyen himself probably never was dishonest, but he did nothing to hinder members of his administration from enriching themselves. In 1922 the Radicals won the election again, and when that term expired Irigoyen was again elected president in 1928. By then he was seventy-six years old and probably senile. He was unable or unwilling to sign papers or handle the routine of his office. Not only did he have no more program than he had had in 1916, but the corruption was worse. When the world depression hit Argentina in 1930, exports declined drastically, the value of the peso dropped, unemployment grew, the cost of living went up. By then the Radical Party was stealing the elections it could no longer win fairly and using other illegal methods to stay in power.

The end came in September 1930, when the army overthrew the government and put General José F. Uriburu, an extreme conservative, into the presidential office. The Radicals had missed their opportunity and their fourteen years in office ended. They were not to have another chance to control Argentina for twenty-eight years. This was a milestone in Argentine history, for it marked the first time since the establishment of constitutional government in the 1860's that the army had brought about a change in government by force of arms.

The revolution of 1930 was probably supported by the majority of the population, but it was controlled by a small group of military officers. Democracy had shallow roots in Argentina and it was natural for a majority of the Argentines to look to the revolutionary government for a solution of the country's pressing problems. General Uriburu declared a state of siege as soon as he took control and governed as a dictator. Using the by then customary methods of intervening in the provincial governments, controlling the elections, and annulling any election whose result he did not like, Uriburu turned the pattern of Argentine government back to what it had been before 1916. In 1931, in an election in which the Radicals were not permitted to participate, General Agustín P. Justo, a Conservative, was elected president.

Although Justo canceled the state of siege and released the political prisoners Uriburu had jailed, he governed as a dictator. The landowners seemed to think they could return to the "good old days." The depression led the government to organize a sort of controlled economy in which only the landowners who sold meat to England really benefited. Thus another opportunity to begin an attack upon Argentina's basic problems was missed. Quickly most of those who had hailed the revolution began to look upon the years of Radical government with nostalgia. Meanwhile, the Radical Party had degenerated to the point where it, too, became a conservative organization, happy with the state of affairs. But social changes were taking place which were to have important consequences.

Most important was the change in the composition of the Buenos Aires working class. With the shutting off of mass immigration by the 1930 world depression, the working class became more homogeneous. As the years passed it came to include fewer and fewer immigrants, more and more native-born sons of immigrants. These Argentines did not accept the socialism of their parents and the Socialist Party declined in strength. At the same time, the world depression was stimulating the growth of manufacturing in Argentina. When England and the rest of Europe could no longer afford to import large quantities of Argentine meat and wheat, Argentina found itself with little foreign exchange with which to buy Europe's manufactures, and small factories began to spring up in Argentina to meet the demand for manufactured goods that could no longer be imported. Thousands upon thousands of farm workers flocked to the city, a new type of immigrant from a tradition different from that of the European immigrants. By the time World War II began, the relation of forces was so changed that the landowning oligarchy, although it controlled the government, had little support in the country. The government simply refused to recognize that new groups had developed which were entitled to share in political power. In addition to the growth of the working class, a new class of industrialists had grown up. Pendle points out that in 1941, of the hundred persons paying the highest income tax, only ten were large landowners. The others were "manufacturers of textiles, beer, bags, and shoes; financiers and importers; operators of mines; owners of casinos, cinemas and radio stations."[2]

Thus the policy of the government and the intransigence of the landowning oligarchy led to a situation ripe for another revolution. In 1938 Roberto M. Ortiz, a rich lawyer, became president. He, like all Conservative presidents before him, was elected in a managed election, but, like Sáenz Peña, Ortiz tried to introduce honest elections. As he did so, more and more Radical and Socialist Party members were elected to Congress and to positions in the provincial governments. This frightened the Conservatives, who favored neither democracy nor honest elections.

Fate cruelly intervened just as World War II began. Ortiz was blinded by diabetes and forced to turn over his office to the vice-president.

---

[2] *Ibid.*, p. 88.

This was not only a great personal tragedy for Ortiz, but a bitter misfortune for Argentina, since it gave power to a sympathizer of Nazi Germany just as the Nazis were at the crest of their conquering advance. As is common in the United States, Argentina had elected a balanced ticket in 1937. The president was an honest, liberal Conservative. His vice-president, Dr. Ramón S. Castillo, was a dishonest, reactionary Conservative. Taking over the presidency, he immediately clamped controls on elections. When the United States entered World War II in December 1941, Castillo declared a state of siege and governed under its shelter until he was overthrown. Under Castillo, the pseudo democracy of Argentina reached one of its low points. Political frustration among the majority of the population turned many against the democratic system, which, as operated by the Conservatives, produced tyrannical government. The war created shortages, a rising cost of living, and much unrest. Most Argentines were probably sympathetic to the Allies, but the government kept Argentina "neutral" and seemed to favor the Nazis. When Castillo tried to install as his successor an extremely wealthy, feudal-minded sugar-plantation owner, Robustiano Patrón Costas, the army once again marched the troops out of their barracks and without firing a shot took over the government, to the applause of a majority of the people.

For two years the officers vied with each other for the seats of power until a colonel, Juan Perón, took over and ushered in an era that was to alter the whole course of Argentina's history and, by ruining its economy, make it even more difficult to set up stable, democratic political institutions after he had passed from the scene. What distinguished the group of officers who took control of Argentina's government in 1943 from the group headed by General Uriburu in 1930 was that the 1943 group was organized and had a program. The *Grupo de Oficiales Unidos* (GOU, the Group of United Officers) consisted of extreme nationalists, many of whom sympathized with the Axis powers during World War II. The Argentine army had been trained by German military missions since 1900, and many Argentine officers had studied at military schools in Germany and Italy. Juan Perón had served as a military attaché in Italy and taken courses at the Universities of Bologna and Turin. Not much is known about the actual functioning of the GOU, but it is known that the group was organized and looked upon itself as destined to lead Argentina to a position of rightful leadership in Latin America.

From 1943 to 1946 three different generals served as president of Argentina, but the power lay in the hands of the GOU and increasingly in the hands of Perón. The new regime functioned as a dictatorship. It dissolved the Congress and put "interventors" into control of the prov-

inces, the universities, and the trade unions. Political parties were outlawed. Newspapers were put under government control. Many democratic political leaders were exiled and jailed. These repressive actions
cost the military government its first popularity. If it had continued as it
started, it would have been just another military regime; but this was a
military government with a difference, and the difference was Juan Perón.

When the military government took over, Perón was made chief of
the secretariat of the Ministry of War and president of the National
Labor Department. At that time the National Labor Department was a
very minor government bureau, and no one heard much of Perón. But
Perón and his advisers evidently realized that the new government
needed more support than its military base, and utilized the Labor Department to take over the organized labor movement. Perón invited the
leaders of the important trade unions to a meeting and asked them
what the workers wanted; he then used his powerful position to get it
for them. In short order organized labor won a social security system,
higher wages, government help in organizing workers, the construction
of housing for workers, paid vacations, and other benefits the labor movement had been struggling to achieve for decades. But at the same time,
Perón gathered into his own hands all the machinery of collective bargaining. He encouraged employers and union leaders to come to his
office to settle disputes, and when workers chose to strike instead of
seeking Perón's aid, he sent troops to break the strike. He also helped
organize new labor unions. As the number of organized workers increased, Perón had his Labor Department converted into a ministry and
combined the trade unions into one national organization, the General
Confederation of Labor. In 1945 he completed the process by having a
rule issued under which only unions registered with the government
could sign valid collective bargaining contracts or use the facilities offered
by the Ministry of Labor. At the same time, the law provided that only
one union could be recognized in each industry in each area. With this
law Perón was able to destroy all unions that refused to be dominated
by him and soon was the controlling force in the organized labor movement. But it must be remembered that the workers did achieve higher
wages, better working conditions, and new fringe benefits during this
period.

On August 19, 1945, for the first time since Pearl Harbor, the state
of siege was lifted and an election was announced for February 1946.
The return of civil liberty was celebrated in Buenos Aires by a demonstration in which 400,000 marched "for the Constitution and for Freedom." The government immediately reimposed the state of siege and

began arresting its opponents. Violence broke out and the university students went on strike. On October 9, 1945, another revolt took place in which the officers, jealous of Perón's increasing prominence, forced him to resign his positions. By then he was vice president of the republic and Minister of War as well as Minister of Labor and Social Welfare. Perón was arrested and imprisoned on an island in the Río de la Plata. This was a dramatic moment in Argentina's political history. With the victory of the Allied forces in World War II, a wave of enthusiasm for democratic government was sweeping the world. The new group of army officers who took control of the government, however, failed to understand what was happening. Many of Perón's new laws benefiting labor were repealed. To make matters worse, many of the employers announced they would not pay wages for October 12, which Perón had just made a legal holiday. To many workers the overthrow of Perón meant the loss of all the gains they had made. In addition, although censorship was abolished and all political prisoners were released, the civilian political leaders failed to take advantage of the situation by making some kind of arrangement with the army officers. They did not realize that they could take over the government. While they hesitated, Perón's supporters acted. Led by his friend Eva Duarte and the trade-union leaders, the workers began to demonstrate. By truck, train, and on foot, thousands of workers, especially from the meat-packing centers, came to demonstrate their support for Perón. Riots broke out. Stores and factories closed. The army could have defeated the demonstrators, but the officers hesitated to use force and finally released Perón. Perón then became the dominant force in the government and put his friends in all key positions. Eva Duarte became his wife and a new period began.

Perón did not take an official position after October 17, but became a candidate for president. He organized the Labor Party; he split some Radicals away from their party and ran one of them as vice-president; and he campaigned as a defender of the working class. All of the traditional political parties supported the Radical Party candidate, Dr. José P. Tamborini. Tamborini turned out to be a poor candidate and his campaign failed to impress the majority of voters. Perón used all the tricks of the demagogue and invented a few of his own, including a governmental decree at the end of 1945 ordering all employers to pay their workers a Christmas bonus of one month's wages. He talked about social reform and Argentine nationalism while his opposition talked of democracy and dictatorship. In addition, Perón was helped by the nationalist resentment aroused when the United States issued a "Blue Book" two weeks before the election which attacked the *de facto* government of Argentina for cooperating with the Nazis. Perón utilized this episode to picture himself as the great leader of Argentina standing up against the "Colossus of the North." Perón's supporters and the government instigated some violence against the opposition, which made their campaigning difficult, but the election itself was peaceful and the votes were apparently honestly counted. Perón won handily, and his followers won large majorities in both houses of Congress.

Why did Perón win the election? The best explanation is that he convinced a majority of the working class that he would improve their conditions. In addition, the Catholic hierarchy seems to have helped him. One of the first actions taken by the military government in 1943 had been to decree that instruction in the fundamentals of the Catholic faith must be given in the schools, regardless of the wishes of the child or his parents. This reversed a long-standing policy of secular education in Argentina and naturally made the church hierarchy sympathetic to the military government. During the electoral campaign, a pastoral letter was read in Catholic churches all over the country which, without endorsing any candidate, warned all Catholics not to vote for any candidate or party that opposed religious instruction in the public schools. Since Perón favored religious instruction and Tamborini opposed it, this was equivalent to supporting Perón.

Once in power as the legally elected president, Perón made a heroic attempt to create South America's first truly totalitarian regime. He never completed the job, but he went a long way toward his goal. He adopted some of the techniques used by European totalitarians to build mass support so he could stay in power with a minimum use of force. Perón's regime was notable for an extreme nationalism, the fostering of the leadership principle, the strengthening of the national government until it intervened in almost every aspect of life, the creation of a militant party organized around Perón as the all-powerful leader, intolerance of any opposition, and the retention of the forms of democracy without preserving any of its substance.

What Perón seemed to be trying to do, in addition to staying in power, was to make Argentina "strong" by freeing it from foreign economic influence. To achieve this, he paid the country's foreign debt with credits accumulated during the war and purchased or confiscated railroads, the telephone system, port facilities, grain elevators, mines, and industrial plants. To strengthen Argentina further, Perón pushed industrialization. He set up the Argentine Institute for the Promotion of Trade as a government corporation which bought the country's agricultural and pastoral products at low fixed prices and sold them overseas for as much as the traffic would bear. By 1953 the Institute was handling 63 percent of Argentina's exports and 20 percent of its imports. The profits were supposed to be used for purchasing machinery to further industrial production. Perón also set up five-year plans to systematize his development program and other reforms.

Unfortunately for Argentina, Perón's program had many weaknesses. The lack of democratic controls made large-scale peculation and graft inevitable, and much of the money that was supposed to go toward industrialization was wasted or stolen. In addition, the emphasis upon industry, combined with low fixed prices for farm products, led to a drop in the production of grain and cattle. There is some evidence that the increase in urbanization and higher wages for workers increased domestic consumption of grains and meat and helped to decrease the amount of these products available for export, thus cutting the amount of foreign exchange earned. At the same time, inflation rapidly made its effects felt. By 1948–49 the economic situation was already bad, and it continued to get worse until Perón was overthrown in 1955.

Under Perón, industrial production did increase, but since Argentina is not naturally endowed with all the raw materials needed for industry, the developments were frequently expensive and inefficient. Some of Perón's other enactments had great permanent effect upon the country. He granted women the vote. He initiated many long-needed social reforms. He increased the size of the armed forces and their budgets, as well as giving the officer corps many privileges. He built up an armaments production industry. In 1953, in an attempt to strengthen the economy, Perón signed a treaty with the Chilean government setting up an economic union between the two countries. This pact was supposed to coordinate production in both countries and reform customs and exchange regulations. Although Paraguay, Nicaragua, and Ecuador joined the economic union, it never succeeded in accomplishing anything before Perón was overthrown and the treaty was forgotten.

Perón never established as tyrannical a regime as Rafael Trujillo and some others have done in Latin America, but in his struggle to stay in power he violated all of the human rights guaranteed by the Argentine constitution. The jailing and torturing of political opponents, the breaking up of meetings, and the censoring, intimidating, and closing down of critical newspapers were regular features of life under Perón. He had Congress pass a law that made it a crime to speak disrespectfully of the president and his regime. This law of *desacato* (disrespect) was used to imprison many, including elected members of the Congress.

Perón and his propaganda experts tried to create an official doctrine, which they called *justicialismo*, but despite all the pamphlets and books published about it, it is difficult to say just what *justicialismo* was. Neither capitalism nor communism, but supposedly a third force incorporating the best of these two competing systems, *justicialismo* was to bring the Argentine people social justice, economic freedom, and political sovereignty. The evidence of history seems to be that Perón achieved none of these goals. He led Argentina toward autarky, exacerbated the relations between classes, strengthened the military, and bankrupted the country.

Perón had a new constitution adopted in 1949 so that he could continue to hold the presidency for succeeding terms. He was reelected in 1951, in a contest in which the opposition had little opportunity to campaign, but in 1955 the army overthrew his government. The end came for Perón when the Catholic church joined his other opponents. As we have seen, the church originally looked with favor upon his regime. Perón regularly had priests give their blessings to *Peronista* Party and trade-union meetings. Pope Pius XII decorated Perón and received his wife in a private audience. But in the 1950's, when the government began to force schoolteachers to teach that *Peronismo* was the one true faith of all Argentines, the church hierarchy stirred in protest. Slowly it began to oppose Perón, and as it opposed him, he retaliated with more laws to which the church objected. In 1954 illegitimate children were made equal under the law to legitimate children, grounds for divorce were established (there had previously been none, and there are none today), and provincial governments were given the right to establish legal houses of prostitution. These measures led to increased conflict between the church and the government. As the church protested, the government silenced Catholic periodicals, priests were imprisoned, religious processions were prohibited. Radicals and Socialists, who opposed Perón, began to swell the crowds at church affairs and religious processions. There were clashes between the police and the crowds. Finally Perón began the process to disestablish the church. Two bishops were expelled from the country. The Vatican excommunicated those responsible for this act without mentioning any names.

A few hours after the excommunication was announced on June 16, 1955, naval aircraft bombed the government offices in Buenos Aires but failed to kill Perón. He succeeded in crushing this revolt, but in the riots that accompanied it nine churches and a cardinal's home were burned by *Peronista* supporters, and the situation grew increasingly tense. Another revolt on September 19, 1955, was successful. Perón took refuge on a Paraguayan gunboat in the harbor of Buenos Aires and was allowed to leave the country.

A military junta took control of the government. Its first leader was General Eduardo Lonardi, but he proved to be excessively influenced by the Catholic hierarchy, an extreme nationalist with little interest in democracy. A bloodless coup d'état on November 13, 1955, deposed him and another group of officers led by General Pedro Aramburu took control of the country.

Under Aramburu, Argentina returned as far toward normality as could be expected under the circumstances. Perón had left the country virtually bankrupt. Despite his emphasis upon industrialization, per capita production had increased only about 3.5 percent in the ten years before he was overthrown. The acreage planted in wheat was down almost one-third, in corn one-half, in flaxseed by three-fourths, as compared with the period before World War II. Inflation was increasing and the net gold and foreign-exchange reserve held by the Central Bank had gone down from 5,646 million pesos in 1947 to 1,485 million pesos at the end of 1955.

The governments that followed Perón were faced by a permanent crisis as the cost of living soared and riots, revolts, strikes, bombings, and other disturbances became commonplace. Much of the difficulty could be attributed to the fact that about one-fourth of the population continued to be sympathetic to Perón. The Communists took advantage of the situation by infiltrating all of the trade unions controlled by the *Peronistas* and carrying on continuous agitation for higher wages and against the United States. The Aramburu government abrogated Perón's constitution of 1949 and reinstated that of 1853. A free press returned. The *Peronista* Party was banned from political activity and interventors took control of the *Peronista* trade unions, but the workers who had benefited from Perón's regime continued to look upon him as their leader. The Radical Party split into two competing organizations, the Intransigent Radicals and the People's Radicals (*Union Cívica Radical del Pueblo*, or UCRP), thus making it more difficult for either to win a majority vote. The *Peronistas* cast blank votes during most elections. In 1957, 24 percent of the ballots cast were blank; in 1960, 25 percent; in 1962, 34 percent.

Arturo Frondizi, the leader of the Intransigent Radicals, made a determined effort to win the *Peronista* voters to constitutional government by running for president on a platform that pledged him to govern for the benefit of all of Argentina's people. The *Peronistas* were persuaded, and their ballots went to him in the election of February 23, 1958, which was a fair and honest election, except for the fact that the *Peronistas* were not permitted to present candidates. Frondizi received 4.1 million votes and took office May 1, 1958.

Frondizi managed to stay in office until March 29, 1962, despite thirty-five attempts by the military to overthrow his government. During his four years in office, he faced a continual series of crises, but by skillful political maneuvering he managed partially to revive the economy and set the country on the road toward constitutional government. His most spectacular success was in stimulating the production of petroleum, so that a drain of $300 million U.S. a year to buy gasoline abroad was stopped. During his administration industrialization was fostered, many of the controls on exchange were abolished, and foreign investment was encouraged. Yet he could not win the support of all sections of the population for a concentrated effort of austerity to save the country's economy from the chaos into which twelve years of *Peronismo* had plunged it. The workers, the rich, the military, the government employees, the landowners, the industrialists, all thought someone else ought to sacrifice. Frondizi tried to have all government employees put in an eight-hour day and quit all their outside jobs. He had little success in this, or in his other attempts at economizing. When the *Peronistas* won a plurality in local elections on March 18, 1962, the military arrested Frondizi and installed a new *de facto* president.

Frondizi had tried to govern constitutionally, but the military hierarchy insisted on a veto over his actions. After so many years of dabbling in politics, with and without Perón, many of the military men seemed to believe that the armed forces had a special role to play as guardians of the constitutional order and supreme authorities on the course of the nation. The officers were willing to let Frondizi govern the country, but within limits set by the armed forces. This pressure kept Frondizi's government in a continual state of crisis. He had begun his term by appointing the first civilian Minister of Defense the country had ever had, but the military refused to accept him and the civilian minister was forced out of office after a year to become ambassador to Uruguay.

Argentina's basic problem was that its old form of economic and political organization broke down around 1910 and no viable new system had replaced it. Perón and his followers only aggravated the situation; they did not create it. Argentine agriculture had never been modernized. Technically inefficient and based on tremendous holdings, it perpetuated a class of intransigent rich who were a bulwark of the status quo. Argentina's traditional economy, based on production of cereals and meat for a world market, which was able to support 10 million people, did not suffice for a population of more than 20 million. The great rise in population in the twentieth century, combined with a rise in the urban standard of living, had increased domestic consumption until Argentina just did not have enough cereals and meat to export to earn the exchange needed to pay for imports. Thus Argentina, which had failed to industrialize in the past, did not have the income to do so when industrialization became imperative. In addition, the nationalistic furore that accompanied Perón's purchase of foreign enterprises helped to cut off the inflow of industrial capital. At the same time, a swollen bureaucracy and the inefficient state-owned enterprises produced a constant government deficit. In buying the English railroads, Perón saddled the government with a new drain on its finances. Railroads were having difficulties in all parts of the world as buses, trucks, cars, and airplanes cut into their passenger and freight business. Yet Perón, to further his ideas of autarky, bailed out the British railroad owners just as their business was declining, and the number of Argentine railroad employees increased tremendously as the railroads became another field for patronage. And so the deficits mounted.

Frondizi tried everything he could think of to improve the situation. The United States government helped him with large loans and credits, but he failed to win a majority of Argentine power groups to his side. He concentrated on the country's economic problems, evidently believing that any improvement in this area would win him the support of the majority of the population. And there is some evidence that his Intransigent Radical Civic Union was getting stronger as the years passed, for the party scored some spectacular victories in provincial elections. And the *Peronistas* did not win a majority vote in 1962, though the election gave them the largest minority voting block. Of 9,295,136 votes, the *Peronistas' Frente Justicialista* received 2,934,497 votes (31.7 percent); the Intransigent Radicals won 2,458,542 (26.4 percent); and the UCRP won 1,832,119 (19.7 percent). If Argentina had used an electoral system that created a majority, such as a system of second elections, as in France, perhaps the crisis could have been avoided. As it was, the *Peronistas* won nine governorships and 45 of the 192 seats in the Chamber of Deputies. This the army could not countenance; it imprisoned Frondizi when he refused to resign, canceled the elections, and indefinitely recessed the Congress.

The military installed José María Guido, an Intransigent Radical who was provisional president of the Senate, as *de facto* president, but the real control of the government fluctuated between two factions of officers, the "Blues" and the "Reds," until October 1962. At that time, the Blues defeated the Reds in an armed struggle and purged the armed forces of all officers sympathetic to the Reds. The Blues favored a return to constitutional government, and they organized an election in 1963. Meanwhile, the situation in Argentina became more chaotic than ever. In the first thirteen months after Frondizi was arrested, Argentina had five Ministers of the Interior, three Ministers of Foreign Affairs, four Ministers of

Defense, three Ministers of Economics, five war secretaries, three air secretaries, four navy secretaries, and five treasury secretaries. The economy continued to decline; in that period bankruptcies increased 46 percent, the cost of living went up 50 percent, the peso dropped 67 percent, and the gross national product declined 3.9 percent.

A new election law and new rules regulating political parties went into effect for the election of July 7, 1963. Proportional representation was introduced to give all legal political parties an opportunity to participate in the electoral colleges and in the new legislature. The *Peronista* parties were banned from electing executive officers (the president and provincial governors), but were allowed to elect members of the electoral colleges and of the various legislative bodies. In one day, 21,173 positions were to be filled by election.

The 1963 election produced a weak government, because no party won anything near a majority. Ten different candidates competed for the presidency and almost fifty parties nominated candidates for the various other positions. When the votes were counted, it was discovered that the People's Radical Civic Union (UCRP) had the largest vote, but this was only about 25 percent of those cast for president. Public opinion was so much in favor of constitutional government that a majority of the presidential electors cast their ballots for the People's Radical candidate, Arturo Illía, who thus became the new president for the 1963–69 term and took office on October 12, 1963.

Argentina's new experiment in constitutional government lasted until June 1966. Illía turned out to be a weak president and his government simply drifted. The cost of living rose about 63 percent in two years. The only decisive step Illía took, canceling the oil-production contracts signed by President Frondizi, turned out to be a disaster. From self-sufficiency in petroleum production, Argentina found itself forced to import almost $100 million U.S. worth annually. The budget deficit each year was enormous, unemployment went up, and the economy failed to grow fast enough to help matters. What Argentina needed was a vigorous government that understood that the country had passed from an agricultural economy to an industrialized economy, and that therefore the other factors in society had to change. The People's Radicals had no program to meet the problems of the country. Things became so bad that, as Professor John Harrison reported, "the prevailing, almost overwhelming attitude toward the civilian administration of Arturo Illía in November, 1965, was one of either lassitude or distaste."[3] To make his situation more

---

[3] John P. Harrison, in *A Report to the American Academic Community on the Present Argentine University Situation* (Austin, Tex.: Latin American Studies Association, 1967), p. 17.

precarious, President Illía got into a dispute with Lieutenant General Juan Carlos Onganía and lost the support of the Blue faction of the military in November 1965. Onganía had been the commander of the motorized cavalry whose tanks had defeated the Red militarists in October 1962. When he resigned his position, Illía's fate was sealed. When the army took over in June 1966, the coup, according to Professor Harrison, "was either actively supported or not opposed by perhaps as much as 90 percent of the population."[4]

When the military expelled President Illía from the Casa Rosada (the Pink House, the home of Argentina's presidents), General Onganía moved in. The Congress was dissolved. The governors and the legislatures of the provinces were expelled from office. The National Election Board was dissolved. All political parties were illegalized and their property was confiscated. The military government then began to introduce the changes it thought Argentina needed. It was suggested that it would take the military five or ten years to organize the country. A sort of puritanical wave of repression was launched against sex. Coeducation was abolished in all Buenos Aires primary schools. Prices were raised on railroad tickets and freight charges to end the tremendous deficits of the railroads. The military tried to cut down the size of the bureaucracy. The mayor of Buenos Aires alone fired 8,500 employees in the last six months of 1966. A new contract was signed with two oil companies from the United States to increase oil production.

One of the military government's most controversial actions was to end the autonomy of the country's public universities. The universities had been financed by the government, but controlled by councils made up of members of the faculty, the student body, and the alumni. Many students and professors were active politically, and some were Communists and other kinds of absolutists. It is reported that one of the senior military officers became infuriated with the University of Buenos Aires when, during a ceremony at the statue of Julio A. Roca near a building of the Faculty of Natural Sciences, a group of students hurled insults and tomatoes at President Illía and disrupted the ceremony. By Law 16912, issued by the military government on July 29, 1966, university autonomy was abolished. The police aroused great criticism by breaking into a university building and beating up and arresting many students and professors who had barricaded themselves inside.

Argentina is still governed by a military dictatorship that expects to remain in office indefinitely. The military claim they are going to reor-

---

[4] *Ibid.*, p. 18.

ganize the economic and political machinery of the country, accelerate the growth of the economy, stop the growth of Peronism, and eliminate Communist and other subversive groups. Most of the population seems to have accepted the military government and life goes on. Although the political parties are "illegal," most are functioning as educational discussion groups.

The armed forces use up a large amount of money that could be used for more productive purposes. The government is always short of funds, but with the officers of the military controlling the country, no one even suggests cutting the military budget. As time has passed, various sectors of the population have become disenchanted. The labor unions struck to achieve their demands, but the strikes were smashed by the government. It is impossible to forecast the future of Argentina or to guess when constitutional government will be reintroduced.

The Formal Constitutional Framework

Argentina is being governed without a constitution, although the exact status of the constitution of 1853 under which President Illía governed is in doubt. The military government of President Onganía has taken to itself all executive and legislative power, and it has purged the Supreme Court.

Argentina has not had as many formal constitutions as the other Latin-American republics. When the Illía government was overthrown, the Argentine constitution was the oldest constitution in all of Latin America. Argentine dictatorships in 1861, 1930, and 1943 had managed to function without abrogating the constitution. Juan Perón produced a new constitution in 1949 only because he wanted to extend his term in office "legally." The revolutionary government headed by General Aramburu abrogated Perón's constitution and reintroduced the 1853 document. The dictatorship that succeeded President Frondizi operated under the 1853 constitution, and it is possible that this charter will again become the country's guideline when constitutional government is eventually restored.

The Argentine constitution of 1853 is very similar to that of the United States; many of its articles, in fact, are almost verbatim translations from the United States document. It provides for a representative, republican, federal system with the power divided between the national and provincial governments. The national government consists of a strong executive headed by a president, a bicameral legislature, and a series of independent courts headed by a Supreme Court of Justice. Theoretically the three branches of government are independent and equal, but the president is granted powers that make the executive the dominant branch of government. With the power to declare a state of siege in case of emergency, the president can rule with virtually absolute authority. The authors of the Argentine constitution feared the effects of a strong executive and instituted an elaborate system of checks and balances to limit his powers, but their efforts were negated by the president's power to declare a state of siege.

The Argentine constitution is a much longer document than the United States charter from which it was copied because of Argentine efforts to enumerate the exact functions of each branch of the government instead of leaving areas of undefined authority, as is the case in the United States. The constitution specifies that the federal government supports the Roman Catholic church and that the president exercises the rights of national patronage.

Who Participates in Politics

Until about 1890, political participation in Argentina was limited to the landowners and the upper classes in the cities. Through the Conservative Party, these groups operated an oligarchical type of government in which all elections were controlled. Toward the end of the century, the developing middle class began to take an interest in politics which culminated in the organization of the Civic Union in 1889. At about the same time the immigrants began to organize anarchist and socialist groups in Buenos Aires, which led to the organization of the Argentine Socialist Party in 1894. The activities of these two new parties stimulated more political participation, particularly in the cities, and when a fair election law was adopted in 1912, mass participation in political affairs began, especially in the cities. From 1916 to 1930 there was a spirited rivalry between the Conservative and Radical Parties which eventually involved the majority of the population in the country's political life. The *Peronista* demagoguery brought the workers of the country more deeply into politics than ever before, and by the time the Perón regime was overthrown the overwhelming majority of adults were participating in politics by voting. In the 1958 election, 9,971,201 were registered to vote and 9,063,498 went to the polls to cast their ballots. In 1963, 11,354,026 were registered and 9,717,657 voted.

There is some doubt, however, that the mass voting was based on real political interest. A study of political behavior made in Buenos Aires discovered that only 29 percent of those polled were really interested in politics, 28 percent were rather indifferent, and 43 percent were totally uninterested.[5] The same study came to the conclusion that the higher up in the social scale a person was, the more interest he took in politics; in the lowest class, 62 percent were totally uninterested.[6]

Under the law that governed elections, voting was secret and compulsory for all citizens in good standing between eighteen and seventy except those who could prove physical disability. The insane, members of the armed forces and police, and persons who had lost their voting privilege by being convicted of certain types of crime could not vote. Workers had to be given time off with pay to vote.

Penalties for not voting were rather severe in theory but were not enforced. The penalties included fines, disqualification from holding public office for a year, and loss of the privilege of transacting any business with the government for six months after the election unless the voter's registration booklet showed that he had paid the fine imposed for not voting. Any public employee who failed to check the registration booklet of any person entering his office during the six months after elections was fined 300 pesos.

The Electoral Machinery

The electoral law passed in 1912 provided for the secret ballot, a system of limited voting to give minorities representation in the legislature, and compulsory voting and registration. Elections were to be held on a Sunday to obtain the largest possible vote. The first honest election on a national scale saw the opposition Radical Party win power in 1916. Unfortunately, the Radical Party degenerated in office and began to cheat in elections, just as its predecessors had done. The years of crisis from 1930 to 1955 saw few honest elections, but those held after 1955 have been fairly conducted. Under Perón, a peculiar system had developed in which votes were counted as cast, but the opposition was not allowed to carry on an effective campaign. Through gerrymandering, violence, and intimidation, Perón created a situation in which he could afford to have the votes honestly counted since he was sure of the results.

The electoral law of April 22, 1957, was carefully drawn up to thwart all the methods of frustrating the popular will that had been devised during previous years. A decentralized system was set up in which the only national apparatus is an agency charged with drawing up the

---

[5] José Luis de Imaz, *Motivación electoral* (Buenos Aires: Instituto de Desarrollo Económico y Social, 1962), pp. 3–4.

[6] *Ibid.*

national register of voters and seeing that its parts get to the appropriate electoral subdivisions. There are two groups of electoral officials in each province, the national capital, and the territories. An electoral judge and his staff handle all matters concerning electoral administration except the election itself. An electoral committee made up of judges of the national and provincial courts is organized in each of the electoral districts to handle the actual election. This body appoints the officials of the voting precincts, recounts the votes after they have been forwarded from the precinct officials, and announces who has been elected.

The polls are open from eight A.M. to six P.M. and the recognized political parties are entitled to have poll watchers at each polling place. Detailed regulations are intended to safeguard the secrecy of the ballot. Each precinct can have no more than 250 voters, except those located in cities with more than 30,000 population, where the maximum number of voters is 300. All troops, except those on duty guarding the polls, remain in their barracks. No political meetings, public spectacles, or athletic contests can be held on election day, nor can any liquor be sold until three hours after the polls have been closed.

Although voting is secret, Argentina has not adopted the Australian ballot. Each party prepares a ballot that must be approved by the provincial electoral officials and the government prepares an envelope. The voter enters the polls and is given an envelope, whereupon he enters a room where he sees stacks of each party's ballots. He picks whichever he chooses to use, votes, and puts the ballot into the envelope, which he seals and deposits in the ballot box. An interesting provision of the Argentine electoral law permits the poll watchers of the recognized political parties to accompany the postal official who carries the precinct ballot box to the provincial capital to assure themselves that there is no tampering along the route. Their transportation is paid from public funds.

Argentina's electoral system seemed to be producing honest results if one can judge by the fact that the party in power lost most of the by-elections after 1958. The 1962 revisions of the electoral law were intended mainly to introduce proportional representation and preserve the system set up in 1957. All observers were convinced that the 1963 election gave a fair reflection of the opinion of Argentina's voters. Both the 1962 and 1966 military coups were organized because the military officers did not like the way the Argentines voted.

Political Parties

Most commentators believe that the Conservative Party, which controlled Argentina until 1916, was a true political party, although not a mass organization. Other scholars disagree. One study published in 1918 described the Argentine party system at that time as follows:

> There are in the Argentine no political parties, in the American sense of the word. There are at election time three outstanding groups—the friends of the president in the capital and of the governors in the provinces; the opposition, made up of those fighting official influence; and the neutrals, who take little interest either in politics or elections and who are apt to form the chief portion of the population.[7]

While this is not a really accurate description of the situation in 1918, it is true that the political parties functioning then had great weaknesses and were in part to blame for the crisis that began about that time and has not yet been overcome.

The political parties functioning in Argentina until World War II were the Conservative, the Radical, the Socialist, and a small Communist party. All became corrupt and weak. By 1967 so many new parties had developed that it was almost impossible to keep track of them all. Thirteen parties nominated presidential candidates in 1958, and this does not include the *Peronistas* and the Communists, who had substantial support but were not permitted to participate in the election. In 1963 there were ten candidates for president and twenty-six political parties participating in the election campaign. Close to a hundred legally recognized parties participated in the elections of 1957, 1958, 1960, 1962, and 1963.

There has been no dominant political party in Argentina since Perón was overthrown, as the elections since 1957 have demonstrated. This is due in part to the 1956 law regulating parties, which made it easy for a party to participate in elections. A new party seeking recognition must state that it will maintain the representative, federal, republican form of government, choose a nonpersonal name for itself, and guarantee freedom of application and participation to any qualified voter. In addition, a party must present a petition signed by 4 percent of the registered voters in each province. To make it easier for small parties to participate in the 1963 elections, this requirement was relaxed to a minimum of 300 registered voters in districts having less than 100,000 registered voters, and 200 signatures in districts having less than 50,000 registered voters. To preserve its registration, a party had to get 3 percent of the votes cast in an election in each province where it was registered. The only other restriction, inserted to prevent Communists, Fascists, and Juan Perón's

---

[7] Charles Seymour and Donald Paige Frary, *How the World Votes* (Springfield, Mass.: C. A. Nichols Co., 1918), p. 274.

followers from participating, prohibited parties from depending on foreign organizations for support.

Another reason for the multiplicity of parties in Argentina is the unintegrated character of the society. There is not enough class interest, nationalist feeling, or ideological unity among the various sections of Argentina's population to enable a majority to combine their efforts for anything.

The government of President Onganía illegalized all political parties and took over their offices and property, but most have continued to function as "education" or "discussion" groups. There seems to have been a tendency for the bigger parties to get bigger in the years since 1957, with only four groups making respectable showings in the 1965 election, but it is impossible to forecast the future of Argentina's party system until a new constitutional system is created and political parties are permitted to function freely.

The largest minority in the country, according to the 1965 election, the last held, consisted of the followers of Juan Perón, who participated in the election under the name Popular Union. While Perón controlled the country, his *Peronista* Party was a large and impressive political machine. Based on the trade unions, it had some of the features of the totalitarian one-party systems, but never achieved a monopoly of political power. After Perón was expelled from the country, a whole series of neo-Peronist parties attempted to capture the votes of the workers, but none was very successful. Some were agencies of Perón and received money and guidance from him. Others were trying to be Peronist without formal connections with Perón. To control these movements, Perón finally set up an organization known as the Supervisory Council of *Peronismo*. From 1957 to 1963 the Peronist vote could usually be estimated by the number of blank ballots cast. (Perón sent instructions to his followers to vote that way.) In 1957 there were 2,115,861 blank ballots; in 1958, when many Peronists voted for Frondizi, there were 815,492 blank ballots; in 1960 there were 2,155,532; in 1962, when the Peronists were on the ballot, they received 1,592,446 votes. In 1963 the total blank vote was 1,827,464, but this is an inflated figure since the Frondizi faction of the UCRI also cast blank ballots. In addition, neo-Peronist parties that participated in the election, against the advice of the national leaders of *Peronismo*, won 628,000 votes, 6.5 percent, and elected sixteen members of the Chamber of Deputies. In 1965 the Popular Union, the group recognized by Juan Perón, received 31 percent of the votes cast and elected thirty-six deputies. In addition, the neo-Peronist parties received 7 percent of the votes, keeping their sixteen seats in the Chamber. What will happen to the Peronist political parties cannot be forecast, but since Juan Perón still has the support of about 38 percent of the voters nearly fifteen years after his overthrow, is would be unrealistic to expect them to disappear within the foreseeable future.

The People's Radical Civic Union (UCRP) won about 30 percent of the votes cast in 1965, and about 25.1 percent of the votes in 1963. The People's Radicals apparently won the support of many of the voters who in previous years supported the traditional conservative parties. Its policies are economically conservative and nationalistic. Generally speaking, the UCRP represents those who visualize an Argentina not much different from what it has been in the past. It is very strong among the middle class.

The only other party that won more than 5 percent of the votes in 1965 was Arturo Frondizi's Movement of Integration and Development (MID). The MID is most of what is left of the Intransigent Radical Civic Union (UCRI), the faction of the old Radical Party which followed Frondizi when the party split after Perón was overthrown. The UCRI was the country's leading party when Frondizi was president and had the support of about 25 to 30 percent of the voters. The UCRI favored democratic government, a strong executive, rapid industrialization, government intervention in the economy, and allowing the Perón-influenced parties and trade unions to participate legally in the political life of Argentina. When Frondizi was in jail before the 1963 election, the UCRI split, with Oscar Alende becoming leader of one faction and Frondizi of the other. In 1965 the MID received 7 percent of the votes and elected fifteen deputies. The UCRI received less than 5 percent of the votes.

Among the other parties that were important in the past but failed to get as much as 5 percent of the votes in 1965 was the National Federation of the Parties of the Center, which consisted of traditional conservatives. Several Catholic parties have participated in recent elections, but the largest one, the Christian Democratic Party, made a good showing only in 1958.

The Socialist Party of Argentina has split into several factions over the issue of Fidel Castro and the Communists. The more democratic-minded faction, the Democratic Socialist Party, takes a dim view of Castro and fights *Peronistas* and Communists in the trade unions impartially. The other faction, the Socialist Party of Argentina, is sympathetic to Castro and makes determined efforts to win the support of former *Peronistas*. It is difficult to estimate the strength of the various Socialist parties, but the combined Socialist vote in 1963 was only 5.6 percent of the total, and in 1965 was less than 5 percent.

Argentina has had a Communist party for many decades. Most scholars think it is the second largest Communist party in the Western Hemisphere (after that of Cuba). In 1958, the only election in which it was allowed to present candidates, it received 191,583 votes, but it is more powerful than this vote indicates. Like all Communist parties, this one operates through a series of front organizations, so it is difficult to know who the Communists are. For many years now, the Communists have been working closely with the Peronists and the pro-Castro Socialists. Some scholars think the Communists can never assume importance in Argentina because of the *Peronista* movement, but all observers agree the Argentine Communist Party is a well-organized and sizable group. Its greatest strength is among university professors and students and the sons of the upper and middle class.

Much of Argentina's political difficulty could have been avoided if the country had ever developed a viable party system. There have always been too many parties. There seems to have been a consolidation in recent years, and perhaps the next time elections are held only a few will participate.

Pressure Groups and Public Opinion

Argentina has a well-developed pressure-group system and an alert public opinion, but the political parties have never succeeded in articulating the various groups to create a stable political system. More than 90 percent of the population is literate, and of all the Latin-American countries, only Uruguay has a greater per capita newspaper circulation than Argentina. In 1960, when the population was just short of 21 million, there were 128 daily newspapers with a total circulation of 3,247,004, or about 155 copies of daily newspapers sold per 1,000 inhabitants. In addition, thirteen monthly magazines have a circulation of over 100,000 each. About thirty newspapers in languages other than Spanish appear, catering to the various foreign groups in the population. The morning newspapers are world-famous and have the largest circulation, except for *La Razón*, the most widely read afternoon paper. *La Prensa, La Nación, Clarín, El Mundo*, and *La Razón* sell from 170,000 to 400,000 copies each. The Buenos Aires dailies are the most important and are read in all parts of the country.

The pressure groups are well organized and make their opinions known through propaganda, demonstrations, strikes, and petitions. Probably most important during the past thirty years have been the armed forces, which include the largest army in Latin America except for Cuba's militarized population. All males are supposed to serve one year in the armed forces, after which they remain ten years in the trained reserves, followed by ten years in the National Guard, followed by five years in the territorial guard. This compulsory military service gives Argentina a military force much greater than it needs for defense and much greater than its economy can support. With about 100,000 in the army, 250,000 in the trained reserves, 25,000 in the navy, and 10,000 in the air force, it took between 25 and 35 percent of the total budget from 1947 to 1957 to support the military establishment. Some scholars estimate that even these figures are low, and that in recent years 40 percent and perhaps more has gone to the armed forces.

The 7,000 officers are the most important section of the armed forces in voicing the demands of the military. Since 1930, secret societies have proliferated among the officer corps; Perón's original basis of power was one of these, the GOU. In the 1960's, the most important groups have been the Blues, or legalists, and the Reds, sometimes called the *Golpistas* or *Gorilas*. The military officers seem to look upon themselves as the final arbiters as to whether a government is functioning constitutionally, and in 1930, 1943, 1955, 1962, and 1966 they removed the president from office because he did not meet with their approval. The armed forces function as a sort of state within a state. They have their own stores, hospitals, schools, factories, housing projects, clubs, and other institutions. It would appear that this privileged position pushes the armed forces to interfere in government, as any effort to cut their share of the budget endangers their special privileges.

The second most important group in Argentina probably consists of the British-oriented landowners and associated interests revolving around the exploitation of meat and grain. Originally organized into the Conservative Party, this traditional oligarchy now functions through a number of parties.[8] It has been successful in preventing the full industrialization of the country and the breakup of the large *estancias*. Composed in large part of the members of the "older" families with Spanish names, many of this group inherited their wealth and are sentimentally associated with the British business representatives in Buenos Aires. This is a dying class, but until the large *estancias* are broken up it will continue to exert influence. In recent years this group has been associated with the army officers of the Red group.

Some writers rate the organized working class as the second most

---

[8] In one study of the upper class in Buenos Aires made at the beginning of 1959, 86 repondents belonged to or were most sympathetic to the following political parties: National Democratic Party, 6; UCRP, 4; Federation of Parties of the Center, 13; Federal Party, 2; Independent Civic Party, 30; Conservative Democratic Party of Buenos Aires, 1; Conservative Party, 13; Popular Conservative Party, 2; UCRI, 2; and Socialist Party, 1 (De Imaz, *La Clase alta de Buenos Aires* [Buenos Aires: Universidad de Buenos Aires, 1962], p. 66).

important pressure group in Argentina, but recent history does not warrant this conclusion. In recent years about 2.5 million workers have been affiliated with various trade unions, about 44 percent of all Argentine wage and salary earners. Since the military government "intervened" the General Confederation of Labor in 1955 after the fall of Perón, the trade unions have not succeeded in establishing a national federation capable of speaking for all organized workers. The national spokesmen for the workers are committees representing blocs of unions, with the 62 Bloc, the 32 Bloc, and the 19 Bloc the most important. The 62 Bloc is led by neo-*Peronistas*; the 32 Bloc is led by the "democratic leaders" and is affiliated with ORIT; the 19 Bloc is dominated by Communists. Generally the 62's and the 19's have cooperated, but most of the larger unions have been affiliated with the "democratic" bloc. In 1956 the 32 Bloc had almost 1.5 million members; the 62 Bloc had about 800,000. Since then there has been much fluctuation, with individual unions changing sides as new officers were elected, now cooperating with other blocs and at other times conflicting with them.

The main weapon of the trade unions has been the strike, although many of the *Peronista* unions have also been very active politically. Under a law passed in 1958, government supervision of union elections has tended to create a leadership representative of the members' desires, but occasional banning of *Peronistas* from the ballot has prevented stability. The agricultural and pastoral workers are least organized, the strongest unions being those of the railroad workers, the commercial employees, the government employees, the metalworkers, and the clothing workers.

The Catholic church retains a strong influence in Argentina and the country remains one of the few that does not permit divorce. During President Frondizi's term in office, the church was allowed to found universities, thus ending the government's monopoly of higher education. Yet most observers think the Catholic church exercises less influence in Argentina today than it did in the past. When General Lonardi briefly headed the first post-Perón government, the influence of the Catholic church was at its highest point, and the papal flag flew alongside that of Argentina as the victorious troops marched into Buenos Aires. Lonardi's removal from office drastically cut the influence of Catholic nationalists in the new government. Yet the provision that only a Catholic can be president remains in the unobserved constitution and the church continues to be an important force in Argentine life. There is much doubt as to how Catholic the Argentine population is. One study of political behavior conducted with rigorous scientific methods found that in a sampling of ten voting precincts, only 29 percent were practicing Catholics; 52 percent were baptized but nonpracticing Catholics, 7.5 percent were Jews, 9 percent were nonbelievers, and 2.5 percent were members of other religious groups.[9]

Both the *interiores* and the *porteños*, the two regional groups, remain important, but the dominant group is still the population in and around Buenos Aires. Most new industries continue to be located in and around the capital city.

Civil Liberties

The Argentine constitution contains the usual list of personal guarantees to be found in practically all constitutions, but these rights have not been observed during most of the period since 1930. When President Frondizi took office, for example, one of his first acts was to get an amnesty law passed under which about 41,000 persons were freed from jails. Yet even President Frondizi could not remain in power while permitting civil liberty; various groups, particularly the rightists, Communists, and *Peronista*-led trade unions, created so much chaos that he was forced to declare a state of siege. It is this constitutional power given to the president and to the Congress which negates many of the constitutional rights given to individuals. It is a vicious circle. When liberty is the rule, bombs are exploded, strikes disrupt the economy, or individuals win elections who do not enjoy the confidence of powerful groups in the armed forces or in the executive. A state of siege is then declared, but the cause of the bombs or the strikes continues. As has been mentioned previously, there does not seem to be enough consensus about the aims of Argentine society to permit the various groups and classes to settle their disputes peaceably. As this is written, the government of President Onganía is ruling without a constitution, although normal freedom of speech, press, and assembly are permitted. How long this will continue is anybody's guess.

The Executive

The Argentine executive under the 1853 constitution was a president elected by an electoral college selected by proportional representation. An absolute majority of the electoral college was needed, and if no candidate received this majority, the Congress chose by an absolute majority between the two who received the highest votes in the electoral college. The president had a six-year term and could not be reelected until six additional years had elapsed. To be a president one had to be born in

[9] De Imaz, *Motivación electoral*, p. 25.

Argentina or, if born abroad, the child of native-born Argentine citizens, a member of the Roman Catholic church, at least thirty years old, with an annual income or salary of at least 2,000 pesos. A vice-president, who had to have the same qualifications, was elected at the same time as the president and succeeded to the office upon the illness, absence from the capital, death, resignation, or removal from office of the president. If both the president and vice-president were unavailable, the office devolved upon the provisional president of the Senate, then upon the president of the Chamber of Deputies, and then upon the president of the Supreme Court. When the presidency was filled by one of these three, the constitution required that a new election should be called within thirty days, but the only time this actually happened, in 1962, this provision was not observed. Unlike most Latin-American constitutions, that of Argentina did not include a long list of those ineligible to be president.

The president had wide constitutional powers, including the general administration of the country, the execution of the laws, wide appointment powers, the conduct of foreign affairs, and the power to approve or veto all legislative acts of the Congress. After 1930, the Argentine executive also developed the habit of issuing decree laws. In addition, with the consent of the Senate the president could intervene in the affairs of the provinces by replacing the governor and could impose a state of siege. In recent years the power of intervention was extended to include national governmental offices, trade unions, and economic enterprises. The president nominated bishops of the Catholic church from a list of three names proposed by the Senate, and approved or withheld approval, with the consent of the Supreme Court, of all "decrees of the councils, bulls, briefs, and rescripts of the Supreme Pontiff of Rome." General Onganía, like all *de facto* presidents before him, continues to exercise these religious powers.

All acts of the president had to be countersigned by one of his ministers, but since he alone appointed and removed all cabinet ministers, this was no limitation upon him. Thus the Argentine president was a very powerful executive who dominated the legislature, the courts, and local government. The great limitation upon the president in recent decades has been the veto power the military officers have arrogated to themselves. During Arturo Frondizi's years in the presidency he never succeeded in getting complete control of the government, even though the constitution made him the commander in chief of the armed forces.

The president had a cabinet of eight ministers to assist him. Ministers were responsible for their actions and had the right to attend sessions of the Congress and take part in the debates without the right to vote. The president and his ministers theoretically had almost complete control of the government administration, as there was no formal appointing or dismissal procedure for government employees.

Because of the extensive educational system, the civil service is a well-trained group of persons, but it has never been very efficient. Government employees are traditionally appointed for political purposes, and it was only in January 1958 that an agency was set up to control them; it was November 1958 before a classification scheme was drawn up and put into effect. President Frondizi tried to cut the number of employees by dismissing and pensioning about 200,000 persons, but he never succeeded in his efforts. Many of the government employees have other jobs and do not devote their best efforts to their government work. Equipment and office procedures are outmoded and there is much red tape. In 1963 the Ford Foundation made a $100,000 grant to develop the program of training and research in public administration of the Superior Institute of Public Administration. President Onganía's government also announced that it would improve the public service and decrease its size.

The Legislative Power

Argentina's legislative power rested in a Congress consisting of a Senate with two members for each province and the Federal District (forty-six in 1964) and a Chamber of Deputies consisting of one member for each 85,000 inhabitants or fraction of not less than 42,500. Each province had a minimum of two deputies, with 192 being elected in 1963. Senators from the provinces were elected by the provincial legislatures. The two senators from the Federal District were elected by an electoral college chosen for that purpose. The senatorial term was nine years, with one-third of the membership elected every three years. Members of the Chamber of Deputies were elected by the D'Hondt system of proportional representation, but all parties receiving less than 3 percent of the votes cast in a district were not included among the parties receiving seats. Deputies served for four years, with half elected every two years. Both deputies and senators could be reelected indefinitely. The number of deputies from each province was set after every census.

To be a deputy one had to be twenty years old, a citizen for at least four years, and a native of the province from which elected or a resident of that province during the two years preceding the election. To be a senator one had to be thirty years old, a citizen for at least six years, and a native of the province from which elected or a resident therein during the two years before the election. Another constitutional provision, which had fallen into disuse, required a senator to have an annual income or salary of at least 2,000 pesos. Regular members of the clergy were barred by the constitution from being members of the Congress.

The Congress met each year from May 1 to September 30, but the president could extend the session or convoke extraordinary sessions. It had all of the powers usually given to a legislature. The Chamber of Deputies had the initiative about laws relating to taxes and the recruiting of troops, but in all other respects the two houses had equal power over legislation. The Chamber had the power to impeach the president, the vice-president, cabinet ministers, and judges, but the Senate tried those impeached and had to vote by a two-thirds majority to punish. No president has ever been impeached. The Senate had to approve certain appointments to high office made by the president as well as the president's declaration of a state of siege, but the president's wishes were always followed.

The Argentine Congress did not play too important a role after constitutional government broke down in 1930. It had a formal procedure for considering legislation in committees and in the houses which enabled it to function as a truly deliberative body. The two houses considered legislation separately; there were no joint committees to consider differences between the houses. If a bill passed in one house was amended in the other, it went back to the first house for approval by an absolute majority. If the changes were rejected, the bill went back to the revising house, and if the changes were accepted by a two-thirds majority there, the bill returned again to the other house, where it required a two-thirds vote to reject the amendments a second time. Bills could be vetoed by the president, but his veto could be overridden by a two-thirds vote on roll call in both houses, whereupon the bill became law. The Congress, however, immediately had to publish in the press the names and votes of those voting, as well as the objections raised by the president in his veto.

The list of perquisites received by members of the Congress was long, headed by immunity from arrest, which could be lost only by a two-thirds vote of the member's house. The members of the Congress did not get individual offices, but each party was given space in the legislative building in proportion to the size of the party faction, as well as a number of employees paid by the Congress to help the party caucuses.[10] The Congress had a large staff of about 2,000 career employees who assisted the members. Each member of the Congress received a salary of 50,000 pesos a month ($292 U.S. in 1965, the last full year the Congress func-

---

[10] In 1963, for example, the UCRP in the Chamber had two secretaries and eighteen office employees, while the Socialist Party had one secretary and one office employee.

tioned), a pension, free postage, telegram and telephone service, and free transportation to and from his district (one airplane ticket and two train tickets each month), in addition to free license plates for his car. Each house had a medical doctor in attendance for its members as well as a restaurant that served meals at minimum prices. A supply service sold food to the members at low prices. The Library of Congress provided an information service. In addition, the deputies and senators from outside the Federal District received the right to rent an apartment in buildings owned by the government at a fixed rental of 3,700 pesos a month ($21.64 U.S. in 1965). Each committee of the two houses had assigned to it a secretary and from two to seven office employees. All of the employees of the Congress were career civil servants, but the party groups had the right to select which employees would be assigned to their party offices.

The Chamber of Deputies elected a member as its president for a one-year term and the Senate elected a provisional president to preside when the vice-president of the republic was not available. All other officials of both houses were employees. The 1963 electoral law, which introduced proportional representation, was intended to strengthen the Congress by making its membership more representative. It did not function long enough for any conclusions to be drawn as to how this affected the operation of the legislature.

Public Finance

Argentina has a budgetary system so complicated that it is almost impossible to discover how much money is spent for the various functions of government. The budget law itself never contains totals of any kind, but authorizes expenditures according to the source of the funds, and the entire published budget for one year makes a book larger than the New York City telephone directory. The budget is prepared by the executive and presented to the legislature by the president, but during the decades after 1930 the legislature had little control over the budget. In many years the president's recommendations reached the legislature so late that there was little time to consider them. In addition, the custom of dividing the budgeted items into "normal" income and "special" income, combined with the deficits incurred almost regularly, made Argentina's financial position most mysterious. In 1966, for example, the deficit amounted to 107.5 billion pesos (about $595 million U.S.), a fantastic amount. During recent years the deficits have been due in large part to heavy losses by the government-owned railroads.

The inflation that has plagued Argentina in recent decades has helped to increase the budget totals rapidly. In 1947 the total was roughly 8.53 billion pesos; in 1948, 15 billion; in 1950, 17 billion; in 1955, 40 billion; in 1957, 60.9 billion; in 1962–63, 199.7 billion; and in 1966, 419.7 billion.

Tables 1 and 2, summarizing the budget of 1962–63, when the peso fluctuated from a high of 1.71 U.S. cents to a low of 0.72 cents, gives a rough idea of where the money comes from and where it goes. As the figures make clear, Argentina devotes far too much of its income to its military and spends far too little for more productive purposes. Not enough is known about the amount the military spends, but one study seems to indicate that from 1947 to 1957 military expenditures went

TABLE 1
REVENUE OF ARGENTINA, FISCAL YEAR 1962–63
(000,000 Omitted)

Source	Amount in Pesos	Percent of Total
Income tax	$20,846	10.77%
Sales tax	19,309	9.98
Excise and customs taxes	15,760	8.14
Surcharges and miscellaneous charges	31,693	16.38
Stamp and other miscellaneous taxes	21,175	10.94
Income from government decentralized organizations	58,069	30.00
Other income	26,683	13.79
Total	$193,535	100.00%

TABLE 2
EXPENDITURES OF ARGENTINA, FISCAL YEAR 1962–63
(000,000 Omitted)

	Amount in Pesos	Percent of Total
National defense	$30,119	15.09%
Education and justice	17,034	8.55
Public debt	14,535	7.30
Communications	5,985	3.01
Health and social assistance	4,781	2.40
Ministry of the Interior	4,519	2.27
State enterprises	21,139	10.58
Government decentralized organizations	56,935	28.48
Miscellaneous	44,662	22.32
Total	$199,709	100.00%

from 24.80 percent of the total budget to 32.61 percent. At the same time the percentage devoted to education went from 16.84 percent in 1947 to 15.93 percent in 1957.

Argentina's tax system is just as bad as its expenditures. There seems to be widespread evasion of taxes, especially those on income. One study made by the Central Bank in 1960 showed that about 62 percent of the national income was not declared for tax purposes. One of the stated aims of the Onganía government is to balance the budget and to improve the system of tax collection.

Argentine Federalism

Argentina's constitution set up a federal republic that today consists of twenty-two provinces, a federal capital district (Buenos Aires), and the territory of Tierra del Fuego, which includes the Argentine part of Tierra del Fuego, some islands in the south Atlantic, and the Argentine Antarctic sector.[11] Federalism has never worked well in Argentina. The conflicts of the first fifty years of the republic between Buenos Aires and the interior saw the provinces dealing with each other at times as if they were foreign nations. When the constitution was written, provisions for federalism were included in frank imitation of the United States and in recognition of the already existing differences among the provinces. They were given the residual powers including primary education, the colonization of provincial lands, and the establishment of municipal and other local government, but the constitutional grant of power to the national government was so broad that little was left to the provinces. The federal government was given the power to "intervene in the territory of a province in order to guarantee the republican form of government or to repel foreign invasions, and at the request of its constituted authorities to support or reestablish them, should they have been deposed by sedition or invasion from another province." As a result of these provisions, Argentina never had a true federalism. The small population of most of the provinces prevented them from even financing their necessary activities without subventions from the national treasury, and the national government soon got into the habit of intervening whenever anyone who disagreed with the president was in control of a province. From 1860 to September 1950 there were about 150 interventions in the provinces, and since 1930 they have been a common feature of gov-

---

[11] Argentina includes the Falkland Islands, which are known there as the Malvina Islands, in the territory of Tierra del Fuego, but the British government has effective control of the Falkland Islands, which it governs as a colony.

ernment, the latest having come after the 1966 coup d'état when the military did not like the elected governors.

Intervention has been so accepted by the Argentine people that there is little debate about it when it happens. The president is supposed to get the consent of the Senate when that body is in session, but there have been cases in which the Senate refused to agree to intervention and the president went ahead with it anyway. Generally the president sends troops to eject the elected provincial governor, legislature, and courts, and a representative of the president, called an interventor, takes over all executive, legislative, and judicial power. Eventually he arranges an election, which is always won by persons favorable to the president.

Intervention has had many serious consequences in addition to negating federalism. Probably most important, it has prevented the strengthening of constitutional government. The political parties could not hold onto power long enough in any province to consolidate a base from which to prepare for the next national election. This prevented the development of a balance between the parties. One had all power, the others had none.

The Provinces and the Cities

Before the 1966 coup, each of the twenty-two provinces was governed under its own constitution, which had to provide for "the republican, representative system, in accordance with the principles, declarations, and guarantees of the National Constitution, insuring its administration of justice, municipal government, and elementary education." Each of the provinces was headed by an elected governor. Nine had bicameral legislatures, thirteen unicameral. Each had its own court system. Most were unable to finance their activities without financial assistance from the national government and only three had populations large enough to give them an important voice in the national legislature. Buenos Aires, Córdoba, and Santa Fe had 88 of the 192 members of the Chamber of Deputies. Adding 35 from the Federal District left only 69 deputies for 19 provinces, or an average of 3.6 deputies per province, with 10 provinces having the minimum of 2. Buenos Aires province alone has 50 deputies, or almost 26 percent of the Chamber.[12] In 1963 four electoral districts—the Federal District and the provinces of Buenos Aires, Córdoba, and Santa Fe—had 69.2 percent of all of Argentina's registered

---

[12] Compare this with the United States, where in a House of Representatives of 435, the largest state, New York, has 43 (about 10 percent) and only five states (Alaska, Delaware, Nevada, Vermont, and Wyoming) have the minimum of one member.

voters and accounted for 71.5 percent of all votes cast in the July 1963 election.

The provinces were not subdivided for purposes of local government. The only local government was in the cities, but the provincial government kept tight control of the city governments. Each was headed by an intendant appointed by the governor. Each had a legislative council elected by the voters. Buenos Aires was the only city with sufficient income to finance its activities, but as a federal district it was controlled by the national government. The intendant here is appointed by the national president with the consent of the Senate. A council of thirty members was elected by the voters to legislate for the capital, but many of the city's services were performed by agencies of the national government. The council imposed taxes and dealt with such subjects as streets, traffic control, public health, markets, jails, and hospitals.

Practically all scholars are in agreement that both provincial and municipal governments in Argentina have been weak and ineffective. Almost all taxes are now collected by the national government, and some of them are shared with the provinces.

The Judicial Power

Under the 1853 constitution Argentina's judicial power was given to a Supreme Court of Justice and a series of lower courts set up by Congress. In addition, each province has its own courts headed by a provincial supreme court. Since the national government enacts almost all law for criminal, civil, commercial, mining, labor, and other codes, most cases have to be tried in national rather than provincial courts, although, as in the United States, persons frequently may choose which court they wish to use. Argentina bases its law upon the code system.

The Argentine Supreme Court consists of five justices appointed by the president with the consent of the Senate. They serve for life during good behavior. Judges of the appellate courts and courts of original jurisdiction are also appointed for life by the president with the consent of the Senate. During all of Argentina's history, judges have been appointed for political reasons and have received low pay. Thus the incoming president always found a court system staffed by supporters of previous governments. Until the Perón era the new governments did not impeach the sitting judges; that was one of Perón's innovations. The revolutionary government in 1955, following his precedent, purged the courts of his appointees, and Frondizi in his turn appointed persons favorable to his viewpoint. President Onganía did the same. The custom of intervening courts thus developed, and there has been much criticism of the judicial system produced by political appointments. Perón also introduced military courts to try his opponents, and this too was copied by the governments that came after him.

The judicial process in Argentina is slow and old-fashioned. Everything is done in writing, and most cases are read rather than heard by the judge. Habeas corpus and *amparo* have developed without being mentioned in the constitution, but the jury system provided by the constitution has never been utilized except in a few provincial courts. The Argentine courts seem to function about as well as most other court systems, but their workings are ponderous, expensive, and slow.

Argentina: A Last Word

Argentina is governed today by a *de facto* military government that has taken to itself all legislative and executive power and is trying to solve the country's problems by executive orders. With the political parties unable to function freely, the only check upon the actions of the government is the power of the organized economic groups. So far the government has proved the stronger in every clash.

Is there any hope that Argentina can develop a stable political system in the foreseeable future? Few scholars are optimistic. The problems that have been tormenting the country since the old system broke down around the time of World War I remain unsolved, and the longer their solution is postponed, the more difficult it will be to create a stable political system. Argentina's population must develop a symbol of authority all can accept, but the constitution is not recognized, no charismatic leader has emerged to attract the support of people in all sections of the population, and nothing else seems to be available to serve as a neutral center around which the nation can rally.

Argentina's basic problem remains the disunity of its population. The gap between rich and poor, between urban and rural, between *Peronistas* and anti-*Peronistas*, between the officers of the armed forces and the civilian political leaders, remains as great as it has ever been. Ex-President Frondizi and his associates think industrialization can be the force to unify the country, but the lack of minerals makes this difficult. Frondizi thought that with the stimulation of petroleum production, a series of large-scale petrochemical plants would produce the materials Argentina needed for expanded industrialization, but the policies of the government of Illía prevented that. Some think the Latin-American Common Market will help, but its progress has been so slow that it has not yet produced any effect. If Argentina's educated population could produce goods for its industrially underdeveloped neighbors, perhaps the economy would spurt forward fast enough to help matters.

The military government probably will do nothing about cutting down the amount of money the military absorbs, thus preventing investment in more productive efforts. What, then, can the future hold for Argentina? The military is talking of a truce in political activity for five or ten years. Meanwhile, the political parties have difficulty functioning and the country's problems remain unsolved. Until someone or something unites a majority of the Argentine population behind a program, it appears as if the impasse in which Argentina has been stalled for decades will continue.

SELECTED READINGS

ALEXANDER, ROBERT J. "Argentina," *Labor Relations in Argentina, Brazil, and Chile*, pp. 139–234. New York: McGraw-Hill Book Co., 1962.

———. *The Perón Era*. New York: Columbia University Press, 1951.

———. "The Stalinists of the Pampas—Argentina," *Communism in Latin America*, pp. 154–76. New Brunswick, N.J.: Rutgers University Press, 1957.

BAILY, SAMUEL L. "Argentina: Search for Consensus." *Current History* 51 (November 1966): 301–6.

BLANKSTEN, GEORGE I. *Perón's Argentina*. Chicago: University of Chicago Press, 1953.

CAMPOBASSI, JOSÉ S., et al. *Los Partidos políticos: Estructura y vigencia en la Argentina*. Buenos Aires: Cooperadora de Derecho y Ciencias Sociales, 1962.

CASTAGNO, ANTONIO. *Los Partidos políticos argentinos*. Buenos Aires: Roque de Palma, 1959.

GÓMEZ, ROSENDO A. "Intervention in Argentina, 1860–1930." *Inter-American Economic Affairs* 1 (December 1947): 55–73.

HOROWITZ, L. L. "Modern Argentina—The Politics of Power." *Political Quarterly* 30 (October–December 1959): 400–10.

IMAZ, JOSÉ LUIS DE. *La Clase alta de Buenos Aires*. Buenos Aires: Universidad de Buenos Aires, 1962.

———. *Los que mandan*. Buenos Aires: Eudeba, 1964.

———. *Motivación electoral*. Buenos Aires: Instituto de Desarrollo Económico y Social, 1962.

JOHNSON, JOHN J. "Argentina," *Political Change in Latin America*, pp. 94–127. Stanford, Calif.: Stanford University Press, 1958.

KANE, JOSEPH P., ed. *Argentina Election Factbook, July 7, 1963*. Washington: Institute for the Comparative Study of Political Systems, 1963.

KENNEDY, J. J. *Catholicism, Nationalism, and Democracy in Argentina*. Notre Dame, Ind.: University of Notre Dame Press, 1958.

KENWORTHY, ELDON. "Argentina: The Politics of Late Industrialization." *Foreign Affairs* 45 (April 1967): 463–76.

MACDONALD, AUSTIN F. "Argentina," *Latin American Politics and Government*, pp. 23–120. 2nd ed. New York: Thomas Y. Crowell Co., 1954.

———. *Government of the Argentine Republic*. New York: Thomas Y. Crowell Co., 1942.

McGANN, THOMAS F. *Argentina: The Divided Land.* New York: D. Van Nostrand Co., 1966.

MARTÍNEZ PAZ, ENRIQUE. "The Influence of the United States on Argentine Institutions." *Bulletin of the Pan American Union* 75 (June 1941): 337–43.

ORFILA REYNAL, ARNALDO. "Evolución y crisis de la política argentina." *Ciencias Políticas y Sociales* (Mexico City) 6 (January–March 1960): 103–40.

PENDLE, GEORGE. *Argentina.* 3rd ed. London: Oxford University Press, 1963.

———. "Argentina: The Past behind the Present." *International Affairs* 38 (October 1962): 494–500.

POTASH, ROBERT A. "Argentine Political Parties: 1957–1958." *Journal of Inter-American Studies* 1 (October 1959): 515–24.

———. "Argentina's Quest for Stability." *Current History* 42 (February 1962): 71–76.

———. "The Changing Role of the Military in Argentina." *Journal of Inter-American Studies* 3 (October 1961): 571–78.

RANIS, PETER. "Background to the 1965 Argentine Elections." *World Today* 21 (May 1965): 198–209.

A Report to the American Academic Community on the Present Argentine University Situation. Austin, Tex.: Latin American Studies Association, 1967.

RODRÍGUEZ, MEDARDO. "Frondizi, the Army and the Peronistas." *Reporter,* April 12, 1962, pp. 23–25.

RODRÍGUEZ ARRIAS, JULIO C. "Experiencia argentina en organzación y métodos para el mejoramiento de la administración pública." *International Review of Administrative Science* (Brussels) 23 (1957): 185–99.

ROMERO, JOSÉ LUIS. "La Crisis argentina: Realidad social y actitudes políticas." *Política* (Caracas), no. 1 (September 1959), pp. 81–96.

———. *A History of Argentine Political Thought.* Stanford, Calif.: Stanford University Press, 1963.

ROWE, JAMES W. *The Argentine Elections of 1963: An Analysis.* Washington: Institute for the Comparative Study of Political Systems, 1964.

ROWE, L. S. *The Federal System of the Argentine Republic.* Washington: Carnegie Institution, 1921.

SILVERT, K. H. "The Costs of Anti-Nationalism: Argentina," *Expectant Peoples: Nationalism and Development,* pp. 347–72. New York: Random House, 1963.

SNOW, PETER G. *Argentine Radicalism.* Iowa City: University of Iowa Press, 1965.

———. "The Evolution of the Argentine Electoral System." *Parliamentary Affairs* 18 (Summer 1965): 330–36.

———. "Parties and Politics in Argentina: The Elections of 1962 and 1963." *Midwest Journal of Political Science* 9 (February 1965): 1–36.

SURREY, STANLEY S., and OLDMAN, OLIVER. "Report of a Preliminary Survey of the Tax System of Argentina." *Public Finance* 16 (April 1961): 155–82, 313–40.

U.S. DEPARTMENT OF COMMERCE, INTERNATIONAL PROGRAMS BUREAU. *Federal Tax System of Argentina.* World Trade Information Service, 67–76 (December 1961).

WHITAKER, ARTHUR P. "The Argentine Paradox." *Annals of the American Academy* 334 (March 1961): 103–12.

———. *Argentine Upheaval.* New York: Frederick A. Praeger, Inc., 1956.

———. "Left and Right Extremism in Argentina." *Current History* 45 (February 1963): 84–89.

———. *The U.S. and Argentina.* Cambridge: Harvard University Press, 1954.

ZALDUENDO, EDUARDO. *Geografía electoral de la Argentina.* Buenos Aires: Ediciones Ancora, 1958.

URUGUAY

International boundary
Departamento boundary
National capital
Departamento capital
Railroad
Road

0   10   20   40 Miles
0 10 20   40 Kilometers

30
58   56   54   30

Uruguaiana

BRAZIL

Monte
Caseros
Bella Union
Río Cuareim
Artigas

ARTIGAS

Belén

ARGENTINA

Río Arapey Grande

Livramento
Rivera

SALTO

Salto

RIVERA

Río Daymán

Río Tacuarembó

Bage

Tacuarembó

Aceguá
32
32

PAYSANDÚ

Río Queguay Grande

TACUAREMBÓ

Río Yaguarón

Concepción
del
Uruguay
Paysandú

Pampa

Río Negro

Melo

CERRO LARGO

Jaguarão

Young

Río Negro

RÍO NEGRO

Paso de
los Toros

Dam

EMBALSE DEL
RÍO NEGRO

DURAZNO

Río Branco

LAGOA
MIRIM

Santa Clara

TREINTA

Fray
Bentos
Mercedes

Río San Salvador

Río Negro

Durazno

Sarandí
del Yi

Treinta y Tres

Y

Cebollatí

Uruguay

SORIANO

Trinidad

FLORES

José Pedro
Varela

TRES

Río Cebollatí

ROCHA

Chuy
34

Carmelo

FLORIDA

LAVALLEJA

Minas

Rocha

PUNTA DEL DIABLO

34

COLONIA

SAN JOSÉ

Florida

Río Santa Lucía

ISLA
MARTÍN GARCÍA
(claimed by Argentina
and Uruguay)

Rosario

San José

Colonia

CANELONES
Canelones

MALDONADO

La
Paloma

ATLANTIC

BUENOS
AIRES

RÍO DE LA PLATA

MONTEVIDEO
MONTEVIDEO

Maldonado
Punta del Este

OCEAN

La
Plata

ARGENTINA

BOUNDARY REPRESENTATION IS
NOT NECESSARILY AUTHORITATIVE

58   56   54

— 23 —

URUGUAY:

A Troubled Democracy

Uruguay presents an enigma to scholars. Why has South America's smallest republic developed so differently from its neighbors? Beginning as a backward, unimportant, and greatly underpopulated province of the Spanish colonial empire, Uruguay has become one of the most equalitarian societies in the world and certainly the most equalitarian society in Latin America. It has one of Latin America's finest educational systems, health and welfare services equaled in few other places in the world, and an economy dominated by the government. When problems arise, the Uruguayans do not seek easy solutions in civil wars or military dictatorships; like the civilized people they are, they change their form of government or elect the opposition to office, and try to find solutions to their problems through political activity. Despite serious problems, the Uruguayans enjoy one of Latin America's highest standards of living and a high life expectancy of 70.5 years.

No satisfactory explanation has ever been presented as to why Uruguay developed this way. Those who believe in the great-man theory of history attribute Uruguay's development to the work of José Batlle y Ordóñez, but this interpretation does not explain why Uruguay produced this great leader, or why it was willing to follow where he led. Others attribute Uruguay's uniqueness to the European character of its population, but Argentina has almost the same kind of population and has developed quite differently. Still others seek an explanation in Uruguay's size, in its soil, in many other factors. None of these alone explains the country's development. The student will have to decide for himself what has made Uruguay Latin America's most advanced political and social democracy.

A National Profile

With an area of 72,172 square miles, Uruguay is dwarfed by its giant neighbors, Brazil and Argentina. With Brazil to the north Uruguay shares a 622.8-mile boundary. To the east is the Atlantic Ocean. To the south is the Río de la Plata, and on the west there is a 269.5-mile boundary with Argentina. Uruguay is a land of gently rolling, grass-covered hills. All of the territory is occupied, although the density of population is much greater around Montevideo than in the northern part of the country. Seventy-three percent of the territory is used for pasture, 12 percent is planted in crops, 2 percent is in forest, and the rest consists of water, wasteland, and urban development. Most of Uruguay's soil is poor. Very fertile soils are found, but in most areas the topsoil is shallow and much of it is subject to erosion. The most modern methods of farming are not universally accepted. The climate is mild. Rainfall of about forty inches annually is sufficient for agriculture, although drought from time to time affects production.

Uruguay's population was estimated by its government in 1967 at 2,845,700; 72.6 percent of the population was urban, with about 46 percent concentrated in and around the capital city, Montevideo, the country's only really large city. All other cities have less than 60,000 inhabitants. The population of Uruguay is very homogeneous, about 90 percent being of European descent, mainly Spanish and Italian. The remaining 10 percent of the population are *mestizos*. Uruguay has Latin America's lowest birth rate, 21.5 per 1,000 inhabitants, and its lowest growth rate, 1.3 percent in recent years.

Uruguay has a reputation as an equalitarian society, and income distribution by social strata compares very favorably with that of other Latin-American countries. There are, of course, rich and poor, and 5 percent of the families receive about 27 percent of the national income. At the lower end of the income scale, 60 percent of all families receive 23 percent of the national income. Social services are highly developed, including medical insurance, child welfare, old-age pensions, and insurance against industrial injury, illness, and unemployment. Education is free at all levels, including the university, is secularly controlled and coeducational, and is compulsory in the primary grades; 26.5 percent of total central government expenditures went for education in 1965. Public health is highly developed and a fairly good transportation system knits the country together. Sections of the rural population, especially in the north, remain poverty-stricken, poorly educated, and relatively backward, but this includes only a minority of the population. The majority of Uruguayans are urbanized and educated and enjoy a fairly high standard of living in comparison with their Latin-American neighbors. Uruguay has proportionately more telephones than any other Latin-American country, and more television sets than any except Argentina. There are more miles of highway in Uruguay than in all except four of the Latin-American countries, and the Uruguayans own more cars, trucks, and buses than Chile, with a population almost four times as large.

Spanish is the official language and is spoken by everyone except a few of the newest immigrants. Since 1919 church and state have been completely separated, and it is believed that Uruguay has the smallest proportion of Catholics in all Latin America, although accurate statistics are not available. The best estimates are that about 50 percent are Catholics; the rest are freethinkers, Protestants, and members of other religious groups. Separation of church and state is strictly enforced and the public school curriculum contains no religious education.

Uruguay has one of the most literate populations in Latin America, with only 9.7 percent of those over fifteen years of age illiterate in 1963. Most of the illiteracy is a heritage of the past, as the illiteracy rate for those fifteen to thirty-five years old was only 3.6 percent.

Militarism is no problem in Uruguay. The armed forces include between 10,000 and 15,000 men, but a uniform is seldom seen in public and national defense receives a small percentage of government expenditures —8.5 percent in 1961, for example.

Until recent years, Uruguay was an agricultural country with stock raising the most important activity (about 70 percent of total farm output). Industrialization has been fostered by a protective tariff and import restrictions in recent decades. Of the total labor force, 19.6 percent is in agriculture and mining, 27.8 in manufacturing and construction, and 52.6 percent in services and other tertiary activities. Unemployment runs around 12.8 percent. Uruguay's principal exports are canned and frozen meat, wool, and hides. Much of the country's economic difficulties in recent years have been due to the position of wool on the international market. From 1955 to 1965, wool went down from 56 percent of the country's exports to 47 percent.

Tourism has become Uruguay's most important industry after livestock and agriculture because of the beautiful beaches stretching for 200 miles along the Río de la Plata and the Atlantic Ocean. Argentines and Brazilians make up the largest number of visitors, although people come from all over the world to enjoy Uruguay's vacation resorts.

Uruguay is an important banking center. Its four government and sixty-three private banks, with about 500 branches, hold a great deal of foreign money in secret numbered accounts. Industrialization is handicapped by the smallness of the local market and the lack of extensive mineral resources; the principal products are canned meat, textiles, and consumer products. With the ocean at its door, Uruguay has never developed either a sizable fishing industry or a large merchant fleet.

During recent years Uruguay has suffered from inflation, an adverse balance of payments, government deficits, and crippling strikes. Politics has become very hectic as the form of government was changed and the political parties split into many factions in the disputes over what to do. One of the factors contributing to the unfortunate situation has been the country's great dependence upon the world prices of wool and meat, the most important exports. Some observers blame the country's social welfare system, claiming that the provisions for pensions and welfare payments are more elaborate than a poor country can afford, but the welfare system did not cause Uruguay's crisis. It was the collapse of the economy, which most competent scholars attribute to mismanagement and the vagaries of the world market. Uruguay simply did not modernize its productive apparatus through the years, and suddenly the country was faced with an agricultural system that was not productive enough to support it. During the 1950's and 1960's, strenuous efforts have been made to diversify the economy, but the problem continues to plague the country.

Although Uruguay's people have a higher standard of living than prevails in the rest of Latin America, it is not high enough to provide everything that the high educational and cultural levels have led the population to demand. This is why there have been so many strikes and labor difficulties in the 1960's. Another serious problem in Uruguay is the wide gap between life in Montevideo and conditions in the rest of the country. Practically all of the cultural opportunities and the political, economic, and other power of the country are concentrated in Montevideo. It is believed that Uruguay's capital contains a larger percentage of its country's population than is true of any other city in the world.[1] This preponderance of the capital gives Uruguay serious problems of social disorganization and prevents the country from developing its resources more rapidly. It is because these are problems that can be solved that

---

[1] See the chart in Russel H. Fitzgibbon, *Uruguay, Portrait of a Democracy* (New Brunswick, N.J.: Rutgers University Press, 1955), p. 108.

most scholars are optimistic about Uruguay's future and rate it as Latin America's most advanced country.

The Development of Modern Uruguay

The "Oriental Republic of Uruguay," so called because of its location on the east bank of the Uruguay River, marked the meeting place of Spanish and Portuguese expansion during colonial days, and as a result it was the scene of a struggle between the two great imperial powers during the seventeenth and eighteenth centuries.

In 1603, Hernando Arias, then governor of La Plata, shipped 100 head of cattle and 100 horses to Uruguay and let them run wild and multiply. After these herds grew to vast numbers, the Argentine gauchos began to cross the river to kill the cattle for their hides. These gauchos roamed over the land, never staying long in one place, but their activities attracted the Buenos Aires merchants, and slowly settlements developed on the river's edge. When the Portuguese built a fort at Colonia on the Río de la Plata opposite Buenos Aires, it jeopardized the business of the Spanish merchants, and an active military struggle began between the Spanish and the Portuguese. The unsettled conditions produced by the almost constant military struggle did not make Uruguay a very choice place for those seeking a home. By the time of independence the population of the area was consequently very low, the best estimates for 1820 being about 60,000 people. These 60,000, however, were a trifle more cosmopolitan than the inhabitants of the average Spanish colony. In addition to the mixture of Spaniards, Portuguese, Indians, and *mestizos*, a sprinkling of French, English, and other Europeans had entered the country from the non-Spanish ships that visited Montevideo from time to time. George Pendle writes of the *Lady Shore*, an English ship carrying female convicts and recruited soldiers to Australia which came to Montevideo after the soldiers had mutinied. "Many of the women," Pendle writes, "seem to have settled quite happily in burghers' homes."[2]

During the struggle for independence, Uruguay was considered one of the provinces of Argentina, but the continued rivalry between Argentina and Brazil combined with British interests to create Uruguay as a buffer state between South America's two largest countries. With the Treaty of Montevideo, signed on October 3, 1828, both Brazil and Argentina renounced their claims to the area, and with the promulgation of the constitution of July 25, 1830, the *República Oriental del Uruguay* began its independent existence.

---

[2] George Pendle, *Uruguay*, 3rd ed. (London: Oxford University Press, 1963), p. 13.

Until 1903, Uruguay was the scene of an almost continuous series of civil wars, dictatorships, foreign wars, and invasions. At one time Montevideo was besieged for nine years, and only the British fleet kept the residents of the city from starving. During this period of turmoil, the articulate section of the population became divided into two factions. Those who adopted the name of *Blancos* (Whites) were basically the landowning oligarchy of the interior who stood for the continuation of the traditional Spanish semifeudal system, support for the Catholic church, and cooperation with Argentina as a counterweight to Brazil. The other faction, which adopted the name of *Colorados* (Reds), was composed largely of the coastal and urban population in and around Montevideo. It opposed the church and the semifeudal land system and favored cooperation with Brazil to strengthen Uruguay's position against Argentina.

Despite the almost constant civil strife from 1830 to 1903, the country developed as Europe's demand for food products stimulated the production of sheep and cattle. Increased production led to the improvement of the transportation system as English capital financed railroads to carry the meat, wool, and hides to Montevideo, where they were loaded on ships for Europe. The increased production also attracted immigrants from Spain, Italy, France, Switzerland, Britain, Germany, Argentina, and Brazil. The population increased rapidly, rising from 131,969 in 1852 to 307,480 in 1860, and to 915,647 in 1900.

As the country developed and the population increased, a new spirit entered Uruguayan politics which was best expressed by José Batlle y Ordóñez. Batlle was the leader of a progressive faction of the *Colorado* Party which started the country on a new course that was to culminate in a democratic nation-state. Two factors are usually mentioned as most important in influencing this change in Uruguay: the immigrants, and the *Colorados'* and *Blancos'* habit of signing "pacts" that divided the country between the two parties.

Many of the immigrants who came to Uruguay in the nineteenth century settled in and around Montevideo. Because this was the stronghold of the *Colorado* Party, the immigrants naturally gravitated to it after they entered politics. These people were not interested in the traditional Uruguayan political struggles. Many of them became small businessmen, who wanted peace so that business could flourish. Others brought anarchist and socialist ideologies with them from Spain and Italy. Thus by the beginning of the twentieth century the *Colorado* Party included many who wanted to see an end to the chaotic political struggles and civil wars that had gone on so long. At the same time, the middle and working classes were growing proportionately larger, and these too tended to support the *Colorado* Party or the newly established Socialist Party.

What has been called the "pacts between the parties" developed because neither the *Colorados* nor the *Blancos* were ever able completely to destroy the other party during the decades of civil war. Thus under certain situations the two parties signed agreements that almost resembled treaties. The first of these came in 1851, but the most important was probably that of 1872, which gave the *Blancos* control of four departments while the *Colorados* kept control of all the other departments and the national government. In 1897 another agreement increased the *Blanco* control to six departments. These pacts demonstrated to the country that the two parties could coexist, thus strengthening the trend toward constitutional government. The pacts are also the origin of the idea, so strong in Uruguay, that a minority party deserves to have some representation in the government. By 1900 Uruguay had almost a million people, a flourishing economy, and some practice in solving political problems by agreement instead of by civil war, though civil war was by no means unknown.

José Batlle y Ordóñez became the leader of the *Colorado* Party, and after being elected president in the same way his predecessors had been, by an indirect election in 1903, he was able to change the course of Uruguayan development. He faced an armed revolt by the *Blancos* as soon as he took office. This revolt was crushed in bloody battles, and few dreamed then that the peace treaty signed on September 1, 1904, marked the last attempt to change Uruguay's government by means of civil war. Since then, constitutional government has been the rule except for a lapse in 1933 caused by the world depression and another in 1942 caused by World War II. Even then there was no civil war.

José Batlle y Ordóñez was one of the most remarkable political leaders Latin America has yet produced. He led Latin America's first social revolution in the early years of the twentieth century. After he had put down the bloody revolution of 1904, he proposed that the *Colorado* Party change its structure by democratizing itself. Even more unusual, he convinced the *Colorado* Party that it ought to become a disciplined organization with a formal program, and that love for Uruguay should be the driving force behind the party instead of the mere desire for power that had motivated politics in Uruguay until then. He favored democracy, social justice, and government ownership of important sections of the economy.

During his first term he could not accomplish much because of the civil war and its aftermath, but he left the presidency retaining the support of a majority of the country's voters. Reelected president in 1911, he sponsored the legislation that began to transform the country. An eight-hour working day, compensation for industrial accidents, and government inspection of factories improved working conditions. The death penalty was abolished. The nation entered upon a program of public ownership of certain economic activities, including banking and insurance.

But Batlle's most important accomplishment was in laying the groundwork for the transformation of the political machinery to provide democratic stability. He thought that Uruguay's problems were rooted in excessive power in the hands of the president of the republic. At the beginning of the twentieth century, the Uruguayan president dominated the legislature and the Supreme Court and selected his successor, who took over the reins of government after a managed election. All the opposition could do was either accept the situation or revolt after each new president was installed. Batlle decided that if the president were stripped of his power and if strong ideological political parties were created, the cycle of revolution, disorder, and dictatorship would automatically come to an end. His proposal was so novel, however, that he never could get it adopted while he was alive. He suggested that a plural executive take the place of the president, and in 1913 he began advocating this step through his newspaper, El Día. He was opposed by almost all political factions, including most of his own party at first, but in 1951, long after he had died, the system was adopted.

Meanwhile, in 1917, delegates to a constitutional convention were elected to reform the 1830 constitution. To Batlle's surprise, his followers failed to gain a majority. He then threatened to run for a third term as president, and this so appalled the Blancos that they agreed to limit the powers of the president, whereupon Batlle agreed not to run again.

The constitution of 1919, therefore, included a new type of presidency, but one so peculiarly organized that it was doomed to failure. The new system, instead of creating a plural executive, divided the executive power between a president, who was authorized to handle only those matters thought to be political, and a National Council of Administration. The president, elected by direct vote for four years, controlled foreign relations, national defense, agriculture, and certain other matters. The National Council of Administration controlled the administration of education, health, public works, industrial relations, and the preparation of the budget. The National Council consisted of nine members serving for six years, with three elected by direct vote every two years, two from the party receiving the most votes, one from the party receiving the second highest vote. This device brought the two largest parties into the government and prevented any one person from controlling the entire government, but the system split the administration in such a way that its functioning was impaired when crisis struck, as the world depression of 1929 was to demonstrate. Yet this system has great symbolic importance, for it marked the real beginning of democracy in Uruguay as the citizens grew accustomed to the idea of representatives of opposing political parties sitting around a table talking to each other, instead of shooting at each other, as had been the pattern of the past. At the same time, the new constitution democratized the country by providing for the direct election of the Chamber of Representatives, for autonomous goverment on the local level, for secret elections, and for the complete separation of church and state.

The new constitution worked well during the 1920's, when the post–World War I prosperity provided a market for Uruguay's production. But the depression demonstrated that the divided authority of the 1919 constitution could not manage the problems produced by the collapse of the prices of the country's exports. Unfortunately for Uruguay, Batlle y Ordóñez was dead by then, and the president, Gabriel Terra, refused to try to solve the problem by constitutional means. On March 31, 1933, using his authority over the armed forces, he organized a coup d'état and established a dictatorship. Terra abrogated the constitution, used troops to prevent the General Assembly from meeting, imposed censorship, governed by decree, jailed and exiled his opponents. By Latin-American standards, it was a rather mild dictatorship, but it broke the pattern of orderly constitutional government the country had enjoyed since 1903.

In 1934 Terra organized a constitutional convention that produced the constitution adopted by plebiscite on March 21, 1934. The new constitution abolished the National Council of Administration and transferred its powers to the president. To limit the president's power, the new constitution gave the second largest party in each election a preferred position. The president had to appoint three of his nine ministers from among the members of the party receiving the second largest vote in the presidential election, and the second party automatically received 50 percent of the seats in the Senate, no matter how many votes it had won. It thus was given the power to block any legislation it opposed.

Having organized the government in the manner he preferred, President Terra had the constituent assembly extend his term in office for four more years, during which he generally ignored his new constitution and governed by decree. Neither armed revolt nor attempted assassination moved him to restore democratic government. Yet he did not try to stay in office after 1938, when his second term in office expired. His successor was his brother-in-law, Alfredo Baldomir, who tried to reintroduce democratic government by pardoning all political prisoners and by reinstituting, by decree, the National Council of Administration, thus restricting his own authority. The beginning of World War II brought fresh problems to the little country, including the organization of a Fascist party financed by the German embassy. President Baldomir found himself unable to act because of the veto power the *Blancos'* control of 50 percent of the Senate gave them. In addition, the *Blancos* seemed to favor the Nazi cause, while the *Colorados* favored the Allies.

As a result of these problems, President Baldomir again broke the constitutional system, in 1942, by postponing the elections scheduled for the spring of that year. He expelled his three *Blanco* cabinet ministers, although he had no constitutional power to do so, he abolished the Congress, and he governed by decree. By November 1942 President Baldomir had everything organized and succeeded in electing his chosen successor, Juan José Amezaga, a rich lawyer. At the same time, he submitted to the voters constitutional amendments to abolish the National Council of Administration, which he had revived, and introduce proportional representation to the Senate. With the adoption of these amendments, constitutional government returned to Uruguay, and since then no unconstitutional governmental changes have taken place.

During the years after the death of José Batlle y Ordóñez, the *Colorado* Party had split into a great number of bitterly quarreling factions. The party kept winning the presidency in the elections every four years because of the unusual system of voting, which in effect combined the party primary election and the final election in one vote. The candidate who received more votes than any other candidate of the same party received credit for all of the votes cast for all of the party's candidates. Under this system, a *Colorado* won the presidency in each election until 1950. In that year the president, Andrés Martínez Trueba, revived the idea of a plural executive to avoid the terrific competition for the presidency provoked by the system in use. Luis Herrera, the leader of the *Blanco* Party, agreed to support a new constitution embodying the plural executive, apparently having given up hope of ever winning the presidency, for by this time the *Colorados* had been in power since 1865. This cooperation between the leaders of the two most important parties won a majority for the new constitution in a plebiscite, and in 1952 a nine-member National Council of Government became Uruguay's executive. This was a true plural executive, in contrast with all previous arrangements.

During the 1950's Uruguay was shaken by an economic crisis that led to the first victory ever won by the *Blanco* Party in a national election. The crisis began with the collapse of Uruguay's export trade and was aggravated by Perón's ban on travel to Uruguay by Argentine tourists. This cut off about 100,000 visitors a year at the same time that exports to the United States went from $129 million in 1950 to $12 million in 1957, while imports were rising from $32 million in 1950 to $55 million in 1957. This crisis brought inflation, class conflict, and a slowing down of the economy. At the end of 1957, two United States meat packers (Armour and Swift) and a British company ended their operations in the country, throwing many thousands out of work.

The bad economic conditions led to agitation to abolish the plural executive and reintroduce a single president, but when this proposition was placed on the ballot, in 1958, it failed to receive a majority. In that election, however, the *Blancos*, for the first time in ninety-three years, won control of the executive power, by charging the *Colorados* with mismanagement and ineffectiveness at a time when the country was suffering severe inflation, unemployment, and a generally deteriorating economic situation. More fundamental to the *Colorados'* fall from power than what the *Blancos* said, however, was the condition of the *Colorado* Party itself. By 1958 the party leadership had grown old and bureaucratized. It had also run out of ideas. Batlle's program was revolutionary before World War I, but as the country became more urban and more industrialized, repetition of the old slogans no longer sufficed. A new day had dawned and the party leadership was unable to meet its challenge. The party's problems were complicated, of course, by the economic situation. At the same time, there was a change in the composition of the population, particularly in Montevideo. With the ending of immigration, the continuing influx of newcomers was composed of people from the rural areas, people who traditionally voted for the *Blanco* Party.

On March 1, 1959, the *Blancos* took control of the government, but the party was divided within itself and its three main factions even had difficulty in agreeing on the members of the national executive. In addition, the worst floods of the twentieth century hit Uruguay in 1959. Among other damage, one of the country's power plants was destroyed, and electricity had to be rationed. As a result, the *Blancos'* margin of victory fell sharply by the time of the 1962 election. From a majority of about 120,000 votes in 1958 it dwindled to about 24,000 in 1962. The *Blancos* abolished some of the controls over the economy which the *Colorados* had instituted and pushed through the country's first income-tax law.

The *Blanco* measures did not solve the country's problems, since only a complete modernization of the economic system could do that. Uruguayan farmers simply had not increased productivity through the years, and agricultural production was not large enough to finance the country's imports. One indication of Uruguay's ills can be seen in the enrollments in the various university faculties. In 1960, of all students registered, 28.7 percent were studying law, 19.3 percent medicine, 12.4 percent economic sciences, 8.2 percent architecture, 6.8 percent the humanities, but only 2.84 percent agronomy and 1.24 percent veterinary science; this in a country whose chief industries and exports are based on sheep and cattle raising.

Most serious of Uruguay's immediate problems was an inflation that cut the value of the country's monetary unit, the peso, from 4 to the United States dollar to 85.40 to the dollar in about fifteen years. This caused the cost of living to rise rapidly, in 1966 alone by 50 percent. At the same time, the *Blancos* who made up the executive proved unable to formulate policies adequate to the situation. To complicate matters, after Fidel Castro came to power in Cuba in 1959, a sizable *Fidelista* movement developed. Uruguay was far enough away from Cuba so that its *Fidelistas* did not become disenchanted with what was happening in Cuba, as occurred in Central America and northern South America. The Communists and the *Fidelistas* combined to foment great unrest in Uruguay. Strikes and political demonstrations became common.

Again the suggestion was made that a strong single executive would be able to solve the problem. This proposition had been defeated in the elections of 1958 and 1962, but when it was again submitted to the voters in 1966, they voted in favor of the constitutional change. At the same time, they gave the majority of their votes to the *Colorado* Party, and a retired general, Oscar Daniel Gestido, became the first president under the new constitution.

President Gestido was inaugurated on March 1, 1967. Uruguay was in a deep crisis. President Gestido instituted an austerity program, but was faced with mass strikes that disrupted production. Food shortages developed. At one time about 200,000 government employees were out on strike or conducting slowdowns or sitdowns to obtain a 40 percent wage increase. In August of 1967, the situation became so critical that the President banned all imports in a desperate effort to stop the loss of foreign exchange. In December 1967 Gestido died suddenly, bequeathing the presidency and its problems to his vice-president, Jorge Pacheco Areco, a former newspaper editor. Pacheco has continued and broadened the austerity program initiated by Gestido. As prices continued to rise, Pacheco replaced all but one member of his twelve-man cabinet and clamped a total freeze on wages and prices, with stiff penalties for violators. Workers responded with new waves of strikes, but a poll conducted in July 1968 showed overwhelming popular support for Pacheco's measures. The country's traditional freedom allows the few Communists to cause much disruption, but most competent observers think the government will win its struggle to enforce an austerity program. Thus, under the presidential system as under the plural executive, Uruguay's crisis continues. Many critics attribute the country's problems to its welfare system. The *Miami Herald,* for example, said just this, editorially, in 1967: "Uruguay falters because it is the most advanced welfare state in the world."[3] According to these critics, all Uruguay has to do is end some of its pension systems, welfare payments, paid holidays, and other welfare measures to recover its economic health quickly.

The country's real problem, however, is one of production. All the welfare provisions do is to distribute the country's income in a more equalitarian manner. If the productive system could be revived, especially if per capita and per acre productivity in agriculture and livestock could be raised, Uruguay would soon be on its way to economic health. Another solution is to develop new sources of income, perhaps fishing or more intensive labor industries. Meanwhile, the country remains Latin America's leading welfare state. That the voters have been able, through a referendum, to adopt a plural executive and then abolish it and to vote out of office a party that had been in power over ninety years, then eight years later go back to the traditional party, leads some scholars to be optimistic about Uruguay. No matter how dark the economic and political picture may look, the fact that the Uruguayans have learned to attack their problems politically gives hope for the future. To change from one of Latin America's most backward countries to one of its leaders was no mean achievement, and just as the Uruguayans were able to solve their problems in the past, they should be able to overcome their current dislocations.

The Formal Constitutional Framework

Uruguay is governed under the constitution that was adopted in November 1966 and went into effect on March 1, 1967. This is the country's fifth constitution. Its first went into effect on July 18, 1830, and served for eighty-eight years, although many of its provisions were ignored during most of the nineteenth century. A second constitution came into force on

---

[3] "Critical Ills of Uruguay," *Miami Herald,* August 9, 1967, p. 6a.

March 1, 1919, as a result of Batlle's efforts to introduce a plural executive. This one lasted until April 19, 1934, when a new fundamental document was produced. In 1951, the struggle to establish a plural executive culminated in the creation of yet another constitution.

The plural-executive experiment lasted from 1951 to 1967. When it proved incapable of leading the country out of its economic morass, Uruguay's voters decided to return to a presidential system. Alongside the president, there is a bicameral legislature and a Supreme Court of five members which has the power to declare laws unconstitutional by reason of form or content.

The 1967 constitution created a very strong presidency. In addition, it took away some of the legislature's power to initiate legislation and provided for automatic approval of bills under certain conditions when the Assembly fails to act. A central bank was created by the new constitution, and all social security funds were incorporated into one national social welfare bank. The term in office had been four years; this was changed to five years in the new constitution.

The 1967 constitution is very long and detailed and carries over much of the 1951 document. An interesting clause states that Uruguay shall "strive for the economic and social integration of the Latin-American states." Another requires that all treaties concluded by Uruguay shall contain a clause "to the effect that all differences which may arise between the contracting parties shall be settled by arbitration or other peaceful means." Military personnel committing common offenses are to be tried by ordinary courts.

It is impossible to forecast how long Uruguay's fifth constitution will remain in force, but its people have given a splendid demonstration of how to change a constitution peacefully. The struggles in Uruguay are electoral, and they have produced a body of voters who know what their constitution is and who take a keen interest in the way it functions.

How the Constitution Is Amended

Amendments to the Uruguayan constitution can be proposed by 10 percent of the citizens inscribed upon the National Civic Register, by two-fifths of the full membership of the General Assembly, or by a national constituent assembly, which is organized when a majority of the General Assembly approves a proposal made by senators, representatives, or the executive power. In any case, to be adopted the amendment must receive a majority vote of the electorate, which majority must equal at least 35 percent of all registered voters.

A special provision refers to "constitutional laws," which are passed by a two-thirds vote of the full membership of each house and ratified by an absolute majority of the electorate.

Who Participates in Politics

Since 1946, when women voted for the first time, practically all adults are eligible to vote, including foreigners who have lived in the country for fifteen years, and the overwhelming majority of the adult population votes and participates in the country's political life. Registration and voting are compulsory, but failure to vote is not punished. A voting registration card is necessary, however, in order to transact certain business with the government and to be admitted to the university.

In 1962, 1,519,684 persons were registered to vote and 1,171,020, 77 percent of those registered, voted. This amounted to 46 percent of the total population. By 1966, 1,659,039 were registered. To vote one must be a citizen at least eighteen years old who has resided in the country for at least three months before registering. (Citizenship is acquired automatically after fifteen years of residence.) The mentally incapacitated and criminals sentenced to the penitentiary are ineligible to vote. The list of registered voters is kept by the National Electoral Office and is permanent; thus citizens need to register only once. The Uruguayans take a great interest in politics and all political parties function continuously. Most newspapers are politically controlled and the majority of the Uruguayan population can be said to be actively participating in the country's political life.

The Electoral Machinery

Uruguay has a very complicated electoral system, but all observers consider the results to be fair reflections of the voters' wishes. In 1966 there were 208 different tickets, which presented thirteen presidential candidates and a total of about 200,000 candidates for all offices. This was one candidate for every eight voters. Some of the complication in the electoral system is due to the practice of electing all officials, national and local, at one time. In the 1966 election, for example, it was necessary to elect a president, 31 senators, 99 representatives, 97 members of departmental councils, 623 members of departmental juntas, and 171 members of the departmental electoral juntas. A second factor leading to complications is the use, since 1924, of what is known as the double simultaneous ballot, an electoral system unique in the world. Invented by a Belgian named Borelly, the electoral system combines into one process what in the United States are primary and general elections. Each voter casts a ballot for the political party he favors, the *lema*, and at the same time for the party faction he favors, the *sublema*. When the votes are counted, the party receives all of the votes cast for all of its factions. The positions are then divided among the various party factions, except for the presidency, which goes to the candidate of the faction receiving the most votes in the winning party. To help the voters keep track of the various *lemas* and *sublemas*, the electoral court assigns numbers to them, and through the years the numbers have become as well known as the names of the parties.

Elections are supervised by an autonomous electoral court of nine members. Five of the members of the electoral court are selected by the General Assembly by a two-thirds vote. The other four members are selected by the General Assembly as representatives of the political parties, with two coming from the largest faction of the largest party and two from the largest faction of the second largest party. The electoral court is elected at the beginning of each legislative term. It directs the work of a national electoral office; sets standards for registration of voters and for elections; registers political parties and candidates; decides how the government subsidy to political parties is to be distributed; tabulates the votes; and can even annul an election by a vote of six members, if the six include three of the five impartial members.

Under the national electoral court are departmental electoral juntas of nine members, elected by a system of proportional representation in each department. The departmental juntas select the polling places, appoint a three-member balloting commission and an actuary for each polling place, and in general supervise the electoral activity in their departments.

Political Parties

Although thirty-eight political parties nominated candidates for the General Assembly from 1926 to 1958, Uruguay has had a well-functioning two-party system since democratic government became the practice at the beginning of the twentieth century. The *Colorado* Party and the National Party (which is always referred to as the *Blanco* Party) always receive about 90 percent of the votes cast. Three small ideological parties have some importance, but they receive only about 10 percent of the total votes. All other parties are unimportant. They appear on the ballot because it is very easy to be recognized as a political party, the only requirement being a minimum of fifty citizens who register their desire to be a party.

The *Colorado* and *Blanco* Parties grew out of the two factions that arose during the chaotic civil wars of the nineteenth century. The *Colorados* were reputedly more liberal and anticlerical than the *Blancos,* but in practice there was little difference between the two organizations. The *Blancos* were a little stronger in the northern part of the country, the *Colorados* in Montevideo, but both had supporters in all parts of the country and among all groups in the population. With the introduction of democratic government and the need to appeal to the voters, the two parties came to have similar programs, though the *Blancos* were generally more conservative than the *Colorados* on economic and social questions. With the development of well-organized permanent factions representing clearer ideas, this confusion continued, for both parties had members of all shades of opinion. The *Colorado* Party was the dominant group in Uruguay from about the middle of the nineteenth century to the 1950's, but since then the two parties have been more even in strength, with slight variations from election to election.

Both parties contain many factions. The most important *Colorado* factions during the 1966 election campaign were Lists 15, 123, 515, 99, 315, and 10. Oscar Gestido, who became president, was the leader of List 123. List 15 is thought to be a more liberal group than the other *sublemas,* and was the largest faction in the *Colorado* Party from 1946 to about 1960. Much of its appeal was to organized labor and the lower classes. List 99 consisted of a group within List 15 that became sympathetic to Fidel Castro. The group was infiltrated to some extent by the Communists, but it never obtained a very large vote.

The National Party's main factions are the *Unión Blanca Democrática,* the orthodox *Herreristas,* the National Popular Movement, and Blue and White. The divisions within the *Blanco* movement are basically matters of personality, each faction favoring its own leader. The National Party won the elections of 1958 and 1962 after being a sort of permanent opposition for more than ninety years, but its failure to make any headway against the country's problems, which led to defeat in 1966, probably means that the party is doomed to opposition status.

Of the three minor parties, the Communist party, because of its international connections, is the most important. It has always been well financed, but has been unable to make real progress in Uruguay's democratic atmosphere. Since 1962 it has been participating in elections as part of a front organization it created to take advantage of Fidel Castro's popularity, the Leftist Front of Liberty (*Frente Izquierda de*

Libertad, or FIdeL.) It is split between pro-Chinese and pro-Soviet factions.

Since 1872 devout Catholics have functioned through an organization called the Civic Union, which never was able to win mass support. In the early 1960's the Civic Union split into the Christian Democratic Party and the Christian Civic Movement. The first is a more progessive-minded group, but neither has won many votes.

A Socialist party has functioned since 1910, but its capture by pro-Communist elements in the 1960's has practically destroyed the organization. The traditional Socialists, led by Emil Frugoni, tried to recapture the party in 1966 by use of a *sublema,* but received fewer votes than the pro-Communist group. The Socialist party appeared on the ballot in 1962 and 1966 as the Popular Union.

TABLE 1

VOTES CAST FOR THE URUGUAYAN PARTIES AND GOVERNMENT SUBSIDY RECEIVED BY EACH TO HELP FINANCE THE ELECTION CAMPAIGN IN 1958

Party	Votes Received	Pesos Received
National Party		
Sublema Dr. Luis A. Herrera	241,939	$1,203,242.97
Unión Blanca Democrática	230,649	1,147,094.05
Sublema Intransigente	26,522	131,902.71
No *sublema* specified	315	1,566.60
Total National Party	499,425	$2,483,806.33
Colorado Party		
Sublema Batllismo (List 15)	215,881	1,073,971.15
Sublema por los Ideales de Batlle (List 14)	154,110	766,455.11
Sublema Unidad Batllista	8,514	42,342.95
No *sublema* specified	557	2,431.96
Total *Colorado* Party	379,062	$1,885,201.17
Civic Union	37,625	187,121.62
Socialist Party	35,478	176,443.87
Communist Party	27,080	134,677.83
Democratic Reformist Movement	19,979	99,362.20
Renovating Movement	6,325	31,456.32
Passive Classes and Social Security Party	142	706.21
Revolutionary Workers' Party	142	706.21
Labor Party	52	258.61
Trade Union Workers' Front	52	258.61
Pesos left over	. . .	1.02
Total all parties	1,005,362	$5,000,000.00

It is comparatively easy to become registered as a political party in Uruguay, as only 500 members are needed, and one can get on the ballot as an "accidental" party with only 50 members. It is also relatively easy to set up a *sublema* within one of the existing parties. The parties are financed by the money they can get from their members and by a government subsidy that is divided among the parties in proportion to the number of votes they received in the last election. In 1958, for example, 5 million pesos were appropriated for this purpose, and each party was given 4.973 pesos for each vote it received. All of the parties try to maintain headquarters in the various parts of the country, with the *Colorados* probably having the largest number of these clubhouses. The party headquarters serve as social and service centers in addition to being used for political activity. Many party members rely on the leaders to help them with the paperwork needed to secure pensions and other services in a highly bureaucratic country.

Pressure Groups and Public Opinion

Uruguay's small size and the concentration of population in and around Montevideo make it easy for public opinion to influence the government. The press is dominated by the daily newspapers published in Montevideo. Uruguay has the highest per capita distribution of daily newspapers in Latin America. All the dailies are political and partisan to the cause of their publishers, and each faction of every party seems to have its own organ. The most important *Colorado* papers are *El Día*, *Acción*, *El Diario*, and *La Mañana*. The National Party newspapers are *El País*, *El Plata*, *El Nacional*, and *El Debate*. The Socialists publish *El Sol*, the Communists *Época* and *El Popular*, the Christian Democrats *El Ciudadano* and *BP Color*. Montevideo's radio and television stations are also important in supplying information.

The proportional representation system and the mass literacy have contributed to the growth of a large number of special-interest groups. Sometimes a pressure group nominates candidates and acts like a political party, but generally the pressure groups have contact with both the *Colorado* and National Parties. In this sense, Uruguayan politics resembles that of the United States, for both parties try to appeal to all groups. The representatives of the pressure groups try to impress their points of view upon the executive, the legislature, and the important officials of the various government agencies and industries. Their activity is much the same as that carried on by similar groups in other democratic countries. They issue propaganda, distribute leaflets, organize parades and demonstrations, send letters and delegations to decision-makers.

Among the most important pressure groups are the government corporations, which have developed vested interests and exert pressure to preserve their positions. Since the government corporations handle a substantial part of the country's economic affairs, they are in a powerful position. Many are monopolies. Other very important pressure groups are the representatives of landowners and agriculture. Business and banking are well organized.

Labor unions have grown in power in recent decades, but are weakened by their division along political lines. The largest federation, the Confederation of Workers of Uruguay (CTU), is dominated by the Communists and has about 90,000 members. The Confederation of Workers of Uruguay (CSU) is affiliated with the ORIT and has about 10,000 members. Other unions are dominated by the Christian Democrats and the anarchists. The unions are very active politically, since most of their members work for the government directly or indirectly.

Neither the Catholic church nor the armed forces, so important in most Latin-American countries, is an important pressure group. General Gestido was elected president not because he had the support of the armed forces, but because he was a member of the *Colorado* Party and proved to be an effective administrator after he left the army.

The extensive pension system has produced associations of retired persons who lobby for higher pensions. The students and intellectuals play the usual important roles of the articulate. The Christian Democrats, the Communists, and the Socialists seem to have the support of most of the university students, who function through the University Students' Federation of Uruguay.

Because Uruguay is a true democracy, the pressure groups tend to line up with either the *Colorado* or the *Blanco* Party. Politics thus becomes an effort to win the support of the most important groups.

Civil Liberties

The Uruguayan constitution spells out in great detail all of the rights guaranteed to the people. These include all the civil liberties found in the most democratic constitutions of the world. Freedom of speech, assembly, religion, and property are guaranteed. An accused person has the right to legal assistance at all stages of a judicial proceeding. No one may be punished or imprisoned without due process of law. There are clauses specifying that the government and its agencies are civilly liable for injuries caused to anyone during the performance of public services, and administrative tribunals are established to protect the citizen's rights in such cases.

All observers are agreed that the Uruguayans enjoy great liberty. There is no censorship, and anyone, Communist, Fascist, or crackpot, can participate in elections, issue propaganda, and seek converts. The constitution does not grant the executive the wide state-of-siege powers so common in other Latin-American countries, and what power is given "to take prompt measures of security in grave and unforeseen cases of foreign attack or internal disorder" is limited by the need to report the action taken to the General Assembly within twenty-four hours. This power has been little used in Uruguay. Social rights are also spelled out in the constitution, including such statements as that every citizen has a right to "decent housing." Illegitimate children are declared equal before the law to other children, and women have the same legal rights as men.

The Executive Power

It is difficult to describe the functioning of the Uruguayan executive because it has not had its present form long enough for any pattern to have emerged. During the twentieth century the form of the executive has been changed regularly as attempts were made to create one in harmony with the ideas of Batlle y Ordóñez. From 1951 to March 1, 1967, the executive was a nine-man National Council of Government. It had been thought that group decisions would be more balanced than those of one man, but in practice all that the system produced was indecision and stalemate.

The constitutional changes of 1966 made the executive a president elected for a five-year term. He may not be immediately reelected. The president is to act in conjunction with his ministers individually or as a group; when the ministers function as a group, the body is known as the Council of Ministers. The position of the president is neither that of the traditional strong president so common in Latin America nor that of the prime minister in a parliamentary system, but combines features of both.

The president appoints the Council of Ministers, but the members of the council have the power to take action opposed by the president. In addition, the president is limited by the constitution in appointing ministers, for he "shall allocate the Ministries to citizens who, by reason of their parliamentary support, are assured of permanency in office." In the legislature elected for the 1967–72 term, the President's party has a majority, but what will this measure mean if an opposition party wins a majority of the legislature? Does this mean the president is to be a figurehead? Only experience will tell.

The president, acting with the Council of Ministers, has all the usual powers of the executive in a democratic state. These include command of the armed forces, the enforcement and proclamation of laws, the power to veto bills passed by the General Assembly, the right to introduce legislation into the Assembly, and the power to appoint and remove many officials, sometimes with the approval of the Senate. The president supervises the preparation of the budget and concludes and signs treaties, which must be ratified by the legislature. The president has exclusive power to introduce legislation dealing with wage increases for government employees, price control, and social security.

The president has one great power that will strengthen his position: in an emergency he can send bills to the legislature with the stipulation that, if they are not acted upon within a fixed time limit, they will automatically become law. And if there is a real deadlock between the executive and the legislature, the president can dissolve the Assembly and call new elections. The new Assembly will then, by an absolute majority of its members, decide the issue.

The Uruguayan public service includes about a fifth of the labor force, because the government operates many economic enterprises. Most are run by twenty-two government corporations, which are independent of the president, except that he appoints their boards of directors. Many operate at a loss, and at times are used for patronage. Yet Uruguay has a fairly good public administration. It is reasonably honest and based on rules that tend to protect the workers. Personnel is generally recruited between the ages of eighteen to twenty-five, through examinations that may be written or oral, qualifying or competitive. Once a six-month probationary period has been served, the employees tend to remain in their positions until they retire on pension. It is all but impossible to discharge an employee after he has served his trial period.

To protect the citizens from the bureaucracy, there is a Contentious-Administrative Tribunal of five members which has jurisdiction over all disputes involving administrative acts.

The Legislative Power

Uruguay's legislative power rests in a General Assembly consisting of a ninety-nine-member Chamber of Representatives and a thirty-one-member Senate, both elected by a system of proportional representation on a double simultaneous ballot for five-year terms. Alternates are elected at the same times as the regular members; thus there are no by-elections. For the Senate, the whole country is considered one election district, and the senator heading the list that receives the most votes within the party receiving the most votes becomes the president of the Senate and of the General Assembly. For the Chamber of Representatives, the electoral court distributes the seats among the departments on a population basis every five years, with each department getting a minimum of two seats.

To be a senator one must be at least thirty years old. To be a representative one must be at least twenty-five years old. Reelection is permitted and some members serve for long periods. Neither house has precedence over the other, and there is some fluctuation in membership; that is, representatives run for the Senate and vice versa. Most members of the Assembly live permanently in Montevideo, although some of the representatives make an effort to keep in contact with their departments. They receive a moderate salary, which is set by the previous Assembly before they are elected. For the 1959–63 Assembly, the salary was 2,200 pesos per month (approximately $198 U.S.). The members of the Assembly receive the customary immunity to prosecution for their speech and activities. They are not supplied with either offices or assistants, but the most important leaders sometimes are provided with these by their parties. Many pay their secretaries' salaries from their own funds.

Officials of the executive, judicial, and electoral powers and members of department boards and councils are not eligible to be representatives or senators, but most of them can become candidates if they resign their positions three months before an election. Civil and military employees can serve if they resign their positions. Pensioned government employees and university teachers are exempt from this prohibition. All members of the Assembly are prohibited from participating in enterprises contracting work or services with any public agency or government department and from representing third parties before the government departments or other public agencies.

The Assembly begins its sessions on March 15 each year and sits until December 15. During an election year, adjournment comes on October 15 and the new session begins the following February 15. A Permanent Commission, composed of four senators and seven representatives, plus their alternates elected by proportional representation, headed by a senator of the majority party, is elected each year during the first fifteen days of the session. The Permanent Commission represents the Assembly when it is not in session and has the power to convoke the legislature in special sessions.

The Uruguayan General Assembly meets jointly or in its separate chambers, according to the business to be transacted. The most important duties of the joint session include the election of the Supreme Court of Justice, of the electoral court, of the Contentious-Administrative Tribunal, and of the Tribunal of Accounts; the settling of disputes about legislation upon which the two houses disagree; and the granting of pardons. When the joint session meets to consider controversial legislation, a two-thirds majority is needed to decide the issue. Ministers have the right to attend sessions of the General Assembly, of either house, of the Permanent Commission, or of the permanent standing committees, and may take part in the debate but have no vote. Ministers must present themselves before the chamber requesting their presence by a resolution of one-third of the full membership. Ministers may also be questioned in writing.

The Uruguayan legislature follows a formal procedure in considering legislation and utilizes a system of permanent committees to consider each bill. There are no joint conference committees to settle disagreements; a constitutional procedure can be followed, or the two houses meet together to settle the issue by a two-thirds vote. The legislature usually meets in the afternoon, and after a recess for dinner may meet again until late at night. The public is permitted to attend sessions, and many interest groups attend in force when legislation in which the group is interested is under discussion.

The Senate spends a great deal of time considering nominations for appointments to and removals from office submitted to it by the executive. In other respects, the two chambers have equal powers and duties. Most observers consider the Uruguayan legislature a true deliberative body. It conducts investigations and seriously considers the business before it. Party discipline is rather weak because of the nature of the parties.

The president has veto power over legislative actions, including an item veto, but the legislature can override the veto by a three-fifths majority. The legislature can accept an item veto by a simple majority or reject the bill completely. The Supreme Court can also declare a law passed by the Assembly unconstitutional in form or content. The president's new power to dissolve the legislature and call elections may change the way the legislature functions in the future. The purpose of the constitutional changes of 1967 was to enable the government to act decisively at times of crisis. These provisions presuppose that the president will act decisively if the legislature is unable or unwilling to pass a bill; only experience will determine how any president will use these powers. It is very likely that the effect will be to strengthen party discipline; if this is so, the president and the other party leaders should be able to work out a program for the country.

Public Finance

Uruguay operates under the principle of a continuous budget; that is, the amounts of the previous year remain in force unless expressly changed. This, combined with the great inflation of the 1950's and 1960's and the various devaluations of the peso, makes it almost impossible to compare the budget from year to year. Generally, the government gets about 10 percent of its income from customs duties, about 30 percent from direct taxes, about 20 percent from other taxes, and about 40 percent from other sources.

In 1963 the government spent its money in the following way: for general administration, 9.6 percent; for defense, 8.6 percent; for courts, police, and jails, 8.7 percent; for education, 20.9 percent; for public health, 9.8 percent; for social security and welfare, 24.7 percent; for agriculture and other economic services, 1.9 percent; for transport and communications, 6.7 percent; and for service of the public debt and miscellaneous, 9.1 percent.

Uruguay certainly has a budget much different from most other Latin-American countries, and it has one weakness: practically nothing is spent for economic development, and most of the money is spent for education, public health, and social security and welfare.

Local Government

Uruguay is a unitary state divided into nineteen departments that are granted certain powers of self-government. All public security services, however, are under a chief of police appointed by the president of the republic. Legislative and supervisory functions in each department are entrusted to a departmental board, which has sixty-five members in the department of Montevideo and thirty-one members in each of the other departments. Executive functions are entrusted to a departmental council with seven members in Montevideo and five members in each of the other departments. Members of both bodies are elected for five-year terms and serve without pay. The councils are modeled on the old National Council of Government. The party receiving the most votes gets four of the seven seats in Montevideo and three of the five seats in each of the other departments. The other seats go to the party getting the second highest vote. The seats on the departmental board are distributed among the various parties in proportion to the votes they receive.

In urban communities outside of the departmental capital, local councils can be set up consisting of five members appointed by the departmental board. The five members are appointed on the basis of the proportional representation of the political parties on the departmental board.

The departmental boards and councils and local councils exercise the powers of local government given to them by the constitution, including the power to tax, spend, supervise local public services, and oversee public health and primary, secondary, preparatory, industrial, and artistic education.

The Judicial Power

Uruguay's judicial system consists of a Supreme Court of five justices and subsidiary tribunals. Justices of the Supreme Court are elected by the General Assembly by a two-thirds vote of the full membership for ten-year terms, and are ineligible for reelection until five years have passed after leaving office. A justice of the Supreme Court must be at least forty years old and must have practiced law for ten years or served for eight years in the judiciary or as a government attorney. The Supreme Court appoints all of the lower court judges, those of the Court of Appeals with the consent of the Senate or the Permanent Commission.

Below the Supreme Court there are appellate courts; *juzgados letrados*, which would correspond to United States district courts; and, at the bottom of the hierarchy, 227 justices of the peace. The Supreme Court makes up the budget for the judicial system, but it must be approved by the legislature, and there has been some criticism that the legislature has not voted enough money for the courts.

Members of the Contentious-Administrative Tribunal, which settle disputes arising from administrative actions, must have the same qualifications as justices of the Supreme Court.

Most observers feel the court system in Uruguay provides justice of high quality. There is no death penalty, and provisions are made to finance trials for those without funds. The jury system is not used in Uruguay.

Uruguay: A Last Word

Uruguay is living through a period of change which has brought with it a severe economic crisis. From 1950 to 1964, agriculture's share of the gross domestic product fell from 22 percent to 15.3 percent, while industry's share rose from 17.8 percent to 23.3 percent. During these years of change, the plural executive created by the 1951 constitution proved incapable of meeting the needs of the country. Change in one aspect of life always requires changes in other aspects, or serious problems arise. The plural executive could not agree on a course of action. Matters were complicated in 1958 when the *Blanco* Party won control of the executive and legislative branches of the government for the first time in the twentieth century. As inflation, unemployment, an adverse balance of payments, and other serious problems arose, the *Blanco* leadership floundered.

As has happened many times before, Uruguay sought a civilized road out of its predicament. The voters decided in a referendum to change the form of their government once again, and at the same time gave the *Colorado* Party a majority vote. Thus today Uruguay faces the future with a new type of government controlled by a political party that was out of power for eight years.

What is happening in Uruguay has great significance for all of Latin America. If Uruguay's new government can lead the country to economic prosperity and development, the power of democracy will have been demonstrated. The solutions offered by Fidel Castro and his Soviet and Chinese friends will be a lot less appealing if Uruguay demonstrates there is another way to achieve progress. On the other hand, if the new government fails, Uruguay is liable to collapse into military or Communist dictatorship.

One can only judge the future by the past, and the Uruguayans have demonstrated an ability to overcome their difficulties. The creation of what is one of Latin America's most highly developed states in a relatively poor area was a great achievement. Uruguay leads all the other Latin-American republics in many statistical indexes, including those of education. It is highly probable, therefore, that the country will find a way out of its troubles and emerge again as a stable, democratic, progressive country whose ever changing political system will be capable of articulating and fulfilling the wishes of the population.

SELECTED READINGS

ALEXANDER, ROBERT J. "Communism in Uruguay," *Communism in Latin America*, pp. 135–48. New Brunswick, N.J.: Rutgers University Press, 1957.

FABREGAT, JULIO T. *Elecciones del 30 de Noviembre de 1958*. Montevideo: Asamblea General del Uruguay, 1962.

———. *Los Partidos políticos en la legislación uruguaya*. Montevideo: Medina, 1949.

FITZGIBBON, R. H. *Uruguay: Portrait of a Democracy*. New Brunswick, N.J.: Rutgers University Press, 1954.

———. "Uruguay: A Model for Freedom and Reform in Latin America?" In *Freedom and Reform in Latin America*, edited by Fredrick Pike. Notre Dame, Ind.: University of Notre Dame Press, 1959.

HALL, JOHN O. *La Administración pública en el Uruguay.* Montevideo: Instituto de Asuntos Interamericanos de los Estados Unidos de América, 1954.

HANSON, SIMON G. *Utopia in Uruguay.* New York: Oxford University Press, 1938.

JOHNSON, J. J. "Uruguay," *Political Change in Latin America,* pp. 45–65. Stanford, Calif.: Stanford University Press, 1958.

KITCHEN, JAMES D. "National Personnel Administration in Uruguay." *Inter-American Economic Affairs* 4 (June 1951): 45–53.

MACDONALD, AUSTIN F. "Utopian Uruguay," *Latin American Politics and Government,* pp. 476–503. 2nd ed. New York: Thomas Y. Crowell Co., 1954.

"A New Constitution for Uruguay." *Bulletin of the International Commission of Jurists,* no. 29 (March 1967), pp. 37–45.

PENDLE, GEORGE. *Uruguay.* 3rd ed. London: Oxford University Press, 1963.

RAMA, CARLOS. *Las Clases sociales en el Uruguay.* Montevideo: Ediciones Nuestro Tiempo, 1960.

———. "La Crisis política uruguaya." *Combate* 1 (March–April 1959): 3–8.

SANGUINETTI FREIRE, ALBERTO. "Social Legislation in Uruguay." *International Labour Review* 59 (March 1949): 271–96.

TAYLOR, PHILIP B. "The Electoral System in Uruguay." *Journal of Politics* 17 (February 1955): 19–42.

———. *The Executive Power in Uruguay.* Berkeley, Calif.: privately published, 1951.

———. *Government and Politics in Uruguay.* Tulane Studies in Political Science, vol. 7. New Orleans: Tulane University, 1960.

———. "Interests and Institutional Dysfunction in Uruguay." *American Political Science Review* 54 (December 1962): 62–74.

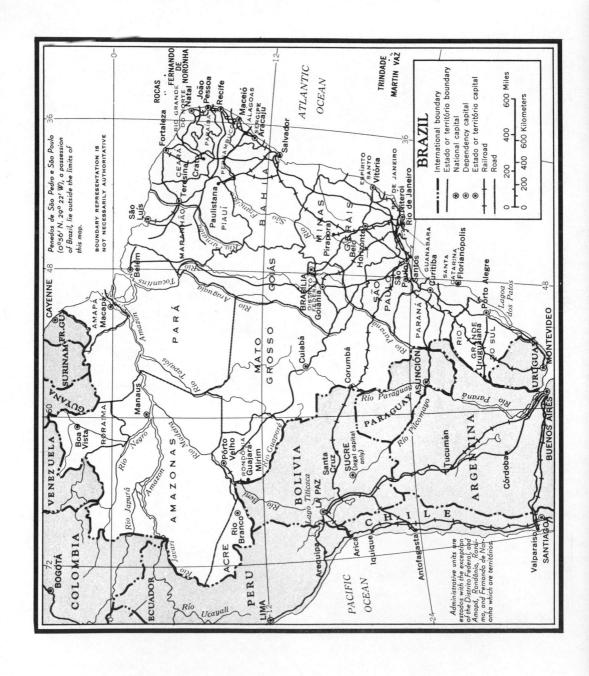

BRAZIL

International boundary
Estado or território boundary
National capital
Dependency capital
Estado or território capital
Railroad
Road

0   200   400   600 Miles
0   200 400 600 Kilometers

Penedos de São Pedro e São Paulo
(o°56' N, 29° 22' W), a possession
of Brazil, lie outside the limits of
this map.

BOUNDARY REPRESENTATION IS
NOT NECESSARILY AUTHORITATIVE

Administrative units are
estados with the exception
of the Distrito Federal, and
Amapá, Rondônia, Rorai-
ma, and Fernando de Nor-
onha which are territórios.

ATLANTIC
OCEAN

PACIFIC
OCEAN

TRINDADE
MARTIN VAZ

FERNANDO
DE
NORONHA
ROCAS

VENEZUELA
COLOMBIA
ECUADOR
PERU
BOLIVIA
CHILE
ARGENTINA
PARAGUAY
URUGUAY
GUIANA
SURINAM (FR. GU.)

BOGOTÁ
CAYENNE
Boa Vista
RORAIMA
Manaus
AMAPÁ
Macapá
Belém
MARANHÃO
São Luís
Teresina
PIAUÍ
CEARÁ
Fortaleza
Crato
Paulistana
RIO GRANDE DO NORTE
Natal
João Pessoa
PARAÍBA
Recife
PERNAMBUCO
Maceió
ALAGOAS
SERGIPE
Aracaju
Salvador
BAHIA
Rio São Francisco

PARÁ
Rio Tocantins
Rio Araguaia
MATO GROSSO
Cuiabá
GOIÁS
BRASÍLIA
DISTRITO
FEDERAL
Goiânia
MINAS GERAIS
Pirapora
Belo Horizonte
ESPÍRITO SANTO
Vitória
RIO DE JANEIRO
Niterói
Rio de Janeiro
GUANABARA
SÃO PAULO
São Paulo
Santos
PARANÁ
Curitiba
SANTA CATARINA
Florianópolis
RIO GRANDE DO SUL
Pôrto Alegre
Lagoa dos Patos
Rio Uruguai
URUGUAIANA

AMAZONAS
Rio Negro
Rio Japurá
Rio Branco
Rio Madeira
Rio Purus
Rio Juruá
Rio Javari
Amazon
Rio Tapajós
ACRE
RONDÔNIA
Pôrto Velho
Guajará-Mirim
Rio Guaporé
Rio Paraguay
Corumbá
ASUNCIÓN
Rio Pilcomayo
Rio Paraná
Rio Paraná
Tucumán
Córdoba
BUENOS AIRES
MONTEVIDEO

LIMA
Arequipa
Arica
Iquique
Antofagasta
Valparaíso
SANTIAGO
LA PAZ
Lago Titicaca
SUCRE
(legal capital only)
Santa Cruz
Rio Beni
Rio Ucayali

72 60 48 36
0 12 24 36 48 12

—24—

BRAZIL:

The Giant of the Future

Brazil is a land of the future because it is changing so fast that it is practically impossible to keep track of all that is happening there. The total population is increasing rapidly, education and health improve each year, industrialization is proceeding at a rapid rate. The rapid change, however, has not yet produced a stable political system of the kind needed in the modern, interdependent, complicated world produced by a half century of wars and revolutions. Brazil's problems are especially difficult to solve because through the years change came at different rates of speed in various parts of the country and in various aspects of the cultural pattern. Change came much more quickly in the south than in the north, and in the west changes have come very slowly. The economic system has changed much more rapidly than the ingrained habits of the people. A political system developed very slowly over a period of four centuries, characterized by the dominance of an entrenched landed aristocracy, cannot easily be replaced by the democratic institutions of the modern nation-state. It is this that makes Brazil's motto, "Order and Progress," only an ideal for some future time, not a present reality.

A National Profile

Stretching for 2,680 miles from north to south and 2,690 miles from east to west, Brazil is a giant among nations. Its 3,286,473 square miles are equal to 1.7 percent of the area of the globe, 5.7 percent of the world's total dry land, and nearly half (47.3 percent) of South America. Bounded on the southeast, east, and northeast by the Atlantic Ocean, Brazil touches all of the other South American countries except Ecuador and Chile. Its 4,600 miles of coastline and 9,700 miles of land frontier enclose areas with many different climates, soils, and altitudes. Most of Brazil is either a plain or a plateau, only 3 percent of its area being above 3,000 feet. Fifty-seven percent is from 650 to 3,000 feet above sea level and 40 percent has an altitude of less than 650 feet. Its location gives Brazil one of the most extensive river systems in the world. About 27,000 miles of these rivers are navigable, and as a result much of Brazil's traffic is via river boat. Large ocean liners go 1,042 miles up the Amazon River to Manaus to pick up cargo, and fairly sizable vessels continue up the river to Iquitos, Peru, 2,300 miles from the Atlantic Ocean.

The various parts of Brazil differ greatly. To the north is the Amazon River basin, an immense tropical area that includes 42 percent of Brazil's area, but only about 4 percent of the population, who produce only 2 percent of the national income. Most of the Amazon basin is a dense tropical rain forest. Various useful products are gathered from the forests, rubber being the most important. There are lumber and fishing industries. Manganese is the most important resource of the area.

Brazil's northeast consists of a very fertile coastal plain and a subtropical, semiarid section. The northeast contains 11 percent of the country's area but 22 percent of the population, who produce 9 percent of the national income. As these figures demonstrate, poverty is the rule in the northeast. This was a prosperous agricultural area during colonial days, but productivity declined as soil became eroded and a tradition-bound society prevented development. A few minerals are produced here, but the main export, in addition to agricultural products, is people, who leave for other parts of Brazil in search of a better life.

Although the coastal strip running north from Rio de Janeiro contains only 15 percent of the country's area, 34 percent of the total population live here and produce 36 percent of the national income. Agriculture is important, and the largest part of the country's dairy industry is found here. Mining, some industry, and the country's largest steel mill are also located here.

Stretching west to Bolivia and Paraguay is the west-central region, a greatly underpopulated plateau where 4 percent of the population live on 22 percent of the country's area and produce 3 percent of the national income. To the south lie the states of São Paulo, Santa Catarina, Paraná, and Rio Grande do Sul. Although this includes only 10 percent of Brazil's area, it contains 36 percent of the population. This is the richest and most modernized and industrially developed section of the country, producing 50 percent of the national income. It is here that the heaviest European and Asiatic immigration came during the last half of the nineteenth century and the first half of the twentieth. Cotton, coffee, wheat, rice, tobacco, corn, and fruits are produced in large quantities. Coal mining and cattle raising are important, and most of the country's factories are in this area.

The great differences in the density of population, economy, wealth, social organization, levels of education and literacy, and political habits in the five areas of Brazil help in large part to explain the country's difficulty in achieving stability. Brazil is not a homogeneous unit, and each of the parts leads a different kind of life. Brazil's population in mid-1968 was 90,193,000, which made it the world's eighth most populous nation. The population is very unevenly distributed, with most Brazilians living in a belt extending inland from the coast from thirty to sixty miles. The population has been growing at a rate of about 3.1 percent; about half is urban. Brazil's size and large population prevent any one city from dominating the country, although São Paulo and Rio de Janeiro are by far the most important.

Brazil's population is the product of one of the most interesting experiments in racial mixture the world has ever seen. Intermarriage between the Portuguese and the Indian began in the first days of the colony and has continued ever since. Gilberto Freyre, one of Brazil's leading scholars, suggests that because the dark-skinned Moors who ruled Portugal for so long were the more cultured, richer, and dominant, many Portuguese came to discard any prejudice against the darker-skinned people that they may once have entertained. It is impossible to judge the exact racial composition of Brazil's population on the basis of the available statistics, but the government considers the population to be 60 percent white, 20 percent mulatto, 10 percent *mestiço*, 8 percent Negro, and 2 percent Indian. The main contributors to the melting pot were the aboriginal Indians (about 50,000 to 100,000 remain, living a tribal life), the Portuguese colonists, the Negro slaves brought from Africa, and the nineteenth- and twentieth-century immigrants, most of whom were Portuguese, Italian, German, Polish, and Japanese. This list does not exhaust the kinds of people who came to Brazil. United States southerners after the Civil War established colonies in Brazil; Korean, Chinese, and all kinds of Europeans helped to populate it. During the last few decades, the government has been trying to push the assimilation of its immigrants. This policy, especially the emphasis on use of the Portuguese language, was adopted during the Second World

War, when the German Nazis, Italian Fascists, and Japanese nationalists organized groups of their nationals as potential fifth columns. Portuguese is the official language, but many of the immigrants continue to speak their native tongues. Although discrimination for color is illegal, most of the top stratum of Brazil's society is white and most of the Negroes are poor.

Church and state are constitutionally separated in Brazil, but the Catholic church is powerful. The great majority of Brazilians are nominally Catholic, but many, especially in the upper classes, are agnostics or freethinkers whose Catholicism is limited to the main *rites de passage:* christening, marriage, and death ceremonies. Education has been improving at a rapid rate since 1945, but the educational system is still very deficient. In 1966 about 39 percent of the population over fifteen years of age was illiterate, and many of the rest were functional illiterates. The urban areas have much better educational facilities than the rural, where some districts are as much as 66 percent illiterate. In 1964, only 66 percent of the children between seven and fourteen were enrolled in a school. There is a very high dropout rate, which complicates the picture. Brazil's thirty-seven universities, among the best in Latin America, had about 125,000 students in attendance, but the dropout rate was high there also, and only about 20,000 graduated each year during the 1960's. Public health levels in Rio and São Paulo are equal to those of large cities in the United States, but the rural areas suffer from tropical diseases and malnutrition. Fifteen thousand of Brazil's 25,000 physicians practice in the urban areas, creating a severe shortage in the rural areas.

Brazil has traditionally been an agricultural country, but it is changing its economic organization rapidly. From 1939 to 1956, while population increased 50 percent, the real product increased 108 percent, thus raising per capita income by 3.2 percent annually compounded during the period. Yet the standard of living continues to be low and most of the development has taken place in only a few places, particularly São Paulo, Rio de Janeiro, and Minas Gerais. The construction of a new capital at Brasília, an attempt to turn the country's attention toward its underdeveloped heartland, is helping to open up new areas. By the 1960's, industrial output was about even with agricultural output: agriculture produced 23 percent of the gross domestic product in 1964, industry 22.5 percent.

There is much potentially good farmland not yet exploited. Ownership of the farmland being utilized is extremely concentrated, thus creating much rural poverty. Of the country's 3,350,000 farms in 1960,

1 percent, each larger than a thousand *hectares*, included about half of all the farmland. An agrarian-reform law was passed in 1964 to improve the situation, but not much has yet been accomplished. By progressive taxation, expropriation, and land settlement, it is hoped to transform the productivity and tenure of the land. The principal agricultural states are in the south, which is also the most industrialized part of the country. The state of São Paulo alone produces about 50 percent of the total agricultural production. Brazil's principal agricultural products are coffee (48 percent of world production and 56 percent of the total value of Brazil's exports in 1960), cotton, cacao (Brazil is the second largest cacao producer in the world), sugar cane, and food crops. Many different kinds of trees are exploited for lumber, food oils, gums, resins, and waxes. Livestock provides a living for many persons.

Industrialization has progressed very rapidly since 1940, but is concentrated mainly in São Paul (60 percent of the total production), Minas Gerais, and Rio de Janeiro. Hydroelectric power is well developed, 4.4 million kilowatts being produced in 1960. Brazil's mineral wealth has never been adequately surveyed or developed, but it is known that there are abundant mineral resources which include important deposits of iron ore, manganese, tungsten, nickel, chrome, titanium, tantalum, berilium, lithium, zirconium, bauxite, and meerschaum. There are small deposits of tin, zinc, lead, and copper. Only about half the needed coal is produced. Important radioactive minerals, including uranium, have been located. Brazil produced only about a third of the petroleum it needed in 1965, although it has large resources not yet exploited. Much of Brazil's industry is partially or completely owned by international corporations or foreign nationals, which helps to create the nationalist fervor that has been a feature of the country during recent decades. Foreign ownership is substantial in the automobile, pharmaceutical, machinery, and chemical industries. Important parts of the country's industry are owned in whole or in part by the government. Petrobras, the government-owned petroleum-producing monopoly, is the largest single industrial corporation in all of Latin America. The government also is part owner of the country's largest steel mill, Volta Redonda, and of airlines, railways, hydroelectric power plants, and merchant shipping.

Brazil's great problems are an uneven pattern of development and population and a social system that condemns most of the people to poverty. At least 50 percent of all Brazilians have no sanitary facilities and 47 percent do not have an acceptable water supply. Conditions are particularly bad for the millions who inhabit the *favelas*, the jungles of rickety packing-case hovels that surround the cities, especially Rio de

Janeiro. In the northeast, most of the population lives in an almost permanent state of crisis due to the lack of sufficient water and to soil erosion. This creates a stream of farmers moving to the cities of the south to swell the *favelas*. A serious inflation during the years since the Second World War has aggravated the problem. Yet Brazil has fantastic possibilities. Its underdeveloped natural resources, including fertile soil, mineral deposits, and potential hydroelectric power, are tremendous. Its size gives it the potential to become a great world power inhabited by hundreds of millions of people. It needs only to create effective political, economic, and social institutions capable of developing its potential. Why so large and richly endowed a land has such serious problems will become clear as its historical development is reviewed.

The Development of Modern Brazil

Brazil has always been a little different from its Spanish-speaking neighbors, both as a colony and as an independent state. When the Portuguese first came to the area in the sixteenth century, they found a vast land inhabited by about a million Indians with no readily apparent sources of wealth. At that time, Portugal possessed exceedingly rich colonies in India, the Pacific islands, and Africa, and as a result the mainstream of Portuguese colonization went to places other than Brazil. A few Portuguese came to look for the gold and silver the Spaniards were finding in their part of America, a few government officials were sent in, and some criminals and other undesirables were shipped to Brazil by the government. During the second half of the sixteenth century the production of sugar began, and for over a century northeastern Brazil supplied most of the European market. Since the scattered Indians were unable to supply the labor the Portuguese refused to do, millions of African Negoes were brought as slaves to work on the sugar plantations and to contribute one of the main elements in modern Brazil's population. Thus the basis was laid for the Portuguese colony of Brazil, and by the seventeenth century it was a flourishing producer of agricultural products.

Brazilian society was more self-reliant than any in the rigidly controlled Spanish colonies. The French attempt to establish themselves on the coast south of the Amazon and the Dutch occupation of the coastal area from Bahia to Guiana from 1621 to 1661 helped to strengthen local Brazilian patriotism, as the Portuguese struggled successfully to eject their European rivals. In the same way, the Brazilian war to destroy the republic of Palmares, organized by ex-slaves (1633–95), strengthened the self-reliant spirit of the Brazilian upper classes. An especially self-confident group developed in São Paulo: the people variously known as the *Paulistas, Mamelucos,* and *Bandeirantes.* This was probably the most dynamic group in colonial Brazil. Restless, ever on the move, the *Paulista* wanderers extended Portuguese Brazil west of the line of demarcation with the Spanish colonies and helped to begin the settlement of a vast area. They established the cattle empires of southern Brazil, discovered the gold and diamonds of Minas Gerais, and stimulated a flow of colonists.

By the end of the colonial period Brazil had a population of close to 4 million, about two-thirds of them Negroes and mulattoes. Society was dominated by a landowning aristocracy living in almost feudal splendor, independent of the central colonial government, self-sufficient, each landowner all-powerful within his domain. The landowners exercised military, political, and economic power, and dominated the small towns and cities. Next in importance was a commercial middle class made wealthy by trade and smuggling. At the bottom were the Negro slaves. The intermixture of the races created a substantial mulatto group, many of whom were artisans rather than laborers. The church was weak in colonial Brazil, as each large landowner tended to have his own church on his estate, which he controlled as effectively as he did every other aspect of life. Many of the priests were sons of the aristocracy.

Brazil began its independent career peacefully and has not been tormented as much as its Spanish neighbors by militarism and civil wars. As in the Spanish colonies, Brazil's independence was a result of Napoleon's conquest of the Iberian peninsula. The transition was peaceful because the British navy transported the prince regent of Portugal to Rio de Janeiro, where he set up his court and created the Kingdom of Brazil in 1808. The period of the Kingdom of Brazil saw much development, for this was now the center of the Portuguese empire. When John VI returned to Portugal in 1820, the opposition to a return to colonial status led John VI's son, Pedro I, to set up an independent state, the Empire of Brazil, in 1822. In 1831 Pedro I abdicated in favor of his five-year-old son, who became emperor as Pedro II in 1840 and ruled until 1889, when a republic was established. Brazil probably had the best and most stable government in Latin America during the nineteenth century, and developed the political habits which have continued until the present day.

In the years of the empire, Brazil was governed under the constitution of 1824, which provided for a limited monarchy in which the emperor was aided by a two-house legislature and a council of state. The legislature consisted of a lower house elected every four years and a senate composed of persons appointed for life by the emperor from a list prepared by electors. The emperor also appointed his council of state and was able to dissolve the legislature and make most of the appointments in the government service.

Brazil made great advances under the empire, and especially under Dom Pedro II. Although the government continued to be dominated by the landowning oligarchy, its territory was expanded, its economy was developed, its transportation system was improved, its population jumped as the expanding economy stimulated large-scale immigration, its commerce increased, and its educational system was improved. During this period two political parties developed, the Conservative and the Liberal. These were not true political parties in the modern sense; they were groups of representatives of the landowning aristocracy, the commercial interests, the coffee barons, and the mineral producers. The emperor was able to dominate both "parties," and he alternated them in office. Thus two strong groups developed, consisting basically of the "ins" and the "outs," both reflecting the interests of the same upper class and both personalistic and based on family ties. The foundations laid by these parties in the nineteenth century remained strong in the twentieth; the same type of political organization continued, especially in the rural areas. The Republican Party, made up mainly of intellectuals and members of the emerging middle class, was organized in 1871. It favored ending the empire and slowly grew in importance.

Although Brazil made much progress under Dom Pedro II, there was much dissatisfaction with his rule, based in large part on the centralizing tendencies of the national government. The large landowners, who were traditionally used to running local affairs, did not like the authority of the state governors appointed by the Emperor, and continuously pressed for self-government of the municipalities and the states. In 1873 the Emperor alienated the devout Catholics by jailing a group of priests who enforced papal decrees without the consent of the government, a practice forbidden by the constitution. When the slave owners withdrew their support of the Emperor after a law freed their slaves in 1888, there was nothing that could prevent the overthrow of the empire. Thus the empire was destroyed, not by those who wanted a more progressive organization of the country, but by those who wanted to preserve an antiquated social structure that no longer fitted the modern world emerging at the end of the nineteenth century.

To complicate matters further, those who established the republic foolishly abandoned the parliamentary system to which the people had grown accustomed during the empire and adopted a constitution modeled on that of the United States, with a strong president as the dominant figure. The bicameral legislature was continued and the federal principle was adopted. As is customary in Latin America, the federal government was given the power to intervene in the states in a number of circumstances. The 1891 constitution also contained a bill of rights which guaranteed freedom of speech and the press, trial by jury, religious toleration, the abolition of the death penalty, the separation of church and state, the civil status of marriage, and the secularization of education. Yet democracy was not emphasized and the franchise was limited. Basically, the landowning aristocracy and the commercial interests dominated the government, with the military as a third force of some importance.

The federalism of the early years of the republic was a peculiar kind, for the political leaders never really understood that the federalism of the United States was a joining together of previously independent units. Brazil's federalism was designed to decentralize a unified empire. As the system operated, the landowning aristocracy developed a sort of political machine which ran each state. The governor became the most important figure, and through his control of the state government he dominated the electoral process. The members of the national Congress were more like delegates from the states than national leaders, for their positions depended upon the state governor and his political machine. The national president, who controlled patronage, gave his favors to those congressmen who helped him, and thus a tight system developed. Since São Paulo and Minas Gerais were the richest and most important states, the custom developed of rotating the presidency between the leading politicians of these two states.

From 1891 to 1930 no true national political parties existed. What were called political parties were simply groups of individuals who controlled each state. All elections were controlled to guarantee the election of the political machines' candidates. Civil liberty was a myth except in half a dozen of the largest cities, and even there the efficacy of the constitutional guarantees was relative. Competition was limited to coalitions of the landowning families jockeying for position.

During the years, the economy grew, the population rose, and industry began to develop, especially during and after World War I. The newer methods of transportation and communication were introduced. A boom in rubber created a new elite of wealth, and coffee became the chief element in economic life. As newer groups began to emerge and as the cities grew, much dissatisfaction was expressed with the political system. Electoral reform became the campaign issue of the opposition and several armed revolts were attempted during the 1920's. Finally, in 1930, the system broke down when the effects of the world depression were added to the old discontent.

In 1930 the term of President Washington Luiz, former governor of São Paulo, came to an end, and now it was the turn of the governor of Minas Gerais to be president. But Luiz decided that only Julio Prestes, the governor of São Paulo, was capable of leading the nation through the depression. Many Brazilians were disturbed by this. Were São Paulo's politicians planning to dominate the government completely? The leaders of Minas Gerais in particular were alienated by this action, and helped to organize a "Liberal Alliance" which supported Getulio Vargas, governor of Rio Grande do Sul, for president. When Julio Prestes was declared elected after the usual controlled election, Vargas led a revolution that succeeded in overthrowing the government of Washington Luiz and installed himself in the president's palace. With this event the constitution of 1891 and the system of government based upon it were destroyed. A new era began for Brazil, the era of Getulio Vargas, who was to dominate the country until his death in 1954.

Getulio Vargas came to office as a radical reformer. He claimed he would sweep out corruption and break the hold of the traditional politicians on the government. He would further industrialization, Vargas claimed, and enable the workers to achieve a better life. His twenty-four-year rule did not produce a stable or democratic governmental system, but he did foster the development of Brazilian nationalism, which transformed most of the country's population into a cohesive whole, and broke the power of the state political machines, which had been interested only in their local situations and never became part of truly national organizations.

Vargas abrogated the constitution of 1891 and governed by decree in the first years of his regime. He ejected large numbers of elected officials and intervened in the governments of many of the states. This centralization of power stimulated São Paulo's leaders to revolt in 1932, but after heavy fighting Vargas' troops won out. The revolt, however, led Vargas to organize a constitutional convention, which produced the constitution of 1934, a serious attempt to improve the governmental machinery of Brazil and to lay the foundations for democratic government. Under this constitution the president was severly limited in what he could do, and an independent electoral court was created to organize fair elections. Vargas, however, after getting himself elected by the Congress as the first president under the new constitution, abrogated it in 1937 when his term was about to expire. Introducing a new constitution (O

Estado Novo) which outlined a sort of corporate state, Vargas then proceeded to ignore this constitution, too, and ruled as a dictator until 1945. He cooperated with the United States in World War II and sent a 25,000-man division to Italy, where it distinguished itself in the fighting. He improved labor conditions, built many public works, improved education, and made a serious attempt to improve public administration. Would all of this development have come without Vargas? Probably; with Vargas, it came under a dictatorship that imprisoned and exiled its opponents and censored the press.

Despite all of Vargas' reforms, he never really changed the organization of Brazil's government. Though industry was encouraged and a government-controlled labor movement grew up, the government continued to be a machine in the service of an aristocracy.

When the war ended, the enthusiasm for democracy that was sweeping the world affected Brazil, and Vargas was ejected from office by the armed forces. The president of the Supreme Court became acting president and presided over an election that saw General Eurico Gaspar Dutra, Vargas' minister of war, elected as the candidate of the newly organized Social Democratic Party (PSD) over an air force general nominated by the National Democratic Union (UDN), composed of Vargas' organized opponents. The election of General Dutra demonstrates the importance of healthy political parties to the functioning of democratic government. Vargas had abolished all political parties, and through his censorship and emergency powers had prevented all except the totalitarian parties, the Communists and Integralists (Fascists), from functioning. Therefore, when elections were held in 1945, the strongest of the new political parties turned out to be the PSD, which included within its ranks most of the followers of Vargas and the remnants of the old pre-Vargas state political machines. Yet the PSD did not win a majority of the seats in the national legislature, and President Dutra's administration began as a coalition government. When it developed that Dutra and the PSD really only wanted to continue the existing status quo without Vargas in the presidency, the coalition dissolved and Dutra completed his term opposed by a majority of the Congress.

The Dutra administration accomplished little. The Communist Party, which had won a substantial vote in the 1945 elections, was banned from the ballot on the constitutional grounds that it was the agency of a foreign power. Little else of importance was accomplished during Dutra's five-year term. It was demonstrated that Brazil could be governed constitutionally, without censorship of press or radio, as efficiently and as well as under Vargas' dictatorship. A new constitution was adopted in 1946 which was another version of the 1934 charter. It provided for a federal republic headed by a president serving a five-year term with a division of powers between the national and state governments. Control of elections was given to an independent electoral tribunal and the customary civil liberties were listed. But the two powers that help to frustrate democracy in Brazil were continued in the new constitution: the president could suspend constitutional guarantees and he could intervene in the affairs of the states.

In 1946, during Dutra's administration, the Volta Redonda steel mill, financed in part by the United States, began production, and many new factories were built. But the Dutra administration failed to do anything decisive about the poverty and misery in which so large a proportion of the people lived. Nothing was done to break up the tremendous latifundia, little was done to improve the educational system, and the postwar recession saw the beginning of an inflationary trend that was to hamper Brazil's development. It is of course not strange that Dutra and the PSD failed to set Brazil on a new course. They represented the same oligarchy that had been governing Brazil since the organization of the colony, and although industrialists and urban political leaders were more prominent in the government than had been the rule before 1930, basically the organization of Brazil was the same as it had always been.

The result was that in 1950 48.7 percent of the voters accepted the demagogic promises of Getulio Vargas again and elected him constitutional president of the republic as the candidate of the Brazilian Labor Party. Although Vargas did not win a majority of the votes cast, he won more than any other candidate. By 1950 Brazil's political parties had proliferated to such an extent that Vargas was supported by three parties; the second candidate, Brigadeiro Eduardo Gomes, was supported by three parties, the most important of which was the UDN; and the third candidate was supported by the PSD and five other parties. Vargas' supporters did not win a majority of either house of the Congress and he had to organize a coalition cabinet in order to obtain some cooperation from the legislature.

As constitutional president from 1951 to 1954, Vargas was a different man from the energetic dictator of 1930–45. By 1951 he was sixty-seven years old, a tired old man who apparently had sought election to demonstrate the unfairness of his expulsion from office. Having won vindication, he did practically nothing about the country's main problems: inflation, the need to develop transportation and oil production, the need to improve education and to institute land reform. His weak and haphazard leadership plunged the country into a serious institutional crisis. Graft ran rampant and scandals in high places were frequent. A most important sign of unrest in the country was the election as mayor of São Paulo of an unknown schoolteacher, Jânio Quadros, who won against the combined efforts of President Vargas and his political parties and of Adhemar de Barros, the political boss of the state of São Paulo. Quadros' victory was followed by a wave of strikes by São Paulo's industrial workers in protest against the continuous inflation.

The Korean War stimulated the inflation in Brazil, and in addition Vargas was faced by a whole series of natural catastrophes that demanded strong leadership, yet the government seemed unable to do anything. Drought came to the northeast, floods to the Amazon valley; freezing temperatures in the south and central area damaged the important coffee crop; power shortages hampered industry and electricity had to be rationed. Yet industrialization continued, and Vargas permitted freedom of press and speech. This was not a dictatorship, but the liberty and chaos gave the Communists a golden opportunity to take advantage of the misery of the masses. Riots and strikes swept the country. In June 1954 an unsuccessful attempt was made to impeach Vargas.

The Vargas government finally collapsed in August 1954 and Vargas either committed suicide or was killed. The immediate stimulus came when persons in the President's bodyguard apparently tried to assassinate Carlos La Cerda, a newspaper critic of Vargas and an important leader of the UDN. La Cerda was not killed, but an air force officer walking at his side was, and this so enraged the air force officers that on August 23, 1954, the armed forces issued an ultimatum to Vargus: resign or be evicted. Vargas resigned and was dead the next day, by whose hand is unclear.

Vargas had been elected by a coalition made up of his Labor Party (PTB) and two other parties; the vice-president who succeeded him, João Café Filho, represented the Social Progressive Party (PSP), a small organization without much following in the country. He had to govern, therefore, without the support of most of the country's more important groups. The problems he faced required action, but it was impossible for him to do very much, and the energies of the nation's political leaders went not toward the success of the government, but into the campaign to elect a new president in 1955.

The presidential election of 1955 demonstrated how disunited Brazil's voters were; again no candidate received a majority of the votes. Juscelino Kubitschek and João Goulart, the candidates for president and vice-president of a coalition made up of the Social Democratic and Labor Parties, received the largest vote, 35.63 percent of the total cast. The UDN candidate, General Juárez Távora, received 30.26 percent of the votes cast, and Adhemar de Barros, nominated by the Social Progressive Party, received 25.77 percent; 8.28 percent of the votes went to Plinio Salgado, the Integralist leader of the 1930's, now operating through an organization known as the Popular Representation Party.

Not only would the new president and vice-president take office without the support of a majority of the voters, but they faced virulent opposition from all those groups and forces that had opposed Getulio Vargas. Kubitschek and Goulart were the inheritors of Vargas' power, for Vargas had started both the Social Democratic Party and the Labor Party. The Social Democratic Party consisted basically of all the "ins," the political functionaries who had achieved power during the Vargas regime. Many, especially the older ones, had been part of the local political machines that flourished during the years before 1930. The Labor Party consisted of the government-controlled and -manipulated trade unions and included some opportunistic politicians who were trying to achieve a following by being "radicals." Goulart was the classic example. He was a rich ranch owner from Rio Grande do Sul who became a "labor leader" when Vargas appointed him Minister of Labor.

A great furore arose after the 1955 election to prevent Kubitschek and Goulart from taking office. A suit was filed asking the Supreme Court to declare that a winning candidate needed a majority of the votes cast, but the court refused to agree with this interpretation of the constitution. Things became so hectic that during November 1955 the country had three different presidents as the various forces struggled to dominate the government. The armed forces officers, however, insisted that Kubitschek take office, and they had the power to enforce their wishes. Thus once again Brazil inaugurated a president who did not have the support of a majority of the voters or of the members of the legislature.

President Kubitschek was a product of the Social Democratic machine in the state of Minas Gerais, and he continued the type of government the country had had since 1945. He juggled the political forces, made demagogic speeches, and pushed industrialization, but he never touched the real problems of Brazil: poverty, agrarian reform, constitutional reform. A spectacular drop in coffee prices from ninety-five cents a pound in 1954 to forty-two cents in 1958 complicated his problems greatly. Inflation increased yearly, and with it the cost of living. Kubitschek's main claim to fame was his successs in pushing the development of a new capital for Brazil in an attempt to turn the country's energy to exploitation of its unused interior. At fantastic costs in money and energy, which stimulated the inflation and were accompanied by great corruption, a new city was carved out of the wilderness in the state of

Goiás about six hundred miles from the coast. Despite the achievement of constructing Brasília, the new capital, Kubitschek's government accomplished little for Brazil. As a result, in 1960, for the first time in the country's history, the opposition candidate, Jânio Quadros, was elected president.

As we have seen, under the electoral system then in use the elected president and vice-president could come from opposing parties. This happened again in 1960; although Jânio Quadros had all of the reformist groups in the country behind him, João Goulart, the candidate of the Labor Party and a representative of the old Vargas machine, was reelected vice-president. After achieving prominence as mayor of the city of São Paulo, Quadros had been elected governor of the state of São Paulo. Nominated for the presidency by the UDN and other reformist parties, he won a sweeping victory, although he did not get a majority (44.78 percent of the votes cast). Taking office on January 31, 1961, Quadros began his term as if he would reorganize all of Brazil. He attempted to reform the public service by insisting that all government employees quit their other jobs and devote full time to their work. He tried to reorient Brazilian foreign policy and he tried to reform the tax structure. He had great difficulty in instituting all these reforms, and on August 25, 1961, Quadros either resigned or was forced out of office by the armed forces. No explanation or hypothesis so far offered really explains what happened; probably the most logical explanation is that Quadros resigned in a fit of pique, never expecting that his resignation would be accepted. But it was, and he left the country. Under the constitution, when Quadros resigned Goulart became president, but the forces that had elected Quadros did not relish having Goulart in control of the executive power. To complicate matters, on the day Quadros resigned, Goulart happened to be in Communist China, and opposition to his assuming the presidency was so great that Brazil was on the verge of civil war. A compromise was reached, however, under which Goulart was allowed to become president, but a constitutional amendment stripped the presidency of most of its powers and transferred them to a cabinet responsible to the Chamber of Deputies. Thus a new experiment in parliamentary government began in Brazil.

The parliamentary system lasted for a year before another constitutional amendment returned the executive power to the president. During that year Brazil was in constant crisis, because the compromise reached in September 1961, when Goulart took office, did not really satisfy any of the important political forces. Under the constitutional amendment, the president was given the power to appoint the prime minister, who then had to receive a vote of confidence in the Chamber of Deputies. The Chamber sitting in 1961 had been elected in 1958 and represented a different balance of voting strength among the political parties than was represented in the 1960 election won by Quadros. As a result of this combination a holdover Chamber and an unpopular president opposed to the parliamentary system—the system did not have a chance to demonstrate its worth. Goulart kept appointing prime ministers who shared his disapproval of the parliamentary system. Thus a country in profound political crisis was being governed by a president who wanted power but had none and a cabinet with power it do not want.

By the end of 1962 the parliamentary system was dead and Goulart was in control of Brazil. Goulart was a product of the Vargas regime, and like Vargas seemed to be interested in only one thing—power. But he was much less capable than Vargas, and was venal and corrupt besides. When Goulart turned to the Communists for support, they soon infiltrated the government and many mass organizations. Inflation grew until it became institutionalized, reforms were forgotten, and a permanent crisis settled over Brazil as the political leaders spent their time getting ready for the 1965 election. By March 1964 the crisis had deepened into chaos. The inflation grew worse every day, strikes and minor violence became commonplace, and many began to fear Brazil would degenerate into anarchy.

President Goulart suddenly proposed that the crisis be solved by amending the constitution to give the vote to illiterates, permit easier land reform, and, most controversial of all, shift some of the legislature's power to the president and permit him to be reelected. These proposals frightened many Brazilians, especially those who were perturbed by the Communist advisers Goulart had placed in key positions. When 1,400 leftist sailors and marines staged a revolt because the leaders of a propaganda organization backing Goulart's proposals had been arrested and Goulart supported the revolting military men instead of the officers who had arrested them, a real revolt began. Supported by most of the governors of the important states, the armed forces took over the government and Goulart fled to Uruguay on April 2, 1964. With Goulart gone, his support disappeared, and the army arrested many thousands for being "Communists, Communist sympathizers, and left-wing supporters."

When the Congress refused to give the leading army officers as much power as they wanted, on April 9 the Supreme Military Revolutionary Command issued an "institutional act" which conferred great power upon the president. The institutional act provided that a new president and vice-president would be elected by the Congress; that all bills sent to the Congress by the president had to be considered within thirty days or they would go into effect as if approved; that only the president could introduce bills creating or increasing public expenditures; that the president could, in any of the cases foreseen in the constitution, decree a state of siege or prolong it for a maximum of thirty days. Even more controversial, the act provided that for six months, all guarantees of tenure for all government positions, national, state, and local, whether elective or appointive, would be suspended. In other words, the new government could purge anyone from any level of government during the following six months. And most controversial of all, a process was created under which the political rights of any person could be suspended for ten years without judicial review.

The military having instituted the institutional act by decree, the Congress accepted it and on April 11, 1964, elected General Humberto Castelo Branco as president until January 31, 1966. The public demonstrated great enthusiasm and sympathy for the new government as it began its work by setting up a coalition cabinet which included members of the Social Democratic Party, the National Democratic Union, the Christian Democratic Party, independent technicians, and high officers of the armed forces. The new government took office pledged to reform. It was anti-Communist, and on May 12, 1964, it broke relations with Fidel Castro's government in Cuba.

The new government removed from office 9,000 elected and appointed officials and stripped 378 individuals of their political rights. Among those who lost their political rights for ten years, including the right to run for office, were former presidents and governors, national congressmen and diplomats. The army was also purged. The Social Democratic Party went into opposition when its leader, ex-President Kubitschek, lost his political rights. The great majority of the population, however, including members of most of the important political parties and pressure groups, accepted the new government as a lesser evil than the chaotic situation during Goulart's term in office.

On July 22, 1964, the Congress approved a series of constitutional amendments intended to help create a viable government for Brazil. President Castelo Branco's term in office was extended until March 15, 1967, to enable the new system to be firmly established. The amendments had the same objective, to help create a government supported by a majority of the population and thus strong enough to be able to govern. The amendments provided that the president, vice-president, deputies, and senators would all be elected simultaneously; the presidential and vice-presidential terms were reduced from five years to four; the president and vice-president must be candidates of the same party and must receive a majority of the votes cast, or the Congress, by an absolute majority, would have to confirm the election of the candidates who had received a plurality; if the Congress failed to confirm their election, then a runoff election would be held in thirty days. Further "institutional acts" were pushed through the legislature in 1964, 1965, and 1966. The electoral system was reorganized. All the political parties were abolished and two new ones were set up, one supporting the government, the other opposing it. The relations between the states and the federal government were changed to make the central government the dominant force.

The measures taken by the military government were all intended to stop the inflationary spiral, further economic development, and create a viable and stable governmental system. Many of the incompetent, politically appointed civil servants were discharged and replaced by trained administrators and technicians. Almost all observers have been favorably impressed with the improvement in the efficiency of the government agencies. Seriousness and honesty seem to be the rule. The rate of inflation was slowed down by the austerity measures introduced, and by May 1967 the wholesale price index actually dropped 0.7 percent for the first decline in many years. Economic development continued and the development of the Amazon valley was pushed rapidly for the first time in the country's history. A drive was begun to diversify agriculture by paying selected farmers to destroy their coffee trees.

By 1966 it was clear that the dominance of the old aristocracy was doomed. The question to be answered was whether a viable political party system could be developed which would be able to articulate the demands of the new forces created by industrialization and urbanization. Labor unions were growing stronger and trying to assert their independence of the Ministry of Labor. Peasant leagues and various kinds of farm workers' organizations were developing in all parts of the country. The middle classes of the cities were becoming more vocal and better organized with each passing year.

Most observers thought the military men were doing rather well, but in 1965 the opposition, centered in the Social Democratic and Labor Parties, succeeded in electing the new governors of Minas Gerais and Guanabara. This upset the military officers, and again the constitution was changed, this time to make the next election of governors and the president indirect. Under the new rule, the electoral college selected General Artur da Costa e Silva as the new president on October 3, 1966, for a four-year term beginning March 15, 1967. When he took office, he appointed a cabinet which began to ease some of the restrictions of the previous government. At the same time, a new constitution went into effect which contained most of the changes the institutional acts had introduced.

Brazil thus began a new era in its development in 1967. Whether the events from 1964 to 1967 should be called a revolution or a counterrevolution cannot yet be determined. The changes during these years may enable the political machinery to meet the needs and demands of the ever increasing number of Brazilians; if it cannot, a real revolution may come.

The Formal Constitutional Framework

Brazil is governed under the constitution of March 15, 1967, which describes the United States of Brazil as a representative, federal republic in which all power emanates from the people and is exercised in their name. This is Brazil's sixth constitution, although only four of the six had any significance.

The 1967 constitution was produced by the military government, which thought that only a complete restructuring of the political machinery could bring Brazil stability. The previous constitution had made it almost impossible for a government to function effectively. Each of the branches of government had a different term in office. The president served for five years, the senators for eight years, the deputies for four years, and the Supreme Court justices for life. In addition, the president and the vice-president could be members of different parties. As the system operated from 1946 to 1964, no party, group, or individual ever was able to lead the government in formulating a consistent policy. The military leaders who wrote the new constitution, therefore, tried to include clauses to prevent future deadlocks.

Under the 1967 constitution, the president and vice-president are elected on a joint ticket by an electoral college composed of the national legislature and delegates elected by the state legislatures. The term in office is four years, the same as that for the Chamber of Deputies. A presidential candidate must get a majority vote in the electoral college or an additional vote is to be taken.

Although an attempt was made by the writers of the constitution to avoid some of the problems created by the 1946 constitution, it remains a rough copy of the United States presidential system. No attempt was made to create states capable of balancing each other in order to make federalism work, and the states as a group were not given the power to balance the power of the central government, which is clearly dominant.

The 1967 constitution is typical of Latin-American constitutions in that it is much too long, containing a great deal of detail that could have been omitted. Such controversial issues as the denial of divorce and such useless hopes as that the government will foster scientific and technological research are included in the document. It is difficult to forecast how long the constitution will endure, but it probably will be replaced by another when the military regime that sponsored it loses control of the government.

How the Constitution Is Amended

It is relatively easy to amend Brazil's constitution; all that is required is a vote by an absolute majority of the Congress in two sessions, the first vote to be taken within sixty days after the introduction of the proposed amendment. Amendments can be proposed by one-fourth of the members of the Chamber of Deputies, by one-fourth of the members of the Senate, by the president of the republic, or by a majority vote in more than half the state legislatures. No amendment can be considered to abolish federalism or the republican form of government, nor can the constitution be amended during the time the country is under a state of siege.

Who Participates in Politics

Until fairly recently, most Brazilians did not effectively participate in politics. The peculiar form of federalism that prevailed until 1930 was based upon a system of managed elections so that for all practical purposes the president was chosen by a caucus of the members of the Congress. This system prevented the growth of strong political parties capable of attracting the new groups that began to develop after the First World War. Under Vargas, the general public had little opportunity to participate in the country's political life. Even the labor movement, which Vargas helped to organize, was not an independent force, but only another group manipulated by the government.

After 1945, an attempt to govern Brazil democratically failed because the Brazilians did not have the social institutions a modern pluralistic society needs to organize and articulate group interests. In addition, the refusal to grant the vote to illiterates disfranchised more than half of the adult population. To vote one had to be literate, eighteen years or older, in possession of political rights, and able to speak Portuguese. The electoral law required registration of all voters except those over seventy years of age, invalids, those who were out of the country, and women who were not employed. All who registered were required to vote under penalty of a fine, but this regulation was never strictly enforced.

There was much sentiment for granting the vote to illiterates, and in 1964 illiterates were finally granted the right to vote in municipal elections. Many observers have pointed out that some of the illiterates had always voted. Professor Leslie Lipson quotes the *Corréio da Manhã* of May 1953 as giving the number of illiterates registered to vote as two million.[1] The denial of the vote to illiterates had many effects, one of which was to strengthen the power of the rural oligarchy. Since all representation in the Chamber of Deputies was based on population, those who did vote actually were selecting the representatives of those who did not vote. Illiteracy was always greater in the rural areas than in the urban areas, and the oligarchy preserved its power on the basis of the small vote in the rural areas.

A little less than half of the adult population participated in elections most of the time after 1945. By the 1960's, the higher literacy rate was being reflected in the number of voters. In 1945, 16.1 percent of the population was registered to vote and 13.4 percent actually voted. In the 1960 election, 21.9 percent of the population was registered to vote (15,543,332) and 17.7 percent voted. By 1966, nearly 23 million were registered, about 27 percent of the population. In the cities the proportion that votes is much higher than in the rural areas. Whether the efforts to create a more effective party system will bring the masses into active political participation cannot be forecast.

The Electoral System

One of the aims of the 1930 revolution was to win a reform in the electoral system, and this was reflected in the 1946 constitution, many of whose electoral provisions are continued in the 1967 document. In order to take the administration of elections out of partisan control and to create a system as fair as possible, control of all elections is given to a Supreme Electoral Tribunal (TSE). The TSE consists of seven persons. Two judges of the Supreme Court, two from the Federal Court of Appeals, and one from a Federal District court are elected by their fellow judges; the other two members are lawyers appointed by the president of the republic from a list of six who are nominated by the Supreme Court. The members of the TSE serve for two years and can be elected

---

[1] Leslie Lipson, "Government in Contemporary Brazil," *Canadian Journal of Economics and Political Science*, 22 (May 1956): 191.

for two consecutive terms. Alternates are elected at the same time and in the same way as the regular members.

The TSE supervises all matters concerning elections, and its decisions cannot be challenged in any other court except on grounds of alleged unconstitutionality or the denial of a writ of habeas corpus or writ of security, which can be appealed to the Supreme Court. The TSE has the power to register political parties and cancel their registration, to set up the electoral divisions of the country, to register the eligible voters, to fix the dates of elections when they are not already set by constitutional or legal provisions, and to handle all matters pertaining to nominations, qualifications of candidates, printing of ballots, counting votes, apportioning the seats in the proportional representation contests, ruling on charges of fraud, and issuing credentials to those elected.

Under the Supreme Electoral Tribunal there are regional electoral tribunals, one in each state capital and in the Federal District, and others in certain territorial capitals. The states and territories are divided into electoral districts, each containing a large number of polling places, under the supervision of an electoral judge. In each polling place a local judge is in charge of the election. The state, district, and local electoral tribunals are made up of both judges and laymen, all appointed in a manner similar to the method used in selecting members of the Supreme Electoral Tribunal.

All candidates for office must be nominated by a legally recognized political party. The cost of campaigning is so high in most areas that only the rich can participate. Until August 30, 1955, ballots were prepared by the political parties and the government provided official envelopes. In 1955 a single ballot prepared by the government was introduced for the offices of president and vice-president. In 1956 the single ballot was extended to include all other elective offices except those for the Chamber of Deputies and the state legislative assemblies. In 1962 it was extended to all federal and state offices in the states of São Paulo and Guanabara and in capitals of 100,000 or more population, and later was extended to all elections there. Even with the single ballot supplied by the government, the voter must write in the name or the number of his choice in the proportional election for the national Chamber of Deputies and for the state legislature. The introduction of a single official ballot for all elections throughout Brazil is being widely advocated.

Voters in Brazil register with the electoral judge of their locality at least thirty days before an election, and he assigns them to an electoral district, which contains from 50 to 400 electors. On election day a five-member board appointed by the electoral judge supervises the local election, assisted by two secretaries appointed by the president of the local board. Each of the registered parties can have one watcher at each polling place, who can, if he wishes to do so, accompany the ballot box to the regional electoral tribunal and watch the counting of the votes. Police are placed at the disposal of the board, but they remain 100 meters away from the polling place unless summoned by the board to keep order.

The polls are open from 8 A.M. to 5 P.M. on election day. Upon entering the polling place, the voter presents his registration certificate, signs his name in a register, receives an open envelope and a ballot, goes into a curtained booth, votes, puts the ballot in the envelope, and drops the envelope in the ballot box. The president of the local board then signs the voter's registration certificate as proof that he has voted. When the polls close, the president seals the ballot box and sends it together with the written comments of the party observers to the regional electoral tribunal, where the votes are counted. Brazil's size and poor communications system account for lengthy delays in reporting the results of elections, for it takes days for the ballot box to arrive at the regional electoral tribunal from some of the out-of-the-way places.

The only seriously undemocratic feature of the electoral system from 1945 to the 1960's was the disfranchisement of the illiterates. The only political group banned from the ballot was the Communist Party, which lost its registration in 1947 under the constitutional clause banning parties that advocate the overthrow of democratic government or function as agents of a foreign power. Much criticism was made of the high cost of campaigning, but this is a phenomenon of all mass societies, and not peculiar to Brazil. Most observers reported that the electoral system gave fair results, the only serious weakness being the controlled vote in certain isolated rural areas.

Under Castelo Branco's government, revisions were made in the system to improve its functioning. The new electoral system is intended to give the voter a meaningful choice when he votes, but it is impossible to say how the new system will work until it has been tried. The most controversial change was to make the election of the president and vice-president indirect.

Political Parties

Brazil's leaders were never able to construct a political party system capable of preserving the stability of the governmental institutions. During the years of the empire, the traditional Conservative and Liberal Parties so common in all parts of Latin America in the nineteenth century developed. Both parties represented the upper classes, the Conservative Party speaking primarily for the landowners of the north and the Liberal Party representing basically the commercial interests and the coffee growers and mine owners of the south. Neither survived the imperial system. After the Paraguayan War, a Republican Party developed, pushing for the institution of the republican form of government. Led by intellectuals and middle-class elements, the party prospered, and during the first decades of the republic it was Brazil's only party. Yet there was no real national party organization in Brazil. Rather, in each state the political leaders in power coordinated their efforts through an organization that had the name Republican in it. In Minas Gerais, it was the *Partido Republicano Mineiro*, in São Paulo the *Partido Republicano*. The president of the republic was able by his use of patronage to dominate all the state parties, since they were the mechanism through which the spoils of office were distributed.

All of these state parties disappeared during the fifteen years that Vargas governed Brazil. The only parties of importance during this period were the Communist and Fascist (Integralist), but Vargas smashed both of them in the late 1930's. Therefore, when free elections were finally announced in February 1945, it was necessary to begin organizing new political parties. As a result of the lack of experience with sound political parties, all those developed after 1945 were weak and torn by factionalism. None was a true national political party; all of them were coalitions of groups of politicians from the various states. None had a worked-out program to solve Brazil's problems; all kept splitting, forming alliances, reorganizing, and splitting again until it was almost impossible to keep track of all the groups calling themselves political parties. Many times a party would nominate or support the candidacy of individuals who were not members of the party.

Since no party was ever strong enough to win a national election, the custom developed of formal alliances between the parties, and this spread to the state and congressional level. Many times the alliances combined apparently contradictory groups, and it was common to see Party A combining in one state with Party B against Party C and Party D while in the next state Party D would combine with Party A to oppose the alliance of Parties B and C. Sometimes the struggle between the factions within a party would be more vicious than that between the parties. By the time of the 1962 election, four major and ten minor parties were active, thirteen legally registered and the Communist Party, which functioned through capturing local units of all the other parties. No one ever really had a majority and all governments were minority governments. Some of the election results were ridiculous. In São Paulo in the 1960's, for example, the 115-member state legislature was divided among the members of eleven parties, with the largest having thirteen seats and the smallest seven. After the 1962 election, the national Chamber of Deputies had members of thirteen different parties divided as follows: Social Democratic, 119; National Democratic Union, 97; Labor Party, 104; Social Progressive, 23; Republican, 10; Social Labor, 6; Liberator, 5; National Labor, 11; Republican Labor, 3; Brazilian Socialist, 5; Christian Democratic, 19; Popular Representation, 3; and Labor Renovation Movement, 4. It was, of course, impossible to obtain a firm majority with this kind of party lineup. Brazil is composed of various kinds of states and has a varied economy and great regional differences, but these splits were not on class lines or ideological lines or even, in many cases, on regional lines. Many of the differences were over personality and other unimportant details.

With the military dominating Brazil's government, all the political parties are passing through a period of crisis. One of the goals of the new electoral system introduced by the military was to force the creation of a strong two-party system. Toward that end the number of supporters a party had to have in order to be recognized was increased to 3 percent of the electorate. In addition, a party must have organized groups in at least one-fourth of the *municipios* in at least eleven states. And once recognized, a party must poll at least 3 percent of the votes cast in a national election or elect at least twelve federal deputies from at least seven states or lose its recognition.

Of the parties functioning after 1945, the strongest was the Social Democratic (PSD). The PSD was organized by Vargas when he was forced out of office in 1945 and it remained in power, usually in a coalition of some kind, from 1945 to 1964, except for the few months when Quadros was president. Despite its name, the PSD was a conservative group based on the remnants of the old state Republican Party machines, which Vargas had incorporated into his dictatorship. Basically, the PSD consisted of the "ins," traditional political leaders, rural landowners, and some of the urban businessmen. It was particularly strong in Minas Gerais. It had no formal membership or dues-collecting machinery, being financed by donations from industrialists, bankers, and landowners. It never had a definite program and seemed to be more interested in patronage than in policy. It contained a large number of factions.

The second largest party during most of the 1945–65 period was the Democratic National Union (UDN), founded by those who opposed Vargas as an all-inclusive force to get him out of office in 1945. After

losing three consecutive presidential elections, it supported Jânio
Quadros in 1960, to put into office the first real opposition candidate
ever to gain the presidency in Brazil. With a strong following among
the intellectuals, industrialists, and urban businessmen, the UDN was a
liberal party seeking more democratic government, industrial development, better education, and the other classic liberal aims. It was the
chief target of the Communists, who looked upon the UDN as their
worst enemy. It had many factions, and some of its members cooperated
with Vargas from 1950 to 1954, while others opposed him. Most of its supporters cooperated with the military in 1964 to expel Goulart from the
presidency.

The third most important party was the Labor Party (PTB), a
nationalistic organization created by Vargas as a personal political
machine based upon the government-controlled trade unions. Very similar to the original *Peronista* Party of Argentina, after Vargas' death the
party floundered, with labor leaders, Communists of several varieties, and
many demagogues and opportunists trying to capture it to advance their
political ambitions. It never was a true labor party; its strongest base was
in Rio Grande do Sul, an essentially rural state, and its outstanding
leader was João Goulart, a millionaire landowner. Through its connections with the Ministry of Labor, however, its leaders were able to
mobilize some urban support. Some observers in the early 1960's thought
it might become the spokesman for the urban poor, but it had not by
1964, when the military took over the government.

Of the minor parties, the largest was the Social Progressive Party
(PSP), formed in 1946 by the fusion of three small groups. The PSP was
basically the personal electoral machine of Adhemar de Barros, a rich
businessman who liked to be in politics but refused to subordinate himself to any political party. The PSP was strongest in São Paulo, where
Adhemar de Barros was twice elected governor, and in the northeast. Another important minor party was the Republican Party, which was
strongest in Minas Gerais and Bahia. This consisted primarily of those
of the old-time political leaders who did not enter the PSD or the UDN.
It was very nationalistic and favored free enterprise and a reduction of the
federal bureaucracy. The Liberator Party (PL) was the former state party
of Rio Grande do Sul. Controlled by the local aristocracy, through electoral deals with other local groups it managed to maintain sufficient
strength to stay on the ballot. It favored the parliamentary form of
government.

There were many groups using the name Labor, most of which had
split off from the PTB, including the National Labor Party (PTN), the

Republican Labor Party (PRT), the Social Labor Party (PST), and the Workers' Reform Movement (MTR). The Brazilian Socialist Party (PSB) was founded in 1946 by the unification of a socialist faction that split off from the UDN and a group of ex-Communists and ex-Trotskyites who had rallied around the publication *Vanguarda Socialista*. The PSB made some gains in the mid-1950's, when it helped to elect Jânio Quadros, a member of the Christian Democratic Party, as mayor of São Paulo and then as governor of the state. It supported democratic government and socialist reforms, but was squeezed between the Communists and the PTB. It won some support among trade unionists, but never became a major force. Francisco Julião, the leader of some of the northeastern peasant leagues, was a member of this party.

The Christian Democratic Party (PDC) was a Catholic party that failed to gain much support. Affiliated with the Union of Christian Democratic Parties of Europe and Latin America, it favored a liberal policy orientated to the social doctrines of the Catholic church.

The Popular Representative Party (PRP) was an extremely reactionary organization founded by Plinio Salgado, who formerly headed the Brazilian Fascist organization, the Integralists, which was important in the late 1930's. The PRP had only minor importance, devoting its efforts to propagandizing for "the sacred defense of Christ and the Fatherland," the corporate state and organic democracy. Its main strength was in southern Brazil; in the 1955 election it received 713,411 votes.

In a class by itself was the Brazilian Communist Party (PCB), one of the largest Communist parties in all America. Banned from the ballot in 1947, it had a field day after that as its members infiltrated practically all the other parties and the governmental services. It participated in elections by capturing the local machinery of other parties and by making deals with unscrupulous politicians. Greatly aided by the misery and poverty of so many of the Brazilians, which it was able to exploit demagogically, it carried on an extensive propaganda campaign and operated hundreds of front organizations and published a large number of newspapers and other periodicals. The military-dominated government of General Castelo Branco tried to destroy the Communist Party, with what success it is impossible to tell.

Brazil had far too many parties, of course, which reflected the unintegrated and varied character of its population. General Castelo Branco tried to unify the parties by his new electoral code and forced the amalgamation of all the members of the legislature into two groups, which became the basis for a new party system. The government supporters became the National Renovating Alliance (*Arena*) and the opposition took the name Brazilian Democratic Movement (MDB). *Arena* included most of the UDN and PSD, and many of the members of the minor parties. In 1966 it had within its ranks all of the country's governors, a majority of the members of the national Congress, and a majority of the members of all state legislatures except that of Guanabara. The president of *Arena* was Senator Daniel Krieger, a former member of the UDN.

The MDB included most of the old Labor Party, a minority of the PSD, some of the Christian Democrats, and members of all the other parties including the UDN. Its national president was Senator Oscar Passos, a former leader of the PTB. Both MDB and *Arena* are temporary unifications of the supporters and opponents of the government and it is impossible to forecast their future. Efforts are being made to reconstitute the UDN, the PSD, the PTB, and the PDC, but the success of these efforts depends upon how well the new two-party system functions.

Pressure Groups and Public Opinion

With the multiparty system in use from 1945 to 1964, the dynamic element in political life was provided by two traditional forces, personality and pressure groups. Of the two, probably because of the great size of the country, the pressure groups were the most important. The roles played by individuals such as Vargas, Quadros, La Cerda, and Goulart testify to the importance of the dazzling personality. The high illiteracy rate tended to allow public opinion to be dominated by the educated and well-to-do. Radio seemed to reach more people than newspapers, and television was becoming important in the largest cities. About 1,200 newspapers are published in Brazil, of which about 250 are dailies. The Monday *O Globo* of Rio de Janeiro is believed to have the largest circulation of a daily, 293,250, but the average for the largest dailies is only between 100,000 and 200,000. About thirty-seven important magazines are issued regularly, the most important being *O Cruzeiro* of Rio de Janeiro, which has the highest circulation of any magazine published in Latin America, about 600,000 in Brazil and 250,000 copies in a Spanish edition.

The most important groups exercising an influence in political life are the armed forces, the aristocracy of wealth, and the Catholic church. The officers of the armed forces play a peculiar role in Brazil because, despite their great power, until 1964 they never themselves took control of the government machinery. They tended to act as a sort of court of last resort, as the group that decided what should be done during moments of crisis. It was the officers of the armed forces who instituted the republic in 1889, helped destroy the first republic and put Getulio Vargas in as president in 1930, expelled Vargas from office in 1945 and again in 1954, insisted that a parliamentary system be introduced in 1961, and expelled Goulart from office in 1964. Some observers believe that the officer corps tends to favor democracy because it consists in large part of persons who come from Rio Grando do Sul and the northeastern states, that is, the smaller states and those that are less well developed economically. The large states of São Paulo and Minas Gerais are less well represented, apparently because boys from these states have more economic opportunities open to them.

Professor Robert Alexander goes so far as to suggest that the younger army officers since the First World War have represented a definite ideological current that resembles the *Aprista*-type political parties in other Latin-American republics. He names this movement *tenentismo*, and argues that it almost did become a political party and has played a significant role in politics since the 1920's.[2] What can be said is that throughout the history of the republic the armed forces have played an important role and few political leaders have tried to oppose the wishes of the leading officers. Since 1964 a high army officer has been the president of Brazil as the military has tried to reorganize the political and economic machinery of the country. In recent years the officers have seemed to be divided into two main groups. The hard-liners want the military to run the government indefinitely, while the soft-liners want to return the country to constitutional government with competitive political parties. The military club in Rio de Janeiro is an important center for military men, and elections for officers of the club are important indicators of the strength of the various military factions. Out of the 2.5 million boys who reach eighteen each year, about 100,000 are drafted into the armed forces. The total manpower during recent years has been about 200,000. The armed forces receive a substantial portion of the annual budget and will probably remain one of the most important groups in Brazilian society in the foreseeable future.

Church and state have been separated since 1891 and religious tolerance has prevailed, but the Catholic church is by far the strongest religious organization in the country. It has never too openly interfered in politics, but divorce is unobtainable in Brazil and on many issues the Catholic church can prevent any action it opposes. Catholic priests are active in politics and have been elected deputies and senators on all of the important party tickets. The Catholic church has created a series of or-

---

[2] Robert J. Alexander, "Brazilian Tenentismo," *Hispanic American Historical Review*, 36 (May 1956): 229–42.

ganizations through which it can influence public opinion, including labor unions, peasant leagues, student groups, businessmen's associations, and Catholic action groups. The Family Electoral Alliance was particularly active in endorsing candidates for office on the basis of their attitude toward the Catholic church.

The traditional landowning aristocracy based on the fortunes made in past centuries has slowly been losing its dominant position to the new urban rich who derive their wealth from banking and industry, but at the same time the traditional values of the old Brazilian upper class seem to be accepted by the new rich. Although Brazil continues to be a highly stratified society, the most aggressive, intelligent, and well educated, no matter what their background, are able to enter the topmost strata of Brazil's power structure. Ex-President Juscelino Kubitschek and the Klabin and Matarazzo families are good examples. The upper class has lost some of its power, but it still is one of the dominant groups in Brazil. The rich operate through all kinds of interest groups, including the National Confederation of Industries, the National Confederation of Commerce, state federations of industry and commerce, the Brazilian Rural Confederation, and many specialized groups. In many cases the upper classes are able to affect policy by having representation on the semiautonomous government agencies, such as the Brazilian Coffee Institute and the Social Service Syndicate Fund.

A middle class has developed rapidly in Brazil during recent decades, consisting of government employees, white-collar workers in commerce, and professionals. This group has not yet been organized well enough to enable it to have an important voice in affairs, but it is increasingly making itself heard. Much of the push to improve education comes from the middle class, which would like its children to have the opportunity to develop into professionals. Since only literates vote, the educated middle class represents an important proportion of the votes cast in elections, and the university students, most of whom come from this class, have played an increasingly important role as the formulators of radical demands upon the government.

Labor is comparatively weak in Brazil, primarily because the Vargas regime in the 1930's set up a system that for all practical purposes made the organized labor movement a branch of the Ministry of Labor. As a result, of the 17,117,362 gainfully employed listed in the 1950 census, not more than 3 to 4 million were claimed as members by the functioning trade unions, and the actual number of members was probably less. The unions have little scope for independent activity because the government dominates the workers' relations with the employers through a compli-cated system of paternalistic legislation.

Probably most unwise is the law under which all employed persons, whether members of trade unions or not, pay a "syndical tax" which amounts to one day's pay each year for every worker except those in agri-culture, the government, and domestic service. This tax is deducted from a worker's wages and paid by his employer to the Bank of Brazil, which pays 60 percent to a local union, 15 percent to a federation of unions, 5 percent to a national confederation, and 20 percent to the Social Service Syndicate Fund, which is controlled by a commission with representa-tives from the government, employers, workers, and professionals. Only one union is permitted to function in each occupational class, and no union can function unless it is recognized by the Ministry of Labor. Thus the Ministry of Labor has effective control over all unions, as it can cut off a union's income by withdrawing recognition. In addition, since all workers must pay the syndical tax, most fail to join unions, and many who do refuse to pay dues, since they consider that they are already paying dues with their syndical tax.

In the early 1960's the National Confederation of Industrial Work-ers, with about 2 million members, was the largest confederation in Brazil. The National Confederation of Commercial Workers claimed 1.2 million members, the National Confederation of Land Transport Work-ers 500,000. All three were affiliated with the ORIT and the Interna-tional Confederation of Free Trade Unions, but the law did not permit the creation of a single national united trade-union organization. The close connection between the Ministry of Labor and the unions enabled Vargas and after him Goulart to utilize workers as the base for their power. Yet no really healthy trade-union movement ever developed, and it probably will not until workers are free to organize outside of the pa-ternalistic network of laws designed by Vargas and Goulart. In the 1960's Catholic trade unions were organized to add another element to the struggle, and the Communists, the Catholics, the followers of Vargas and Goulart, and the officials of the Ministry of Labor all competed to control the trade unions, each group for its own purpose.

The rural population, except for the large landowners, has never had much to say in the formulation of public policy. It was not until 1963 that rural workers were given the legal right to organize unions and that the benefits of the existing labor legislation were extended to rural labor. There are many different types of farm workers, ranging from the paid worker on the industrialized coffee and sugar plantations to the cowboy

and the subsistence farmer who clears the land by burning and scratches
out a living with a hoe. A high proportion of the rural population is illiterate and has no access to such amenities as schools and public health
centers. In recent years, attempts have been made to organize peasant
leagues by the Catholic church, Communists, intellectuals, and labor
leaders, and the leagues have attracted much attention as a potential
force for a Castro-type revolution, but basically the rural population has
little political effectiveness. The extreme concentration of landownership, with perhaps 15 percent of the landowners controlling about 85 percent of the registered landholdings, tends to keep the rural worker in a
subordinate condition.

Civil Liberties

The Brazilian constitution guarantees all of the civil liberties its writers
could think of: those typical of the last century, taken from the 1891 constitution, and the newer social rights so popular in this century, taken
from the 1934 document. Nevertheless, the president can declare a state
of siege for sixty days when faced with grave disturbance or the menace of
grave disturbance, or in case of war. Under a state of siege the executive has the powers, among others, to arrest, hold, and banish persons; to
censor correspondence and news media of all kinds; to suspend freedom
of assembly; to search private homes; and to intervene in public service
enterprises.

Civil liberties, however, are generally respected, particularly in
the cities. There is no death penalty except under military law during
time of war with a foreign country. Even the Communists, although their
party cannot participate in elections under its own name, have functioned
freely most of the time, and until 1964 hundreds of Communist periodicals were published. Speech, the press, radio, and television were all free
from interference from 1945 to 1964, and the average Brazilian felt free
to do and say what he pleased. The institutional act of 1964 allowed the
new government to jail many suspected or actual Communists and to
take away the political rights of many, including some of the leading political figures of the postwar period. The military did about as it pleased
until 1967. It is impossible to forecast what will happen under General
Costa e Silva's new constitutional government.

The Executive

The Brazilian executive is a president who serves for a four-year term and
may not be immediately reelected. From 1945 to 1964 the presidential

term had been five years. Under the 1946 constitution, the president was elected by direct vote. Much of the political turmoil of the 1950's and early 1960's was caused by the fact that a president did not need a majority of the votes to be elected, and that the vice-president did not have to be elected from the same party as the president. The Castelo Branco government, by decree, had the president and vice-president elected by the Congress in 1966, and the new constitution instituted a system of presidential election under which presidents are elected by a special electoral college, which is composed of all members of the Congress plus a group of special delegates selected by the state legislatures. Each state names at least three members of the electoral college; states with more than 500,000 registered voters name an extra member. The candidates for the presidency must be nominated by a registered political party and receive an absolute majority of the electoral-college vote, unless no candidate receives a majority in two ballots; in that case, whoever receives the highest vote on the third ballot is declared elected. President and vice-president are to be elected on a party ticket.

Since 1946 the president has been an extremely strong executive and the 1967 constitution extends his powers, especially by giving him exclusive initiative in the introduction of legislation pertaining to public finance and national security. The constitutional grant of power is very broad, including the powers of declaring a state of siege and intervening in the states. In addition, the president can issue decrees and regulations which for all practical purposes are new laws. The president controls the bureaucracy and has extensive appointive and removal power. His power of item veto strengthens him in relation to the Congress, which needs a two-thirds majority to override his vetoes.

The size of the country has helped to prevent any real personal dictatorship, and the president is limited in various ways in what he can do. The Congress may reject the legislation and many of the appointments he suggests, and can impeach the president. The Supreme Court can declare the president's decrees and actions unconstitutional. The armed forces are a powerful check upon the president, even though he is the commander in chief.

Nevertheless, the president remains the key figure in Brazilian government. During the years after 1930, his office has been strengthened by the creation of various administrative commissions and boards which advise the president, coordinate matters, help keep the president in touch with affairs, and study broad policy questions. The members of a cabinet of sixteen act as advisers to the president and administer the work of the government. One of the weaknesses of the executive in Brazil has been the proliferation of specialized administrative agencies, advisory boards, foundations, autonomous bodies, and mixed corporations. It is estimated that in addition to the agencies in the president's office and the sixteen ministries, there are about thirty organizations of various kinds directly responsible to the president, including such agencies as the General Staff of the Armed Forces; the Administrative Department of the Public Service (DASP), an extremely complicated organization which supervises the civil service and has certain budgetary controls; the National Security Council; the Development Council; the Tariff Commission; and various regional organizations such as Sudene, the body that is trying to develop the northeastern part of the country. About forty other organizations are connected with the president or are supposed to be coordinated by his office or that of a minister, including the Bank of Brazil, the government monopolies such as Petrobas, the petroleum monopoly, and many others. The new constitution apparently strengthens the office of the president, but only time will tell how these new provisions will work out.

Most scholars have commented about the size of the bureaucracy, its inefficiency, the graft that permeates many agencies, and the lack of clear lines of authority and responsibility. Many of the ministers, directors, and the president are so involved with administrative details that they cannot devote time to the larger problems of coordination and planning. In addition, since most government employees were appointed on a patronage or family basis, inefficiency has been notorious. A centuries-old tradition against delegating authority causes delay, and the habit of putting everything in writing creates a constant stream of papers, all of which require signatures and stamps. In 1962 there were about 500,000 jobs grouped into 3,000 classes in the federal civil service which were supposed to be filled by merit examinations, but only about 12 percent were filled in this way. The basic legislation on the merit system was introduced during the Vargas era, and the opponents of Vargas oppose the whole idea on the principle that no system of Vargas' can be very good. The DASP possesses legal responsibility in the areas of the budget, organization and management, personnel, training, and the control of public buildings, but in practice it does whatever the incumbent president wants it to do, and none from 1945 to 1964 tried to strengthen the civil service system. Some studies seem to demonstrate that in each agency a "workhorse" group seems to do the work and the rest of the employees just get in the way or take up space. All supervision is political, and many supervisors, to make their jobs secure, insist on signing all papers and keeping information to themselves, so no one else knows what is going on.

Since 1936, when the Federal Council of the Civil Public Service was set up, many attempts have been made to develop a modern administrative system, but not much has been achieved. A Brazilian School of Public Administration is functioning with assistance from such organizations as the United Nations and the United States AID. In the 1960's the University of Southern California School of Public Administration sent a group of public administration specialists to Brazil under an AID contract to advise in this field. The problem of improving the public service is very serious, for in 1958 there were 1,194,858 government employees: 246,852 in the federal government, 317,867 employees of the states, 185,632 municipal employees, 179,762 employees of the national government corporations, 247,528 in national defense and public security, and 17,217 miscellaneous. Perhaps 50 percent of the budget goes to personnel, and all observers comment on the favoritism, nepotism, patronage, lax discipline, and thievery. It is too soon to say whether the efforts of Presidents Castelo Branco and Costa e Silva to improve the system will have permanent effects, although most observers have been favorably impressed with the results of their reforms in the public administration.

Public Finance

Brazil's budget is compiled by a budget commission located in the Ministry of Finance. It is presented to the Congress by the president and must be adopted within four months. If the Congress fails to act by the deadline, the budget as presented automatically becomes law. The fantastic inflation that Brazil has suffered during recent years makes deficit financing common. The inflation has been speeded by the issuance of treasury bonds or new paper money to meet government deficits. Thus the cruzeiro, Brazil's monetary unit, went from 19 to the United States dollar in 1945 to 1,850 to the dollar in June 1965. By late 1965 it was around 2,250 to the dollar when the government issued a new monetary unit, the new cruzeiro, to try to control the inflation.

Naturally, the total budget has risen astronomically as a result of the inflation. From about 179.5 billion cruzeiros in 1960, the total budget receipts reached the amount of more than 4.678 trillion cruzeiros by 1966. The budget for 1966, shown in Tables 1 and 2, is typical of Brazilian budgets during recent years. As the figures demonstrate, Brazil receives too large a portion of its income from indirect taxes, which fall most heavily upon the poor. It receives 23.51 percent of its income from income taxes. Until 1964 there was much dissatisfaction with the income-tax laws, and evasion of payment was widespread. One of the achieve-

TABLE 1

ESTIMATED REVENUE OF BRAZIL, 1966

(000,000 Omitted)

Source	Amount in Cruzeiros	Percent of Total
Taxes		
On imports	Cr$357,986	7.65%
On consumption	1,895,000	40.50
On income (of persons and corporations)	1,100,000	23.51
On stamps, etc.	457,200	9.77
On electricity	183,000	3.91
On minerals	2,437	.05
On rural land	2,700	.06
Miscellaneous	19,477	.42
Governmental property	36,065	.77
Governmental industry	36,648	.78
Miscellaneous income	290,000	6.20
Receipts of capital (loans)	298,394	6.38
Total	Cr$4,678,907	100.00%

ments of the military government was to increase the collection of these taxes. The rates go from 3 percent on annual incomes of 2,131 new cruzeiros to 50 percent on all income above 68,160 new cruzeiros. There is a withholding tax on wages and salaries. The expenditures reflect many of the reasons for Brazil's problems. Only 9.69 percent of the expenditures in 1966 went for education and culture, but 21.40 percent went for the armed forces.

The Legislative Power

Brazil's legislature is a Congress consisting of a 66-member Senate and a 409-member Chamber of Deputies. Each state has three senators. Deputies are allotted to the states in accordance with their population, one deputy for each 300,000 inhabitants, but each state has a minimum of seven deputies. Each territory has a minimum of one deputy. Those states with populations greater than 7.5 million receive another deputy for each million persons over that amount. This method of apportionment means that the smaller, least populated states are always overrepresented. Some scholars attribute much of the turmoil of the 1950's and 1960's to the unrepresentative character of the legislature, which tended

TABLE 2

ESTIMATED EXPENDITURES OF BRAZIL, 1966

(000,000 Omitted)

	Amount in Cruzeiros	Percent of Total
Legislature		
Chamber of Deputies	Cr$37,544	0.80%
Senate	18,770	0.39
Tribunal of Accounts	5,356	0.11
National Economic Council	879	0.02
Executive		
President	408,429	8.70
Administrative Department of Public Service (DASP)	5,700	0.12
General Staff of Armed Forces	5,333	0.11
Ministry of the Air Force	269,765	5.72
Ministry of Agriculture	177,338	3.76
Ministry of Education and Culture	457,432	9.69
Ministry of Finance	793,381	16.80
Ministry of the Army	500,195	10.60
Ministry of Industry and Commerce	10,136	0.21
Ministry of Justice	110,147	2.33
Ministry of the Navy	234,700	4.97
Ministry of Mines and Electricity	337,483	7.15
Ministry of Foreign Relations	94,069	1.99
Ministry of Health	202,604	4.29
Ministry of Labor and Social Security	63,035	1.34
Ministry of Roads and Public Works	939,158	19.90
Judiciary	47,631	1.00
Total	Cr$4,719,085	100.00%

to become a bulwark of the status quo. The Congress reallocates the seats after each census.[3]

One-third of the senators are elected one year and two-thirds four years later, all for eight-year terms. Deputies are elected by a complicated system of proportional representation for four-year terms. Under the sys-

[3] The division of seats in the 1960's was Acre 7, Alagôas 9, Amazonas 7, Bahia 31, Ceará 21, Espírito Santo 8, Goiás 13, Guanabara 21, Maranhão 16, Mato Grosso 8, Minas Gerais 48, Pará 10, Paraíba 13, Paraná 25, Pernambuco 24, Piauí 8, Rio de Janeiro 21, Rio Grande do Norte 7, Rio Grande do Sul 29, Santa Catarina 14, São Paulo 59, Sergipe 7, and the territories of Amapá, Roraima and Rondônia one each. Under the provisions of the 1967 constitution the total membership of the Chamber will probably decrease by at least 100 members the next time a census is taken and seats are redistributed. The figures above are based on the provisions of the 1946 constitution, which provided one member for each 150,000 persons, with the same minimum of seven for each state.

tem introduced by Castelo Branco, all elections for the legislature and
the presidency will be held at the same time, every four years. Both deputies and senators can be reelected. Alternates are elected at the same time
as the regular members to take their places in case of need.

All Brazilians in possession of their political rights are eligible to be
members of the national Congress. Deputies must be over twenty-one
years of age, senators over thirty-five. To prevent conflict of interest, constitutional rules ban congressmen from taking other positions in the
government, either appointive or elective, on the national, state, or municipal level, except that congressmen may serve as members of the president's cabinet, secretaries of state, interventors, or *prefeito* of the national
capital. In addition, congressmen cannot be the owners, directors, or employees of enterprises negotiating contracts with the government. If a
member of the Congress is absent from more than half the sessions of his
house without permission, he can lose his seat. The Congress meets in the
capital at Brasília from March 1 to June 30 and from August 1 to November 30 each year, and in special session upon the call of the president
of the republic or of one-third of the membership of either chamber.

Although the 1946 constitution gave Brazil's national Congress a
great deal of power, it was not able to exercise that power effectively.
Some scholars think this was because the weighted system of representation in the Chamber combined with equal representation in the Senate
to give the less populous and underdeveloped states too much representation. In addition, since all representation in the Chamber of Deputies
was based on population, but only the literate were supposed to vote,
the deputies from underdeveloped states always represented oligarchic
interests rather than a majority of their states' people, who had no vote,
while the representatives of the areas with high literacy (São Paulo, Rio
de Janeiro, etc.) were responsible to most of their population but were
relatively underrepresented in the Chamber. This is not to say that the
legislature was the puppet of the executive, but rather that the legislature did not exercise the full powers it had. Some observers think this
was because no party ever was able to elect a majority of the membership
and it proved to be impossible to organize the legislature effectively for
serious action. This was clearly demonstrated during the parliamentary
period from 1961 to 1963, when the "powerless" president was able to
dominate the "all-powerful" legislature. It was seen again after Goulart's
ouster, when the new executive was able to obtain consent to its new
"institutional acts" although the majority of the members of the legislature probably were opposed to their adoption. The constitution requires
that all congressional committees be set up on a basis of proportional

representation, and this further tends to prevent the emergence of a solid majority in control of either house. If the two-party system becomes accepted this will change, but it is impossible to forecast the future of the party system.

Congress is thus primarily a sounding board for the members, some kind of limited check upon the executive, and a forum for debate rather than the ultimate formulator of public policy. The legislature was made even weaker than it had been by the 1967 constitution. The most important change was to put a time limit of forty-five days upon each house for the consideration of bills submitted by the president of the republic. If after ninety days the proposed bill has not been acted upon, then it automatically becomes law as submitted by the president. At the same time, the allotment of seats was changed by doubling the number of people represented by each deputy. Under the new constitutional provisions the ministers of state have the power of participating in the committees and meetings of the Congress at any time to debate and defend bills concerning their ministries.

The new powers given to the president under the constitution of 1967 allow him to recess the Congress whenever they disagree, and this was done in 1966 when a dispute arose between the Congress and President Castelo Branco. Under the new constitution the president is clearly the dominant figure and the Congress has become a very weak check upon what he can do.

The Judicial Power

Since Brazil had courts before its present governmental system was created, it simply incorporated them into the republican constitutional system. Thus, ordinarily all cases begin in the lowest state court and then progress upward to the highest state court. Then if there is any federal or constitutional question involved, the case can be appealed to the Federal Court of Appeals, from which it can go to the Supreme Court, if necessary. The Supreme Court consists of sixteen justices appointed by the president with the consent of the Senate. The president appoints all other federal judges in the same way. The judges of the state courts, by constitutional provision, secure their positions by examination. All judges have life tenure upon good behavior, but must resign at seventy or upon proven disability. All judges can, of course, be impeached by the corresponding legislature.

In addition to the regular court system, special courts have been created to handle military, electoral, and labor matters, but all these

are federal courts. Brazil's courts have the constitutional power of judicial review and have exercised it to check the legislative and executive
powers.

Brazilian Federalism

Brazil's constitution sets up a federal republic which today consists of
twenty-two states, three territories, and a federal district in which the
national capital, Brasília, is located. Although federalism has been a
feature of Brazil's constitutional system since 1889, the system never
worked properly, and much of the political struggle has revolved around
what the relation of the states and the central government ought to be.
Federalism in Brazil does not work well because most of the states are
not viable political units. As a result, the political leaders from São
Paulo, Minas Gerais, and one or two other states have been able to
dominate the national government. In the 1960's, for example, the state
of São Paulo contained 18.28 percent of the country's population and
only 2.91 percent of the total area, yet its people paid about 41 percent of
the total income tax collected and cast 25 percent of all votes in national
elections. Most states had to depend upon grants in aid from the central
government, which supplied patronage and finances. The central government needs the political support of the state officials and thus the
states become building blocks which are used to build up national
power.

Some observers have described Brazil as a country dominated by
its south, with the north and west in the position of colonies. This is an
extreme statement, but it is impossible to consider the twenty-two states
as equals. In the presidential elections of 1945, 1950, 1955, and 1960,
from 50 to nearly 60 percent of the votes were cast in only four states:
São Paulo, Minas Gerais, Guanabara, and Rio Grande do Sul. And of
the presidents elected, Vargas came from Rio Grande do Sul, Kubitschek
from Minas Gerais, Quadros from São Paulo. All were former governors
of their states. (General Dutra's geographical origins, of course, were of
no consequence.)

Many efforts have been made to overcome the imbalance between
the states, but none has worked. Since 1946 there has been an effort to
build up the underdeveloped areas of the country by means of regional
organizations. These include the Amazon Valley Authority, the Northeast Development Agency, the Tocantins-Araguaía Valley Authority,
the San Francisco Valley Commission, and the Economic Development
Agency for the Southwest Frontier.

The constitutional division of powers between the national and state governments gives the national government control over national security, foreign and interstate commerce, the currency, and the postal service. In addition, the national government has the sole right to legislate in the fields of civil, commercial, penal, electoral, aviation, and labor law. It also regulates the practice of the technical and liberal professions, operates the ports, and has the power to expropriate property.

There is not much left for the states, even though they do have the residual powers, for there is little the federal government does not do. The most populous states have managed to develop activities and build up their power, but most of the Brazilian states are dependent upon the federal government. It is not to be wondered at that Brazil's states have difficulty; the same is true in the United States, Canada, and all other federal systems. Yet the extreme powers granted the federal government in Brazil, including the right to intervene in the states, makes them very weak partners in the Brazilian federation. In addition, the constitutional division of powers can be changed by the national Congress, thus negating one of the basic requirements of federalism.

The Structure of the States

Each Brazilian state sets up its constitution and governmental machinery, but all are roughly similar to those of the national government. The executive is a governor elected by a direct secret vote for four years. The legislature is a unicameral body elected by proportional representation for four years. Generally, the states exercise only such powers as the national government has failed to utilize, including the regulation of public safety, welfare, sanitation, local justice, and education. The states are further hindered by their weak financial position, and except for São Paulo and one or two others, all are dependent upon national grants in aid, which give the federal government much control over their actions. The federal territories are directly administered by the national government. They have little importance, as all are very lightly populated. The Federal District is administered by a *prefeito* appointed by the president with Senate approval and a council elected for a four-year term.

The Municipalities

For purposes of local government, all states and territories are divided into municipalities (*municipios*), which are roughly the equivalent of United States counties, containing both rural and urban areas. In 1960 there were 3,112 municipalities. The national constitution establishes the principle that municipalities shall be autonomous, and this is repeated in all state constitutions. The national government has the constitutional power to intervene in any state that abrogates the autonomy of the municipality.

In all Brazilian states, the municipal government resembles the strong mayor-council system in the United States. The voters elect a *prefeito*, who resembles a mayor in the United States, and a council (*câmara de vereadores*) of from five to fifty members. The council is elected for a four-year term by the list system of proportional representation, with one *vereador* for each 2,000 inhabitants, and has the power to legislate on all matters of purely local interest. It thus deals with such subjects as taxes, fees and fines, city planning, zoning and building inspection, streets and parks, water supply, sewers, garbage, public markets, hours of business for commercial establishments, and public utilities. The municipal councils also are responsible for certain aspects of education, public health, sanitation, and social services in cooperation with the federal and state governments. The councils have limited police power. They exercise some control over the *prefeitos* and provide certain services for the rural sections of their areas.

The *prefeito* is the titular head of the municipality. He appoints employees, makes up the budget, and has a veto over the decisions of the council. The municipal government has its seat in one of the urban areas within the municipality. The municipality is further divided into districts (*distritos de paz*), which center around population nuclei other than that in which the municipal government is located. Each district is headed by an elected *vice-prefeito* who is responsible to the *prefeito*. Towns and cities are not themselves incorporated, the municipality being the effective unit of local government.

Both the national and state governments exercise controls over the municipalities. On the national level, the control is primarily financial, as the national government makes grants for various purposes to the municipalities. The states make various rules that the municipalities must observe, and in some states the state auditors check the municipalities' financial records. Some states have set up departments of municipal affairs which aid the municipalities with various kinds of technical services, such as training personnel or lending road-construction equipment.

In the territories, municipal government is provided by *prefeitos* appointed by the territorial governor. The tendency during recent decades has been to centralize most activity in the national government at the same time that efforts have been made to expand the functions and scope of municipal government. The nature of the relations between federal, state, and municipal governments is very complex and varies greatly depending upon the level of development of the state and the municipality. The mass illiteracy and poor transportation system in vast areas create a situation in which most of the rural municipalities are dominated by the local agricultural oligarchy. This is in great part a heritage of colonial days, when slavery created a powerful aristocracy that grew accustomed to ordering the lives of lesser folk.

Brazil: A Last Word

In 1967 Brazil began a new attempt to operate constitutional political machinery, but many scholars were skeptical that this attempt would be any more successful than the previous ones. Brazil's fundamental problem is that it is not an integrated nation-state. In many ways it resembles France, for, like the French, the Brazilians have never been able to agree on the kind of political system the country ought to have. Thus the symbols of constitutional and democratic government were adopted, but not the reality. Perhaps, as some scholars have suggested, the unintegrated character of the society has continued for so long that the culture has come to include a tolerance for chaos, which permits life to go on with little change even when the government ceases functioning.

Brazil's people have one very admirable characteristic: an ability to compromise. Despite the six constitutions, military interventions in government, terrible inflation, and abject poverty of so many Brazilians, no serious civil war has ever taken place, and very few Brazilians have been killed in political struggles. At the same time, the fantastic contrasts between the rich and the poor, the north and the south, the urban and the rural have prevented the development of any real concensus. Regionalism remains a strong factor. With the population about half rural and half urban, apparently no advances will be made until the processes of urbanization and industrialization have proceeded further.

Brazil seems to demonstrate that urbanization and industrialization do stimulate changes within a political system, but in Brazil, as economic development spurred the growth of new groups within the society, the archaic electoral system prevented the democratization of the government. At the same time, the size of the country, the vast differences between its parts, and the poor communication and transportation systems prevented any one political party or group of any other kind from setting up a dictatorship or gaining the support of a majority of the population, or even of all who voted. Thus every president of Brazil represented a minority, and the Congress represented a series of minorities whose interests were balanced during the legislative struggle. In this situation, the officers of the armed forces came to consider themselves the only representatives of the country as a whole. Whenever a deadlock arose in the government, the military intervened to enforce a solution.

Political development is so difficult to foster that it is impossible to forecast the future of Brazil. Some observers even doubt that the money spent to create Brasília was a wise investment. The economic heart of Brazil remains the São Paulo–Minas Gerais–Rio de Janeiro triangle. Putting the political center of the country in an undeveloped, primitive wilderness brought some development to the jungles of Goiás, but it will be decades before the investment in Brasília will begin to bring returns. If the millions poured into Brazília had been spent instead for education, roads, public health, and/or agrarian reform, greater results probably would have been achieved more quickly.

Brazil needs to continue its industrialization, develop its untapped resources, reform its agricultural system, knit its vast area together with railroads and highways, improve public health, and educate its illiterates. All of these things will cost vast sums of money and require an effective public administration to plan and execute the programs. Whether Brazil can raise the money and develop the administrative machinery needed, only time will tell. The country has the resources, both natural and human, and judging from the country's course since independence, the political development probably will come.

SELECTED READINGS

ALEXANDER, ROBERT J. "An Interpretation of Brazilian Politics." *Social Sciences* 26 (October 1951): 202–14.
————. "Brazil," *Labor Relations in Argentina, Brazil and Chile*, pp. 25–136. New York: McGraw-Hill Book Co., 1962.
————. "Brazilian Tenentismo." *Hispanic American Historical Review* 36 (May 1956): 229–42.
————. "Luis Carlos Prestes and the Partido Communista do Brasil," *Communism in Latin America*, pp. 93–134. New Brunswick, N.J.: Rutgers University Press, 1957.
————. "The Organized Workers in Brazil," *Organized Labor in Latin America*. New York: Free Press, 1965.
AN AMERICAN IN BRAZIL. "President João Goulart and Brazil." *Antioch Review* 23 (Fall 1963): 313–30.
ARINOS DE MELLO FRANCO, AFONSO. "The Tide of Government from Colony to Constitutional Democracy." *Atlantic* 197 (February 1956): 152–56.

————. *Curso de diréito constitucionál brasiléiro.* Rio de Janeiro: Revista Forense, 1958.

AZEVEDO, FERNANDO DE. *Brazilian Culture.* New York: Macmillan Co., 1950.

BISHOP, ELIZABETH, and the editors of *Life. Brazil.* New York: Time, Inc., 1962.

BONILLA, FRANK. "A National Ideology for Development: Brazil." In *Expectant Peoples: Nationalism and Development,* edited by K. H. Silvert. New York: Random House, 1963.

"Brazil: Economic Problems and Political Solutions." *World Today* 19 (November 1963): 476–84.

BUSEY, JAMES L. "Brazil's Reputation for Political Stability." *Western Political Quarterly* 18 (December 1965): 866–80.

CARVALHO, ORLANDO M. *A Crise dos partidos nacionais.* Belo Horizonte: Kriterion, 1950.

COMACHO, J. A. *Brazil: An Interim Assessment.* New York: Royal Institute of International Affairs, 1962.

COSTA PINTO, L. A. "Economic Development in Brazil; Its Sociological Implications." *International Social Science Journal* 11 (1959): 589–97.

DALAND, ROBERT T., ed. *Perspectives of Brazilian Public Administration.* In John W. Donner Memorial Publication Fund publication no. 26. Los Angeles: University of Southern California at Los Angeles, 1963.

DAUGHERTY, CHARLES; ROWE, JAMES; and SCHNEIDER, RONALD, eds. *Brazil Election Factbook Number 2, September, 1965.* Washington: Institute for the Comparative Study of Political Systems, 1965.

DELL, EDMUND. "Brazil's Partly United States." *Political Quarterly* 33 (July–September 1962): 282–93.

DONALD, CARR L. "Brazilian Local Self-government: Myth or Reality?" *Western Political Quarterly* 13 (December 1960): 1043–55.

DOS PASSOS, JOHN. *Brazil on the Move.* Garden City, N.Y.: Doubleday & Co., 1963.

FERRARI, FERNANDO. "Panorama político del Brasil." *Combate* 4 (March–April 1962): 9–13.

FREYRE, GILBERTO. *The Mansions and the Shanties: The Making of Modern Brazil.* New York: Alfred A. Knopf, Inc., 1963.

————. *The Masters and the Slaves.* New York: Alfred A. Knopf, Inc., 1964.

————. *New World in the Tropics.* New York: Alfred A. Knopf, Inc., 1959.

FURTADO, CELSO. "Brazil: What kind of Revolution?" *Foreign Affairs* 41 (April 1963): 526–35.

————. *Diagnosis of the Brazilian Crisis.* Berkeley and Los Angeles: University of California Press, 1965.

————. "Political Obstacles to Economic Growth in Brazil." *International Affairs* 41 (April 1965): 252–66.

HARRIS, MARVIN. "Government and Politics," *Town and Country in Brazil,* pp. 179–207. New York: Columbia University Press, 1956.

HOROWITZ, IRVING LOUIS. *Revolution in Brazil.* New York: E. P. Dutton & Co., 1964.

HUMES, SAMUEL, and MARTIN, EILEEN M. "Brazil," *The Structure of Local Governments throughout the World,* pp. 342–46. The Hague: Martinus Nijhoff, 1961.

JAMES, HERMAN GERLACH. *The Constitutional System of Brazil.* Washington: Pan American Union, 1923.

JAMES, PRESTON. "Forces for Union and Disunion in Brazil." *Journal of Geography* 38 (October 1939): 260–66.

JOHNSON, JOHN J. "Brazil," *Political Change in Latin America: The Rise of the Middle Sectors,* pp. 153–79. Stanford, Calif.: Stanford University Press, 1958.

JORDAN, HENRY P. "Brazil: From Dictatorship toward Constitutionalism." In *Foreign*

Governments, edited by Fritz Morstein Marx. New York: Prentice-Hall, Inc., 1962.

LANDAU, G. D. "School for Public Servants." *Americas* 8 (November 1956): 12–15.

LIMA, ALCEU AMOROSO. "An Interpretation of Brazilian Politics." *Social Science* 26 (October 1951): 202–14.

LIPSON, LESLIE. "Government in Contemporary Brazil." *Canadian Journal of Economic and Political Science* 22 (May 1956): 183–98.

LOPES MEIRELLES, HELY. "O Regime municipál brasiléiro." *Revista de Administracão Municipál* 11 (September–October 1964): 461–65.

LOWENSTEIN, KARL. *Brazil under Vargas*. New York: Macmillan Co., 1942.

MACDONALD, AUSTIN F. "Brazil," *Latin American Politics and Government*, pp. 121–99. 2nd ed. New York: Thomas Y. Crowell Co., 1954.

MADAY, BELA C., *et al. U.S. Army Area Handbook for Brazil*. Department of the Army pamphlet no. 550–20. Washington: U.S. Government Printing Office, 1964.

MANCHESTER, ALAN K. "Brazil in Transition." *South Atlantic Quarterly* 54 (April 1955): 167–76.

————. "Constitutional Dictatorship in Brazil." In *South American Dictators during the First Century of Independence*, edited by A. Curtis Wilgus. Washington: George Washington University Press, 1937.

PAULSON, BELDEN H. *Local Political Patterns in Northeast Brazil: A Community Case Study*. Land Tenure Center research paper no. 12. Madison: University of Wisconsin, 1964.

PETERSON, PHYLLIS. "Brazil: Institutionalized Confusion." In *Political Systems of Latin America*, edited by Martin C. Needler. Princeton: D. Van Nostrand Co., 1964.

RONNING, C. NEALE. "Brazil's Revolutionary Government." *Current History* 51 (November 1966): 296–300, 309–10.

SCHNEIDER, RONALD, ed. *Brazil Election Factbook Number 2, Supplement, November, 1966*. Washington: Institute for the Comparative Study of Political Systems, 1966.

SCHURZ, WILLIAM LYTLE. *Brazil, the Infinite Country*. New York: E. P. Dutton & Co., 1961.

SIEKMAN, PHILIP. "When Executives Turned Revolutionaries." *Fortune* 70 (September 1964): 147–49, 210, 214, 216, 221.

SKIDMORE, THOMAS E. *Politics in Brazil 1930–1964: An Experiment in Democracy*. New York: Oxford University Press, 1967.

SMITH, T. LYNN. *Brazil, People and Institutions*. Rev. ed. Baton Rouge: Louisiana State University Press, 1963.

————. "The Giant Awakes: Brazil." *Annals of the American Academy of Political and Social Science* 334 (March 1961): 95–102.

SOARES, G. A. D. "El sistema electoral y la reforma agraria en el Brasil." *Ciencias políticas y sociales* (Mexico) 8 (July–September 1962): 431–44.

TORRES, J. C. DE OLIVEIRA. *A formação do federalismo no Brasil*. São Paulo: Companhia Editora Nacionál, 1961.

U.S. DEPARTMENT OF LABOR. *Labor in Brazil*. Bureau of Labor Statistics report no. 191. Washington: U.S. Government Printing Office, 1962.

VIANA, ARIZIO DE. *Budget Making in Brazil*. Columbus: Ohio State University Press, 1947.

WACHHOLZ, PAUL F. "The Army of Brazil." *Army Information Digest* 14 (September 1959): 48–51.

WAGLEY, CHARLES. "Brazil." In *Most of the World*, edited by Ralph Linton. New York: Columbia University Press, 1949.

————. "The Brazilian Revolution: Social Change since 1930." In Richard N. Adams *et al., Social Change in Latin America Today, Its Implications for United States Policy.* New York: Harper & Row, 1960.

————. *Brazil: Crisis and Change.* Headline Series no. 167. New York: Foreign Policy Association, 1964.

————. *An Introduction to Brazil.* New York: Columbia University Press, 1963.

WALKER, HARVEY. "Federalism in Brazil." *State Government* 18 (March 1945): 43–44.

WIARDA, HOWARD J., and WIARDA, IÊDA S. "Revolution or Counter-Revolution in Brazil?" *Massachusetts Review* 8 (Winter 1967): 149–65.

WYCKOFF, THEODORE. "Brazilian Political Parties." *South Atlantic Quarterly* 56 (Summer 1957): 281–98.

YOUNG, JORDAN M. "Some Permanent Political Characteristics of Contemporary Brazil." *Journal of Inter-American Studies* 6 (July 1964): 287–301.

BOLIVIA

62

58

Corumbá

54

20

Fortín Ingavi

16

20

Rio Paraguay

BRAZIL

15

Fuerte
Olimpo

Mariscal
Estigarribia   Minas-cué

Puerto
Guaraní

La Esmeralda

Rio

Filadelfia

Puerto
Sastre

Bella Vista

Rio

Verde

Puerto
Casado

1

Pedro
Juan
Caballero

Ponta Porã

BRAZIL

Rio

Pilcomayo

Horqueta

Rio Paraguay

13

Rio Paraná

Concepción

24

14

Puerto Ybapabó

2

24

Rio

Teuco

San Pedro
Rosarió

ARGENTINA

Rio

Pilcomayo

San
Estanislao

5

10

Villa
Hayes

17

ASUNCIÓN

Caacupé

3

Coronel
Oviedo

Hernandarias

Foz do Iguaçu

11

Paraguarí

Villarrica

4

9

Formosa

Rio

Bermejo

Caazapá

6

12

Pilar

San Juan
Bautista

7

Rio

Alto

Paraná

8

Desmochados

Encarnación

Resistencia

Corrientes

Posadas

Uruguay

ARGENTINA

28

28

62

58

BRAZIL

54

BOUNDARY REPRESENTATION IS
NOT NECESSARILY AUTHORITATIVE

ADMINISTRATIVE DIVISIONS

DEPARTAMENTOS

1. Concepción
2. San Pedro
3. Cordillera
4. Guairá
5. Caaguazú
6. Caazapá
7. Itapúa
8. Misiones
9. Paraguarí
10. Alto Paraná
11. Central
      (capital: Asunción)
12. Ñeembucú
13. Amambay
14. Presidente Hayes
15. Boquerón
16. Olimpo

17. CAPITAL NACIONAL

PARAGUAY

━━━ International boundary
─·─·─ Departamento boundary
⊛ National capital
○ Departamento capital
╫╫╫ Railroad
─── Road

0   25   50   100 Miles
0   25 50   100 Kilometers

——25——

PARAGUAY:

The Politics of Isolation

Paraguay, surrounded as it is by larger, more developed states, has always tended to be a backwater. Since its only connection with the outside world until recent years was via the Paraná and Paraguay Rivers, it was inevitable that Argentina, at the mouth of Paraguay's pathway to the sea, would come to dominate the country economically. In addition, Paraguay has suffered more from international wars than any other Latin-American state. Today Paraguay is conspicuous as the home of the only surviving old-fashioned Latin-American *caudillo* dictatorship.

A National Profile

Paraguay is a landlocked, isolated country in the center of South America, bounded on the west by Bolivia, on the north and east by Brazil, and on the south by Argentina, with an area of 157,047 square miles. The Paraguay River divides the country into two distinct sections. Between the Paraguay and Paraná Rivers lies 39 percent of the country's area, inhabited by 95 percent of the population. For all practical purposes this is Paraguay, a fertile, well-watered area, most of which can be used for agriculture or cattle raising. West of the Paraguay River is the region known as the Chaco, a low-lying area variously covered with swamps, dense jungle, and dry wasteland, containing 61 percent of the country's area but only about 5 percent of the total population (about 67,500 in 1964). Quebracho wood is produced here and a few agricultural products, but most of the land is unused and probably cannot be developed without the expenditure of exceedingly large amounts of money. The most important of the Chaco's inhabitants are 30,000 or so Indians, many of whom continue to live as their ancestors did before them, and 10,000 or so Mennonites who came from Europe and North America to live in isolated colonies, practically independent of the national government.

Paraguay's population on July 1, 1966, was estimated to be 2,094,000. The rate of increase has been about 2.6 percent in recent years, low for Latin America. This is due in large part to the exodus of hundreds of thousands for political and economic reasons. Perhaps 600,000 Paraguayans live in the neighboring countries, about 400,000 in Argentina, the rest in Uruguay and Brazil. There is only one large city, Asunción, the capital, which had 305,160 residents in 1962. About 64.2 percent of the population was rural in 1965. Most of the country's people live within a radius of sixty miles from Asunción. During the nineteenth-century dictatorships the Spanish aristocracy was all but exterminated. Many Italian, French, Spanish, English, and German immigrants came after 1870, and with only a few exceptions intermarried with the older inhabitants. As a result, about 94 percent of the population are *mestizos*, about 3 percent almost pure Indians, another 3 percent European and Oriental.

Although Spanish is the official language, most of the people also speak Guaraní and perhaps 50 percent use no Spanish at all. Illiteracy was very widespread in the past, but the rate has gone down in recent years. About one-third of the total population remains illiterate and about 23 percent of the children of school age were not in school during 1963. There is a very high dropout rate and the average child receives only a year or two of schooling. Roman Catholicism is the official state religion and most of the people consider themselves Catholic. Health and welfare are primitive. Many diseases that have been controlled in other Latin-American countries (leprosy, tuberculosis, and malaria) are endemic in Paraguay.

Paraguay has traditionally been an agricultural country, since its main resources are grazing land, farmland, and forests. Despite its unused fertile soil, about one-fourth of the food required by its people has been imported in recent years; the best land is devoted to producing crops for the world market. The backwardness of Paraguay is usually attributed to the very unequal pattern of land ownership, the inadequate road system, the population's low income, and the isolation of the country. All this has been complicated by the very poor government the country has had. During the 1960's, an effort to improve the economy by developing new activities has resulted in lowering the proportion of the gainfully occupied in agriculture. Cattle production is the most important industry, with most of the meat being exported. In 1962, 52 percent of the workers were in agriculture, 19 percent in industry, 7 percent in commerce, 3 percent in public service, and the rest in services and other activities. About 5 percent of the labor force was unemployed. The leading crops are cotton, sugar, rice, tobacco, tannin, vegetable oils, and *yerba mate*. The small amount of manufacturing, which accounts for about 16 percent of the national income, is confined to processing some of the agricultural production and producing a few consumer goods. The hydroelectric potential of the rivers has not yet been developed. Raine estimates that 50 percent of the country's productive land is owned by foreigners.[1] Yet the land-tenure system is even worse than this would suggest. In 1959, when there were 149,489 farms in Paraguay, 7,789 of them, or 5.2 percent, were larger than fifty *hectares* each and contained 93.8 percent of all the country's farmland (15,914,334 *hectares* of the 16,965,485 total). Most farmers are sharecroppers and there is much squatting and land grabbing. Much of the population survives on subsistence agriculture.

Transportation is very poorly developed. In 1965 the whole country had 2,964 miles of roads, only 292 miles paved. Fifty-five percent of the road network has been built since 1960. Housing is extremely primitive. In 1962, 65 percent of all homes consisted of a single room lacking the most basic facilities. There is only one public water supply and sewage system in the whole country, located in Asunción, and it services only 40 percent of the city's population.

In general Argentina's economic development has been so much further advanced than Paraguay's that it has been able to dominate the economy of its poorer neighbor. In recent years, roads and railroads have been built to give Paraguay an exit to the Atlantic through Brazil, but this has only given the Brazilian economy a chance to compete with that of Argentina.

The Development of Modern Paraguay

"No country of Latin America has had a more bizarre history, or experienced greater suffering at the hands of domestic tyrants and foreign foes, than Paraguay," Professor Hubert Herring wrote.[2] Its isolation, its climate, its native people, and the European conquerors who arrived during the sixteenth century all contributed to that bizarre history.

When the first Portuguese and Spanish explorers came to what is

---

[1] Philip Raine, *Paraguay* (New Brunswick, N.J.: Scarecrow Press, 1956), p. 277.
[2] Hubert Herring, *A History of Latin America from the Beginnings to the Present,* 2nd ed. (New York: Alfred A. Knopf, Inc., 1961), p. 710.

now known as Paraguay, they found the area inhabited by about 200,000 Guaraní Indians who had already come into contact with the Inca empire to the west. The Spaniards first came to Paraguay in their search for a way across the continent, but they soon turned their attention to seeking a path to the riches of the Inca empire. As early as 1524, Aleixo García, a Portuguese adventurer, had brought back some silver stolen from the Incas. The news of this source of wealth stimulated the Spaniards to fortify Paraguay in order to keep the Portuguese out and to develop a route to Peru. Thus, by 1537, Asunción had been established to become the center from which the whole Río de la Plata area was to be conquered by the Spaniards. Buenos Aires, Santa Fe, and Corrientes were all founded by expeditions that started from Asunción.

Asunción's relative isolation developed an independent and proud population. By 1544 the first revolution against authority had taken place. In the 1720's, the great revolt of the *Comuneros* almost expelled Spanish authority.

In its first century Paraguay developed two distinct cultural patterns. In and around Asunción a Spanish, *mestizo*, and Indian population lived, with a latifundia type of agriculture dominant in the region. In the southeastern part of the area, the Jesuit order created a series of towns in which about 100,000 Indians lived under the paternalistic dictatorship of the Jesuit priests. Continuously attacked by the latifundia owners of Asunción, who wanted the Indians to be their serfs, and by the slave traders from Brazil, the Jesuit colonies received their death blow when, in 1767, the Spanish king expelled all Jesuits from Spanish South America. Two hundred years of domination by the Jesuits helped to foster a docility among the Indians which seems to have prevented them from readily accepting industrial society. The Jesuits left little else behind except some ruins; Paraguayan culture in the twentieth century is far more Guaraní than Catholic.

By 1617 the authorities in Spain had evidently decided that a useful route to Peru could not be created through Paraguay and turned their backs on Asunción in favor of Buenos Aires. After that the colony declined until it became a backwater defensive outpost, used only to keep the Portuguese out of Spanish territory. The people of Asunción resented the creation of the vice-royalty of the Río de la Plata in 1776 and became even more independent and proud in their isolation. Thus, when Buenos Aires became independent of Spain in 1810, the Paraguayans not only refused to become part of the United Provinces of the Río de la Plata, but defeated an Argentine army sent to compel their adherence to the newly independent state centering on Buenos Aires.

As a result, in 1811 Paraguay started out as an independent state, although it had neither the population, the economic development, nor the cultural training needed to prosper independently. Its people had never governed themselves, most of the area was unpopulated, the boundaries of the country were very indefinite (which later led Paraguay into two international wars), and the isolation in which most of its people lived inevitably doomed them to backwardness. Soon after independence, a dictatorship gained control of the country and in the process created a pattern of government which has continued to this day.

Paraguay's first tyrant was Dr. José Gaspar Rodríguez Francia, who became dictator for life in 1816 and remained in power until his death in 1840. Francia was obsessed with a fear of Argentinians and all other foreigners, and isolated Paraguay from contact with its neighbors. In their isolation, with no foreign trade or immigration permitted, the modern Paraguayan people emerged as one of the most completely amalgamated groups in America. Francia ran a one-man show. He completely dominated every aspect of life, and the government was so involved in the country's economic life that some writers describe Francia's regime as socialistic. But it was a government based on force and terror, and people who objected were either murdered or jailed. Francia's policies produced a type of economic autarky that inevitably doomed the country to a low standard of living, although it did foster self-reliance and local production. Much of Francia's energies and the government's budget were expended in creating a large army.

Francia's dictatorship, of course, did little to prepare the Paraguayans to govern themselves. No newspapers or books could be published; education was nonexistent; all opposition was crushed; travel within and out of the country was strictly controlled. Francia ran everything. Thus no one else was allowed to learn how to administer the government, and when he died, anarchy naturally followed until a new dictator emerged in the person of Carlos Antonio López. López is reputed to have become the richest man in Paraguay while he was president, but he was a paternal soul and he did try to improve conditions in Paraguay. The embargo on foreign trade was ended, attempts were made to develop the country's resources, and British engineers were brought in to begin the construction of one of South America's first railroads. Various new industries were established, education was fostered, and young men were sent to Europe for training. As these positive steps were taken, however, López became involved in disputes with the neighboring countries and the United States, and began to devote more and more of the country's resources to strengthening his powerful army.

When López died in 1862, his son Francisco Solano López inherited both his wealth and his power. Within three years Paraguay was at war with Brazil, Uruguay, and Argentina. It was insane to believe that little Paraguay could defeat three more highly developed, larger neighbors, but for five years Solano López fought on in a senseless war in which most of the male population was exterminated by disease and enemy troops. It was only after the death of the dictator on the battlefield, in 1879, that the war finally ended, with Paraguay exhausted and part of the territory it claimed taken over by Argentina and Brazil. Out of a population of 525,000 in 1865, only 221,079 remained alive in 1870. Of this number only 28,746 were adult males.

Had the victors in the war annexed all of Paraguay's territory, South America might have one less problem today. The rivalry between the Brazilian and Argentine governments, however, preserved Paraguay as an independent state. The armies of occupation remained in Paraguay for six years, but did little to stabilize conditions in the country, and the people still possessed none of the prerequisites necessary for the creation of any kind of stable government. Furthermore, the three men who had dominated Paraguay had prevented the emergence of any class or individuals capable of governing. As a result, when the invading armies left Paraguay, no stable government could be established. It is estimated that from 1870 to 1932, thirty-three executives tried to rule the country, about one every two years. In this chaotic situation, revolutions and coups d'état were the normal ways of changing government, and the efforts made to stimulate immigration were severely handicapped. Many attempts were made to settle colonists from the United States, Australia, England, and other countries. Practically all failed, except for the religious colonies set up by Mennonites in the 1920's. The population grew slowly from 1870 to 1932; the economy developed a little; and the first political parties emerged. It is possible a more viable organization of society might have eventually developed, but just as Paraguay seemed to be entering into the modern world it became involved in another war, this time with Bolivia.

As with the War of the Triple Alliance, the Chaco War was caused by Paraguay's poorly demarcated boundaries. After Bolivia lost its outlet to the Pacific Ocean, its governments were interested in reaching the Paraguay River to have an outlet to the Atlantic. Paraguay resisted this effort, and in 1932 the war began to decide who would control the almost empty Chaco between Bolivia and Paraguay. Although the Chaco was an unpopulated, desolate region, not itself worth fighting for, the Paraguayans discovered intense nationalistic feelings toward the area and were able to defeat the better-armed Bolivian troops. The Paraguayans were all lowlanders, used to the climate in the Chaco; the Bolivian highland Indians were at a great disadvantage. The fighting ended in 1935 with Paraguay in control of most of the Chaco, and the treaty of 1938 confirmed Paraguay's possession.

The history of modern Paraguay begins with the end of the Chaco War. Before that time nothing resembling constitutional government had developed. During the Argentine-Brazilian occupation, the educated people had coalesced around two political parties, the *Colorado* and the Liberal. The *Colorado* Party was a conservative organization founded in 1874 by General Bernardino Caballero, a war hero who dominated the country for thirty years, until 1904. His opponents, led by Juan Silvano Godoi, created the Liberal Party, which came to power in 1904 by means of an armed assault on the government and held control until the termination of the Chaco War. Neither party was much more than a mechanism to control the government, and there was little difference between their ways of governing.

The first attempts to redirect the course of Paraguayan development came after the Chaco War ended. Just as in Bolivia, the war veterans returned home with dreams of changing their country. Led by a war hero, Colonel Rafael Franco, the organized war veterans, the university students, and the intellectuals revolted and captured control of the government on February 17, 1936. The new holders of power began a land-redistribution program, passed the country's first social legislation, including a labor code, and made determined efforts to develop good relations with Paraguay's neighbors. At the same time the *Febreristas*, as the new group was called, exiled many of their opponents, just as they themselves had been exiled by previous governments. Their efforts were too radical for Paraguay, too sharp a break with the past, and in August 1937 the government was overthrown by a new revolt.

In 1938 Paraguay was still living in the eighteenth century. The whole country had 136 miles of roads. Most of the population consisted of illiterate peasants scratching out a living through subsistence agriculture. After Colonel Franco and the *Febreristas* were expelled from office, therefore, a period of instability followed. In 1939 General José Félix Estigarribia, the candidate of the Liberal Party, became president. Estigarribia discovered that his restoration of political liberty brought strikes, conspiracies, and general chaos. Therefore, in February 1940, he declared himself dictator of Paraguay, abolished all liberty, and tried to implement some of the radical *Febrerista* ideas, including land redistribution, highway construction, economic and monetary reform, and intervention by the government in many economic matters. At the same time, he had a new constitution drawn up which was to be in true harmony with the country's past by setting up a very powerful authoritarian state in which the executive had ample power to govern. It is impossible to say whether Estigarribia could have developed constitutional government, for three weeks after the constitution went into effect he was killed in a plane crash.

From 1940 to 1948, Estigarribia's war minister, General Higinio Morínigo, ran Paraguay in a dictatorial fashion. Some economic development took place as the United States and Brazil supplied lend-lease and other loans and grants and as World War II scarcities increased the demand for Paraguay's exports. But he did little to lay the groundwork for a constitutional system, and most of the democratically minded political leaders lived in exile. After the war ended, Morínigo slackened his dictatorship and allowed the exiles to return. Some *Colorados* and *Febreristas* were taken into the cabinet to create a coalition government. But this relaxation only provoked attempts to overthrow the government, and by January 1947 the attempt at a coalition government ended. In March 1947 a serious civil war began in which *Febreristas*, Communists, and Liberals cooperated in an attempt to overthrow Morínigo's government. After six months of fighting the revolt was put down. During the years of dictatorship and fighting, Morínigo had built up the *Colorado* Party as a means of obtaining some popular support. In 1948 a *Colorado* political leader, Juan Natalicio González, became president, but the *Colorados* soon split into two factions. Eventually the army, working with one of the *Colorado* factions, obtained control of the government and set up the system that still continues today. It is a type of one-party state in which the armed forces serve as the most important support of the government. The *Colorado* Party is used to give the dictatorship an aura of respectability, since all other parties are illegal most of the time. After May 1954, General Alfredo Stroessner became the dominant figure in the dictatorship. In managed elections he was elected president in 1954, 1959, and 1964; all of the opposition parties refused to participate.

Since the constitution permitted only two terms for the president, in 1967 Stroessner organized a constitutional convention to create a new constitution, which allowed him legally to run for the presidency again. The election for delegates to the convention saw 441,912 votes cast, with the *Colorado* Party receiving 68.7 percent of the votes and eighty seats in the convention. The Liberals received 20.9 percent of the votes and twenty-eight seats; the Liberal faction that cooperates with Stroessner had 6.1 percent of the votes and eight seats; the *Febrerista* Party had 2.7 percent of the votes and three seats; 1.6 percent of the votes were spoiled. In addition to permitting Stroessner to have two more presidential terms, the new constitution added a Senate to the legislature and increased the size of the Supreme Court. The new constitution came into force on August 25, 1967, and on February 11, 1968, Stroessner was reelected for a new term. The only campaign posters seen during the preelection period were those boosting Stroessner. On August 15, 1968, Stroessner was inaugurated for his fourth term as president of the republic.

Under Stroessner there has been some economic development, much of it financed by grants and loans from the United States, other countries, and international organizations. Roads have been built to connect Paraguay with Bolivia and Brazil; colonization has been fostered and some immigrants have been attracted; a plush tourist hotel has been built in Asunción. There is no doubt that economically the country is better off than it was in the past. At the same time, however, the country has lived under a state of siege almost continually. Most of the political parties have been illegalized most of the time, and an incredible number of invasions, revolts, and riots have taken place. Stroessner has tried to be a "progressive" dictator and has talked much of the need to prepare Paraguay for democratic life. Despite his promises, however, whenever any threat to his power has emerged, Stroessner has smashed it. Every once in a while the opposition parties have been permitted to function, but whenever they began their activities, riots and demonstrations would break out, and as the evidence of mass opposition to Stroessner became apparent, the government reintroduced the state of siege.

There was some relaxation of Stroessner's dictatorship in 1968, and in March of that year the President came to the United States as a state visitor. From 1942 to 1968 the United States had given Paraguay about $57 million in aid plus about $3 million in military aid and training. In May of 1968, Paraguay joined Argentina, Bolivia, Brazil, and Argentina to set up an organization for the joint development of the Río de la Plata basin. Thus Paraguay in 1968 seemed to be entering a period of change. With the relaxation of the dictatorship and the new emphasis upon economic development, it is possible this change may become accelerated and lead to fundamental reorganization of the political system.

The Formal Constitutional Framework

Paraguay is governed under the constitution of August 25, 1967. Paraguay has had a relatively small number of constitutions; the constitution of 1967 is only the fifth. Yet even these five have never really been observed.

The constitutional "governmental regulations" of Dr. Francia's epoch were never observed at all. Neither was the constitution of 1840. Under the invading armies of the Triple Alliance, a new constitution was instituted in 1870. This was modeled after that of the United States and Argentina, and created a system of checks and balances between a powerful bicameral legislature and a president. Of course, it too was never really observed.

General Estigarribia thought that since Paraguay had always been dominated by a strong executive, he would produce a constitution that reflected reality and thus institute true constitutional government. Unfortunately, as we have seen, he died in a plane crash three weeks after the constitution of 1940 went into effect and never had a chance to make it operative. His successors operated under a state of siege most of the time and paid little attention to the constitution. The fate of Stroessner's new constitution cannot be forecast. For all practical purposes we can say that Paraguay has never really lived under constitutional government.

Who Participates in Politics

Most Paraguayans have never been able to participate effectively in the political process since the establishment of the "republic." Practically all elections have been rigged, or only one candidate has been permitted to run. The state of siege under which most presidents have governed Paraguay has prevented nonelectoral political activity. There probably is more political activity by Paraguayans outside of the country than within it.

Until recent years, only literate men could vote, and this regulation is reflected in the number of votes recorded. In 1953, for example, 39,982 votes "elected" Federico Chávez president (he was the only candidate). General Stroessner has increased the electorate by giving both women and illiterates the vote. In 1963, 638,000 votes were cast, but the election was just as firmly controlled as all past elections had been, with the state of siege suspended only for the one day of voting. In 1968, 897,455 persons were registered to vote in the presidential election and Stroessner received 463,811 votes. This is the largest turnout in Paraguay's electoral history. Of course, again the state of siege was suspended only for the day of voting, and the opposition parties had little opportunity to campaign freely.

Much of the political participation takes the form of developing contacts. With about 64 percent of the population rural, politics remains a pastime for a few people in Asunción.

The Electoral Machinery

As has been pointed out, there has never been a fair election held in Paraguay. The six-man Central Electoral Board which is in charge of the electoral machinery is a part of the executive. In 1963 it was composed of four members of the *Colorado* Party and two of the Liberal Party, who were members of the party faction cooperating with General Stroessner. That year was only the second time in the history of the republic that two candidates were on the ballot for the presidency. Voting is obligatory. It is interesting to note that the receipt given voters at the polls is needed to buy or sell property, to engage in commercial enterprises, and for other purposes. And it is almost impossible to vote for anyone but the official candidate. Paraguay still uses the system in which one selects a ballot provided by the party and puts it into an official envelope. It is always easier to use the *Colorado* ballot, and a lot safer.

Political Parties

Paraguay's first political parties were organized in the period after the War of the Triple Alliance, when the articulate section of the oligarchy became divided into the *Colorado* and Liberal Parties. The *Colorado* Party (founded 1874) controlled the government from 1876 to 1904, when a coup d'état expelled it from office and the Liberals (founded 1887) took over. The Liberals kept control until the February 1936 revolution expelled them from office and ushered in the modern period of Paraguayan politics. In 1937 the Liberals returned to power, to be expelled again in 1940. After a period during which Higinio Morínigo operated a personal dictatorship, the *Colorados* returned to power in 1947 and retain control at this writing.

There was no significant difference between the *Colorado* and Liberal Parties during the period from 1876 to 1936, and some suspect there is none at the present time. Both have always operated dictatorially when in power. Both have always had conservative and liberal factions within their ranks, and both have done little to involve the masses in politics, although many peasants, by tradition, have supported one or the other of the parties.

The *Colorado* Party (its legal name is the National Republican Association) was the only legal party in Paraguay from 1947 to 1962. During that period it took on most of the characteristics of the type of party found in a totalitarian state and became a powerful arm of the dictatorship. It was well organized and was controlled by the same figures during most of the period. Most of the government employees were recruited as members of the party and each government employee "donated" 5 percent of his salary as dues. General Stroessner has controlled the party as he has controlled everything else in Paraguay. A group of dissident *Colorados* functions outside Paraguay as the Popular *Colorado* Movement, but it does not have much support inside Paraguay.

The two leading opposition groups are the Liberal and the *Febrerista* Parties, which cooperate through the National Paraguayan Union, which also includes a few *Colorados*. The Liberal Party greatly resembles the *Colorado* Party, except that it talks more radically from exile. It was founded as an attempt to achieve fairer elections and much of its ideology came from Europe's revolutionary movement of 1848. In power, the Liberals acted just as undemocratically as the *Colorados*, and by the time of the Chaco War they were discredited among the masses. They still talk of representative and responsible government, but most Liberals seem to visualize a future for Paraguay not much different from the past, except that it will have the liberty necessary for the Liberal Party to win control of the government. In 1962 General Stroessner persuaded a small group of Liberals, operating as the Liberal Renovation Movement, to become his "loyal opposition," and in 1963 this group participated in the election and received the twenty minority seats in the legislature. Most observers feel this tiny group will disappear if a free election is ever held.

The *Febrerista* Party developed out of the group of Chaco War veterans who put Colonel Franco into office after the 1936 revolution. During their eighteen months in power the *Febreristas* stimulated the organization of labor unions, began an agrarian-reform program, and sought to stimulate the economy. But they were too radical for Paraguay and did not have an organization strong enough to hold power. After being expelled from office, however, these people slowly developed a sound party structure both within Paraguay and in exile, modeled after the style of the other indigenous revolutionary parties in Latin America. They refined a program that calls for a radical reorganization of Paraguay along democratic lines and became a powerful organization. The *Febrerista* Party is a member of the League of Popular Parties and of the Socialist International. The only other party of any importance is the Communist Party, founded in the 1920's, which has operated under a series of different names during the years. In 1946–47 it was permitted to function legally, but since then it has been outlawed most of the time. A Christian Democratic Party was established in 1965 but it boycotted the 1967 and 1968 elections.

It is difficult to estimate the strength of the various parties. After the 1968 election the parties lined up in the legislature as follows: *Colorados,* forty seats in the Chamber and twenty in the Senate; Liberals, sixteen in the Chamber and nine in the Senate; the Liberal faction that cooperates with Stroessner received three seats in the Chamber and one in the Senate; the *Febreristas* have one seat in the Chamber. The Communist and Christian Democratic Parties are not represented.

Parties are known by their colors in Paraguay. The *Colorados* wear red ties, the Liberals blue, the *Febreristas* green.

Public Opinion and Pressure Groups

Public opinion does not have much opportunity to express itself in Paraguay, but whatever opinion is heard comes from Asunción, which completely dominates the country. Only 46,000 newspapers circulated daily in 1961, less than the number of daily newspapers in Nicaragua, which has a smaller population and a higher rate of illiteracy. None of Asunción's daily papers is really independent, but the most widely read is *La Tribuna* (about 30,000 daily), the most independently controlled newspaper.

Pressure groups do not have much scope for activity. The most important group, of course, is the armed forces, which consumes a high proportion of the country's budget. In 1959, for example, Juan de Onís, writing in the *New York Times,* estimated that

> of a budget of 2,627,000,000 guaranies (about 21 million U.S. dollars) it is calculated that forty percent goes to the armed forces, which total 12,000 men. From the $1,500,000 Defense Ministry to the officers' casino and the new barracks of the cavalry division it is evident that the army is being taken care of. Staff officers may obtain credit for housing or business from an official bank. Army officers also have an interest in the booming meat export industry.[3]

It is estimated that there have been 23,000 men in the armed forces during recent years.

Labor unions are weak and the peasants are unorganized. There are no other substantial organizations of any kind to function as pressure groups, although the Liberal and *Febrerista* Parties function as pressure groups, particularly in their exile activities.

---

[3] Juan de Onís, "Paraguay's Chief Coddles His Army," *New York Times,* February 19, 1959, p. 8. © 1959 by The New York Times Company. Reprinted by permission.

Civil Liberties

Although Paraguay's constitution lists "rights, obligations, and guarantees" for its population, including the right to meet peacefully, to petition the authorities, and to publish, in practice the citizens have no rights. It is common to read such reports as "the brutality of the police shocked Paraguay"[4] or "the blue-eyed Latin dictator slaps down ruthlessly any overt act of opposition to his regime."[5] Nor is General Stroessner acting differently than most of his predecessors. Ever since Dr. Francia set up his dictatorship, liberty has been absent from Paraguay.

Things have been so bad in recent decades that perhaps a fourth of the Paraguayan population has left the country. Not all are fleeing oppression; many have left to seek better economic opportunities in Argentina and other neighboring countries. But the dictatorship which keeps the economy stagnant contributes to the exodus.[6] From time to time General Stroessner will relax the dictatorship or even cancel the state of siege under which the country usually lives, but the iron fist is always there, ready to clamp down again on anyone rash enough to exercise his theoretical rights.

The Executive

The Paraguayan executive is a president elected for a five-year term by direct suffrage. He can be reelected for a second term. To be president one must be a natural citizen, over forty years old, and a Roman Catholic. There is no vice-president. If the president dies, the Minister of the Interior convokes the National Assembly (the legislature and the Council of State meeting together), which selects a new president. If more than two years of the late president's term have gone by, the new president finishes the five-year period. If less than two years have gone by, an election is called within two months to select a new president. When Estigarribia died, this procedure was not followed; when Chávez left office it was. What is done in Paraguay depends upon the situation at the moment.

Both traditionally and constitutionally, the president is an extremely powerful executive. In addition to all the powers a constitutional executive usually has, he can declare a state of siege, he can dissolve the legislature, and he appoints practically all government officials with little check

---

[4] "Paraguay: Clubs and Sabers," *Newsweek*, June 5, 1961, p. 53.

[5] Al Burt, "Freedom in Paraguay: Doing as You're Told," *Miami Herald*, May 30, 1962, pp. 1, 18a.

[6] See, for example, the Associated Press dispatch headlined "Stifled Paraguay Exports . . . People," *Christian Science Monitor*, June 12, 1962, p. 6.

from anyone. Certain of his appointments must be approved by the legislature or the Council of State, but this has been no check upon him, since
he freely appoints most of the members of the Council of State and can
dissolve the legislature. In addition, the legislature must make a decision
on all proposals sent by the president during the session or the proposal
becomes law automatically when the legislature adjourns. When it is not
in session, the president can issue "decrees with the force of law" if the
Council of State approves and if he submits them to the legislature for
approval when it reconvenes.

The president is assisted by a cabinet of eleven ministers. All presidential acts must be signed by a minister, but this does not serve as a
check on the president, since he freely appoints and removes all ministers.
An unusual feature of government in Paraguay is the Council of State,
which also advises the president and exercises other powers. Consisting of
the cabinet members, the archbishop of Paraguay, the rector of the university, one representative from commerce, one from manufacturing, two
from agriculture and stock raising, the president of the Bank of the Republic, and two representatives of the armed forces holding the rank of
colonel or higher, the Council of State theoretically has a great deal of
power. It approves or vetoes the president's decree laws, advises him on
foreign affairs, consents to or rejects the appointment of Supreme Court
justices, diplomatic representatives, and promotions in the armed forces,
and advises on financial and economic matters. The Council of State
could be an important organ of government, since it represents the dominant groups in Paraguayan society, but it is controlled by the president,
since he appoints a majority of the members, and it does nothing not in
harmony with his wishes. It has been suggested that General Estigarribia
wanted to set up a sort of corporate state. If he did, it never worked out
that way.

Public Administration

As would be expected in a country with a government as personal as that
of General Stroessner, there is no formal civil service system. Whatever
laws are on the books are ignored, and practically all employees of the
government obtain their positions for political reasons. No central body
supervises the employees; each ministry has its own personnel department, headed by a presidential appointee. It is thought that this is pur-
posely done to prevent the emergence of a strong bureaucracy as a threat
to the monopoly of power in the hands of the president. At the same time,
the public servants receive comparatively good treatment in return for

their continued support. There are about 50,000 government employees. They can retire with a pension of 92 percent of their last salary after thirty years of service. They receive vacations with pay, sick leave, and other benefits.

In an attempt to improve the functioning of the Paraguayan government, the United States has supplied technical assistance in public administration since 1952. A Paraguayan School of Public Administration has functioned in Asunción since 1959 with United States technicians as part of the faculty. The United States has provided money for books and equipment for this school and has brought Paraguayans to the United States and Puerto Rico for training as professors in public administration. Other United States technicians have served as advisers in the Ministry of Public Works, the Tax Administration, and other departments of the government. Nevertheless, public administration remains inefficient and backward because of the dictatorial character of the government. Friendship and monetary influence make papers move in Paraguay, and the administration is kept decentralized to allow the dictatorship more extensive power.

The Legislative Power

Until 1967 Paraguay's legislative power was supposed to be a unicameral Chamber of Representatives of sixty members elected for five-year terms. In the new constitution of 1967 a Senate of thirty members and eighteen alternates was introduced, and the legislature was given the power, by a two-thirds majority of both houses, of rejecting the budget or overriding the president's veto. The Chamber of Representatives still has sixty members. Both houses are selected by a system of proportional representation which gives two-thirds of the seats in each house to the party receiving the most votes; the other third of the seats is divided among the other parties participating in the election.

Until 1963, all representatives belonged to the *Colorado* Party. In the February 1963 election, the Renovation faction of the Liberal Party was given the twenty minority seats because it was the only part of the opposition willing to participate in the election. The whole country is one electoral district, with the parties presenting lists of names. The legislature meets in regular session from April 1 to August 31 each year, but the president can disband the session at any time or call the legislature into session when it is adjourned.

The Paraguayan legislature is granted thirteen powers by the constitution, but five of them can be exercised only "on the initiative of the

Executive Power." Contrary to most constitutions, that of Paraguay covers the executive before the legislature, and there is no doubt that those who wrote the constitution intended the legislature to be weak. In actual practice, it is a rubber stamp for General Stroessner. Practically all bills are initiated by the executive, who also has both a general veto and an item veto power. Since there almost never is any real opposition permitted, and since practically all bills are initiated by the executive, there is little dispute and the legislature acts as a bill-passing agency.

Legislators are granted parliamentary immunity by the constitution, but they get few other privileges except a salary. No offices are provided; there are no caucus rooms for the party groups; there is no restaurant; there is no legislative reference service; there is no library for the legislature. Since 1957 the *Colorado* legislators have had offices in the party headquarters, a large building in the center of Asunción. Members of the other parties must get along without offices or provide their own.

Public Finance

Paraguay's expenditures and income have risen very rapidly in recent years as attempts were made to develop the country. Total revenue was only 704 million guaraníes in 1954; by 1955 it was ₲975.6 million; by 1960, ₲2,083.8 million, and by 1964, ₲4,183,300,380, or $33,466,403 U.S. (the guaraní is worth $0.008). Most of the country's income came from indirect taxes; in 1964, only 9.32 percent came from taxes on income. About 11 percent of the income came from United States loans. The budget for 1964, given in Tables 1 and 2, shows the pattern of income and expenditures during recent years. It is typical of Paraguay that the largest single expenditure was 17.21 percent of the budget for national defense. Adding 3.75 percent for police, that means almost 21 percent of a small budget is going to the armed forces, while education receives only 14.83 percent and health 5.55 percent.

Local Government

Paraguay is a unitary state and for all practical purposes there is no local self-government. All power in the subdivisions of the country is exercised by officials appointed by the national executive. For administrative purposes, the country is divided into sixteen departments, which are divided into 143 districts, which are divided into *compañías* and sometimes into *colonias*. In twelve of the departments a *delegado de gobierno*, a sort of glorified police officer, represents the national government. The national

TABLE 1
ESTIMATED REVENUE OF PARAGUAY, 1964

Source	Amount in Guaranies	Percent of Total
Import taxes	₲705,686,600	16.87%
Export taxes	44,049,000	1.05
Inheritance and gift taxes	11,324,760	0.27
Income taxes	390,000,000	9.32
Various consumption and transaction taxes	584,715,240	13.98
Liquor and alcohol taxes	120,000,000	2.87
Real estate taxes	200,000,000	4.78
Post office (stamps, etc.)	25,774,460	0.62
Taxes for pensions	125,000,000	2.99
Consular fees	163,342,500	3.90
Sales taxes	329,000,000	7.86
Miscellaneous special laws, traffic fines, lottery, government services	78,527,300	1.88
Miscellaneous taxes and fees	947,530,120	22.65
Loans from U.S.A.	330,750,000	7.91
U.S. agricultural surpluses	127,600,400	3.05
Total	₲4,183,300,380	100.00%

capital and the three Chaco departments have no *delegado de gobierno*.

In each district a populated place is designated the capital. A municipal council (*junta municipal*) and a *comisario,* a police official, both appointed by the national executive, make their headquarters there and handle traffic, law and order, public health, sanitation, and other matters. Generally, the councils consist of five members and a secretary without vote. The president of the council and the secretary receive small salaries; the other members serve without salary. Usually the *comisario* with his squad of soldiers becomes the most powerful local official. Other officials found in each district, all appointed from Asunción, are the tax collector, the telegraph operator, and the justice of the peace. In certain places that have been designated first-class cities, the president of the republic appoints an *intendente municipal,* a sort of mayor who handles the city's affairs. Asunción and a few other cities have in addition city councils which are supposed to be elected by the city's residents (there has been only one election of this type, in 1965).

Since Paraguay has no true local government, the population cannot learn how to govern itself in preparation for the day when national dictatorship is abolished. The only elections, except for those held in the cities once in a while, are those held every five years for the president and the legislature. Moreover, all local appointees in recent decades have been

TABLE 2
ESTIMATED EXPENDITURES OF PARAGUAY, 1964

	Amount in Guaranies	Percent of Total
General services		
General administration	₲375,911,720	8.19%
Órgano del Estado	51,650,000	1.12
Justice	91,748,550	2.00
Fiscal administration	160,910,440	3.50
National defense	790,337,130	17.21
Police	172,320,940	3.75
Foreign relations	114,327,240	2.49
Total general services	₲1,757,206,020	38.26%
Cultural and social services		
Labor	3,650,800	0.08
Health	254,750,940	5.55
Education	681,119,880	14.83
Religion	12,026,800	0.26
Social welfare	9,960,070	0.22
Social assistance	12,566,000	0.27
Housing	2,028,400	0.04
Total cultural and social services	₲976,102,890	21.25%
Economic services		
Industry	10,452,970	0.23
Commerce	2,407,970	0.05
Transportation	691,646,025	15.06
Public works	6,060,410	0.13
Mineral resources	2,152,000	0.05
Communications	50,224,330	1.09
Tourism	2,146,800	0.05
Agriculture and livestock	78,106,380	1.70
Forests, hunting, and fishing	1,757,300	0.04
Cooperatives	534,000	0.01
Economic development	221,000,000	4.82
Total economic services	₲1,066,488,185	23.23%
Miscellaneous		
Service on public debt	218,928,930	4.77
Other obligations	573,640,000	12.49
Total miscellaneous	₲792,568,930	17.26%
Total budgeted expenditures	₲4,592,366,025	100.00%

members of the *Colorado* Party or of the tame opposition so the *Colorados* and their friends are the only ones getting any administrative experience.

The autonomous Mennonite colonies in the Chaco, by agreement with the national government, control their own affairs and enforce Paraguayan law. However, the Mennonite boys are not subject to the draft into the armed forces. Each colony has its own town meeting and elections of officials by the heads of families, the most important being the members of the *Amt* (a sort of town council) and the *Obershulze*, a sort of governor. The Mennonite colonies have been described as theocratic, but the people do govern themselves, even though their church is the center of their life. The various Mennonite colonies are not officially connected with each other in any way, and each one deals directly with the national government. Some scholars think that when roads knit the country together, the Mennonite system of local government could become the model for local government in other communities.

The Judicial Power

The Paraguayan judicial system, like every other part of the government, is dominated by the president, who appoints the five justices of the Supreme Court for five-year terms with the approval of the Council of State and the judges of the lower courts with the approval of the Supreme Court. Most observers feel that Paraguay's judicial system not only is subservient to the legislature, but is very inefficient, since it works only with written testimony, which must be presented on a special taxed paper. Thus cases drag through the courts for years as the judges try to assess the ever growing files of documents. In the entire country there were only 256 judges in 1960, including 207 justices of the peace at the lowest level, 31 regular district judges of various kinds, 12 Appeals Court judges, 3 in the Tribunal of Accounts (a special court dealing with administrative matters and public funds), and the 3 members of the Supreme Court. Since all judges serve five-year terms coterminous with that of the president, there are few disputes between the two powers.

Article 17 of the constitution gives the courts the power of judicial review, but they never exercise this power. No juries are used. Paraguay is one of the few countries in Latin America which still permit capital punishment.

Paraguay: A Last Word

The tragedy of Paraguay is that it probably could be a paradise if its ruling oligarchy stopped trying to preserve the status quo created so many centuries ago. The mild climate, plentiful rainfall, and fertile soil in the eastern section of the country could combine with a hard-working people to produce a prosperous country. But the refusal of the ruling oligarchy to relax the centuries-old dictatorship prevents full development. The oligarchy lives in a dream world. When President de Gaulle of France visited Paraguay in 1965, the joint communiqué issued by Stroessner and de Gaulle reaffirmed "the ideals of liberty and democracy held by their two countries and governments."

Despite such statements, Paraguay has never known either liberty or democracy and does not know them today. The economic development that is taking place is insufficient to bring the kind of rapid change the country needs, and one can only expect Paraguay to continue to stagnate until some group gains power which is determined to modernize the country. The only faint hope at the present time seems to be the *Febre-rista* Party, which, because its leaders have lived in exile for so long, has developed an intelligent program for revolutionizing the country. Yet the *Febrerista* Party suffers all the handicaps of an exile organization. It never has enough money to function well and it is continuously faced with internal fights as its various factions struggle to control the party.

A more hopeful development has been the stimulation of immigration by hard-working Korean and Japanese peasants. By 1966 over 7,000 Japanese had been settled on the land, and each month during 1966 about thirty-five Korean families entered the country. That appears to be the only solution for Paraguay: to populate the empty land and to create new economic enterprises.

SELECTED READINGS

ESCUELA PARAGUAYA DE ADMINISTRACIÓN PÚBLICA. *Manual del Gobierno Paraguayo.* Asunción, 1963.

FRIEDENBURG, DANIEL M. "Report from Paraguay." *New Leader* 48 (November 8, 1965): 5–7.

HICKS, FREDERIC. "Politics, Power, and the Role of the Village Priest in Paraguay." *Journal of Inter-American Studies* 9 (April 1967): 273–82.

LEWIS, PAUL HECTOR. "The Politics of Exile: The Case of the *Partido Revolucionario Febrerista,* Paraguay's 'Left.'" Ph.D. dissertation, University of North Carolina, 1965.

LOTT, LEO B. "Paraguay." In *Political Systems of Latin America,* edited by Martin C. Needler. Princeton, N.J.: D. Van Nostrand Co., 1964.

MACDONALD, AUSTIN F. "Paraguay," *Latin American Politics and Government,* pp. 504–24. 2nd ed. New York: Thomas Y. Crowell Co., 1954.

MAFFIODO, SALVADOR V. *Gobierno y administración del Paraguay.* Asunción: Escuela Paraguaya de Administración Pública, 1961.

PENDLE, GEORGE. *Paraguay, a Riverside Nation.* 2nd ed. London and New York: Royal Institute of International Affairs, 1956.

"Quo Vadis Paraguay?" *IUSY Survey,* no. 1 (1967), pp. 12–13, 16.

RAINE, PHILIP. *Paraguay*. New Brunswick, N.J.: Scarecrow Press, 1956.

UNIÓN NACIONAL PARAGUAYA. *El Tirano Stroessner ante la conciencia democrática de América*. Buenos Aires: Junta Central Coordinadora del Exilio, 1960.

————. *La Tragedia paraguaya: Datos para el análisis de la gestión gubernativa del tirano Stroessner*. Buenos Aires: Junta Central Coordinadora del Exilio, 1961.

————.*Un Pueblo en lucha por la libertad*. Buenos Aires: Junta Central Coordinadora del Exilio, 1960.

WARREN, HARRIS GAYLORD. *Paraguay: An Informal History*. Norman: University of Oklahoma Press, 1949.

——26——

EPILOGUE

Reviewing the political systems of the twenty Latin-American states, one is struck by the difficulty all have had in creating stable systems of any kind. Military dictatorships, constitutional democracies, autocratic republics, and empires have all been tried many times, but none has ever brought stability. The oldest continuously functioning government in Latin America is that of Mexico, which dates from 1917; eleven of the twenty Latin-American states are governed under constitutions created in the 1960's. Is there any logical explanation for the political instability these dates represent?

It has been customary to attribute Latin America's political instability to such factors as the racial background of the people, the tropical climate of much of the region, the Iberian cultural heritage, or interference from the United States and Europe. These theories are not so popular as they once were since the emergence of the many new states of Asia and Africa has demonstrated that political instability is not an exclusively Latin-American characteristic. Evidently certain conditions are necessary for the establishment of a stable political system, and whatever the factors are, they are missing in Latin America, Asia, and Africa. Constructing a political system that functions well is one of the most difficult challenges facing any group of human beings. Constructing one that is stable and also responsive to the wishes of the people involved is even more difficult, if we may judge by the small number of those in existence.

> The political system [writes David Easton] looks like a vast and
> perpetual conversion process. It takes in demands and support as
> they are shaped in the environment and produces something out of
> them called outputs . . . The outputs influence the supportive sen-
> timents that the members express toward the system and the kinds
> of demands they put in.[1]

Comparing Latin America's political systems with Professor Easton's
model, one notices immediately that in practically all of the Latin-
American states only a fraction of the population has been involved in
the workings of the political system. Some have been outside the political
system because they were physically separated by jungles and other natural barriers—the Jíbaro and other Indian groups of the Amazon basin,
for example. Other groups have been kept from participating by such legal measures as literacy or property requirements. Others, and by far the
largest number, were kept out of the political system by custom and tradition developing out of the colonial organization of society. Under systems
of chattel slavery and latifundia agriculture, neither slaves nor peons
were supposed to have demands. Their function was to work to make
their lords and masters more prosperous, and they were expected to accept this situation as the natural order of things; and this idea was so
imbedded in the Latin-American culture that it continues to influence
the way people act in the twentieth century. In a country as advanced as
Chile, only 9.6 percent of the population voted in the presidential election
of 1938, and as late as 1963 only 26.76 percent of the population voted.
If this is the situation in Chile, what kind of political participation can
there be in countries with large numbers of non-Spanish-speaking Indians, or in Haiti, where 90 percent of the population does not speak
French, the language of the government?

A country can function with a political system in which large sections of the population are not allowed to make demands upon the system
only as long as the cultural pattern trains people not to participate in the
country's political life. The conversion process in the political system
then takes in the inputs from the acceptable groups and creates outputs
for their benefit, ignoring the rest of the population. What happens, however, when radio, television, urbanization, industrialization, airplanes,
and all the other modern means of transportation and communication
begin to bring to the groups excluded from political life an awareness of
the possibilities of the modern world? The groups traditionally out of

---

[1] David Easton, *A Systems Analysis of Political Life* (New York: John Wiley & Sons,
1965), p. 29.

politics immediately enter the game. They begin to make demands upon the political system by means of demonstrations, riots, and violence, and they begin to join or to create political parties, trade unions, and other secondary organizations. Many, seeing that the political system contains no process by which their demands can be taken into consideration, turn to attempts to change the governmental structure.

It is this that makes Latin-American politics so chaotic, that creates conditions in which governments are so often overthrown and new constitutional arrangements continuously appear. The groups outside of the political system clamor for admittance and the old traditional power holders try to exclude them. This is why Argentina has a military dictatorship and why Brazil is dominated by its military. In both of these countries there are large groups (the Peronists in Argentina, the illiterate in Brazil) who have been unable to win full participation in the political system, and the determination to keep these groups out of the political system leads to a breakdown of the system and to dictatorship. Since World War II the excluded groups have been able to win the right to participate in some countries, and it is these countries—Venezuela, Mexico, Chile, Costa Rica—which have been making the most progress. Political stability will come to the Latin-American republics when all of the people in each country win full political participation.

Another characteristic of the Latin-American states well worth noting is that they have been subjected to an exceptionally large amount of outside interference. Many of the Latin-American republics were not viable political units at the time they were created, and were tempting booty for the world's adventurers, including European and American states, international financial corporations, and individuals ready to fight on any side of any argument for the proper pay. The adventurers and soldiers of fortune were a particularly troublesome element in Latin America. William Walker is probably the best known, but the number of professional soldiers who helped keep Latin America in turmoil is long, stretching from soldiers of the wars of independence such as Lord Cochrane to such contemporary figures as Che Guevara and Régis Debray. These international adventurers helped win independence and contributed to the chaos that followed. Some remain national heroes today; some are forgotten footnotes in obscure books.[2]

All political systems receive inputs from outside the system, but Latin America has been subjected to far more of them, and much stronger

---

[2] Ivan Lamb, a United States citizen, for example, hired himself out as a soldier in Nicaragua, Mexico, Guatemala, Brazil, Colombia, Honduras, and Ecuador. See *The Incurable Filibuster, Adventures of Colonel Dean Ivan Lamb* (New York: Farrar & Rinehart, 1934).

ones, than any system can comfortably accommodate. A United Fruit Company or a Standard Oil Company or a W. R. Grace & Co. may control larger financial resources and be more powerful than the political system into which it is inserting its demands. Most unsettling to the Latin-American state is the fact that it cannot control what the extrasocietal environment is inserting into the political system. Chile's economic disruption following a German chemist's laboratory synthesis of Chile's most important export is a case in point. So is the difficulty some countries are having with the adventurers financed and inspired by the Soviet Union, China, and/or Cuba.

In each of the twenty Latin-American states, the type of indigenous culture and the kind of invaders who came in the sixteenth century combined with geographic conditions to create a cultural pattern. After 400 years, the mixture in each unit had become unique. All had combined Indians, Europeans, and Negroes with a dash of Oriental, but by the twentieth century the resultant mixture was not a "Latin American," but a Brazilian, a Haitian, a Costa Rican, an Argentine. In each country, the political system that had developed was different from that of its neighbors, as its people were different, and its economy, and its cultural pattern. It is for this reason that all of the writings on Latin America which try to describe the "average" legislature or executive or political party are exercises in futility. The Latin Americans are Latin Americans in the same sense that Europeans are Europeans. No one, however, would try to combine the governments of Finland and France, Switzerland and Sweden, Great Britain and Germany into a classification called the European political system.

This is not meant to give the impression that all Latin-American political systems differ from each other in like degree; the differences between Nicaragua and Honduras, for example, are certainly less than those between Paraguay and Mexico. But there are sufficient differences among the twenty political systems that any valid generalizations about political behavior in Latin America will have to be based upon something much more fundamental and important than the fact that all of the twenty republics are located in the Western Hemisphere, or that all were once colonies, or that the majority of the people are Spanish-speaking Roman Catholics.

If, in Professor Easton's terminology, we view "political life as a system imbedded in an environment to the influence of which the political system itself is exposed and in turn reacts,"[3] then we cannot be very opti-

---

[3] Easton, *Systems Analysis*, pp. 17–18.

mistic about the future of Latin America's political life. Even though we live in an ever changing, dynamic world, the various political units into which we have divided the world are all subject to their environments, and these are not changing fast enough. Mexico is the classic example. Located next door to the United States and subject to all the pressures almost 200 million people living in the most powerful country in the world can exert on their neighbors, Mexico, nearly sixty years after a bloody revolution, still has been unable to modernize its institutions fast enough to incorporate all of its population within the society, and at least 40 percent of the Mexicans still remain outside the political system, in some cases continuing to live in much the same fashion as their ancestors did hundreds of years ago.

Another example of the difficulty of changing people's ways comes from Chile. There, after President Frei won election with the greatest majority a presidential candidate ever had, he tried to increase efficiency in production by having everyone work a consecutive shift. This would have avoided the fantastic midday transportation tie-up as practically the entire working population went home for lunch and a siesta. The President was unable to enforce this measure. After a few months of trying, he announced that the nation's work force would return to the old hours of work: 9 A.M. to 1 P.M. and 3:45 to 7 P.M., with an extra evening hour Friday and a half day on Saturday. When people are unwilling to accept a simple change in their lunch hour—and one that would have allowed them more free hours at the end of the day—any really important change becomes earth-shattering. People are creatures of habit and change comes hard.

Any change in Latin America's political systems, therefore, will come slowly. There is a great deal of evidence accumulating that as the so-called underdeveloped countries progress, they do not close the gap between themselves and the economically developed countries, for these have also been changing. It would seem, then, that the economically weaker states will always be at a disadvantage. Yet nothing remains the same; change does come, and each change makes the next one a little easier. It has been suggested that education, the development of new sources of economic wealth, or mass immigration may be the key to change in Latin America. But until the inputs into the Latin-American political systems do change, by whatever means, the outputs will continue to be about as before. As long as a country like Nicaragua is governed as if it were the private property of one family, it will continue to be inhabited by wretched, hungry, and backward people, unproductive and unwilling to accept any political system as permanent.

Another problem in Latin America is what is known in Britain as the "brain drain." The most energetic and, in many cases, the best educated members of the population are drawn to the United States, western Europe, and the service of the international organizations. Each such person lost to a Latin-American state prevents the country from developing as much as it would have if he had stayed home. This is something that Latin America finds almost impossible to avoid. The only thing that will keep people from leaving is the creation of better living, working, and political conditions, but the achievement of these conditions is hampered by the exodus of the very people most capable of bringing them about.

This is, perhaps, not a very optimistic view of Latin America's future, but it is difficult to be optimistic in the face of the reality of Latin America. When one gets out of the capital cities and away from the luxury hotels built by international capital, one sees a Latin America that is backward, underdeveloped, and so lacking in the rudimentary necessities of life that it is extremely doubtful that it can ever raise itself by its bootstraps. What Latin America needs is some kind of shock, some kind of cataclysmic awakening that will move its people to take advantage of the possibilities of the area.

Perhaps the solution to Latin America's problems is to unify the various republics into one or two or three large federal republics. United they may be able to do what they have been unable to do separately: provide the conditions under which their people will be able to unlock the fantastic untapped human and natural resources of the region and make the United States of Latin America the home of a prosperous and happy people.

Index

Index

Martin, Eileen M., 129, 425, 458, 500, 693
Martin, Percy F., 110
Martínez, Álvaro, 117
Martínez M., Alfredo, 60
Martínez Paz, Enrique, 616
Martínez Trueba, Andrés, 628
Martz, John, 385
Masó, Calixto, 289
Matos, Hubert, 271
Matthews, Herbert, 278, 288, 289
Maximilian (emperor of Mexico), 19
May, Stacy, 227
Mears, Leon G., 272
Mecham, J. Lloyd, 53
Medina Angarita, Isaías, 355, 356
Meek, George, 60
Melgarejo, Mariano, 510, 520
Mendershausen, Horst, 425
Méndez Montenegro, Julio César, 79, 80, 88, 90, 93
Méndez Montenegro, Mario, 77, 79, 85, 100
Mendieta y Núñez, Lucio, 53
Mendoza, Carlos Alberto, 251
Menéndez, Andrés, 111
Menges, Constantine C., 571
Mexico, 11–54
  armed forces in, 37
  budget of (tables), 42, 43
  Catholic church in, 37–38
  civil liberties in, 38
  civil service in, 41
  Committees of Moral, Civic, and Material Improvement in, 49
  constitution of, 26–28, 38
    how amended, 28–29
  economy of, 14
  election campaigns in, 30–31
  electoral system in, 29–30
  executive in, 39–41
  federalism in, 46–48
  historical development of, 16–26
  illiteracy in, 14
  judiciary in, 45–46
  legislature in, 44–45
  local government in, 49–50
  organized labor in, 37
  political participation in, 29
  political parties in, 31–35
    Authentic Party of Mexican Revolution, 35
    Communist, 34–35
    Institutional Revolutionary (PRI), 28–36, 39–41, 44, 47–48, 50–51, 112, 264
    National Action, 34, 35, 44
    National Liberation Movement, 34
    National Revolutionary, 24, 31, 39
    National Sinarquista Union, 35
    Nationalist, 34, 35

Mexico—Cont.
  political parties in—Cont.
    People's, 34
    Popular Socialist, 34, 35, 44
    Worker and Peasant, 34
  population of, 13
  public finance in, 41–43
  public opinion and pressure groups in, 35–38
  revolution of 1910 in, 20–22, 26, 34
  structure of states in, 48–50
Milla Bermúdez, Francisco, 140
Mills, C. Wright, 255
Miolán, Ángel, 335n.
Miquelena, Luis, 370
Miranda, José, 53
Mirkine-Guetzevitch, Boris, 481
Miró Cardona, José, 270
Mónagas, José Tadeo, 352
Monahan, James, 289
Moncada, José María, 165
Monge Alfaro, Carlos, 194
Monteforte Toledo, Mario, 100
Montes, César, 87
Moore, D. Ernest, 311
Mora, Manuel, 194, 198, 199
Morazán, Francisco, 59, 68, 110, 136
Moríñigo, Higinio, 704, 707
Morrison, Howard P., 454, 458
Morton, Ward M., 53
Moses, Carl C., 61
Munro, Dana G., 61, 191

Nájera Farfán, Mario Efraín, 100
Napoleon III, 19
Nash, Manning, 100
Navarro Bolandi, Hugo, 227
Needler, Martin C., 53, 129, 157, 183, 226, 251, 311, 458, 500, 570, 717
Neef, Arthur, 54
Nicaragua, 159–84
  armed forces in, 175
  budget of (tables), 180, 181
  civil liberties in, 176–77
  constitution of, 169–70
    how amended, 170
  education in, 160–61
  electoral system in, 171–72
  executive in, 177–78
  history of, 162–69
  interest groups in, 175–76
  judiciary in, 181
  legislature in, 178–79
  local government in, 179–81
  National Guard in, 175
  organized labor in, 176
  political participation in, 170–71
  political parties in, 172–74